THE HISTORY OF
HIGHER EDUCATION

THE HISTORY OF
HIGHER EDUCATION

Major Themes in Education

Edited by
Roy Lowe

Volume IV
The evolving curriculum

Routledge
Taylor & Francis Group

LONDON AND NEW YORK

First published 2009
by Routledge
2 Park Square, Milton Park, Abingdon, Oxon, OX14 4RN, UK

Simultaneously published in the USA and Canada
by Routledge
270 Madison Avenue, New York, NY 10016

Routledge is an imprint of the Taylor & Francis Group, an informa business

Typeset in 10/12pt Times NR MT by Graphicraft Limited, Hong Kong
Printed and bound in Great Britain by
MPG Books Ltd., Bodmin, Cornwall

British Library Cataloguing in Publication Data
A catalogue record for this book is available from the British Library

Library of Congress Cataloging-in-Publication Data
The history of higher education : major themes in education / edited by Roy Lowe.
p. cm.
Includes bibliographical references and index.
ISBN 978-0-415-37854-3 (set) – ISBN 978-0-415-38469-8 (vol. 1, hardback) –
ISBN 978-0-415-38470-4 (vol. 2, hardback) – ISBN 978-0-415-38471-1
(vol. 3, hardback) – ISBN 978-0-415-38472-8 (vol. 4, hardback) –
ISBN 978-0-415-38473-5 (vol. 5, hardback)   1. Education, Higher–History.
I. Lowe, Roy.
LA173.H584 2008
378.09–dc22
2008008884

ISBN10: 0-415-37854-0 (Set)
ISBN10: 0-415-38472-9 (Volume IV)

ISBN13: 978-0-415-37854-3 (Set)
ISBN13: 978-0-415-38472-8 (Volume IV)

Publisher's Note

References within each chapter are as they appear in the original
complete work.

CONTENTS

CONTENTS

ACKNOWLEDGEMENTS

The publishers would like to thank the following for permission to reprint their material:

Oxford University Press for permission to reprint Sir R. W. Livingstone, 'The Need for the Study of Philosophy', in Sir R. W. Livingstone, *Education and the Spirit of the Age*, Clarendon Press, Oxford, 1952, pp. 22–39.

Peter Owen Ltd, London, for permission to reprint Karl Jaspers, 'The Cosmos of Knowledge', in Karl Jaspers, *The Idea of the University*, Peter Owen, London, 1960, pp. 93–110.

Princeton University Press for permission to reprint Ortega y Gasset, José, *Mission of the University*. © 1944 Princeton University Press, 1972 renewed PUP.

Duckworth Publishers and Holmes and Meier for permission to reprint Charles Webster, *The Great Instauration: Science, Medicine and Reform, 1626–1660*, Holmes and Meier, New York, 1975, pp. 155–122.

Oxford University Press for permission to reprint John Twigg, 'The Limits of "Reform": Some Aspects of the Debate on University Education during the English Revolution', *History of Universities*, vol. 4, 1984, Oxford University Press, pp. 99–114.

Oxford University Press for permission to reprint Christopher Stray, 'From Oral to Written Examinations: Cambridge, Oxford and Dublin 1700–1914', *History of Universities*, vol. XX/2, 2005, Oxford University Press, pp. 76–130.

Oxford University Press for permission to reprint Christopher Stray, 'Curriculum and Style in the Collegiate University: Classics in Nineteenth-century Oxbridge', *History of Universities*, vol. XVI/2, 2000, Oxford University Press, pp. 183–218.

Oxford University Press for permission to reprint G. L'E. Turner, 'Experimental Science in Early Nineteenth-century Oxford', *History of Universities*, vol. VIII, 1989, Oxford University Press, pp. 117–135.

Cambridge University Press and Roy Lowe for permission to reprint Roy Lowe, 'Structural Change in English Higher Education, 1870–1920', in Detlef K. Müller, Fritz Ringer and Brian Simon (eds), *The Rise of the Modern Educational System, 1870–1920*, Cambridge University Press, 1987, pp. 163–178.

Blackwell Publishing for permission to reprint T. D. Weldon, 'Modern Greats', *Universities Quarterly* (now *Higher Education Quarterly*), vol. I, 1946–47, Turnstile Press, London, pp. 348–357.

Blackwell Publishing for permission to reprint J. S. Fulton, 'General Education', *Universities Quarterly* (now *Higher Education Quarterly*), vol. V, 1950–51, Turnstile Press, London, pp. 41–48.

R. O. Berdahl and I. J. Spitzberg for permission to reprint Oliver Fulton, 'Modular Systems in Britain', in R. O. Berdahl, G. C. Moodie and I. J. Spitzberg (eds), *Quality and Access in Higher Education: Comparing Britain and the United States*, SRHE and Open University Press, 1991, pp. 142–151.

Oxford University Press for permission to reprint Stephen C. Ferruolo, 'The Paris Statutes of 1215 Reconsidered', *History of Universities*, vol. V, 1985, Oxford University Press, pp. 1–14.

Oxford University Press for permission to reprint Jurgen Herbst, 'American Higher Education in the Age of the College', *History of Universities*, vol. VII, 1988, Oxford University Press, pp. 37–59.

Blackwell Publishing for permission to reprint John U. Nef, 'The Committee on Social Thought of the University of Chicago', *Universities Quarterly* (now *Higher Education Quarterly*), vol. III, 1948–49, Turnstile Press, London, pp. 678–686.

Sheldon Rothblatt, R. O. Berdahl, and I. J. Spitzberg for permission to reprint Sheldon Rothblatt, 'The American Modular System', in R. O. Berdahl, G. C. Moodie and I. J. Spitzberg (eds), *Quality and Access in Higher Education: Comparing Britain and the United States*, SRHE and Open University Press, Buckingham, 1991, pp. 129–141.

Disclaimer

INTRODUCTION

In 1838 William Whewell, a polymath professor at Cambridge, who had argued for many years in favour of 'inductive' approaches to learning, produced his widely influential book *On the Principles of English University Education*. From it is drawn the first extract in this collection whose central theme is the curriculum. In his book, Whewell argued for Classical and philosophical studies and sought to demonstrate the distinctions between theoretical and practical study which need to be made within the university. Both for its arguments and for its impact, it is appropriate that Whewell's rationale generates the first chapter of this volume (Chapter 74), since it initiated arguments that were to resound throughout the following two centuries.

Another giant of the nineteenth century, at least in terms of his impact on the debate on higher education, was John Henry Newman. His book *Discourses on the Scope and Nature of University Education* became the vehicle for an exploration between the claims of religious faith (Newman was, and remained throughout his life, a devout Roman Catholic) and those of scientific enquiry. It encapsulated problems that were at the heart of contemporary discussions on the emergence of the 'modern' university. The extract reproduced here as Chapter 75 is focused on that issue.

These two introductory essays, giving a flavour of the nineteenth-century debate, are followed by four that illustrate mid-twentieth-century concerns. R. W. Livingstone's book *Education and the Spirit of the Age*, published in 1952, epitomised the post-Second World War debate on the curriculum, and his chapter on the need for the study of philosophy (Chapter 76 in this volume) gave a striking illustration of the way in which the postwar spirit of collectivism impinged on thinking about the content of teaching in the universities. In similar vein, Karl Jaspers' *The Idea of the University*, first translated from German in 1960, concentrated on the classification of knowledge, the rise and rationale of subject departments, and the issue of whether some theoretic studies should be given higher esteem than the practical (Chapter 77). José Ortega y Gasset was another who called for 'a new integration of knowledge'. His essay, reproduced as Chapter 78, raised the question of whether an understanding of the sciences in general, and physics and mathematics in particular, was a prerequisite for any meaningful wider understanding in the modern world. Similarly, Adolph Löwe reflected on the role of vocationalism in what he called 'a new cultural education'. Löwe had survived the trenches of the First World War and had moved as a refugee from Frankfurt to Manchester before the appearance of his book in 1940. He was therefore well-attuned to the political realities of the mid-twentieth century and to the ongoing debates on university reform. His lifelong focus was on a rapprochement between economics and sociology, but in the extract selected as Chapter 79 his argument ranged more widely.

These pieces are followed by a number of contributions focused far more on the day-to-day realities of curricular change. John Fletcher's first essay (Chapter 80) provides a fascinating insight into the rise of the college university during the early-modern period, focusing on Scotland but ranging far more widely. Fletcher was one of the best-known historians of European universities during the fifteenth and sixteenth centuries, and his second contribution (Chapter 81), a comparison of developments in England and Germany during the sixteenth century, is an authoritative and fascinating glimpse into curricular reform in Northern Europe at this time. Chapter 82, an extract from Charles Webster's 1975 book, deals with the role of the sciences in general, and mathematics and medicine in particular, at Oxford during the seventeenth-century Puritan revolution. This is twinned with an article by John Twigg (Chapter 83), who, a decade after the appearance of Webster's book, reflected on the necessarily limited nature of the reform of the universities in England during this period.

Another leading researcher whose work has thrown light on what was happening within the universities in Britain is Christopher Stray. Here, in two major articles, both exhaustive in their scope, he details, first, in Chapter 84, the reform of examinations (the shift from the tripos to written examinations) and second, in Chapter 85, the continuing dominance of Classics at Oxbridge. His work, focused on the nineteenth century, is set alongside that of G. L'E. Turner (Chapter 86), who published in the journal *History of Universities* in 1989 on the role of the experimental sciences at Oxford during the nineteenth century, and shows that one side effect of the continuing engagement with the Classics was that the sciences were kept largely at arm's length by the ancient universities. A more wide-ranging analysis of nineteenth-century higher education is made by Roy Lowe, whose chapter on the structural changes taking place in English higher education at this time shows some of the linkages between curricular change and the emergence of a system of higher education (Chapter 87). He was but one of a number of historians who were investigating curricular differentiation in higher education during the late nineteenth and early twentieth centuries and who were also interested in pan-European similarities and trends.

Six contributions deal with curricular trends in England during the twentieth century. First, in Chapter 88, T. D. Wheldon writes on the establishment of Modern Greats at Oxford during the interwar years, reflecting on the trend away from Classical and single subject studies. One of the leaders of the drive, in the years after the Second World War, towards even more generalised study at the universities was J. S. Fulton, who was one of the architects of curricula at Keele, Swansea and Sussex. In his article from the *Universities Quarterly*, 1950, reproduced here as Chapter 89, he offered his rationale for general studies as being at the core of undergraduate curricula. Another key theme in curricular debates at this time was a new vocationalism, and E. E. Robinson, who wrote on the origins of the poly-technics, contributes a chapter which chronicles the evolution from College of Advanced Technology to technical college and then to polytechnic during what might be called in retrospect the Robbins era (Chapter 90). Alongside the polytechnics, the technological universities made their own contribution to curriculum reform and this theme is dealt with in Chapter 91 by Peter Venables, who authored the early and definitive study of these foundations in his book published in 1978. Two further contributions round off this part of the collection. Walter Perry, the first Vice-Chancellor of the Open University, reflects on its unique contribution to curriculum reform in Chapter 92, while Oliver Fulton, in Chapter 93, chronicles the coming of modular systems to Britain during this period.

This volume is completed by four essays that deal with widely differ-ing developments in other countries. In Chapter 94 Stephen Ferruolo, an eminent authority on the late medieval European universities, deals with the impact of the Paris statutes of 1215. In Chapter 95 Jurgen Herbst offers an informed overview of developments in American higher education during the period between the Revolution and the Civil War, a period often described as 'the age of the college'. John Nef's essay on the Committee on Social Thought of the University of Chicago (Chapter 96) reminds us that the mid-twentieth-century concern for over-specialisation was not a uniquely British concern. Finally, Sheldon Rothblatt's address to the Society for Research into Higher Education (Chapter 97), presented in 1990, illustrates the ways in which, in the United States, the development of the world's first mass-access system of higher education involved modularisation at the heart of the curriculum.

OF THE SUBJECTS OF
UNIVERSITY TEACHING

William Whewell

Source: W. Whewell, *On the Principles of English University Education*, West Strand, London: John W. Parker, 1838, pp. 5–51.

Sect. 1.—Of the distinction of practical and speculative teaching

There are two modes of teaching, which, in a general view, may be broadly distinguished from each other. In the one mode the lecturer merely expounds to his audience the doctrines or results belonging to some branch of knowledge; he states the discoveries and speculations of antecedent philosophers, or his own, while the office of the audience is only to attend to him; they have to listen, to receive, think on, and treasure up what the speaker delivers, without being called upon themselves to take any active part; without being required to produce, to test, or to apply the knowledge thus acquired. In another mode of teaching, the learner has not merely to listen, but to do something himself; not merely to receive, but to produce his knowledge:—as when the mathematical student proves the proposition which is enunciated by his teacher, or solves a problem proposed by him;—or when the classical scholar renders Horace or Thucydides into English. The former I call *speculative*, the latter, *practical* teaching. And I must beg the reader to recollect the manner in which I use these terms; namely, with reference to the *mode* of teaching, not the possible application of the *subject* taught. It is because geometry is taught thus *practically*, and not because it is what is commonly called "practical knowledge," that I designate the cultivation of geometry, in the manner which prevails in English Universities, as Practical Teaching. In their marked forms, these two kinds of teaching are very clearly distinguished. Lectures uncombined with any questions or practical demands on the learner, are familiar to us in our own Universities, in those of foreign lands, in the metropolis, and in the provinces; as modes of treating of physics and metaphysics, geology and political economy, taste and politics. All such

4

lectures I speak of as speculative teaching, since they are employed in delivering to the hearer the doctrine adopted by the teacher, in a speculative form. Practical teaching, where the scholar, with voice, pen, or pencil, follows the track pointed out to him, and is constantly brought back into it when he deviates, are still more familiar; for by this method we learn every thing that, in the most peculiar sense, we learn at all. It is by such a process that we become able to read, to write, to cast accounts, to translate Latin and Greek, to speak French and German, to solve equations, to obtain our own results in the highest branches of mathematics. The teaching of mothers and fathers, of schools, and a great part of the teaching of our English Universities, has hitherto been on this practical kind.

Now we may observe, that when we come to such branches of literature and science as are likely to be selected for the matter of University teaching, some of these branches naturally and almost inevitably require to be taught practically, while others as clearly are more fitted for the speculative mode of teaching. Languages and mathematics are of the former kind; but many of the sciences, and those especially which are wide and varied in their topics, those which involve doubtful or newly-established principles, those of which the foundations are constantly undergoing changes, can hardly be taught otherwise than speculatively. Such subjects are, for example, geology, political economy, and, as appears to me, metaphysics. In such subjects as these, the student may listen, and may acquire such knowledge as the teacher possesses; but he is not, and cannot be called upon, as a part of the teaching, to do something which depends on the knowledge thus acquired. He may follow with the clearest apprehension, and it may be with full and well-founded conviction, the views which are presented to him by the teacher; but still he is passive only; he is a spectator, not an actor, in the intellectual scene. He does not interpret and employ a peculiar acquired language, as he does in his classical reading, or his algebraical calculations.

What I have called practical teaching prevails in the Colleges of our English Universities. A large portion of the teaching, in those institutions, has always consisted, as it still does, of exercises, in which the pupil translates his Greek or Latin author, proves his proposition, or solves his equation, in the hearing or under the eye of his tutor; or answers interrogatories, in which he has to produce the knowledge which he has acquired. I believe this to have been the mode of teaching employed among us from the earliest times. In that College, at least, of which I know most, such a method is enjoined in the statutes. Disputations are to be constantly held in the chapel; verses written and affixed in the hall; and the lecturers are to employ half an hour in expounding their author, but a whole hour in examining their class[1]. But besides these practical lectures, we have always had lectures of the speculative kind, delivered by the University professors. Such lectures on history, morals, political economy, law, medicine, anatomy, geology, botany, mineralogy, chemistry, the mechanical sciences, and other subjects, have constantly been going on in our Universities; and have, especially of late years, often excited very great attention. We may, therefore, distinguish our practical and speculative teaching, as *college lectures* and *professorial lectures;*—and such a distinction corresponds to the phraseology commonly in use among us.

It may be said, that with professorial lectures examinations may be combined, and that such lectures may thus be converted into practical teaching. Nor do I intend to deny that, under certain conditions, which I shall afterwards endeavour to determine, this effect may be produced. But without now entering into this subject, I trust that the main features of the distinction, which I am trying to point out, of the two kinds of teaching, are already sufficiently clear.

Now it must be observed that, though all branches of science and speculation, old and new, fixed and moveable, may be made the subjects of exposition in lectures, practical teaching is applicable only to a limited range of subjects;—those, namely, in which principles having clear evidence and stable certainty, form the basis of our knowledge; and in which, consequently, a distinct possession of the fundamental ideas enables a student to proceed to their applications, and to acquire the habit of applying them in every case with ease and rapidity. The ideas of space, of number, of the general relations of grammar and the force of language, are necessary and immutable parts of the furniture of the human mind. And mathematics and languages, which are the developement and working of these ideas, can be practically taught, for we can appeal to these ideas, and familiarize the mind with a series of vast and varied, yet certain consequences, to which they lead. But when we come to the wider physical sciences, we can only present the facts as a matter of observation, and the speculations as dependent on the facts. Here there is no room for acquiring habits of interpretation which can be tested by the teacher. And in sciences which are not physical, as morals or metaphysics, the philosophy of history, or of taste, the instruction is still more inevitably of the speculative kind. The teacher must be content to tell, and the learner to receive, what has been thought, or ought to be thought, on these subjects. He does not, by learning them, acquire a new faculty, which he must practically exercise. Such subjects as I have just described, may, perhaps, without impropriety, be distinguished by the collective title of "philosophy;" and if this be allowed, it will, I think, appear, that *philosophy* is only fitted for speculative, as *mathematical and classical* studies are for practical, teaching. In saying this, I do not at all profess to know, whether I am employing the term "philosophy," in the sense attached to it by other persons, who may have written on the subject; but it may, I think, designate appropriately a large class of studies, all of which admit of the same mode of communication to the student.

In such studies, moreover, even if examinations be added to lectures, they can hardly constitute a practical teaching; for in such instances, the knowledge which lectures convey, is either merely retained in the memory, or is employed as material for further speculation by the student, and is not assimilated and converted into a practical habit of intellectual action. Examinations, therefore, in these cases, may test the goodness of the memory, and the clearness of the apprehension or general faculties; and we may also conceive examinations of a higher kind, that call out the powers of original thought, and detect the activity of talent and genius. But to require proof of mere memory and clearheadedness is not practical teaching, in the same sense as it is so to ascertain that a power of interpretation or calculation has been acquired; and the higher kind of examination which we have mentioned, in which the student is called upon to give evidence of his own speculative talent, presupposes that practical teaching of which we here speak, and is not to be confounded with it. And thus, even with the addition of examinations on subjects of general philosophy, there will still remain, between those studies and the mathematical and classical pursuits of the English Universities, that difference which I describe by calling the former speculative teaching.

Thus the distinction of speculative and practical instruction, which at first sight appears to be a difference of the manner of teaching, is found, on examination, to imply a difference of the subjects taught. When we have determined that we will teach practically, we have decided that we must lecture, not on philosophy, not on metaphysics or speculative morals, or political economy, but on subjects of a different kind;—on the works of Greek and Latin authors;—the properties of space and number;—the laws of motion and force.

Of course, I mean only, that *so far* as we teach practically, we must select such subjects. Nothing prevents us, and as I have said, we have not been prevented, from giving, in addition to our college courses, professorial lectures on all the other subjects which I have mentioned. But it is not on that account the less important to my purpose, to keep the consideration of the two kinds of study distinct. It is obvious also, that, in many cases, the same subject admits of being dealt with in both ways. We may not only ascertain that our pupils can translate Sophocles, but we may present to them the widest speculative views at which critics have arrived, respecting the history and structure of the Greek language, or the Greek drama. We may enter into discussions respecting the metaphysical grounds of the axioms of geometry, the processes of algebra, the laws of motion. Such speculations and discussions are of the highest interest and value; but it is easy to see that they are something in addition to the teaching of Greek and mathematics. They add immensely to the value of the practical acquisition of language and mathematical habits, but they presuppose the acquisition; and when these philosophical views are substituted for the practical instruction, they are altogether empty and valueless as means of education.

But I do not here insist upon this point. In the present section, my object has been to distinguish the two systems, before I compared them. Trusting that the distinction is now sufficiently clear, I proceed to the comparison. And this I shall consider with reference to such points as these:—the effect on the intellectual and on the moral character of those who are educated, and on the general progress of national culture and civilisation.

Sect. 2.—Of the effect of practical teaching on the intellectual habits

The advantages which belong to the study of mathematics, as an intellectual discipline, have been often stated by various persons. I may repeat language which I have already used:—"In mathematics, the student is rendered familiar with the most perfect examples of strict inference; he is compelled habitually to fix his attention on those conditions on which the cogency of the demonstration depends; and, in the mistaken or imperfect attempts at demonstration made by himself or others, he is presented with examples of the most natural fallacies, which he sees exposed and corrected." My Edinburgh reviewer[2] expressed a wish, that these latter "novel assertions had been explained and exemplified;" and obviously, was really at a loss to understand them, although they refer to the daily occurrences of the lecture-room. This is a curious proof how entirely practical teaching is lost sight of, amid the speculations of his school. I may observe, too, as I have done elsewhere,[3] that reasoning, as a practical habit, is taught with peculiar advantage by mathematics, because we are, in that study, concerned with long chains of reasoning, in which each link hangs from all the preceding. "The language contains a constant succession of short and rapid references to what has been proved already; and it is justly assumed, that each of these brief movements helps the reasoner forwards in a course of infallible certainty and security. Each of these hasty glances must possess the clearness of intuitive evidence, and the certainty of mature reflection; and yet must leave the reasoner's mind entirely free to turn instantly to the next point of his progress. The faculty of performing such processes well and readily, is of great value;" and this faculty can hardly be acquired and cultivated in any other way, than by the study of mathematics.

I shall not pursue the consideration of the beneficial intellectual influence of mathematical studies. It would be easy to point out circumstances, which show that this influence has really operated;—for instance, the extraordinary number of persons, who, after giving more than the common attention to mathematical studies at the University, have afterwards become eminent as English lawyers. It would be easy, also, to gather together a "cloud of witnesses," who have spoken with admiration and enthusiasm of mathematics as a discipline of the mind. But this would be a very idle mode of treating the subject; for it might be possible also, to adduce a large bulk of similar testimony on the other side. And what could be inferred from this array of cloud against cloud? Except we can get some clear insight into the subject ourselves, we can never know whether the authors we adduce, are not speaking from views as vague and confused as our own. When any one will point out any other study, as a mode of *practically teaching* reasoning, which he maintains to be preferable to mathematics, we may be tempted to make the comparison; but this has not been done, so far as I know.

It may be said, that mathematical reasoning is but one kind of reasoning, and that the study and practice of this alone, ought not to be spoken of as the cultivation of the reasoning power in general. To this, I reply, that the faculty of reasoning, *so far as it can be disciplined by practical teaching*, receives such a discipline from mathematical study. If, for instance, any one says, "Why do you not cultivate the habit of *inductive* as well as of *deductive* reasoning?" I answer, that the only cultivation of which inductive reasoning admits, is that which is supplied by deductive reasoning. For when we collect a new truth by induction from facts, what is the process of our minds? We acquire a new and distinct view, or hit upon a right supposition; and we perceive that, in the consequences of our new notions, the observed facts are included. The former part of this process, the new and true idea suited to the emergency, the happy guess, no teaching can give the student. All that we can do is, to fix the idea when he has it, and to teach him to test his hypothesis by tracing its consequences. And this, the cultivation of deductive habits does. We cannot teach men to invent new truths; we cannot even give them the power of guessing a riddle. But those who have been inventors, have always had, not only that native fertility of mind which no education can bestow, but also a talent of clearly and rapidly applying their newly-sprung thoughts, in which talent half their power consisted, and which is precisely that faculty which mathematical habits may improve. And the distinctness of the fundamental ideas (a state of thought essential alike to sound reasoning from old truths, and to the discovery of new,) is not unprovided for by the study of mathematics; for thought deductive habits do not *give* distinct fundamental ideas they *demand* them; and, by the constant appeal to such ideas, they fix and develope them. A perception of the truth of mathematical axioms cannot be conveyed into the mind by reasoning; but still, the mathematical reasoner usually sees more clearly than other men, the necessary truth of his axioms.[4] Other persons may have the idea of space, as well as the geometer;—the idea of force and matter, as well as the mechanician; but these ideas shine with a clearer and steadier light in the minds of those who constantly work by such lamps, and therefore, carefully tend and trim them.

Since the study of mathematics is thus useful, not only in teaching habits of deduction, which are exemplified in its proofs, but also in leading men to the distinct ideas which are expressed in its definitions and axioms, we learn a lesson respecting the kind of mathematics which we may most advantageously introduce in our education. For since those clear ideas upon which the several mathematical sciences depend are a valuable mental possession, both on their own account, and as examples of such a class of elements of truth, we ought not to be content with one or two such ideas and their consequences, but should introduce the student to a wider range of mathematical proof. We shall thus succeed best in repressing the evil consequences which might arise from confining ourselves to one kind of reasoning. We ought, therefore, to include in our course, not only pure mathematical sciences, geometry, arithmetic, and algebra, the consequences of the fundamental ideas of space, number, and quantity; but we ought also admit the consequences of other ideas, which lead to rigorous mathematical sciences, such as the ideas of pressure and matter, of rigidity and fluidity, of velocity and force; of which ideas the developments are found in the sciences of Mechanics and Hydrostatics. This maxim I have already urged, in a former publication on this subject.[5] And I rejoice to say, that a recent alteration in the examinations of the University of Cambridge, by which certain portions of Mechanics and Hydrostatics are introduced into the lower Examinations for Degrees, has made our system, what appears to me, on the grounds just stated, a better intellectual education than it was before.

I shall not here dwell upon the intellectual effect of the practical teaching of Greek and Latin, but proceed to consider the effect of the two systems of instruction in another point of view.

Sect. 3.—Of the effect of practical and speculative teaching on the progress of civilisation

If I were to begin by asserting that the progress of civilisation is essentially connected with the prevalent education, the assertion would probably be assented to; but at the same time, it would probably also be understood in so general and indistinct a manner, that no real use could be made of it in our argument. The connexion is, indeed, generally acknowledged; for instance, Dr Diesterweg's pamphlet, in which he so deeply deplores the present diseased condition of the German Universities, (a subject which has recently excited much remark in that country,) is entitled,[6] "The Vital Question of Civilisation." But some definite statement of the nature of this connexion is requisite, in order to enable us to draw any inferences from it. The subject is far too large to be treated generally here; but there is one view of it to which I hope I shall obtain the reader's assent.

Among the elements and indications of civilisation, I think it will be allowed that a generally diffused faculty of *speculative* thought forms a leading point. Such a faculty, and its habitual exercise, forms a main distinction between the most refined and the rudest nations; as, in a broader sense, it does between man and lower animals. For even the brutes have *practical* powers of thought; they have a practical notion of space and force; a practical sense of things good and bad, of things which they may and which they may not do; but man alone has a geometry and a mechanics, an idea of happiness and of a moral law. And the clearness of the ideas which speculation requires and uses, is one of the most essential features of the progress of intellectual refinement. This appears in matters, which at first seem trivial, as, for instance, in the importance attached to correct speaking and writing. Why is it that a false spelling or wrong accent in our own language, is considered a mark of a vulgar, or, at least, unpolished, mind? Why is it that a false quantity, or a false concord, is looked upon with horror by the thorough scholar, as something offensive and ridiculous? Why is it that men are more angry at being accused of bad reasoning than of erroneous opinions? Clearly because all these faults imply an incomplete and ill-conducted cultivation of the speculative faculty, in reference to language or to reasoning. The errors may be trifling, but they seem to disclose faults of intellectual training: they are, in the world of literature and thought, what violations of good breeding are in manners. A single fault of grammar may betray a want of perception of the analogy of language; a single fault of logic may shew that the speaker has no distinct apprehension of the force of demonstration; and when this judgment is formed of him, he immediately appears to sink below the standard point of cultivation and connexion of thought. He is less cultured than those who detect his deficiencies;—less refined in his intellectual character, because he is less distinct and connected in his intellectual habits. And thus we have, in the common judgments of mankind, an evidence that they consider distinctness and clearness of the speculative faculty as one of the elements of civilisation.

But we may take a larger view. Probably all persons will acknowledge, that those nations by whom great advances in knowledge are made, and among whom such advances are widely diffused and well understood, have the pre-eminence in civilisation. Great scientific discoveries, along with a general national interest and intelligence respecting such matters, are circumstances peculiar to the most highly cultured times. Now this consideration will lead us by a different road to the same element of civilisation which we have already pointed out. For by a history of each of the sciences in succession,[7] I have proved, I hope satisfactorily, that their progress depends upon the distinctness of certain fundamental ideas; and that these ideas, being first clearly brought into view by the genius of great discoverers, become afterwards the inheritance of all who thoroughly acquire the knowledge which is thus made accessible. In highly cultered nations, a large portion of society will thus attend to the progress of knowledge; so as to obtain a just view, at least of the general nature of the treasures which are thus placed within their reach, and of the triumphs which their intellectual leaders have achieved. And thus we are again brought to the principle, that distinct speculative ideas generally diffused, are an essential part of our conception of civilisation.

Having reached this point, we have to inquire whether practical or speculative teaching, distinguished as in the preceding section, be the best instrument for that kind of culture on which civilisation thus depends. I do not think it would be difficult to shew, from general considerations, that it is only by the practical teaching of mathematics, that the fundamental ideas of science can become distinct among men in general. But a more interesting mode of deciding this point will be, to look back at the history of the world; for the whole history of the world has been one grand experiment on this subject. Let us take a general view of the result. Our question is, whether practical or speculative teaching most promotes civilisation; which question, as we have seen, may be decided, by inquiring whether an education in *mathematics*, or in general *philosophy*, is most favourable to the progress of science, and to the general diffusion of the knowledge which this progress brings. A rapid survey of the history of education, with this view, will repay us.

Of the Greek education, up to the time of Plato, we know enough to be able to assert, that it was in the main practical teaching. The "music" ($\mu o \upsilon \sigma \iota \kappa \acute{\eta}$) which constituted the principal part of this, was taught unquestionably in a practical manner; and if the occasion admitted, it might be shown, both from the elements which it included, and from the way in which it was conducted, that it had nearly the same effect that the practical teaching of mathematics has, in giving distinctness to the ideas,—independently of its other and collateral influences. But in the time of Aristophanes[8], a change took place in the instruction of the Greek youth. The sophists and philosophers were extraordinarily admired and followed; and to acquire an acquaintance with their doctrines and systems came to be considered as the most essential part of a liberal education. This was still more the case among the Romans, when they attempted to take a place among cultivated nations. Their youth listened to what "Chrysippus and Crantor taught," and were thus supposed to be filled with all learning.[9] The study of *philosophy*, in the general sense, that is, of the moral, metaphysical, and physical doctrines of the framers of universal systems, was, as we know, the highest conception of the Greeks and Romans in their aims at intellectual culture, till civilisation itself sickened and declined. It was so, too, among the Neoplatonists, the schoolmen, the theologians of the middle ages; till in the monasteries there again grew up a method of practical teaching from which the system of the English universities had its origin.

Such is the course of education; now what is the corresponding course of knowledge? The answer is well worth notice. *The progress of science corresponds to the time of practical teaching; the stationary, or retrograde, period of science, is the period when philosophy was the instrument of education.* At the time of Plato, the Greek education had been for a long period virtually mathematical; a fact, of which the very term *mathematics* is the record. At that time the greatest scientific discovery of the ancient world,—the resolution of celestial phenomena into circular motions,—was caught sight of by Plato, and soon after fully brought out by Hipparchus. At a similar stage of Greek culture, although at a later time and in a different country, the science of mechanics was established by Archimedes, on foundations fitted to endure to eternity. What might have been the history of civilisation if the Greek education had continued to be practically mathematical, we cannot tell. Speaking according to human views of probability, perhaps the Greeks might, in that case, have anticipated the discoveries of modern times by a thousand years; and the places of Galileo, and Kepler, and Newton, might have been preoccupied by citizens of Athens and Alexandria. But the speculative study of philosophy prevailed. From that time no material advance was made in science. What great men had already taught mankind, was perverted or forgotten by their degenerate followers. The schools of the philosophers resounded with systems old and new, with wranglings and boastings; but this availed not to urge on the intellectual progress of man, or even to prevent his sliding backwards. The simple geometrical conceptions of the school of Plato were debased and weighed down by a cumbrous apparatus of crystalline spheres. The mechanical truths brought to light by Archimedes, were, like his tomb, overgrown with the rank and unprofitable vegetation of later days, till they were lost sight of; and were not resumed and pursued till a thousand years, and half a second thousand, had elapsed. It is a manifest mistake to ascribe the decay of science to the incursions of the northern nations. Science was dead, and literature mortally smitten, before the external pressure was felt. But the study of speculative philosophy, as the business of cultured men, survived. Still the intellectual world grew darker and darker. "Light after light goes out, and all is night." In vain do the schoolmen of the middle ages build system upon system, as the schoolmen of Athens and Alexandria had done before. The centuries roll on, and bring no day. But in the mean time the religious orders have established among themselves a system of practical teaching. They introduce mathematics into their course with especial attention. The principle of progress is soon felt to be again at work. A Franciscan friar lifts up his voice against the sway of Aristotle, and points to the far-off temple of science, declaring that *mathematics* is its gate and its key.[10] His announcement is found to be true. From the like mathematical schools proceed the luminaries of a new dawn,—Copernicus, Galileo, Kepler, Newton, are the founders of a fresh era of knowledge, because they are well-trained mathematicians. The universities of Europe assume a form in which such a training goes on; thus the cultured classes become capable of receiving and appreciating the great discoveries by which man's intellectual position is advanced; and we reach the present condition of the civilised world.

But we have not yet done with the survey of this great experiment. In one country of Europe the universities give up their habits of practical teaching, and return to the speculative method. They make *philosophy* their main subject. Their professors deliver from their chairs system after system to admiring audiences. The listener may assent or criticise; but he is not disturbed by any demands on his mind, such as the teaching of mathematics gives rise to. And what is the class of men thus produced, in their bearing upon the progress of sure and indestructible knowledge? They are such men as to be utterly incapable even of comprehending and appreciating the most conspicuous examples of the advance of science. Those who are universally allowed to be the greatest philosophers of our own day in the German universities, Hegel and Schelling, cannot understand that Newton went further than Kepler had gone in physical astronomy, and despise Newton's optical doctrines in comparison with the vague Aristotelian dogmas of Göthe respecting colours.[11]

Thus, the experiment on education, which has been going on from the beginning of Greek civilisation to the present day, appears to be quite distinct and consistent in its result. And the lesson we learn from it is this; —that so far as civilisation is connected with the advance and diffusion of human knowledge, civilisation flourishes when the prevalent education is mathematical, and fades when *philosophy* is the subject most preferred. We find abundant confirmation of the belief, that education has a strong influence upon the progress of civilisation; and we find that the influence follows a settled rule: when the education is practical teaching, it is a genuine culture, tending to increased fertility and vigour; when it is speculative teaching, it appears that, however the effect is produced, men's minds do, in some way or other, lose that force and clearness on which intellectual progression depends.

I cannot go on to the next point of my argument without an observation founded on the view which has been presented. It is impossible, after the survey we have just made, not to reflect of what immense importance the question of the two kinds of education is. The reform of the European universities, a subject which is now exciting so much interest in England, France, and Germany, is, in truth, what it has been termed, the Vital Question of Civilisation. Upon the decision of that question may depend, whether Europe, and America, which must follow the intellectual fortunes of Europe, shall, for the next thousand years, be in the condition of the later Greeks and Romans, having for their mental aristocracy, a class of philosophical system-builders, commentators, and mere metaphysicians; or shall go on to exhibit that healthy vigour and constant effort at real progress and improvement, which has characterized this quarter of the globe for the last three hundred years. This is no slight matter. And let no one attempt to make it less momentous, by persuading himself that civilisation must advance;— that we cannot run back into an inferior condition of culture and thought. The history of the world shows that we have no such security. Civilisation, in its best sense, may too surely decline. Greece and Rome had wasted by their own folly almost all that was most valuable in their intellectual inheritance, before the foreign spoiler came. The civilisation of the eastern and southern shores of the Mediterranean, once the fairest spots in the world of literature and art,—where is it, and how is it vanished? It is not enough to say that the barbarising storm of Mahommedan conquest has swept over and destroyed it. The Mahommedans did not barbarise Spain or Persia. And to whatever violent external causes we may ascribe this deplorable change, it shows, at least, that in some countries civilisation takes deeper root than in others; and warns us to use our best endeavour, that, so far as we are concerned, our country and the world may lose nothing of that real civilisation which, combined with morality and religion, constitutes the brightest glory and most precious treasure of the human race.

It is difficult to mark out, even in conjecture, the path of the future progress of mental civilisation. Yet some light we may gather from the history of the past. One idea after another, of those which constitute the basis of science, becomes distinct, first in the minds of discoverers, then in the minds of all cultured men, till a general clearness of thought illuminates the land; and thus the torch of knowledge is handed forwards, thousands upon thousands lighting their lamps at it as it passes on; while still from time to time some new Prometheus catches a fresh light from heaven, to spread abroad among men in like manner. Thus the opening of Greek civilisation was marked by the production of Geometry;—the *idea of space* was brought to a scientific precision. Of that step we still inherit the benefits; for example, all educated Europeans conceive the relation of the various parts and lines on the terrestrial globe with a distinctness in which the rude savage or uncultured boor has no share. The opening of the civilisation of modern Europe was distinguished, in the same way, by the production of a new science,—Mechanics, which soon led to the Mechanics of the Heavens. And this step, like the former, depended on men arriving at a properly-distinct fundamental idea. The *revival of the scientific idea of force* (an idea which had been brought to light by Archimedes, and extinguished again amid the mists of Greek philosophy,) was, as I have elsewhere shown, the essential condition to which this step was due.[12] This idea, too, has now been communicated to persons of education in general, as the general reception of the Newtonian theory of the universe proves; while, at the same time, the very indistinct views which men of considerable cultivation often entertain of the mechanism of the universe, proves that the fundamental ideas on which a clear apprehension of the doctrine of universal attraction depends, have hitherto been very imperfectly diffused through the atmosphere of the literary world. And the cause of this remaining imperfection probably is, that elementary mechanics has not hitherto been made an essential portion of a liberal education, as for centuries elementary geometry has. Nothing forbids us to look forward to the time, when not only this deficiency shall be supplied,[13] but when men's minds shall have been carried much further in the same track. We may imagine a future period of mental culture, when the elements of chemistry and natural history shall be fundamental parts of a good education, as the elements of mathematics now are; and when consequently the ideas on which our knowledge of the composition of bodies, or our estimate of the natural classes of organized beings, depends, shall be as clear in cultivated minds, as the conception of universal attraction is now, in the mind of a thoroughly educated man; or as the conception of the circles of latitude and longitude, in the thoughts of a well-taught child. And if we add to this, the possibility that the ideas which are the bases of sound criticism, morals, and politics, may become equally distinct and equally diffused, by means of an appropriate education, we catch a glimpse of the grand and boundless vista of possible and probable intellectual refinement and civilisation which the future offers.

Whether or not the reader may assent to the view thus presented of the nature and prospects of civilisation, he will, I trust, sympathize with another reflection which offers itself to us at this point of our survey. If the destinies of the highest civilisation of man, be thus closely connected with the progress of truly liberal education; and if it depend upon the constitution and conduct of educational institutions, whether such civilisation shall continue to advance, or shall become retrograde: it is impossible not to reflect, how grave and weighty is the office of those, on whom it falls to found and to put in action new institutions of liberal education, intended to meet the requirements of present and future ages. To do this, is a great, and we may say, a solemn task. Those who are engaged in it, must act as men building for eternity. We see no reason to believe otherwise, than that this great nation, hitherto so highly favoured with outward and inward gifts, (and with it, its vigorous progeny, which, while peopling and civilising the other side of the globe, is involved in the intellectual fortunes of its parent,) is destined by Providence for an advance yet to be long continued, in civilisation and refinement of the best and highest kind. To what consummation the world is reserved by its Governor we know not, nor whether he has decreed, that, before the final close of all things, the brightness of civilised England must wane and become dim, as that of Greece and Rome has done before. But this we know, that it would be the most fantastical presumption of system-making, for any one to predict and reckon in centuries the calculated time and rate of the declension of Britain. We know, too, that if such a declension menaced us, the wisest, as well as the noblest course, would be to seek and apply our remedies in the spirit of considerate and hopeful regard for the future. And surely, even if our final declension were certain, and if we could yet, by our exertions, so retard its progress, that, during the ensuing three hundred years, our condition should be no worse than for the last three hundred years it has been, this were a blessing, and a distinction among the nations of the earth, well worth the best resolves and exertions the nation can bring to the task. When, therefore, we attempt to construct institutions of education for the countless youth of centuries still to come, we enter upon a task full of solicitude and responsibility, but full also of hope and promise. And in this spirit should the office be discharged; all narrow interests, and little jealousies, and limited regards, being laid aside, and the great object itself, the transmission of the best portion of our own culture to the Britons of ages now far removed, being steadily kept in view. With this object we should guard especially against bringing down the standard of our system to the level which transient and partial circumstances, or popular prejudices, may suggest. That education which will secure to the future the civilisation of the past and present, is that which the country really requires; and modes of education which may attract for a moment, but can produce no effect of this kind, are of no value for the real purposes of education, and can satisfy none of the real wants of the age.

But a part of this subject requires a separate section.

Sect. 4.—Of the learned languages as subjects of university teaching

It has appeared in a preceding Section, that the decision of the question, whether our teaching shall be practical or speculative, in the sense already explained, in a great measure decides the subjects taught; since certain subjects only can be made the basis of practical education, and certain other subjects are peculiarly fitted for speculative discussion. But there are some other questions concerning the matter taught, which may be considered here; for instance, the proposal to include in it modern languages and their literature, instead of, or along with, the ancient authors of Greece and Rome; and to introduce the modern sciences, as general physics, chemistry, natural history, and geology, along with pure and mixed mathematics. I will say a word on each of these questions.

It is one of the characters of the present time, alarming to many persons, but, if we use the occasion well, a blessing rather than an evil, that doctrines which have hitherto passed unquestioned, and on which the frame of the institutions of European states is founded, are unscrupulously and rudely assailed. The propriety of the use of what are called the learned languages (Greek and Latin), among the main instruments of education, is a doctrine of this kind. And the question whether, in modern education, these languages are to retain their ancient supremacy,—or whether, on the contrary, the languages and literature of modern Europe are to be placed by their side, or before them,—has been recently discussed with reference to educational institutions, both in this and other countries. In France, for example, this has been the subject of animated debates in the Chamber of Deputies; and that distinguished man of science, M. Arago, is reported, on such an occasion, to have expressed himself to the following effect:—

"I ask for *classical* studies: I require them: I consider them as indispensable; but I do not think that they must necessarily be Greek and Latin. I wish that, in certain schools, these studies should be replaced, at the pleasure of the municipal councils, by a thorough study of our own tongue. I wish that in each college, it should be permitted to put, in the place of Greek and of Latin, the study of a living language. I require even, that this language may be different according to the situation of the place; that at Perpignan and at Bayonne, for example, it may be the Spanish; at le Havre, the English; at Besançon, the German."

He then proceeds to answer certain objections, of which I shall only notice the one which more peculiarly concerns our subject.

"It is urged," he says, "that Greek and Latin must be the principal classical studies, for they are *the true culture of the mind.*"

To this he makes the following reply:—

"What does this mean? Are Pascal, Fenelon, Bossuet, Montesquieu, Rousseau, Voltaire, Corneille, Racine, Molière—the incomparable Molière,—are these writers deprived of the privilege which is so liberally granted to the ancient authors, of enlightening, of unfolding the mind, of touching the heart, of putting in vibration the springs of the soul! God preserve me from insulting you, by refuting in detail a heresy such as this!"

In opposition to the opinion thus expressed, I maintain that Greek and Latin are peculiar and indispensable elements of a liberal education; and it is my business to shew, that the study of the modern authors just enumerated, and of others, however admirable their works may be, does not produce that kind of culture of the mind, which is the true object of a liberal education.

This culture of the mind consists in sharing in the best influences of the progressive intellectual refinement of man. The present age is not independent of those which have preceded it. On the contrary, it is the heir of all the past. Its wealth, intellectual and material, may have been improved in the hands of the present holders, but the value of what we have added is small, compared with the amount of what we found already accumulated. In thought and language, as well as in arts and the products of art, we inherit an inestimable fortune from a long line of ancestors. In literature, we are the children of the early Greeks;

$$Κάὸμου\ τοῦ\ παλαι\ νέα\ τροφή.$$

But thoughts can be inherited, and words, in all their force, transmitted, only by those who are connected with their ancestors in the line of thought and understanding, as well as in the mere succession of time. And how is this connexion of generations, thus requisite to the transmission and augmentation of mental wealth, to be kept up?

The cultivated world, up to the present day, has been bound together, and each generation bound to the preceding, by living upon a common intellectual estate. They have shared in a common developement of thought, because they have understood each other. Their standard examples of poetry, eloquence, history, criticism, grammar, etymology, have been a universal bond of sympathy, however diverse might be the opinions which prevailed respecting any of these examples. All the civilised world has been one intellectual nation; and it is this which has made it so great and pro-sperous a nation. All the countries of lettered Europe have been one body, because the same nutriment, the literature of the ancient world, was con-veyed to all, by the organization of their institutions of education. The authors of Greece and Rome, familiar to the child, admired and dwelt on by the aged, were the common language, by the possession of which each man felt himself a denizen of the community of general civilisation;—free of all the privileges with which it had been gifted from the dawn of Greek liter-ature up to the present time.

What can the best authors of modern days do in the way of filling such an office? Even if their language were universally familiar in cultured Europe, how do they connect us with the past? How do they enable us to read the impress which was stamped upon thought and language in the days of Plato and Aristotle, in virtue of which it is still current? How do they enable us to understand the process by which the language of Rome conveyed the culture, the philosophy, the legislation of the ancient civilised world into the modern? How do they enable us to understand the thoughts and feelings to which they themselves appeal? If the Greek and Latin languages were to lose their familiar place among us, Montesquieu and Bossuet, Corneille and Racine, would lose their force and their charm. Those who read and admire these authors constantly make a reference in their minds to the works of the ancients, which they know immediately or through a few steps of deriva-tion. If this knowledge were taken away, many of the strings would be broken in the instrument on which those artists played. And though, so long as a liberal education continues what it has been, the well-educated diffuse to others a general admiration of the "classical authors" of their own lan-guage; if Greek and Latin were to cease to be parts of general culture, the admiration of the classical authors of England and France would become faint and unintelligent, and, in a few generations, would vanish.

The same may be said of language. The languages of ancient Greece and Rome have, through the whole history of civilisation, been the means of giving distinctness to men's ideas of the analogy of language, which dis-tinctness, as we have seen, is one main element of intellectual cultivation. The forms and processes of general grammar have been conveyed to all men's minds by the use of common models and common examples. To all the nations of modern Europe, whether speaking a Romance language of not, the Latin grammar is a standard of comparison, by reference to which speculative views or grammar become plain and familiar.

And then, as to the derivation of the modern European languages:— Those who are familiar with Greek and Latin cannot but feel, in every sentence they read and write, that the whole history of the civilised world is stamped upon the expressions they use. The progress of thought and of institutions, the most successful labours of the poet, the philosopher, the legislator, have, in thousands of cases, operated to give a meaning to one little word. Those who feel this, have a view of the language which they speak, far more intelligent, far more refined, than those who gather the force of words from blind usage, without seeing any connexion or any reason. What does intellectual culture mean, if it does not mean something more than this? What does it mean, but that insight, that distinctness of thought with regard to the terms we employ, which saves us from solecisms, not by habit but by principle, which shows us analogy where others see only accident, and which makes language itself a chain connecting us with the intellectual progress of all ages.

In what a condition should we be, if our connexion with the past were snapped;—if Greek and Latin were forgotten? What should we then think of our own languages? They would appear a mere mass of incoherent caprice and wanton lawlessness. The several nations of Europe would be, in this respect at least, like those tribes of savages who occupy a vast continent, speaking a set of jargons, in which scarcely any resemblance can be traced between any two, or any consistency in any one. The various European languages appear to us obviously connected, mainly because we hold the Latin thread which runs through them; if that were broken, the pearls would soon roll asunder. And the mental connexion of the present nations with each other, as well as with the past, would thus be destroyed. What would this be but a retrograde movement in civilisation?

In nations as in men, in intellect as in social condition, true nobility consists in inheriting what is best in the possessions and character of a line of ancestry. Those who can trace the descent of their own ideas, and their own language, through the race of cultivated nations; who can show that those whom they represent, or reverence as their parents, have everywhere been foremost in the fields of thought and intellectual progress,—those are the true nobility of the world of mind; the persons who have received true culture; and such it should be the business of a liberal education to make men.

With these views, I cannot conceive it possible that any well-constituted system of University teaching, in any European nation, can do otherwise than make the study of the best classical authors of Greece and Rome, one of its indispensable and cardinal elements. But before I proceed, I cannot refrain from pointing out the evil of making such an element, or any one element alone, too exclusive or too large a part of our system of instruction.

Sect. 5.—Of the necessity of combining classical and mathematical studies as subjects of university teaching

The arguments which we have urged in support of the necessity of the ancient languages as prominent parts of the teaching of our Universities, proceed upon the ground of their usefulness as instruments of mental culture. And this effect has been contemplated, as resulting, not only from the familiarity which the student of classical literature may acquire with the works and style of the brightest periods of ancient civilisation; but also, from the clear views to which he may be led, by such studies, of the principles and history of grammar, language, and literary thought. Now it must not be forgotten, that in classical as in any other literature, the reader who merely flutters through a series of authors such as catch his fancy, who studies them only as a literary amusement, without severe thought, or steady perception of the principles of language and composition, cannot receive from them such a culture as we have supposed; any more than from any other line of reading, suggested and directed by mere caprice and personal taste. Indeed, since principles are disclosed and illustrated by the reading of poets and orators, far more obscurely and vaguely than by most other studies, classical literature so pursued is entirely inefficient for any purpose of genuine mental cultivation. It will only produce a taste, fastidious, indeed, but superficial and arbitrary, without any distinct and developed apprehension of analogies and reasons. And even if the classical authors be studied profoundly and thoroughly, as examples of language, composition, and thought, still they only supply one occasion among many, for the cultivation of the more exact operations of the mind; and in this, or in any other way, the adoption of one instrument alone, for such a purpose, will make the resulting culture extremely partial and deficient. The mode in which this defect may most effectually be remedied, is by combining, with the study of classics, the study of the elementary portions of mathematics. For these severer studies will bring into play that class of intellectual faculties, which the pursuit of elegant literature alone leaves unexercised. We may add, too, that the mental powers so developed will react upon the study of classical authors; and the perception of general relations, of grounds and reasons, even in matters of grammar and taste, will be far more likely to arise in the mind of a student thus disciplined, than in that of the mere elegant scholar. Every person of mathematical cultivation is necessarily an analyst of conditions and connexions: the analytical power thus awakened will commonly exercise itself upon language, as well as upon mathematical quantity; and thus a familiarity with the best models of composition will become such a discipline of distinct ideas, with regard to the principles of language and thought, as, for our purposes, we require it to be.

The study of elementary mathematics, therefore, along with the study of classical authors, ought to be imperatively required by all Universities. To separate these two branches of study, and to allow students to neglect one of them, because some persons have a taste for one, and some persons for the other, is to abdicate the functions of education altogether. Universities and Colleges do not exist merely for the purpose of enabling men to do what they best like to do; or for the purpose of offering and awarding prizes for trials of strength, in modes selected by the combatants. Their business is the general cultivation of all the best faculties of those who are committed to their charge, and the preservation and promotion of the general culture of mankind. And it is certain, that of all the persons who derive advantage from a University education, none are more benefited than those who, with a great general aptitude for learning, are prevented, by the requisitions of such institutions, from confining their exertions to one favourite channel. The man of mathematical genius who, by the demands of his College or his University, is led to become familiar with the best Greek and Latin classics, becomes thus a man of liberal education, instead of being merely a powerful calculator. The elegant classical scholar, who is compelled, in the same way, to master the propositions of geometry and mechanics, acquires among them habits of rigour of thought and connexion of reasoning. He thus becomes fitted to deal with any subject with which reason can be concerned, and to estimate the prospects which science offers; instead of being kept down to the level of the mere scholar, learned in the literature of the past, but illogical and incoherent in his thoughts, and incapable of grappling with the questions which the present and the future suggest. To neglect to demand a combination of these two elements, would be to let slip the only machinery by which Universities, as the general cultivators of the mind, can execute their office.

Sect. 6.—On the sciences as subjects of university teaching

From what has already been said of the use of mathematics in University education, it will easily be inferred, that we cannot find, in any of the more modern physical sciences, any thing that can fitly be substituted for that study. The effect of the clear insight of geometry or mechanics cannot be efficiently replaced by sciences which exhibit a mass of observed facts, and consequent doubtful speculations, as geology; or even by other sciences, as chemistry and natural history, which, though they involve philosophical principles, can only be learnt by presenting numerous facts to the senses. But though such sciences cannot do the work of mental cultivation, they are highly valuable acquisitions to the student, and may very beneficially engage his attention during the later years of his University career. For although they do not constitute the *culture*, they belong to the *information* of the well-educated man; though his habits of thought must be *formed* among other subjects, they may be beneficially *employed* on these. And it is advantageous for the general sympathy and mutual understanding of the cultivated part of mankind, that such persons should have many subjects of common interest.

But we may say much more than this. A considerable general knowledge of the modern progressive sciences, is as requisite to connect the educated man with the future, as a thorough acquaintance with ancient literature is to connect him with the past. Except he know what has been done and is doing, in the way of extending our knowledge of earth, its elements, and its inhabitants, how can he judge what are the probable prospects of our knowledge? And if he be indifferent to this, how can he feel that interest in the future fortunes of his race, which becomes a person of his lofty extraction? Some insight into the progressive sciences is an essential part of a liberal education, in any large sense of the term.

This consideration is in some measure connected with the choice of our course of mathematical reading. For mathematics has been one of the great instruments of the progress of the physical sciences; and the constant use of this instrument, and the efforts to make it more effective, lead to frequent modifications of its form and expansions of its powers; and thus occasion, from time to time, changes in the current system of mathematics. This change, so far as the use of mathematics in education is concerned, is an evil rather than a good: for in our design we do not wish our pupils to possess mathematics principally as information, nor even as an instrument, although in that way it is of great advantage to many persons; but as an intellectual discipline; and this end is best answered by teaching the stable system of a demonstrative science. But at the same time we must recollect, that we cannot give to our mathematical studies their true dignity, without showing the place they hold in the progress of science; and, for the reason which we have mentioned, namely, in order to nourish in our more advanced pupils an interest in that progress, we do not hesitate to introduce to them all new mathematical methods, which have a prominent and permanent importance. But this is salutary to the more advanced pupils only. No deviation from the plain instructive circle of ancient elementary mathematics is fitted for the first stages of the student's University progress. The mode in which his elementary mathematical studies best produce their effect upon him is, when they are presented in the luminous simplicity in which the Greek intellect contemplated them, not when they are disguised and obscured by being translated into the modern language of symbols. To learn this language, (a valuable lesson for the mind, if it be rightly taught,) is best made an ulterior step in the student's advance.

But the physical sciences are useful, not only as belonging to the information of the educated man, but also as supplying him with examples of Inductive Reasoning. The general rules and conditions of such reasoning have hitherto been very imperfectly pointed out; but a knowledge of the sciences gives any one the means of speculating for himself on the subject;— a subject of the strongest interest with reference to the future progress of knowledge. I have already said, that a practical instruction in Inductive Reasoning is not possible, except so far as it depends on the cultivation of the Deductive Faculty. We may lead men to feel the force of demonstration, but we cannot teach them to discover new truths. And I may repeat my observation, that the value of this practical teaching of the reason by means of mathematics may be much enhanced by a proper selection of our mathematical studies;—namely, by not confining ourselves to pure mathematics, and, least of all, to the pure mathematics of symbols. On the subject, considered in this point of view, I, a little while ago, published a few remarks, under the title of "Thoughts on the Study of Mathematics, as a part of a Liberal Education;" and as these remarks may serve to illustrate further what is here said, I reprint them at the end of the present book.

It will be observed, that I intentionally omit, at present, all reference to professional education; and, consequently, to lectures, examinations, and degrees, in Divinity, Medicine, and Law. All such studies should be subsequent to the intellectual culture of which I now speak; and the professions to which these studies belong will derive the greatest part of their real dignity and refinement, from their being built on such a foundation. I omit, also, all consideration of what is called "practical knowledge," such as civil engineering, practical arts and trades, and the like; which are sometimes recommended as useful elements of education. If these are wanted as professional knowledge, they must be learnt, as, in fact, they are learnt, among professional men and practical applications. If they are wished for as information, they stand on the same ground as the higher physical sciences, of which we have spoken above, so far as the arguments there employed are applicable to them. But this "practical knowledge" can never stand in the place of a really liberal education, nor in the smallest degree supersede the necessity of the studies we have pointed out, if such an education be our object.

Sect. 7.—On the moral effect of practical and speculative teaching

Besides the communication to the student of the matter taught, there are certain collateral effects of the two kinds of teaching, which are well worthy of notice. I will speak briefly of a few of these.

Mathematical doctrines are fixed and permanent; no new system of geometry can supersede the old. The old truths will always be true, and always essential. Not only so, but even the old books remain in use. Euclid has never been superseded, and never will be so without great detriment to education. And if Archimedes had written a treatise on Mechanics, in extent and form similar to that of Euclid on Geometry, such a work would probably have been one of our best instruments of education at the present day.

In *philosophical* doctrines, on the contrary, a constant change is going on. The commentator supersedes the original author, or at least becomes equally important: the systematiser is preferred to him who first threw out the same thoughts in a less regular form. Or else a revolution takes place: the old system is refuted; a new one is erected, to last its little hour, and wait its certain doom, like its predecessor. There is nothing old, nothing stable, nothing certain, in this kind of study. Change is constantly taking place; change is constantly looked for. Novelty is essential, in order to command attention or approbation. The ship sails on; old objects glide back; the point of view changes. The student knows, or at least cannot but suspect, that his teacher and his teacher's creed are but for a day; and that what is demonstrated to be true, will be found hereafter to be a truth so imperfect, that it is best put out of sight.

Now I conceive it cannot be doubted that the mind of a young man employed mainly in attending to teachers of this latter kind, must fail to acquire any steady and unhesitating conviction of the immutable and fixed nature of truth, such as the study of mathematics gives. This constant change in the system of received doctrines must unsettle and enfeeble his apprehension of all truths. He has no time, he has no encouragement, to take up the doctrines that are placed before him, and to study them till he is firmly possessed of them, secure that their certainty and value can never alter. He lives among changes, and has not the heart to labour patiently for treasures that may be ravished from him by the next revolution. The state of Germany, for instance, has of late years been as unfavourable to the intellectual welfare of its students, as the condition of the most unstable government of the East is to the material prosperity of its subjects. A great philosophical conquest is made by Kant, and a universal empire is supposed to be on the point of being established. But Fichte, who began with being a follower of Kant, ends by deposing him. Schelling carries away the allegiance of Germany from Fichte; and then Hegel becomes more powerful than any of his predecessors; and a younger Fichte raises the standard against all these rulers. And thus, with dire shedding of ink, revolution after revolution succeeds.

Now amid all this change and fear of change, how can any man eat tranquilly of the fruit of his own field, under his own vine and fig-tree? How can he cultivate his own thoughts, and possess in a tranquil and even spirit the knowledge and the habits of mind which he has acquired? He cannot feel or relish old and familiar truths, such as mathematical sciences deal with. He cannot be content with such conclusions as can be obtained by the way of demonstration. He becomes almost inevitably himself a wide and restless speculator; criticising what has already been done in philosophy; attempting to guess what will be the next step; and destitute, not only of those clear ideas, and those habits of exact thought, through which alone any real advances in knowledge can be appropriated by the student, but devoid also of that steady belief in the permanent nature and value of speculative truth, which is an essential virtue of the understanding.

Again; another mode in which this speculative teaching operates unfavourably, as I conceive, upon students, is this;—it places them in the position of critics instead of pupils. In mathematical and other practical teaching, the teacher is usually, and almost necessarily, much the superior of his scholar in the knowledge which they cultivate together; and the scholar cannot but feel this, and must consequently be led to entertain a docile and confiding disposition towards his instructor. On the other hand, when a system is proposed, as only offering its claims to him, and asking his assent, which he may give or refuse, he feels himself placed in the situation of an equal and a judge, with respect to his professor. And if, as is very likely to be the case with active-minded young speculators, he goes through several phases of philosophical opinion, and gives his allegiance to a succession of teachers, he can hardly fail to look upon them with a self-complacent levity, which involves little of respect. He will probably think of his masters much as the poet speaks of the objects of his transient admiration whom he chronicles:

> The gentle Henrietta then,
> And a third Mary next did reign,
> And Joan, and Jane, and Audria;
> And then a pretty Thomasine,
> And then another Katharine,
> And then a long *et cetera*.

Now this want of docility, confidence, and respect, when it prevails in the student towards his teacher, cannot, I think, be looked upon otherwise than as a highly prejudicial feeling, and one which must destroy much of the value and usefulness of the education thus communicated.

The difference of the subjects which are recommended by different persons as suitable for University teaching, does in fact depend upon an entire difference in the views and temper of the authors of the recommendations. In the teaching of universities, a spirit of *respect*, or a spirit of *criticism*, may be appealed to. According to the first system, we must select subjects which consist of undoubted truths, and works of unquestioned excellence, and must require the student to familiarise himself with these. Such subjects are mathematical studies, and the best classical authors. According to the other system, we take subjects in which we endeavour to draw the student's attention by our mode of treating them, and to carry his conviction with us by our arguments. In this system, we invite him to inquire for himself; to accept or reject according to his best judgment; to examine all doctrines boldly and thoroughly. This *critical* system it is which rejoices to have *philosophy* for its subject, and has shown alike its vigour and its tendency by the rapid succession of prevalent systems.

I do not at all hesitate to say, that the *respectful* system appears to me the proper line of education. I conceive that the student ought to have, placed before him, something which is of a stable and permanent kind;—in which it is a good mental exercise to struggle with the apparent objections, because it is certain that by effort and practice they may be overcome;—and in which it has been ascertained that admiration is not the result of novelty, or of some transient bearing upon the feelings of the age. The *critical* system seems to me to be properly addressed, not to students who are undergoing education, but to philosophers who have already been completely educated. If this course educate a man for anything, it educates him to be a judge of philosophical systems;—an office which so few Englishmen will ever have to fill, that it does not appear wise or reasonable to make it the main object of our education. Nor can I believe, that to put young men in the position in which that system of teaching places them, at a period of their lives when they ought to be quietly forming their minds for future action, can have any other result than to fill them with a shallow conceit of their own importance; to accustom them to deliver superficial and hasty judgments; and to lead them to take up new systems, with no due appreciation of the knowledge, thought, and gravity of mind, which are requisite for such a purpose.

I believe that this opinion of the effect of the two modes of university education has been confirmed by the actual result. The practical education of the English Universities has produced men fitted for practical life. I need not dwell upon this. I have already noticed how well the training of the college appears to prepare men to become good lawyers. I will add, that I conceive our physicians to be the first in the world, and that I ascribe their excellence mainly to the practical course of general culture which they receive in the Universities; which does what no merely professional education can do; and of which the effects are seen, when the professional employments bring into play the intellectual habits. Our clergy derive inestimable advantages from the cast of their university education; and if clerical education among us be capable of improvement, this certainly will not be brought about by the substitution of the philosophy of Schelling and Hegel for the mathematics of Euclid and Newton. That our Universities educate men to be legislators, statesmen, and magistrates of some practical power and skill, no one can doubt, except he who thinks that this little island has, for the last three hundred years, run an unprosperous course, and held an undistinguished place in Europe. For the fortunes of nations are determined, under Providence, by their practical leaders, and men are formed by their education.

In Germany and France, we are told that there prevails among the young men of the Universities a vehement and general hostility to the existing institutions of their country. I know not how truly this is said; but I conceive that such a consequence may naturally flow from an education which invokes the critical spirit, and invites it to employ itself on the comparison between the realities of society and the dreams of system-makers.

I shall not here prosecute this subject further, since my object is to hasten on to some principles which apply more intimately to that process of instruction which has hitherto existed in the English Universities. But I hope I have made it appear that, distinguishing the two systems of education as I have done, we may, with nearly equal propriety, treat of them as *practical* and *speculative* teaching;—or on the one hand *mathematics* combined with *classics*, and on the other *philosophy;*—or *college* lectures, and *professorial* lectures;—and may look upon them as exemplifying a *respectful* and a *critical* spirit. And I hope I have satisfied the reader that (allowing fully the value and use of philosophy and of professorial lectures in their due place, of which I may afterwards speak,) we could not abandon the practical teaching, the mathematical and classical studies, and the College lectures of our Universities, without great loss to the intellectual training of our youth, without destroying highly beneficial feelings which exist between them and their teachers, and without putting in serious and extensive jeopardy the interests of the civilisation of England and of the world.

Notes

1 Lectorum singuli horam in dies singulos quibus legere tenentur in classe suâ examinandâ consumant; dimidiatam vero in authore interpretando. *Stat. Trin. Coll. Cant. cap. 9mo, De Lectorum Officio.*

2 Review of Thoughts on the Study of Mathematics, p. 127.

3 Mechanical Euclid, with Remarks on Mathematical Reasoning, p. 144.

4 On this subject, see the Remarks at the end of the Mechanical Euclid.

5 Thoughts on the Study of Mathematics; reprinted at the end of this volume.

6 Die Lebensfrage der Civilisation; oder: Ueber das Verderben auf den Deutschen Universitäten.

7 History of the Inductive Sciences, from the earliest to the present Times.

8 See The Clouds.

9 See the beginning of Cicero's Offices.

10 Harum scientiarum porta et clavis est mathematica, quam sancti a principio mundi invenerunt, etc.—Roger Bacon, Specula Mathematica, cap. i.

11 See Hegel's Encyclopædia, and Schelling's Lectures.

12 History of the Inductive Sciences, Book VI. chap. i. sect. 2.

13 Partly for the reasons here suggested, I have published a work on Elementary Mechanics (The Mechanical Euclid), such as I hope may fit that branch of knowledge for taking its due place in education by the side of geometry.

75

CHRISTIANITY AND SCIENTIFIC INVESTIGATION

A lecture[1]

John Henry Newman

Source: John Henry Newman *Discourses on the Scope and Nature of University Education*, London: Dent, 1915, pp. 235–59. Originally published 1852.

This is a time, Gentlemen, when not only the Classics, but much more the Sciences, in the largest sense of the word, are looked upon with anxiety, not altogether ungrounded, by religious men, and, whereas, a University such as ours professes to embrace all departments and exercises of the intellect, and since I for my part wish to stand on good terms with all kinds of knowledge, and have no intention of quarrelling with any, and would open my heart, if not my intellect (for that is beyond me) to the whole circle of truth, and would tender at least a recognition and hospitality even to those studies which are strangers to me, and would speed them on their way; therefore, as I have already been making overtures of reconciliation, first between Polite Literature and Religion, and next between Physics and Theology, so I would now say a word by way of deprecating and protesting against the needless antagonism, which sometimes exists in fact, between divines and the cultivators of the Sciences generally.

Here I am led at once to expatiate on the grandeur of an institution which is comprehensive enough to admit the discussion of a subject such as this. Among the objects of human enterprise,—I may say it surely without extravagance, Gentlemen,—none higher or nobler can be named, than that which is contemplated in the erection of a University. To set on foot and to maintain in life and vigour a real University, is confessedly, as soon as the word "University" is understood, one of those greatest works, great in their difficulty and their importance, on which are deservedly expended the rarest intellects and the most varied endowments. For, first of all, it professes to teach whatever has to be taught in any whatever department of human

29

knowledge, and it embraces in its scope the loftiest subjects of human thought, and the richest fields of human inquiry. Nothing is too vast, nothing to subtle, nothing too distant, nothing too minute, nothing too discursive, nothing too exact, to engage its attention.

This, however, is not why I claim for it so sovereign a position; for, to bring schools of all knowledge under one name, and call them a University, may be fairly said to be a mere generalisation; and to proclaim that the prosecution of all kinds of knowledge to their utmost limits demands the fullest reach and range of our intellectual faculties, is but a truism. My reason for speaking of a University in the terms on which I have ventured, is, not that it occupies the whole territory of knowledge merely, but that it is the very realm; that it professes much more than to take in and to lodge as in a caravanserai, all art and science, all history and philosophy. In truth, it professes to assign to each study, which it receives, its own proper place and its just boundaries; to define the rights, to establish the mutual relations, and to effect the intercommunion of one and all; to keep in check the ambitious and encroaching, and to succour and maintain those which from time to time are succumbing under the more popular or the more fortunately circumstanced; to keep the peace between them all, and to convert their mutual differences and contrarieties into the common good. This, Gentlemen, is why I say that to erect a University is at once so arduous and beneficial an undertaking, viz., because it is pledged to admit without fear, without prejudice, without compromise, all comers, if they come in the name of Truth; to adjust views, and experiences, and habits of mind the most independent and dissimilar; and to give full play to thought and erudition in their most original forms, and their most intense expressions, and in their most ample circuit. Thus to draw many things into one, is its special function; and it learns to do it, not by rules reducible to writing, but by sagacity, wisdom, and forbearance, acting upon a profound insight into the subject-matter of knowledge, and a vigilant repression of aggression or bigotry in any quarter.

We count it a great thing, and justly so, to plan and carry out a wide political organisation. To bring under one yoke, after the manner of old Rome, a hundred discordant peoples; to maintain each of them in its own privileges within its legitimate range of action; to allow them severally the indulgence of national feelings, and the stimulus of rival interests; and yet withal to blend them into one great social establishment, and to pledge them to the perpetuity of the one imperial power;—this is an achievement which carries with it the unequivocal token of genius in the race which effects it.

"Tu regere imperio populos, Romane, memento."

This was the special boast, as the poet considered it, of the Roman; a boast as high in its own line, as that other boast, proper to the Greek nation, of literary pre-eminence, of exuberance of thought, and of skill and refinement in expressing it.

What an empire is in political history, such is a University in the sphere of philosophy and science. It is, as I have said, the high protecting power of all knowledge and science, of fact and principle, of inquiry and discovery, of experiment and speculation; it maps out the territory of the intellect, and sees that the boundaries of each provinces are religiously respected, and that there is neither encroachment nor surrender on any side. It acts as umpire between truth and truth, and, taking into account the nature and import- ance of each, assigns to all their due order and precedence. It maintains no one department of thought exclusively, however ample and noble; and it sacrifices none. It is deferential and loyal, according to their respective weight, to the claims of literature, of physical research, of history, of metaphysics, of theological science. It is impartial towards them all, and promotes each in its own place and for its own object. It is ancillary, certainly, and of neces- sity, to the Catholic Church; but in the same way that one of the Queen's judges is an officer of the Queen's, and nevertheless determines certain legal proceedings between the Queen and her subjects. It is ministrative to the Catholic Church, first, because truth of any kind can but minister to truth; and next, still more, because Nature ever will pay homage to Grace, and Reason cannot but illustrate and defend Revelation; and thirdly, because the Church has a sovereign authority, and when she speaks *ex cathedra*, must be obeyed. But this is the remote end of a University; its immediate end (with which alone we have here to do) is to secure the due disposition, according to one sovereign order, and the cultivation in that order, of all the provinces and methods of thought which the human intellect has created.

In this point of view, its several professors are like the representatives of various political powers at one court or conference. They represent their respective sciences, and attend to their private interests respectively; and, should dispute arise between those sciences, they are the persons to talk over and arrange it, without risk of extravagant pretensions on any side, of angry collision, or of popular commotion. A liberal philosophy becomes the habit of minds thus exercised; a spaciousness of thought, in which lines, seemingly parallel, may converge at leisure, and principles, recognised as incommeasurable, may be safely antagonistic.

And here, Gentlemen, we recognise the special character of the Philosophy I am speaking of, if Philosophy it is to be called, in contrast with the method of a strict science or system. Its teaching is not founded on one idea, or reducible to certain formulæ. Newton might discover the great law of motion in the physical world, and the key to ten thousand phenomena; and a similar resolution of complex facts into simple principles may be possible in other departments of nature; but the great Universe itself, moral and material, sensible and supernatural, cannot be gauged and meted by even the greatest

31

of human intellects, and its constituent parts admit indeed of comparison and adjustment, but not of fusion. This is the point which bears directly on the subject which I set before me when I began, and towards which I am moving in all I have said or shall be saying. I observe then, and ask you, Gentlemen, to bear in mind, that the philosophy of an imperial intellect, for such I am considering a University to be, is based, not so much on simplification, as on discrimination. Its true representative defines, rather than analyses. He aims at no complete catalogue or interpretation of the subjects of knowledge, but at following out, as far as man can, what in its fulness is mysterious and unfathomable. Taking into its charge all sciences, methods, collections of facts, principles, doctrines, truths, which are the reflexions of the universe upon the human intellect, he admits them all, he disregards none, and, as disregarding none, he allows none to exceed or encroach. His watchword is, Live and let live. He takes things as they are; he submits to them all, as far as they go; he recognises the insuperable lines of demarcation which run between subject and subject; he observes how separate truths lie relatively to each other, where they concur, where they part company, and where, being carried too far, they cease to be truths at all. It is his office to determine how much can be known in each province of thought; when we must be contented not to know; in what direction inquiry is hopeless, or on the other hand full of promise; where it gathers into coils insoluble by reason, where it is absorbed in mysteries, or runs into the abyss. It will be his care to be familiar with the signs of real and apparent difficulties, with the methods proper to particular subject-matters, what in each particular case are the limits of a rational scepticism, and what the claims of a peremptory faith. If he has one cardinal maxim in his philosophy, it is, that truth cannot be contrary to truth; if he has a second, it is, that truth often *seems* contrary to truth; and, if a third, it is the practical conclusion, that we must be patient with such appearances, and not be hasty to pronounce them to be really of a more formidable character.

It is the very immensity of the system of things, the human record of which he has in charge, which is the reason of this patience and caution; for that immensity suggests to him, that the contrarities and mysteries, which meet him in the various sciences, may be simply the consequence of our necessarily defective comprehension. There is but one thought greater than the universe, and that is the thought of its Maker. If, Gentlemen, for one single instant, leaving my proper train of thought, I allude to our knowledge of the Supreme Being, it is in order to deduce an illustration bearing upon it. He, though One, is a sort of world of worlds in Himself, giving birth in our minds to an indefinite number of distinct truths, each ineffably more mysterious than anything that is found in this universe of space and time. Any one of His attributes, considered by itself, is the object of an inexhaustible science; and the attempt to reconcile any two or three of them together,—love, power, justice, sanctity, truth, wisdom,—affords matter for an everlasting controversy. We are able to apprehend and receive each divine attribute in its elementary form, but still we are not able to accept them in their infinity, either in themselves or in union with each other. Yet we do not deny the first, because it cannot be perfectly reconciled with the second, nor the second, because it is in apparent contrariety with the first and the third. The case is the same in its degree with His creation, material and moral. It is the highest wisdom to accept truth of whatever kind, wherever it is clearly ascertained to be such, though there be difficulty in adjusting it with other known truth.

Instances are easily producible of that extreme contrariety of ideas, which the contemplation of the Universe inflicts upon us, such, as to make it clear to us that there is nothing irrational in submitting to apparent incompatibilities in that teaching which we have no thought on that account of denying, Such, for instance, is the contemplation of Space; the existence of which we cannot deny, though its idea is able, in no sort of posture, to seat itself (if I may so speak) in our minds;—for we find it impossible to say that it comes to a stop anywhere; and it is incomprehensible to say that it runs out infinitely; and it seems to be unmeaning, if we say, that it does not exist till bodies come into it, and thus is enlarged according to the accident.

And so again in the instance of Time. We cannot place a beginning to it without asking ourselves what was before it; yet that there should be no beginning at all, put it as far off as we will, is simply incomprehensible. Here again, as in the case of Space, we never dream of denying the existence of what we have no means of understanding.

And, passing from this high region of thought (which, high as it may be, is the subject even of a child's contemplations) when we come to consider the mutual action of soul and body, we are specially perplexed by incompatibilities which we can neither reject nor explain. How it is that the will can act on the muscles, is a question of which even a child may feel the force, but which no experimentalist can answer.

Further, when we contrast the physical with the social laws under which man finds himself here below, we must grant that Physiology and Social Science are in collision. Man is both a physical and a social being; yet he cannot at once pursue to the full his physical end and his social end, his physical duties (if I may so speak) and his social duties, but is forced to sacrifice in part one or the other. If we were wild enough to fancy that there were two creators, one of whom was the author of our animal frames, the other of society, then indeed we might understand how it comes to pass that labour of mind and body, the useful arts, the duties of a statesman, government, and the like, which are required by the social system, are so destructive of health, enjoyment, and life. That is, in other words, we cannot adequately account for existing and undeniable truths except on the hypothesis of what we feel to be an absurdity.

33

And so in Mathematical Science, as has been often insisted on, the philosopher has patiently to endure the presence of truths, which are not the less true for being irreconcilable with each other. He is told of the existence of an infinite number of curves, which are able to divide a space, into which no straight line, though it be length without breadth, can even enter. He is told too of certain lines, which approach to each other continually, with a finite distance between them, yet never meet; and these apparent contrarieties he must bear as he best can, without attempting to deny the existence of the truths which constitute them in the Science in question.

Now, let me call your attention, Gentlemen, to what I would infer from these familiar facts. It is, to urge you with an argument *à fortiori:* viz., that, as you exercise so much exemplary patience in the case of the inexplicable truths which surround so many departments of knowledge, human and divine, viewed in themselves; as you are not at once indignant, censorious, suspicious, difficult of belief, on finding that in the secular sciences one truth is incompatible (according to our human intellect) with another or inconsistent with itself; so you should not think it very hard to be told that there exists, here and there, not an inextricable difficulty, not an astounding contrariety, not (much less) a contradiction as to clear facts, between Revelation and Nature; but a hitch, an obscurity, a divergence of tendency, a temporary antagonism, a difference of tone between the two,—that is, between Catholic opinion on the one hand, and astronomy, or geology, or physiology, or ethnology, or political economy, or history, or antiquities, on the other. I say, that, as we admit, because we are Catholics, that the Divine Unity contains in it attributes, which, to our finite minds, appear in partial contrariety with each other; as we admit that, in His revealed Nature, are things, which, though not opposed to Reason, are infinitely strange to the Imagination; as in His works we can neither reject nor admit the ideas of space, and of time, and the necessary properties of lines, without intellectual distress; really, Gentlemen, I am making no outrageous request, when, in the name of a University, I ask religious writers, jurists, economists, physiologists, chemists, geologists, and historians, to go on quietly, and in a neighbourly way, in their own respective lines of speculation, research, and experiment, with full faith in the consistency of that multiform truth, which they share between them, in a generous confidence that they will be consistent, one and all, in their combined results, though there may be momentary collisions, awkward appearances, and many forebodings and prophecies of contrariety, and at all times things hard to the Imagination, though not, I repeat, to the Reason. It surely needs no great boldness to beg of them,— since they are forced to admit mysteries, even in the actual issue itself, in the truths of Revelation, taken by themselves, and in the truths of Reason, taken by themselves,—to beg of them, I say, to keep the peace, to live in good will, and to exercise equanimity, if, when Nature and Revelation are compared with each other, there be, as I have said, discrepancies,—not in

34

the issue, but in the reasonings, the circumstances, the associations, the anticipations, the accidents, proper to their respective teachings.

It is most necessary to insist seriously and energetically on this point, for the sake of Protestants, for they have very strange notions about us. In spite of the testimony of history the other way, they think that the Church has no other method of putting down error than the arm of force or the prohibition of inquiry. They defy us to set up and carry on a School of Science. For their sake, then, I am led to enlarge upon the subject here. I say then, he who believes Revelation with that absolute faith which is the prerogative of a Catholic, is not the nervous creature who startles at every sudden sound, and is fluttered by every strange or frightful appearance which meets his eyes. He has no sort of apprehension, he laughs at the idea, that anything can be discovered by any other scientific method, which can contradict any one of the dogmas of his religion. He knows full well, that there is no science, but, in the course of its extension, runs the risk of infringing, without any meaning of offence on its own part, the path of other sciences: and he knows also, that, if there be any one science which, from its sovereign and unassailable position, can calmly bear such unintentional collisions on the part of the children of earth, it is Theology. He is sure, and nothing shall make him doubt, that, if anything seems to be proved by astronomer, or geologist, or chronologist, or antiquarian, or ethnologist, in contradiction to the dogmas of faith, that point will eventually turn out, first, *not* to be proved, or, secondly, not *contradictory*, or thirdly, not contradictory to anything *really revealed*, but to something which has been confused with Revelation. And if, at the moment, it appears to be contradictory, then he is content to wait, knowing that error is like other delinquents; give it rope enough, and it will be found to have a strong suicidal propensity. I do not mean to say he will not take his part in encouraging, in helping forward the prospective suicide; he will not only give the error rope enough, but show it how to handle and adjust the rope;—he will commit the matter to reason, reflection, sober judgment, common sense; to Time, the great interpreter of so many secrets. Instead of being irritated at the momentary triumph of the foes of Revelation, if such a feeling of triumph there be, and of hurrying on a forcible solution of the difficulty, which may in the event only reduce the inquiry to an inextricable tangle, he will recollect that, in the order of Providence, our seeming dangers are often our greatest gains; that in the words of the Protestant poet,

> The clouds you so much dread
> Are big with mercy, and shall break
> In blessings on your head.

To one notorious instance indeed it is obvious to allude here. When the Copernician system first made progress, what religious man would not have been tempted to uneasiness, or at least fear of scandal, from the seeming contradiction which it involved to some authoritative tradition of the Church and the declaration of Scripture? It was generally received, as if the Apostles had expressly delivered it both orally and in writing, that the earth was stationary, and that the sun was fixed in a solid firmament which whirled round the earth. After a little time, however, and on full consideration, it was found that the Church had decided next to nothing on questions such as these, and that Physical Science might range in this sphere of thought almost at will, without fear of encountering the decisions of ecclesiastical authority. Now, besides the relief which it afforded to Catholics to find that they were to be spared this addition, on the side of Cosmology, to their many controversies already existing, there is something of an argument in this circumstance in behalf of the divinity of their Religion. For it surely is a very remarkable fact, considering how widely and how long one certain interpretation of these physical statements in Scripture had been received by Catholics, that the Church should not have formally acknowledged it. Looking at the matter in a human point of view, it was inevitable that she should have made that opinion her own. But now we find, on ascertaining where we stand, in the face of the new sciences of these latter times, that, in spite of the bountiful comments which from the first she has ever been making on the sacred text, as it is her duty and her right to do, nevertheless she has never been led formally to explain the texts in question, or to give them an authoritative sense which modern science may question.

Nor was this escape a mere accident, or what will more religiously be called a providential event, as is shown by a passage of history in the dark age itself. When the glorious St. Boniface, Apostle of Germany, great in sanctity, though not in secular knowledge, complained to the Holy See that St. Virgilius taught the existence of the Antipodes, the Holy See apparently evaded the question, not indeed siding with the Irish philosopher, which would have been going out of its place, but passing over, in a matter not revealed, a philosophical opinion.

Time went on; a new state of things, intellectual and social, came in; the Church was girt with temporal power; the preachers of St. Dominic were in the ascendant: now at length we may ask with curious interest, did the Church alter her ancient rule of action, and proscribe intellectual activity? Just the contrary; this is the very age of Universities; it is the classical period of the schoolmen; it is the splendid and palmary instance of the wise policy and large liberality of the Church; as regards philosophical inquiry. If there ever was a time when the intellect went wild, and had a licentious revel, it was at the date I speak of. When was there ever a more curious, more meddling, bolder, keener, more penetrating, more rationalistic exercise of the reason than at that time? What class of questions did that subtle, metaphysical spirit not scrutinise? What premiss was allowed without examination? What principle was not traced to its first origin, and exhibited in its most naked shape? What whole was not analysed? What complex idea was not elaborately traced out, and, as it were, finely painted for the contemplation of the mind, till it was spread out in all its minutest portions as perfectly and delicately as a frog's foot shows under the intense scrutiny of the microscope? Well, I repeat, here was something which came somewhat nearer to Theology than physical research comes; Aristotle was a somewhat more serious foe then, beyond all mistake, than Bacon has been since. Did the Church take a high hand with philosophy then? No, not though it was metaphysical. It was a time when she had temporal power, and could have exterminated the spirit of inquiry with fire and sword; but she determined to put it down by *argument;* she said: "Two can play at that, and my argument is the better." She sent her controversialists into the philosophical arena. It was the Dominican and Franciscan doctors, the greatest of them being St. Thomas, who in those mediæval Universities fought the battle of Revelation with the weapons of heathenism. It was no matter whose the weapon was; truth was truth all the world over. With the jawbone of an ass, with the skeleton philosophy of pagan Greece, did the Samson of the schools put to flight his thousand Philistines.

Here, Gentlemen, observe the contrast exhibited by the Church herself, who has the gift of wisdom, and even the ablest, or wisest, or holiest of her children. As St. Boniface had been jealous of physical speculations, so had the early Fathers shown an extreme aversion to the great heathen philosopher whom I just now named, Aristotle. I do not know who of them could endure him; and, when there arose those in the middle age who would take his part, especially since their intentions were of a suspicious character, a strenuous effort was made to banish him out of Christendom. The Church the while had kept silence; she had as little denounced heathen philosophy in the mass, as she had pronounced upon the meaning of certain texts of Scripture of a cosmological character. From Tertullian and Caius to the two Gregories of Cappadocia, from them to Anastasius Sinaita, from him to the school of Paris, Aristotle was a word of offence; at length St. Thomas made him a hewer of wood and drawer of water to the Church. A strong slave he is; and the Church herself has given her sanction to the use in Theology of the ideas and terms of his philosophy.

Now, while this free discussion is, to say the least, so safe for Religion, or rather so expedient, it is on the other hand simply necessary for progress in Science; and I shall now go on to insist on this side of the subject. I say, then, that it is a matter of primary importance in the cultivation of those sciences, in which truth is discoverable by the human intellect, that the investigator should be free, independent, unshackled in his movements; that he should be allowed and enabled, without impediment, to fix his mind intently, nay exclusively, on his special object, without the risk of being distracted every other minute in the process and progress of his inquiry, by charges of temerariousness, or by warnings against extravagance

37

or scandal. But in thus speaking, I must premise several explanations, lest I be mistaken.

First, then, Gentlemen, as to the fundamental principles of religion and morals, and again as to the fundamental principles of Christianity, or what are called the *dogmas* of faith,—as to this double creed, natural and revealed,—we, none of us, should say that it is any shackle at all upon the intellect to maintain these inviolate. Indeed, a Catholic cannot help having regard to them; and they as little impede the movements of his intellect, as the laws of physics impede his bodily movements. The habitual apprehension of them has become a second nature with him, as the laws of optics, hydrostatics, motion, dynamics, are latent conditions which he takes for granted in the use of his corporeal organs. I am not supposing any collision with dogma, I am but speaking of opinions of divines, or of the multitude, parallel to those in former times of the sun going round the earth, or of the last day being close at hand, or of St. Dionysius the Areopagite being the author of the works which bear his name.

Nor, secondly, even as regards such opinions, am I supposing any direct intrusion into the province of religion, or of a teacher of Science actually laying down the law *in a matter of Religion;* but of such unintentional collisions as are incidental to a discussion pursued on some subject of his own. It would be a great mistake in such a one to propose his philosophical or historical conclusions as the formal interpretation of the sacred text, as Galileo is said to have done, instead of being content to hold his doctrine of the motion of the earth as a scientific conclusion, and leaving it to those whom it really concerned to compare it with Scripture. And, it must be confessed, Gentlemen, not a few instances occur of this mistake at the present day, on the part, not indeed of men of science, but of religious men, who, from a nervous impatience lest Scripture should for one moment seem inconsistent with the results of some speculation of the hour, are ever proposing geological or ethnological comments upon it, which they have to alter or obliterate before the ink is well dry, from changes in the progressive science, which they have so officiously brought to its aid.

And thirdly, I observe, that, when I advocate the independence of philosophical thought, I am not speaking of any *formal teaching* at all, but of investigations, speculations, and discussions. I am far indeed from allowing, in any matter which even borders on religion, what an eminent Protestant divine has advocated on the most sacred subjects: I mean "the liberty of Prophesying." I have no wish to degrade the professors of Science, who ought to be Prophets of the Truth, into mere advertisers of crude fancies or notorious absurdities. I am not pleading that they should at random shower down upon their hearers ingenuities and novelties; or that they should teach even what has a basis of truth in it, in a brilliant, offhand way, to a collection of youths, who may not perhaps hear them for six consecutive lectures, and who will carry away with them into the country a misty idea of the half-created theories of some ambitious intellect.

Once more, as the last sentence suggests, there must be great care taken to avoid *scandal*, or of shocking the popular mind, or of unsettling the weak; the association between truth and error being so strong in particular minds, that it is impossible to weed them of the error, without rooting up the wheat with it. If then there is the chance of any current religious opinion being in any way compromised in the course of a scientific investigation, this would be a reason for conducting it, not in light ephemeral publications, which come into the hands of the careless or ignorant, but in works of a grave and business-like character, answering to the mediæval schools of philosophical disputation, which, removed as they were from the region of popular thought and feeling, have, by their vigorous restlessness of inquiry, in spite of their extravagances, done so much for theological precision.

I am not then supposing the scientific investigator to be *coming into collision with dogma;* nor venturing, by means of his investigations, upon any interpretation of Scripture or upon other *conclusion in the matter of religion;* nor *teaching* even in his own science, instead of investigating; nor to be careless of *scandalising the weak;* but, these explanations being made, I still say, that a scientific speculator or inquirer is not bound, in the course of his researches, to be every moment adjusting his course by the maxims of the schools or by popular traditions, or by those of any other science distinct from his own, or to be ever narrowly watching what those external sciences have to say to him; being confident, from a generous faith, that, however his line of investigation may swerve now and then, and vary to and fro in its course, or threaten momentary collision or embarrassment with any other department of knowledge, theological or not, yet, if he lets it alone, it will be sure to come home, because truth never can really be contrary to truth, and because often what at first sight is an *exceptio*, in the event most emphatically *probat regulam*.

This is a point of serious importance to him. Unless he is at liberty to investigate on the basis, and according to the peculiarities, of his science, he cannot investigate at all. It is the very law of the human mind in its inquiry after and acquisition of truth, to make its advances by a process which consists of many stages, and is circuitous. There are no short cuts to knowledge; nor does the road to it always lie in the direction in which it terminates, nor are we able to see the end on starting. It may often seem to be diverging from a goal into which it will soon run without effort, if we are but patient and resolute in following it out; and, as we are told in ethics to gain the mean merely by receding from both extremes, so in scientific researches error may be said, without a paradox, to be in some instances the way to truth and the only way. Moreover, it is not often the fortune of any one man to live through an investigation; the process is one of not only many stages, but of many minds. What one begins, another finishes; and a true conclusion is at length worked out by the co-operation of independent schools and the perseverance of successive generations. This being the case, we are obliged, under circumstances, to bear for a while with what we feel to be error, in consideration of the truth in which it is eventually to issue.

The analogy of locomotion is most pertinent here. No one can go straight up a mountain; no sailing vessel makes for its port without tacking. And so, applying the illustration, we can indeed, if we will, refuse to allow of investigation or research altogether; but, if we invite reason to take its place in our schools, we must let reason have fair and full play. If we reason, we must submit to the conditions of reason. We cannot use it by halves; we must use it as proceeding from Him who has also given us Revelation; and to be ever interrupting its processes, and diverting its attention by objections brought from a higher knowledge, is parallel to a landsman's dismay at the changes in the course of a vessel on which he has deliberately embarked, and argues surely some distrust either in the powers of Reason on the one hand, or the certainty of Revealed Truth on the other. The passenger should not have embarked at all, if he did not reckon on the chance of a rough sea, of currents, of wind and tide, of rocks and shoals; and we should act more wisely in discountenancing altogether the exercise of Reason, than in being alarmed and impatient under the suspense, delay, and anxiety which, from the nature of the case, may be found to attach to it. Let us eschew secular history, and science, and philosophy for good and all, if we are not allowed to be sure that Revelation is so true, that the altercations and perplexities of human opinion cannot really or eventually injure its authority. That is no intellectual triumph of any truth of Religion, which has not been preceded by a full statement of what can be said against it; it is but the *ego vapulando, ille verberando*, of the Comedy.

Great minds need elbow-room, not indeed in the domain of faith, but of thought. And so indeed do lesser minds, and all minds. There are many persons in the world, who are called, and with a great deal of truth, geniuses. They had been gifted by nature with some particular faculty or capacity; and, while vehemently excited and imperiously ruled by it, they are blind to everything else. They are enthusiasts in their own line, and are simply dead to the beauty of any line *except* their own. Accordingly, they think their own line the only line in the whole world worth pursuing, and they feel a sort of contempt for such studies as move upon any other line. Now, these men may be, and often are, very good Catholics, and have not a dream of anything but affection and deference towards Catholicity, nay perhaps are zealous in its interests. Yet, if you insist, that in their speculations, researches, or conclusions in their particular science, it is not enough that they should submit to the Church generally, and acknowledge its dogmas, but that they must get up all that divines have said, or the multitude believed upon religious matters, you simply crush and stamp out the flame within them, and they can do nothing at all.

This is the case of men of genius: now one word on the contrary in behalf of master minds, gifted with a broad philosophical view of things, and a creative power, and a versatility capable of accommodating itself to various provinces of thought. These persons, perhaps, like those I have already spoken of, take up some idea and are intent upon it;—some deep, prolific, eventful idea, which grows upon them, till they develop it into a great system. Now, if any such thinker starts from radically unsound principles, or aims at directly false conclusions, if he be a Hobbes, or a Shaftesbury, or a Hume, or a Bentham, then, of course, there is an end of the whole matter. He is an opponent of Revealed Truth, and he means to be so;—nothing more need be said. But perhaps it is not so; perhaps his errors are those which are inseparable accidents of his system or of his mind, and are spontaneously evolved, not pertinaciously defended. Every human system, every human writer, is open to just criticism. Make him shut up his portfolio; good! and then perhaps you lose what, on the whole and in spite of incidental mistakes, would have been one of the ablest defences of Revealed Truth (directly or indirectly, according to his subject) ever given to the world.

This is how I should account for a circumstance, which has sometimes caused surprise, that so many great Catholic thinkers have in some points or other incurred the criticism or animadversion of theologians or of ecclesiastical authority. It must be so in the nature of things; there is indeed an animadversion which implies a condemnation of the author; but there is another which means not much more than the *piè legendum* written against passages in the Fathers. The author may not be to blame; yet the ecclesiastical authority would be to blame, if it did not give notice of his imperfections. I do not know what Catholic would not hold the name of Malebranche in veneration; but he may have accidentally come into collision with theologians, or made temerarious assertions, notwithstanding. The practical question is, whether he had not much better have written as he has written, than not have written at all. And so fully is the Holy See accustomed to enter into this view of the matter, that it has allowed of its application, not only to philosophical, but even to theological and ecclesiastical authors, who do not come within the range of these remarks. I believe I am right in saying, that, in the case of three great names, in various departments of learning, Cardinal Noris, Bossuet, and Muratori, while not concealing its sense of their each having propounded what might have been said better, nevertheless it has considered that their services to Religion were on the whole far too important to allow of their being molested by critical observation in detail.

And now, Gentlemen, I bring these remarks to a conclusion. What I would urge upon every one, whatever may be his particular line of research,—what I would urge upon men of Science in their thoughts of Theology,—what I would venture to recommend to theologians, when their attention is drawn to the subject of scientific investigations,—is a great and firm belief in the sovereignty of Truth. Error may flourish for a time, but Truth will prevail in the end. The only effect of error ultimately is to promote Truth. Theories, speculations, hypotheses, are started; perhaps they are to die, still not before they have suggested ideas better than themselves. These better ideas are taken up in turn by other men, and, if they do not yet lead to truth, nevertheless they lead to what is still nearer to truth than themselves; and thus knowledge on the whole makes progress. The errors of some minds in scientific investigation are more fruitful than the truths of others. A Science seems making no progress, but to abound in failures, yet imperceptibly all the time it is advancing, and it is of course a gain to truth, even to have learned what is not true, if nothing more.

On the other hand, it must be of course remembered. Gentlemen, that I am supposing all along good faith, honest intentions, a loyal Catholic spirit, and a deep sense of responsibility. I am supposing, in the scientific inquirer, a due fear of giving scandal, of seeming to countenance views which he does not really countenance and of siding with parties from whom he heartily differs. I am supposing that he is fully alive to the existence and the power of the infidelity of the age; that he keeps in mind the moral weakness and the intellectual confusion of the majority of men; and that he has no wish at all that any one soul should get harm from certain speculations to-day, though he may have the satisfaction of being sure that those speculations will, as far as they are erroneous or misunderstood be corrected in the course of the next half century.

Note

1 This Lecture, which was never delivered, was addressed to the School of Science.

THE NEED FOR THE STUDY
OF PHILOSOPHY

R. W. Livingstone

Source: R. W. Livingstone, *Education and the Spirit of the Age*, Oxford: Clarendon Press, 1952, pp. 22–39.

> Whatever the world thinks, he who hath not much meditated upon
> God, the human mind and the Summum Bonum, may possibly
> make a thriving earthworm, but will certainly make a sorry patriot
> and a sorry statesman.
>
> Bishop Berkeley

Intellectual and spiritual disorder, and, in its train, a creeping paralysis of moral standards, as the beliefs that in the past created and supported them grow progressively weaker—so one might diagnose the sickness of our generation. It affects international relations as well as the individual life, for with the loss of its fundamental beliefs a civilization loses cohesion. Till recently a common belief, varying in detail but fundamentally the same, underpinned the peoples of Western civilization. Today they have to build their co-operation on the shifting sands of self-interest and on the remains of an historic tradition. I suggested in my last chapter that the agencies which have contributed most to our condition are rationalism and liberalism; a rationalism which destroys and does not construct and a liberalism divorced from any guiding purpose. What is the prognosis for the patient? Can we form any idea how things will develop?

We may note that our predicament is not new. It is not the first time in history that new ways of thought have shaken or shattered current views of life. Certain ages—the fifth century B.C. in Greece, the Renaissance in Europe, are obvious examples—develop an intense activity of thought, and its impact strikes violently on traditional beliefs and accepted standards and throws them into confusion. A revolution breaks out. In the intellectual and spiritual, as in the political sphere, revolutions follow the same

43

course. At first everything is in disarray; the old order seems destroyed, the familiar landmarks disappear in the storm; 'men's hearts fail for fear and for expectation of the things which are coming on the earth'. Then gradually the storm subsides. After it things are different but the changes, however considerable, are far less fundamental than they seemed at first, for the human mind comes to terms with them and imposes its natural rhythms on life. So no doubt it will be with us. Liberty and reason, which are mainly responsible for our disorders, are in themselves wholly admirable. There is no occasion for despair; what has happened to us has happened before, and some light may be thrown on our problem by an age which had an experience closely parallel to our own. How parallel the following passages taken from its literature show.

Here is agnosticism. 'I cannot determine whether the gods do or do not exist, or what is their character: there are many obstacles to such knowledge —the obscurity of the subject and the shortness of human life.' Here is relativism. 'Man is the measure of all things.'[1] 'There are no such things as beauty and ugliness, justice and injustice: and so in general—nothing has an absolute existence: convention and habit determine human conduct: no single thing is this rather than that.'[2]

Here is a materialist theory of the universe.

Fire and water, and earth and air, owe their existence to nature or chance, and not to design; and the bodies which come next in order—earth, sun, moon, stars—have been created by means of these absolutely soulless agents, which drifted together accidentally, following their own natural laws, and produced all the heavens and their contents, and in due course, animals and plants. Neither Mind, nor God had anything to do with it: it was the work of nature and chance alone. Art, the subsequent and late-born product of these causes, herself as perishable as her creators, has since produced certain toys, with little real substance in them, such as music and painting and their companion arts. The only arts which produce anything of serious value are those which co-operate with nature, such, for example, as medicine, gymnastic and agriculture. Politics has something in common with nature, but is mainly artificial; while legislation is entirely so, and is based on assumptions which are not true. As for the Gods, they have no natural or real existence, but are artificial, conventional creations and vary from place to place, according to the convention which established them. There is no such thing as natural justice: but men are always disputing about justice and altering it; and the alterations which are made by art and by law have no basis in nature, but are valid only for the moment and at the time at which they are made.[3]

Here are power politics. 'Justice is no more than the interests of the stronger party.'[4] 'You know and we know that the question of justice only arises between disputants equal in strength, and that the strong do what they can and the weak submit.'[5]

> Laws are made by the masses who are weak, and in what their laws praise or censure they have themselves and their own interests in mind. So the attempt to get the better of the masses and keep them in their place is called injustice. But Nature herself indicates that it is just for the better and the more powerful to dominate the worse and the weak, and she shows in many ways, both in the human and in the animal world, that justice consists in the superior dominating and getting the better of the inferior.[6]

Here is pessimism. 'Nothing is certain except that birth leads to death and that life cannot escape Ruin.'[7] Here is unrestrained hedonism. 'Pleasure is good, even if it results from the most unseemly sources: even if the act is unnatural, the pleasure to which it gives rise is good and desirable.'[8] So far as their mood and content goes, these words might belong to our own epoch, though the writers are more frank and ruthless than most moderns would be; but in fact they all come from the fifth or fourth centuries B.C., and express views widely current at the time.

The disease is obviously like our own and it is due to the same cause—a sudden flaring-up of thought, the greatest in human history. Between 600 and 500 B.C. in a primitive, superstitious, ignorant world, some Greeks conceived the idea that the universe can be rationally explained and understood, and there appeared among heavy surrounding clouds a patch of the clearest sky, in which one of the great lights of the human firmament, truth, shines as brightly as it has ever shone since; the spirit of science came into the world, full-grown.

As with us, its impact was first felt in the field of cosmology, with such revolutionary effect that by the middle of the fifth century B.C. Leucippus argued that the universe was composed of atoms in infinite space. From cosmology (again, as with us) reason passed to religion, morals, and politics, and there too turned the light of criticism on accepted beliefs. The formula with which it operated was the contrast between nature and convention, or what Plato calls 'Art', and some of the results can be seen in my previous quotations. Nature, it was argued, knows nothing of good and bad, or of religion, or of the laws of the state; all these are man-made, created by convention, by 'art', and with no natural authority of their own.

A society where such views are widely current might seem to be sliding into moral chaos, and indeed it is such chaos that is revealed in the famous chapters of Thucydides[9] which describe the class-war in Greece. Yet in fact Greek civilization did not founder, but lasted on, through political collapse, for another 800 years and was the foundation of the æsthetic, moral, and intellectual life, first of the kingdoms of the successors of Alexander and then of the Roman Empire.

The recovery was due in the first place to a young man who in later life described the Athens of the early fourth century in these terms: 'When I considered the type of men engaged in politics and the condition of the laws and of morality, the more difficult appeared the task of good government. Traditions of conduct and the observance of the law were degenerating with surprising rapidity.' These words might have been written today, and a modern philosopher might come to Plato's conclusion, that little could be done through political activity and that the remedy lay in 'surveying the question of political justice and the whole human problem from the standpoint of a true philosophy'.[10] To the working out of such a philosophy Plato devoted his life. Taking up the contrast between 'nature' and 'convention' which the materialists had used to argue that religion and morals were human figments with no basis in nature, Plato answered that the soul is as 'natural' as matter and that it, and not matter, is the original and directing force in the universe; that virtue so far from being a 'convention' is 'natural' to human beings. 'Goodness is the health, beauty, and well-being of the soul, and evil is its disease, disfigurement, and weakness';[11] and the ultimate reality in 'nature' is an eternal world beyond the senses, from which the visible world draws all its meaning and value.

The importance of Plato is not only in his doctrines but in the fact that he saw that a doctrine was necessary, and that the cure for the distempers of the time was 'to survey political justice from the standpoint of a true philosophy': this involved finding such a philosophy: failing that, men would continue to walk without a guide in the perplexities and confusions of moral relativism. Plato gave to his times—and to after times—a clear principle by which men could order their conduct and judge between right and wrong. It might almost be said that he created the idea of living by principle. Certainly after his day the ancient world never lacked philosophies of life, founded on a definite intellectual basis. Within fifty years of his death the great philosophies of Greece which lasted on into the Roman Empire were in existence—Platonism in its various forms, Stoicism, Cynicism, Aristotle and the doctrines of the Peripatetic School, Epicureanism. The existence of these philosophies, dominant over the lives of men, is as characteristic of the ancient world, as the absence of equivalents for them is characteristic of our own.

My argument is that fifth-century Athens suffered from a malaise of intellectual and spiritual confusion, resembling our own and like it due to the impact of science and reason on accepted religions and moral beliefs, and that the progressive rot was stayed when Plato set himself to find a clear philosophy of life. He did not indeed establish a uniform creed for the

Greek world, but he divined and initiated the way of advance. He saw that once reason has replaced the rule of use and wont, men must have a rational theory of the universe and base their conduct on it, and he thought such a theory out. Others followed his example and produced their interpretations of the world and systems of conduct founded upon them. This did not bring uniformity of belief but it did give educated men definite bases for an intelligent and rational life. After Plato, Greek thought was divided between his spiritual descendants and the materialist creeds of which Epicurus was the most famous representative, but it was free from the drift and confusion of the age of the Sophists.

We are the spiritual contemporaries of that age, but our Plato has not yet appeared. The Christian has indeed a clear philosophy of life: so has the good Marxist—he knows what to believe and how to behave, and in countries behind the Iron Curtain he is brought up to believe and behave as he should, and marches to his preconceived goal with a steady step and unwavering purpose, which the Western world envies but finds hard to emulate, living, as much of it does, on the broken meats of a view of life which it neither disbelieves nor holds with firm conviction. Things will get no better—indeed they will get worse—until we clear our minds, decide what we do believe, or at least what we are prepared to take as a working hypothesis by which to live. We might well follow the advice which Plato gave to his contemporaries.

> I feel myself, and I daresay that you have the same feeling; how hard and indeed impossible is the attainment of any certainty about questions such as these in the present life. And yet I should regard a man as a coward who did not test what is said about them to the uttermost, or whose heart failed him before he had examined them on every side. He should persevere until he has achieved one of two things: either he should discover the truth about them for himself, or learn it from others: or, if this be impossible, I would have him take the best and most irrefragable of human theories, and let this be the raft upon which he sails through life—not without risk, as I admit, if he cannot find some word of God which will more surely and safely carry him.[12]

Apart from a minority, we have not yet found our certainty, or, in default of it, taken to a raft: for though we are becoming aware of the danger of drowning we have not yet considered how to avoid it. That is natural. For hundreds of years—to change my metaphor—the peoples of the West have been walking through country signposted and fenced by the precepts of a religion which they accepted. Perverse or adventurous spirits might indeed break from the road and wander where their fancy led them. But the great majority followed the beaten track, kept within the fences, and so were protected from the precipices of the difficult and broken country through which the human way leads. They had a feeling of security and—something more—an inner sense that they were on the right path. If they kept to the highroad, it would lead them safely to their destination, and if they needed more direction they could refer to the map which the Church provided. We live in a different world. The main road indeed is still there and those who follow it reach the haven where they would be. 'Adducit eos in portum desiderii eorum'. But people have broken through the fences, defaced the signposts, and questioned the accuracy of the map. The situation is changed: we can no longer live like our forefathers by use and wont, for their validity is denied. Where then shall we turn?

We should expect help from education. If it does not send out its pupils into life with at least the rudiments of a philosophy of living, it has not given them what they most need. But education has not taken this, the most important part of its duty, seriously. We have not yet fully woken up to our predicament, still less to the steps necessary to meet it; we still act as if we were living in a world supported by a common belief and accepted standards. We do not realize that we are back in the moral confusion of the Greek 'Age of the Sophists'. A good boarding-school does indeed habituate its members to certain standards, certain habits of conduct, and sometimes it imparts a definite philosophy of life: and the same is true of some day-schools. The provision in the Education Act of 1944 that 'religious instruction shall be given in every county school and in every auxiliary school' at least shows awareness of the need and makes it possible to meet it. But old habits are difficult to discard, it is easier to provide new machinery than to get it used, and the higher stages of our education suffer from a specialization which even in its own field increasingly squeezes out more general interests. In how many universities is it possible to take philosophy or religion as part of the prescribed course; in other words, in how many is there an opportunity for the student to think methodically under competent guidance about the ultimate problems of the universe and of life? But if so, what has become of the blessed word 'integration'? What are we doing to correct the fragmentation of studies which we deplore, or to prevent a university from being a mere concourse of specialisms which are hardly on speaking terms with each other? And—more important still—are our students, to whom professedly we have given the highest and completest education available, likely (so far as anything the university has done for them) to have any view of the nature of the world into which they are going or of the right way to behave in it, or even to have realized that such a view is desirable for rational living?

My suggestion therefore is that some study of either philosophy or religion or of both should be an element in any university education. It is sometimes held that the study of literature can serve this purpose and be the best road to a philosophy of life; and the reasons given for this view are that it is a criticism of life by writers of genius, that it is more intelligible and attractive to the ordinary person than philosophy, and that everyone reads it. The first two of these arguments are sounder than the last. It is a rash assumption that even university students read widely or seriously outside their special subjects. But apart from that, literature is unsuitable for this particular purpose. There are indeed poems—the *Divina Commedia*, the *Prelude*, and the *Testament of Beauty* are examples—which expound in an unsystematic way a definite philosophy of life. But literature is not in its nature rational; rather it is the expression of an infinite variety of insights and emotions. In it men of genius or high talent have recorded their feelings about life, their visions, their ideals, their passions, love and lust and hatred, hope and despair, cynicism and magnanimity. The only constant element in it is literary power, the gift of expression, a quality which sometimes, not very accurately, is called beauty. Apart from this, it is a chaos of many emotions and in reading it we are exposed to the impact of this chaos. Walt Whitman, speaking of himself, was describing literature when he wrote;

> Do I contradict myself?
> Very well then, I contradict myself,
> I am large, I contain multitudes.

Poets and novelists pour out their feelings and the air is full of these arrows, winged with imagination, these suggestions, some healthy, some harmless, some dangerous. Poets are indeed apt to see farther and to feel more deeply than most philosophers and therefore can help us to richer and profounder views; but if we are looking for anything that can be called a rational philosophy of life, we might as well try to extract it from the collection of pictures in the National Gallery as from this vast miscellany of human emotions which is called literature. If we want a rational theory of life, it is to philosophy or religion that we must turn.

It is absurd to ignore in education the religion which, whether it is regarded as the source of truth and life, or as an *ignis fatuus* that has misled mankind, has been the greatest spiritual force in our history. Some knowledge of it is necessary, if we wish to understand Western civilization; and those who reject Christianity will find it an advantage to know more of its creed than many of them do. If we compare it in importance with some other subjects which are accepted as essentials of the curriculum, we shall be astonished— if anything in education could astonish—at the neglect with which it is treated, and at the consequent ignorance of it shown by many persons who are supposed to be educated.

But in what form are people to be introduced to it? My own belief is that the important thing—certainly the first step—is to give people an idea of Christ and of the Christian life, and if I had to teach Christianity, I should try to make two things vivid to my pupils; to make them see Christ as a person living a human life in the actual world of His day, and I should tell them that Christians believe that in the Gospels we see as much as we are ever likely to know of God, and that at any rate we see the way He behaves when He comes into the world. Then I should try to give them an idea of the early Christian communities as one gets a glimpse of these in the Acts of the Apostles and still more in the passages of St. Paul's letters, where he passes from theology to practical rebuke and advice. Here we see Christian communities in big cities, and St. Paul trying to teach men and women living in the atmosphere of the pagan world, many of them lately pagans themselves, how to behave in their own homes and in their relations to each other, what virtues to follow, what sins to avoid. I think that this might serve as an introduction to Christianity and to the Christian way of life; and it would have the advantage of being concrete, a picture of Christianity embodied in action. Afterwards would come dogma, theology, the intellectual formulations of religious belief.

We should begin, I believe, with religion, and in religion with Christianity. But only less important is the study of natural religion and natural morals, which both logically and historically are prior to revealed religion. The relation of man to the universe and the problem of his conduct in it would exist if there were no such thing as religion; and, in history, Plato and Aristotle, the Stoics and the Epicureans preceded Christ, and Christianity adopted, adapted, and enriched a rational system of ethics which it found already existing. To ignore natural religion and morals in any attempt to build up a philosophy of living is like studying medicine without a knowledge of physiology.

Something perhaps might be done to make the best of both worlds and to combine the study of religion and philosophy on the general lines suggested in the Report of the Indian University Commission (1948–9), of which I quote the relevant recommendations.[13]

'We recommend
(1) that all educational institutions start work with a few minutes for silent meditation,
(2) that in the first year of the Degree course lives of the great religious leaders like Gautama the Buddha, Confucius, Zoroaster, Socrates, Jesus, Samkara, Rāmānuja, Madhva, Mohammed, Kabir, Nānak, Gāndhi, be taught,
(3) that in the second year some selections of a universalist character from the Scriptures of the world be studied,
(4) that in the third year, the central problems of the philosophy of religion be considered.'

These proposals have many merits. They start with religion in the concrete, in the study of those who have lived it and of the books in which its spirit is embodied, and one learns more about religion from meeting it in the flesh than from abstract arguments about it (naturally in a Christian country the emphasis here will be different from that in the Indian Report). But they go on to the philosophical approach, which is wisely deferred till the end of the university course when the student is maturer, and, having acquired some knowledge of actual religions to which the philosophy can be related, will be more aware of what he has to consider. Above all they are an attempt to attack the problem (as we have not yet attacked it) seriously and rationally; a refusal to treat the most important subject in the world as if it was indifferent; an insistence that it is the concern of all higher education.

But to return to the question of the study of philosophy for the purposes of which I have spoken. Some people argue that it is not the business of the university to provide its students with a definite view of life. That is no doubt true; but is it satisfactory that they should go out into the world without one, that they should have no rational basis for their ideas of good and bad, right and wrong, and that the university should wash its hands like Pilate and say that such matters are none of its concern? Yet does not this fairly describe the attitude of nearly all universities today? Could they not at least do something to help their students to form views of their own? That is what is wanted. It is not a question of indoctrination; the university, unless it is denominational, professes no creed except the belief in truth and knowledge. But it is, I maintain, part of its business to see that all its students get at least an opportunity of thinking about the most important of all problems, not merely in casual talks among themselves, but methodically and under intelligent guidance. This does not mean that those who teach or lecture on these subjects will or should urge any definite views on their students. Most teachers have and express definite views on their subjects, but they teach objectively, without becoming propagandists for their own theories. So it should be with religious studies; so it is already with philosophy.

I do not, of course, suppose that the study of philosophy is a panacea for our ills. Men can be brought to its waters, but they cannot be compelled to drink—to listen, to understand, and to think out a rational theory of conduct for themselves. Even when they do so, a variety of theories will emerge, not a universal creed. And when people have a theory, they do not always act upon it.

As Aristotle remarked:

> No one can have the remotest chance of becoming good, unless his actions are good. But most men instead of acting rightly, take refuge in discussing virtue and fancy that they are being philosophers and that this will make them good men. They are like invalids, who listen attentively to their doctors but do not carry out any of their prescriptions. That kind of philosophy will no more

produce spiritual health, than this mode of treatment will lead to physical health.[14]

And, in any case, philosophical systems, however powerfully they may influence an educated minority, leave the mass of mankind untouched. It is religion, not philosophy, that reaches and moves humanity and satisfies its needs. Yet the uses of philosophy, if different, are not less real. It clears the mind, it forces people to think, it makes them realize the importance and value of having a fixed principle by which to test and guide and strengthen conduct, and it sets them on the road of finding such a principle.

We must be clear what kind of philosophy we need for such a purpose. Naturally if we are looking for a rational theory of life, it is to moral philosophy that we should turn. But it must be a different kind of philosophy from that to which the modern world is accustomed. The subject is in bondage to the contemporary habit of specialism. Its most characteristic and most distinguished products are books and articles which only experts wish to read or are able to understand. Philosophers write for philosophers —an appreciative but small audience—and for no one else. Innocent and unconscious imitators of the devils in Milton,

> Apart they sit retired
> In thoughts more elevate, and reason high . . .
> And find no end, in wandering mazes lost.

When they turn to ancient philosophy, they are often more interested in Plato and Aristotle than in the problems in which Plato and Aristotle were interested. Though these are justifiable activities, they do not help us—at any rate directly. But philosophy may be studied and written from a different angle, and ethical systems are or may sometimes be intended to guide intelligent men in the practical business of living. It has been so in the past. Plato and Aristotle wrote works which were at once landmarks in the history of thought and at the same time books which any intelligent man could read, and which were written—especially the *Republic*—with contemporary problems and the practical needs of men in mind. Later the Stoics and Epicureans wrote with the same end in view and the lives of innumerable Greeks and Romans show that they achieved their purpose. Among the moderns Bentham, Mill, and T. H. Green aimed at providing men with theories by which they could live. It should be possible to write a book on moral philosophy, such as the preface of Lowes Dickinson's *Meaning of Good* contemplates. 'The problems I have undertaken to discuss have an interest not only philosophic but practical; and I was ambitious to treat them in a way which might perhaps appeal to some readers who are not professed students of philosophy.' The thing has been done, can be done again, and badly needs doing.

Notes

1 Protagoras, fr. 1. 4.
2 Diog. Laert. ix. 61.
3 Plato, *Laws*, 889 (tr. Taylor).
4 Id., *Republic*, 338.
5 Thucydides, v. 89.
6 Plato, *Gorgias*, 483.
7 Critias, fr. 49.
8 Diog. Laert. ii. 88 (Aristippus).
9 Thucydides, iii. 82 f.
10 Plato, *Letters*, 325 f.
11 Id., *Republic*, 444.
12 Plato, *Phaedo*, 85.
13 i. 303.
14 Aristotle, *Ethics* ii. 4, 5.

77

THE COSMOS OF KNOWLEDGE

Karl Jaspers

Source: K. Jaspers, *The Idea of the University*, London: Peter Owen, 1960, pp. 93–110.

In origin, the various sciences grew from practical experience, from the art of healing, from surveying, from the workshops of builder and painter, from navigation. The unity of science is a philosophical idea. In practice the philosophical ideal of unity became the search for a single organic body of knowledge. So began the co-operation of all branches of learning toward a common goal.

Practical instruction, dating back to time immemorial, is concerned not with the whole or the purity of knowledge, but only with the particular skill required for a particular occupation. By contrast, scientific instruction in accordance with the ideal of the university seeks to guide us to the foundations of all knowledge by the light of the idea of unity. It encourages a particular skill to uncover those roots which join it to the single whole of science, so that its deeper meaning and full range may become apparent.

The university must always meet the needs of the practical occupations. In this respect it resembles the ancient training schools. But it adds something totally new when it meets these needs by way of defining their place within the whole of knowledge.

Thus, from one point of view, the university resembles an aggregate of professional training schools isolated from one another, or an intellectual department store with an abundance of goods for every taste. But from another point of view, it is clear that this is mere appearance since, if true, the university would simply disintegrate. The very existence of the university stands for that oneness and wholeness of all knowledge which alone enables us to know in the broader sense of the term.

The wholeness of knowledge, however, presents us with the task of classifying all knowledge. The departmental divisions appear to but do not in fact coincide with this classification. Though they can never really coincide they must be related to one another.

The course catalogue of any large university will suffice as a first guide to the kinds of different subjects in existence. We find that the university is divided into faculties and these in turn into departments divided by subject —in almost endless variety. Clearly the course catalogue as a whole is the product not of a master plan, but of a slow process of historical accretion.

The classification of knowledge

Since the idea of knowledge as a cosmos does not stem from practical application but from philosophy, its vitality is tied to the diffusion of philosophical awareness throughout the university.

From the very start, the idea of knowledge as a unity has given rise to different systems of classifying the various fields of knowledge. Classifications abound. None of them, however, can claim absolute truth and validity. Definitive classifications have always reflected someone's proud conviction of having hit upon the whole and absolute truth of things.

As "absolute" truths definitively formulated here and now have succeeded one another, the necessary relativity of all systems of classification has become increasingly clear. Our faculty of understanding has been emancipated. The educational power of knowledge has ceased to be identical with a fixed world outlook and ontology. It is replaced by our realization that our capacity for learning new things is infinite.

To assume that one has the one final and correct classification of studies is to pretend that a given field of knowledge can be defined and localized with the help of certain fixed, absolute points. Conversely, to attempt to relate a given field to the whole of knowledge involves pushing inquiry to those depths where that field appears as a microcosmic replica of the whole of knowledge. For there is almost no significant fact which is not at some point related to the whole of knowledge in that it is either illumined by its context or itself in turn illumines that context.

Knowledge is usually classified according to some pair of opposites. Thus there are:

(1) Theoretical and practical studies. Theoretical studies are concerned with a given subject as an end in itself; practical studies are concerned with the subject as a means toward the realization of practical ends.
(2) Empirical sciences and purely rational sciences. Empirical sciences deal with real objects in space and time. Pure sciences deal with concepts which are intelligible once they can be independently derived. Mathematics is unique among the sciences in that it deals solely with ideal objects.
(3) Natural sciences and cultural sciences. The object of empirical sciences can be grasped in two ways. It can be grasped from without like matter or understood from within like the human mind. The natural sciences

explain things from without through laws of causation or mathematical constructs; the cultural sciences or humanities understand from within by ascertaining purpose and meaning.

(4) Sciences concerned with general laws and historical sciences, the former seeking the universal, the latter, the particular and historical unique.

(5) Basic sciences and auxiliary sciences. Basic sciences seek to learn by reference to the whole of knowledge, hence become representative of the whole and therefore universal in character. Auxiliary sciences either collect material or assemble knowledge for a particular practical purpose.

In each of these pairs the opposing principles of scientific understanding complement one another. They can but briefly isolate themselves, for in isolation each becomes sterile. In practice, each pair of opposites asserts itself simultaneously, there being no way of dividing them neatly and permanently into opposites.

The concrete sciences are united only by the object which they seek to approximate with every method at their disposal. They no more fit into a fixed classification scheme than do the widening and intersecting circles caused by pebbles tossed into a pool. But then these widening circles may conceivably be classified according to the relative nature and position of the pebbles involved. Thus, sciences may be ranked in the order of their intrinsic priority where each level depends on the next lower one, as in the order physics, chemistry, psychology, sociology. This would be a series of sciences seeking the universal. Or cosmic history, world history, life history, human history, European history. This would be a series of studies concerned with what is unique and individual. Whatever our system of classification, it is always predicated on a single pair of opposites and to that extent not all-inclusive. Further examination would show that such schemes can never illumine more than single sciences, and imperfectly at that; that genuine classification is unattainable. At best, a given scheme has pragmatic relevance to a specific area of actual research.

Usually the unity of any given scheme is furnished by that particular science which this scheme favours. There is good reason for the fact that almost every science has at one time or another declared itself the only genuine, all-inclusive and absolute science. The reason is that every true science constitutes a single whole. Error ensues only when the wholeness of one science is allowed to obscure the equally autonomous wholeness of other sciences. One-sided emphasis on a particular science impoverishes science as a whole.

The unity of all knowledge is an ideal. Every classification is a provisional attempt to translate this ideal into reality from a particular point of view and in terms of a particular intellectual and historical situation. To that extent every scheme is false.

Academic departments

No single principle governs the organization of disciplines at a university. No one man has planned this classification with the knowledge of the whole picture in mind, as in the case of industrial division of labour. On the contrary, there have arisen a number of separate intellectual movements each aiming individually at the whole of knowledge. The particular sciences have remained such independent wholes. They do not lie next to one another like the separate drawers of a filing cabinet, but overlap, and interrelate without necessarily intermingling. They communicate without blurring into one another, guided by the vision of an infinitely large single body of knowledge. The essence of the university is concerted yet unregimented activity, a life of diversity yet inspired by the ideal of wholeness, the co-operation yet independence of many disciplines.

Departmentalization still in use today dates back to the medieval period. The three upper faculties were theology, jurisprudence and medicine. A fourth or lower faculty was added—the liberal arts, today's philosophical faculty. (The meaning of these faculties has changed as the meaning of research has changed. For the last 150 years the number of faculties has at times been increased, then again reduced to the old number. Today there are usually five, because the old philosophical faculty has been broken up into two faculties, one of mathematics and natural sciences and one of liberal arts.)

These faculties claim to mirror faithfully the cosmos of sciences. They represent the whole of human knowledge. They arose from the practical needs of intellectual work, not from theoretical schemes of classifying the sciences. The continuing validity of these faculties today, after centuries of radical change in our environment, our knowledge, and our research, attests to the truth of their original conception. Theology, jurisprudence and medicine cover permanent areas of inquiry: understanding of religious revelation, of statute law, both private and public, and of the nature of man. The study of these subjects is meant to train ministers, judges, administrators and physicians for their practical careers. They all need at least logic and philosophy as a common foundation.

The sciences of theology, jurisprudence, and medicine aim for an end itself no longer scientific, the eternal salvation of the soul, the general welfare of people as members of society, and bodily health respectively. Paradoxically then, these sciences originate outside the scientific realm. They work with assumptions which though themselves not scientific, impart substance, meaning and purpose to science. Theology is concerned with revelation approached in three ways: through the history of the holy scriptures, through the church, through dogma, and verified in terms of contemporary faith. Jurisprudence is concerned with rationalizing and standardizing statute law as produced and validated by the power of a given state. Medicine is concerned with preserving, fostering and restoring the health of human beings, and is based on an inclusive knowledge of human nature.

Each of these scientific disciplines is entirely based on nonscientific premises. Each must seek to shed light on these premises. For without them it loses all meaning, as shown by the following typical phenomena.

Theology touches upon the supra-rational realm but through rational means. Now, instead of rationally developing the meaning of revelation, theology can develop a passion for "the absurd." Self-contradiction is then supposed to confirm the very truth of an assertion; the enslavement of reason to confirm the very truth of faith; and arbitrary submission to an authority, even though in reality it exists in the world in the form of judgments and expressions, which are supposed to be the true way of life. Brutality, fanaticism, inquisitions, and lovelessness—these make up this theological fury.

Conversely, revelation, the basis of faith, may be lost. Faith is then equated with rational doctrine and deduced from reason alone. But as revelation, the historical foundation of faith is lost, faith itself is lost. Reduced to unrestricted rational thinking, it ends up in unbelief.

Jurisprudence bases itself upon the reality of the positive legal order. This order of statute law is to be made meaningful, coherent, and consistent. Natural law, though by no means a fixed standard, provides a guiding idea of what is right or wrong. Without this foundation, jurisprudence sinks into the abyss of total arbitrariness. Statute law then is valid simply because backed up by state power. Self-contradiction and injustice cease to be valid counter-arguments. Illegality is legally sanctioned, and thought itself bows before the law of force.

Conversely, a jurisprudence concerned only with natural law and without any reference to actual statute law becomes meaningless too.

Medicine is premised on the will to advance the life and health of all men as human beings. This ideal admits of no qualification. First and foremost, the desire to help and heal concerns itself with individuals. It concerns large groups only in so far as individuals profit, and no individual is physically harmed.

Yet, medical interest in health is as ambiguous as the concept of physical health itself. The task of medicine involves conflicting tendencies. It becomes meaningless both where the individual's inalienable right to physical health is abandoned, and where the meaning of physical health becomes a convenient but over-simple stereotype.

Once a particular racial or physiological type is preferred to man as a whole, a motive exists for doing harm to the life and health of individuals for the supposed benefit of some particular group as a whole. Thus, persons presumed to have large chances of transmitting unfavourable hereditary traits have been forcibly sterilized, and in the name of euthanasia the mentally ill have been murdered.

In the three so-called higher faculties, the ideas of reason, natural law (justice), and life and health are standards indispensable to research, if it is to retain any meaning. But in revelation, positive law, and human nature dark powers remain which we can endlessly illuminate but never fully understand, and it is these that endow research with substance and life.

The philosophical faculty enjoys a unique position. Originally, it did not prepare for a specific profession but prepared solely for the higher faculties (theology, jurisprudence and medicine). Today, the function of the philosophical faculty has changed from a preparatory to a fundamental one. The philsophical faculty embraces all other branches of knowledge. The three remaining faculties derive their intellectual substance from contact with the basic disciplines comprised in the philosophical faculty (the faculty of arts and sciences). Thus from the viewpoint of research and theory alone, the philosophical faculty by itself comprises the whole university. Any classification of knowledge which includes everything contained in the philosophical faculty is complete.

In the course of the nineteenth century, the philosophical faculty lost both its uniqueness and its unity. It split up into a faculty of mathematics and natural sciences, on the one hand, and humanities, on the other, from which, in turn, a social science faculty branched off. One came to think of the faculties as existing side by side rather than forming an organic whole. In this way, the idea of the oneness of the university was lost. The university became an aggregate, an intellectual department store.

Several motives entered into this split-up: the size of the old faculty which included more professors than all the other three faculties combined; the schism between the natural sciences and the liberal arts which entailed estrangement, lack of understanding and mutual disdain; and the need to train people for different professions such as teaching, chemistry, physics, geology, and agriculture.

The reunification of the university, which stems from an awareness of the cosmos of the sciences, cannot simply mean restoring things to their medieval unity. The whole content of modern knowledge and research must be integrated: broadening the scope of the university must initiate a genuine unification of all branches of learning.

The expansion of the university

In the modern world the university keeps establishing institutes and teaching organizations designed to meet the changing requirements of society. Thus, areas of specialized technical training or entirely new curricula for professional courses of study require special ways of teaching. Nothing can stop the continuing expansion of the university. This process has meaning, because all human activity involves knowledge. Wherever there arises a demand for knowledge the university is responsible for forging ahead in the new field and teaching it.

Not infrequently the net result was a meaningless aggregate of totally unrelated fields. Astronomy and business administration, philosophy and hotel management find themselves equals in this intellectual "department store."

To ignore the presence of these newcomers is nothing but useless snobbery. The idea of the university requires that the university be open to new ideas. There is nothing which is not worth knowing about, no art which does not involve a form of knowledge. Only by unifying these various new lines of inquiry can the university do justice to them. The university is called upon to preserve the scientific spirit by transforming and assimilating the new materials and skills and integrating them in the light of a few leading ideas.

There are two ways in which the curriculum may be broadened by increasing the number of subjects offered. On the one hand, science differentiates itself in the natural course of its growth. In this process each new phase remains an integral whole comparable to the propagation of life. In this way, psychiatry as well as ophthalmology achieved an independent status within medicine itself, because they developed both subject matter and scientists of universal significance. Conversely, legal medicine does not qualify as an independent field, but is a collection of technical skills and "know how." Similarly, the status of dental medicine, as well as the medicine of ear, nose and throat, is dubious because the organs concerned lack universal implications. These fields lack the over-all significance of internal medicine, psychiatry or ophthalmology. Public health, too, enjoys a dubious status. Although outstanding representatives of this field have rightly held professorships, the field itself has its practical and technical limitations; it lacks a really challenging idea. The mere fact that people working in the field of public sanitation have made contributions to bacteriology does not suffice to enrol public sanitation in the ranks of the basic sciences. To give detailed answers to the questions raised here would require further study and expert knowledge in the fields concerned. We are here concerned only with the principle: the split-up of sciences into new fields of study is desirable to the extent that a given new field can, in turn, develop into an integral whole in touch with universal ideas and so remain a basic science.

Alternatively, science can grow if new materials and skills enter into it from without. They demand admittance because they can make a valuable contribution to the cosmos of the sciences. Thus, for example, the content of the cultures concerned explains why Indic and Chinese studies are basic sciences; African and prehistoric studies are not.

Whenever the university expands it must keep its sights set on the unity of knowledge, on the daily task of revalidating this unity, in two ways. Throughout all change, the university must retain its awareness of the basic sciences and of the hierarchy both of basic as against auxiliary sciences and of instruction through research as against mere factual and technical instruction.

The expansion of the university is a problem which relates to its very survival in the modern world. New ideas must be recognized and made part of the whole of the university. It is yet to be seen whether the university is equal to the new world, whether it can accept it and serve it, whether the new knowledge and the new abilities can be permeated with the spirit without which they are, strictly speaking, meaningless.

Theology, jurisprudence and medicine, traditionally the three upper faculties, address themselves to areas of human existence that have remained unchanged for thousands of years. Nonetheless, they do not cover the whole of modern existence. This is evident if one considers the large variety of institutions of higher learning which have been founded outside the confines of the university itself, such as technological institutes, agricultural colleges, veterinary colleges, teachers' colleges, schools of business administration, schools of mining, etc. Is their mere existence not proof that the life of the university has failed in important respects? Does not the establishment of these independent institutes violate the idea of the university?

It is significant, indeed, that these establishments tend to duplicate some of the work of the university, that they have a natural tendency to expand into a university so that, for example, we find all the liberal arts, up to and including philosophy, being taught at technical institutes. More often than not, however, even the presence of outstanding scholars in the humanities has not been able to produce anything more than an empty educational routine bereft of the vitality and strength which comes only with creative scholarship. Thus, these scholars frequently feel as exiles. Could it be that there is some connection between the growing emptiness of modern life and this growth of diverse specialized schools? Is there a way which would lead back from the superficiality of specialism, the general aimlessness, the dilemma of diverse special schools, to some new unity? Whatever possibility exists hinges upon the extent to which vast new areas of human life can be incorporated in the university. Medicine, jurisprudence and theology, the three traditional branches of learning, no longer suffice as they did for the medieval world. Yet, progress cannot be achieved by simply increasing the number of departments. One cannot just add a new department whenever a new field has been opened up somewhere on a large scale. Even highly specialized departments must relate to a genuinely important sector of human life.

This is not a new idea. In 1803, for example, the local government established in Heidelberg "a department of political economy" and incorporated it temporarily into the philosophical faculty. This department included forestry, urban and rural economics, mining and surveying, civil engineering, architecture, assaying, and police organization, "everything that concerns the knowledge, preservation, development and proper maintenance of public administration." All that eventually remained of these arts and sciences was what came to be known as economics. Clearly the department failed to encompass a genuine self-contained sector of human life. The reference to public administration served as a utilitarian container for various unrelated jobs, but failed to provide a unifying ideal.

Yet, here were the roots of an important later development, which became a factor in the public mind only gradually in the course of the nineteenth century. This is technology, which, as is becoming ever clearer, is the sole really new field. Although technology is ages old, and has developed through thousands of years, until the end of the eighteenth century it remained a part of handicraft. Hence it remained basically unchanged and part of man's daily life within his natural environment. Then, during the last 150 years, technology made an incision deeper than all the events of world history over the past thousands of years, as deep perhaps as that caused by the discovery of tools and of fire. Technology has become an independent giant. It grows and advances. It brings about a unified and planned exploitation of the globe, an exploitation which is financially profitable. Trapped in the spell of technology, men seem no longer capable of controlling what originated as their own works. Technology has a claim to our basic concerns equal in objectivity to that of theology, jurisprudence and medicine, a claim which was not fully recognized until it compelled our attention amid the catastrophic changes and events of recent history. For it is technology which has now taken over the job of moulding man's natural environment, of transforming human life even as it transforms nature and the technical world.

To expand the university by creating a fourth faculty next to the three upper faculties, theology, jurisprudence and medicine, poses a real challenge. Technology represents an entirely new and developing area of human life. Unclear as is the ultimate effect of technology upon human existence, it is involved in a development at once planned and chaotic.

We all observe the drastic changes of our immediate environment. Apartment house and public building, road construction and traffic management, transportation and communication, the furnishing of kitchen, desk and bed, the supply of water, gas and electricity—all of which spell the difference between our modern environment and earlier ones, are held together not only by utilitarian considerations, or by the agency of the natural sciences, but by the novel concept of man's transformation of his natural environment.

Still, this novel conception of human life and the enormous apparatus dedicated to its maintenance have so far failed to crystallize into a controlled and permanent pattern. The restless march of technological change on a gigantic scale makes us stagger between ecstasy and bewilderment, between the most fabulous power and the most elementary helplessness.

Everything seems to flow into the one great stream of technological organization which for reasons which escape adequate historical understanding began to flow 150 years ago and to this day continues to swell steadily, flooding everything. Today, we feel that this colossal phenomenon must stem from metaphysical sources, that all must accept its objectives at pain of extinction. It seems as if there is something that is bound to awake even though still half asleep, something that until now has remained silent behind the great mass of ingenious technological devices, something dimly perceived by a few individuals like Goethe and Burckhardt who reacted to it with a mixture of horror and distaste.

Perhaps, the best interests of the intellectual life as well as of technology are served by making the university their mutual meeting place. Perhaps then, technology and the confusion which has resulted from it would be infused with meaning and purpose. Perhaps then, out of the idea of the university would grow an openness, truthfulness, up-to-dateness in which this idea would prove itself. Thus the university would in effect be transforming itself.

Only a revival of the old idea of the university could make scholars feel the magnitude of their task to the point where the creation of a new technical faculty would benefit the university as a whole. But the university as a whole would have to share in this rededication if it is to have a chance of promoting a general rebirth. The university's great task would be to create a truly comprehensive awareness of our age in terms of the sum total of knowledge and practical skills of which the integration of the technical faculty is only one aspect.

Along with the incorporation of a school of technology other changes would become essential. Above all, the old philosophical faculty must be reunified. The division into the natural sciences and the humanities must be overcome. Only reunification can impart sufficient force to the basic theoretical disciplines to counteract the increased impact and scope of the practical disciplines. This reduces the danger that its continued isolation at the university will slowly drive the natural sciences into the camp of technology and medicine, leaving the other faculties to cherish precious memories in aesthetic isolation without vigour and relevance.

More than that, it would necessitate reintroducing into the sciences the concept of hierarchy, which distinguishes between basic and auxiliary disciplines.

A technical faculty would be something new at the university. It would have to be more than just a new faculty or school. It would have to get the university to do something entirely new. The university must face the great problem of modern man: how out of technology there can arise that metaphysical foundation of a new way of life which technology has made possible. It is impossible to predict which disciplines will provide the strongest impulses to this end, once scholars and scientists have begun to realize this task in close and constant intellectual co-operation.

Technology is an autonomous discipline which like any other field is prone to certain grave and specific errors once it loses sight of its own presuppositions. Thus, theology was shown to be prone to lapse deliberately from the secret of revelation into absurdity and witch hunting; jurisprudence to lapse from its concern with statute law into legal rationalization of lawless brutality and licence; medicine to lapse from its essential duty to heal, to euthanasia and the killing of the insane. Similarly, technology either does or does not live up to its ideals. We have heard about inventors who in their old age were overcome by horror at the realization of the evil they had unwittingly and indirectly brought about by their discoveries. We have heard about the emptiness of certain kinds of technical work, the arbitrary nature of its goals, the pointlessness of mere competence as such. Yet the foundation of all technical activity is the profoundly informed will to develop more fully man's existence in this world.

A technical faculty can serve no more than the medical one as a mere annexe to the philosophical faculty. It has its own independent area of existence and its own practical task. Still, like medicine it is grounded intrinsically and pedagogically in the basic sciences which are part of the philosophical faculty.

The following are the most immediate consequences of the proposed change: as the university absorbs the institute of technology, the need for duplicating physics, chemistry and mathematics is removed. The history of ideas, history of art, economics and political science would also become part of the philosophic faculty. The needs of technology would impart fresh life to the philosophic faculty as a whole. For the basic disciplines would more consciously focus on the common horizon of theoretical inquiry. Their teaching would be directed to the common problems of medicine, technology and teaching. It is difficult to say how this will manifest itself in the personality of the individual scholar. Quite possibly, teaching will stress the historical development of scientific and mathematical insights and in this way carry over the unity of the philosophical faculty into the individual sciences.

All told, both university and technical institutes stand to profit from unification. The university would grow richer, more inclusive and more modern. Its basic problems would be infused with new life. Conversely, the technological world would become more contemplative as the problem of its meaning becomes a matter of serious concern. Its self-affirmation and its limits, its over-optimism and its tragic disappointments would all be placed in a deeper context.

It is exceedingly important, however, to recognize the independence and universality of the technical world as a modern phenomenon without drawing the empty conclusion that a great many other departments are warranted by the same token. In no case can the study of agriculture, forestry, business administration, etc., be considered as faculties of equal status with the technological faculty. These are specialties, pure and simple, without a truly comprehensive subject. Still, they must not be excluded from the university.

The university is free to teach whatever is teachable provided it distinguishes sharply between research subjects and auxiliary subjects such as those mentioned above. Research subjects cover disciplines whose content and level of achievement merit incorporation into the university itself. The other group of subjects does not merit incorporation, but affiliation only to the university, at least for the time being. Their teachers and students will work in the atmosphere and framework of the university without belonging to it in the narrower sense.

The university faculty member differs from the teacher of affiliated subjects (like agriculture, business administration, etc.) in that he is judged not only on his teaching performance but on the merit of his self-directed research. The faculty member engaged in research differs from his technical assistant in that he is concerned with the basic problems and their meaning. The technical assistant limits himself to the collection of facts, auxiliary work, and certain well-defined preliminary objectives.

A higher education is a prerequisite for an ever-growing number of jobs. We have the choice of either ignoring this need from a misplaced and unrealistic sense of caste or else of doing something to help meet it. If we choose the second path (carefully and step by step, as is only reasonable) the difficult question arises whether there really is an enduring need at the university for isolated "service" skills. We have to decide if our common interests are really served by specialized intellectual techniques, a kind of second order manual labour, a mere routine efficiency without a corresponding vision of the whole; or if this is pernicious in the long run, even though, for the time being at least, we must learn to put up with it. Does the university embody the aspirations of *all* men and is it therefore called upon ultimately to accept all applicants and to elevate to a higher level each and every branch of human knowledge and technique? Or does it contain an esoteric element, forever intelligible only to a minority?

We must not allow ourselves to be deceived by the inevitable demands of those who oppose the idea of intellectual hierarchy. Their claims are premature. Equality of intellectual status cannot be decreed. It can only be earned through patient and individual effort and growth. Nor must we be deceived by the dream that all people can achieve the noblest function of humanity. This is a utopian dream which is not realized simply by assuming that it exists already when, in fact, no one knows or is capable of knowing to what extent it can be realized. A temporary solution is that the university set up schools which are affiliated with but not actually part of the university. The university must maintain its aristocratic principles if it is not to fall prey to a universal lowering of standards. The actual incorporation of affiliated schools into the university is not a matter of decree. It can only be accomplished by allowing these schools to grow into intellectual maturity in their own way. If this is done, then the actual incorporation is no more than a formal recognition of an accomplished fact.

78

CULTURE AND SCIENCE

José Ortega y Gasset

Source: José Ortega y Gasset, *Mission of the University*, London: Kegan Paul, Trench, Trubner and Co., 1944, pp. 63 72.

If we review in substance the distinction between profession and science, we find ourselves in possession of a few clear ideas. For example, medicine is not a science but a profession, a matter of practice. Hence it represents a point of view distinct from that of science. It proposes as its object to restore and maintain health in the human species. To this end, it appropriates what it finds useful: it goes to science and takes whatever results of research it considers efficacious; but it leaves all the rest. It leaves particularly what is most characteristic of science: the cultivation of the problematic and doubtful. This would suffice to differentiate radically between medicine and science. Science consists in an urge to solve problems; the more it is engaged in this occupation, the more purely it accomplishes its mission. But medicine exists for the purpose of applying solutions. If they happen to be scientific, so much the better. But they are not necessarily so. They may have grown out of some millennial experience which science has not yet explained or even confirmed.

In the last fifty years, medicine has allowed itself to be swept off its feet by science; it has neglected its own mission and failed to assert properly its own professional point of view.[1] Medicine has committed the besetting sin of that whole period: namely, to look askance at destiny and strain to be something else—in this case, pure science.

Let us make no mistake about it. Science, upon entering into a profession, must be detached from its place in pure science, to be organized upon a new centre and a new principle, as professional technics. And if this is true, it must certainly have an effect on the teaching of the professions.

Something similar is to be said of the relations between culture and science. The difference between them seems to me clear enough. Yet I should like not only to leave the concept of culture very definite in the mind of the reader but also to show what basis it has. First, the reader must go to the trouble of scrutinizing and reflecting upon the following résumé—which will not be easy: culture is the system of vital ideas which each age possesses; better yet, it is the system of ideas *by* which the age lives. There is no denying the fact that man invariably lives according to some definite ideas which constitute the very foundation of his way of life. These ideas which I have called "vital", meaning ideas by which an age conducts its life, are no more nor less than the repertory of our *active* convictions as to the nature of our world and our fellow creatures, convictions as to the hierarchy of the values of things—which are more to be esteemed, and which less.[2]

It is not in our hands whether to possess such a repertory of convictions or not. It is a matter of inescapable necessity, an ingredient essential to every human life, of whatever sort it may be. The reality we are wont to refer to as "human life", your life and the next fellow's, is something quite remote from biology, the science of organisms. Biology, like any other science, is no more than one occupation to which some men devote their "life". The basic and truest meaning of the word *life* is not biological but biographical: and that is the meaning it has always had in the language of the people. It means the totality of what we do and what we are—that formidable business, which every man must exercise on his own, of maintaining a place in the scheme of things and steering a course among the beings of the world. "To live is, in fact, to have dealings with the world: to address oneself to it, exert oneself in it, and occupy oneself with it."[3] If these actions and occupations which compose our living were produced in us mechanically, the result would not be human life. The automaton does not *live*. The whole difficulty of the matter is that life is not given us ready made. Like it or not, we must go along from instant to instant, deciding for ourselves. At each moment it is necessary to make up our minds what we are going to do next: the life of man is an ever-recurrent problem. In order to decide at one instant what he is going to do or to be at the next, man is compelled to form a plan of some sort, however simple or puerile it may be. It is not that he *ought* to make a plan. There is simply no possible life, sublime or mean, wise or stupid, which is not essentially characterized by its proceeding with reference to some plan.[4] Even to abandon our life to chance, in a moment of despair, is to make a plan. Every human being, perforce, picks his way through life. Or what comes to the same, as he decides upon each act he performs, he does so *because* that act "seems best", given the circumstances. This is tantamount to saying that every life is obliged, willy-nilly, to justify itself in its own eyes. Self-justification is a constituent part of our life. We refer to one and the same fact, whether we say that "to live is to conduct oneself according to a plan", or that "life is a continuous justification to oneself". But this plan or justification implies that we have acquired some "idea" of the world and the things in it, and also of our potential acts which have bearing upon it. In short, man cannot live without reacting to his environment with some rudimentary concept of it. He is forced to make an intellectual interpretation of the world about him, and of his conduct in it. This interpretation is the repertory of ideas or convictions to which I have referred, and which, as it is now perfectly evident, cannot be lacking in any human life whatsoever.[5]

The vast majority of these convictions or ideas are not fabricated by the individual, Crusoe-wise, but simply received by him from his historical environment—his times. Naturally, any age presents very disparate systems of convictions. Some are a drossy residue of other times. But there is always a system of live ideas which represents the superior level of the age, a system which is essentially characteristic of its times; and this system is the culture of the age. He who lives at a lower level, on archaic ideas, condemns himself to a lower life, more difficult, toilsome, unrefined. This is the plight of backward peoples—or individuals. They ride through life in an ox-cart while others speed by them in automobiles. Their concept of the world wants truth, it wants richness, and it wants acumen. The man who lives on a plane beneath the enlightened level of his time is condemned, relatively, to the life of an infra-man.

In our age, the content of culture comes largely from science. But our discussion suffices to indicate that culture is not science. The content of culture, though it is being made in the field of science more than elsewhere, is not scientific fact but rather a vital faith, a conviction characteristic of our times. Five hundred years ago, faith was reposed in ecclesiastical councils, and the content of culture emanated in large part from them.

Culture does with science, therefore, the same thing the profession does. It borrows from science what is vitally necessary for the interpretation of our existence. There are entire portions of science which are not culture, but pure scientific technique. And vice versa, culture requires that we possess a complete concept of the world and of man; it is not for culture to stop, with science, at the point where the methods of absolute theoretic rigour happen to end. Life cannot wait until the sciences may have explained the universe scientifically. We cannot put off living until we are ready. The most salient characteristic of life is its coerciveness: it is always urgent, "here and now," without any possible postponement. Life is fired at us point-blank. And culture, which is but its interpretation, cannot wait any more than can life itself.

This sharpens the distinction between culture and the sciences. Science is not something by which we live. If the physicist had to live by the ideas of his science, you may rest assured that he would not be so finicky as to wait for some other investigator to complete his research a century or so later. He would renounce the hope of a complete scientific solution, and fill in, with approximate or probable anticipations, what the rigorous corpus of physical doctrine lacks at present, and in part, always will lack.

The internal conduct of science is not a *vital* concern; that of culture is. Science is indifferent to the exigencies of our life, and follows its own necessities. Accordingly, science grows constantly more diversified and specialized without limit, and is never completed. But culture is subservient to our life here and now, and is required to be, at every instant, a complete, unified, coherent system—the plan of life, the path leading through the forest of existence.

That metaphor of ideas as paths or roads (*methodoi*) is as old as culture itself. Its origin is evident. When we find ourselves in a perplexing, confused situation, it is as though we stood before a dense forest, through whose tangles we cannot advance without being lost. Someone explains the situation, with a happy idea, and we experience a sudden illumination—the "light" of understanding. The thicket immediately appears ordered, and the lines of its structure seem like paths opening through it. Hence the term *method* is regularly associated with that of enlightenment, illumination, *Aufklärung*. What we call to-day "a cultured man" was called more than a century ago "an enlightened man", i.e. a man who sees the paths of life in a clear light.

Let us cast away once for all those vague notions of enlightenment and culture, which make them appear as some sort of ornamental accessory for the life of leisure. There could not be a falser misrepresentation. Culture is an indispensable element of life, a dimension of our existence, as much a part of man as his hands. True, there is such a thing as man without hands; but that is no longer simply man: it is man crippled. The same is to be said of life without culture, only in a much more fundamental sense. It is a life crippled, wrecked, false. The man who fails to live at the height of his time is living beneath what would constitute his right life. Or in other words, he is swindling himself out of his own life.

We are passing at present, despite certain appearances and presumptions, through an age of terrific *un-culture*. Never perhaps has the ordinary man been so far below his times and what they demand of him. Never has the civilized world so abounded in falsified, cheated lives. Almost nobody is poised squarely upon his proper and authentic place in life. Man is habituated to living on subterfuges with which he deceives himself, conjuring up around him a very simple and arbitrary world, in spite of the admonitions of an active conscience which forces him to observe that his real world, the world that corresponds to the whole of actuality, is one of enormous complexity and grim urgency. But he is afraid—our ordinary man is timorous at heart, with all his brave gesticulations—he is afraid to admit this real world, which would make great demands on him. He prefers to falsify his life, and keep it sealed up in the cocoon of his fictitious, oversimplified concept of the world.[6]

Hence the historic importance of restoring to the university its cardinal function of "enlightenment", the task of imparting the full culture of the time and revealing to mankind, with clarity and truthfulness, that gigantic world of to-day in which the life of the individual must be articulated, if it is to be authentic.

Personally, I should make a Faculty of Culture the nucleus of the university and of the whole higher learning.[7] I have already sketched the outline of its disciplines. Each of these, it will be remembered, bears two names: for example "The physical scheme of the world (Physics)". This dual designation is intended to suggest the difference between a cultural discipline, vitally related to life, and the corresponding science by which it is nurtured. The "Faculty" of Culture would not expound physics as the science is presented to a student intending to devote his life to physico-mathematical research. The physics in culture is the rigorously derived synthesis of ideas about the nature and functioning of the physical cosmos, as these ideas have emerged from the physical research so far completed. In addition, this discipline will analyse the means of acquiring knowledge, by which the physicist has achieved his marvellous construction; it will therefore be necessary to expound the principles of physics, and to trace, briefly but scrupulously, the course of their historical evolution. This last element of the course will enable the student to visualize what the "world" was, in which man lived a generation or a century or a thousand years ago; and by contrast, he will be able to realize and appreciate the peculiarities of our "world" of to-day.

This is the time to answer an objection which arose at the beginning of my essay, and was postponed. How—it is asked—can the present-day concept of matter be made intelligible to anyone who is not versed in higher mathematics? Every day, mathematical method makes some new advance at the very base of physical science.

I should like the reader to consider the tragedy without escape which would confront humanity if the view implied here were correct. Either everyone would be obliged to be a thorough physicist, devoting himself, dedicating his life,[8] to research in order not to live inept and devoid of insight into the world we live in; or else most of us must resign ourselves to an existence which, in one of its dimensions, is doomed to stupidity. The physicist would be for the man in the street like some being endowed with a magical, hieratic knowledge. Both of these solutions would be—among other things—ridiculous.

But fortunately there is no such dilemma. In the first place, the doctrine I am defending calls for a thorough rationalizing of the methods of instruction, from the primary grades to the university. Precisely by recognizing science to be a thing apart, we pave the way to the segregating of its cultural elements so that these may be made assimilable. The "principle of economy in education" is not satisfied by extruding disciplines the student cannot learn; it requires economy in the teaching of what remains to be taught. Economy in these two respects would add a new margin to the learning capacity of the student, so that he could actually learn more than at present.[9] I believe, then, that in time to come no student will arrive at the university without being already acquainted with the mathematics of physics, sufficiently at least to be capable of understanding its formulas.

70

Mathematicians exaggerate a bit the difficulties of their subject. It is an extensive one but, after all, it is always expressible in definite terms to anyone who "knows beans". If it appears so incomprehensible to-day, it is because the necessary energy has not been applied to the simplifying of its teaching. This affords me an opportunity to proclaim for the first time, and with due solemnity, that if we fail to cultivate this sort of intellectual effort —effort addressed not to descriptive analysis, after the usual manner of research, but to the task of simplifying and synthesizing the quintessence of science, without sacrifice of its quality or substantialness—then the future of science itself will be disastrous.

It is imperative that the present dispersion and complication of scientific labours be counterbalanced by the complementary kind of scientific activity, striving towards the concentration and consolidation of knowledge. We need to develop a special type of talent, for the specific function of synthesizing. The destiny of science is at stake.

But, in the second place, I deny roundly that in order to grasp the fundamental ideas—the principles, the methods of procedure, the end results—of any science which has fundamental ideas to offer, the student must necessarily have had formal training and become familiar with its techniques. The truth is quite otherwise. When a science, in its internal development, proceeds towards ideas which require technical familiarity in order to be understood, then its ideas are losing their fundamental character to become instruments subordinate to the science, rather than its substance proper.[10] The mastery of higher mathematics is essential for *making* the science but not for understanding its import for human life.

It happens, at once luckily and unluckily, that the nation which stands gloriously and indisputably in the van of science is Germany. The German, in addition to his prodigious talent and inclination for science, has a congenital weakness which it would be extremely hard to extirpate: he is *a nativitate* pedantic and impervious of mind. This fact has brought it about that not a few sides of our present-day science are not really science, but only pedantic detail, all too easily and credulously gathered together. One of the tasks Europe needs to perform with dispatch is to rid contemporary science of its purely German excrescences, its rituals and mere whims, in order to save its essential parts uncontaminated.[11]

Europe cannot be saved without a return to intellectual discipline, and this discipline needs to be more rigorous than those which have been used or abused in other times. No one must be allowed to escape. Not even the man of science. To-day this personage conserves not a little of feudal violence, egotism and arrogance, vanity and pontification.

There is need to humanize the scientist, who rebelled, about the middle of the last century, and to his shame let himself be contaminated by the gospel of insubordination which has been since then the great vulgarity and the great falsity of the age.[12] The man of science can no longer afford to be what

71

he now is with lamentable frequency—a barbarian knowing much of one thing. Fortunately the principal figures in the present generation of scientists have felt impelled by the internal necessities of their sciences to balance their specialization with a symmetrical culture. The rest will follow in their steps as sheep follow the leading ram.

From all quarters the need presses upon us for a new integration of knowledge, which to-day lies in pieces scattered over the world. But the labour of this undertaking is enormous; it is not to be thought of while there exists no methodology of higher education even comparable to what we have for the preceding levels of education. At present we lack completely a pedagogy of the university—though this statement seems untrue at first.

It has come to be an imminent problem, one which mankind can no longer evade, to invent a technique adequate to cope with the accumulation of knowledge now in our possession. Unless some practicable way is found to master this exuberant growth, man will eventually become its victim. On top of the primitive forest of life we would only add the forest of science, whose intention was to simplify the first. If science has brought order into life we shall now have to put science in order, organize it—seeing that it is impossible to regiment science—for the sake of its healthy perpetuation. To this end we must vitalize science: that is, we must provide it with a form compatible with the human life by which and for which it was made in the first place. Otherwise—for there is no use in entrenching ourselves behind a vague optimism—otherwise science will cease to function; mankind will lose interest in it.

And so you see that by thinking over what is the mission of the university, by seeking to discover the consequent character of its cultural disciplines (viz. systematic and synthetic), we come out upon a vast horizon that spreads quite beyond the field of pedagogy, and engages us to see in the institution of higher learning an agent for the salvation of science itself.

The need to create sound syntheses and systematizations of knowledge, to be taught in the "Faculty of Culture", will call out a kind of scientific genius which hitherto has existed only as an aberration: the genius for integration. Of necessity this means specialization, as all creative effort inevitably does; but this time, the man will be specializing in the construction of a whole. The momentum which impels investigation to dissociate indefinitely into particular problems, the pulverization of research, makes necessary a compensative control—as in any healthy organism—which is to be furnished by a force pulling in the opposite direction, constraining centrifugal science in a wholesome organization.

Men endowed with this genius come nearer being good professors than those who are submerged in their research. One of the evils attending the confusion of the university with science has been the awarding of professorships, in keeping with the mania of the times, to research workers who are nearly always very poor professors, and regard their teaching as time stolen away from their work in the laboratory or the archives. This was brought home to me by experience during my years of study in Germany. I have lived close to a good number of the foremost scientists of our time, yet I have not found among them a single good teacher[13]—so let no one come and tell me that the German university, as an institution, is a model!

Notes

1 On the other hand, when medicine has devoted itself to its proper function of curing, its work has proved most fruitful for science. Contemporary physiology was launched on its career, early in the last century, not by the scientists but by the physicians, who turned aside from the scholasticism that had reigned over eighteenth century biology (taxonomy, anatomism, etc.) to meet their urgent mission with pragmatic theories. See Emanuel Radl, *Geschichte der biologischen Theorien*, vol. II (1909), a book which seems the more admirable with the passing of time.

2 [EDITOR'S NOTE] Cf. Ortega's *The Modern Theme*, p. 76: "Culture is merely a special direction which we give to the cultivation of our animal potencies."

3 I have borrowed this formula from my essay *El Estado, la juventud y el carnaval*, published in *La Nación*, of Buenos Aires, December 1924, and reprinted in *El Espectador* (VII).

4 The sublimity or meanness of a life, its wisdom or stupidity is, precisely, its plan. Obviously our plan does not remain the same for life; it may vary continually. The essential fact is that life and plan are inseparable.

5 It is easy to see that when an element of our life so fundamental as this self-justification functions irregularly, the ailment which ensues is grave. Such is the case with the curious type of man I have studied in *The Revolt of the Masses*. But the first edition of that book is incomplete. A prolonged illness prevented me from finishing it. In the later editions [not yet appeared, Oct. 1944–ED.] I am adding the third part of the study, analysing more in detail this formidable problem of "justification", and thus adding the finishing touch to that book's investigation into this very prevalent phenomenon.

6 On this subject in general see *The Revolt of the Masses* in its next edition [not yet published, Oct. 1944–ED.], where I deal more in detail with the specific ways in which the people of to-day are falsifying their lives: for example, the naïve belief that "you have to be arbitrary", from which has issued in politics the lie of Fascism, and in letters and philosophy, the young Spanish "intellectual" of recent years.

7 [EDITOR'S NOTE] The form of this proposal has been objected to by readers of the manuscript on the ground that it gives too much responsibility and too much power to one group. The American college or university might better seek to solve the administrative problem through a committee representative of the whole faculty, serving as the spearhead for the reform yet democratically stimulating and co-ordinating the initiative arising from all parts of the institution. Another committee of the whole faculty might be made responsible for improving the conditions for research; and each professional department might appoint a committee of appropriate academic and community representatives to examine how the occupational training can be oriented towards a richer service to society. This adaptation of Ortega's basic idea has been elaborated in the editor's forthcoming book on cultural education and intercultural synthesis, tentatively scheduled to be published in 1945 by Harper and Brothers.

8 It is to be noted that any dedicating of oneself, if it is real, means the dedication of one's life and nothing less.

9 Precisely because of the efficiency in the teaching, a greater power to learn is called into action.

10 In the last analysis, mathematics is wholly instrumental in character, not fundamental or substantial in itself—just as is that branch of science which studies the microscope.

11 Do not forget, in seeking to grasp the implications of this opinion, that the writer of it owes to Germany four-fifths of his intellectual possessions. I am more conscious to-day than ever before of the indisputable, towering preeminence of German science. The question alluded to has nothing to do with this.

12 The great task of the present age, in the field of morality, is to convince common men (uncommon men never fell into the snare) of the inane foolishness which envelops this urge to revolt, and make them see the cheap facility, the meanness of it; even though we may freely admit that most of the things revolted against deserve to be buried away. The only true revolt is creation—the revolt against nothingness. Lucifer is the patron saint of mere negativistic revolt.

13 Which does not mean that none exist; but it does indicate that the combination does not occur with any dependable frequency.

OUTLINES OF A POSSIBLE SOLUTION

Adolph Löwe

Source: A. Löwe, *The Universities in Transformation*, London: Sheldon Press, 1940, pp. 21–47.

The sociological approach has so far directed our critical analysis. For the problems thus discovered we can hope to find a solution only if we succeed in defining our educational aims in terms appropriate to the new society in formation. In other words, to discover the criteria for a present-day university education we must, first of all, form a general idea of the social order we are heading for, and of the position which the "educated man" is to hold in it.

In doing so, I shall refrain from committing myself to any particular social philosophy. My aim is not to postulate a new society in accordance with the aspirations of one of the political movements, but rather to read in the actual transformation of the last decades the general features and tendencies which are likely to determine the social order of the future.

1. The new society

The main data for any coming European and, in particular, English civilisation can be deduced from the cardinal changes referred to above: the end of the political and economic expansion of Western Europe, a transformation of our material and psychological technique, and the need for new forms of social integration, both national and international. Whatever the reaction of English society to these new data may be, the historical phase ahead of us will be a period of radical social change. We may take it for granted that, in view of the magnitude of the social groups and technical means involved, these changes cannot be left to individual trial and error, but require collective guidance and rational planning. I leave it undecided whether, in the distant future when Western society has readjusted itself to the new conditions, collective planning will still be required in all essential spheres of life.

It is quite possible that a new spontaneous conformity may develop and that the social character of the individuals may become strong enough to replace, as the driving force of the cultural process, the collective machinery which is necessary for the period of transition. We may even regard it as a cardinal aim of the new education to promote such a development. Yet at present we are concerned only with the period of transition the duration of which will certainly extend over more than one generation.

For this period of transition, and under the conditions assumed, the rôle of the academic graduate can be clearly defined. From whatever social strata the *political* leaders of the nation may be recruited, the *administrators* in the new society will have to be educated in the universities. To state that this has already been so in the past would not do justice either to the ever-growing range of administrative activity up to date, or to the new responsibilities, intellectual and moral, which will fall to the future social functionaries. Even before the war, more and more spheres of the economic and cultural life of the nation were being drawn into the network of planned organisation. The war itself is bound to increase this tendency, and even to divest many liberal professions of their "private" character. It is more than probable that the formidable problems of reconstruction with which we shall be faced after this war are going to strengthen rather than to weaken the forces making for control and administrative regulation.

All the symptoms mentioned which point in the direction of a planned society are visible in most Western countries. On the continent they have widely assumed the rigid form of centralised dictatorship in the service of any but humanistic ends. Yet it would be very misleading, and even highly dangerous, to confound the perverted manifestation of a universal development with the meaning and trend of this development itself. The appropriate reaction of a liberal country like England to the universal tendency towards planning cannot consist in clinging obstinately to the social organisation of a past age. The true task lies rather in the direction of shaping this evolution in accordance with the traditions and values of a democratic society. This, however, implies that the ultimate end of planning must be a new order of freedom, while the means are to be sought in spontaneous co-operation from below rather than in conformity enforced from above.

It is at once obvious that, in such a planned democracy, the education of the social functionaries is of the utmost importance. The wider the administrative power is to be diffused, and the more of it is to be delegated from the centre to regional and functional nuclei of self-government, the higher the level of rationality and morality must be both of the holders of ultimate authority and of the subordinate organs. Professional specialisation is certainly one precondition for the proper exercise of these extensive functions. Yet what will be required is, above all, imagination, enterprise and a strong sense of responsibility, all of them qualities very different from those of the professional routine mind. For this reason, the future administrator will be able to fulfil his specialist task only if he is fully conscious of the structure and aims of society at large. To be able to plan, one has to foresee the secondary consequences of one's actions. Nothing else is meant when we say that "theory" has to guide "practice" in all but the simplest undertakings. But theory in the social field rests on the understanding of the psychological and institutional mechanisms of the cultural order as a whole, and of one's own position in it. It is in this sense that the educated person of the coming age can perhaps be defined as the "enlightened expert", and since the key positions of social planning on every level will be the centres of social responsibility, the "enlightened expert" may rightly be taken as the ideal pattern of a democratic ruling class.

We should grossly underrate the magnitude of the transformation ahead of us if we were to assume that the new intellectual *élite* could be produced according to a simple blueprint devised in anticipation of the social changes themselves. The solution of the educational problems will mature only gradually during and through the bigger work of social reconstruction. All we can expect to achieve in the near future is such rebuilding of our educational framework as is necessary to stimulate the creative forces and to encourage experiments in accordance with the needs of our age of transition.

2. Vocational education

To do so will be least difficult in vocational education. As was shown above, for more than a generation the universities have been yielding to the growing demand for vocational training. They have done so to such an extent that the most popular of all complaints directed against modern university education is concerned with its "over-specialisation". Put forth as an isolated grievance, this attack is hardly fair. It is often directed against certain modern specialisms by the representatives of traditional subjects which are in themselves no less specialised. The complaint is justified only if it arises from a new insight into what makes an educated man in the modern world. But even so, the trend towards vocational specialisation cannot be reversed, since it corresponds to the higher stage of social differentiation for which we are heading. The task is one of discovering a method of specialisation which makes vocational study grow out of the understanding and experience of the cultural process as a whole.

From this point of view we should even admit that specialisation has not yet advanced far enough. Up to the present it has been more or less confined to the training in the "liberal" professions of clergy, teachers, lawyers, doctors and technicians, while the particular intellectual qualities required for social planning have hardly been trained in specialist courses. With the one exception of Economics, none of the subjects which are sometimes labelled as the "New Humanities" has secured its legitimate place in the English universities. Psychology, Sociology, Political Science, Public

Administration and even Business Administration play a rather subordinate part in the syllabus of most degree courses, yet it is these subjects in particular which will have to shape the intellectual outlook of the future social functionary. The fact that some of these New Humanities form, at the same time, an indispensable element for a new cultural education will be demonstrated below. In the same context the necessity for certain changes in the method of vocational training will have to be stressed.

3. A new cultural education

There are many details of a reform of vocational education which I propose to pass over at this stage. Indeed, we need hardly worry about its further development. The extension and intensification of vocational study are so much in line with the spontaneous demands of the age that it will "pay" in every sense of the word, and will therefore look after itself. Our true concern must be with a new *cultural* education which is both to balance and to underpin vocational education. We have discussed above some of the reasons why this is the field in which the English universities, like their opposite numbers in pre-war and Republican Germany, have lagged behind during the last generation. We must now deduce from our general assumptions as to the trend of social development what the content of a new cultural education should be.

The general definition of the aims of cultural education, given above, still holds good. Its task is one of interpreting the structure and dynamics of the modern world, both in its natural and social aspects. To do so the new cultural education must be *substantial* and not only formal. In other words, it will have to deal with the concrete matter of the cultural objects and not only with the abstract methods applied by the analysing subjects. At the same time it must be concrete in another sense, in so far as it has to interpret not only the "perpetual existence" of man, but also the *topical* situation in which modern mankind in general and the Western nations in particular find themselves.

In thus defining the new task, we have implicitly rejected any attempt to solve the problem in the traditional forms of the classical and philosophical education of the nineteenth century. Certainly there exists a great heritage of philosophical knowledge and general wisdom, handed down to us from the Ancient World and elaborated by the work of 2000 years of thought and speculation. It is also true that the fundamental values embodied in this heritage, such as liberty, justice, the value of the personality and the claim of all to the "good life", have lost nothing of their original importance, as is equally true of the values contained in the Christian message. But these abstract values and criteria have not yet found their concrete explication appropriate to the modern situation. The pattern of ancient society, so well suited for nineteenth-century England, has become quite unreal in modern mass society living under the strain of social reconstruction. An interpretation of the modern world in terms of the psychology, sociology and the concrete valuations of Plato or St Thomas must necessarily overlook or misjudge the very features which distinguish our age from the City State or from Medieval Society. Before we can apply the eternal criteria to our civilisation we must understand its structure and evolutionary tendencies by using the appropriate scientific categories.

These simple considerations will keep us out of the quarrels in which some of the representatives of Greats and traditional philosophy are involved with the extremists among the scientific specialists. The champions of the Old Humanities are right in attacking the unenlightened outlook of the narrow specialists. But the latter are equally right in rejecting the obsolete hypotheses and antiquated patterns of thought on which so much of the traditional interpretation of Nature and Society is based. Our future intellectual leaders will not be able to understand, and still less to plan, even a small fraction of social life unless they know how to link together the various aspects of their experience into a unity of knowledge. But they can carry out this process of linking together only if they have learnt to make use of the findings of the specialist sciences and, at the same time, have acquired some direct experience of, say, the particular benefits and strains arising from industrial life, of nature as re-shaped by technique, of social responsibility as increased by the new potency of planning.

The new understanding of the cultural process will have to be based on theoretical knowledge of the crucial facts, on practical experience in a representative section of modern life, and on the acquirement of intellectual and moral criteria. Accordingly the organisation of cultural education in the universities will have to be carried out on three levels.

(a) The interpretation of modern culture

The interpretative task will devolve mainly on three groups of specialisms: on History, on the New Humanities and, after a fundamental re-organisation, on the Language Departments. English education has always acknowledged the cultural function of the teaching of *History*. Yet many History Departments will have to overcome serious weaknesses in their syllabus before the old tradition can be revived under modern conditions. To my knowledge, in most universities the teaching of History still concentrates on political history on the one hand, and English history on the other hand. Neither European history as a whole, including at least America, nor the wider aspects of social and cultural history plays any significant rôle in the ordinary routine. It is doubtful whether this "isolationist" method meets the demands even of vocational education, if we consider the kind of History teaching we should like to see introduced in our schools. At all events, for the purpose of cultural education in the universities, it is certainly the universal rather than the sectional approach to the evolution of the human race which should form the students' general outlook. In this context Anthropology too has a definite function to fulfil.

If History opens up the longitudinal view, the scientific cross-section through modern society is provided by the *New Humanities*, aided by Geography. But we have to admit that the present organisation of the teaching of Psychology, Sociology, Politics and Economics serves the task of cultural education only imperfectly. This is especially true of Psychology and Economics, which are primarily organised according to the requirements of professional training and research, with a definite emphasis on the technical problems. Since the significance of these specialisms for vocational education is bound to increase, the existing organisation of teaching should by no means be scrapped. But it will have to be supplemented by courses which are expressly designed for the purpose of cultural education. This means that, in such courses, the technicalities of the subject will have to recede behind the big outlines and the crucial problems. It means further that the cultural courses based on these specialisms will have to be planned as an organic whole which reflects the totality of modern life in its various aspects.

In contrast with America or pre-Hitler Germany, *Psychology* and *Sociology*, the essentially "synthetic" subjects among the New Humanities, hold only a minor position in the present organisation of academic teaching in Britain. This has not always been so. It can be claimed that, in the Schools of Cambridge and of the Scottish Moralists, the Social Sciences developed in this country as both a humanistic and a synthetic study of man in society. This great tradition was interrupted during the nineteenth century, on the one hand by the more abstract turn which academic Philosophy took, and on the other hand by the growing preponderance of Economics in study and practice. To revive the synthetic tradition on the modern level of empirical knowledge in all the related specialisms, Psychology and Sociology should be given a central place in the organisation of postgraduate education.

The new social pattern of a planned order will crystallise around, though, we hope, not ossify within, the various national states. Therefore the study of individual civilisations, based on Language and Literature, forms one main instrument in interpreting modern culture. By transforming the *Language Departments* into Departments of National Civilisations, we shall have to attempt for our age what Ancient Greats achieved for antiquity. In these "synthetic" courses the primary interest will be not philological but cultural in the widest sense, including the political and economic history and the social structure of the country in question. Though some knowledge of the respective language is indispensable, for certain texts the use of translations may be preferable. What matters is, first of all, a broad understanding of institutions and spirit, and all means available should be used for this purpose.

It is hardly necessary to emphasise that one of these potential Departments of National Civilisation, and the most important of all of them, is the

Department of *English* Language and Literature. To interpret to the student his own national civilisation as a living pattern, which takes shape in political and social institutions no less than in the evolution of the vernacular and the works of art, literature and philosophy, is one of the cardinal aims of cultural education. The complementary task of determining the place which one's own national civilisation holds in the supra-national network of social and cultural relations, falls to the study of Universal History and of the New Humanities.

I am less certain as to the position which falls to the *Natural Sciences* in cultural education. There is the danger of superficiality if this range of subjects with very different methods is to be included. On the other hand, some knowledge of, say, Biology or Theoretical Physics would not only widen the Arts students' outlook but, at the same time, open to them a detached point of view outside the social field where personal "standpoints" constantly colour interpretation. This is, of course, even more true of the study of Mathematics.

(b) The training of experience

The opportunities of a university to bring its students into contact with social reality are limited. I shall return to this point later on, when I have to discuss the meaning of moral education under modern conditions. Here I would only point to the necessity of breaking down the barrier which to-day separates theoretical instruction and *practical apprenticeship* in the process of vocational training. The ways in which this artificial separation can be overcome are manifold, and have been widely explored in the United States. There for financial reasons a large number of students are compelled to take up practical work of some kind during their university years. Yet there are strong educational reasons which should, *e.g.*, induce a medical student to work for some time as an ambulance man or in another part of our social service system. In the same way, a law student might do work in business or as a lower clerk, not to mention the students of the teaching profession who, as a rule, test their teaching ability at a time when their choice of profession can no longer be altered. Much more valuable are, of course, experiments like the organisation at Cincinnati University, where most Departments have established systematic co-operation with the civil administration, the leading firms, the social services, etc., of the City. Theoretical instruction and practical work are combined according to a well-thought-out plan for each Department, and so vocational training becomes a living experience for the student, and is itself made the starting-point for his synthetic understanding of social life.

The quest for concrete experience could be satisfied in a more general way by introducing an obligatory "practical year" for all school-leavers intending to proceed to a university. Such an arrangement would break through both the scholastic and the social exclusiveness which, at present, separates the academic youth from the realm of action and from the other groups of society. It is certainly neither healthy nor truly humanistic to spend the first twenty to twenty-five years of one's life in nothing but receptive intellectual activity. At the same time, the university shirks an important part of its responsibilities if it confines its work to training immature minds for professional life. Practice is as much a preparation for theory as is theory for practice, and adult education, on different levels of age and experience, is a paramount task of the contemporary university.

(c) The teaching of "criteria"

On the Continent the establishment and critique of *rational and moral criteria* are regarded as the domain of Philosophy. During the last generation this view has prevailed also in England, though it is not quite in accordance with the tradition of Oxford Greats. Here History and literary education have always played a part equivalent to Philosophy. It seems to me that English civilisation has always used for its approach to Metaphysics the intuitional method of literary appreciation rather than the rational method of Philosophy. This may again be connected with the firm tradition in which the cultural life of the country developed during the last centuries, and may therefore change with the growing need for rational reorientation. Even so, literary and artistic education will always have a special function to fulfil in the formation of taste and sensibility which are critical faculties of particular importance in a highly mechanised and organised civilisation. It is true that, to serve as an instrument of cultural education, the academic teaching of art and literature would itself have to be reformed. But beginnings have been made, and at different places (Cambridge, Manchester, Kelham) a young generation consciously tries to use literary criticism for this wider task.[1] The rationalist objection against the literary approach that it is not likely to furnish "exact" results is no longer convincing, in view of the doctrinal anarchy which prevails in Philosophy.

This modern "chaos of values", which characterises all Arts subjects dealing with criteria, requires, perhaps, special consideration. We know that agreement on fundamentals and conformity of valuation cannot be restored by intellectual effort only. Still less should we try to bring about such unification from outside by organising the new university as a Church. Nothing but the process of cultural evolution itself can establish a commonly accepted table of values, and the universities would sin against their true spirit, and would ultimately frustrate their cultural mission, if they were to force this development. The university and the student within it must accept the existing struggle of competing ideologies as the background for their work. This by no means implies that this work has to confine itself to an exposition and immanent criticism of the various doctrines. Such a kind of "scientific objectivity" is, at best, a crude form of self-deception which, by its false pretences, corrupts the sense of both intellectual and moral honesty. During the present historical phase of transition, no university teacher should claim the possession of the complete truth. All he can, and should, achieve is the highest possible degree of *truthfulness*. This, however, can be attained only if he frankly professes what the natural scientist calls his "personal equation". For the same reason William James and Dewey, Frazer and Freud, Nietzsche, Bergson and Maritain, Kierkegaard and Tolstoi may be as important for cultural education as is the study of Plato and Kant.

A note on "Modern Greats"

The principle of co-ordination which should apply to the various specialisms extends also to the relationship between the interpretative and the normative part of cultural education. In other words, the courses in Philosophy and Literary Criticism will have to form an organic whole with the study of History, of the Modern Humanities and of the individual Civilisations.

In this connexion attention must be directed to a very interesting experiment in cultural education which has been made in recent years. I am referring to the Oxford Honour School of Philosophy, Politics and Economics, popularly known as "Modern Greats". More than a decade's practical experience makes this course an object-lesson of the various problems with which reform within the prevailing teaching organisation is faced.

The general idea underlying the "Modern Greats" School seems excellent. Formed after the pattern of Ancient Greats, it tries, on the one hand, to combine the interpretative and the normative elements and, on the other hand, to substitute a group of inter-related subjects dealing with the chief domains of modern civilisation for the heaping up of disconnected fragments of knowledge which characterises so many other Honours courses. One could certainly think of other possible combinations of Arts subjects, or of the inclusion of a general science subject such as Biology. But, in principle, the linking together of Philosophy with a more general and a more specialised subject of the Modern Humanities is as promising for cultural education as any other combination.

Yet at this point certain difficulties arise. As organised at present, Modern Greats not only has to serve the aims of cultural education but is, at the same time, the main course for the specialist training in Economics at Oxford. Thus for the majority of Modern Greats students cultural and vocational education are being squeezed into a three years' course. No wonder that many of them look at the philosophical and the political part of their education as an appendage of secondary importance to, if not as a diversion from, what they regard as their main subject of study. An even greater dilemma arises for the teacher in Economics. Since he is expected to provide a thorough vocational training he is bound to stress the technical aspects of his subject at the expense of the humanistic ones.

Some important lessons are to be drawn from this experience. As will be shown below, cultural education can be organised in either of two ways. On the one hand, general courses can be offered irrespective of the vocational interest of the students which is to be satisfied in specialist courses at a later stage. On the other hand, vocational education itself can be "humanised" by extending the specialist courses to bordering fields of study of particular cultural significance. It is not easy to say which way the Modern Greats School actually pursues. Originally designed as a modern parallel to Ancient Greats, the course seems to serve primarily the aims of cultural education. But the prevailing method of teaching in Economics is not quite in harmony with the humanistic tendencies of the Oxford tradition in Philosophy and Politics. Conversely, these latter courses include too small a range of topics and are, at the same time, planned on too big a scale, as would be appropriate were they only to supplement the vocational study of Economics. The solution lies probably in creating a new vocational course in Economics to which the treatment of the technical problems and the training in research would have to be transferred. Then Modern Greats could present a truly synthetic course in modern civilisation in which the principal human problems would be analysed from different angles according to a well-coordinated plan.

4. Moral education

To speak in general terms about a new form of moral education is extremely difficult. Some conclusions can be drawn from what was said above about the combination of theoretical and practical training. Certainly, less than any other, moral education admits of institutional organisation. It is bound up with that unity of theoretical postulates and practical experience which characterised the later nineteenth century. This unity has been broken up, and the prevailing scepticism and radicalism are chiefly due to the clash between the high-sounding words which fill the lecture-room and most of our orthodox text-books, and the practice of business life, party politics and international relations. Therefore we find ourselves in the paradoxical situation where we should first have to change reality before we could hope for a wholesome influence on the outlook and behaviour of the younger generation, and yet we cannot change reality unless, by some educational agency, an *élite* has been formed which acts in the new spirit.

It is true, experience in both the theoretical and practical world is the only way of breaking through this vicious circle. But we must not blind ourselves to the fact that aiming at the right kind of experience is a very difficult undertaking. Here Mr Paton's book again tells us a good deal about frustrated attempts made by the present student generation. As in all fields of life, superficial contacts may prove worse than complete seclusion. The globe-trotter who poses as the promoter of international understanding is more dangerous than the average nationalist who, at least, has genuine experience of one of the problems hampering international understanding. In the same way, the truly trained scientist, narrow as his outlook may be, is yet a more useful member in the hierarchy of the modern division of labour than is the superficial busybody who acts as president of half a dozen Student Societies.

Fundamental as moral education will be for the formation of a new *élite*, the task which falls to the universities in this respect will primarily be one of *providing opportunities* for true experience and initiative. I am not at all sure whether, under the perspective of modern life, the Ancient Universities really have much greater opportunities in this field than the Modern. College life has certainly great advantages. But I wonder whether these advantages are more than potential to-day. From the little I know about it, I have not formed the impression that consciousness of a joint purpose generally permeates the members of a college. This can arise only from important and durable contacts with the outside world, based on serious responsibilities, for instance such as the pupils in Kurt Hahn's[2] school are taking upon themselves. If the members of the different colleges were to become joint guardians of various social activities in their university towns, the original idea of the University Settlements could be revived in a modern and collective form. It is at once obvious that the Modern Universities have, in principle, the same or even greater opportunities for these experiments, both in town and country districts. But the popular cry for more residential halls in the Modern Universities once again stresses form at the expense of substance. Life in the existing halls seems of great benefit to the private comfort and, perhaps, the intellectual study of their residents. But the average student coming from these places is, as a personality, hardly above the rest.

It is not so much the master builder as the master mind whose services are required for moral education in the described sense. If I compare my experience in Germany and casual impressions formed in Switzerland, Holland and America, with my English experience, I am compelled to say that the human contacts between student and staff form the most striking contrast. This may again be different in the Ancient Universities where members of the staff live in the college. But I very much doubt whether the problem is one of external provisions mainly. A certain reluctance to form intimate relationships in the continental or American sense is bound up with what is still regarded in England as proper social intercourse. This friendly aloofness has very great advantages in ordinary life and, by working with psychological traffic lights, contributes much to the smooth operation of business in the widest sense. But is it the best possible way in which the mature person can guide the young in a period of transition, when the problems and failures of the age are constantly reflected in the problems and failures

85

of the individual? All this is part of a big chapter which would have to deal with the qualities and duties of a modern university teacher. Since we cannot presuppose his existence, all our plans in the moral field should be very cautious.

All that has been said so far against the overemphasis on loose associations without a definite purpose makes also the value of the many Student Societies questionable. Their immense number cannot deceive us about the fact that, like the soldiers who act a huge army on the stage, it is always the same few dozen people who turn up in various disguises. Matters are somewhat different in the political Societies, particularly on the Left. But again the normal procedure seems rather anarchic, and only a reflection of party life itself in its contemporary decline.

However discordant this conclusion may be with past English tradition, we must realise that the spontaneous growth of innumerable voluntary groups will not by itself satisfy the needs of a changing world. Excellent as this social technique is in a society held together by a stable framework of institutions and ideas, a much more purposeful technique and a different kind of leadership are required under the new conditions. It is in this field that English tradition will have to be amalgamated with continental and American experience, and may to its advantage even try out some of the totalitarian experiments. But the cardinal question is whether this country will again become conscious of a cultural mission, as it was conscious in the seventeenth and the nineteenth centuries. This question will be answered in fields much wider than the educational, and only then shall we know what kind of moral temper the nation will transmit to the universities, and in response receive back from them.

5. Social problems of the modern university

Numerous grave problems arise from the *new social stratification* of the student body. Besides France, England is the only European country where no serious graduate unemployment has developed yet. This is, at first sight, surprising, since the number of students has increased by about 80% above the level of 1910. This percentage increase almost equals that of Germany between 1910 and 1932 which led there to a graduate unemployment of more than 50,000 persons. The solution of the riddle lies in the absolute figures. Of 100,000 persons in this country only about 110 are students, while the corresponding figure in Germany was above 200 in 1932.

It can easily be shown that this overcrowding of the universities in post-war Germany was due largely to economic distress and social dislocation, in the same way as the relatively low figures in England reflect the stability of the middle-class position in the non-academic occupations until quite recently. Now it is very doubtful whether this stability will outlast the present war, irrespective of its military and political outcome. The grave financial inroads which the conduct of the war is bound to make upon the accumulated wealth of the business classes may easily induce them to seek a spurious economic security for their children in an academic profession. For political no less than for educational reasons, the post-war development will have to be watched very carefully and, if necessary, strict measures controlling the admission will have to be taken if the disastrous situation of post-war Germany is to be avoided.

This necessity is, however, in flagrant conflict with the demands for educational *equality of opportunity*. The present lack of this opportunity is so much the object of popular complaint that we need not enlarge upon it. Yet the measures which are usually proposed for the cure of this evil partly neglect the truly social aspect of the problem. In theory to-day everyone is agreed that each child with intellectual ability above the average should find his way to the highest stages of the educational ladder, and an increase in the number of scholarships and bursaries is regarded as the necessary but also the sufficient condition for the fulfilment of this postulate. Important and unassailable in itself as this argument is, it pays attention only to that side of the question which is primarily, though not wholly, a question of individual ascent. Against this policy it has been objected that, far from establishing educational equality, it will only deprive the lower classes of their more intelligent members and, by absorbing the rising individuals into the social *milieu* of the upper classes, will consciously or unconsciously establish an alliance between intelligence and wealth.

Promoting the social ascent of the "geniuses" of the lower classes is a matter of *individual* emancipation. Quite different is the postulate of *social* emancipation which wants to distribute the key-positions in society equally among the different social groups and classes. A stricter selection of those aspirants who come from the upper classes would, unfortunately, be no solution of this problem. No nation is so abounding in Alpha and Beta students as to be able to fill all professional posts with them. A very considerable number of Gamma students will always have to be trained in our universities, and the difficult question arises how we can mix this average group according to the demands of social equality. So long as wealth is the only criterion of selection for this group the university will not be a democratic place of education, nor will the professions for which it educates conform to the democratic criterion. Bad as the result of this state of affairs has always been from the point of view of social ethics, it may not have prejudiced very seriously the working of the social machinery during the liberal age. In the approaching age of social planning this defect may actually endanger social stability because of the increased power of the academically trained minority and the inevitable suspicion with which the masses will examine the process of their selection.

Clearly as I see the problem, I have at the moment no solution to propose. It will probably have to be sought in a reform of the school system.

The entrance to secondary education will have to be democratised in such a way as to exclude a fair number of those pupils who to-day are admitted and dragged through simply because their parents can afford to pay. Such a reform would, of course, presuppose a re-organisation of the system of school examinations. The present prevalence of memory knowledge and set-book cramming would have to give way to tests of intellectual initiative. But these are matters for another book.

Notes

1 *e.g.*, see Brother Every's book in this series.
2 Kurt Hahn, *Education for Leisure*, Oxford, 1938.

80

THE COLLEGE-UNIVERSITY

Its development in Aberdeen and beyond

John M. Fletcher

Source: J. J. Carter and D. J. Withrington (eds) *Scottish Universities: Distinctiveness and Diversity*, Edinburgh: John Donald, 1992, pp. 16–25.

At the Siena conference of 1988 to discuss the history of academic colleges, an attempt was made to list the various types of colleges established in universities before the close of the seventeenth century. The college-university was then noted as one distinctive type.[1] It was apparent, however, that no serious attempt had been made to consider the reasons for the emergence of this institution or to discuss the difficulties it experienced and the legacy it bequeathed. The first college-university, described by Rashdall as a 'new form of university',[2] was established at Sigüenza in 1489. Foundations at Aberdeen (1495) and at Alcalá (1499)[3] followed shortly afterwards, establishing, particularly in Spain, the acceptability of this type of institution. For the British Isles, the most important college-university was erected as Trinity College, Dublin, in 1592.[4] The reasons for the sudden appearance of several examples of this special type of university in the last decades of the fifteenth century will concern us later. It is difficult to trace any direct link between the three earliest foundations. William Elphinstone, when he planned the establishment of King's College in Old Aberdeen, can hardly have had any knowledge of the changes that had taken place at a relatively obscure college in Sigüenza. For Alcalá the stated model was not Sigüenza but the College of Saint Bartholomew at Salamanca.[5]

The organisation of a college-university, as its name suggests, involved in a variety of ways some amalgamation of the functions of the college and the university. It was not always clear exactly what was intended here. As late as 1821 the position of Trinity College was ambiguous; George IV on his visit to Dublin agreed to receive the university but not the college! A judicious alteration to the wording of the invitation on this occasion resolved the difficulty, but it was still occupying the minds of legal experts advising the Royal Commission on Trinity College in 1907.[6] The bond between college and university was cemented by the role allocated to the head of the college; he was given some important statutory position in the administration of the university. At Alcalá the early statutes record unequivocally that one person should be both head of the college and rector of the university.[7] At Aberdeen, the offices of principal of King's College and rector of the university were separated but the principal, by the terms of the founder's charters, always held one of the three keys of the university chest;[8] no financial decision, therefore, could be implemented without his knowledge and consent. It is possible that the role of the head of the college was perceived differently according to whether the founder envisaged that the future members of his university would include those living outside college jurisdiction.

The college-university was also different from other contemporary institutions in that it attempted to include in one complex all the various buildings required for the activities of a university. Fortunately the survival of several of these early complexes enables us to examine more clearly the intentions of the founders. From such evidence and from an inventory of residential accommodation made in 1542, it would seem that King's College, Aberdeen, provided a chapel, a library, a refectory with kitchen and storerooms, a lecture hall, and rooms for some twenty-four masters and students.[9] Since the hall, chapel or refectory could be used for university meetings and formal ceremonies, all the essential needs of staff and students could be supplied within this one college. However, such an arrangement would assume that numbers attending the university remained small and unchanging, and that the existing buildings and accommodation would continue to satisfy their requirements.

That three college-universities appeared over such a short space of time and in both Spain and Scotland would lead us to believe that some common factors were influencing founders at this date. It could be argued, from the example of Aberdeen, that the college-university represented the best use of limited resources in an economically backward area. The founder was compelled to provide the necessary university buildings and accommodation in the absence of private support from wealthy patrons or from families with money enough to pay for their sons' residence. Control over the endowments of a small university could be better arranged when the head of a college had complete oversight of all its buildings and residential accommodation. Whatever were the motives of Elphinstone, they could not necessarily be attributed to other founders. The rich cardinal-archbishop of Toledo, primate of Spain, was certainly not restricted by limited resources when he established his college at Alcalá. It was a much larger institution than King's College, with support for thirty-three collegiales, twelve capellani, thirteen cameriste and an undetermined number of portionists.[10] As will be noted below, Ximenes' later measures to endow further his new university were not the actions of a man constrained by poverty.

Perhaps more important in influencing founders at this date was a growing concern for the maintenance of law, order and discipline within the
university community. As the early history of the universities of Paris, Oxford
and Bologna had shown, tensions between privileged masters or students and
aggrieved townsmen frequently ended in violence. Rival elements amongst
masters and students themselves also often resorted to open street warfare;
one of the earliest Oxford statutes attempted to bring peace to the quarrelling Irish and members of the northern Nation.[11] The expansion of universities in the fourteenth and fifteenth centuries spread this problem and an
awareness of it. The magistrates of Brussels and Barcelona were so afraid of
violence from undisciplined students that they strongly opposed attempts
by state governments to establish universities in their cities.[12] This problem
stemmed partly from an inability of early university authorities to control
masters and students. When their members lived in rooms rented from
townsmen, universities could do little to monitor the behaviour of students
or prevent those accused from quitting the university speedily with their
possessions; any aggrieved party was left without adequate remedy or compensation. The need to survey student behaviour and to apprehend criminal
elements became more serious when universities were accused in the fifteenth
century of harbouring heretics, especially followers of Wyclif and Hus. In
Spain efforts to cleanse the kingdom of Jews and Moslems, a policy supported also by the founder of the University of Alcalá, encouraged concern
for the stricter control of student activities. 'New Christians' were banned
from attendance at the University of Sigüenza in 1497.[13] It is understandable that benefactors at the close of the fifteenth century wished to support
a system whereby all or most students and masters lived in colleges under
the supervision of a principal. Not only could such students be closely
observed, but the threat of expulsion from their accommodation and seizure
of any property could be real deterrents against misbehaviour.

The need to harbour resources and control students was a very real requirement, but less tangible influences on founders of the college-university
may have been the desire both to strengthen college life and to enhance
developments already seen earlier in universities. College founders in the
middle ages held the view that the collegiate life was superior to that of
the individual. Probably derived from an early respect for the common life
of the religious, this belief was reinforced by an awareness of the practical
advantages — interaction with other students and perhaps masters, the possibility of financial and moral support, access to a common library, experience
of administration — that collegiate life could bring. The college-university,
by requiring all members of a university to adopt the collegiate life, could
be seen as reversing that damaging tendency towards individualism and
selfishness that many prominent academics saw amongst their contemporaries.[14] Also, the institution of this new type of university could be seen as a
logical extension of what had gone before. Whereas the earliest universities

had been little more than gatherings of masters and students utilising what rooms and shelter they could find, by the close of the middle ages students were expecting more facilities. New foundations of the late fourteenth and early fifteenth centuries were often equipped from their beginnings with purpose-built lecture rooms, libraries and chapels. Such ranges of buildings survive today, as for example at Cracow where the Collegium Maius took its present form largely in the fifteenth century. Earlier foundations, Salamanca, for instance, now also acquired such groups of buildings. There was a movement away from seeing the university as a collection of students towards regarding it as a collection of buildings. Several universities, especially those in the Holy Roman Empire, that needed to attract qualified teaching staff, provided special colleges to accommodate their lecturers. It would seem a logical extension of these developments to expect the founder to provide *all* the buildings required by masters and students on one site. This would mean adding to the now usual chapel, library, and lecture rooms accommodation for teachers and students and the necessary refectory, kitchen and ancillary buildings to support this. The college-university perhaps arose from both a development of earlier precedents and as a response to difficulties that these foundations were experiencing.

Yet it may be argued that the college-university was itself already out-of-date at the time of its inauguration. Changes in the pattern of student and staff recruitment to the late medieval and renaissance universities made the concepts that lay behind the establishment of such college-universities no longer generally acceptable. Historians have correctly drawn attention to the changes in the curriculum that accompanied the reception of the New Learning by the European universities. The attack on scholastic logic and scholastic theology, the encouragement of the study of classical Latin and Greek grammar and the literature of Rome and Greece, the emergence of Hebrew as a university subject, efforts to 'purify' the study of law and medicine, certainly greatly changed the appearance of the curriculum of all universities. Such changes did little to affect the structure of these institutions. The universities could offer the new or remodelled subjects without altering their faculty, administrative or teaching structures. The same lecture rooms and the same buildings could accommodate and cater for students of these different subjects. The survival of so much of medieval terminology, of medieval academic organisation and of so many medieval buildings shows how the older universities could adopt the renaissance curriculum without a radical change in their form and appearance. They could not, however, adapt to major social changes at this date without abandoning some of their important and cherished characteristics. It is in this area, we may suggest, where the serious pressures for radical change originated; these pressures especially affected the college-university.

Firstly, we must consider the changing role of married students and lecturers. This has attracted little attention from historians of the medieval universities, perhaps intimidated by the harsh comments on women found in college statutes and by the much quoted judgment on a married student of Vienna 'uxorem duxit versus in dementiam'.[15] In fact, many universities assumed that there would be married students, masters and doctors amongst their members and, especially in the fifteenth century, made provision for the protection of their wives and families. No full investigation of the position of such married men within the universities has been made, but it is interesting to note that it was the role of the scholar or wife as a trader protected by university privileges that attracted the attention of the local civic authorities. Scattered references to this concern in the fifteenth century indicate that the number of married men within the universities was sufficient to provoke these authorities to take action. At Oxford, for example, in 1459 an agreement between the university and the town defined the types of privileged persons allowed to remain within the jurisdiction of the university. It was expressly stated that scholars having 'a wyf and household within the precinct of the Universite' and engaging in trade were to pay the same charges as other burgesses of the town.[16] Again, at Freiburg at the close of the fifteenth century, the presence of married students, masters and doctors was continually souring relations between town and university.[17] If students did not intend to pursue a career in the church there was no reason why they should remain celibate. Civil lawyers and physicians in particular could find lucrative employment in lay society. Moreover, with the end of compulsory celibacy in countries that accepted the protestant Reformation, the necessity for theologians to refrain from marriage if they wished to follow a career in the church was here ended. The universities of the sixteenth century, especially in the protestant area of northern Europe, had to recognise that some of their members, especially their older masters and doctors, would be married with wives and probably children and servants to support.

The university colleges of northern Europe had to make an important reassessment of their position as this situation became more common. Already an occasional individual and unmarried member of a college had attempted to retain his fellowship and yet live outside the premises: a master of the Sorbonne in 1481 had his own house and complained that he could not sleep in the college because his books were kept at his home.[18] Even when the original numbers for which colleges were founded were reduced, the standard of comfort left much to be desired, and it is understandable that the more prosperous of university masters preferred to acquire their own privacy and accommodation. If such masters and doctors were married with families, it would be impossible to house them in colleges with very limited accommodation and rules for common meals in hall. The acceptance of such a situation implied the end of collegiate life as the medieval universities had known it; especially for the teaching staff. Some colleges, such as those at Oxford and Cambridge, survived with an uneasy compromise, allowing their heads to marry while the fellows had to remain celibate. Most had to abandon gradually any requirement that teaching staff should share a collegiate life. The universities sometimes accepted the need to cater for the children of such staff; Freiburg already in 1480 allowed the legitimate sons of its regent masters and doctors to matriculate without charge.[19]

If these changes threatened the existence of such colleges, they posed an equally serious threat to the survival of the college-universities. It would seem that Elphinstone, himself a trained lawyer with considerable experience of continental universities, was aware of this problem. He required his legal and medical teaching staff to live not in his college but in separate houses in Old Aberdeen. Probably the possibility that his university would have to recruit married men with families to fill some at least of these posts had already occurred to him. He also allowed his grammarian to live outside the college; many humanist teachers were married and preferred to work outside institutions with a clerical tradition.[20] Presumably students of civil law and physicians, the most likely to be married, received their instruction in these separate houses and so did not disturb the routine of the younger members of the college. Even when Trinity College, Dublin, was founded by a protestant monarchy, the medieval insistence on celibacy for its fellows was maintained. Clearly, both King's College and Trinity College would be in some difficulties when others, apart from lawyers and physicians, demanded the right to marry and yet retain their fellowships.

In fact, neither institution seems to have been able to cope satisfactorily with this situation. At the date of the Nova Fundatio for Aberdeen in 1583 there seemed no possibility of allowing any of the twelve bursars to marry and retain his scholarship. The position of the principal and the four regents is not clear. The statutes speak of the wives and daughters of the masters, so presumably these were to be allowed to marry. However, the same statutes require all members on the foundation except the grammarian to live in the college, but prohibit all women from entering! Are we to imagine that it was expected that the wives of the masters would live apart from their husbands and outside the college? The position is very unclear and it is possible that all provisions of the Nova Fundatio were not followed at King's College.[21] It does seem, however, that any attempt to require celibacy from the teaching staff had been by this date abandoned. At Trinity College, the formal prohibition of marriage remained binding on fellows until 1840. However, many fellows simply ignored this; in 1811, when action was taken to impose the regulation strictly, sixteen out of the twenty-five fellows were married.[22] It is apparent that the problem of accommodating married fellows was never satisfactorily resolved by either of these northern college-universities until more recent attitudes rendered any attempts to impose celibacy on teaching staff obsolete.

The second factor which seriously challenged the character of the college-universities was simply their need to expand. The difficulty here was how to maintain a growing university population all or mostly resident in one set of buildings. At Sigüenza, the college-university seems to have been very small and limited in its outlook; it provided for only a rector and twelve collegiales, following the pattern set by Christ and his disciples. One lecturer in theology and one in philosophy were established; the collegiales were forbidden to study canon law, although after 1505 they could begin such a course after six years' preparatory work.[23] Expansion at Sigüenza seems neither to have been anticipated nor greatly desired. The position was much different at Alcalá established by the ambitious and powerful Ximenes. Here, the instant success of the university and its reputation brought a sudden influx of students: 'plurimi . . . ad praefatum nostrum collegium et universitatem . . . confluunt', as the 1513 statutes declare.[24] Supported by its generous and wealthy founder, the university proceeded to establish no fewer than eighteen new colleges, twelve to accommodate 154 students, six to accept a further 72.[25] However, the authority of the head of the original college, instituted by the early statutes, was maintained by allowing him the right to remove the principals of these new colleges at will: 'ad nutum rectoris a mobile'.[26] In this way the university was assisted in its efforts to maintain a totally residential membership under the authority of the rector.

At Aberdeen we have seen that a number of students and teaching-staff was expected to live outside the college from the early days of its foundation. By the terms of the Nova Fundatio, as we have noted, all members of the foundation except the grammarian were required to reside in college. This unequivocable demand was made more understandable by the abolition of the posts of canonist, civilian and medical lecturer by the same Nova Fundatio, for these were the teachers allowed to live out-side the college by the original university statutes.[27] No doubt the pres-sures on the college-university to expand its intake had been dampened by the depressed state of Scotland during the sixteenth century and then much reduced by the foundation of Marischal College in New Aberdeen in 1593. Even so, the requirement of residence could not be maintained, as the records of the 1619 visitation show, probably because the numbers entering the university exceeded the rooms available in the college; thirty-eight students entered in 1604 so that some sixty or seventy undergraduates required accommodation in each year of the early seventeenth century.[28] Certainly, later in the century, some students were allowed to live outside the college, to which they returned for their evening meal and for a period of study before leaving when the gates were closed.[29] Nevertheless, attempts were made again in 1724 and 1753 to enforce residence in college and the taking of meals at the common table.[30] The constant repetition of these requirements is in itself an indication that residence could not be enforced. Indeed, it is difficult to see how, without further building, expen-sive beyond its financial resources, the college-university could maintain such a requirement.

The need to enforce residence at Trinity College, especially in the first two centuries of its existence, was much more evident. The college had been founded to discourage the Irish from travelling to the continent for their education. It was expected to promote the protestant cause in a country that had so far proved largely resistant to its evangelism. Accordingly it was recognised that the best method of influencing the young was to place them under strict control in residential accommodation. Here their behaviour, morals and religious observances could be monitored as well as their academic progress supervised. Early humanist educators in Italy and elsewhere had stressed the importance of boarding, and the Jesuits were also to emphasise the role of residential education. The college-university in Dublin was expected not only to bring higher education to Ireland but also to convert the sons of Catholic families that it hoped to attract. In this way a strong and influential protestant party could be formed. Accordingly, the provision of residential accommodation was seen as an essential part of this ambitious scheme. Trinity College, therefore, made strenuous efforts to maintain its residential character. Conditions in Ireland during the sixteenth and seventeenth centuries did not favour the expansion of higher learning, nor did the turbulent and violent relations between the Catholic and protestant elements encourage an increase in Catholic participation in the expansion of a protestant college. Pressure on space at Trinity College was not a serious problem while such a situation existed in Ireland. Following the victory of William at the Battle of the Boyne in 1690, and the establishment of a virtually unchallenged English rule, an increasingly prosperous aristocracy and bourgeoisie sent its sons in growing numbers to the college. Between 1765 and 1790 the annual intake of students rose from around one hundred to about double that number,[31] and the college was unable to provide accommodation for this very considerable increase. By 1775 only 225 from a total of 598 could be found rooms in college buildings.[32] A greater number of entrants produced also an increase in the teaching staff employed. Nor could these new professors be accommodated in college: by 1830 there were thirteen professors who did not hold fellowships.[33] Inevitably this situation produced divisions within both the student and the teaching community. Despite its energetic building programme, Trinity College was unable to maintain a policy of complete residence for its staff and students as soon as more peaceful and prosperous times persuaded more young men to seek entrance.

The college-universities of Old Aberdeen and Dublin were, therefore, both forced to abandon one of their essential characteristics, the insistence on residence by most staff and students, in face of pressure of numbers and hostility to this concept especially by married members. Space does not allow a closer examination of the later history of college-universities in Catholic areas of Europe, but several important differences may here be emphasised. Firstly, the survival of religious houses in university towns there provided a means of recruiting both students and lecturers to the universities without the necessity of providing residential accommodation. Such members would be expected to reside in the houses of their appropriate order; nor was there a problem of married entrants here. Secondly, and more importantly, the spread of the Jesuit order in Catholic Europe brought a new stimulus to older universities but also encouraged the foundation of new institutions, several of which later acquired the status of universities. Often the Jesuits were able to realise most of the ambitions of the college-university: their buildings were frequently large and well-endowed, as a perambulation of the site of the Clementinum in Prague today still shows. The lecturers, being members of the order, were required to be resident and celibate; they encouraged students to be resident; finally, they were usually able to offer a complete programme of study in arts subjects, in theology and, less successfully, in canon law.[34] The success of the Jesuit order in attracting and in teaching students is perhaps a belated justification for the concept of the college-university. It must also be remembered that for students wishing to follow their studies at university by a career in the church, celibacy was still required in Catholic areas. Pressure on accommodation from married students was, accordingly, not so great a problem in these parts of Europe. Nevertheless, however successful the Jesuit revival of the college-university, social and political changes in the late eighteenth century in Catholic areas were working against the continuance of such institutions. The demand for an education free of clerical control and designed to produce graduates to serve a secular state was an essential feature of the Enlightenment. Like their predecessors, the college-universities of the Jesuits could not for long resist such pressures.

From this introduction to some aspects of the comparative study of the college-universities, it will be apparent that there are many further features of the development of these interesting institutions that deserve attention. Although college-universities emerged at an inopportune time, especially in northern Europe, problems associated with their peculiar constitutions remained to occupy the attention of their administrators for many centuries. It was not until 1836 that King's College, Aberdeen, reported that for several years past there had been no demand for a public table, and only in 1826 that it was noted that no students lived in the college.[35] For some three hundred years here the college authorities, it seems, had struggled to maintain one of the essential principles of the college-university.

At the close of the nineteenth century the universities of Europe reacted in various ways to the demands of women's organisations for equal treatment. Admission was first conceded, then the right to attend lectures and take examinations, and finally permission to take degrees and play a full part in university affairs. However, at Trinity College, the university buildings belonged to the college and were situated in its grounds. The university fought a strenuous and sometimes humorous campaign to keep out women,

97

raising such profound objections as the impossibility of constructing a ladies toilet in the college. It was not until 1968 that women were elected to college fellowships and only in 1972 allowed to reside in college rooms.[36] Was this perhaps the last desperate effort of the college-university to maintain its unique character?

Notes

1 See J. M. Fletcher, 'The History of Academic Colleges: Problems and Prospects', in D. Maffei, H. de Ridder-Symoens (eds), *I collegi universitari in Europa tra il xiv e il xviii secolo* (Milan, 1991).
2 H. Rashdall, *The Universities of Europe in the Middle Ages* (new ed., Oxford, 1936), ii, 105.
3 *Ibid.*, ii, 318–320 (the revised foundation date is taken from L. J. Macfarlane, *William Elphinstone and the Kingdom of Scotland 1431–1514: the Struggle for Order* [Aberdeen, 1985], 105–106).
4 The latest of many histories of Trinity College is that by R. B. McDowell and D. A. Webb, *Trinity College Dublin 1592–1952. An Academic History* (Cambridge, 1982).
5 Rashdall, *Universities*, ii, 106.
6 The problems concerning Trinity College are noted in C. Maxwell, *A History of Trinity College Dublin 1591–1892* (Dublin, 1946), 6 n.6.
7 'Unus sit caput et rector totius collegii et universitatis': *Constitutiones insignis collegii sancti Ildephonsi* (Alcalá, 1716), 2.
8 Macfarlane, *Elphinstone*, 358.
9 *Ibid.*, 326–39.
10 The early documents are printed in *Constitutiones . . . Ildephonsi*.
11 S. Gibson, *Statuta Antiqua Universitatis Oxoniensis* (Oxford, 1931), 84.
12 See the discussion in J. M. Fletcher, 'Welcome stranger or resented intruder? A reconstruction of the foundation of the University of Aberdeen in the context of European university development in the later middle ages', *Aberdeen University Review*, 180 (1988), 311.
13 Rashdall, *Universities*, ii, 105 n.3.
14 See, for example, the attack on Oxford bachelors of law who wished to be known as masters 'propter lucrum et superbiam' in 1435: H. E. Salter, *Registrum Cancellarii Oxoniensis 1434–1469* (Oxford, 1932), ii, 356.
15 Rashdall, *Universities*, ii, 242 n.4.
16 H. Anstey, *Munimenta Academica* (London, 1868), i, 347.
17 See the repeated disputes in the first volume of the unpublished Senatus Protocollum in the Freiburg University Archives.
18 'Difficile enim esset ei penoctare in collegio et habere libros suos in domo quam habet in vico': R. Marichal, *Le Livre des Prieurs de Sorbonne (1431–1485)* (Paris, 1987), 245.
19 Freiburg Protocollum Senatus, i, f.78v.
20 Marfarlane, *Elphinstone*, 339, 378.
21 The Nova Fundatio is discussed in R. S. Rait, *The Universities of Aberdeen* (Aberdeen, 1895), 108–117, and in D. Stevenson, *King's College, Aberdeen, 1560–1641: from Protestant Reformation to Covenanting Revolution* (Aberdeen, 1990).
22 McDowell and Webb, *Trinity College*, 107.
23 I. Montiel Garcia, *Historia de la Universidad de Sigüenza* (Maracaibal, 1963), ii, 12, 20, 59, 81.

24 *Constitutiones . . . Ildephonsi*, 104.
25 The arrangements are noted in *Constitutiones . . . Ildephonsi.*
26 *Ibid.*, 106.
27 Rait, *Universities of Aberdeen*, 114.
28 *Ibid.*, 126, 120.
29 *Ibid.*, 156.
30 *Ibid.*, 200.
31 McDowell and Webb, *Trinity College*, 86.
32 *Ibid.*, 115.
33 *Ibid.*, 110.
34 See, for example, the interesting study of the Jesuits at Fulda, Würzburg, Ingolstadt and Dillingen in E. Schubert, 'Zur Typologie gegenreformatorischer Universitätsgründungen', in H. Rössler and G. Franz (eds), *Universität und Gelehrtenstand 1400–1800* (Limburg, 1970), 85–105.
35 Rait, *Universities of Aberdeen*, 223–24.
36 McDowell and Webb, *Trinity College*, 353.

CHANGE AND RESISTANCE TO CHANGE

A consideration of the development of English and German universities during the sixteenth century

John M. Fletcher

Source: *History of Universities* I (1981): 1–36.

During the sixteenth century, the universities of northern Europe reacted to criticisms of their structure and curricula more searching than any other attack they had received since the thirteenth century. The censures of humanists, which perhaps could be dismissed at the close of the preceding century as the comments of a few talented but exceptional individuals, were now taken up by considerable numbers of influential scholars and supported by the prestige of Erasmus himself. Controversies in Germany, such as that surrounding the rivalry of Pfefferkorn and Reuchlin, publicised the arguments of the supporters of the New Learning, perhaps against the wishes of some of them; in England, Oxford and Cambridge received new colleges whose founders, Fisher, Fox and Wolsey, were pledged to encourage the study of classical learning. As the breach between Protestants and Catholics in northern Europe widened, universities again found their traditional liberties and curricula challenged. The luxury of a free university could not be tolerated by any ruler wishing to stifle resistance in his own dominions and fearing for the safety of his throne. By the close of the century, supporters of the Reformation and the Counter Reformation looked to the universities they controlled to produce learned defenders of their different beliefs. The reaction of the universities of England and Germany to these challenges will reveal something of the different characteristics of the universities and the societies in which they functioned.[1]

It is not possible to speak of a humanistic 'programme' for the reform of the northern universities. Some humanists approached the universities with wide experience of the curricula of several different institutions at which they had studied: Thomas Linacre, for example, knew of the state of the faculties of arts and medicine at Oxford, but also of the situation at the universities of Rome and of northern Italy where he had studied. The arrangements he made for his lectureships at Oxford and Cambridge show how he had profited from this experience.[2] Others had for many years been absent from academic life; Jakob Sturm in 1522 confessed that he had studied at Heidelberg only grammar and logic and that eighteen years ago. He nevertheless criticises the university's teaching of both arts and theology, not understanding that the use of a new translation of Aristotle, which he recommends, had in fact been accepted by the Faculty of Arts two years earlier.[3] Some humanists reacted violently against the curriculum of the universities; others were prepared to see some value in contemporary studies which they wished only to modify or extend. The early disagreement, for instance, between Erasmus and Colet about the recognition of Aquinas's importance is well known.[4] Most humanists contented themselves with general attacks on 'Scotists', 'Thomists', 'sophisters' and such like, or, as Conrad Celtis at Vienna,[5] attempted to set up rival institutions of further education outside the control of the universities. Even Erasmus thought that the conservatives were too strongly entrenched in the northern universities. He showed little interest in specific proposals for wholesale reform, writing, perhaps naively, 'ego nunquam futurus sum huius autor tumultus'.[6]

Occasionally, however, prominent humanists were asked to address themselves to the reform of certain universities and faculties, and were so compelled to put forward detailed expression of their views. In 1522 the prominent scholar and humanist Jakob Sturm supplied to the Chancellor of the Elector Palatine proposals for the reform of the University of Heidelberg. He complains that at the university lecturers teach from unsuitable translations of Aristotle so that neither lecturers nor students understand what has been written. Students, he argues, are required only to have heard, or to have 'completed' the study of the Aristotelian texts. This programme is to be abolished. In its place, grammar is to be taught from the best authors together with rhetoric and 'quae ad bone ac expedite dicendum conferunt.' Logic, Sturm proposes, should be taught not from texts which contain 'dregs of sophistry' but from such authors as Trapezuntius or Rudolfus Agricola, himself buried at Heidelberg; Petrus Hispanus, 'barbaricus ille', is to be replaced by Julianus Caesar. Despite his previous mention of 'the most eloquent philosopher', Sturm can only write condescendingly of Aristotle that he *may* be taught: 'non displicet', but the new translations are to be used. Physics and Ethics are to be studied from the *Paraphrases* of Jacobus Faber Stapulensis. More highly qualified teachers of mathematics are required, and a lecturer should be appointed to teach Greek and to give a daily lecture on some 'good author' of oratory or poetry.[7] These proposals for the modification of the arts course contain the usual references to contemporary authors supported by the humanists and the usual tactless and inconsiderate language found too often in humanistic diatribes against their opponents. More seriously, the implementation of these proposals would replace a course bound together by the common use and teaching of basic concepts of logic and philosophy with a programme of no unity, where the subjects seem to have no obvious relationship one with the other and appear to represent an uneasy compromise between classical studies and remnants of the medieval curriculum. Certainly the earlier aim of introducing the student to a study in depth of Aristotelian philosophy would, by these proposals, be abandoned.

For the Faculty of Theology, Sturm confesses his lack of knowledge but suspects that Heidelberg shares the failings of other German universities: an exclusive reliance on scholastic doctors and Peter Lombard. These authors are to be repudiated and relegated to the convents of the Franciscans and Dominicans who may teach them to those who wish to attend. Instead, the faculty is to appoint two lecturers to teach the Old and New Testaments, and especially the Epistles of St. Paul. The early Greek and Latin Fathers are also to be taught. In law and medicine, Sturm has not a great deal to suggest except to hope that the Chancellor himself can advise the university. Other humanist critics here content themselves with demanding better translations and a clearer attention to the literal exposition of the text. It is clear that, for the humanists, the chief opposition to their reform proposals was expected to come from the faculties of arts and theology: the theologians were thought to be especially hostile to change. 'Reformacio a theologis incipienda est', wrote Spiegel of Heidelberg, 'quam tamen omnium maxime oppugnabunt'.[8] Yet these were the faculties that were strongest in the northern universities. In Germany the numerical predominance of the artists was overwhelming even if their constitutional strength did not always reflect this; at Oxford and Cambridge, the faculties of theology and arts were not only numerically and constitutionally powerful, but they could justly claim that the European reputation of both universities, and especially Oxford, rested on their achievements. It is not surprising that, in face of such potential opposition, humanists in both Germany and England attempted to utilise pressure from external sources to compel universities to accept their programmes of reform.

Pressure on the universities from Catholic or Protestant sources did not represent so serious a threat to their traditional character. Rulers, churchmen, local government representatives and city authorities were usually more concerned to establish their authority over their own universities than to interest themselves in details of curricular reform. However, once this authority had been recognised, it was not difficult for the dominant party, especially when led by some such dynamic personality as an Oecolampadius at Basel or a Melanchthon at Wittenberg, to encourage a reform programme within the university. However, such reforms in general affected two faculties only: canon law and theology. The Faculty of Canon Law was of no concern to Protestants and was usually quickly abolished. Both Protestant and later Catholics reformers were concerned to adjust the curriculum of the Faculty of Theology in their own favour. Protestants were generally hostile to the medieval authorities and sought to replace them with a deeper study of the Bible and the early Fathers. Catholics, especially after the Council of Trent, were compelled to be more selective in their choice of medieval authorities. A greater respect and reliance on Thomas Aquinas replaced the more diverse studies of the fifteenth century universities. It is clear that the Protestant attitude to the studies of the Faculty of Theology had many similarities to that of the humanists. Indeed, many of the early Protestant reformers of theological faculties were themselves supporters of the New Learning and it is difficult to disentangle one reforming strand from the other.

By the close of the sixteenth century, the reactions of the German and English universities to these proposals for change were revealing interesting differences. The German universities showed a readiness to accept speedy and frequent changes in their structure and curriculum; such changes were not simply of minor importance but often involved a drastic reshaping of the particular university. Space will not allow a full examination of each faculty of each university, but it will be useful to consider in detail one faculty of a major university. For our purposes, the University of Wittenberg, founded in 1502 before the full impact of humanistic and Protestant criticism was felt, will act as a convenient barometer to test the reaction of German universities. Within this university, changes in the Faculty of Arts structure and curriculum will enable us to plot the progress of reform proposals in an area where they were chiefly felt.

The University of Wittenberg promulgated its first set of statutes for the Faculty of Arts in 1504, basing them almost word for word on those of the Faculty of Arts at Tübingen.[9] The 1507 lecture list shows that there were twenty five lecturers in the faculty which, as at Tübingen, was organised to provide two *viae*. There were already lectures being given on certain Latin classical texts. In 1508, only four years after the acceptance of the first statutes, the faculty was reorganised and new statutes provided: three *viae*, Thomist, Scotist and Occamist, were established and three hours of humanistic lectures were given daily. By 1518, Greek and Hebrew lectures were organised and the new translation of Aristotle was being used; in the following year it was proposed to end lectures in the Thomist *via* and erect a lectureship on Ovid. In 1523, Melanchthon arranged for the introduction of declamations, two in each month; these were reorganised in 1538. A further issue of statutes to the faculty was made in 1545 when ten lectureships were named: two of these were in Latin poetry and Cicero, one was in grammar, based on the reading of recent or classical authorities, one was in Greek, and another in Hebrew. The movement away from the medieval curriculum that still characterised the statutes of 1504 is already significant. The five lectureships that cover the traditional areas of study are also in some cases associated with more recent texts in these fields. Shortly after the university celebrated its first centenary, a further detailed reorganisation of the Faculty of Arts was made by the Elector Christians II in 1606. From these regulations, we learn that the faculty had eight official lecturers: in Hebrew, Greek, oratory, poetry, dialectic, physics, ethics, and mathematics. Lectures on history were also given, but as an adjunct to the central programme. The century, therefore, had seen a profound modification of the traditional course in arts. New subjects and new texts have been introduced. The study of logic, which had earlier underpinned the entire arts course has now become simply one of a number of special subjects: indeed, the Elector in 1606 seems to regard logic as essentially a tool to protect students from the arguments of Jesuits and Calvinists: 'von den fallaciis Jesuitarum et Calvinianorum'. The major texts of Aristotle, Euclid, Ptolemy and a few others continue to be studied, as the sixteenth century here had as yet found no substitute. At the beginning of the seventeenth century, the Faculty of Arts seems to be moving towards the modern situation where the faculty consists of a number of independent disciplines, each claiming to be virtually self sufficient.[10]

This readiness of the Faculty of Arts to accept frequent and radical change can also be found in other faculties and in the university as a whole at Wittenberg. New statutes for the higher faculties and for the university are regularly promulgated. These, for instance, reorganised the Faculty of Theology on Lutheran principles and established the use of recent Italian commentaries in the Faculty of Medicine. Apart from major changes introduced in this way, there was a steady stream of investigations into the university which often produced legislation modifying aspects of teaching, discipline or procedure. It is especially interesting to see at Wittenberg that new Electors often used the occasion of their accession to issue charters of refoundation to the university, introducing various minor changes at the same time. In 1555, the new Elector August von Sachsen, for example, introduced formal examination of books and papers in theology by a panel of lecturers before permission to print them was granted. The university seems to have been under continuous pressure to ensure that its curriculum was up to date and that its lecturers were carrying out their duties properly. Problems presented by innovations, such as that raised by the use of Ramist texts, were quickly dealt with and the decisions embodied in formal legislation.

Other German universities have a similar history during the sixteenth century. Ingolstadt adopted new statutes for its Faculty of Arts in 1519–20 and again in 1539. Here also religious pressure produced changes in the Faculty of Theology; the lecture lists of 1575 show how for a strongly Catholic university the Bible and the works of Thomas Aquinas now dominated the curriculum.[8] A reorganisation of the University of Rostock followed the acceptance of the *Formula Concordiae* in 1563; a further *Formula Concordiae* followed in 1577 and the Duke's visitation of 1599 introduced more changes.[12] The University of Basel had a stormy history in the first half of the sixteenth century; Bonjour speaks of a 'reconstruction', *Neubau*, of the university in the 1530's. Between 1540 and 1591 the Faculty of Arts received four sets of statutes.[13] Universities such as Basel were by their geographical and political associations in the forefront of the struggle between Protestants and Catholics and the supporters of traditional and new methods of learning. No German university, however, could escape some of the repercussions of the struggle and all reacted quickly to the consequent academic turmoil.

Such ready and speedy reaction was not entirely new and did not cease with the close of the sixteenth century. Several German universities had at the end of the medieval period been prepared to accept fundamental changes in their curriculum and structure: the University of Tübingen, for example, received statutes for its Faculty in Arts in 1477, probably, in 1488, in 1505, and in 1536.[14] Even more remarkable was the radical revision of its curriculum undertaken by the Faculty of Arts at Freiburg in 1490. The earliest statutes of the Freiburg faculty probably date from 1463, so that within less than thirty years the original faculty structure was abandoned and the organisation as recommended by the nearby University of Tübingen was introduced.[15] The new statutes did not simply modify existing practices but departed considerably from the original requirements, allowing, for example, teaching according to the *via antiqua* previously forbidden by the faculty. After the close of the sixteenth century, German universities continued to respond to changes by modification of their statutes: at Ingolstadt, for example, new statutes were promulgated for the Faculty of Theology in 1605, for the Faculty of Arts in 1649, and for the whole university in 1642.[16] The acceptance by German universities in this period of the need to modify their curricula and structure was, therefore, only part of a general willingness to respond to criticisms in a positive manner, shown both before and after the sixteenth century.

The English universities, at least when superficially examined, do not appear to share these characteristics. At Oxford during the later medieval period and the early years of the sixteenth century there was much discussion not of the need to change the statutes of the university but of the need to codify them. Frequent complaints were made of those ambiguities in the statutes which were forcing students and masters to incur the charge of perjury since they had sworn to obey or enforce legislation which was often apparently self contradictory. Several prominent personalities were approached by the university and offered the task of producing a coherent code that all could accept. Nothing was achieved. University committees appointed for the same purpose also failed to resolve the problem.[17]

Throughout this important period, therefore, the University of Oxford was governed by a number of obsolescent statutes, amended by the occasional *ad hoc* pieces of legislation. In fact, the university appears to have operated very much according to a system of 'custom and practice', where the statutes were regarded as offering only a general guidance to what was taught, how it should be taught, and to what requirements were expected of students for the various university qualifications. When compared with the university Grace Books, which give exactly what programme students were following for their different degrees, the statutes are clearly shown to give a very incomplete picture.[18]

During the reign of Edward VI an attempt was made to provide the university with a comprehensive code of statutes.[19] This code presents many problems: it was never officially entered in the university register and may not have been properly enforced; its provisions are frequently vague and sometimes appear to contradict the practice of the university as we know it at this date. It does, however, indicate how many problems had previously arisen from the chaotic state of the university statutes: a final section notes the considerable number of points where the university was doubtful as to the correct procedure to follow and attempts to resolve these difficulties. Shortly afterwards, in 1556, another code was presented to the university by Cardinal Pole.[20] This, in turn, was quickly superseded by the *Nova Statuta* issued by Queen Elizabeth in 1564–5.[21] Apart from occasional legislation to deal with specific problems, the university remained content with this code until the much fuller and more detailed legislation of Archbishop Laud was received in June 1636.[22] Under the Laudian code, the university was to be governed until the reforms of the nineteenth century.

How far were these changes a reaction to the proposals of the sixteenth-century reformers and how far did they modify the medieval structure and curriculum of the University of Oxford? The traditional constitution of the university was not seriously disturbed by these arrangements; the artists, therefore, retained their dominant position in Congregation. It was not until the acceptance of the Laudian code that the authority of Congregation was emasculated by the requirement, then made mandatory, that important business should be discussed by a meeting of Heads of Houses, the so called Hebdomodal Council, before its submission to Congregation. The faculty structure of the university remained unaltered, although here the disappearance of the monks and friars must have seriously weakened the Elizabethan faculties of theology and law. Degrees in Canon Law ceased to be awarded after the restoration of the Protestant ascendency under Elizabeth, although mention of the subject was retained in some official documents. In the 1601–2 list of fees chargeable by the bedels and the registrar, for example, payments by canon lawyers are still recorded;[23] in 1569 two Fellows of Merton College were admitted 'ad studium iuris civilis et canonici'.[24] A determination to exclude all but members of the Anglican Church from Oxford produced the legislation of Elizabeth's reign preventing the admission to degrees and to the university of those refusing to accept the Thirty Nine Articles of the Church of England.[25]

Changes in the content of the curriculum were also made by these statutes. In medicine and law they were of little significance: as in Germany the traditional authority of Galen and Hippocrates and the Corpus Iuris Civilis is accepted because no adequate substitute has been found. Attempts, for example, by Linacre to amend the study of medicine at Oxford had concentrated on efforts to enforce the literal interpretation of the accepted texts rather than on moves to replace them.[26] For theology, the Elizabethan statutes order the replacement of all references to the *Sentences* by references to some book of the Bible. There was, in fact, no need to exclude the other medieval scholastic authorities since they had never been mentioned by name in the university statutes. Otherwise both students for the bachelor's degree and the doctorate are instructed to follow the earlier regulations: 'vetera sua et antiqua statuta observabunt.'

As with the German universities, the crucial area for estimating the impact of reformers' theories was the Faculty of Arts. The Elizabethan statutes, the unprinted university Grace Books and the Laudian code show that the traditional complex series of academic exercises, in the Parvisus, the ordinary disputations, in the disputations *apud Augustinenses*, and during Determination was maintained. Modifications to these exercises affect only details of their procedure; university legislation, in fact, is concerned more to strengthen their position in the curriculum, and to punish breaches of statutes requiring their performance.[27] Reforming influence was, however, evident in the acceptance by the faculty of declamations. These first appear in the code presented to the university under Edward VI,[28] but they are not mentioned in the Elizabethan and the Laudian statutes as requirements for either degree in arts; they appear in the Laudian code under those statutes made for the regulation of the halls.[29] Isolated references in the university Grace Books and college records of the reign of Elizabeth reveal that declamations were made,[30] but the evidence is scanty and seems to suggest that the university did not regard declamations with the concern of the German universities. Already in 1539, for example, the University of Ingolstadt, in its statutes for the Faculty of Arts, devoted a complete, detailed, separate section to declamations in contrast to the scattered references in the later Oxford Edwardian statutes.[31] A few years beforehand, in 1536, the University of Tübingen had, under the heading '*De rhetoricis exercitiis*' provided a programme: 'ita progredientibus studiis iuventutis ad integras Declamationes devenietur'.[32]

The pressure of the reformers was, however, felt most heavily in attempts to change the content of the curriculum of the Faculty of Arts. Here, the ancient division of the subjects of study of the faculty into the seven liberal arts and three philosophies had been accepted by medieval universities. By the close of the fifteenth century, the divisions were becoming blurred as, for example, when logicians discussed concepts of natural philosophy, and specialisation, especially in astronomy, was developing. Nevertheless, the arts course at most medieval universities provided instruction in each of these ten areas of study. By the close of the sixteenth century, as we have seen, the German universities had abandoned any pretence to organise their teaching under these traditional headings, introducing new subjects, such as Greek, Hebrew and poetry, and abandoning earlier studies, especially metaphysics. The Oxford codes, on the contrary, maintain the earlier division. The Elizabethan statutes regulating the lectures to be given by the masters of arts begin by instructing 'vetera statuta . . . observabunt' and continue to name six of the seven traditional subjects, grammar, rhetoric, logic, arithmetic, geometry and astronomy on which 'ordinaria' are to be given. The sole omission is music. As for the three philosophies — named as 'tria philosophorum genera' — the practices of the older statutes are to be retained.[33] At the same date, another statute allocates the length of time for which each subject is to be studied: here all seven liberal arts and three philosophies are mentioned.[34] The contemporary evidence of the practice of the faculty shown in the university Grace Books confirms that this division of studies was still a reality: lists of nominated lecturers show that the ten subjects of the arts and philosophies were at this date expected to be covered.[35] The same records, however, also indicate that the lecture in music was frequently abandoned,[36] an interesting comment on the wording of the Elizabethan Statute: a reluctance to abandon the medieval arrangement combined with a realisation that it could not be completely accepted.

The most striking aspect of the departure, in German universities, from the older curriculum in arts was, of course, the incorporation of Greek and Hebrew lecturers into the teaching establishment. At Oxford, the foundation of the Regius Professorships in these two subjects had provided regular instruction, but the introduction of these subjects into the formal arts curriculum seems to have been hesitant. The Edwardian statutes appear to require all bachelors of arts to attend Greek lectures, but then, in a later note add 'ad lectionem Graecam ne obstringuntur'.[37] No mention of a compulsory attendance is made in the Elizabethan *Nova Statuta*, but these do require the Greek lecturer to read four times in each week.[38] In 1576, however, the bachelors are specifically required on pain of fine to attend the Greek lecture.[39] As was probably the case in Germany, the Hebrew lecturer was intended to benefit most the students of theology, and it was masters of arts who had not opted to study law or medicine who were compelled to attend his lectures.[40] The Laudian Statutes give a summary of the situation in the early seventeenth century: the arts student is required to attend lectures on the Greek language, the three philosophies and five of the seven liberal arts; music and arithmetic are omitted, but geometry is mentioned twice in the list.[41] Compared to the radical changes in the curricula of most German universities, Oxford in the late sixteenth century has only slightly modified the form of its traditional programme.

This would not necessarily mean that the faculty's studies remained unchanged: new texts could be used without any change in the title of the appropriate subject. The list of prescribed texts in the Edwardian Statutes introduces Plato, Pomponius Mela, Pliny, Strabo, Cicero, Quintilian and Hermogenes into the curriculum: a strange hotch-potch to mix with Aristotle, also recommended, and characteristic of the disorganised nature of this particular code. There is little concession here to the literary tastes of humanist reformers. Two different statutes of the early years of Elizabeth's reign offer a more coherent programme and prescribe first Linacre, for grammar, Cicero, for rhetoric, and Gemma Frisius or Tunstall for arithmetic in addition to the older authorities, Aristotle, Porphyry, Boethius, Euclid, Witelo, John of Hollywood and Ptolemy. The second statute adds Vergil, Cicero, and Horace for grammar, Oronce Fine for geometry, and the *Republic* of Plato for moral philosophy.[42] The impact of humanist criticism has, therefore, been felt in the subjects areas of grammar and rhetoric, and, to some extent, in mathematics, but the greater part of the arts course is still being taught from the traditional authorities. It would appear that in its formal legislation — and we shall return to this limitation later — the Faculty of Arts has been unsympathetic to humanist criticism.

We have examined the structure and content of the Oxford curriculum. Now a brief comment on the method of providing lectures must be made. In the German universities, the traditional regency system had been virtually abandoned, especially in the higher faculties, before the close of the fifteenth century. By a process which was to continue into the sixteenth century these universities came to recruit their teaching staff from a body of lecturers who expected salaried chairs. Apart from providing financial security for the lecturer and often a cheaper course for the student, such a system prevented the automatic continuance of teaching concepts and could enable those appointing to chairs to introduce new subjects and new methods. Clearly once reformers had obtained influence over such appointments, they would be in a strong position to impose on the universities their own supporters and eventually their own policies. The control over the teaching staff at Oxford was, therefore, a crucial issue. Here the tenacity of the regency system is very marked. Despite obvious failings, it continued to provide the great part of the teaching for the Faculty of Arts where student numbers demanded many lecturers. In the higher faculties the problem was not so acute: here the Lady Margaret lecturer in theology the Regius Professors in theology, medicine, civil law and Hebrew, and the Linacre lecturers in medicine could provide for the much smaller group of students. From about 1550, the university registers show how the regency system in the Faculty of Arts was modified: gradually the requirement that all new masters should lecture was withdrawn and replaced by the practice of demanding from each newly created master a sum of money which was used to pay a certain number of masters who then provided the necessary lectures.[43] In perhaps a typical fashion, the statutory requirement to act as a regent was not withdrawn, and indeed was embodied in the Laudian Code; then graduates had to place a caution in the hands of the Vice-Chancellor, and could recover this only at the end of their first year of regency.[44] Only after the close of the century were university lectureships in the traditional arts subjects established, and these were at first in geometry, astronomy and moral philosophy rather than in those subjects usually associated with humanist scholars. Even more remarkable was the continuance at Oxford throughout the sixteenth century of some reliance on the bachelors to provide part of the teaching in the Faculty of Arts. It was not until 1584 that the traditional cursory lecturers of the bachelors, stated to 'have bin divers times read very unprofitably', were abandoned. Even after this date, six 'sollemne' lectures were still required of the bachelor; this obligation to lecture was repeated in the later Laudian Statutes. As late as 1584, the traditional cursory lectures were still required from bachelors of law, medicine and theology also.[45] The statutory lectures at Oxford were provided at the close of the sixteenth century in a manner that had largely been abandoned in Germany before the end of the fifteenth century.

We are fortunate at Cambridge in that the university received the code of statutes that was to survive until the nineteenth century during the reign of Elizabeth, in 1570.[46] The new statutes certainly made considerable modifications to the traditional structure of the university. The 'democratic' authority of Congregation and the Proctors was now curbed by a committee consisting of the Vice-Chancellor and the heads of houses exercising control through a reformed 'Caput' on which the regent masters were given only one seat. The programme in the Faculty of Arts prescribed for the bachelor's degree the study of rhetoric in the first year, dialectic in the second and third year, and philosophy in the fourth year. For the master's degree, philosophy, astronomy, optics and Greek were required.[47] The derivation of this pattern from the seven liberal arts and three philosophies of the medieval arts curriculum is clear, although the Cambridge regulations are not so sharp in their divisions as those of Oxford: astronomy and optics probably can be associated with the earlier geometry, arithmetic and astronomy; music, as at Oxford, seems to have dropped out of the arts course; grammar is not mentioned. In fact, music seems to have played little part in the formal academic life of the university: there are notes of two degrees only in music awarded between 1542 and 1589.[48] The last degree in grammar of the century was awarded in 1548.[49] The sole obvious humanistic influence here is the introduction of compulsory Greek. For the higher faculties, little detailed information is given: as at Oxford, the basic texts in medicine and civil law remained unchanged, canon law, of course, had ceased to be taught after the reassertion of the Protestant supremacy, and theology was purged of its Roman Catholic elements and the teaching of Hebrew was introduced. The absence of precise information on many important subjects is no doubt explained by a final section which includes the note that, although all statutes contrary to Holy Scripture, the royal injunctions and these new regulations are to be void, others are to retain their authority: 'reliquis suo robore permansuris'.[50] As is shown by the internal struggle at Cambridge in the years following the promulgation of these statutes, their chief impact was felt in the transfer of constitutional supremacy to the heads of houses, and this is certainly what the Queen and her advisers wished.

If reforming plans seem to have had little affect on the structure of the faculties and their programme of instruction, we have to consider whether the content of teaching shows any such influence. The Elizabethan statutes name certain texts to be read in the public schools.[51] For philosophy the *Problemata, Moralia* or *Politica* of Aristotle, or Pliny or Plato are required; for cosmography Mela, Pliny, Strabo or Plato; for arithmetic Tunstall or Cardanus, for geometry Euclid; for astronomy Ptolemy; for logic the *Elenchi* of Aristotle or the *Topica* of Cicero; for rhetoric Quintilian, Hermogenes or one of the orations of Cicero; for Greek Homer, Isocrates, Demosthenes, Euripides or some other classical authority together with instruction in the language. In the higher faculties, theologians are to teach only — *tantum* — the Holy Scriptures, the Hebrew lecturer the language from the scriptures alone, lawyers, the civil law code and the law of the English church which, says the statute, is about to be edited, and the physicians the works of Galen and Hippocrates. It is interesting to see that this statute repeats, often almost word for word, the relevant statute issued by Edward VI.[52] As compared with the list of texts in arts given for Oxford in the *Nova Statuta*, this for Cambridge shows interesting differences: there is not such a close adherence to the traditional division of the course into the liberal arts and philosophies, and more contemporary and classical texts are prescribed. Nevertheless, those authorities, Aristotle, Euclid, and Ptolemy, studied in the medieval Faculty of Arts still retain their place. The movement away from the medieval curriculum, although more marked than at Oxford, has still not, from this statutory evidence, gone as far as we found in Germany.

In other, related, respects Cambridge also stands half way between Oxford and Germany. It retains the medieval faculty structure, the traditional long course in arts, and the complex disputations of the Faculty of Arts. But the abandonment of the traditional regency system as a method of supplying lecturers seems to have gone much further than at Oxford by the close of the century. Already, in 1518, Sir Robert Rede had left money to provide for annual payments to three lecturers in philosophy, logic, and rhetoric.[53] In the early years of the century, the university established a lectureship to guarantee instruction in arithmetic, music, geometry, optics, and astronomy; from 1504–5 regular payments are made by students about to take the lower degree in arts 'pro lectura mathematica'.[54] At the same date, we have references to the payment of a 'Terence' lecturer by the university and of other payments to those lecturing 'ordinarie'.[55] The money for such official lecture-ships came apparently from the payments made by masters seeking dis-pensation from their duties as lecturers during necessary regency; the Grace Books record at this time many such dispensations 'pro gratia de non legendo'. At Cambridge, therefore, the university itself seems to have taken the lead in dismantling the traditional regency system in the Faculty of Arts; no mention of the masters' duty to give ordinary lectures is made in the Elizabethan statutes. During the sixteenth century, the bachelor's respons-ibility to give cursory lectures was also abandoned; this is not noted in the Elizabethan statutes. For the higher faculties, lectureships provided by the Lady Margaret and, perhaps, 'per dominum Husy',[56] in theology, by Thomas Linacre in medicine, and by the crown in divinity, Greek, civil law, Hebrew, and medicine, provided salaried readers to replace the earlier necessary regents. In comparison to Oxford, Cambridge seems far more ready to adopt the teaching system of the continent and to end its depend-ence on the medieval method of recruiting lecturers from its own new graduates. Perhaps a smaller university than Oxford faced the same diffi-culties of those of the German universities.

Regency was, however, retained and indeed extended during the sixteenth century. The Elizabethan statutes required of each master in arts at his graduation a commitment to a five year period of regency.[57] This arrange-ment was probably to ensure that there would be sufficient disputants available for the bachelors from those masters who chose to remain at the university: the words of the statute, in fact, continue to insist that each regent shall dispute in his turn throughout the period of regency. As at Oxford, declamations were made a compulsory part of the curriculum, but firmly placed in the statutes: bachelors were required by the Elizabethan statute to declaim for one hour each week and arrangements were made for the organisation of the programme and the punishment of those who refused to comply.[58]

The universities of Germany and England appear, therefore, to have reacted to the reforming pressures of the sixteenth century in markedly different ways. On the Continent, universities seemed ready and indeed eager to accept radical changes in their structure and curriculum, under-taking regular and searching examinations of their performance and quickly embodying new educational methods and material in their official regula-tions and statutes. Cambridge University showed itself at an early date prepared to accept the innovations of the Continent regarding the provi-sion of teaching, but was less ready to abandon totally the medieval course in arts; its early constitution had, however, been seriously modified by the close of the century. Oxford clung tenaciously to the regency system and to the bachelor's lectures, retaining these, if in a revised form, as the most important method for the provision of official teaching in the Faculty of Arts. The structure of the university and its constitution were not seriously altered during the century. Apart from necessary changes in the study of canon law and theology to accompany the restored Protestant supremacy, the official curriculum was only slightly modified. Humanistic influence was restricted to a hesitant acceptance of declamations, the reception of some new texts in certain subjects, and the introduction of Greek and Hebrew. The seven liberal arts and the three philosophies were still recognised as the most convenient method of dividing the studies of the artists. It will be interesting to consider why the universities responded to the pressure to reform in different ways, and, in the case of the English universities, how far their official programme is a true guide to their actual reaction to the educational proposals discussed during the century.

The differences between the development of English and German universities during the century must in part be explained by the character of the German foundations at the close of the medieval period. Despite the claims of these universities to be founded 'ad instar studii Parisiensis', it quickly became obvious that the constitution of that large, cosmopolitan and greatly respected university could not be reproduced in the small, provincial and newly established foundations of Germany. By the close of the fifteenth century all but the few very large universities had abandoned the 'nation' structure so important at Paris, had been forced to attract their teaching staff by the offer of salaried positions, even in the Faculty of Arts, and had lost most of the traces of that 'democratic' system of government by regent masters found in the early northern universities that derived their inspiration from Paris. The German universities were also unable to attract a steady and numerous intake of students into the higher faculties: here promotions were irregular and infrequent. Students of theology, law and medicine preferred to receive their training in the more famous and, perhaps, more socially attractive schools of France and Italy. Accordingly, the typical German university of the late fifteenth century drew its student body, almost all studying arts, mainly from its territorial surroundings, and was controlled by a small council composed of salaried lecturers, most of whom owed their position to the influence of the local secular authority which had usually been responsible for the establishment of the university. In such a situation, it was not difficult to introduce radical change. There was no entrenched, organised body to defend the status quo, especially after the removal of the religious from the universities in areas that espoused the Protestant cause. An appointed, salaried lecturer determined on reform had a powerful voice in the council of the university; if the secular power was pledged to the reform of the university, it would be difficult for the council to resist his wishes. These factors will be considered in more detail later. Nor were the changes in the German universities purely structural. It is interesting to see that many of them inserted into their programme of studies contemporary or near contemporary texts on which lectures are to be given. This is especially noticeable in the Faculty of Arts. At Vienna, for example, Marsilius of Inghen's *Consequentie* appear in the lists of books read in 1390;[59] the works of Petrus Hispanus are widely prescribed. At Ingolstadt the commentaries of John Eck on Aristotle were required in the 1519/20 statutes 'ubi tandem in lucem venerint'.[60] German universities, therefore, were not only well structured to respond to demands for change, but also were already accustomed to accept considerable alterations in their constitution and curriculum by the early sixteenth century.

In contrast, the universities of Oxford and Cambridge had in essence determined their structure and curriculum before the foundation of the first university in the Empire. Statutory changes in the late fourteenth and fifteenth century are here introduced to adapt and develop a working system that is in no need of radical alteration. These features that, in 1500, distinguish the organisation of the English universities from most of their counterparts, the long course in arts, the complex series of academic exercises required for the M.A. degree, the importance of Determination, the dominance of the Faculty of Arts in their constitutions, the importance given to the study of theology, and the reduction of the role of the nations in the administration of the universities, were then already sanctified by the usage of at least two centuries. Furthermore, it could be claimed, especially by scholars of the University of Oxford, that this organisation had enabled the English universities to build up an enviable reputation in the fields of logic, science, and theology: in these areas the works of English scholars were consulted, prescribed, and respected throughout Europe. In fact, this very success may have produced an attitude of mind amongst many prominent scholars within the universities which made them reluctant to accept untried and radical changes that would entail the abandonment of an old and successful tradition.

Such reluctance would have been hardened by the awareness that changes were being supported by scholars who had themselves generally been influenced by study abroad or who were foreigners. During the late fourteenth and fifteenth centuries, the studies of both English universities take on a far more parochial nature than at an earlier date. Scholars in arts and theology at the close of the medieval period in England relied for the greater part of their material on works produced by their fellow countrymen of a few generations earlier. Lecturers in the Faculty of Arts at this date quote regularly from Burley, Grosseteste, Scotus, Bradwardine, Mylverly, Alyngton, Wyclif and others; theologians are deeply indebted especially to Scotus. The logical systems used at the two universities are named specifically as the '*Usus Oxoniensis*' and the '*Usus Cantabrigiensis*'. European contemporaries, especially in Italy, castigated the English logicians and theologians for their over dependence on sophistry and subtlety: such scholars were the 'barbari britanni' with their 'logica britannica', made more horrible to Italian ears by the peculiar sounds of such surnames as Heytesbury, Swineshead, or Strode.[61] The absence of foreign contemporary work in

English collections of the fifteenth century strongly indicates that Oxford and Cambridge scholars believed that they had a lot to teach to but little to learn from their European counterparts in logic and theology. Even the great disputes that marked the quarrel of the '*moderni*' and the '*antiqui*', the two philosophical '*viae*', that are so marked a feature of fifteenth century German university life, seem totally absent in Oxford and Cambridge. Such a group of scholars, convinced of the superiority of their own traditions and system and unfamiliar with the learning of continental universities, would not readily accept reform proposals that owed much to foreign influence.

The universities of Germany were much more ready to accept foreign influence. Many of them, of course, owed their origins to the flight of German scholars and students from the universities of Paris and Prague in the late fourteenth and early fifteenth centuries. It was inevitable that they should look to foreign universities for guidance especially in their early, formative, years. German students travelled easily to Italy and France; many of them returned to their native universities and brought with them attitudes of mind learned abroad. Since the German universities failed to develop reputable schools of law, medicine and theology, lecturers in these faculties had usually been trained in Italy or France, or were themselves Frenchmen or Italians. The close connections thus maintained with the schools of northern Italy, in particular, brought into important positions in the German universities scholars who were not merely skilled in law and medicine, but who were also supporters of the New Learning. The first rector of the University of Freiburg, for example, was Matthaus Hummel von Villingen, 'den eben aus Pavia heimgekehrten Magister artium, Doktor der Medizin und des kanonischen Rechtes'.[62] Such scholars, especially those qualified in medicine and law, quickly became not only influential in the administration of the university but also closely in touch with the local secular prince or council and his or their families. It was not difficult for the views of such foreign trained scholars to carry great weight in the formulation of policies concerning the future development of their universities.

Certainly, one of the most important factors encouraging the German universities to respond sympathetically to the reform movements of the sixteenth century was the awareness that failure to do so might result in a loss of students, with the consequent diminution of the important role of the university in the economic life of a small city or community. At the beginning of the sixteenth century, Germany was well endowed with universities, and others, the most significant at Wittenberg, Marburg, and Jena were added during the century itself. It was not difficult for groups of students dissatisfied with what one university offered to transfer their allegiance to another. Those in charge of German universities were acutely aware that they must consider student demand and student preferences when planning their teaching programme. Innovations that proved successful at one university were quickly noted by others, especially when a withdrawal of students indicated that the new model was preferred. Jakob Spiegel urged his opinion on reform at Heidelberg in 1522 by noting the success of mathematical lectures at Vienna: scio ego, quantum fame Viennensi studio peperit duarum lecturarum in mathematica a Maximiliano institucio.[63] Appeals for the provision of finance for a lectureship in mathematics at Wittenberg in 1545 are supported by references to the success of such lectureships at Tübingen, Leipzig, Greifswald and Rostock: 'ist auch andern universiteten ein gut exempel gewesen'.[64] In the struggle to attract well qualified teaching staff and viable student numbers, German universities could not afford to ignore the preferences, however dictated by current fashion, of younger, vociferous scholars. Here, students could 'vote with their feet' and compel university authorities, faced with a declining student intake, to pay attention to their demands. The Dean of the Faculty of Arts at Heidelberg, supporting in 1520 the use of the new translation of Aristotle, argued that it would benefit both the university and the world of learning, but also noted that other universities had reformed their teaching in this way, and that young students had been attracted by this: 'adulescentes emendata sequuntur'.[65] Shortly afterwards, Wimpfeling warned Heidelberg that opposition to reform by the theologians would ruin the university, making it similar to Cologne, whose scholars 'feces istas et quisquilias seminarunt', while other universities produced theologians able to speak and preach with eloquence. The installation of Reuchlin as Professor of Greek and Hebrew at Tubingen produced an appeal in 1521 from the Heidelberg Faculty of Arts for a similar prestigious appointment — the name of Erasmus was suggested. It was noted that students were deserting Heidelberg: 'partim . . . ad Tübingense gymnasium, partim ad alia secesserunt'.[66] Clearly, Heidelberg believed that it could not afford to allow this advantage to remain with its rivals.

This situation became particularly acute in Germany with the foundation of new universities in the sixteenth century. Not only did the competition for students become sharper, but the new centres offered a different curriculum often strongly influenced by the more outspoken of the radical critics of the existing system. At Wittenberg, for example, the 1507 list of lectures offered by the Faculty of Arts shows that already Sulpitius had been adopted as the set text in grammar and that some specially appointed lecturers 'in humanis litteris' were covering classical and contemporary humanistic material.[67] The establishment, shortly afterwards, of endowed chairs in Greek and Hebrew further emphasised the university's concern for the New Learning. The influence of Wittenberg, spread especially through the writings and statements of Philip Melanchthon, was strongly felt in the later foundations of Marburg, Königsberg, and Jena. These new universities, closely associated with both the humanist and the Protestant reform movement, must have seemed to many young German students to offer the very latest in higher education. It is interesting to see that even a relatively recent foundation such as Wittenberg could be affected by the establishment of a nearly new university. Caspar Eberhard complained, in 1574, that the teaching of medicine at Wittenberg was in need of improvement; the attraction of Jena had proved too strong for Wittenberg's medical students: 'die studiosi medicine nach Jena zihen'.[68] Such references indicate how successful reform of an older university or the foundation of a new centre on progressive lines could compel other institutions to examine their own curricula in an attempt to retain staff and students they might otherwise lose. Of course, this aspect of academic life in Germany was not confined to the sixteenth century. The foundation later of such innovatory universities as Halle or Berlin in turn led to an attempt by other German universities to absorb their successful educational philosophy. The movement of staff and students throughout the German university system in the sixteenth century and later encouraged an awareness of new teaching methods and a readiness to adopt those found successful in attracting good staff and students.

The unusual situation in England, where two universities enjoyed a monopoly of higher education, did not pass unnoticed. Sir Humphrey Gilbert, around the year 1572, in his *Queen Elizabeth's Academy*, pointed out that the country needed other institutions that would produce men of such education that they could serve the state in a more adequate manner. The Inns of Court to some extent did provide an alternative education for those seeking official preferment, and, of course, were more conveniently situated in London, near to the seat of government. Sir George Buck, in 1612, spoke of London as having 'the thirde universitie of England' and assigned to the Inns of Court pride of place amongst the capital's colleges and schools. However, it is Professor Charlton's view that the role of the Inns of Court in providing anything more that a narrow legal education must not be exaggerated.[69] Critics of the English universities did have one important success in the establishment, significantly in London, of Gresham College, but this did not happen until 1598 and did not infringe the monopoly held by Oxford and Cambridge in the award of degrees. In England, therefore, the established universities did not have to face serious competition from other institutions or have to come to terms with any new university embodying a radically different approach to the curriculum.

Indeed, the universities could argue that their popularity with students indicated that there was little demand for new institutions or a different educational philosophy to that which they offered. Professor Stone has argued that 'between the early 1550s and the 1580s, there took place an enormous expansion' in the numbers attending both universities. Even the slump that lasted from about 1590 until about 1615 was followed by a further 'huge expansion' and 'unprecedented boom' in the 1620s and 1630s.[70] Since the Puritan critics of the Elizabethan Church of England were as yet for the most part included within the Anglican faith, the restrictive religious legislation of the universities served to exclude only prospective Catholic students. Both universities continued to attract endowments: the early sixteenth century foundations or refoundations at Cambridge of St. John's College, Trinity College, and Christ's College were joined by Emmanuel and Sidney Sussex Colleges before the close of Elizabeth's reign; at Oxford, Brasenose College, Corpus Christi College and Christ Church were joined by Trinity College, St. John's College, and Jesus College. The disturbances of the Reformation period had passed, and the reign of Elizabeth saw both Oxford and Cambridge able to retain the confidence and patronage of those seeking higher education or wishing to encourage it.

Certainly the increase in admissions to the universities would have justified the creation of a new foundation. It has been estimated that in the years 1500–1530, between 120 and 220 freshmen entered Oxford university; between 1570 and 1600 the number of entrants had climbed to around the 400 mark.[71] Serious problems must have arisen from the need to cater for this increase in numbers, and especially from the sudden, greater, demand for accommodation and teaching supervision. Had the universities been unable to resolve these problems, the pressure for new foundations would have perhaps been more acute. However, this rise in numbers was accompanied by, and probably stimulated, the admission of students to those colleges which had previously been almost entirely graduate, and the provision of internal teaching on a larger scale. The evolution of the colleges as we know them today at Oxford and Cambridge was responsible for important changes in the character of both universities. These changes have been noted and discussed at length by historians. What has not previously been suggested is that this process may have blunted the demand for the erection of another one or more universities and so postponed the establishment of the University of London for a further two centuries.

One of the most important factors that could have encouraged a more positive official attitude to reforming ideas in the two English universities was at this date absent. During the eighteenth century, the sharpest criticism of Oxford and Cambridge came from scholars in the Scottish universities. Not only could they point with pride to the achievements of Aberdeen, St. Andrews, and especially Glasgow and Edinburgh in promoting and spreading the philosophy of the Enlightenment, but they could point also to the many able English students at universities north of the border, and the serious decline in student numbers at Oxford and Cambridge.[72] In the sixteenth century, however, Scotland was still a foreign and frequently enemy country. Its universities, especially that of Glasgow, were badly damaged by the struggles that accompanied the Reformation in Scotland; Edinburgh University was not founded until 1585. However, what happened during the next century is instructive. The three ancient Scottish universities in the late sixteenth century revised their constitutions and teaching arrangements in response to reforming ideas; the challenge of the new university at Edinburgh was a stimulus to the acceptance of change. By the close of the seventeenth century, Scottish universities were poised to benefit from new scientific, social, and political philosophies derived, paradoxically, from English sources, but largely ignored by English universities. When government policy drove out of the Anglican church, and so out of the English universities, a large body of nonconformists, the Scottish universities were also able to recruit many talented Englishmen denied higher education in their own country. The very lack of competition and challenge in sixteenth century England perhaps spread in the English universities a confidence that began to appear as complacency.

It could also be argued that the time for new foundations in England was not propitious. The frequent investigations of the universities by the governments of Henry VIII, Edward VI and Mary had indicated the concern of these rulers to ensure acquiescence in their policies. Once the Reformation controversy began to affect England and involve the central authority, we would expect that interest in the reform of the universities on academic grounds alone became a subject of little urgency. In the early years of the century, humanistic reformers had attempted, with some success, to recruit the support of members of the royal family. The Lady Margaret Beaufort, mother of King Henry VII, was herself responsible for the refoundation of God's-house as Christ's College and for much of the initiative for the foundation of St. John's College, at Cambridge. The influence of the prominent humanist, John Fisher, Bishop of Rochester, confessor to the Lady Margaret, was here vital to the success of these projects, especially as the Lady Margaret died before the adequate establishment of St. John's College. However, this early royal support seems to have considerably decreased during the reign of Henry VIII. Prominent humanists, More and Fisher, were executed for opposition to the royal policy; financial support for the Lady Margaret's foundation of St. John's College and for the Wolsey inspired foundation at Oxford was not overgenerous; neither university benefited greatly from wealth accruing to the crown from the dissolution of the monasteries despite losing its important religious colleges and students. The great humanist spokesman, Erasmus, wrote against Luther and his Reformation. Prof. McConica has shown how the influence of humanists at court continued beyond this crisis,[73] but the possibility of their urging a monarchy faced with serious internal and external problems towards a radical reform of the universities seemed remote.

The careful reestablishment of the Protestant supremacy and the relative tranquility of the reign of Elizabeth, especially after the removal of the threat of a Spanish invasion, would, we might expect, reopen the question of university reform. The universities, however, purged after a few years of their Catholic elements and, after the imposition of religious tests, admitting only members of the Anglican Church, were expected by the government to be defenders of the religious settlement. Any proposal for radical reform, or especially any scheme to establish a new university, would inevitably weaken support at Oxford and Cambridge for the government and produce internal disquiet within the universities: a pre-run of the long, bitter and complex struggle of the nineteenth century was the very thing that an Elizabethan government was concerned to avoid. Nor were the benefits of reform or of a new foundation obvious to the government. Very quickly, and especially after the danger of a Catholic revival had disappeared, the Elizabethan settlement came under attack from radical reformers looking to Geneva and Calvinism for their inspiration. Many prominent young intellectuals in the universities demanded further progress towards some type of Presbyterian church. In face of this criticism, the government and the Anglican church stressed the importance of compromise, the middle way, and, to its opponents, the value of the more conservative interpretation of biblical evidence on the administration of the church and the duty of the laity and parish clergy to follow the guidance of its bishops. Any new or reformed university, it might be suggested, would attract those very radical elements that were opposed to the Elizabethan settlement. Indeed, the government had encountered trouble with radicals at Cambridge and had placed, in 1570, control of the university in the hands of a conservative oligarchy. Such a government could be expected to regard concessions to any radical element with some disquiet; arrangements for higher education would, it might be thought, more safely be left unchanged.

In the one action where it did break radically with tradition in the organisation of higher education, the motives of the Elizabethan government are made clear. Elizabeth provided Ireland with her first university with the foundation, in 1591, of Trinity College, Dublin. The antecedents of this action are interesting. In 1569 the Lord Deputy and Council in Dublin declared that a university was required for the 'reformation of the barbarisme of this rude people',[74] and the Queen herself noted that the new university would dissuade young men from travelling to France, Italy, and Spain 'whereby they have been infected with Popery and other ill qualities and so become evil subjects'.[75] Trinity College, unlike Oxford and Cambridge, could accept Catholic students. Here, in a country with a hostile, Catholic majority, radical Protestant scholars could be allowed some authority; the early Provosts of Trinity College were supporters of the Puritan movement. Provost Travers, appointed in 1594, had, in fact, been one of the major Puritan critics of the Anglican church, and we can probably view his promotion as an attempt to get out of England a dissenter whose abilities would be useful to the government in the different environment of Catholic Ireland. In its early years, the college was under financial constraint and disturbed by rebellion in Ireland. Nevertheless, a graduation ceremony could be held in 1601.[76] For its academic organisation, the college was allowed to select suitable statutes based on those of Oxford and Cambridge;[77] in an interesting concession to national and humanistic feeling, lectureships in Irish, Hebrew and mathematics were established.[78] It would appear that where radical measures were necessary to attract reforming staff and make concessions to a hostile, nationalistic population, the Elizabethan government was ready to consider the foundation of a university of a new type. However, the inspiration behind the erection of Trinity College seems to have been essentially political: the need to placate and reconcile to Protestantism an important section of the Irish population. In England, where no such pressures were experienced, the government gave support to conservative elements in both universities prepared to uphold the Elizabethan religious settlement. Nor were the attractions of this small if distinguished college, in a land ravaged by rebellion for much of the first fifty years of its foundation and far from the centres of English social life, scholarship and patronage, able to prove sufficient to draw students and scholars in any numbers away from Oxford and Cambridge or to present a challenge to the curriculum of either university.

There was also important internal pressure at Oxford, and to a lesser extent at Cambridge, in defence of the traditional curriculum, especially in arts, that was absent in the German universities. We have noted how the early claims of the German universities to be modelled on the great University of Paris were quickly modified. In no area is this more noticeable than in the failure of the German universities to build up reputable and well attended faculties of theology. At Heidelberg, between 1404 and 1449 the names of forty-five students who obtained the doctorate in theology are recorded;[79] at Tübingen, in the period of its greatest reputation between 1477 and 1507, only forty degrees in theology, to bachelors and doctors, were awarded.[80] Even at such a large university as Vienna, where the numbers of masters lecturing in arts annually approached and once exceeded one hundred in the middle of the fifteenth century, it was usual to grant each year only one or two doctorates in theology.[81] In 1516, the University of Wittenberg reported to the Elector the numbers of students promoted during the past years: in seven years only ten doctorates in theology had been awarded, and eight of these had been presented in two years; during the same period sixty-seven bachelors had been given the master's degree in arts. Moreover, most of these successful theology students were members of religious orders; only one of the doctorates noted above as being gained at Wittenberg was won by a secular scholar.[82]

Although the sixteenth century was a time of continual theological controversy between Protestant and Catholic and between Lutheran, Calvinist and Anglican, this does not seem to have stimulated students to enter the German faculties of theology in greater numbers. In areas that accepted the Protestant doctrine, the dissolution of religious houses brought a sudden reduction in those studying theology. Eulenburg has produced some interesting figures for various German universities in the sixteenth century, and concludes: 'Die theologischen Würden sind immer nur ganz selten verliehen worden'.[83] In some universities, the salaried lecturers in theology seem to have found their duties not too onerous; at Wittenberg in 1577, the Elector's Visitors found that in the Faculty of Theology 'würd wenig gelesen'.[84] Most

German students were content to obtain an arts degree; the few who remained to study theology rarely completed the course and obtained the doctorate.

The English universities had theological faculties of great antiquity. By the close of the medieval period, the fame especially of the Oxford faculty, even though 'tainted' with the 'indiscretions' of Ockham and Wyclif, attracted students from many parts of Europe. Moreover, at both Oxford and Cambridge, a considerable number of those proceeding to degrees in theology were seculars who had first received their training in the Faculty of Arts, usually that of the university granting them the higher degree. In this way a close link was forged between the two faculties in the English universities, and sufficient masters still advanced to the study of theology to enable the Faculty of Arts to be regarded as a training ground for the later study of theology. In the German universities the connection was weak, and the overwhelming majority of students never considered an academic career stretching beyond one of the arts degrees. We may suggest that this close link between arts and theology in England helps to explain why much of the medieval curriculum in arts, especially at Oxford, was retained in the formal statutes of the universities. It could perhaps be argued that the humanistic course of studies, designed to produce a cultured, eloquent graduate with interests that were predominantly literary, was not the best training for a student intending to pursue a further degree in theology. Of course, certain parts of the humanistic programme were valuable to theologians and appreciated by them: a competence in the Greek and Hebrew languages, a knowledge of textual criticism and classical Latin grammar. These were, in fact, the very subjects welcomed at an early date at Oxford and Cambridge. Such a curriculum in arts as found in the German universities of the late sixteenth century represents an independent training in 'liberal studies' rather than a deliberate effort to underpin a later course in the Faculty of Theology. German theologians in the universities were too few in number to be concerned about this development, which only continued a trend noticeable in the later Middle Ages. In England, the traditional close connection between the faculties and the number and importance of the theologians ensured that the requirements of the Faculty of Theology were at least formally defended by the universities.

Theologians, of course, were needed by both Catholic and Protestant interests in the sixteenth century to defend their particular case and to attack that of their opponents. Since many of the Catholic protagonists were trained to use certain of the medieval scholastic authorities, it was impossible for the Protestant supporters to ignore totally the texts used by the opposition. A steady trickle of medieval texts enters Oxford and Cambridge libraries during the reign of Elizabeth. It is perhaps possible to explain away as chance acquisitions the reception of gifts of such material: of Bonaventura, Scotus, Ockham, Alexander de Hales, Dorbellus and others given by William Marshall to Merton in 1583; it is more difficult to explain the deliberate purchase by the same college of an expensive copy of the *Summa* of Thomas Aquinas in 1591.[85] N. R. Ker has spoken of 'the new interest in the medieval schoolmen and in Catholic theology' in the later years of Elizabeth's reign.[86] Together with these theological works came commentaries on the Aristotelian texts used in the medieval Faculty of Arts; Thomas Savile purchased for Merton College while in Italy the commentaries of Iohannes Grammaticus on the *Priora, Posteriora, Physica, De Generatione et Corruptione*, and the *De Anima*, and other commentaries by Alexander and Eustratius.[87] That such books were read at Merton is shown by the special permission given to Daniel Bond, Fellow of the college, to borrow from the library in 1575 copies of Versor on the *Ethics*, Aquinas on the *Politics*, and Versor on the *Politics*.[88] England was dependent for its supply of trained theologians on two universities only. At a later date, in the eighteenth and nineteenth centuries this obsession at the universities, and especially at Oxford, with the defence of the Anglican Church and the importance of theology began to appear outmoded and an obstacle to the introduction of new subjects and different programmes of study. In Elizabeth's reign, the necessity to justify a peculiar *media via* against the criticisms of both Catholics and more radical Protestants was a real need which the universities could not ignore. The attraction of theology to the devoted academic was still strong enough to ensure that the Faculty of Arts, in the formal statutes of the universities, had to accept some direct and traditional responsibility for the production of a master qualified to move into the Faculty of Theology armed with some of the weapons that his opponents were in the future also to use against him.

It is apparent, from the frequent indirect references already made, that the attitude of the secular authority to the reform of the universities was a major, perhaps the decisive, factor in determining the speed of change. There is no doubt that humanistic influence was strong at the royal and princely courts both in England and in Germany. Once it became fashionable to have available secretaries able to write in elegant, Ciceronian Latin, and orators able to produce eloquent speeches larded with quotations from obscure classical authorities, then the humanists found ready employment. Aeneas Sylvius Piccolomini at Vienna, Florentius von Venningen at Heidelberg, Thomas More and Richard Pace at London are just a few examples of prominent humanists who held important posts at court. Lawyers and medical doctors trained in Italy were welcomed by rulers who needed their technical skills: Thomas Linacre was physician to Henry VIII; Matthias Hummel acted as physician to the house of Austria. Of a salaried lectureship in law established at Heidelberg and first occupied in 1498 by Johann von Dalheim, doctor of the University of Siena, it has been noted that 'der Inhaber sollte in erster Linie dem Hofe als kurfürstlicher Rat verpflichtet sein'.[89] The humanists' view of education as designed to produce the articulate, cultured man of the world was itself attractive to the nobility of the North who seem to have envied the manners and polish of their Italian contemporaries; such an education seemed to offer more than the earlier linguistic, logical and philosophical training of the medieval universities. In their efforts to ensure university reform, humanists sought and usually received the help of the secular power.

In Germany this was a very valuable asset. Most universities were small, of recent foundation, and heavily dependent on financial support from the local secular power. Usually they had been established as territorial universities by a prince, duke, city, or other temporal authority to serve the region in which they were situated, to provide a supply of trained civil servants, teachers and officials, and to attract a few well qualified lecturers in law, medicine and theology who would assist the local ruler and adorn his court. Claiming rights derived from their ancestors who had founded the university, rulers did not hesitate to interfere in the details of academic life and regulate the affairs of the university. This is clearly seen at Heidelberg in 1452, where Friedrich I, after listing the names of his predecessors and their concern for the university, imposes a complete set of reforms 'umb besserunge willen desselben unsers studiums.'[90]

Long before the controversies of the sixteenth century, the German universities were accustomed to accept a scale of interference from the secular authority that was not known in England. It is significant that the only statutes that originated directly from royal pressure in fifteenth century Oxford were those of 1420 concerned with the preservation of law and order, a subject which might be regarded as of royal concern. The English universities, unlike most of those of Germany, were not situated in the capital of the state, near the centre of political and social power, where the necessity of secular control was more apparent and more easily obtained. Even when royal interference in the affairs of the English universities became more frequent in the sixteenth century, we must suspect that the motive for this was not to ensure the reform of the university on humanistic lines, but to make certain that elements hostile to the crown's policy were expelled and that the future actions of the university would be in support of that policy. The Elizabethan statutes at Cambridge, as we have noted, left untouched the essential features of the curriculum but confirmed a fundamental change in the character of the government of the university. The Laudian Statutes of 1636 in the same way preserved intact much of the medieval curriculum at Oxford, but withdrew control of the university from the regent masters.

If this was the real motive behind royal interference in the English universities, we may suggest that references to curricular change by the crown must be received with some scepticism. The Royal Injunctions of 1535 issued to the University of Cambridge contain several interesting references to material used in the faculties of arts and theology. Aristotle, Rudolfus

Agricola, Philip Melanchthon, Trapezuntius and others unnamed are to be read; 'the frivolus questions and obscure glosses' of Scotus, Burley, Trombetta, Bricot, Brulifer and others are to be avoided. The study of canon law is to end, and also the use of any theologian who had written on the *Sentences*. Students are urged to cultivate 'polite learning'. Named colleges were instructed to establish daily lectureships in Latin and Greek.[91] There are a number of interesting features about these Injunctions. The style and wording, with their ridiculing of scholastic works, their reference to 'polite learning', and their condemnation of theological works on the *Sentences*, are typical of humanistic criticisms of the traditional university curriculum. The references to the works of Bricot, Trombetta, and Brulifer are also somewhat puzzling. These scholars wrote only in the late fifteenth and early sixteenth centuries; it is difficult to estimate how far their works were so popular in the English universities as to be named together with the earlier and well read authorities, Scotus and Burley. Certainly, they were known in England, but we have only scant references to the ownership, sale or purchase of their books at this date.[92] We may doubt whether the Royal Injunctions represent a correct view of what texts in logic were used at Cambridge at this date. What is, on the contrary, quite clear is that the authors named were amongst those most hated by the northern humanists.[93] The 'scotistae' at Cambridge had already been criticised by Erasmus.[94] The recommended texts, Agricola, Melanchthon, and Trapezuntius were also popular with the northern humanists; we have already found their logical writings recommended to the German universities. Since there are so few references to the condemned recent writers before 1535, it is difficult to estimate how far the prohibition was effective, but it certainly did not prevent the circulation in Cambridge of other proscribed texts, the medieval commentators on the *Sentences*. To give just a few examples, they occur in the 1556–7 catalogue of the University Library,[95] in a contemporary catalogue of the library of Corpus Christi College,[96] and in the library of Bishop Lancelot Andrews.[97] Many of these and other contemporary lists of books owned by Cambridge scholars or in Cambridge collections contain various logical writings of Scotus and Burley, and also some of the traditional texts used earlier for the study of canon law. The Royal Injunctions may have prevented the delivery of official lectures on certain texts, but they did not remove from Cambridge collections much medieval material which, therefore, remained accessible to those who wished to read it. It would certainly seem an exaggeration to see these Injunctions as heralding 'the final triumph of the Humanists';[98] as we shall indicate below, these academic changes that we see occuring in Elizabethan Cambridge as at Oxford owe little to royal intervention and more to slower and more significant movements.

We must argue, therefore, that the Royal Injunctions of 1535 do not represent a sudden and unusual royal interest in the internal affairs of the university. They seem to represent more the last important attempt by humanists at court to promote a radical change in academic education at Cambridge. Prof. McConica has emphasised the role of another generation of humanists around Thomas Cromwell after 1534.[99] As Chancellor and Royal Visitor of the University, Cromwell had an ideal opportunity to impose humanist concepts; this, we may suggest, was the driving force behind the detailed academic arrangements of the Injunctions. But, with Cromwell removed from power and the government concerned with more pressing affairs, hopes of a full humanistic victory again receded. We are not yet able to evaluate the full significance of the Royal Injunctions, but we may tentatively suggest that they must be consigned to those other, earlier efforts of the London court humanists to use the royal authority to effect drastic change; which efforts achieved only partial success and failed to alter significantly the structure and curriculum of either English university.

It has been suggested that the formal legislation of the German universities during the sixteenth century showed that they were prepared to accept regular and radical change, that at Cambridge there was some resistance to such reform, and that, at Oxford, there was a reluctance to see the medieval structure and curriculum of the university seriously modified. We have indicated reasons for these differences of approach, and suggested that, especially at Oxford, the need to prepare students for a period of further study in theology and an assumption that many would find a career in the church assisted in maintaining the traditional course in arts. However, the English universities could not stand totally aloof from developments on the Continent. The rapid spread of books now more easily and cheaply available from the printing presses of the Continent, the absence of any large production of material of predominantly English origins with the failure to establish in England any successful, prosperous and long lasting press, the strong contacts made with their continental colleagues first by Renaissance scholars and then by Protestants seeking support and sanctuary in Germany and Switzerland, to some extent brought England out of that intellectual parochialism that seemed to be developing in the later Middle Ages.[100]

Of more importance in affecting the studies of Oxford and Cambridge, was the changing character of the student intake at the close of the sixteenth century. Scholars may disagree on the nature and extent of the infiltration of the sons of the nobility and gentry into the English universities, but there can be little doubt that by the time of Elizabeth's death both Oxford and Cambridge were accepting many students of high social standing who were not concerned to pursue a career in either the church, law or medicine, but whose chief ambition was to obtain a liberal education before they devoted themselves to the administration of their estates, the service of their local community, or the pursuit of office in the central government.[101] For such students, the traditional curriculum was unsuitable; many had little interest in obtaining any academic qualification; the university became a sort of finishing school for them before entry on an active political and social life.

Perhaps it was inevitable, with the absence of any other institutions of higher education of similar prestige, that the gentry should look to Oxford and Cambridge to provide for its sons, but the movement was welcomed at the universities. Such students brought honour and gifts to the colleges: Merton College, in 1595, allowed Francis, the son of John Wolley, a member of the Queen's council, dining rights in hall; in 1598 the college received from Francis 'a white playne standing French cup' engraved with his name and the family arms.[102] Those taking charge of such young men were paid for their services and also obtained contact with rich patrons who could repay their concern in later life. For such students there existed alongside the formal curriculum of the university an alternative course designed to cater for their specific interests. Despite their adherence to older ways and older forms, the English universities could not ignore what their German contemporaries had already found: that there was a demand for a reformed curriculum by students who were prepared to attend such universities and pay for their education.

We find, therefore, at Oxford and Cambridge, a readiness to teach the Greek and Latin classics, modern languages, Ramist logic, Hebrew, history, and such subjects not emphasised, ignored or proscribed by the formal legislation of the universities.[103] At this date the two systems seem to have co-existed, although there are signs that some formal lectures especially of the universities were not well attended.[104] The seventeenth century continued to be a period of theological debate, and the numbers of those taking lower degrees in theology rose in the period 1610–39 to heights probably never reached before or since.[105] While this situation remained, it could be argued that an arts course of the traditional type was of value. Perhaps when theological controversy declined, interest in the traditional form of education at Oxford and Cambridge also waned. The English universities were then, in the eighteenth century, left with a formal curriculum ignored by most students. We must, however, be careful not to read back the hypocrisy, corruption and inefficiency of some practices of the later universities into the Elizabethan period.

In one respect, in both Germany and England, there was a definite change in the curriculum of the arts faculty. The later Middle Ages had seen the development, especially at Oxford, of numerous tractates dealing with aspects of logic under such headings as *suppositiones, ampliationes, consequentie, obligationes* and so forth. Such works were widely read in the German universities, often in convenient summary form,[106] or in a series of often anonymous texts brought together in booklet form.[107] In England selections from these collections were later printed as the *Oxford Logic*, or the Oxford and Cambridge *Libelli Sophistarum*.[108] Several substantial works based on this logic were produced, especially at Oxford where such writers as Dumbleton and Heytesbury produced influential books that subsequently were incorporated into the curriculum of many European universities. This material seems to fall out of favour in both England and Germany in the late fifteenth century. In some cases we can date the withdrawal of specific texts as at Leipzig when a decision of 1496 ordered the rejection of a text 'quia parum fructus in se habeat.'[109] In most universities, however, the process appears to have been gradual. There had already been complaints of the time spent on the study of logic in the arts course,[110] and the introduction of new subjects such as Greek into the curriculum in the sixteenth century must have put even greater pressure on the time available for teaching, especially as the original length of the arts course had, by this date, been reduced in most continental universities to a period of three or four years. These factors, together with the known dislike of 'sophistry' by many humanist propagandists, probably helped to force such logic out of the curriculum. The process by which this happened is obscure, and further research is needed to clarify many points, but for most students at the end of the century, the 'sophismata' familiar to the medieval student had ceased to be a significant part of the arts curriculum.[111]

Finally, in considering the development of German and English universities during this period, we must be careful not to fall into the trap of accepting much contemporary criticism of these institutions. This is not the place to discuss fully one of the fundamental issues concerning this century, but most historians of universities have assumed that the arguments of the humanists were valid: that their philosophy offered a better education than that of their medieval predecessors. This assumption must be challenged. Perhaps an education based on a thorough study of the classics was equally as narrow as that based on the writings of commentators on Aristotle. Perhaps the humanist training did not fit scholars to accept much of the scientific and technological discoveries of the late seventeenth, eighteenth, nineteenth and twentieth centuries. Perhaps the emphasis on style and polish produced graduates better known for the manner in which they expressed their thoughts rather than for the content of that thought. A sympathetic history of the opposition to the infiltration of humanistic educational concepts into the universities remains to be written. When this is done, it may show that more academics than one might expect had reservations about the validity of the humanists' arguments. Certainly it seems that, at Oxford at least, a powerful group of masters and doctors was reluctant to break completely with the past. Because of the peculiarities of the situation in England, discussed above, their attitude was able to influence strongly the history of academic development in Tudor England. We must be careful, therefore, before we assume that in Germany the humanists' educational philosophy was welcomed by academics or regarded generally as progressive. When more detailed evidence is available, it may appear that the new values were imposed on reluctant universities by external political and social pressure, stronger in Germany than in England. Opposition to humanism may have been more powerful in both countries than has been generally recognised and the grounds for that opposition can perhaps be today more readily understood and appreciated. Moreover, to the twentieth century reader, the humanists' readiness to use the authority of the secular power often to impose change upon the universities will appear somewhat disturbing. When such aspects of the academic changes of the century are considered, the humanists case may appear less convincing and their methods of achieving their aims less attractive.

References

1. It is not my intention to provide full bibliographies for this important field which has attracted the attention of many scholars during this century, but the more recent lines of argument may be here briefly indicated. The German universities, many of which have recently celebrated their anniversaries with commemorative publications, are well served for general histories, but we might especially mention here M. Grossmann, *Humanism in Wittenberg 1485–1517*, Nieuwkoop, 1975, and L. Boehm, 'Humanistische Bildungsbewegung und mittelalterliche Universitätsverfassung', in *The Universities in the late Middle Ages*, eds. J. Ijsewijn and J. Paquet, Louvain, 1978. There has been great interest shown in the social structure of the Renaissance German universities as indicated by such works as R. A. Müller, *Universität und Adel. Eine soziostrukturelle Studie zur Geschichte der Bayerischen Landesuniversität Ingolstadt 1472–1648*, Berlin, 1974. Controversies in the early sixteenth century German universities have been refreshingly surveyed by J. H. Overfield in his 'A New Look at the Reuchlin Affair', *Studies in Medieval and Renaissance History*, 8 (1971): 165–207, and 'Scholastic Opposition to Humanism in Pre-Reformation Germany', *Viator*, 7 (1976): 391–420. The University of Cambridge has not been properly examined for this period, but a preliminary study has been made by L. Jardine in her short account 'Humanism and the Sixteenth Century Arts Course', *History of Education*, 4 (1975): 16–31. The history of the sixteenth century University of Oxford is now being studied by a group of scholars working for the Official History of the University. The fate of scholastic logic in the English universities has been tentatively examined in articles by L. M. De Rijk, 'Logica Cantabrigiensis. A Fifteenth Century Cambridge Manual of Logic', *Revue Internationale de Philosophie*, 113 (1975): 297–315; 'Logica Oxoniensis. An Attempt to Reconstruct a Fifteenth Century Oxford Manual of Logic', *Medioevo*, 3 (1977): 121–64, and E. J. Ashworth, 'The *Libelli Sophistarum* and the Use of Medieval logic Texts at Oxford and Cambridge in the Early Sixteenth Century', *Vivarium*, 17 (1979): 134–58, but these must be used with care in view of our lack of knowledge of the fourteenth and fifteenth century manuscript tradition. J. K. McConica has extended the debate with his 'Humanism and Aristotle in Tudor Oxford', *English Historical Review*, 94 (1979): 291–317. I have indicated in the notes to this essay only those works directly relevant to my argument or from which I have drawn material.
2. See my essay 'Linacre's Lands and Lectureships', in *Linacre Studies. Essays on the Life and Work of Thomas Linacre c 1460–1524*, ed. F. Maddison, M. Pelling, C. Webster, Oxford, 1977.

3. E. Winkelmann, *Urkundenbuch der Universität Heidelberg*, 2 vols., Heidelberg, 1886, 1: 214, 213.
4. Described by Erasmus in his letter to Jodocus Jonas 1521. P. S. Allen, ed., *Opus Epistolarum Des. Erasmi Roterodami*, 12 vols., Oxford, 1906–58, 4: 520.
5. The attempt is discussed fully in G. Bauch, *Die Reception des Humanismus in Wien*, Breslau, 1903.
6. Allen, *Opus Epistolarum*, 4: 33.
7. Winkelmann, *Urkundenbuch*, I: 214–6. The reading by Winkelmann of 'Julianus Caesar' is puzzling. Is 'Johannes Caesarius' intended?
8. *Ibid.*, p. 218.
9. References to the documents noted here and below may be found in W. Friedensburg, *Urkundenbuch der Universität Wittenberg*, I, 1502–1611, Magdeburg, 1926.
10. Terence Heath, in an important article 'Logical Grammar, Grammatical Logic, and Humanism in Three German Universities', *Studies in the Renaissance*, 18 (1971): 9–64, emphasises that the humanist view of grammar denied any connection between the study of grammar and logic, and so began the process of divorcing one subject from the other. Once the Faculty of Arts ceased to accept the role of linguistic logic as an influence pervading all subjects, the unity of the faculty appeared to have little justification.
11. The documents are printed in K. von Prantl, *Geschichte der Ludwig-Maximilians-Universität in Ingolstadt, Landshut, München*, 2 vols., Munich, 1872, vol. 2.
12. The history of the university is to be found in O. Krabbe, *Die Universität Rostock im 15. und 16. Jahrhundert*, Rostock, 1854.
13. E. Bonjour, *Die Universität Basel*, Basel, 1960, pp. 121, 151.
14. Printed in R. von Roth, *Urkunden zur Geschichte der Universität Tübingen aus den Jahren 1476–1550*, Tübingen, 1877.
15. The statutes are printed and discussed in H. Ott and J. M. Fletcher, *The Mediaeval Statutes of the Faculty of Arts of the University of Freiburg im Breisgau*, Notre Dame, 1964.
16. Printed in Prantl, *Ludwig-Maximilians-Universität*, 2.
17. The attempts to reform the statutes are discussed by Strickland Gibson in his Introduction to *Statuta Antiqua Universitatis Oxoniensis*, Oxford, 1931, pp. xlv–xlix. See also the article by E. Mullally, 'Wolsey's Proposed Reform of the Oxford University Statutes: A Recently Discovered Text', *Bodleian Library Record*, 10 (1978); 22–7.
18. The relationship between the Statutes and the Grace Books is further discussed in my forthcoming study of the Oxford Faculty of Arts at the close of the Middle Ages.
19. Printed in Gibson, *Statuta Antiqua*, pp. 341–60.
20. *Ibid.*, pp. 363–75.
21. *Ibid.*, pp. 378–88.
22. The Laudian Statutes have been edited by J. Griffiths, *Statutes of the University of Oxford codified in the Year 1636 under the Authority of Archbishop Laud*, Oxford, 1888.
23. Gibson, *Statuta Antiqua*, pp. 467, 481.
24. J. M. Fletcher, ed., *Registrum Annalium Collegii Mertonensis 1567–1603*, Oxford Historical Society. New Series, vol. 24, Oxford, 1976, p. 15.

25. Gibson, *Statuta Antiqua*, p. 409 etc.
26. Discussed in Fletcher, 'Linacre's Lands and Lectureships', above note 2.
27. A more detailed investigation of these exercises will be presented in my forth-coming study of the Tudor Faculty of Arts for the official history of the University of Oxford.
28. Gibson, *Statuta Antiqua*, pp. 344, 348, 359.
29. *Laudian Statutes*, pp. 50, 270.
30. Discussed in my forthcoming essay.
31. Prantl, *Ludwig-Maximilians-Universität*, 2: 185–6.
32. Roth, *Universität Tübingen*, pp. 389–90.
33. Gibson, *Statuta Antiqua*, p. 378.
34. *Ibid.*, p. 390.
35. E.g. Oxford University Archives, Reg. I, ff. 213^v, 214.
36. E.g. *ibid.*, f. 205.
37. Gibson, *Statuta Antiqua*, pp. 344, 358.
38. *Ibid.*, p. 381.
39. *Ibid.*, p. 408.
40. *Ibid.*
41. *Laudian Statutes*, p. 271.
42. Gibson, *Statuta Antiqua*, pp. 378, 389–90.
43. The process is traced in more detail in my forthcoming essay.
44. *Laudian Statutes*, p. 103.
45. Gibson, *Statuta Antiqua*, p. 431. *Laudian Statutes*, p. 58.
46. The statutes may be consulted in *Documents relating to the University and Colleges of Cambridge*, 3 vols., London, 1852, 1: 454–95.
47. *Ibid.*, p. 459.
48. John Venn, ed., *Grace Book Δ*, Cambridge, 1910, pp. 28, 148.
49. *Ibid.*, p. 48. See also K. Bartlett, 'The Decline and Abolition of the Master of Grammar: An Early Victory of Humanism at the University of Cambridge', *History of Education*, 6 (1977): 1–8. Whether the failure to create a separate Faculty of Grammar on humanistic lines can be described as a 'victory of humanism' is perhaps questionable.
50. *Documents*, 1: 495.
51. *Ibid.*, p. 457.
52. John Lamb, ed., *A Collection of Letters, Statutes and other Documents from the MS. Library of Corpus Christi College Illustrative of the History of the University of Cambridge during the period of the Reformation*, London, 1838, pp. 124–5.
53. Charles H. Cooper, *Annals of Cambridge*, 5 vols., Cambridge, 1842–1908, 1: 301–2.
54. *Documents*, 1: 382–3. Mary Bateson, ed., *Grace Book B, Part 1*, Cambridge, 1903, p. 199.
55. *Grace Book B, Part 1*, pp. 232, 237.
56. *Ibid.*, p. 232.
57. *Documents*, 1: 459.
58. *Ibid.*, p. 465.
59. Joseph Aschbach, *Geschichte der Wiener Universität im ersten Jahrhunderte Ihres Bestehens*, Vienna, 1865, p. 142.

60. Prantl, *Ludwig-Maximilians-Universitiät*, 2: 161.
61. See, for example, the essay by Cesare Vasoli, 'Intorno al Petrarca ed ai logici "moderni" ', in *Antiqui und Moderni*, Berlin, 1974, pp. 142–54.
62. Johannes J. Bauer, *Zur Frühgeschichte der theologischen Fakultät der Universität Freiburg i. Br., (1460–1520)*, Freiburg im Breisgau, 1957, p. 11.
63. Winkelmann, *Urkundenbuch*, 1: 218.
64. Friedensburg, *Urkundenbuch*, 1: 254.
65. Winkelmann, *Urkundenbuch*, 1: 213.
66. *Ibid.*, p. 217; 2: 76.
67. Friedensburg, *Urkundenbuch*, 1: 16.
68. *Ibid.*, p. 394.
69. K. Charlton, *Education in Renaissance England*, London, 1965, pp. 169–95.
70. Lawrence Stone, 'The Size and Composition of the Oxford Student Body 1580–1910', in Lawrence Stone, ed., *The University in Society, 1, Oxford and Cambridge from the 14th to the Early 19th Century*, Princeton, 1974, p. 17.
71. *Ibid.*, p. 91.
72. These points are well presented in their Scottish context in A. C. Chitnis, *The Scottish Enlightenment. A Social History*, London, 1976.
73. James K. McConica, *English Humanists and Reformation Politics under Henry VIII and Edward VI*, Oxford, 1965, ch. 6.
74. C. Maxwell, *A History of Trinity College Dublin 1591–1892*, Dublin, 1946, p. 3.
75. *Ibid.*, pp. 5–6.
76. W. B. S. Taylor, *History of the University of Dublin*, London, 1845, p. 16.
77. *Ibid.*, p. 8.
78. *Ibid.*, p. 24.
79. Gerhard Ritter, *Die Heidelberger Universität*, Heidelberg, 1936, 1: 85, n. 2.
80. Johannes Haller, *Die Anfänge der Universität Tübingen 1477–1537*, Stuttgart; 1927, p. 62.
81. Aschbach, *Wiener Universität*, pp. 355, 296.
82. Friedensburg, *Urkundenbuch*, 1: 78–9.
83. Franz Eulenburg, *Die Frequenz der Deutschen Universitäten*, Leipzig, 1904, pp. 233–6. See also pp. 312, 315, 318.
84. Friedensburg, *Urkundenbuch*, 1: 406.
85. Fletcher, *Registrum Annalium 1567–1603*, pp. 163–4, 273.
86. N. R. Ker, 'Oxford College Libraries in the Sixteenth Century' *Bodleian Library Record*, 6 (1959): 498.
87. Fletcher, *Registrum Annalium 1567–1603*, p. 248.
88. *Ibid.*, p. 75.
89. Ritter, *Heidelberger Universität*, p. 445.
90. Winkelmann, *Urkundenbuch*, 1: 161.
91. The Injunctions are conveniently summarised in J. B. Mullinger, *The University of Cambridge from the Earliest Times to the Royal Injunctions of 1535*, Cambridge, 1873, p. 630.
92. For instance, in contemporary Oxford inventories (A. B. Emden, *A Biographical Register of the University of Oxford A.D. 1501 to 1540*, Oxford, 1974, pp. 716, 732, 742), in John Dorne's Day Book (See under "Index" in Montague Burroughs, ed., *Collectanea: Second Series*, Oxford, Oxford Historical Society, 1890, pp. 463–77), and in the Warden's study at Canterbury College, (W. A.

Pantin, *Canterbury College Oxford*, Oxtord, Oxford Historical Society, 1947, 1: 61).

93. For the views expressed by Erasmus and Beatus Rhenanus, see Allen, *Opus Epistolarum*, 2: 550; 5: 102.

94. *Ibid.*, 1: 467 etc.

95. J. C. T. Oates and H. L. Pink, 'Three Sixteenth-Century Catalogues of the University Library', *Transactions of the Cambridge Bibliographical Society*, 1 (1952): 315 (Aquinas), 324 (Scotus).

96. J. M. Fletcher and J. K. McConica, 'A Sixteenth Century Inventory of the Library of Corpus Christi College, Cambridge', *Trans. Camb. Bib. Soc.*, 3 (1961): 191 (Aquinas), 192 (Bonaventura, Scotus).

97. D. D. C. Chambers, 'A Catalogue of the Library of Bishop Lancelot Andrewes (1555–1626)', *Trans. Camb. Bib. Soc.*, 5 (1970): 106 (Biel), 114 (Major, Marsilius, Mayronnes), etc.

98. Mullinger, *Cambridge*, p. 631.

99. McConica, *English Humanists*, ch. 6.

100. I have here benefited from advice from Julian Deahl, now working on the study of logic in England in the later medieval period.

101. See, for example, the discussion in M. H. Curtis, *Oxford and Cambridge in Transition 1558–1642*, Oxford, 1959, ch. 3; Stone, 'Oxford Student Body', pp. 24–8, and H. Kearney, *Scholars and Gentlemen, Universities and Society in Pre-Industrial Britain 1500–1700*, London, 1970.

102. Fletcher, *Registrum Annalium 1567–1603*, pp. 317, 202 n. 1.

103. For Greek and Latin see Curtis, *Oxford and Cambridge*, ch. 4. For modern languages and Hebrew, see Fletcher, *Registrum Annalium 1567–1603*, pp. 43, 317. For Ramist logic see Curtis, *Oxford and Cambridge*, p. 118. For history, see ibid., p. 120.

104. See, for example, Curtis, *Oxford and Cambridge*, pp. 96–9.

105. Stone, 'Oxford Student Body', p. 22.

106. For example, the popular *Summulae Logicales* of Petrus Hispanus.

107. For example, Worcester Cathedral MS. F. 118; New College, Oxford, MS. 289.

108. London 1497, ca. 1499, etc. For a full list of editions see Ashworth, 'The *Libelli sophistarum*', cited above in note 1.

109. The text 'Lectio Loicae Hesbri' (i.e. Heylesbury's *Logic*) was replaced by 'Liber rhetoricorum Aristotelis'. F. Zarncke, *Die Statutenbücher der Universität Leipzig*, Leipzig, 1861, p. 22.

110. For example, at Oxford in 1412 'cum a logicalium lectura artentur nimis diu iudicio plurimorum' (Gibson, *Statuta Antiqua*, p. 216).

111. Preliminary work on the relationship between the study of logic and the progress of humanistic studies has now begun. Charles B. Schmitt's careful and sensible observations in 'Philosophy and Science in Sixteenth-Century Universities: Some Preliminary Comments', *The Cultural Context of Medieval Learning*, eds. J. E. Murdoch and E. D. Sylla, Dordrecht, 1975, are a valuable contribution. For Oxford, James K. McConica's 'Humanism and Aristotle in Tudor Oxford', *English Historical Review*, 94 (1979): 291–317 is a perceptive introduction. For Cambridge, L. Jardine's 'The Place of Dialectic Teaching in Sixteenth-Century Cambridge', *Studies in the Renaissance*, 21 (1974): 31–62, and her 'Humanism and Dialectic in Sixteenth-Century Cambridge: A Preliminary

Investigation', in *Classical Influences on European Culture A.D. 1500–1700*, ed. R. R. Bolgar, Cambridge, 1976, are weakened by her lack of knowledge of the type of logic studied in late medieval English universities and her assumption that the curriculum here followed that of Europe in its reliance on such authors as Petrus Hispanus. Our knowledge of the interaction between late medieval and sixteenth century concepts of logic will be greatly improved when Julian Deahl publishes his study of late medieval logic at Oxford. In the meantime, the work of Dr. Schmitt and Prof. McConica in particular indicates that many late sixteenth century scholars avidly read Aristotle and his contemporary commentators, but did not all reject earlier medieval commentaries such as those of Scotus and Aquinas. Little enthusiasm, however, was expressed for the 'modistae' 'sophisters' and 'summulistae' of the fifteenth century.

82

Excerpt from
THE GREAT INSTAURATION
SCIENCE, MEDICINE AND
REFORM 1626–1660

Charles Webster

Source: C. Webster, *The Great Instauration: Science, Medicine and Reform, 1626–1660*, New York: Holmes and Meier, 1975, pp. 115–22.

Science and medicine in academic studies before 1640

In an assessment which must be allowed to have considerable authority, Oxford's restoration chancellor Lord Clarendon admitted that, notwithstanding the general barbarism of the interregnum, Oxford had during that period 'yielded a harvest of extra-ordinary good and sound knowledge in all parts of learning'.[1] This was an opinion shared by all but the severest high-church critics of the parliamentarian regime, who, once reinstalled in the universities, embarked upon a course of retribution which precluded acknowledging any grain of merit in the offending Presbyterian and Independent parties. Clarendon's estimate is confirmed by the well-informed Anglican and royalist physician Walter Charleton, an eye-witness who extolled 'The noble successes of those Heroicall Wits among our Country-men, who have addicted themselves to the Reformation and Augmentation of Arts and Sciences, and made a greater Progresse in that glorious design, than many ages before them could aspire to.'[2] Oxford and the London College of Physicians were singled out for special mention in Charleton's eulogy of his countrymen's contribution to the various facets of experimental science. This rise of experimental natural philosophy at the universities impressed many other observers, eliciting comment in orations delivered during the interregnum by academics of many persuasions. Clarendon was probably impressed by the increasing reputation of the scientific virtuosi, but intellectual vitality was not the only reason for the debt of the restoration to the natural philosophers who rose to prominence during the interregnum.

They had proved to be exemplary guardians of the academic institutions moulded by Archbishop Laud.

In order to arrive at a balanced view of the role of science and medicine in the universities during the Puritan Revolution it is necessary to draw attention to the conditions prevailing in the earlier part of the century. There is considerable divergence of opinion on this subject. At one extreme it is felt that the period of Laudian dominance was characterised by intellectual stagnation, which was effectively counteracted by parliamentarians, to allow free flowering of the new philosophy.[3] Others would claim that the new science became firmly rooted in the Laudian universities and that this tradition was merely maintained during the subsequent upheavals.[4] Both points of view rely on substantially the same sources of evidence: the autobiographical and apologetic writings of Ward, Wilkins and Wallis, and the 'Directions for a Student' attributed to Richard Holdsworth. All of these documents were composed after 1640, but they have been cited as guides to earlier educational attitudes, a purpose for which they must clearly be used with the greatest caution.

Whatever view is taken about the rise of science in the universities, it must be appreciated that the 'sciences' which captured the imagination of Brian Twyne at the beginning of the seventeenth century had little in common with those pursued by the students of John Wilkins fifty years later. In the course of that time each facet of science developed and metamorphosed. The new systems of Telesio, Campanella, Descartes and Gassendi greatly diversified the conceptual approach to natural philosophy. Most of the experimental activities, mathematical problems and philosophical debates recorded by Wallis for the originators of the Royal Society would have been foreign to the experience of natural philosophers at the beginning of the century. Developments of this kind cannot be ignored when assessing the intellectual atmosphere in the English universities. Accordingly it is as frivolous to deny that there were any substantially new developments after 1640 as it is to assert that puritanism provides a sufficient explanation for the change.

It is not possible to enter into a discussion of academic response to the sciences without some reference to the problems of definition. It is for example important to bear in mind that the term 'university' is customarily used for an institution and the statutory activities of its members, but that it may also be legitimately applied to cover the wider, informal activities of the community of scholars associated with the institution. In the seventeenth century at least it was possible for individuals to play an institutional role little related to their private intellectual life. The universities may therefore be assessed according to various standards. The institutional structure, statutory teaching regulations, and examination mechanisms seem the most obvious basis on which to make a judgement. But this evidence usually provides only limited and superficial indications about the scope of formal education. At the other extreme, we possess considerable information about the informal intellectual activities of the university in the wider sense. Between these two extremes of university life lies the *terra incognita* of tutorial studies and independent student enterprise. Some tutors would have taken the fullest advantage of any opportunity of introducing their students to the latest intellectual developments; ambitious students took the initiative themselves, sometimes even against their tutors' advice. In view of the fragmentary preservation of student records, our estimation of general tutorial response to the growth of the sciences must be largely speculative.

The scientific disciplines which could be most readily assimilated into university studies were medicine and mathematics. The former had a venerable history as a postgraduate discipline, while the latter was a potentially important constituent of the liberal arts curriculum. In addition, natural philosophy received some attention during the later stages of the arts course. The exact role intended for these subjects is not easy to determine. The statutes were specific and detailed, but these complex documents are extremely difficult to interpret. In some cases, later statutes were intended to complement the earlier, while in others they were to supplant them. The two universities differed slightly in their requirements, but some tuition was offered in arithmetic, geometry, music, cosmography, and astronomy.[5] Under the Laudian code at Oxford, arithmetic, geometry and music were stipulated for undergraduates, while at Cambridge only natural philosophy was authorised. Thus during the four-years preparation for a BA, little attention to mathematics and natural philosophy was required, particularly at Cambridge. During the subsequent three years of study for an MA, these subjects assumed greater importance. Both universities required some reading in astronomy, geometry and natural philosophy.[6] The stipulated texts for these studies were predominantly classical, or later didactic works based on obvious classical sources. The texts of Euclid, Galen, Ptolemy, or Aristotle were often an excellent starting-point for wider investigations, but there is little indication that the average student was made aware of the changing horizons of scientific knowledge. Pedagogical routine increasingly stood in the way of a flexible and creative approach to the sciences in both English and continental universities.

Student notebooks probably give a reliable impression about the general tone of formal studies.[7] They confirm the dominance of standard classical texts and exhibit a degree of formalisation and didactic simplification characteristic of the systematic but desiccated textbooks of the protestant scholastics. By their capacity to administer precisely to the statutory requirements of undergraduates, rather than by genuine intellectual appeal, the scholastic textbooks of the seventeenth century gained a tenacious hold which was only slowly overcome by textbooks representative of the new philosophy. Even in the eighteenth century, Tristram Shandy could be made to remark with simulated astonishment that his father 'had never in his whole life [had] the least light or spark struck into his mind, by one single lecture upon Crakenthorp or Burgersdicius, or any Dutch logician or commentator'.[8] But virtue was not entirely absent from these writings. Besides their sharp disputes on logical and ethical questions, such authors as Alsted and Ramus made distinct moves away from Aristotelianism, preparing the ground for more eclectic approaches to education and philosophy. Both Alsted and Ramus were successful textbook writers in natural philosophy and mathematics, but they were inclined to overreach themselves in their enthusiasm for comprehensiveness.[9] The restlessness of a young intellectual with a desire to escape from scholastic values, but without clear insight into a means of emancipation, is instanced by Nathaniel Carpenter. His *Philosophia Libera* was a work on natural philosophy explicitly intended to undermine Aristotelian orthodoxy, but whose author was totally imprisoned by scholastic concepts and terminology.[10]

Those who were tempted to explore neglected areas of knowledge found little encouragement, incentive or guidance. Brian Twyne's father warned him against premature reading of medical works.[11] None the less, Twyne accumulated medical books and quickly moved into even more disputed territory, studying mathematics and astrology under Thomas Allen of Gloucester Hall, at a time when 'astrologer, mathematician and conjurer were accounted the same things'.[12] With this danger in mind Ascham had warned against too great an interest in mathematics, while the most active exponents of this subject, Dee, Allen and the Harriot circle, earned notoriety as 'juglers'.

Under these circumstances the serious student of mathematics was an isolated figure, often displaying an almost religious devotion and enthusiasm for his new-found interest. The most influential mathematics teacher of this period, William Oughtred, described his mathematical apprenticeship in fervent terms:

> 'I redeemed night by night from my naturall sleep, defrauding my body, and inuring it to watching, cold, and labour, while most others tooke their rest. Neither did I therein seek only my private content, but the benefit of many: and by inciting, assisting, and instructing others, brought many in to the love and study of those Arts, not only in our own, but in some other Colledges also.'[13]

Oughtred's new obsession gave him intense satisfaction, which he transmitted to younger disciples. Through such ardent advocates as Oughtred, mathematics became available to a small but active 'sect' of academics. It reached a wider audience through Oughtred's textbook, *Clavis mathematica* (1631), which greatly enhanced the status of the subject. The astronomer William Gascoigne reported that he turned to Oughtred's book after he had failed to obtain guidance in mathematics at Oxford.[14] Many other provincial gentlemen shared Gascoigne's experience. Even those who spent many years at university were likely to find that mathematics was a neglected subject, its appearance in the notebooks of Twyne being an exception.[15] John Wallis was exceptionally fortunate in attending Felsted School, where the rudiments of arithmetic were taught. He regretted that 'this was my first insight into Mathematicks, and all the teaching I had'. At Cambridge he found that mathematics was thought appropriate to seamen and artisans, no assistance being available in 'what books to read, or what to seek, or in which method to proceed'. Of the two hundred students at his college Wallis knew only two who possessed reasonable skill in mathematics. He knew that mathematics was thriving in London among the mathematical practitioners, with whom he was soon able to associate, owing to his decision to leave university and enter the ministry.[16] Seth Ward at Sidney Sussex College had similar experiences; upon finding mathematical books in the college library, he was unable to find any Fellow able to help him. This position was only remedied when his ejection in 1644 led to his association with the London mathematicians and with William Oughtred.[17]

Such biographies suggest that before 1640 colleges at Oxford and Cambridge placed very little emphasis on mathematics and virtually none on experimental science. As Costello concludes, the neatness and convenience of their existing arrangements insulated them 'from any obligation to rethink the old curriculum in terms of the busy findings of the new mathematics and the New Science'.[18] There appears to have been a willingness to surrender these subjects to the London mathematical practitioners, or to the professors of Gresham College. The close interrelationship between scholars and practitioners in London may have convinced most academics that mathematics was irrelevant to liberal education in the universities. This attitude continued to prevail until the middle of the nineteenth century.

The medical faculties offered an alternative basis for the assimilation of science into higher education. If natural philosophy had been neglected in arts studies, there were no counter-attractions to deflect the student from its study during the long period of preparation for an MD.[19] The capacity of medical studies to lead to productive research in a wide range of scientific problems is illustrated by the careers of Gilbert and Harvey. However, their personal success was not due to the vitality of English medical schools. The medical schools at Padua, Bologna, Leyden and Montpellier had become centres of humanistic learning, anatomy, natural history and clinical training. Their counterparts at Oxford and Cambridge were not active in these directions, although Thomas Linacre and John Caius attempted to bridge the gulf between English, and continental medical education. Each university had been furnished with a Regius professor in medicine since the reign of Henry VIII. Linacre endowed medical lectureships at both Oxford and Cambridge, but these never became properly functional. A few colleges had medical fellowships; Caius was exceptional in establishing two at his college.[20]

Before 1640 the English medical faculties appear to have adopted an extremely traditional approach to medical education. The professors were orthodox and almost uniformly undistinguished. Considering the extreme length envisaged for medical studies, the statutory provisions were vague and fragmentary. Nothing like a comprehensive medical curriculum emerged. Thus when as regularly happened a dispensation was granted so that requirements might be reduced, no dilution of standards was involved. The essential ingredients were lectures and the study of small sections of the Galenic and Hippocratic corpus. The occasional revisions of the statutes betrayed no significant response to developments in humanistic medicine.[21]

There was no move towards the kind of clinical teaching adopted in certain Italian medical schools. More surprisingly, dissection appears not to have been practised more than sporadically although the Edwardian statutes prescribed two anatomies for each incepting MD. Various graces were passed to prompt more active attention to dissection, but to little avail.[22] The disputation subjects for this period reflect the intellectual tone of the medical faculty. Most disputations related to elementary Galenic and Hippocratic tenets. Diet, alcoholic drinks and exercise were discussed in the frequent questions on regimen. There was also considerable discussion about the correct practice of phlebotomy and purgation. In one exceptional instance Robert Fludd debated the virtues of chemical therapy (1605). Discussion of points of anatomy was almost unknown, while physiological questions were general and elementary. Edmund Deane was asked whether respiration was necessary to sustain life; others were asked about the nutritive functions of blood. Humoral pathology and the doctrine of temperaments were the basic components of these disputes.[23] Medicine was evidently a literary study, but its practical aims should not be overlooked. The knowledge acquired from the texts studied at university was intended as a substantial foundation for medical practice.[24]

The numbers graduating in the medical faculties fluctuated widely before 1640. Occasionally the faculties must have hovered on the edge of extinction, since in some years no MB or MD was granted. For the period 1620–1640 Oxford produced an average of 2.5 MBs and one MD each year, while the equivalent figures for Cambridge were 1 and 1.5. The medical faculties of both universities were important as licensing agencies, granting incorporations to physicians with foreign MDs, and dispensing licences for practice 'pro regnum Angliae'. Incorporation was uncontroversial, since it was primarily intended to supply a qualification for membership of the College of Physicians. However, the College asserted that its position was being undermined by physicians who were using the university licence as an excuse to practise in London.[25] Furthermore, the College believed that the universities were unduly generous in granting medical licences. Soon after his appointment as Regius professor at Cambridge, Ralph Winterton 'observed and grieved to see sometimes a Minister, sometimes a serving man, sometimes an Apothecary admitted to a licence to practice in Physick'.[26] Both he and his predecessor were anxious to confine the grants of licences to those possessing a classical education but, according to the College of Physicians, arbitrary licensing continued.[27] Licences for the practice of medicine may have been given indiscriminately in a few cases, but at least as far as the Oxford records show, licences were almost invariably given to physicians having an MB or MD qualification.

For a more substantial medical training it was customary for medical students to visit one of the major continental universities. This expedient offered an insight into the full complexities of humanistic medicine. Foreign travel also served to familiarise English scholars with continental developments in mathematics and natural philosophy. Strong links were often forged between English and foreign physicians, which were maintained after the English scholars returned home, thus ensuring that they continued to be exposed to the most recent debates and advances in their specialities. The taste for continental medical education had been firmly established by the humanists in the first part of the sixteenth century. Linacre returned from Italy with a considerable reputation as a translator of Galen. His example was followed by Caius, who even incorporated a provision for such peregrinations in the statutes of his college. Caius had known Vesalius at Padua and later he collaborated with Conrad Gesner in compiling his *Historia animalium*. When faced with Vesalius's revisions of Galen however he reacted in favour of tradition. By contrast, Thomas Mouffet, who also visited Gesner in Switzerland, became an advocate of Paracelsus. Exposure to continental influences led to diversification of outlook within the medical profession, but it was an extremely long time before the new ideas became reflected in educational practice.

Notes

1 *History of the Rebellion*, ed. W. D. Macray (Oxford, 1847), iv, p.284. For a similar estimate in an oration delivered in 1654 by Vice-Chancellor Owen, see *The Oxford Orations of Dr. John Owen*, ed. P. Toon (Linkinhorne, 1971), p.15.
2 Charleton (46), p.33.
3 'A Note on the Universities', Hill (149), pp.301–14.
4 Curtis (69), pp.227–60; P. Allen, 'Scientific Studies in the English Universities of the Seventeenth Century', *JHI*, 1949, *10*: 219–53; also B. J. Shapiro, 'The Universities and Science in Seventeenth Century England', *Journal of British Studies*, 1971, 10: 47–82. Shapiro suggests that 'Universities had shown continuous interest in science, that Puritan intervention did not significantly alter the pattern of scientific concerns . . .'. For a valuable review of sources, see Frank (106).
5 Curtis (69), pp.86–90.
6 Gibson (116), pp.xcii–xcvi, 378.
7 W. J. Costello (61); H. Kearney (170), pp.77–90, 102–9.
8 Laurence Sterne, *The Life and Opinions of Tristram Shandy*, Chapter XIX. For an earlier remark of a similar satirical nature, see Joseph Glanvill, *Plus Ultra*

(London, 1668), p.118. For the neo-scholastics, see P. Miller (189), pp.102–4, 510–12; N. W. Gilbert, *Renaissance Concepts of Method* (New York, 1960); P. Dibon, *La philosophie néerlandaise au siècle d'or: Tome I* (Paris, 1954). For a review of recent research, see C. B. Schmitt (256). For textbooks, Patricia Reif, 'The Textbook Tradition in Natural Philosophy 1600–1650', *JHI*, 1969, *30*: 17–32.

9 W. J. Ong, *Ramus: Method and the Decay of Dialogue* (Cambridge, Mass., 1958).

10 Madan (184), iii, p.312.

11 Letter from Brian Twyne to Thomas Twyne, 6 July 1601, Bodleian MS, Gr. Misc. d. 2, fols. 40r–41v; quoted from *Bodleian Quarterly Record*, 1926/9, *5*: 217.

12 Aubrey, i, pp.26–9.

13 Oughtred, *The Circles of Proportion* (London, 1633), appendix, 'The Just Apologie', sig. A4v–B1r. A. J. Turner (293), draws attention to the importance of instruments in seventeenth-century mathematical education. Aubrey noted that 'countrey people did beleeve that he [Oughtred] could conjure' and that 'He was an astrologer and very lucky in giving his judgements on nativities': Aubrey, ii, pp.108–9. For further consideration of this subject, see Thomas (281), pp.349–54.

14 Gascoigne 'Left both Oxford and London before [he] knew what a proposition in geometry meant': Letter to Oughtred [1640], Rigaud (245), i, p.35.

15 W. J. Costello (61), pp.102, 149.

16 Scriba (257), pp.26–7, 29–30. See above, pp.40–1.

17 Walter Pope (223), pp.9–10, 16.

18 Costello (61), p.148.

19 The precise length of time spent in preparation for an MD is difficult to estimate. According to the statutes, after obtaining an MA in seven years, an MD was confirmed after a further four to seven years. However, in almost all cases, graces were obtained to reduce this period of study. For a brief survey of this topic, see P. Allen, 'Medical Education in Seventeenth-Century England', *J. Hist. Med.*, 1946, *1*: 115–43.

20 Curtis (69), pp.152–5; Costello (61), pp.128–35; Macalister (182).

21 Gibson (116), pp.ciii, 346, 379; Clark (48), ii, part 1, pp.123–9.

22 Macalister (182), pp.10–11.

23 Clark (48), ii, part 1, pp.189–94; Univ. Oxon. Arch., Congregation Registers 1623–1640.

24 This contradicts the opinion of the editor of the Oxford registers: 'The faculty of Medicine . . . had already lost touch with the requirements of professional study, and presented very much the features which it has at the present day [1885]'. Clark (48), ii, part 1, p.123.

25 For the sources of the statistics quoted, see below, note 153. Averages are given to the nearest 0.25 per cent. G. Clark (50), i, pp.112–13; 209–10.

26 C. Goodall (119), p.443. Letter to the College of Physicians, 25 August 1635.

27 Clark (50), i, pp.260–1.

Bibliography [edited]

(46) Charleton, Walter. *The Immortality of the Human Soul Demonstrated by the Light of Nature. In two Dialogues* (London, 1657).

(48) Clark, A. and Boase, C. W. *Register of the University of Oxford*, 2 vols. (Oxford Historical Society, Oxford, 1885–9).

(50) Clark, G. *A History of the Royal College of Physicians of London*, 2 vols. (Oxford, 1964–6).

(61) Costello, W. J. *The Scholastic Curriculum at Early 17th Century Cambridge* (Cambridge, Mass., 1958).

(69) Curtis, M. H. *Oxford and Cambridge in Transition, 1558–1642* (Oxford, 1959).

(106) Frank, R. G., Jr. 'Science, Medicine and the Universities of Early Modern England: Background and Sources', *History of Science*, 1973, *11*: 194–216; 239–69.

(116) Gibson, Strickland (ed.) *Statuta Antiqua universitatis Oxoniensis* (Oxford, 1931).

(119) Goodall, Charles. *The Royal College of Physicians of London, founded and established by Law* (London, 1684).

(149) Hill, C. *Intellectual Origins of the English Revolution* (Oxford, 1965).

(170) Kearney, H. *Scholars and Gentlemen. Universities and Society in pre-Industrial Britain 1500–1700* (London, 1970).

(182) Macalister, A. *The History of the Study of Anatomy in Cambridge* (Cambridge, 1891).

(184) Madan, F. *Oxford Books*, 3 vols. (Oxford, 1895–1931).

(189) Miller, P. *The New England Mind: The Seventeenth Century* (Cambridge, Mass., 1939).

(223) Pope, Walter. *The Life of the Right Reverend Father of God, Seth, Lord Bishop of Salisbury* (London, 1697).

(245) Rigaud, S. P. (ed.) *Correspondence of Scientific Men of the Seventeenth Century*, 2 vols. (Oxford, 1841).

(256) Schmitt, C. B. *A Critical Survey and Bibliography of Studies on Renaissance Aristotelianism 1958–1969* (Padua, 1971).

(257) Scriba, C. J. 'The Autobiography of John Wallis', *Notes & Records of the Royal Society*, 1970, *25*: 17–46.

(281) Thomas, K. *Religion and the Decline of Magic* (London, 1971).

(293) Turner, A. J. 'Mathematical Instruments and the Education of Gentlemen', *Annals of Science*, 1973, *30*: 51–88.

83

THE LIMITS OF 'REFORM'

Some aspects of the debate on university education during the English Revolution

John Twigg

Source: *History of Universities* 4 (1984): 99–114.

On the question of university reform, the English Revolution flattered to deceive. It is certain that revolutionary governments regarded educational reform as vital; their favourite educational theorist, Samuel Hartlib, wrote that 'this Endeavour alone, or nothing, will be able to work a Reformation in this our Age'.[1] Encouragement was given to reformers such as Hartlib, Dury and Comenius, attempts were made to propagate the Gospel in remote and backward regions, the universities were purged, Trinity College Dublin was reformed, and a new University college was founded at Durham, yet these grand schemes produced little that was deep-rooted and lasting.[2] Certainly the pressures of war and revolution hampered the reformers, and many hopes were dashed at the Restoration, but in this essay I wish to advance the tentative hypothesis that the ostensible 'failure' of revolutionary governments to implement far-reaching change was perhaps in part because the intellectual preconditions for such change were not yet present, and many modern notions of 'reform' may be out of place in the seventeenth century.

Firstly, many contemporaries perceived the universities' role in society in narrowly political terms. This was possibly due in part to the changes in the function of the universities during the sixteenth century, particularly the greater emphasis on a learned clergy, and the influx of the gentry, a process which Curtis describes as the 'Englishing' of the universities: they were brought into a closer relationship with the specifically English cultural and social environment.[3] Oxford and Cambridge products permeated the influential quarters of English society and institutions.

The Duke of Newcastle commented that 'it is a great matter in a state or kingdom, to take care of the education of youth, to breed them so, that they may know first how to obey, and then how to command and order affairs wisely'.[4] This was echoed by two leading authorities on educational theory, writing over a century apart: in 1570, Roger Ascham noted that 'the good or ill bringing up of our children doth as much serve to the good or ill service of God, our prince and our whole country as any one thing doth beside'; in 1678 Christopher Wase observed that 'Now that universities flourish, and schools are in many populous towns erected, from these places of public education especially, persons are sent into all parts of the land engaged in the strictest bonds of allegiance'.[5] These defences of the conservative, not innovative, rôle of education were supported by Henry Burton and John Aubrey, both of whom saw education as a means of maintaining a static social order.[6] The humanist ideals of educational thinkers were compromised by such demands throughout the Tudor and Stuart period, but it is difficult to imagine how it could have been otherwise.[7]

Change and innovation in the universities were therefore considered potentially dangerous instruments of social disintegration; in 1610 the Earl of Northampton complained that too many young men left the universities to 'go up and down breeding new opinions'.[8] This danger was particularly apparent after the Revolution and was expressed most notably in the writings of Clarendon and Hobbes. These are well known and do not require repetition here, except in one respect: both believed that the universities were 'not to be cast away, but to be better disciplined'—in other words, that there were no fundamental weaknesses in the universities as institutions, but only failings in the hearts and minds of the individuals who studied there.[9] This 'personalisation' of the university question was common in contemporary writings; at its worst, it engendered philistinism: the Duke of Newcastle believed that 'wise men rather than learned, should be chosen heads of schools and colleges'; but it is also very important in understanding the attitudes of seventeenth-century reformers, as will appear below.[10]

If significant reform, in anything approaching the modern sense, were to be accomplished at the universities, then a deeper investigation of the role of the university in society was required. Recognition of the need to go beyond the 'political' and 'personal' themes cited above was contained in some contemporary literature, but was for the most part merely implicit. The description of the universities as 'nurseries' or 'fountains' of church and commonwealth was employed so frequently by commentators of all kinds that it became a cliché: contemporaries were aware of the universities' importance, but employed a well-worn expression which avoided the need for deeper analysis.[11] There was some confusion over the question, and certainly no coherent approach or attitude. For example, in 1632 Sir Edward Cecil naively suggested that the universities should teach 'the brave exercise of horsemanship' in order to improve the quality of the nation's cavalry, for 'who may better do it than the Universities, which are ordained for the learning of all manner of virtues?'.[12] Although Cecil misunderstood the nature of contemporary university education, he was suggesting a means for enhancing the relevance of the universities to society, albeit within the narrow context of the dominant social élite.

Such confusion was due in part to the limited impression of university education which contemporaries received. In 1622 John Brinsley wrote that the views of many were distorted by the examples of those who had not used their time at university to good advantage, and returned home 'almost as rude as they went thither'.[13] Such attitudes were encouraged by the élitism of university members, as expressed in Isaac Barrow's description of scholarship as 'a calling which, being duly followed, will most sever us from the vulgar sort of men, and advance us above the common pitch', and by the impression of the luxurious existence enjoyed there, described by William Fleetwood as a life of 'perfect Ease and Liberty', with 'all the Helps, and all the Encouragements that We can want or wish for'.[14] This made the 'personalised' attitude a natural channel for hostility.

The attitudes of the Stuarts, and of the different revolutionary régimes, towards the universities, are made much clearer when understood in this light. Charles I's policy was summed up in a letter from Chancellor Holland to the University of Cambridge in 1635 requiring the university authorities to secure from their members 'a fitting obedience of their superiors at home, as they may not take the liberty to importune his Majestie with needles complaints'.[15]

This emphasis on discipline and, wherever possible, nonintervention, was followed by revolutionary governments. The purges of Oxford and Cambridge in the 1640s were not in essence 'reformist' measures: that of Cambridge in 1644–5 was brutal, but hastily conceived and executed because of the exigencies of the civil war; at Oxford, where there were no such urgent pressures, the parliamentary visitation was muddled and incoherent, with no clear aims or methods.[16] Such purges of the politically and religiously disaffected formed part of the first stage of revolutionary governments' strategy for higher education. The second stage was the promotion of new schemes.[17] Existing beliefs made the first stage easy, but did not provide adequate conceptual framework for the second.

This becomes more apparent when we examine certain features of the university debate during the Revolution. Firstly, there was no truly great intellectual contributor to dominate the debate. Many Puritans regarded Francis Bacon as an intellectual figurehead; unfortunately, Bacon left no all-embracing scheme for educational reforms behind at this death. The concept of the 'Great Instauration' was of paramount importance for subsequent Puritan thought, but it degenerated easily into a slogan. As Webster has shown, Puritans accorded a near-canonical status to Bacon's works, but the dominant influences were, paradoxically, the vague schemes of the *New Atlantis*, which was left incomplete. The fully-fledged Baconian educational doctrine propounded by Comenius in the 1640s was only a 'somewhat mystical version' of this.[18]

Secondly, although the educational debate took on a new momentum and sense of urgency after 1640, the heady optimism of the early revolutionary years following the collapse of censorship was perhaps more conducive to inchoate and impulsive ideas about reform, rather than coherent and rational planning. There was a 'reform movement' of sorts, but not in any organised sense, and those who called for reform represented a wide variety of opinions. Some well known examples of the different shades of thought illustrate the hypothesis of the limits of 'reform'.

Attacks on the universities were not new; they grew out of traditional English anticlericalism. None of the writers of the 1640s and 1650s could outdo the Elizabethan separatist Henry Barrow in extreme expressions: he had attacked university learning as profane, ungodly, idolatrous, venal and superstitious; he thought university members idle and claimed that the ban on marriage there led to sodomy, concluding that the universities had 'a popish original', and should be abolished. It is significant that a selection of Barrow's writings, entitled *The Pollution of Universitie-Learning* was published in 1642, and his arguments seemed quite up to date.[19] It should also be noted that Barrow's method, based on invective rather than reasoned argument, was common to many writings of this period, which fostered a predominantly negative attitude.

This is particularly evident in the writing of Samuel How, one of the first major contributors to the revolutionary debate. The threat which 'radicals' such as How posed to the existing order came as much from their persons as from their writings: in the 'radical movement' there was a strong leavening of artisans (How was a cobbler) and *déclassés* (such as the New Model Army chaplain Hugh Peters). Not only were How's arguments unoriginal, they were also similar to those of respectable men in society; How would have endorsed Fulke Greville's view: 'What then are all these humane Arts, and lights, but seas of errors? In whose depths who sound, Of truth finde only shadowes, and no ground', but How's prose style was less elegant and his person more dangerous to the social hierarchy, expressing a subversive strand in English life and thought which stretched back to Lollardy.[20]

His arguments were to be repeated, with individual idiosyncracies, by most of the radical pamphleteers. These do not require repetition here, except in certain respects relevant to this argument. The dominant emphasis of How's book was on the teaching of the Holy Spirit; it did not adopt a philosophical or scholastic method, which is not surprising, but relied on examples from the Bible — not the ambiguous Old Testament, but the New, particularly the writings of St Paul, who became something of an intellectual figurehead for many radicals. At the heart of the New Testament examples was the fact that Christ and the Apostles were unlearned in any worldly sense.[21]

147

The main point at issue was the 'gift of tongues', when the Apostles received the power of speech in many languages.[22] Defenders of universities used this as an illustration of the need for clergymen to have knowledge of different tongues, which by implication meant a need for traditional university education. To this straightforward, standard interpretation How presented an equally standard retort: the gift of tongues came directly from God, and history was full of examples of worldly learning which had conveyed no spiritual benefits.[23]

This question was at the heart of the debate on university education, but the different polemicists did not explore it in depth. How's approach cited here is typical: he never came to grips with the rôle of language in scriptural exposition, resting his case on the stark contrast between human and spiritual teaching. He was an iconoclast, but had no plans for reform. The dogged refusal to explore such vital questions, and the over-simplification of issues in order to present them in black-and-white terms is characteristic of the debate. The argument did not develop and pamphlets repeated the same themes incessantly: the Quakers, for example, were certainly regarded as radicals by contemporaries, but echoed traditional prejudices about the pride and sinfulness of man, the 'inordinate desire for knowledge', and the need to abolish the clergy.[24]

Such developments as there were tended to be inspired by political changes nationally. John Dury's *Motion Tending to the Publick Good*, published in 1642, was moderate, and sought only to add improvements to the existing educational system; this was in keeping with the irenic spirit which directed his work and writing. However, by 1645 his sermon *Israel's Call to March Out of Babylon*, which was influenced by the experience of the civil war, was speaking in directly apocalyptic terms of purging the universities of the 'gibberidge of Scholastical Divinity . . . the language of corrupt humane reason'.[25] Dury gave no details of what he envisaged, but the change in tone was significant: the carefully reasoned and elaborate plan of 1642 had given way to a harangue. This was an expression of despair: strong language had to be used to whip up enthusiasm where logic had failed. With the advent of the Commonwealth, Dury felt more confident and he drew up detailed schemes for the future in his *Reformed School*.[26]

The belief that the Revolution might be ushering in the Millenium could encourage optimism and more explicit writing, in contrast to the old-fashioned underground literature of such as How. There were some who wanted genuinely radical change: Hugh Peters proposed 'That Academies may be set up for Nobility and Gentry, where they may know piety and righteousnesse, as wel as gallantry and Courtship . . . and that shorter ways to learning may be advanced, and that godlinesse in youth give them place in Colledges before letters and importunitie of men'.[27]

This egalitarian notion was extended to the entire social order by the communist Gerrard Winstanley, whose *Law of Freedom* viewed learning in starkly utilitarian terms. Winstanley thought constructively about the rôle of the universities in society: he saw the existing institutions as economically useless and socially divisive. In his ideal society, learning was to be an adjunct to trade, so that 'after children have been brought up at schools to ripen their wits, they shall then be set to such trades, arts and sciences as their bodies are capable of'.[28] Because he did not view education in isolation from the entire social order, Winstanley may be seen as the most 'modern' idealist from this period, but he was an isolated thinker.

The contrast between old-fashioned slogan-mongering and the more advanced ideals of such as Winstanley is particularly apparent in the work of William Dell, one of the most famous radical critics of the universities.[29] Dell's language, particularly his identification of human learning with Antichrist, was extreme, but he regarded himself as a traditionalist, heir to a line of critics of the universities which included Wycliff, Hus and Luther. He followed Barrow in seeing popish remnants in the universities' customs and teaching and followed standard radical practice in claiming that the clergy used their education as an excuse to exalt themselves unjustly over the people.[30]

Dell's self-evident desire to be seen as the harbinger of the new reformation resulted in a spate of works on the subject of university education in the years 1653–4, most of which were vigorous, straightforward polemics.[31] There was one crucial exception to this: in 1654 he published a short pamphlet entitled *The Right Reformation of Learning*, which was out of character in that it put forward constructive plans for a new educational system. The work showed strong sympathy with Winstanleyan ideals, especially concerning the practical utility of education, but Dell had no plans to change the social order, merely to increase the number of schools, which was neither new nor specifically radical.[32] Dell's other works were almost exclusively religious in aims and argument, whereas *The Right Reformation* concentrated on the practical aspects of education, as if Dell were trying to step beyond the confines of radical polemic; religion appeared only indirectly in the book. Dell's educational system was designed to free young men from 'that ease and idleness, which fills the hearts of University-Students with many corruptions, and noisome lusts, whilst they fill their heads only with empty knowledge and foolish notions; whereby neither can God be glorified, nor their neighbour profited'.[33]

It was not clear how God was to be glorified: under the scheme which Dell propounded, learned clergy would be made redundant, and their places be taken by part-time lay preachers, but these preachers would also have to be learned. It is clear that the learning which Dell envisaged was not old-fashioned scholasticism and Graeco-Roman philosophy, and he did believe that even the highest education should be socially relevant, but his failure to define the kind of learning which would benefit a lay preacher apart from the study of Scripture, which was open to any literate man, rendered his position ambiguous. Dell knew what he disliked, but was confused as to what should take its place.

The concluding section of the work recognised this pitfall, and Dell repeated that human learning could have a place only among purely earthly matters, but he maintained the existing ambiguity by reaffirming the value of an improved faculty of reason and sober learning to the extent of saying that, even if all men could not be Christians, they should at least be taught to live like men.[34] This is quite out of tune with his other writings. Hill notes that Dell was far from antagonistic towards learning in *The Right Reformation*, but does not stress sufficiently its unique place among his output.[35]

The idea that Dell may have been depressed, defeatist, or was attempting some sort of tactical compromise is unlikely from what is known of his character. But when his career is examined in detail, a possible answer emerges: in his messianic zeal — his utterance of the old slogans — Dell yielded to nobody, but he was less enthusiastic about some of the implications of more advanced thought, especially where reorganisation of the entire social order was suggested. Dell had been among those sectaries whom Hill describes as 'Masterless Men', who would not accept authority, but by the time he wrote *The Right Reformation*, he was no longer *déclassé*, as in his days as an outspoken chaplain in the New Model Army: he had acquired a comfortable parish living in Bedfordshire, where he settled down with his wife and children, and, incredibly, was also master of Caius College Cambridge; he had too much to gain from the existing social order.[36]

More moderate and practical thinkers were arguably more likely — in theory — to create intellectual preconditions for *viable* reform; however, many men of intellect and perception would go no further than admitting that something was wrong with the universities. Robert Greville attacked 'Criticall, Cabalisticall, Scepticall, Scholasticall Learning: which fils the head with empty, aeriall, notions, but gives no sound food to the Reasonable part of man', but he used this merely as an argument against episcopacy.[37] Richard Baxter also commented on the limited value of human learning: 'When I have studied hard to understand some abstruse admired book . . . I have but attained the knowledge of human imperfection, and to see that the author is but a man as well as I'.[38] But he would say no more on the subject.

A particularly interesting group of commentators on university questions were those Presbyterian divines who received masterships at Cambridge after the parliamentary purge of 1644–5. At first sight, it appears that their new position moderated their attitudes towards the universities, but closer examination reveals that they were not hypocrites like Dell, but had never held any constructive ideas about university reform; their previous utterances had been empty rhetoric. The most consistent speaker of this group was Thomas Hill, who became master of Trinity in 1645. His interest in university matters predated his appointment by some years and is shown in the fast sermons he delivered to the Long Parliament. In 1642 he noted that religion and learning were mutually dependant and drew attention to the continued use of Laudian ceremonies at Oxford and Cambridge; a year later he called for their 'purging and pruning'.[39] In another sermon he described the land's three main failings as: the lack of valid ordination, the insufficiency of maintenance for the clergy, and the decay of schools and universities. A close watch should be kept on the three 'chiefe springs' of the nation: the universities, the Inns of Court, and the families of the nobility; England could 'never expect pure streams, whilst the Fountains continue full of mud'.[40] However, whilst affirming the importance of godliness, he also defended traditional learning, on the grounds that 'Religion is the greatest Mysterie in the world. In any ordinary trade, before a man can bee acquainted with the secrets of it, you bind him Apprentice for six or seven years; truly, there are so many mysteries in Religion, that require the service of divers Apprentishipps to bee well acquainted with them'.[41] He did not therefore seek changes in the university structure, but merely the abolition of a few bad habits and a change in personnel; once this was accomplished, normal life and godliness would resume. Only once was he more detailed: in April 1644, preaching before the Corporation of London, he called on citizens to improve the quality of their schools, and to provide more scholarships and exhibitions for the most gifted pupils to go on to university; this too was well within the existing system.[42]

Herbert Palmer, intruded master of Queens' Cambridge in 1644, also recognised that the universities had an important role to play in national regeneration. In 1646 he observed that a constant supply of 'Ministers and Builders' from Oxford and Cambridge was essential for the nation's well-being; it would 'make way for all the rest, and make all other things prosper'. He had made a similar plea to the House of Commons in 1643 to 'Secure youth in the Universities, and Schools, with the utmost care; and even in Parents houses, what you can, specially the poorer sort. The young ones are the hopes or the bane of the Church and State in the next 20, or 10, or 7 years'. But both in 1643 and 1646 Palmer called solely for abolition of old and unnecessary statutes and oaths; like Hill, he saw reform in terms of the removal of the most cumbersome features of the old superstructure, rather than major institutional change.[43]

Anthony Tuckney, later to be master of Emmanuel and St John's colleges respectively, compared the universities to diseased bodies which needed medicine, and saw reform as a mixture of better 'Nurserie' for the patients (in other words, financial help for the universities) and 'Chirurgerie', by which he meant a purge of unsound members.[44] John Arrowsmith, intruded master of St John's, spoke in his fast sermon of 12 March 1645 of the violent changes recently effected and the need to return to normality, 'lest Cambridge become as a cottage in a vineyard, as a lodge in a garden of cucumbers', and two years later he called on the House of Commons to 'give incouragement to learning, and continue nursing fathers to the nurseries of it', again thinking in terms of support for the recently purged university, not of reform.[45] Richard Vines, the new master of Pembroke Hall, took a consistently sympathetic and traditional stance: in November 1642 he urged parliament never to let the universities suffer, and in March 1645, with the benefit of firsthand experience, merely translated this into more specific terms by asking that financial burdens on the University of Cambridge be lifted, 'that learning may not be starved'.[46]

All these men expressed normality at least implicitly in terms of a *status quo ante* with different personnel, which was what the purges of Oxford and Cambridge were designed to achieve. Herbert Palmer felt that more could be done and called for further reforms to prevent inertia setting in, for spiritual regeneration, and for the provision of more preaching ministers, but he was vague about what should be done in practice. His absence at the Westminster Assembly and death in 1647 may have prevented him from demonstrating his ideas in his own college.[47] Ralph Cudworth, the new master of Clare, was the only intruded head to give much thought to the quality of learning in abstract terms. His fast sermon in March 1647 invited the House of Commons to 'promote ingenious learning, and cast a favourable influence upon it'. By this he meant not only the learning which 'furnisheth the pulpit', of which they were already well aware, but also 'that which is more remote from such popular use, in the several kinds of it, which yet are all of them, both very subservient to religion, and useful to the commonwealth'. He wanted men to have a greater understanding of nature as well as of languages and philology, so that they would learn more both of the workings and the Word of God. Knowledge was prized highly, but was not an end in itself; one of the nation's main failings was that 'we naturally prize truth more than goodnesse, knowledge more than holinesse', and Cudworth was particularly contemptuous of 'bookish Christians, that have all their religion in writings and papers, think they are compleatly furnished with all kinds of knowledge concerning Christ . . . as if religion were nothing but a little book-craft, a mere paper-skill'.[48] Yet Cudworth did not introduce reforms.

Even a sophisticated intellectual critic like John Milton had little to offer that was constructive and realistic. Milton echoed Hartlib, to whom his book *Of Education* (1644) was dedicated, by calling educational reform one of the 'greatest and noblest designs that can be thought on, and for the want whereof this nation perishes'.[49] But the vehemence of his language and the candid expression of his hatreds masked a basic traditionalism in his outlook, drawn from Renaissance humanism.

He adopted the standard view of the universities' opponents that the knowledge of languages was not an end in itself, but his main complaint of existing university methods was that languages were not taught well enough, and the curriculum of the ideal academy that he devised included a substantial amount of language teaching.[50] Although Hill has argued that Milton was closely connected with the contemporary radical underground, in this work he distanced himself from much of contemporary radicalism by his obvious intellectual snobbery.[51] Whereas How had been concerned that education failed to serve the needs of the people, Milton's complaint was that it was no longer adequate for the intellectual élite. Milton had long been obsessed with the need to defend intellectual freedom against all enemies, and he was afraid of the clergy slipping back into 'the sacerdotal ignorance of a former age'.[52]

Milton's academy was closely modelled on classical forms, aiming to fit men 'to perform justly, skillfully and magnanimously all the offices, both private and public, of peace and war', and, like the Romans, Milton was seeking to educate a patrician order.[53] His curriculum would have been too much for any but the exceptionally gifted, and Milton was out of touch with the realities of education, and of English society; his academy was as other-worldly as that of Plato, by which it was influenced, and provides a good example of the naive optimism of the Hartlib school at that time.

Two of the most able critics of the universities were John Hall and John Webster. Hall had failed to get a fellowship at St John's College, Cambridge, and turned to political journalism in the late 1640s, but when he wrote on the university question in 1649, he showed himself superior in argument to the usual bigoted pamphleteer. Like so many contemporary commentators, he was at his best when describing the inadequacies of the existing system, but his analysis was penetrating. He criticised the parliamentary purge of Cambridge in 1644–5 for having 'reached no further then Politicall aimes, it removed many persons of a more thriving and consistent growth in learning, then it either left there, or planted in their steads; it medled not at all with a view of reformation of those fundamental constitutions, on whose happy or weak designations, the interest and prosperity, the decay and ruin of such litterary Republicks principally depends'.[54]

He also wrote of the need for financial reform, for fewer fellowships (in order to encourage academic competition), for honours and rewards to the most innovative and creative minds, for copyright libraries in the universities, and for the more serious encouragement of individual skills, efforts and specialisations.[55] It is clear that Hall recognised that the universities had become less useful to society, by being élitist, isolated and introspective, and failing to utilise the real talents of their students.[56] He described the inadequate social animals produced by the existing system as 'detestable quacking Empricks, lewd, and contentious, Gownmen, or ignorant mercenary Divines'.[57] But Hall did not press home these tentative ideas of greater social integration; he was above all a patriot, concerned that the universities should help to re-establish national prestige, and learning was still designed to lift selected individuals from out of the masses, not to raise the general level of education.[58]

There is a strong sense of realism in John Webster's *Academiarum Examen* of 1653, a detailed, comprehensive critique of university studies and practices.

Webster did not indulge in grandiose visions; his book was dedicated to John Lambert, the favoured recipient of several of the Revolution's more practical schemes. Webster was anxious to dissociate himself from the essentially negative attitude of many of the radical critics: 'he that would raise himself by the ruins of others, or warm himself by the burning of Schools, I wish him no greater plague than his own ignorance'.[59] His aims were avowedly limited: he did not wish 'to traduce nor calumniate the Academies themselves, but only the corruptions that time and negligence hath introduced there, but simply to attempt . . . some reformation, not eradication of their customes and learning'.[60] In some respects, this view was close to that of the intruded Presbyterian masters; it was a conservative mode of thought. Webster recognised the dangers of university élitism: 'those that teach in the Academies are but as others, and *homo* is a common name to all men', and that the universities had become isolated, creating a false impression of uniform quality among their graduates and maintaining that a university education qualified its recipient automatically for higher things.[61]

Webster's proposed reforms went no further than improving the existing curriculum, despite hoping that every graduate would have 'his honour according to his industry and proficiency'.[62] The need for more meaningful integration of the universities into society at large was only implicit in his work, and the strength of his attack came not from any adventurous new schemes of reform, but from his detailed and informed criticism of existing methods and the fluency and clarity of his arguments, which stood out in sharp relief from the repetitive bombast of so many of the pamphleteers.

The strength of the reformers' ideas can also be tested by examining some of the prominent defences of the existing order. To a critical, intellectual observer, these seem unimpressive: most of the defenders stuck rigidly, even thoughtlessly, to the best-tried arguments; yet it has already been shown that they were not unique in this, and because their opponents usually posed old questions, they had little need of new answers.

Their commonest device was that of mud-slinging. Thomas Hall said that 'to seek the destruction of humane learning is the badge and practice of wicked men I never read in History, Sacred or Divine, of any but wicked men that did ever oppose it'. Seth Ward described Dell as 'an angry fanatick man, who wanting himselfe such Academicall Learning as would become his relation, would needs persuade others against it', and he bracketed Webster with the Levellers.[63]

The defenders treated attacks on the universities as attacks on the whole body of the church.[64] This was quite consistent with the accepted view of the universities' role as being 'to fit men thence for the work of the Ministry'.[65] Such an approach meant that there could be no major compromises, but there were some who admitted minor failings. Robert Boreman admitted that 'in these tumultuous, disordered times, some dirt has gotten into our

Fountaines, and mingled it selfe with our pure streams; but, what was ever in all Ages, we hope will not with aggravations be charged upon us, as the onely fault of ours'.[66] Joseph Sedgwick argued that justifiable criticisms could be countered if university authorities would 'maintain strictnesse of discipline, profitablenesse of study and reality of learning'.[67] Both Boreman and Sedgwick demonstrate the 'personalised' approach to university problems which was shared with so many thinkers of various types. Seth Ward, who disliked the ingrained attitudes of students and the gentry towards education, had only limited sympathy for traditional methods, but suppressed this feeling because he feared that even moderate and reasonable suggestions were a smokescreen for the destructive radical fringe.[68]

On the main issues the defenders were intransigent, and sometimes evasive. Sedgwick, for example, pushed the questions of the Spirit's teaching and the value of languages into the background, and emphasised the need for national peace and unity; his claim that university degrees were a public witness to known and approved learning was ostentatiously blind to the reformers' complaints.[69] Edward Waterhouse's *Humble Apology* of 1653, a bigoted and élitist tract, reduced learning to the role of a guardian of social status, and simplified the debate to a choice between education and anarchy.[70] Yet in the context of contemporary beliefs, there was little more that could have been required of him; he and the other defenders were true to the most widely accepted attitudes towards the universities.

This study has not sought from these few selected examples to establish a new orthodoxy concerning the university debate during the Revolution, but merely to present one facet of the debate which has not been stressed. Although the Revolution ushered in a wave of new visions, many of the ideas expressed were traditional, but with a new opportunity for expression. Attitudes towards the universities were not yet ready to progress further; we should not blame revolutionary governments for doing 'so little'; they were consistent with the ideas of their age. Some of the reformers may have been correct in asserting that the universities were not doing enough for society as a whole, but they were doing all that was required of them within the traditional concepts of the social hierarchy. The reformers failed to produce clear and widely acceptable concepts of the university-in-society to challenge these orthodoxies, and until they did so there could be no accepted need for reform. Seventeenth century governments left the universities alone because they saw no need for social change; the universities guarded their independence to avoid being caught up in change of any sort. Their relative isolation from society prompted criticism, but also helped to shield them from its full effects.

References

1. John Dury, *The Reformed School* (London, 1651), A3–4.

2. M. R. James, *Social Problems and Policy during the Puritan Revolution, 1640–60* (London, 1930), chapter 7; C. Hill, *Change and Continuity in Seventeenth-Century England* (London, 1974), chapter 1; H. R. Trevor-Roper, *Religion, the Reformation and Social Change* (London, 1972), 237–293; T. C. Barnard, *Cromwellian Ireland* (Oxford, 1975), chapter 7; C. E. Whiting, *The University of Durham* (London, 1932), pp. 16–29; G. B. Tatham, *The Puritans in Power* (Cambridge, 1913), chapters 4 and 5; J. D. Twigg, 'The Parliamentary Visitation of the University of Cambridge, 1644–5', *English Historical Review* xcviii (1983), 513–528.
3. M. H. Curtis, *Oxford and Cambridge in Transition* (Oxford, 1959), pp. 49–51.
4. Margaret, Duchess of Newcastle, *The Life of the Duke of Newcastle* (London, 1915), p. 152.
5. D. Cressy, *Education in Tudor and Stuart England* (London, 1975), p. 18; C. Wase, *Considerations concerning Free Schools as Settled in England* (Oxford, 1678), pp. 33–4.
6. J. E. Stephens (ed), *Aubrey on Education* (London, 1972), p. 10; J. C. Davis, *Utopia and the Ideal Society* (Cambridge, 1981), p. 101.
7. Cressy, 'Educational Opportunity in Tudor and Stuart England', *History of Education Quarterly* 16 (1976), pp. 303–6.
8. C. Russell, *The Crisis of Parliaments* (Oxford, 1977) p. 269 and n.
9. Edward Hyde, Earl of Clarendon, *Works* (London, 1751), pp. 313–333; T. Hobbes, *Works* (London, 1840), VI, pp. 168, 192, 233, 236–7.
10. *Life*, p. 153.
11. Curtis, p. 172; there are countless examples in contemporary literature.
12. C. H. Firth, *Cromwell's Army* (London, 1962), pp. 6–7.
13. John Brinsley, *A Consolation for our Grammar Schools* (London, 1622), p. 8.
14. I. Barrow, *Theological Works* (Oxford, 1818), III, pp. 69, 74; W. Fleetwood, *A Sermon Preached before the University of Cambridge in Kings-College Chapel* (Cambridge, 1689), pp. 20–2.
15. Cambridge University Library, Guard Book CUR 11, 1.
16. See footnote 2.
17. James, pp. 321–2.
18. C. Webster, *The Great Instauration* (London, 1975), p. 25; A. M. Quinton, *Francis Bacon* (Oxford, 1980), p. 74.
19. H. Barrow, *Writings* (London, 1962), pp. 349–352; P. K. Christianson, *Reformers and Babylon* (Toronto, 1978), pp. 84–5.
20. Webster, p. 19.
21. S. How, *The Sufficiency of the Spirit's Teaching without Human Learning* (London, 1816), pp. 7, 12–14, 19–32; see Acts 17.15–34; 19.19; I Cor. 1.17; 2.10–14; 3.18–19; 8.1–2; Romans 1.22.
22. Acts 2.1–4.
23. How, pp. 38, 44, 45, 69.
24. William Penn, *No Cross, No Crown* (London, 1930), pp. 96–8, 101–107; R. Schlatter, 'The Higher Learning in Puritan England', *Historical Magazine of the Protestant Episcopal Church*, 23 (1954), pp. 175–6.
25. *A Motion Tending to the Publick Good* (London, 1642), *passim; Israel's Call to March out of Babylon* (London, 1646), p. 48.
26. *The Reformed School* (London, 1651).

27. H. Peters, *A Word for the Armie. And two words to the Kingdome* (London, 1647), p. 11.
28. G. Winstanley, *The Law of Freedom and Other Writings* (London, 1973), pp. 361 5.
29. His writings on the universities are best summarised in C. Webster, 'William Dell and the Idea of University', in M. Teich and R. Young, (eds.), *Changing Perspectives in the History of Science* (London, 1973), pp. 110–126.
30. W. Dell, *A Plain and Necessary Confutation* (London, 1654), introduction, p. 24.
31. *A Plain and Necessary Confutation; A Testimony from the Word against Divinity-Degrees in the University* (London, 1654); *The Testimony of Martin Luther upon the whole matter* (London, 1654).
32. *The Right Reformation of Learning* (London, 1654), p. 29.
33. *Ibid.*
34. *Ibid*, pp. 29–30.
35. C. Hill, 'The Radical Critics of Oxford and Cambridge in the 1650s', in J. W. Baldwin and R. A. Goldthwaite (eds), *Universities in Politics*, (London, 1972), p. 120.
36. C. Hill, *The World Turned Upside Down* (London, 1975), pp. 41, 42, 59, 94; E. C. Walker, *William Dell, Master Puritan* (Cambridge, 1970), pp. 57–68, 104–6.
37. W. Haller, *Tracts on Liberty in the Puritan Revolution* (Columbia, 1934), II, p. 53.
38. R. Baxter, *The Autobiography of Richard Baxter* (London, 1974), p. 114.
39. T. Hill, *The Trade of Truth Advanced* (London, 1642), pp. 42, 49–50; *The Militant Church Triumphant* (London, 1643), p. 23.
40. *The Season for Englands Selfe-Reflection, and Advancing Templework* (London, 1644), p. 37; *The Right Separation Incouraged* (London, 1645), pp. 33–4.
41. *The Good Old Way* (London, 1644), pp. 11, 36.
42. *Ibid*, pp. 44–5.
43. H. Palmer, *The Duty and Honour of Church-Restorers* (London, 1646), pp. 36–7, 44, 55; *The Necessity and Encouragement of utmost venturing for the Churches Help* (London, 1643), pp. 51–2, 54.
44. A. Tuckney, *The Balme of Gilead* (London, 1643), p. 25.
45. J. Arrowsmith, *Englands Eben-ezer* (London, 1643), dedication; *A Great Wonder in Heaven* (London, 1647), p. 40.
46. R. Vines, *Caleb's Integrity* (London, 1643), p. 31; *The Happinesse of Israel* (London, 1645), p. 25.
47. Palmer, *Duty*, pp. 13–14, 17, 37, 44–6, 55; he was one of the Assembly's assessors, see S. W. Carruthers, *The Everyday Work of the Westminster Assembly* (Philadelphia, 1943), p. 45.
48. R. Cudworth, *A Sermon preached before the Honourable House of Commons* (Cambridge, 1879)), pp. 6, 7, 10.
49. J. Milton, *Milton on Education*, ed. O. M. Ainsworth, (New Haven, 1928), p. 21.
50. *Ibid*, pp. 53, 56–62.
51. C. Hill, *Milton and the English Revolution* (London, 1977), pp. 93–115.
52. Hill, p. 36; Ainsworth, p. 215.
53. Ainsworth, pp. 55–8.
54. J. Hall, *An Humble Motion to the Parliament of England* (Liverpool, 1953), p. 5.

55. *Ibid*, pp. 29–31.
56. *Ibid*, p. 17.
57. *Ibid*, p. 27.
58. *Ibid*, pp. 8, 14–16.
59. J. Webster, *Academiarum Examen* (London, 1653), introduction.
60. *Ibid*.
61. *Ibid*, introduction, pp. 3, 91.
62. *Ibid*, pp. 95–110, *passim*, 109.
63. T. Hall, *Vindiciae Literarum* (London, 1654), p. 21; S. Ward, *Vindiciae Academiarum* (Oxford, 1654), pp. 6, 17.
64. Ward, 3; R. Boreman, *The Triumph of Learning over Ignorance*, (London, 1653), p. 2.
65. J. Sedgwick, *A Sermon preached at St Maries* (London, 1653), p. 12.
66. Boreman, p. 13.
67. Sedgwick, p. 15.
68. Ward, p. 50.
69. Sedgwick, pp. 2, 5, 7, 12, 25.
70. E. Waterhouse, *An humble Apologie for Learning and Learned Men* (London, 1653), pp. 91, 188.

84

FROM ORAL TO WRITTEN EXAMINATIONS

Cambridge, Oxford and Dublin 1700–1914

Christopher Stray[*]

Source: *History of Universities* XX(2) (2005): 76–130.

Reading maketh a full man, conference a ready man, and writing an exact man.
Francis Bacon, *Of Studies* (1597)

Why, Sir, I think every man whatever has a peculiar style, which may be discovered by nice examination and comparison with others.
Samuel Johnson, 13 April 1778[1]

The history of examinations in Britain remains a relatively unexplored field. The standard works by Montgomery and Roach are largely concerned with the great expansion of examinations in the nineteenth century: the period when the examination seemed to be almost a miracle cure for social ills, though its rampant spread generated a backlash in the second half of the century.[2] In this paper I have chosen to focus on the development of examinations in the two ancient English universities from the beginning of the eighteenth century: the period which witnessed the emergence from an oral context of the written forms of assessment which were taken for granted by the late nineteenth century.[3] The paper concentrates on Cambridge and Oxford because in this period, their practices were central to English educational practice as a whole. Evidence is also adduced from Trinity College Dublin, an influential, if marginal institution which at the beginning of the nineteenth century had as many students as Cambridge. Other institutions could, and should, be investigated, if overall patterns of examination are to be explored, rather than just those in universities. To take a single example, the Royal Military Academy at Woolwich employed both oral and written examinations in the eighteenth century. Monthly and termly written exams were held to fix places in classes, and a final one of several days determining rank in the promotion order. Public viva voce exams are recorded from 1764; by the 1850s they had become rehearsed exhibitions.[4] In a sense the Academy is atypical, since the amount and intensity of assessment can be related to the central place of seniority in careers in the armed forces: a group of cadets graduating together were of the same seniority, and so needed to be ranked within it.[5] But it is only by surveying a range of such cases that the boundaries of the typical can be established.

This example raises the question, to what extent were the forms of assessment developed in Oxbridge similarly the product of institutionally specific imperatives? The comparison of Oxford and Cambridge should throw some light on this point. The latter is highlighted in the paper, for the simple reason that it was the dominant site in the shift from oral to written examination. The degree to which this process is embedded in the history of these two institutions complicates the task of describing it, especially as, in the period with which I am concerned, they grew more unlike each other in many ways. But it is a fruitful complication, since it enables us to see how traditions of examination are in part the products of specific institutional contexts.

The poet in the examination room

Let me begin with a worm's-eye view: a student's experience, towards the end of the period, of both oral and written assessment. On 25 November 1870 Arthur Hilton, a student in his second year at Cambridge, wrote to his mother, 'It is the most disagreeable business I ever was in for. Most of my friends are in a very despondent way'.[6] Hilton was referring to the 'Little-Go'—an intermediate examination covering a wide range of subjects—which that year was held on 5 December. In his final year, he edited and largely wrote a short-lived periodical called *The Light Green* which included several verses on the subject of examinations. One of them, *The Vulture and the husband-man*, has the Little-Go as its subject. The poem's title is explained in its epigraph, which quotes Dr Johnson's definition of a vulture as a bird which *plucks* its victim limb from limb, and of a husbandman as one who makes his living from the *plough*. 'Pluck' and 'plough' were student slang at Oxbridge for failure in examinations; the vulture and the husband-man are the invigilating examiners.[7] The poem, which Hilton ascribed to 'Louisa Caroline', is modelled on Lewis Carroll's *The Walrus and the Carpenter* (published the previous year in *Through the Looking-Glass*), and very aptly: for the mixture of subjects included in the Little Go resembled Carroll's miscellaneous list 'of shoes—and ships—and sealing wax, Of cabbages—and kings'. The poem begins:

> The rain was raining cheerfully,
> As if it had been May,

> The Senate-House appeared inside
> Unusually gay;
> And this is strange, because it was
> A Viva-Voce day.

Later stanzas portray the grilling of the candidates, two at a time, by the examiners, who give them all fail grades.

The point of this stanza is that it was the oral part of the examination which students feared most. Just why this was, is made clear by another of Hilton's poems. *The Heathen Pass-ee*[8] deals with a written examination in which he imagines himself not as candidate but as invigilating examiner. The 'pass-ee' is a comprehensively-equipped cheat who is caught, searched and divested of his 'passing aids':

> In the crown of his cap
> Were the Furies and Fates
> And a delicate map
> Of the Dorian States,
> And we found in his palms, which were hollow,
> What are frequent on palms—that is dates.

In this case the examination is the final examination for the Ordinary (pass) degree, which Hilton sat in 1872. This is the mundane world below that of the high-flying honours student; a world in which memory aids, both legitimate and illegitimate, were very much at home.[9] Many of the Pass-ee's coevals will have sought to carry into the examination hall the kind of information he was found to possess; though in their heads, rather than in their caps or on their palms. What makes the Pass-ee a cheat is precisely that he has written down what others may have stored in memory, perhaps by a mnemonic scheme.[10] Questions on William Paley's *Evidences of Christianity* (1802) were included in the Previous Examination from its inception in 1824, and continued to be set until December 1920, generating summary volumes and also 'Paley cards': printed cards bearing mnemonic verses. For example, Paley's eleven proofs of the authenticity of Scripture were summarised as follows:

> Quoted, sui generis, vols, titles, publicly, comment.
> Both sides, without doubt, attacked, catalogue, apocryphal.[11]

Hilton describes in the poem the looks of alarm which pass between the narrator and another invigilator when they see 'Tom Crib' (the Pass-ee) 'flooring the paper at twenty past three' (the real-life examination would have begun at 2 pm and lasted three hours).[12] Both that brief interaction, and the divesting of Crib's examination aids which follows it, exemplify the range of social relationships which may obtain within the process of examination. This is not just a black box which receives inputs of knowledge and generates a rank ordering of individuals. It is a situated complex of social action of which the formal rules are only a part, in which informal rules also exist, and in which both are in practice negotiable. This is true of both oral and written examinations, but more obviously so of the former.[13]

All the information carried by the Pass-ee is written. The subject of *The vulture and the husband-man*, on the other hand, is a viva voce examination—where all the Pass-ee's devices would have been useless. The candidates have already finished their written work: as the poem continues,

> The men were sitting sulkily,
> Their paper work was done,
>
> . . .
>
> The papers they had finished lay
> In piles of blue and white.[14]

The system of assessment these verses reveal is a mixture of oral and written examination, but by the 1870s the role of the viva voce was very limited. Its regular use in Cambridge university examinations was confined to the Little Go, and that only until the regulations were changed in 1882; in college examinations, it had already disappeared.[15] Yet oral examination had once been the only mode of assessment used. When, how and why did the shift to written examinations take place?

Viva! The heyday of oral examination

In medieval Oxford and Cambridge all examinations were public, oral and in Latin. The community of MAs was assumed to be involved, and any of its members could challenge a candidate for the BA degree. Fixed ritual forms were followed: challenge and defence, often in a sequence which involved several challengers. The award of a degree followed an 'act' in which a student had to debate in public with a senior member. This was preceded during his student career by disputations in which he was expected, on different occasions, to perform both as 'opponent' (advancing an argument) and as 'respondent' (challenging an argument put by another student). These disputations were also public, and enabled junior students to gain a sense both of how they were conducted and of the range of eristic tactics which might be employed. The same applied to the final 'acts', from which those who were some way from graduating could learn how to cope when they reached that stage.[16] Accounts of actual disputations are not common, but it is clear that they typically began with an opponent declaring support for an author and the respondent criticising this:

162

Opp. Recte statuit X de Y . . . [X's views on Y are correct]
Resp. Recte non statuit X de Y . . . [No they are not][17]

The economy of the oral examination was different from that of the written. Its verbal jousting, which might go on for two hours or more, constituted a public negotiation not just between examiner and examinee but between several participants, since students were disputing with one another and with any graduates who might choose to intervene.[18] Examination and adjudication took place at the same event, and apart from any notes which were taken, and such written theses which happened to be preserved, no record survived beyond the memory of participants except for the official record of success or failure.[19] What is clear is that disputations were often dramatic, exciting and unpredictable events. As Costello remarked, to call them 'debates between students' was 'like describing a Spanish bullfight as the killing of a cow'.[20] Morgan, similarly, suggests that 'for their enthusiastic observers they seem to have constituted a form of academic bloodsports or the equivalent of the vitriolic review of a later time'.[21] The volatile nature of such occasions was captured in an account by Symonds D'Ewes of a music act at Cambridge in 1620. The sophister who carried it out began by playing a tune on his viol; and having defended his position successfully against three opponents, he played another piece, presumably in a triumphant strain. The Moderator there upon observed that 'ubi philosophia desinit, ibi incipit musicus [where philosophy leaves off, there music begins]', which D'Ewes thought 'a very pretty jest'.[22]

The public involvement of the academic community carried with it an element of risk. Inappropriate speech could not easily be prevented, and students who sought to distinguish themselves in other than officially condoned ways sometimes took their acts down informal paths. Where these involved allusive criticism of individuals or institutions, there was little that could be done to stop them on the spot.[23] Perhaps to act as a kind of lightning conductor for such undergraduate energies, a licensed fool (at Oxford called Terrae filius, 'son of the earth') was appointed each year to deliver a comic or satirical speech. On occasion, the Terrae filius himself overstepped expected bounds. In 1669 John Evelyn heard the speech of the Oxford Terrae filius and was shocked by his 'tedious, abusive and sarcastical rhapsody . . . It was rather licentious lying and railing than genuine and noble wit'.[24] (The Terrae filii of 1591 and 1632 had been expelled because of their speeches; that of 1713 had his speech publicly burnt by order of Convocation. After this the office, perhaps unsurprisingly, lapsed.[25])

The Cambridge equivalent of the Terrae filius was 'Mr Tripos'. The title came from the role played in degree disputations by a BA who sat on a three-legged stool. As well as engaging questionists in disputations, Mr Tripos composed a satirical Latin poem which was circulated during the ceremony.

He thus had both to speak and to write, unlike his Oxonian equivalent. The earliest surviving verses (also, confusingly, known as 'triposes') are those of 1583.[26] Some of these tripos verses were censured on their appearance, e.g. one of 1789, which gave an account of a prize fight. None of the several verses which dealt with contemporary political topics in the 1790s, however, seems to have caused trouble to the authorities.[27]

At both universities, oral disputations survived into the nineteenth century.[28] In his *Reminiscences of Cambridge*, Henry Gunning gives an account of his own act, held in 1787, which allows us a glimpse of the situational contingencies which might arise. He was alarmed to find that he had been chosen to open the proceedings; but disappointed to discover that since he was not thought to be a very promising student, he had been assigned two obscure undergraduates to debate with. Towards the end of his opening argument, his voice began to fail, but he recovered, and easily disposed of his opponents' arguments. He was then congratulated by the examiner, having clearly done better than was expected of him.[29] Coming first on such a public occasion brought with it heightened stage fright; those who came later might be able to gauge an examiner's mood. Learning about testing, then, might take place not only in earlier disputations, but in the earlier stages of one's own final test. In this kind of interactive assessment, the character and ability of those playing the other parts were crucial. Gunning's opponents came from the ranks of the lower-achieving students. This was an advantage in that it made it easier for him to show them up during the debate; but he clearly felt it as a kind of insult that he had not been given better (i.e. more able) opponents. The ranking of a victory, then, depended in part on the stature of those one defeated. The moderator who selected Gunning to lead off the disputations was a fellow of his own college, and may have chosen Gunning as a mediocre but reliable student who could be counted on not to lose his head in the unsettling first few minutes of the proceedings.

Of the few detailed accounts we have of disputations, most come from the period of Gunning's examination.[30] From these it is clear that the public argument, when subjects were proposed as theses, might be preceded by private negotiations. Subjects chosen were liable to be refused for a variety of reasons. Doctrines which were seen as self-evident or almost so were not usually allowed, since they made life impossible for the opponent. Thus the moderators would not normally allow statements from Euclid to be advanced; though exceptionally in 1818 a 'questionist' [finalist] was allowed to 'keep' [take part in an act] in the eleventh book. Theses regarded as immoral or heretical were also liable to be barred. In 1762 William Paley (later the author of the textbooks of moral philosophy and theology studied by several generations of Cambridge undergraduates) proposed as one of his questions for debate that hell's punishments were not eternal ['Aeternitas poenarum contradicit Divinis attributis?']. Soon afterwards, he came to see the Senior Moderator in alarm. The master of his college, who was also Dean of Ely, had made it clear that he did not want such a disturbing thesis defended in public. The moderator, Richard Watson, invited him to insert the word 'non' in his title. Hence on the day, Paley advanced the converse of his original thesis—leaving his opponent to defend the theologically risky position.[31] Hoskin's account of this episode represents it as a tussle between Paley and the university, portrayed as an impersonal body ('pressure was applied').[32] Given Hoskin's Freirean exposé of the 'banking model' of education—the unproblematic transmission of fixed knowledge-commodities from one generation to the next—it is ironic that he reinforces the model by assuming consensus among the dons. This was in fact a tussle between liberals and conservatives in which young Paley was, to some extent, a pawn. (A successful pawn, however: he emerged as Senior Wrangler, i.e. top of the first class).

The last survivals of the public, oral world of the medieval university are perhaps to be found in the competing praelections by candidates for chairs. At Cambridge, the last event of this kind appears to have been the competition for the Regius Chair of Greek in January 1906. This was a high-profile event, reported in national newspapers; the praelections were, uniquely, published as a volume by Cambridge University Press.[33] It was, however, also a very local event, since all five candidates were Cambridge men. Although the electors to the chair were no longer the Senate, but the Council, a much smaller body, the praelections were delivered in the Senate House to over a hundred MAs. Later elections to chairs were held under revised statutes, which handed over decision making to subject-specific groups of academics meeting in private.[34] The viva voce element in degree examinations survived, in large part as a device for grading borderline candidates, and after 1920 the introduction of the Ph.D. brought with it an oral examination.[35] Today they are among the relatively few survivals of the world of oral testing.[36]

The origins of the written examination

In his *History of the Study of Mathematics at Cambridge*, Rouse Ball wrote that 'We are perhaps apt to think that an examination conducted by written papers is so natural that the custom is of long continuance. But I can find no record of any (in Europe) earlier than those introduced by Bentley at Trinity in 1702'.[37] When we realise that these originating events took place in Rouse Ball's own college, in his own university, we are entitled to wonder if his loyalty has outstripped his historical imagination. Subsequent investigation, however, with one exception to be mentioned below, has not challenged his conclusion.[38]

Rouse Ball was relying on the life of Richard Bentley written by an earlier fellow of Trinity, James Monk, whose account is as follows:

Hitherto the examinations had taken place in the chapel viva voce, before the Master and eight Seniors [i.e. senior fellows], who are the Electors: Bentley being of opinion that this oral test was not satisfactory in an enquiry so extensive and profound, ordered that the candidates should be examined by each of the electors at his own apartments, whereby an opportunity was given for the performance of written exercises, and time allowed to weigh and compare the respective merits of the young men with suitable deliberation. This method of separate examination, although liable to considerable objections, which were felt both in Bentley's time and subsequently, continued to be the practice of Trinity College for ninety years.[39]

The only contemporary witness we have is John Byrom, who was elected to a scholarship in 1709 (the scholarship examinations seem to have followed the same procedure as those for fellowships). In May of that year, Byrom was examined by the Vice-Master on one day, and on the following Monday and Tuesday by Bentley and two fellows in their own rooms; on the Wednesday he went to the Master's Lodge to 'make theme' (write a [Latin] composition).[40] The procedure was much the same in the 1750s, when Bentley's grandson Richard Cumberland was elected to a fellowship.[41]

Bentley's motive was probably to improve the quality of a fellowship which had been appointed through a mixture of laxness and patronage (including those appointed under James II by royal mandate), but he will also have wanted to make the existing fellows work. In a communal 'act' in the chapel it was all too easy for some of them to be little more than observers.[42] The new arrangement may also have made it easier for Bentley to control the outcome of the examination—not a motive to be discounted in his case. Later in his mastership we find him appointing a layman as chaplain, contrary to statute, and even appointing his son a fellow without examination. It is noticeable in Byrom's account that Bentley himself drew up the list of successful candidates. In about 1720 an unsuccessful candidate for a fellowship, Charles Squire, complained that he had had only

a slight examination from the Master which lasted little more than a quarter of an hour during which he was examin'd as to Greek but in one Greek Epigram of six lines, and as to Latin but in about twelve lines out of Seneca's Tragedies: had some few questions asked him out of Tacitus, and as to other University learning had only some few Superficial Questions asked him in Astronomy, and having been examined also by Dr Colbatch Casuistical Professor and Senior Fellow of the College for three hours and a half together with three others of the candidates in Herodotus, Thucydides,

Aristotle's Ethics and in other Greek as well as Latin History
[gave] the said Reverend Doctor full satisfaction throughout that
examination.

A majority of the senior fellows voted for Squire, but Bentley had decided
for someone else and overruled them.[43]

I mentioned above that Rouse Ball's claim for the primacy of Bentley's
new written examination has gone unchallenged, with one exception. The
exception is Rouse Ball himself. Ten years after his claim was published, he
wrote that he doubted whether the fellowship examination before Bentley's
time had been entirely oral: 'Monk seems to have thought that before this
time [sc. 1702] elections to scholarships and fellowship took place on the
result only of an oral examination in the college chapel . . . I doubt whether
this is correct'.[44] Ball gives no reasons for his doubt, though he earlier
quotes William Lynnet, vice-master in the 1690s, as referring to candidates
producing 'a theme . . . given them by the Master', and 'each one writing his
name his age and his country'.[45] The candidates sat the examination for
three days; on the third day they were brought the theme, and for it were
'excused the 4th [day]'.[46] Lynnet's statement is, in fact, simply an expanded
translation of Chapter XII of the college's Elizabethan statutes (1560),
which laid down exactly this procedure.[47] The only detail Lynnet has added
is the practical detail that the theme is brought to the candidates from
the Master by the chapel clerk. It is thus clear that the fellowship examination contained a written element for well over a century before Bentley's
arrival in Trinity.[48] Where did Monk get his story from? It is impossible
to tell, since he cites no source for his account of the examinations. Certainly there is no relevant decision recorded in the Conclusion Book of
the Master and Seniors. In 1710, when Bentley published a reply to the
charges laid against him by some of the fellows, he dwelt on the lax state of
the college at his arrival, and on his reform of the fellowship examination.
But the only aspect he mentions is that he abolished the custom that the
candidates entertained the fellows at a local tavern from 7 pm till past
midnight for the four nights of their examination—the bill being paid by the
successful candidates.[49]

The conclusion of this cautionary tale, then, is that the Trinity fellowship examinations had included a written element since the passage of the
Elizabethan statutes of 1560. In the sixteenth and seventeenth centuries,
college statutes constituted in effect a detailed instructional manual for the
running of the college, and there is no evidence that they were not in general
adhered to. (By the nineteenth century, Statute XII was adapted by simply
not reading it all out when fellows were elected).[50] Trinity may have held the
first written examination in Europe, but if so it must be dated to 1560 rather
than to 1702—with the proviso that the themes, once written, were probably
then read out before the examining fellows.

Newtonianism and marks:
the rise of the Senate House Examination

It was at about the time of Bentley's arrival, in the 1700s, that the beginnings can be detected of what became known as the Senate House Examination, and later the Mathematical Tripos. This was a university degree examination whose history through the eighteenth century is one of increasingly fine differentiation of grading. Since the sixteenth century, the highest-achieving BAs of each year had been listed in an order of merit (the Ordo Senioritatis); the others were listed separately in college groups.[51] In 1710–11 the higher men were listed in two groups, First Tripos and Second Tripos, and though the terminology changed, this division into two classes persisted in subsequent years. From 1747–8 the list was printed. From 1753 the first class was divided into two, and this was the origin of the distinction between wranglers and senior optimes; the second class consisting of junior optimes. Together these classes represented the three classes of honours, the other candidates being known as 'hoi polloi' (the masses).

Some of the changes in the examination were prompted by external factors. In 1715 the building in which the disputations were held was commandeered to store part of a large library given to the university by George I. A new Senate House was commissioned, but was begun only in 1722, and not finished until 1730. In the interim, when it was difficult to find accommodation for the exercises, the moderators took to interrogating finalists after the acts as a supplementary test. It was these interrogations which increasingly predominated as a basis for classification. Rouse Ball was confident that the interrogation was conducted in English from the outset, though he acknowledged that John Jebb's statement in 1772 that 'This examination has now for some years been conducted in the English language' suggested otherwise. In fact it is clear from a letter of Horace Walpole's describing the examination ('and all this in Latin') that Latin was being used in 1735.[52] The shift relates to the decline in conversational fluency in Latin even in academic communities from the seventeenth century, of which Locke had already complained in his *Essay on education* in the 1690s. We might guess that it took place in the 1750s, when resistance to the use of Latin was gathering force in a wide variety of social contexts.[53] But more importantly, in this local manifestation it probably reflects the increasing impact of Newtonian natural philosophy on the examination in the 1750s and 60s. The new, heavily mathematicized approach was more easily handled in the vernacular.

Isaac Newton's work forms a crucial element in the development of the Senate House Examination. His influence began to spread in the 1690s. One of his chief supporters in Cambridge was Richard Laughton, a well-known tutor. The examination was technically controlled by the two university proctors, but since 1680 this duty had been delegated to two moderators. In

1710–11, however, Laughton, who was proctor that year, decided to take charge of the examination himself. He invited one student to defend a Newtonian thesis, and promised as a reward to insert his name high on the list.[54] He also drew up a series of Newtonian propositions for use in the oral exercises which preceded the examination. It is probably not a coincidence that it was in 1710–11 that the beginnings can be seen of the ranking system which was later to become so fine-tuned: the division of the honours students into two classes.[55]

In the later eighteenth century, the classifying of finalists took place in several stages. The Senate House Examination was administered to groups of students who had been classed in advance. Each college sent in to the moderators a list of its questionists with assessments of their ability, and the students were examined in college groups. This must have made comparison difficult, since each group was of mixed ability. From 1763, however, perhaps to ease this difficulty, they were divided into eight classes by ability, though still on the basis of college officers' opinions. This innovation seems to have been due to Richard Watson, who was moderator in that year. His own account of the change makes it vividly clear why he proposed it.

> I was the second wrangler of my year [1759], the leading moderator having made a person of his own college [St John's], and one of his private pupils, the first, in direct opposition to the general sense of the examiners in the Senate House, who declared in my favour. The injustice which was done me then was remembered as long as I lived in the University; and the talk about it did me more service than if I had been made senior wrangler. Our old master sent for me, and told me not to be discouraged, for that when the *Johnians* had the disposal of the honours, the 2nd wrangler was always looked upon as the 1st.[56]
>
> There was more room for partiality in the distribution of honours, not only with respect to St Johns, but other colleges, *then*, than there is now; and I attribute the change, in a great degree, to an alteration which I introduced the first year I was moderator, and which has been preserved ever since.
>
> At the time of taking their Bachelor of Arts degrees, the young men are examined in classes, and the classes are *now* formed according to the abilities shown by individuals in the schools. By this arrangement, persons of nearly equal abilities are examined in the presence of each other, and flagrant acts of partiality cannot take place. Before I made this alteration, they were examined in classes, but the classes consisted of members of the same College, and the best and worst were often examined together.[57]

Later in the same year, 1763, Watson successfully proposed to the university senate that all MAs, not only as previously those of five years' standing, should be allowed to participate in questioning candidates.[58] This might be seen as acknowledging the growing importance of the young graduates who were now coaching undergraduates in the increasingly dominant mathematical section of the examination, and who might perhaps be expected to be less swayed by college prejudice than their elders.

Of the eight groups into which the questionists were divided after 1763, it was expected that the first two would become wranglers (i.e. first class men), the second two senior optimes (second class), the next two junior optimes (third class), the last two the 'poll' ('hoi polloi').[59] At some point soon after 1763, the classes began to be examined together: the first two, the next four, and the last two.[60] After these preliminary gradings, the questionists were interrogated by the moderators in the (largely mathematical) Senate House Examination. During the second half of the eighteenth century, the Examination began to dominate, leaving the Latin exercises as a mere pre-classifying operation. In 1827 the classes were reduced to four, and in 1838 were abolished; the moderators for 1839 consequently decided not to hold any disputations. Thus ended, at least in the arts faculty, a tradition of oral examination several hundred years old.[61]

A significant step in the shift of emphasis away from the preliminary to the later stages of the examination was taken in 1779, when a system of 'brackets' ('classes quam minimae', i.e. very small groups) was introduced. On the fourth day of the examination, the list of candidates was exhibited outside the Senate House at 8 am, with those who were regarded as roughly equal bracketed together. Those who felt this did not do them justice could then appeal against the classification, and were promptly interrogated anew. A new list was then put up, and this happened several times during the day, until at 5 pm the final order was posted up.[62]

Though the chronology cannot be established with complete certainty, the move away from orality can be traced in outline. By 1772, questions were dictated to students for written answer.[63] From about 1790, some papers (problem papers, set only to the first two classes) were printed, and given to candidates to take away to window seats for solution.[64] The other ('bookwork') papers continued to be dictated until 1828, when new regulations laid down that all papers should be printed, and gave examiners only very restricted power to examine orally. At the same time, the involvement of MAs tailed off, their right to intervene in the examination of candidates being apparently not exercised after 1785; while from 1779 the number of examiners was increased from two to four. Similarly, the right of the vice-chancellor and proctors to nominate 'honorary senior optimes' who could be inserted into the tripos list fell into disuse, to be formally abolished in 1827.[65] The examination was taking on its own existence, separate from that of the university as a whole; and in the process, socio-moral criteria were giving way to cognitive evaluation.[66] Separate from that of the university: or perhaps we should rather say, from that of the colleges. The young MAs allowed to examine after 1763 would often have been the private tutors of the leading candidates, and accusations of partiality were common in the next decades. Of Isaac Milner, President of Queens' College and much in demand as an examiner, it was said that he was impartial except in the case of men from his own college and from Emmanuel. Gunning described Milner as having all the qualities an examiner needed 'praeter aequitatem'.[67] We have already seen how Richard Watson, at least by his own account, suffered from such partiality.

The mixture of oral and written elements in the Senate House Examination at the end of the eighteenth century can be seen in the detailed account printed in the University Calendar for 1802 (at that time in its infancy, and produced by private enterprise).

> Immediately after the University clock has struck *eight*, the names are called over . . . The classes to be examined are called out, and proceed to their appointed tables, where they find pens, ink, and paper provided in great abundance . . . The young men hear the propositions or Questions delivered by the Examiners; they instantly apply themselves . . . All is silence; nothing heard save the voice of the Examiners; or the gentle request of some one, who may wish a repetition of the enunciation. It requires every person to use the utmost despatch; for as soon as the Examiners perceive that any one has finished his paper, and subscribed his name to it, another Question is immediately given.[68]

The treatment of the Examination in the 1802 Calendar perhaps suggests a newly self-conscious pride. It may be that this was fuelled by comparison with the new Oxford examinations, set up by the statute of 1800.[69] Certainly the picture of organized speed and silence in the examination hall must have presented a striking contrast with the public verbal battles taking place in Oxford. The significance of the examination for the university's self-image is indicated by the publicity given to the annual ceremonial at which degrees were conferred. The Senior Wrangler (top of the first class) was awarded his degree first, in a separate ceremony, and was clearly regarded with considerable reverence. What makes the symbolic weight of this apotheosis of competition even clearer is the award of an informal title to the student who came out at the bottom of the honours list (i.e., last of the junior optimes). It was at about this time (*c*. 1800) that he became known as the Wooden Spoon; at the degree ceremony a large spoon was lowered by his fellow-students from the gallery of the Senate House as he received his degree. What was being celebrated was not his (comparative) failure, but the competitive system itself, dominated by a ranking procedure of unparalleled intensity and precision.[70]

Competition between Oxford and Cambridge is a central theme in a letter published anonymously in 1808 by Benjamin Newton, Rector of Norton St Philip in Somerset, and designed to be bound up with the Cambridge University Calendar.[71] The bulk of Newton's book is, as his title declares, a list of those who had gained honours at Cambridge since 1754. This is prefaced, however, by a letter to a local friend who had consulted Newton on which of the ancient universities he should choose for his son. As a good Cantabrigian, Newton was firmly in favour of his *alma mater*, but he goes to some lengths to argue, rather than assert, his case. His main charges against Oxford are (1) that candidates are allowed to choose books on which to be examined—and so they direct the University, rather than the University directing them, (2) candidates are not examined all at the same time, but in separate groups in January, April and June; hence there is no chance to assess comparative merits; (3) candidates offering different numbers of books are examined according to different standards—again, proper comparison is impossible; and finally (4) 'the not hanging up publicly the names of all who take their degrees, from the highest to the lowest, as is done in Cambridge, and greatly encourages the assiduity of the industrious, disgracing, at the same time, laziness, stupidity, and irregularity'.[72] Newton's charges throw into relief a fundamental conflict of institutional style. For the Oxonian examiners, fairness consisted in treating each candidate according to his lights. This meant taking in to account the amount he had read, his hearing (on which see below), in fact any factor of which they might be aware. Comparison with other candidates was inevitable, but the ranking of an individual in relation to the whole body of candidates was unnecessary.

As we have seen, the competing conception of fairness was that all candidates received exactly the same treatment (we might call this formal, as opposed to functional fairness). But as we have also seen, in Cambridge the tide did not turn in favour of this conception until around 1840. The contrast between the two conceptions is clearly closely linked to, though not identical with, the contrast between oral and written examination. It is thus striking that Newton does not raise this latter contrast in his account. One reason is perhaps that he had been an undergraduate in the 1780s, when the formal conception had made relatively little impact. It may also be relevant that his talents lay in classics rather than in mathematics. Though he was himself a 'name in the tripos', in 1783, he was in the middle of the second class (senior optimes); but he won two classical medals, the Browne Medal and the second Chancellor's Medal. Finally, one has to remember that in 1808 the surviving oral elements in Cambridge examinations may have blurred the perception of the oral versus written distinction when the procedures of the two universities were compared, in the end, the truth may be simply that, as Newton himself suggests, the failure of the Oxonians to produce an equivalent of the Cambridge *Calendar* left him in comparative ignorance of their procedures.

The politics of the examination: college versus university

As the Senate House Examination moved away from the old model of orality and general participation, and as its Newtonian mathematical element came to dominate, a reaction occurred in some of the colleges. When John Jebb of Peterhouse proposed in 1772 that university examinations in non-mathematical subjects should be set up, his fiercest opponent was William Powell, master of the largest college, St John's. Powell denounced the scheme as a 'hasty secret trial based on no knowledge of candidates'.[73] His terminology reveals the defence of collegiate *Gemeinschaft* against the threat of an overweening university *Gesellschaft*—a test without an informing social context of teaching and learning. Jebb's proposals were in fact probably inspired by Powell's own examination system at St John's, instituted shortly after his election as master in 1765. Those examinations were largely, if not entirely oral: they took place publicly in the college hall and it was remembered that Powell was 'always there to hear them'.[74] In his proposal, Jebb took care to acknowledge Powell's reform: 'those half-yearly examinations, which Dr Powell, highly to his credit, hath introduced into that society over which he so worthily presides'.[75]

The St John's examinations are documented in a series of examinations books which vividly convey the fellows' concern to be at once strict and fair.[76] They also convey a determination to avoid premature classification, and thus perhaps to defend the collegiate ethos against the passion for ranking embodied in the university examination. It is often difficult to tell if examination is oral or written; the occasional reference to 'answering' is not conclusive. This is a problem with much of the evidence. Consider the case of Charles Darwin, who took the Previous Examination in March 1830. Like Arthur Hilton in the 1870s, he reported a general state of alarm among his contemporaries: 'The men are in a dreadful plight, from fear and anxiety'. He passed his examination on the 24th, but it was a gruelling experience: 'They are very strict, and ask a wonderful number of questions'.[77] Were these oral or written? The official report of October 1829 which had made the examination more rigorous—hence in part the 'fear and anxiety' Darwin's peers felt—had laid down a procedure which included translation, construing (an oral exercise in verbal analysis) and 'answering printed questions'. Candidates were to be employed in translating and answering, and would then be called up individually to construe and explain passages from the books set. In this case, then, the procedure combined oral and written examination.[78] For an earlier period (1772), however, we can be sure of the form of the examination when we read in the St John's examinations book that 'Perhaps Atley might also have been thought to deserve [a prize], if he had spoke louder, as much of his answers as could be heard was very good'.[79] And as in the case of the Previous Examination, we can draw the same conclusion from the remark that 'Bedel and Lord Blantyre construed the

Classic well'.[80] Another clear-cut case is that of a student who was promoted to a higher class in the Senate House Examination of 1787 'because it was considered his position was owing to extreme deafness'.[81] It can not always have been easy to assess allegedly deaf students. William Tuckwell of Oxford remembered the case of 'mad Harry Wilkins', who matriculated in 1840:

> I remember his examinations in the Schools, his inability to hear questions, his cataclysmal answers when they reached him. Probably his deafness was calculated; Liddell, one of the examiners, remarked that the way to make Mr Wilkins hear was to question him on subjects which he knew.[82]

Occasionally something of the procedure employed can be glimpsed: 'Gordon answered very well . . . the first time round in Butler'.[83] In his vivid account of the examination undergone at St John's by William Wordsworth in June 1788, B. R. Schneider describes how 'the examiner, dictating orally, went on from one problem to the next as soon as the fast men had finished'.[84] Even rarer is evidence of discussion between examiners, though on one occasion deafness was an issue here too. In the Previous Examination of 1843, Rooke of Magdalene College was plucked (failed, in Cambridge parlance), much to his surprise. He called on the examiners, one by one, to find out where the line had been drawn between pass and fail. His first target, Matthew O'Brien, referred him to his co-examiner Robert Leslie Ellis. But as Ellis confessed in his diary, 'He passed in my papers & I am too deaf to have been able to follow entirely the marking out of the line. Poor devil—he haunted me all the evening'.[85]

Though there is no space in this paper to discuss school examinations, the St John's evidence provides a convenient link to this separate but related area. The relationship is especially notable in the case of St John's, since the college had a close link with Shrewsbury School, whose headmaster and second master it appointed until quite late in the nineteenth century. Samuel Butler, a fellow of St John's, was appointed headmaster of the school in 1798, and by his retirement in 1836 had made it famous as a breeding ground for classical scholars, most of whom went to St John's. Butler operated a superannuation system in which boys competed for promotion within and between forms each month. There was also a monetary prize system based on 'merit marks'; this latter was introduced on his arrival at Shrewsbury, and unlike several other aspects of school organisation, which he copied from Thomas James of Rugby, seems to have been Butler's own invention.[86] Butler's annual visits to Cambridge for information on the tripos examinations were compared by the Master of Trinity, Christopher Wordsworth, to those of a London milliner to Paris to discover the latest fashion in hats.[87] Here we have school and university examinations operating as a linked pair, each reinforcing the other. And we can be fairly sure that Butler, whose undergraduate career had been spent at St John's, was predisposed to use regular examinations by his experience of the college system.

The role of the individual

The abandonment of disputations by the moderators of 1839 seems to have run counter to the spirit of a Senate report of 1838, which laid down that the disputations should continue, though it also abolished the grouping system, allowing only for distinction between candidates for honours and for ordinary degrees. This illustrates the extent to which the examiners of a year could make policy on the hoof; similar cases at Oxford are discussed below. How important was individual initiative in the shift from oral to written assessment? So far several individuals have figured in significant changes in examination practice: Bentley in 1702, Laughton in 1710, Watson in 1763, Powell in 1765. To these, it has been claimed, we should add William Farish, the first serious student of mechanical engineering in Cambridge, who held the chair of Mechanics from 1811 until his death in 1837. In 1967, T. J. N. Hilken stated that as moderator in 1792, Farish had introduced the practice of assigning marks to individual questions.[88] Keith Hoskin emphasised the importance of such a change, as a significant moment in the development of the fine-tuned marking system.[89] In Hoskin's neo-Foucauldian narrative, this event becomes a crucial one in the emergence of a modern system of control, of 'normatising individuation'. It was 'a most momentous step, perhaps the major step towards a mathematized model of reality . . . The science of the individual was now feasible . . . The blunt weapon of banding yielded to the precision tool of the mark' (ibid).[90]

In his analysis, Hoskin relied on Hilken's account: a short history of engineering at Cambridge written by the then secretary to the faculty. It is not footnoted, but sources are listed for each chapter. Of those given for the account of William Farish, only one makes any reference to marks. This is Farish's obituary in the *Christian Observer*, and the relevant statement is this: 'he was the means of introducing into the University of Cambridge the system of classifying the candidates for a degree according to the number of marks obtained at their examination'.[91] There is no mention here of individual questions. It is in any case likely that impression marking continued to be used for some time; the senior moderator of 1836 claimed that his year of office was the first in which impression marking was not used at all.[92] The only evidence before that date for mark allocation comes from J. M. F. Wright's memoir *Alma Mater*, where he tells us that in the Senate House Examination: 'Printed papers, containing each about twenty questions, are laid before each class, the solution of each question being previously determined upon by the examiners *numerically*. At the close of the examination these numbers are summed up for each examinee'.[93]

If the story of the individual mark were true, Farish would certainly be an apt hero. He was well known for his ingenuity and curious inventions; his self-acting trough for flushing water closets was exhibited at the educational exhibition in South Kensington in 1854, seventeen years after his death.[94] The apparatus at his lectures included a kind of brass Meccano of rods, wheels and so on from which could be assembled a variety of devices. The recombinatory principle this embodies offers, indeed, a perfect parallel to the alleged marking principle. But perhaps this very parallelism should make us cautious. Farish was the kind of mildly eccentric don about whom myths tend to cluster, and until hard evidence is found, we must assume that the story of the unit mark is one such myth.

The role of the individual depends in part on the room for individual initiative proved by the institutional system in which he or she works. In several cases mentioned above, it is clear that the delegated powers of proctors, moderators and examiners could be used quite freely by a determined office-holder. This freedom was finally curtailed in the 1840s in Cambridge, when examination boards were set up to 'stabilize' examinations. Before this, however, some extensions of the de facto curriculum might be created by the personal preference of an examiner in a single year. At Oxford, individual moderators had indulged their preferences for subject matter: 'the importance of Aristotle is said to date from Dr Sheppard, examiner in 1806; of Butler, from Dr Hampden'.[95]

The account of the examinations quoted above from the 1802 Cambridge *Calendar* was based on a pamphlet circulated in 1772 by John Jebb of Peterhouse.[96] Jebb certainly belongs in any list of individuals who made a difference to Cambridge examinations, but his reforming efforts of the early 1770s ended in failure. A crucial element in his proposals for annual university examinations, which would have included classics and religion, is that they were to have been taken by all students. This was aimed at the noblemen and fellow commoners who paid more and were exempted from many of the restrictions suffered by ordinary undergraduates. In proposing this change, Jebb was taking a path also followed by other reformers of the period. His failed reforms have to be seen in the context of, for example, the campaign to remove subscription to the Thirty-Nine Articles as a matriculation requirement. The influential minority of Cambridge men who supported this belonged to the latitudinarian wing of the Church of England, strong there as it was not in Oxford. Richard Watson, whose initiatives I described above, was one of these men, and was in fact a pupil of Jebb.[97] The case of William Paley and his daring thesis on eternal pain belongs to the struggles between this liberal minority and the conservative Anglicans in Cambridge. Several of this group, after the failure of Jebb's reform proposals in the mid-1770s, became Unitarians, as did Jebb himself, who joined the group based on the Essex Street congregation in London. In short, these late eighteenth-century moves towards a fairer system based on universalised principles of evaluation cannot be seen simply as the work of individuals. They arose from a coherent movement of social and religious reform which enshrined an ideological *concept* of the individual.

The last days of the viva voce

By the end of the eighteenth century, many exercises were 'huddled', i.e. carried out in a perfunctory ritual fashion. A common source for ready-made arguments was Thomas Johnson's *Quaestiones Philosophicae* (1735). In addition, manuscript copies of sets of standard arguments were handed down from one undergraduate generation to the next: these were called 'strings' at Oxford and 'arguments' at Cambridge. In some cases these were still in use in the 1830s.[98] William Whewell, later to be Master of Trinity College, Cambridge, kept his acts in 1815. Shortly beforehand he wrote to his friend George Morland, 'it consists in a person getting up into a box to defend certain mathematical and moral questions, from the bad arguments and worse Latin of three men who are turned loose into a separate box to bait him with syllogisms'.[99] Four years later, Whewell acted as moderator for the exercises, and reported to Morland that 'the syllogisms were such as would make Aristotle stare, and the Latin would make every classical hair on your head stand on end'.[100] By the 1830s, the disputations were on their last legs, enlivened only by an occasional outburst of playful virtuosity by a student able to manipulate oral Latin. Thus in 1832, the noted classical scholar Richard Shilleto had fun at the expense of his opponent when he stated the well-worn theme 'Is suicide justifiable?'. 'Quid est suicidium', he asked, 'nisi suum caesio?' (What is suicide but the slaughter of pigs?). Shilleto was at Trinity College and his opponent belonged to its great rival St John's, whose members were commonly nicknamed 'hogs'. The Johnian's Latin was poor, so he opposed Shilleto's argument only with difficulty, and without seeing the joke. The moderator, however, did understand, and shared it.[101] A comparable example can be found in Oxford a decade later: the young Frederick Temple answered Hanswell, an examiner, using phrases from a book published by his tutor Tait, who was also present as an examiner. Tait recognised his own words and looked at Hanswell, who failed to spot the quotations.[102] In both cases, there are layers of complicity and exclusion; what is more, these cut across the institutional boundary between teachers and taught, examiner and examinee.

Such anecdotes remind us of the interactional dynamics which were of the essence of oral examination, but which were hardly possible in a written test. A Cambridge anecdote from the 1860s illustrates these vividly: it concerns John William Strutt, later Lord Rayleigh, Professor of Natural Philosophy and a Nobel prizewinner. Strutt was known to be a brilliant mathematician (he went on to be senior wrangler in 1865), but his (oral) examiners at the multi-subject Previous Examination in 1863 'had some difficulty in finding a question he could answer, so that they could with decency let him pass'.[103] Here the examiners saw their task as one of enabling a student of known ability to progress outside his favoured subject. The contrast between the economy of oral and written examinations, however, must be employed with caution. The written examination, after all, had its social relationships, muted though they were—the quiet requests for repeats or clarification of questions, the surreptitious actions of cheats.[104] As for the emotional atmosphere of examination, the comments of the American Charles Bristed, on a college examination in 1841, encourage a nuanced approach to the contrast between oral and written examination:

> The pen-and-ink system of examination has been adopted partially at Oxford, and almost entirely at Cambridge,* in preference to the *viva voce*, on the ground, among others, that it is fairer to timid and different men. The advantage in this respect is somewhat exaggerated: the excitement, though not so great for the moment, is constant, and the scratching of some hundred pens all about you makes one fearfully nervous. Then, too, any little slips you may make in a *viva voce* may be allowed for, or may even escape observation, but *litera scripta manet*; everything you put down here will be criticised deliberately and in cold blood. Awful idea!
>
> * We had a little *viva voce* in this examination, perhaps equivalent to a twentieth or twenty-fifth part of it.[105]

The same theme is sounded by a much later commentator, writing anonymously in the *Cambridge Review* in 1910:[106]

> By the twitching of shoulders and the responsive creak of chairs you may divine the intense mental concentration that surrounds you. An athlete frowns dreadfully . . . A black man lolls a purplish tongue . . . A red-haired youth is staring intently at a vacant wall . . . Somewhere else a nervous cough, apparently tuberculous, is the irritating symptom of intellectual effort . . . There's a Jew sniffing audibly . . . The room is neither noisy nor silent, but an unceasing succession of small fidgettings which requires a foreground to make it tolerable. The ineffable torment of small unmeaning grunts, creaks, scrapes, grunts and rustlings, exasperates and exhausts one who merely sits in the midst of it for three hours.

Oxford: the non-identical twin

I once passed a morning in the schools at Oxford and came away with a profound conviction of the intense injustice of using oral trials for the purpose of assigning relative rank for which men have toiled for years, and I do not think this conviction will leave me this side of the grave.[107]

As we have seen, the system of disputations at Oxford was very similar to that in Cambridge. The development of degree examinations, however, was rather different. The examination established by a statute of 1800 was to be entirely oral and to be held in public.[108] Ranking by merit ('the Cambridge system') was to be practised, though for the first twelve candidates only (this was soon abandoned in favour of alphabetic ranking). There were however never more than four men to rank; apparently candidates were discouraged by the prospect both of a public challenge to the examiners and of public humiliation if the challenge failed. Rothblatt quotes suggestions of private examinations for dull candidates to avoid public shame.[109] A reform of 1807 created only two classes, each listed in alphabetical order.[110] Later on, the number of classes was increased. The maximum reached was five, of which the fifth was not publicly listed to avoid shaming its members. The examiners of 1832 felt that to be placed in the third or fourth class was 'a *degredation* rather than a *distinction*'.[111]

The Oxford degree examination, then, was strikingly different from its Cambridge equivalent. It provided a public spectacle, and occasionally high drama. In 1810, Sir William Hamilton offered a long list of books for examination, and was grilled for twelve hours over two days in front of a large audience; the event concluded with the thanks of his questioners.[112] In the 1820s, when the level of matriculations rose sharply at both Oxford and Cambridge, the oral examination system began to break down. The number of moderators was limited by statute, as was the number of candidates they could examine in a day. They found themselves working for almost half the year clearing the backlog of candidates. As a result, written examinations were introduced in the later 1820s, and from 1828 printed papers were used.[113] The decisive shift towards written work came with the 1830 examination statutes, which allowed examiners 'to try several persons at the same time, at answering the same questions'.[114] Nevertheless, Oxford retained a considerable viva voce element in its degree examinations. Mark Curthoys has argued that this is related to the powerful local emphasis on religious testing.[115] It is certainly true that questions on divinity loomed large in vivas, which always began with the New Testament: for this part of the examination, both examiner and examinee stood up. On the other hand, it may be that (as Durkheim might have said) it was the social group which was being worshipped, not the god. The oral emphasis, that is, belonged to the tradition of communal academic solidarity preserved by a continuing adherence to debate on logic: the Oxonian version of the medieval curriculum, from which Cambridge had diverged with its emphasis on mathematics.[116] The viva voce examination, then, celebrated the solidarity of a High Anglican academic community whose religious centre of gravity was rather different from that of latitudinarian Cambridge. In 1882, when the new Examination Schools were opened, this shrine to written examination was decorated with a large bas relief of an oral examination.[117] By this time it was rare for vivas to attract audiences, and this trend was reinforced after 1883, when final examinations were rearranged so that vivas took place in the summer vacation. The viva was dropped from classical moderations in 1884 and from Responsions (the Oxonian equivalent of the Previous Examination) in 1890, but at the beginning of the twentieth century, finalists were still being routinely vivaed in every subject except mathematics.[118] The compulsory divinity examination ('divvers'), which was not abolished till 1931, ended with a viva, and by the end of the century (as earlier in the 1820s) the examiners were overwhelmed by rising student numbers. In 1911 they managed to conduct eighty vivas a day, but the system was acknowledged to be a 'blasphemous farce'.[119] The poem 'In memoriam examinatoris cuiusdam' published by Arthur Godley in 1907 summed up the state of play.[120] The dead examiner was himself to face a 'final viva voce' (conducted, of course, in another world). His sober assessments of examination papers produced letter marks —the poem mentions alpha, epsilon, and, written on his tomb, 'β—(?)'. The assessments themselves are however described in numerical terms:

> He did his estimate express
> In terms precise and weighty,—
> And Vice got 25 (or less),
> While Virtue rose to 80.

The contrast of intellectual style between Oxford and Cambridge shows up clearly in the marking schemes adopted in each place. The Cambridge system was based on a strict ranking of numerical marks. There were only two departures from this at university level. First, candidates who did not obtain honours were listed in alphabetical order. (This was applied in 1851 to the third class of the Classical Tripos, but abandoned in 1859 on the ground that it discouraged effort).[121] Second, it was possible to gain more than one hundred per cent for a paper. This could be done if a candidate produced a more elegant solution to a problem than the standard example. This tradition renders rather less bizarre the action of Thomas Evans in giving one of his students 700 marks out of 500, though Evans, who had been prevented from sitting the Classical Tripos by his failure in mathematics, was surely driven by resentment at the mathematicians.[122] In Oxford, marking was usually by Greek letters rather than numbers. As Hartog and Rhodes commented in 1936, this system, which they described as 'common at Oxford, but not elsewhere', reflected a concern with quality rather than quantity.[123] The literal marking system can be related to the Oxonian concern to avoid intensive ranking. A committee of the university's reigning

Hebdomadal Board declared in 1829 that the standard for each class should be 'absolute and positive'. Curthoys comments on this that 'Theoretically, all the candidates could be in the first class, and individual classes could be (and sometimes were) empty'; and he suggests that this system encouraged the use of Greek letter grades.[124] Alpha, beta and gamma provided broad distinctions, while at the same time celebrating the dominance of classics at Oxford, with which that of mathematics at Cambridge contrasted very sharply.

As a practical system, however, the literal scheme could be, and was, employed to make fine distinctions, usually by adding pluses and minuses. It is notable that such schemes were also used in Cambridge outside the degree examination. The few surviving moderators' books for the eighteenth century contain alphabetical marks. In a 1778 book, the marks are recorded as A, a, E, e; each with pluses and minuses for finer gradation.[125] These marks, significantly, are for performance in the disputations. That literal marking was commonly used for these oral performances is suggested by Whewell's statement to the 1850 Royal Commissioners that the disputations were abandoned because of problems in combining their marks with those for written papers.[126] Surviving mark lists for Trinity College scholarships and fellowships for 1791 have mark ranges of a, a^2, a+, a, a−, x^2, x+, x, x−, o; and of +aa, +a, +, + −, +o. Clearly there is an element of improvisation here, but the scheme is algebraic rather than literal, and in this case the papers are written. This collection in fact includes a cautionary notice warning that in the past 'candidates have been in a rush and written badly'.[127] The collegiate evidence at Cambridge, then, supports the linkage between oral examination and literal marking which dominates in Oxford. Bearing in mind the tutorial ethos identified at St John's, Cambridge, we can also link both these to a concern with students as social beings, as opposed to the severely cognitive obsessions of the Cambridge mathematical examination. The only use of literal marking there at university level may have been in the oral element of the Previous Examination. In Hilton's *Vulture and the Husbandman*, the Vulture asks his fellow-examiner,

> 'If seven C's or seven D's
> We give to all the crowd,
> Do you suppose' the Vulture said
> 'That we could get them ploughed [failed]?'[128]

Different kinds of knowledge and genre, as well as of marking, were at home in oral or in written examinations. The 1850 Royal Commission on Oxford, in its historical retrospect, stated that after the 1807 reforms:

> The principal part of the examination seems to have been oral, and [the candidates'] success naturally depended rather on skill and

accuracy in construing the classics than on acquaintance with Philosophy and History . . . the increase in the number of the Candidates had an effect which had not been foreseen. It became necessary that the Examination should be conducted more and more on paper, and therefore knowledge of Philosophy, together with skill in Composition, increased gradually in importance, and perhaps skill in Construing proportionably declined.[129]

Similar effects were noted in mathematics:

Till the year 1820, the subjects of Examination were chiefly such as admitted of Geometrical treatment; and the Examination was conducted viva voce. As the various branches of Analysis were introduced into the Examinations, the viva voce Examination became of less and less importance, and is now almost a form.[130]

'Analysis' refers to the continental algebraic tradition which was resisted in Cambridge, loyal to its Newtonian heritage, until the early years of the nineteenth century. Algebraic analysis began to infiltrate degree examinations around 1820, and probably increased pressure on the oral examinations. It may be this development which was referred to by the leading mathematical coach William Hopkins. In his evidence to the 1850 Royal Commission, Hopkins averred that 'Viva voce was found to be hard to use to convey complex nuances of meaning in questions'.[131] In his own evidence William Whewell, a former supporter of analysis who had backed away from it as he became more conservative, declared that 'Viva voce examination catches out the crammer. It measures quality and competency while written papers produce classification'.[132] Whewell wanted a return to oral examining and geometry because he saw them as the twin pillars of a pedagogic system which effectively tested 'permanent' rather than 'progressive' knowledge— eternal truths rather than research-led knowledge, which he believed was too unstable to form the basis of a liberal education.[133]

By 1850, Whewell was, one might think, in a minority: the day of the written examination had arrived, and since 1828 printed papers had been used. His nostalgia for oral examination could thus be seen as a longing for the return of an academic community in which fairness and mutual trust were relied on; in which moderators were trusted to address different questions to candidates of different abilities, and perhaps because the latter had been roughly pre-classified in the disputations, they would know how to pitch their questions.[134] Whewell turns out, in fact, to have had considerable support for his views. In a series of reports issued between 1853 and 1860, a sub-committee set up by the Board of Mathematical Studies was almost unanimous in urging that oral examination be reintroduced into the Mathematical Tripos. They were convinced that it was a useful technique for appraising candidates whose reading was limited; it also helped to test 'some powers of mind' in more talented students. A third reason offered was that if the examination were conducted in public, 'the preparation would be a useful discipline for much of the work of active life'.[135] The Board hesitated at first to make a formal proposal, apparently unwilling to divert attention from other changes currently being discussed. In its report for 1860 it did finally make such a proposal, but this seems never to have been acted on.

From the late eighteenth century, however, a different notion of fairness was developed by men like Jebb and Watson, one focused on the individual rather than the group. The result was that it came to be felt that the only fair procedure in comparing candidates was to give them all the same questions. It is not coincidental that the emergence of this principle in the Mathematical Tripos, as it was called after 1824, went hand in hand with the decline of the preliminary disputations. In his evidence to the Royal Commission, Henry Philpott stated that in the mid-1820s 'candidates for honours were divided into 6 divisions before the main examination, divided according to the exercises in the public schools, and different questions were for the most part proposed to the different classes. In 1827 the number of such classes was reduced to four, and the Examiners allowed to propose the same questions to different classes as they should think fit. Accordingly all the questions from books for the first 2 days, and all the Problems were made common to all the candidates'. This move, of course, was a major incentive to use printed question papers, which were introduced both in Cambridge and at Oxford in 1828. In both cases, the sheer numbers of students in the 1820s forced change: 'In 1828, the plan of printing the Questions proposed to the Candidates was first introduced. This introduction was necessitated by the increasing numbers of Candidates, and its effect has been beneficial in giving a certain stability to the system of Examinations'.[136] Printed papers in turn will have reinforced the assumption that questions should be standardized. As Philpott told the Cambridge Royal Commission, '[from 1838] the conviction appear[ed] to gain ground by degrees that the relative merits of different candidates can not be fully determined unless they are all tested by the same examination'.[137]

The silent sister: Trinity College Dublin

Trinity, like Oxford, was given new statutes in the 1630s by Archbishop Laud. Unlike Oxford, however, it clung to them in detail, and Laud's injunctions on examinations were still being followed in the early nineteenth century. Another reason for discussing TCD as a comparative case is that unlike Oxford and Cambridge, it was not a collegiate university: indeed it was technically the only college of the University of Dublin. By 1800, it resembled Edinburgh and Glasgow in being a large urban institution, but differed from both them and from Oxbridge in being only minimally residential. By

1830, only about twenty per cent of its students were in college accommodation at any one time; while of the total student body, only about twenty-five per cent came from Dublin. The heart of the student career lay not in collegiate residence (for which there was no requirement) but in the termly examinations; and adequate performance in these could lead by itself to the award of a degree.[138]

Trinity held a wide range of examinations, beginning with an entrance examination: something almost unknown at Oxbridge.[139] Students were examined every term throughout the four-year undergraduate course; in addition there were examinations for scholarships, for medals and for fellowships of the College. In 1830, when Cambridge had largely moved to written and indeed printed papers and Oxford was moving more slowly in the same direction, Trinity's quarterly[140] terminal examinations remained entirely oral, with the exception of the classical theme (written essay), set on one day and submitted the next. At the final (degree) examination, which was simply the last of a long series of such ordeals, those who had gained prizes in terminal examinations were tested more rigorously, and the top scorers in classics and science were each given a medal. The final hurdle, for those who chose to brave it, was the fellowship examination, conducted orally and in public over four days. This covered a wide range, but since the 1750s mathematics and physics had come informally to dominate it. The continuing dominance of oral examining is less surprising when one remembers that moves to written examination at Oxbridge took place at the level of university final degree examinations, in contrast with annual or semi-annual college tests. At Trinity, sole college in its university, students were tested every term: a system resembling Oxbridge college examinations rather than those for *literae humaniores* or *scientia naturalis* at Oxford, or the mathematical and classical triposes at Cambridge.

Even before Bartholomew Lloyd's reforming Provostship of 1831–7, there were protests against aspects of the Trinity examination procedures. In 1824 an anonymous pamphlet was published which both described and criticised the procedure of the fellowship examination.[141] Its printing in both London and Dublin suggested a concern for a wider audience, and this is confirmed by its opening words:

> The rapid extension of education within the last thirty years in these countries, has created a considerable interest in the proceedings of our national seminaries. As knowledge has spread and deepened, public solicitude has extended from the schools to the colleges, and curiosity and inquiry are as alive to the details of a University Examination now, as they were to a debate in Parliament a century ago.

The writer went on to explain that the examination was entirely oral, except for the fourth and last day, which was devoted to (written) themes: 'These are however considered mere forms, and never influence the election'. A sign of their marginality was that the Senior Examiner was present, but not the other examiners.

> The questions to candidates are viva voce in Latin, and they are expected to answer them in the same manner. . . . not only in popular departments, Logic and Ethics, but also in Mathematics and Physics. The Candidates are not allowed the use of the pen, nor any means of describing geometrical constructions, nor of writing algebraic form-ulae; and are required to answer all . . . questions in general terms, and in Latin. These rules necessarily impose great restrictions upon both Examiners and Candidates, and it is to these restrictions that the principal defect of the examinations must be attributed.[142]

The writer helpfully records the questions asked in each two-hour examina-tion; the numbers are typical of oral examination and provide a record of one side, as it were, of a stichomythic exchange. The History examination consisted of sixty questions, while in Ethics 122 were asked. This was clearly a quick-fire procedure, as in Ethics less than a minute per question and answer will on average have been available, and several candidates had to be interrogated.

In 1828 this attack was followed up by an internal critic. Richard MacDonnell, one of the Fellows, published a letter to the Registrar in which he roundly criticised the undergraduate examinations.[143] A particular target was the custom of dividing up the student body between the examiners, so that each group had only one examiner: as a result, two equally qualified candidates in different groups might be given very different marks. MacDonnell did not recommend the abolition of viva voce interrogation, but he urged that it should become a minor part of the examination, to be modelled on the Oxford examinations. The greater part of the examination, he suggested, should follow the pattern now well established at Cambridge: 'Examination by printed lists'. This, he argued, would help to supply an uniformity of standard'.[144] It would also keep the students occupied:

> At present the time in which any individual, not a candidate for honors, is occupied by either of the two Examiners, cannot out of the eight hours exceed ten minutes. Very often two hours pass without a question being put to a large portion of the division. The effect is, that many of the Students pass their time in conversation, drawing with their pencils, or cutting the tables. Our Examination loses much of its solemnity'.[145]

With such comments we gain something of the atmosphere of the oral examination, as conducted for relatively large numbers.[146]

The TCD entrance and scholarship examinations were in this period entirely oral, and as the *Quarterly Journal of Education* pointed out, in the latter case 120 to 130 candidates had to be examined in eight hours: 'far too little for any effective examination of well prepared men'.[147] The height of the writer's scorn, however, is reserved for the annual fellowship examination, which extended over four days, each day having two two-hour sessions. Here the complaints of the anonymous critic of 1824 are repeated: despite the range of subjects (logic, ethics, mathematics, physics, history, Latin, Greek and Hebrew), the whole examination was conducted orally in Latin. This produced the remarkable spectacle (the whole examination being held in public) of candidates translating passages from Latin literature into Latin. It was equally absurd, in its own way, that 'the highest branches of mathematics and physics are required to be expounded *viva voce* without any use of paper whatever'. This was all the more remarkable since over the previous seventy-five years or so, the examination had in practice become dominated by mathematics. In 1855 the Fellows altered the balance of marks to ameliorate this, but they also abolished the use of Latin. A proposal in 1856 to use written papers instead of viva voce questioning for the classical part of the examination was voted down.[148]

The situation at Trinity *c.* 1830 might be described as an Oxonian time warp: the Laudian statutes were clung to, and the adjustments made at Oxford were absent. The de facto domination of the curriculum by mathematics and physics since the mid-eighteenth century in fact represented a shift to a Cambridge model, which had however taken place within a continuing straitjacket of Oxford-style regulations. The shift from a four-to a three-term year in 1834 was described in the *Calendar* as a move from Oxonian to Cantabrigian practice; the anonymous critic of 1824 had referred to the recent publication of the Cambridge Senate House examination papers, and was clearly using them as an implicit point of reference. An important part of the changes taking place in the first half of the nineteenth century, then, was the emergence of a public debate on assessment procedures which involved the comparison of different institutions. The 'peculiar style, which may be discovered by nice examination and comparison with others', on which Samuel Johnson commented in individuals, was now also to be identified and assessed in the case of the institutions which examined individuals.[149]

Conclusion

The aims of the new examination were *to raise and standardize performance*, thus conceding the needs of serious-minded undergraduates who were willing to work methodically under supervision and have their scholarship submitted to a rigorous test.[150]

This innocuous-sounding pronouncement refers to the Senate House Examination (or as Judges anachronistically calls it, the Mathematical Tripos) of the 1750s. It has a definitive, indeed definitional air about it, almost as if it were extruded from an essence of examination. Yet in its assumption of students ready to work, of monolithic aims, in its exclusion of curricular and institutional politics, it is curiously ahistorical.[151] The late-Victorian alarms about the effects of examinations had in a paradoxical sense only confirmed the contemporary sense of their being a perfection of method, the end of partiality. The machine was to be feared for an excess, not for a lack of efficiency. Though their work is much more nuanced, this perspective was to some extent shared by Montgomery and Roach.[152]

Since then there have been two major attempts to view examinations in a broader historical perspective. Sheldon Rothblatt brought to the subject a keen sense of the subtleties of social and cultural change in eighteenth- and nineteenth-century England; this enabled him to situate examination changes in wider contexts.[153] Keith Hoskin sought to provide a Foucauldian account of examinations to stand alongside Foucault's treatment of prisons and hospitals: a study of the emergence of the mark as a finely-tuned grading device.[154] Hoskin's work is stimulating and often perceptive, but as I have argued above, its evidential basis is occasionally shaky. What I have tried to add to the work of Rothblatt and Hoskin is a sense of the institutional contexts of examination history. It is here that comparison of those strikingly non-identical twins, Oxford and Cambridge, is so useful. In the most detailed account we have of early nineteenth-century university examinations, Rothblatt tells a largely Oxonian story, and as Hoskin has suggested, does not 'explain the specifics of the prior Cambridge development'.[155] Much more remains to be done in this area, particularly in the investigation of college examinations.[156] This paper represents no more than a preliminary attempt to move the discussion forward. Evidently some of the evidence needs to be re-examined. We have seen in the case of Bentley's 'reform' (1702) and of the 'fixed mark per question' (1792) that an original assertion for which the evidence is either unavailable or misinterpreted is repeated until it becomes a fixed part of the received narrative. Future students of this area will need to be aware of the ideological or methodological agendas influencing the work of historians, both within and without the institutions whose stories they tell.

A more recent study deserves separate comment, since its title may suggest a more restricted analysis than it actually provides. This is Andrew Warwick's *Masters of Theory: Cambridge and the Rise of Mathematical Physics*.[157] Warwick's book includes, as one might expect, an account of the development of the Cambridge style of mathematics from the late eighteenth to the twentieth century. The subversion of a resolutely Newtonian curriculum through the introduction of continental analysis led to a high-intensity system of teaching and research which produced the work of Maxwell, Larmor and Eddington, and the founding and expansion of the Cavendish Laboratory. In addition, however, Warwick provides a pioneering analysis of the pedagogical developments of the late eighteenth and early nineteenth centuries which underpinned this intellectual production and moulded its style. Central to these developments were the growth of an intensive system of private tuition ('coaching'), and the emergence of an institutional world of written examination and rigorous, fine-tuned marking. This was a world in which students ambitious for success exercised both mind and body at a high level, vigorous physical exercise being seen as part of a unified process of preparation. The winners emerged as perhaps the best-trained mathematicians anywhere; the cost of the system was felt by those who suffered mental or physical breakdown, or both. Warwick provides a detailed and perceptive account of the contrast between this world and that of the oral examination which it superseded. Although he concentrates on the internal structure of the Cambridge system, he includes comparisons between Cambridge and continental universities. A particular strength is his ability to generalize, as a methodological issue, the analysis of the influence of pedagogy on research style: demonstrated in convincing detail for Cambridge mathematics, it can and should be applied to other places and other subjects.[158]

At this point, it may be useful to list the factors which have been most important in the shift from oral to written examinations.[159]

First, the general shift in the second half of the eighteenth century away from socio-moral assessments of members of status groups, toward purely cognitive assessments of individuals.[160] For most of the eighteenth century, it was regarded as normal for honorary optimes to be inserted high in the list at Cambridge (as with Laughton in 1710–11). The decline of this practice, and its subsequent expunging from the official record in the university calendar in the 1790s, indicate a distinct shift in notions of social worth and assessment. This is also evident in the moves of the 1770s to make superior grades of undergraduate (noblemen and fellow commoners) subject to examination discipline. We might link to this the transfer of control of the process of assessment from the community of MAs, and their representatives the Proctors, to the moderators. The latter, originally the proctors' deputies, became examiners in sole charge of proceedings, while the involvement of MAs, who had once been able to join in the interrogation of candidates, gradually disappeared.[161] Paradoxically, a similar development affected the moderators, whose own individual freedom of decision on the running of exams was itself curtailed in favour of examining boards. The power vested in the community of MAs passed to a specialised body of examiners. This shift was entangled with religious and political conflicts which affected Cambridge, where the forces of reform were well represented, much more than at Oxford. The reforming efforts of Jebb and Watson in the 1760s and '70s belonged to a concerted and consistent campaign which began with the petition against subscription to the Thirty-Nine Articles. Exactly how the shift from ascribed to achieved social status (as both fact and ideology) was related in different institutional settings to the shift from oral to written testing is something which remains to be investigated.

Second, the content of the knowledge tested played an important part. The precocious emergence of the rigorous marking system of Cambridge took place in the home of Newtonian mechanical materialism, and dates from the latter's emergence to dominance there in the first half of the eighteenth century. Subject matter and assessment by precise rank order had an elective affinity. The point is highlighted if we compare Cambridge, dominated by mathematics, with Oxford, where classics held sway. The home of humane letters (*literae humaniores*, or 'Greats') used Greek letters for marking. Oxford's association with the public sphere of elite culture helps to explain the minimal public ranking—alphabetic order within classes, and indeed alphabetic marking of examinations. The rhetoric of display was part of the culture of gentlemanly orality, a culture which, as we have seen, persisted longer in Oxford than did its attenuated counterpart in Cambridge.[162] This was a republic of equals, or at least of potential equals. The greater emphasis on culture and character at Oxford was paralleled in the combined moral and intellectual status of the tutorial relationship. The Cambridge system, by contrast, separated moral tutors from 'supervisors' and 'directors and studies'.[163] As we have seen, the later shift to continental (algebraic) analysis at Cambridge in the early nineteenth century also affected methods of assessment, working as it did against effective viva voce examination.

Even within subjects, some kinds of test were difficult or impossible to carry out orally. When they became popular, the oral nature of the examination was eroded and eventually disappeared. We have seen the effect of essays and Latin proses at Oxford in this respect. A similar process can be observed at Westminster School, where the debate between Opponent and Respondent was kept alive by the 'Challenges' conducted for election to scholarships. Pairs of pupils interrogated each other on the translation and analysis of set texts, the victor winning the scholarship. The long history of Challenges reached its final phase in 1855, when Latin prose composition was introduced. The last occasion on which oral competition was wholly decisive was in 1873; by the end of the century, the contest was entirely conducted through written papers.[164]

Third, rising student numbers, first in the 1820s and then at the end of the century, had a significant influence in swamping viva voce procedures.[165] The shift away from general MA involvement meant that large numbers of students had to be examined by small numbers of examiners. It is in the nature of oral examination that an interrogator can only address one examinee at a time. In Oxford in the 1820s, the statutory restrictions on numbers examined led to the collapse of the system. Seventy years later, another rise in student numbers led to the 'blasphemous farce' of hasty and perfunctory divinity vivas.[166] The shift from oral to written can thus be compared with other qualitative changes prompted by quantitative increases.[167]

Fourth, both oral and written examinations were subject to the politics of the institutional contexts in which they took place. These included conflicts between colleges, and between college and university interests. In the period I have considered, the universities were slowly recovering from their marginalization by the colleges earlier in their history. Here the interests of larger and smaller colleges were very different; a fact especially noticeable at Cambridge, where St John's and Trinity were many times larger than their smallest rivals. At the time of Powell's reforms, in the mid-1760s, St John's was the largest college in Cambridge. In many ways, it would be more helpful to employ three categories: small college, large college, university. In Oxford, though colleges differed in size, the differentials were smaller; something which clearly has much to do with Oxford's being a more *collegiate* university. An interesting contrast is provided by the new University of London, founded in 1836 as an examining institution with two colleges, the already-existing University and King's Colleges. As one might expect from its metropolitan, largely bourgeois clientele, the new university followed Cambridge (written) practices rather than those of Oxford.[168]

In this paper I have tried to outline overall trends in the shift from oral to written examination, while allowing for the local effects of institutional structures and ideologies. It is clear that the written examinations introduced at Cambridge in the eighteenth century became a model for other British universities in the 1820s and 1830s. If we look further afield, the chronology of change may suggest a similar pattern. For example, the first mention of written examinations at Yale has been dated to 1830, at Harvard to 1833.[169] It is not at all clear that these events were influenced by British practice. The influence of Cambridge methods on Jefferson's new University of Virginia, however, is beyond doubt. The techniques of written examination were carried there by Cambridge-educated men appointed as founding professors.[170] Within Britain, as we have seen, the importation of examining practices was not uncommon: Oxford gradually adopted Cambridge techniques, while Trinity College Dublin was urged to follow both the English universities. James Booth, educated at TCD in the 1830s, was a keen advocate of oral examination in the discussions of the Society of Arts.[171] The examinations at the East India Company's college at Haileybury, whose staff were mostly Cambridge men, were conducted, from 1807, by written papers.[172] In some cases, change was brought about by the movement of individuals. At Glasgow, the professor of law appointed in 1855 used oral examination, but the first professor of conveyancing, appointed in 1861, introduced written examinations, following the lead of the first professor of the subject at Edinburgh, elected in 1856.[173] Only in the second half of the nineteenth century did Oxford and Cambridge collaborate, when schools examination bodies were set up. Attempts to formulate common rules for assessment were apparently obstructed by the difference in their procedures for reconciling disagreements between examiners. The Cambridge Syndicate's first secretary, Henry Roby, remarked in his memoirs that in Oxford these were called 'idiosyncrasies', in Cambridge 'personal equations'. The terminological difference is characteristic of the difference of intellectual style between the two universities.[174] In his evidence to the 1850 Royal Commission, the celebrated mathematical coach William Hopkins singled out 'definiteness' as leading characteristic of the Cambridge style. Of the textbooks in use there, he stated that:

> Every subject is divided into as many separate propositions, formally enunciated, as it will admit of. Great perspicuity in details is thus secured, but generally at the expense . . . of a comprehensive exposition of general views and principles. . . . The character of the French elementary works [written for the Ecole Polytechnique] . . . is exactly the reverse of our own in the points above mentioned, as is also their system of examination, which, I believe, is entirely *viva voce*.[175]

Hopkins had earlier made much the same point about examinations, adding that the reintroduction of oral examinations would offer a solution; though he recognised that it would be a considerable task to hold such examinations for about 150 candidates each year.[176] The contrast Hopkins points to is strikingly similar to the contrast which has been identified between Oxford and Cambridge.[177] What makes it all the more interesting is that he is comparing the mathematical teaching at two institutions. The contrast is thus analytically independent of the contrast between classical Oxford and mathematical Cambridge: it relates only to the kind of assessment employed.

Several of the points which emerge from the above evidence are neatly summarised in letter of 24 March 1838 from J. W. Lubbock to the Earl of Burlington on the conduct of University of London Arts degree examinations.[178] Lubbock wrote to argue against the use of any viva voce element in the examinations; defining viva voce examination as 'the proposing of questions verbally to each of the candidates separately, as is practised at Oxford, and also on the Continent'. He offered six arguments against the practice:

1 The University charter required that candidates' proficiency should be stated in relation to that of other candidates. This could only be done if all candidates answered the same questions: impossible in viva voce examinations. (Presumably Lubbock was thinking of the vagaries involved in using multiple examiners.)

2   Both candidates and examiners would be inconvenienced by the impossibility of fixing precise time limits for oral examinations.

3   Examiners would need to stay for a considerable time; this would make it hard to find suitable examiners, and expensive if they could be found.

4   The Senate in a new institution like the University needs to know what is being asked in examinations; this would hardly be possible unless the questions are on paper.

5   Students would find it hard to learn in advance what is involved in examinations—something they can do from past papers for written examinations.

6   It would be difficult to draw up rules for regulating oral examinations. The Oxford Calendar is notable for giving no information on the conduct or length of examinations.

This is an interesting mixture of the pragmatic, the administrative and the ideological; the last category needing to be assessed, inter alia, in relation to Lubbock's own mindset.[179] At one point he admits that oral examination has its virtues, as for instance in promoting 'readiness and presence of mind'.[180] But for Lubbock, oral examination can only lead to candidates' being '*classed*', not to having their proficiency ascertained '*in relation to that of other Candidates*'.[181]

It is clear that the changes identified above formed part of larger social and cultural developments.[182] They belong to the wider history of orality and literacy, with which the history of educational institutions has been variously entangled.[183] They can also be looked at as phases in the emergence of systems of power and control, linked to developments in accounting, business, prisons and hospitals. Here a central concept is the Foucauldian notion of 'normatising individuation'.[184] The crucial elements in the changes described above, however, are related to conceptions of individuals and the way in which they should be assessed. The individual emerges from a social nexus in which social status is a vital determinant of the way he or she is treated, and in which he is to a large extent a known quantity, to become a bearer of intellect which is to be assessed on a par with any other.[185] The differential treatment of nobles, fellow commoners and 'honorary optimes' fades away in the face of the examination machine, which treats all candidates equally. Outstanding achievement by the nobly born becomes something unusual which attracts comment.[186] This is surely at least a partial explanation for the remarkable decision at Cambridge in 1881 to allow female students to sit tripos examinations, and to have their results published, albeit in separate lists.[187] What is now a banal assumption, that all candidates should be treated equally, was highly contentious in the late eighteenth century, when John Jebb narrowly failed to introduce into the university examinations for all students, including nobles and fellow commoners.[188] In that case, an Enlightenment agenda reinforced by political and religious radicalism was being proposed, and the narrowness of Jebb's defeat indicates the degree to which the relatively low-church and rationalist academic body differed from that in Oxford, where Jebb's nearest counterpart, John Napleton, was very much a conservative reformer.[189] The whole question of the class basis of recruitment to Oxford and Cambridge is clearly relevant here. This is a notoriously thorny area, both because a large minority of students cannot be classified from the surviving records and because of the difficulty of interpreting the often vague contemporary categories. One point, however, does seem clear: that there was a resurgence of aristocratic entry to Oxford c. 1765–1835.[190] (It might tentatively be suggested that this resonated with the emphasis on confident public display in Oxford oral examinations in the first third of the nineteenth century).

In the oral tradition, individuals were usually interrogated by individuals; when printed papers were introduced, the focus shifted from such one-to-one relationships to the standardized testing of groups. The crucial turning points are reflected in the comments of Henry Philpott to the 1850 Royal Commission on Cambridge, reported above: 'the view gradually gained ground that the relative merits of different candidates can not be fully determined unless they are all tested by the same examination'.[191] Philpott was referring to the late 1830s; the same decade in which Oxford had begun 'to try several persons at the same time, at answering the same questions', as allowed, in the interests of coping with a growing workload, by the 1830 examination statutes. We can locate in the 1830s, then a changing conception of 'equality' and 'fairness' which emerged from the interaction of abstract notions of the way individuals should be treated, institutional pressures on examiners—and perhaps a changing political context in the wake of the 1832 Reform Act. In the half century after this period, a climate of patronage gave way slowly to a climate of access via examination. But although individuals might be treated equally, they were of course usually unequal—as the published marks showed. They were also different from one another in a way that made them more than passive recipients of marks: they made choices. Greats students at Oxford in effect declared which class of degree they were aiming for by the number of set books in which they chose to be examined. In Cambridge, the Mathematical Tripos by the 1850s offered a mass of papers and questions through which ordinary and advanced students took very different routes: 'Two men taking the tripos the same year could answer very different examinations'.[192] In an oral examination, the particular needs and abilities of an individual candidate might be brought out by the examiners—if they saw them, and chose to address them. In a written examination, the candidate was alone with the questions, but could (often) choose between them. In both cases, the examiner had the initiative, but the candidate could, in different ways, influence the outcome.

References

* My thanks to Gill Sutherland for inviting me to write the original version of this paper, and to the following for assistance of various kinds: Jacky Cox, Mark Curthoys, John Fauvel, Jonathan Harrison, Keith Hoskin, James Lawson, Elisabeth Leedham-Green, Richard Luckett, Alice Millea, David McKitterick, Robert McDowell, James Moore, Susan Parkes, Sheldon Rothblatt, Jonathan Smith, Keith Tribe, Malcolm Underwood, Graham Whitaker and Ben Wilbrink.

1. James Bowell, *Life of Samuel Johnson* (Oxford, 1927), ii. 212.
2. Robert J. Montgomery, *The Rise of Examinations as Administrative Devices* (London, 1965); John P. C. Roach, *Examinations 1850–1900* (Cambridge, 1971). For the backlash of criticism, see e.g. Roach, *Examinations*, 257–86.
3. Contemporary references to 'oral examination' are most likely to refer to the activities of dentists. Hence the necessary additional specification in the title of a study of dental education: H. A. Ryding and H. J. Murphy, 'Employing Oral Examinations (Viva Voce) in Assessing Dental Students' Clinical Reasoning Skills', *Journal of Dental Education* 63 (1999), 682–7.
4. H. D. Buchanan-Dunlop (ed.), *Records of the Royal Military Academy, 1741–1892* (Woolwich, 1892); Frederick G. Guggisberg, *The Shop. The Story of the RMA* (London, 1900); Trevor Hearl, 'Military examinations and the teaching of science', in Roy MacLeod (ed.), *Days of Judgement* (Driffield, 1982), 109–51. The annual public viva voce examinations at the East India Company's military academy, Addiscombe, were also carefully staged: there is a vivid description in H. M. Vibart, *Addiscombe, Its Heroes and Men of Note* (London, 1894), 231–4.
5. An order of precedence according to seniority and status of degrees status existed at Cambridge, and was used to determine, e.g. which member of a committee was to chair its meetings. This should be distinguished from the Ordo Senioritatis which from 1499 to 1747 listed the graduates of each year in (rough) order of ability, though the basis of assessment is unclear. See Victor Morgan, with Christopher Brooke, *A History of the University of Cambridge, Vol. II, 1546–1750* (Cambridge, 2004), 518. A similar system obtained at Oxford. The discussion of both by Samuel E. Morison is still useful: *Precedence at Harvard College in the Seventeenth Century* (Worcester, Mass., 1932).
6. Robert P. Edgcumbe (ed.), *The Works of A. C. Hilton together with his Life and Letters* (Cambridge, 1905), 59.
7. Benjamin H. Hall, *College Words and Customs* (Cambridge, Mass., 1856), 355–6; Morris Marples, *University Slang* (London, 1950), 83–4; Sheldon Rothblatt, *The Modern University and its Discontents* (Cambridge, 1997), 190–200; Christopher A. Stray, 'Introduction', *Slang in Nineteenth-Century England* (5 vols, Bristol, 2002), i. v–xviii.
8. Both of Hilton's poems were reprinted in Edward E. Kellett (ed.), *A Book of Cambridge Verse* (Cambridge, 1911), 283–8. 'The Heathen Pass-ee' (1872) is modelled on Bret Harte's 'The Heathen Chinee' (1871).
9. For a brief discussion of the proportions of honours and pass students at Cambridge through the nineteenth century, see Christopher A. Stray, 'Renegotiating Classics: the politics of curricular reform in late-Victorian Cambridge', *Echos du Monde Classique/Classical Views* 42 (ns 7) 3, 449–70, at 458 n. 23. The

percentage of non-honours students had probably sunk below fifty per cent by the early twentieth century. When Sydney Roberts reached Pembroke College in 1907, 'of the eighty-odd freshmen of my year just under half were Pass men'. Sydney C. Roberts, *Adventures with Authors* (Cambridge, 1966), 3.

10. Many such schemes were promoted by their (self-proclaimed) inventors in the 19th century. For a brief survey, see A. E. Middleton, *All about Mnemonics* (London, 1885), 23–48.

11. The 'Paley Card' is mentioned in George O. Trevelyan's *Horace at the University of Athens* (1861), reprinted in his *Interludes in Verse and Prose* (London, 1905), 23. The full title of Paley's work was *Natural Theology, or Evidences of the Existence and Attributes of the Deity, Collected from the Appearances of Nature.*

12. 'Floor' = finish off: Cambridge slang for examination prowess. Tom Cribb (1781–1848), the champion boxer of England, had floored his opponents more literally.

13. For a study of the informal negotiation of marks by staff and students, see Howard S. Becker, Blanche Geer, Everett C. Hughes, *Making the Grade: The Academic Side of College Life* (New York, 1968).

14. Blue paper was supplied to discourage cheating, the colour distinguishing it from any written-on sheets a candidate might import into an examination. (Such paper characteristically has white flecks showing through the blue dye.) When the Society of Arts started its examinations in 1856, it supplied answer sheets with its name printed at the top, 'so as to leave space for the answer to be written on the same sheet'—in reality, surely, to prevent cheating. Frank Foden, *The Examiner. James Booth and the Origins of Common Examinations* (Leeds, 1989), 138.

15. In Trinity College, the last viva voce exam was held in 1861. It is perhaps not coincidental that in the same year the college received new statutes, following the report of the Royal Commission of 1850.

16. Damian R. Leader, *A History of the University of Cambridge, Vol. I: the University to 1546* (Cambridge, 1988), 95–107. An interesting example of a student *not* coping, which also reminds us of the role of written texts in oral examination, is that of Samuel Parr, who in 1781 kept two acts at Cambridge for the degree of LLD. His biographer reported that 'These were fine compositions but not having a complete command over his papers, he bungled in referring to them, and thus embarrassed the disputations'. *The Works of Samuel Parr, with Memoirs of his Life and Writings, and a Selection from his Correspondence*, ed. John Johnstone (8 vols, London, 1828), i. 173. Speaking and writing might also be combined by examiners: J. B. Bury, when examining women viva voce in Oxford, wrote impromptu descriptions of the candidates on the spot. (Aptly, he wrote in Sapphic metre. It was perhaps also apt that a Cambridge man imported writing into an Oxford oral examination.) N. H. Baynes, *A Bibliography of the Works of J. B. Bury . . . with a Memoir* (Cambridge, 1929), 51.

17. See Christopher Wordsworth, *Scholae Academicae* (Cambridge, 1877), 33–42; William W. Rouse Ball, *History of the Study of Mathematics at Cambridge* (Cambridge, 1889), 174–8; Ben R. Schneider, *Wordsworth's Cambridge Education* (Cambridge, 1957) 31–2.

18. Henry Latham, *The Action of Examinations* (Cambridge, 1877), 98.

19. Andrew Warwick, 'A mathematical world on paper: written examinations in early nineteenth-century Cambridge', *Studies in the History and Philosophy of Modern Physics* 29B.3 (1998), 295–320, at 300–1; idem, *Masters of Theory: Cambridge and the Rise of Mathematical Physics* (Chicago, 2003), 118–29. Warwick's book, which I discuss in my Conclusion, is an impressive analysis of the growth of an institutionally-specific pedagogical system which led to a distinctive intellectual style in the nineteenth and early twentieth centuries.

20. William T. Costello, *The Scholastic Curriculum at Early Seventeenth-Century Cambridge* (Cambridge Mass., 1958), 15.

21. Morgan, *History*, 129. The absence of any reference to Costello's *Scholastic Curriculum* in this volume is surprising.

22. *College Life in the Time of James I as Illustrated by an Unpublished Diary of Sir Symonds D'Ewes Bt MP* (London, 1851), 104–5.

23. For a remarkable example, a disputation held in 1614 before James I in which the king himself intervened, see Costello, *Scholastic Curriculum*, 24–6.

24. Jan Morris, *The Oxford Book of Oxford* (Oxford, 1978), 128.

25. The 1713 speech was afterwards published. A speech published in 1733 was not in fact delivered. For these and further details, see Vivien H. H. Green, 'The University and social life', in Lucy S. Sutherland and Leslie G. Mitchell (eds), *Eighteenth-Century Oxford* (*The History of the University of Oxford, Vol. V*, Oxford, 1986), 351–2; and in general, Kristine Haugen, 'Imagined Universities: Public Insult and the Terrae filius in Early Modern Oxford', *History of Universities* 16 (2001), 1–31.

26. A comprehensive account of the Act and Tripos Verses by Dr John Hall is to be published by the Cambridge Bibliographical Society.

27. E.g. the 'Address to Liberty on the fall of the Bastille, July 14, 1789'. For this and other eighteenth-century verses see Christopher Wordsworth, *University Life in the Eighteenth Century* (Cambridge, 1874), 231–44.

28. At St John's College they were last delivered, from written texts, in the 1850s: H. F. Jones, *Samuel Butler. A Memoir* (London, 1920), i. 46–7.

29. Henry Gunning, *Reminiscences of Cambridge* (Cambridge, 1855), i. 74.

30. For examples see William W. R. Ball, *History of the Study of Mathematics at Cambridge* (Cambridge, 1889), 166–9. For earlier disputations, see Costello, *Scholastic Curriculum*, 14–31.

31. Richard Watson, *Anecdotes of Bishop Watson* (2 vols, 2nd edn, London, 1818), 30.

32. Keith Hoskin, 'The examination, disciplinary power and rational schooling', *History of Education* 8 (1979), 135–46, at 139–40.

33. *Cambridge Praelections 1906* (Cambridge, 1906).

34. For a detailed discussion, see Christopher A. Stray, 'Flying at dusk: the 1906 Praelections', in idem (ed.), *The Owl of Minerva: the Cambridge Praelections of 1906* (*Proceedings of the Cambridge Philological Society*, supplementary vol. 28, Cambridge, 2005).

35. For a blow-by-blow account of a 2001 viva voce examination by the examinee, see http://urchin.earth.li/~sax/biochem/vivas/niall.html.

36. The arrival of female students after 1870 led to debate on the proprieties of assessment. Most of this is not germane here, but it is worth mentioning that the pugnacious William Ridgeway complained in 1920 that good-looking female students had an unfair advantage in oral examinations. He even claimed

that a successful female one year had married one of her examiners the next year: *Cambridge University Reporter*, 28 October 1920, 197–8.

37. Ball, *History*, 193.

38. See, for example, Hoskin, 'The examination'; John Gascoigne. 'Mathematics and meritocracy: the emergence of the Cambridge mathematical tripos', *Social Studies of Science* 14 (1984), 547–84; idem, *Cambridge in the Age of the Enlightenment: Science, Religion and Politics from the Restoration to the French Revolution* (Cambridge, 1989); Warwick, *Masters of Theory*.

39. James H. Monk, *Life of Richard Bentley* (2nd edn, 1833), i. 159–60; cf. Ball, *History*, 81.

40. John Byrom, *The Private Journal and Literary Remains* (Manchester, 1854–5), 5–6; quoted by Wordsworth, *Scholae Academicae*, 347.

41. Richard Cumberland, *Memoirs of Richard Cumberland* (London, 1806), 106–110, quoted by Wordsworth, *Scholae Academicae*, 344–6. Cumberland was first quizzed on 'the ancient empires of the world', then given a sheet of Greek written by his examiner, and told to turn it into Latin or English.

42. It is worth noting that only two of the eight senior fellows actually took part in Byrom's examination.

43. Squire's complaint is in Trinity College Library, B.17.15/18.

44. William W. R. Ball, *Notes on the History of Trinity College Cambridge* (London, 1899), 114.

45. Ibid, 99. Themes seem always to have been written compositions: see Foster Watson, *The English Grammar Schools to 1660* (Cambridge, 1908), 442–37; Ian Michael, *The Teaching of English from the Sixteenth Century to 1870* (Cambridge, 1987), 309–16. Rouse Ball gives no source; there is no mention of the matter in his *Cambridge Papers* (Cambridge, 1918), later enlarged and revised as *Cambridge Notes* (Cambridge, 1921).

46. Rouse Ball gives no source for this quotation, nor have I been able to find anything relevant in the Trinity College or Cambridge University archives. He explains in his preface that his book does not pretend to be a scholarly account, for which the reader will soon be able to turn to his colleague A. H. T. Boughey's history of the college. This was never published; the surviving text (Trinity College Library, O.6, 2a–c, 3) contains no relevant information.

47. Caput XII (De sociorum electione): 'quarto in scribendo schemate aliquo, et in carminibus componendis'.

48. To 'make theme' seems always to refer to the writing of a text, though the text could subsequently be spoken 'without book' and the writer quizzed on it (Watson, *English Grammar Schools*, 422–37). In the present case, the excusing of the candidates for theme-making makes it clear that this was a private activity, and so presumably involved writing rather than speaking.

49. Richard Bentley, *The Present State of Trinity College* (London, 1710), 10, 14.

50. See the copy of the College Statutes owned by Christopher Wordsworth, Master 1820–41 (Trinity College Library, N.8.106), which indicate that the statute was 'read only as far as iudicaverint'. The 1560 statutes, amended in 1844, were replaced only in 1861.

51. The function of the Ordo was to facilitate decisions on succession to university posts; in this sense, it can be compared with the seniority lists at the Royal Military Academy.

52. Ball, *History*, 188 n. 2; *The works, theological, medical, political, and miscellaneous, of John Jebb*, ed. John Disney (3 vols, London, 1787), ii. 290; *The Correspondence of Horace Walpole*, ed. Wilmarth S. Lewis, (vols 13–14, New Haven, 1948), 78.

53. Christopher A. Stray, *Classics Transformed: Schools, Universities, and Society in England, 1830–1960* (Oxford, 1998), 21 (where the reference to J. A. W. Gunn's *Beyond Liberty and Property* should be to page 29).

54. In this period, several senior officers of the university had the right to nominate 'honorary senior optimes' for the list. The custom died out only toward the end of the eighteenth century.

55. Gascoigne, 'Mathematics and meritocracy', 574.

56. In the light of Watson's antagonism to St John's, it is interesting to note that as soon as William Powell became master of that college in 1765, he introduced college examinations. Powell may have seen the division into university-wide ability classes as an encroachment on the previous college-based system. (See below for Powell's antagonism to John Jebb's proposals for a university examination in the 1770s.)

57. Richard Watson, *Anecdotes of Bishop Watson* (2nd edn, London, 1818), i. 29–30.

58. Denys A. Winstanley, *Unreformed Cambridge* (Cambridge, 1935), 350 n. 25.

59. 'Optime' came from the moderators' closing words to participants in the acts, when choice of words indicated a rough grading: 'optime disputasti' = 'well disputed!', 'optime quidem . . .' = 'very well indeed'. 'Poll' came from the Greek hoi polloi, the many; though the poll men were in this case in a minority.

60. Peter Searby, in his *History of the University of Cambridge, Vol. III: 1750–1870* (Cambridge, 1997), 178 states that the number of groups was reduced from eight to six, but I believe the references in the sources to six groups are to the honours men: the eight groups minus the two of hoi polloi (see e.g. Winstanley, *Unreformed Cambridge*, 52. The account in the *Cambridge University Calendar* for 1802, xx–xxi, which is based on Jebb's 1772 description, refers to eight classes: six plus the hoi polloi. James M. F. Wright, in his *Alma Mater; or, Seven Years at the University of Cambridge, by a Trinity-Man* (London, 1827), ii. 74, has six classes for honours in 1819. Similarly G. B. Airy said in 1823 that the honours candidates were in six classes (Ball, *Cambridge Notes*, 293).

61. Viva voce examinations were retained in the faculties of Divinity, Law and Physic until the introduction of new statutes in 1858: Henry Latham, *The Action of Examinations* (Cambridge, 1877) 121. There is a useful appendix on the disputations of the period in Charles Wesley, *A Guide to Syllogism: or, a Manual of Logic; Comprehending an Account of the Manner of Disputation now Practised in the Schools at Cambridge; with Specimens of the Different Acts* (London, 1832), 97–133.

62. The grouping is named after the form of the published list; similarly the name of the examination itself, later called the Mathematical Tripos, was derived from the published list, known in the later eighteenth century as 'the Tripos': see Christopher Wordsworth, *Scholae Academicae* (Cambridge, 1877), 16–21.

63. Ball (*Cambridge Notes*, 170–1) has 'c. 1770', but this is clearly an approximation based on the date of Jebb's 1772 account.

64. These were also offered to classes 3–4 in 1800, and to classes 5–6 in 1818: Ball, *Cambridge Papers*, 272, 281, 291. They were known as 'window problems'.

Why carried to window seats? Perhaps because this was where individual candidates had previously been quizzed by MAs who chose to intervene in the examination. But in the middle of winter, before the days of gas lighting, perhaps the window seats were also the best places for inspecting printed papers.

65. They appear in the lists from 1753, though from 1773 at the foot of the list in a group. From 1797 the power was not exercised. The early University Calendars (publication began in 1796) did not print their names, which were restored to the historical record by Joseph R. Tanner's *Historical Register of the University of Cambridge* (Cambridge, 1917).

66. On this shift see Sheldon Rothblatt, 'The student sub-culture and the examination system', in Lawrence Stone (ed.), *The University in Society* (Princeton, 1975), i. 247–303; idem, *Tradition and Change in English Liberal Education* (London, 1976).

67. 'Except fairness': Henry Gunning, *Reminiscences of the University, Town and County of Cambridge since the Year 1780* (2nd edn, London, 1855), i. 85. Queens' and Emmanuel were both centres of Evangelicalism in Milner's time; he himself was a leading Evangelical.

68. Benjamin C. Raworth, *Cambridge University Calendar for the Year 1802* (Cambridge, 1802), xx.

69. Warwick (*Masters of Theory*, 124–5) argues that the insertion of the description in the Cambridge *Calendar* demonstrates the 'relative novelty yet increasing importance' of written exams at this point. It is more likely that it was provoked by the appearance of the very different Oxford examination.

70. In 1799 the Senior Moderator had issued a stern warning about the failure of students from some colleges to reach certain minimum standards (Wordsworth, *Scholae Academicae*, 56); this may have prompted the coinage of the term. (It may be relevant that in 1802, 1803 and 1804 the Wooden Spoon came from Clare College.)

71. *The Names in the Cambridge Triposes, from 1754 to 1807, Both Inclusive, Alphabetically Arranged. With the Prizes Obtained by Each Person, Affixed to their Names. Prefaced by a Short Letter, on the Comparative Merits of the Two Universities, Oxford and Cambridge* (Bath, 1808). The only copy known to me is in the British Library (732 b 16). His authorship is claimed in a manuscript annotation by 'F.W'.; presumably Francis Wrangham, who in 1824 published a similar honours list, *Sertum Cantabrigiense; or, the Cambridge Garland*. Newton's capacity for unbiased reflection is evidenced by the remarks with which he begins his diary for 1816–18, in which he describes himself—height, weight, baldness, proneness to flatulence, moral weaknesses and so on:, *The Diaries of Benjamin Newton, Rector of Wath, 1816–1818, ed.* C. P. Fendall and E. A. Crutchley (Cambridge, 1933), 1–3.

72. Newton, *Names*, vii–ix.

73. Denys A. Winstanley, *Unreformed Cambridge* (Cambridge, 1935), 327–8.

74. Thomas Baker, *History of the College of St. John the Evangelist, Cambridge* (Cambridge, 1869), ii. 1071; Winstanley, *Unreformed Cambridge*, 317. The first examinations took place in December 1765.

75. Disney, *Works of John Jebb*, i. 300. This diplomatic statement follows a declaration that Jebb's proposed reforms stemmed from his experience of the quarterly examinations at Trinity College Dublin: on which, see below.

76. Powell himself seems to have planned to subject noblemen and fellow-commoners to the examinations. Some of the college fellows, whose future careers may have been linked to patronage from noble families, demurred: Edward Miller, *Portrait of a College. A History of the College of St John the Evangelist, Cambridge* (Cambridge, 1961), 69. On two occasions the college examinations book records praise for students who sat the third-year examinations, even though their rank exempted them (St John's College archives, C 15 6.56, 69 [1798 and 1805].)

77. Letters of 13 January and 25 March 1830: *The Correspondence of Charles Darwin: Volume 1, 1821–36*, ed. Frederick Burkhardt and Sydney Smith (Cambridge, 1985), 98, 101.

78. The report of 29 October 1829 is in Cambridge University Archives, CUR 28.11.

79. C 15 6, 5: June 1772.

80. ibid, 49, June 1794.

81. Gunning, *Reminiscences*, i. 80.

82. William Tuckwell, *Reminiscences of Oxford* (London, 1900), 117.

83. St John's College, C 15 6, 89: December 1813.

84. Schneider, *Wordsworth's Cambridge Education*, 28. Schneider gives no source for this statement, but states elsewhere (ibid. 268, n. 31) that all unreferenced statements are drawn from the Examinations Book 1770–1833 (which I have quoted from above). None of them, however, contains any such information; I suspect that it was taken from Jebb's account of the Senate House examination, on which the text in the 1802 University Calendar is based.

85. Robert L. Ellis, MS diary, entry for 13 November 1843: Trinity College Library, Add. Ms. a.218.41. Quoted by permission of the Master and Fellows of Trinity College, Cambridge.

86. Keith Hoskin claimed that Butler introduced internal written examinations in the 1790s—hence presumably on his arrival in 1798 or soon afterwards (Keith Hoskin, 'Examinations and the schooling of science', in Roy MacLeod (ed.), *Days of Judgement* (Driffield, 1982), 224). The school archives, however, contain no evidence of such examinations before 1813. Hoskin's source was apparently Peter Wales, 'Samuel Butler of Shrewsbury School: some aspects of his headmastership, 1798–1836', M.Ed. thesis (Warwick, 1981); but I can find no evidence in it to support Hoskin's case.

87. Samuel Butler, *Life and Letters of Samuel Butler* (London, 1896), i. 9.

88. Thomas J. N. Hilken, *Engineering at Cambridge University, 1783–1965* (Cambridge, 1967), 40. In fact Farish was not a moderator in 1792; he was proctor that year and moderator in 1793. (His duties would have commenced after the Senate House Examination of 1792, but led up to and included the Examination of 1793.)

89. Hoskin, 'The examination', 144.

90. Hoskin was followed by Gascoigne, 'Mathematics and meritocracy', 552; but in his subsequent book, *Cambridge in the Age of the Enlightenment* (Cambridge, 1989), at 205, Gascoigne relied instead on Schneider's *Wordsworth's Cambridge education*, 35. Schneider, however, writing of the late 1780s, claims only that on the first day of the examination 'the moderators strove . . . to discover a general gradation in each class'. Hoskin's account was later taken over by Madaus,

who referred to 'the invention of the quantitative mark by William Farish in 1790, a key development in testing's history' (George F. Madaus, review of F. Allan Hanson, *Testing Testing: Social Consequences of the Examined Life*, in *American Journal of Education* 102 (1994), 222–34, at 230).

91. Anon. [Obituary of William Farish], *Christian Observer* (1837), 611–13, 674–7, 737–41, at 675. A copy of the obituary, together with other sources on Farish, is held in the Old Library, Magdalene College, Cambridge, M 5.29.

92. Ball, *History*, 213.

93. [J. M. F. Wright], *Alma Mater, or, Seven Years at the University of Cambridge* (London, 1827), i. 3.

94. Robert K. Webb, 'William Farish', *Magdalene College Magazine* (1955), 29.

95. *Oxford University Commission* (1852), 63: Hampden was an examiner in 1829, 1831 and 1832.

96. On Jebb, see Anthony Page, *John Jebb and the Enlightenment Origins of British Radicalism* (Westport, 2003).

97. As was James Lambert, one of the leaders of the movement for rigorous fellow-ship examinations at Trinity College in the 1780s: see Jonathan Smith, 'Trinity College annual examinations in the nineteenth century', in idem and Christopher A. Stray (eds.), *Teaching and Learning in 19th-Century Cambridge* (Woodbridge, 2001), 125–6.

98. 'These commodious sets of syllogisms are call'd strings and descend from undergraduate to undergraduate, so that, when any candidate for a degree is to exercise his talent in argumentation, he has nothing else to do but to enquire amongst his friends for a string upon such or such a question, and to get it by heart, or read it over in his cap'. Thomas Amherst, *Terrae filius* no. 20 (Oxford, 1721), 104. For Oxford, see the chapters by Lucy Sutherland and John Yolton in Lucy S. Sutherland and Leslie G. Mitchell (eds.), *Eighteenth-Century Oxford* (*The History of the University of Oxford, Vol. V*, Oxford, 1986); for Cambridge, the early nineteenth-century slang dictionary *Gradus ad Cantabrigiam* (London, 1803), 13 (the book is anonymous, but was probably written by William Paley jr.); Wordsworth, *Scholae Academicae*, 36 n 2. For a surviving set of 'argu-ments', see ibid 368–74; no 'strings' seem to be extant. 'Strings' heads the list of 'ingenious monkish institutions' that Newton reported as 'falling in to decay' at Oxford; the others are 'juraments, walks in the pig-market, wall-lectures and chopping-logic' (Newton, 'Letter', xxvi).

99. William Whewell to George Morland, 3 January 1815: Isaac Todhunter, *William Whewell DD* (2 vols, London, 1876), i. 5.

100. Whewell to Morland, 3 October 1819: Todhunter, *Whewell*, ii. 35.

101. For these disputations, see Ball, *History*, 173–82. Shilleto's act is described on pp. 181–2; Wordsworth (*Scholae Academicae*, 42) gives a different and more detailed account. Though both must have been aware of the joke, neither explains it. 'Caesio' is extremely rare (one would expect 'caedes'); Shilleto may have chosen it deliberately to flummox his opponent and to impress the moderator.

102. Edward G. Sandford, *Memoirs of Archbishop Temple by Seven Friends*, 2 vols (London, 1906), ii. 433. Temple later followed Tait as headmaster of Rugby and then as Archbishop of Canterbury.

103. Robert J. Strutt, *John William Strutt, Third Baron Rayleigh* (London, 1924), 31.
104. Not always surreptitious. For an account of widespread copying and of invigilatorial connivance, see [Thomas Joyce], 'College life at Cambridge', *Westminster Review* 25 (1841), 456–81, at 462.
105. Charles A. Bristed, *Five Years in an English University* (2nd edn, New York, 1852), 71. Bristed was at Trinity College, Cambridge, from 1840 to 1845. Thomas Joyce, who matriculated there in 1836, remembered the annual college examination: 'the bustle at first in the hall, with four hundred men writing and joking at once': 'College life', 470.
106. 'W', 'Vigilans invigilavi', *Cambridge Review* 31 (1909–10), 469–70.
107. Quoted in part and without date by Todhunter, *Whewell*, i. 161. The original is in Trinity College Library, Add. Ms. c 52 105. It need hardly be said that both Whewell and his close friend Jones were Cambridge men.
108. Two grades of examinations were to be held, the severer grade (honours) examination being held in the Easter Term. The first examinations were held on 4 and 15 December 1801, the first honours examination on 2, 7 and 9 April 1802. Oxford University Archives, SP59.
109. Richard Jones to William Whewell, 16 November 1845. William R. Ward, *Victorian Oxford* (London, 1965), 14; cf. George V. Cox, *Recollections of Oxford* (London, 1869), 49; Rothblatt, 'Student sub-culture', 295.
110. Falconer Madan claimed that 'the first Oxford written examination took place in 1802': *Oxford Outside the Guide-Books* (Oxford, 1923), 47. In fact the earliest reference to written examination comes in the 1807 examination statute; it allows written work to be used to supplement viva voce testing.
111. [Augustus De Morgan], 'State of the mathematical and physical sciences at the University of Oxford', *Quarterly Journal of Education* 4 (1832), 191–208.
112. Mark C. Curthoys, 'The examination system', in Brock and Curthoys, *Nineteenth Century Part 2*, 346.
113. J. M. F. Wright's reference (see note 92) to 'printed papers' is puzzling, since his book was published early in 1827 and the Grace to use printed papers did not pass the Senate until November of that year. But Wright had good contacts in Cambridge, and may have been told the decision was certain to be taken.
114. Curthoys, 'Examination system', 247.
115. ibid, 347–8.
116. Gascoigne, 'Mathematics and meritocracy', 573–7. Cf. Charles Bristed's comment on his Trinity College examinations, in the 1840s, that 'The lecturer stands, and the lectured sit, *even while construing* (my italics): Bristed, *Five years*, 18. Bristed was writing for American readers, and the implied contrast may have been with his own previous student experience at Yale. According to the *OED*, s.v. *sit* (v), in Cambridge one sits, in Oxford one stands, for a degree.
117. Brock and Curthoys, *Nineteenth Century Part 1*, 10–11.
118. Curthoys, 'Examination system', 349.
119. Ibid, 358.
120. Arthur D. Godley, 'In memoriam examinatoris cuiusdam', *Oxford Magazine*, 23 January 1907; reprinted in Charles L. Graves and Charles R. L. Fletcher (eds.), *Fifty Poems by A. D. Godley* (Oxford, 1927). Echoing a common examination rubric, the examiner's tombstone is '*on one side only* graven'.

121. Cf. Latham, *Action of Examination*, 510.
122. See Christopher A. Stray, 'Thomas Saunders Evans (1816–89)', in Robert B. Todd (ed.), *Dictionary of British Classicists* (Bristol, 2004), ii. 304–5.
123. Philip Hartog and Edmund C. Rhodes, *The Marks of Examiners* (London, 1936), 154.
124. Curthoys, 'Examination system', 344–5.
125. Trinity College Library, Banks, Challis and Hodson papers: R 2 82.45. It is clear that the grades are thus arranged, as E is mostly used for the lowest group (the poll). Rouse Ball, curiously, lists them as A, E, a, e. Embarrassingly enough for a mathematician, he also adds 5 + 3 + 1 to make 8. See Ball, *History* 168–72; his errors were pointed out by William Chawner, 'The thesis in the disputation of the senior sophs, 1770–1838', in *Fasciculus Ioanni Willis Clark Dicatus* (Cambridge, 1910), 280–2. A similar marking scheme (eleven grades, from A+ to e–) is used in the moderators' book for 1763–4, which indexes all candidates and lists the disputation theses in full: Trinity College Library, R.9.44.
126. *Cambridge University Commission* (1852), i. 272.
127. Trinity College Library, R 2 80.14,20; 81.61.
128. Edward E. Kellett, *A Book of Cambridge Verse* (1911), 287. C and D were fail grades.
129. *Oxford University Commission* (1852), 60–1.
130. *Oxford University Commission* (1852), 63.
131. *Cambridge University Commission* (London, 1852), evidence 239–40. The analytical school is surveyed by Ball, *History*, 117–37; the rise and implications of analysis in Cambridge are dealt with by Warwick, *Masters of Theory*, 66–8.
132. *Cambridge University Commission* (1853), evidence 251.
133. Cf. Whewell's *Of a Liberal Education, with Special Reference to the University of Cambridge* (Cambridge, 1845).
134. In Oxford this was strongly reinforced by the concern to avoid humiliating poor candidates; hence Napleton, who proposed examination reforms there in the early 1770s, suggested that variable standards should be used for students of different abilities. John Napleton, *Considerations on the Public Exercises for the First and Second Degrees in the University of Oxford* (Oxford, 1773), 29.
135. Report (1853), Cambridge University Archives, CUR 28.6.1/18. 10–11. Later reports on the subject are at CUR 28.6.1/28, 30, 31, the last being the 1860 report.
136. *Oxford University Commission* (1852), report 63.
137. *Cambridge University Commission* (1852), evidence 259–60.
138. The basic published source is R. B. MacDowell and R. K. Webb, *Trinity College Dublin 1592–1952: An Academic History* (Cambridge, 1982); 113–29 deal with students and examinations *c*.1830. The nickname 'the silent sister' seems to have been current during the first third of the nineteenth century—the stagnant period preceding Bartholomew Lloyd's reforming Provostship of 1831–7. The phrase appears in an anonymous review of the first published Calendar (1833): *Dublin University Magazine* 1 (1833), 101–10, at 106; cf. Anon., 'The University of Dublin', *Quarterly Journal of Education* 6 (1833), 212. See also W. M. Dixon, *Trinity College, Dublin* (London, 1902), 179, quoting J. P. Mahaffy, 'Trinity College, Dublin', *Macmillan's Magazine* 20 (September 1869), 436–72.

139. Trinity College, Cambridge introduced an informal entrance test in the early nineteenth century. The TCD test was evidently not very rigorous, since the failure rate was between two and three per cent.

140. There were four terms in each academic year; changed to three terms in 1834 by one of Lloyd's reforms.

141. *A Report of the Examination for Fellowships in the University of Dublin* (London and Dublin, 1824). Copies in TCD Library and in Cambridge University Library (Bradshaw Collection). This pamphlet is not referred to by McDowell and Webb, *Trinity College Dublin.*

142. Ibid, ix–x.

143. Richard MacDonnell, *A Letter to Dr Phipps . . . Concerning the Undergraduate Examinations of the University of Dublin* (Dublin, 1828). Copies in Haliday Collection, Royal Irish Academy; Bradshaw Collection, Cambridge University Library. MacDonnell became provost of TCD in 1852.

144. MacDonnell, *Letter*, 8–9. The pamphlet is irregularly paginated: 1–10, 9–27.

145. Ibid, 9 (i.e. the first page 9).

146. A detailed account of the termly classical examinations under the new three-term system was published by John M'Caul: *Remarks on the Course of Classical Study, Pursued in the University of Dublin* (Dublin, 1834), 2–6. Oral and written examination ran in parallel: during a two-hour period in which all candidates had to write a Latin prose, for example, they would be called out one by one to read out aloud passages from their set texts, and quizzed on them.

147. 'The University of Dublin', *Quarterly Journal of Education* 6 (1833), 235.

148. McDowell and Webb, *Trinity College*, 231–2. The abolition of Latin probably explains the wobbling about undergraduate examinations detectable in later Calendars; e.g. 'oral examination shall be retained . . . Latin shall not necessarily be used in any part of the examination'. (*Calendar* 1859, 45).

149. Johnson's remark is quoted above as an epigraph to this article.

150. Arthur V. Judges, 'The evolution of examinations', in James A. Lauwerys and David G. Scanlon (eds), *Examinations* (*World Year Book of Education 1969*) (London, 1969), 23.

151. Cf. Rothblatt, 'Student sub-culture', 280f.

152. See note 1 above.

153. Sheldon Rothblatt, *The Revolution of the Dons. Cambridge and Society in Victorian England* (London, 1968); id., 'Student sub-culture'; id., *Tradition and Change in English Liberal Education* (London, 1976).

154. Hoskin, 'The examination'; id., 'Examinations'.

155. Rothblatt, 'Student sub-culture'; Hoskin, 'The examination', 145. The same might be said of the discussion in Rothblatt, *Tradition and Change*, 119ff.

156. See Jonathan Smith, 'Trinity College annual examinations in the nineteenth century', in id. and Christopher A. Stray (eds), *Teaching and Learning in 19th-Century Cambridge* (Woodbridge, 2001), 122–38; Malcolm G. Underwood, 'The revolution in college teaching: St John's College, 1850–1926', ibid., 107–21.

157. Chicago, 2003. A review appears elsewhere in this issue.

158. I hope to provide a parallel analysis of Cambridge classics in a forthcoming account of the Classic Tripos in the century after its foundation in 1822.

159. Cf. Rothblatt, 'Student sub-culture', 293–4.

160. Cf. the phenomenon of the 'Greek play bishop', appointed for scholarship rather than for social connections. See Michael G. Brock, 'The Oxford of Peel and Gladstone, 1800–1833', in Brock and Curthoys, *Nineteenth Century Part 1*, 15; Stray, *Classics Transformed*, 39, 41, 61.

161. Examiners were appointed by the university senate, which could overrule them; but the rules as they applied to particular situations were far from clear. This confusion is apparent in the controversy over the case of R. P. N. Downing, accused of cheating in 1882: Cambridge University Archives, Vc Ct I 22.

162. Rothblatt's emphasis on the role of Georgian polite sociability is relevant here, although the evidential linkage with specific institutional changes in Oxford is at times lacking. Rothblatt, 'Student sub-culture'; id., *Tradition and Change*.

163. Rothblatt, *Revolution*, 231–5; Christopher A. Stray, 'Curriculum and style in the collegiate university: classics in nineteenth-century Oxbridge', *History of Universities* 16.2 (2001), 183–218. The new University of London followed Cambridge (written) practices rather than those of Oxford: Montgomery, *Examinations*, 58.

164. John Serjeaunt, *Annals of Westminster School* (London, 1898), 162–4, 259. A similar system had obtained at Merchant Taylors' School, but the oral element had disappeared by 1820: F. W. M. Draper, *Four Centuries of Merchant Taylors' school 1561–1961* (London, 1962), 123–4.

165. The point was made for the 1820s by Rothblatt, 'Student sub-culture', 294.

166. Details of changing student numbers in both places and in both periods can be found in Michael G. Brock, 'The careers of Oxford men', in Brock and Curthoys, *Nineteenth Century Part 1*, 477–509, at 481.

167. Compare the development of 'classes', or at least the division of student populations into smaller groups, in the schools of the Brethren of the Common Life in the late 14th century. See David Hamilton, *Towards a Theory of Schooling* (London, 1989), 41–2; Ben Wilbrink, 'Assessment in historical perspective', *Studies in Educational Evaluation* 23 (1997), 31–48.

168. Montgomery, *Examinations*, 58.

169. Mary L. Smallwood, *An Historical Study of Examinations and Grading Systems in Early American Universities* (Cambridge Mass., 1935), 15. Only five institutions are covered: Harvard, Yale, the College of William and Mary, Mount Holyoke, and the University of Michigan.

170. 'There are two public and general examinations in the year . . . These are wholly written, except in the schools of languages, in which they are partly oral . . . This plan of testing and actual and comparative proficiency of the students was introduced into the university of Virginia by Professors Long and Key, according to the model of the Cambridge system'. Anon., 'Education in Virginia', *Quarterly Journal of Education* 4 (1832), 64.

171. Foden, *The Examiner*, 146–7.

172. Keith Tribe, 'Professors Malthus and Jones: Political Economy at the East India College 1806–1858', *European Journal for the History of Economic Thought* 2 (1995), 327–54. ('Jones' was Richard Jones, whose opinion of Oxford examinations is quoted above).

173. David Murray, *Memories of the Old College of Glasgow* (Glasgow, 1927), 231, 235–6. Written examinations had been introduced at Aberdeen in 1833, when the custom of awarding prizes according to the votes of class members was

discontinued: Neil M. Maclean, *Life at a Northern University*, ed. W. Keith Leask (Aberdeen, 1906), 363.

174. Henry J. Roby, *Reminiscences of My Life and Work, For My Family Only* (Cambridge, *c.*1913), 42. Copy in St John's College Library, Cambridge. 'Personal equations' were the differences between reports of single astronomical phenomena by different observers. (This led to the invention of the 'idiometer', a device for discounting such differences.) See Simon Schaffer, 'Astronomers Mark Time: Discipline and the Personal Equation', *Science in Context*, 2 (1988), 115–145.

175. *Cambridge University Commission* (London, 1852), evidence, 244.

176. Ibid, 244.

177. Stray, 'Curriculum and style in the collegiate university'.

178. *Pamphlets Relating to the University of London*, Vol. III, item 3, pp. 2–5. The only copy known to me is in the University of London Library; class-mark JSED/BP4. Lubbock was at the time Vice-Chancellor of the University; Burlington was its Chancellor.

179. See Tim Alborn's article on Lubbock in the *Oxford Dictionary of Biography* (2004), and his 'Public science, private finance: the uneasy advancement of J. W. Lubbock', in *Science and British Culture in the 1830s* (Stanford in the Vale, 1994), 5–14.

180. Not all viva voce examinations promoted 'readiness'. A member of R. C. Jebb's Greek class at Glasgow in the 1870s commented that Jebb 'examined his class in rotation throughout the session', and pointed out 'the defect involved by the virtual notice given to the men of the days on which it would be inexpedient to risk non-preparation'. A. M., 'Our professors: Mr Jebb', *Glasgow University Magazine* 2.3 (8 January 1880), 1–2.

181. Italics in original. Lubbock is referring to alphabetic listing within classes, as at Oxford. Compare William Whewell's summary of the contrast between oral and written examinations: the former measures quality and competency, while written papers produce 'classification'. *Cambridge University Commission* (1852), evidence, 251. Whewell was of course writing from within a Cambridge vocabulary, but in favour of an Oxonian emphasis and against the trend in his own university.

182. See e.g. Gillian R. Sutherland, 'Assessment, some historical perspectives', in Harvey Goldstein and Toby Lewis, *Assessment: Problems, Developments and Statistical Issues* (Hoboken NJ, 1996), 9–20.

183. Two very different discussions are David Potter, *Debating in the Colonial Chartered Colleges. An Historical Survey, 1642 to 1900* (New York, 1944), and Françoise Waquet, 'Parler. La disparition historiographique de la parole magistrale', *Actes de la Recherche en Sciences Sociales* 135 (December 2000), 39–47.

184. See for example Keith W. Hoskin and Richard H. Macve, 'Accounting and the examination: a genealogy of disciplinary power', *Accounting, Organizations and Society* 11 (1986), 105–36.

185. By the 1940s, it was simply impossible for C. S. Lewis to understand how an examiner could test a pupil who was personally known to him: 'The Parthenon and the Optative', in *On Stories, and other Essays on Literature* (London, 1947), 111.

186. Two Cambridge examples: George William Lyttelton, second Baron Lyttelton, Senior Classic in 1838, and John William Strutt, third Baron Rayleigh, Senior Wrangler in 1865.

187. Since the male and female list had common categories (classes), it became evident when women scored higher than men, as in the case of Agnata Ramsay in Classics (1887) and Philippa Fawcett in mathematics (1890). In the latter year a man became Senior Wrangler (top of the first class), but Fawcett was publicly announced as being 'above the Senior Wrangler'.

188. Peter Searby, *History of the University of Cambridge, Vol. III: 1750–1870* (Cambridge, 1997), 163–6; Page, *John Jebb*, 129–50.

189. Vivian H. H. Green, 'Reformers and reform in the University', in Lucy S. Sutherland and Leslie G. Mitchell (eds.), *Eighteenth-Century Oxford* (*The History of the University of Oxford, Vol. V*, Oxford, 1986), 615–18.

190. Mark C. Curthoys and Janet Howarth, 'Origins and destinations: the social mobility of Oxford men and women', in Brock and Curthoys, *Nineteenth Century Part 2*, 571–95, at 586. For Cambridge, still worth consulting is Rothblatt, *Revolution of the Dons*, 29–93.

191. Henry Philpott, *Cambridge University Commission* (1852), evidence, 259–60.

192. David B. Wilson, 'Experimentalists among the mathematicians: Physics in the Cambridge Natural Sciences Tripos, 1851–1900', *Historical Studies in the Physical Sciences* 12 (1982), 325–71, at 337.

85

CURRICULUM AND STYLE IN THE COLLEGIATE UNIVERSITY

Classics in nineteenth-century Oxbridge[1]

Christopher Stray

Source: *History of Universities* XVI(2) (2000): 183–218.

The aim of this paper is to compare two institutions which are in many ways similar but in others strikingly different: nineteenth-century Oxford and Cambridge. It focuses on the content, organization, and status of their classical curricula, and explores the links between these and the social and intellectual styles characteristic of the two universities. These styles are identified both in the comparisons made within the universities, and in the fictional accounts which transmitted them in stereotyped form to a wider public. Such a comparison has the advantage of highlighting the extent to which transmitted knowledge is shaped by specific institutional contexts: academic politics, organizational structures, ideological traditions, and patterns of teaching and learning. In looking at Oxford and Cambridge from this point of view, we need to remember that in the collegiate university a layer of activity—pedagogical and political—has to be allowed for which is absent in most other such institutions. The Oxford battles between the advocates of college-based tutorials and those of a research-oriented professoriate—i.e., between the followers of Benjamin Jowett and Mark Pattison—are well known. In the nineteenth century both universities had professors, but these were not the powerful founders and controllers of seminars, the patrons of pupils who followed their style and their commands which one finds in Germany in this period.[2] In the first half of the century, indeed, many Oxbridge professors did not lecture, and some did not even reside. The university was beginning to take back the original authority which had been usurped by the colleges several centuries before, but the process was by no means complete.[3]

The recognition of 'Oxbridge' as a single institutional world was cemented by the coining of the term by Thackeray in 1849 in his novel *Pendennis*.[4] In a sense the conflated title was timely, since Lord John Russell's government had just appointed a pair of Royal Commissions to investigate the 'state, discipline, studies and revenues' of the two universities. This intervention came as the climax of a long series of intermittent attacks on Oxford and Cambridge, beginning with articles in the *Edinburgh Review* in 1809. The charges were that they were socially and religiously exclusive, had narrow curricula, and were not even very good at what they did teach. As a result of the two Commissions' reports, new honours courses were introduced and old ones reformed, and some religious restrictions were relaxed. The 1850s marked, in fact, the beginning of the period in which the state first intervened seriously in modern times in English education at all levels; Oxford and Cambridge in their present form were shaped by these Commissions and those which followed in the 1870s and the 1920s.[5] In general this process has had a homogenizing effect; yet differences in the extent and nature of state intervention also led to continuing differences in their internal structure, and especially in the relations between colleges and university. Through the process of change initiated by the three Royal Commissions between 1850 and 1925, the Oxford colleges retained more independence than their counterparts in Cambridge, which thus became a more centralized institution than its sibling. It also needs to be pointed out that the 'nationalization' of the ancient universities, while promoting convergence in curriculum and organization, *ipso facto* provoked ideological celebrations of difference. This was surely a potent factor in the publication of Oxford and Cambridge college histories at the end of the nineteenth century.[6]

In the early nineteenth century, other differences were recognizable, most of them the products of the separate routes each university had taken as it developed from its medieval beginnings. After the unsettling of the scholastic curriculum by the impact of the scientific revolution, Cambridge took up the study of mathematics and Lockean epistemology, while Oxford clung to the logic and ethics of Aristotle.[7] The role of mathematics at Cambridge became increasingly important in the eighteenth century as Newtonian natural theology was adopted as a bulwark of the 'holy alliance' between science and Anglicanism.[8] The strength of latitudinarianism promoted a wider range of theological debate than was found in Oxford.[9] Political differences between the two places confirmed those in religion. After the accession of George III in 1760, Whig Cambridge found its relatively favoured position vis-à-vis the throne eroded, as the threat of Jacobitism faded, to be replaced by that of Jacobinism. The threats to the social order posed by Wilkes's followers, by the American rebels, and finally by the French Revolution made liberalism suspect and prompted a move to the right.[10]

Yet if this promoted a convergence with Tory Anglican Oxford, the timing of curricular reform in the two universities led to continuing differences between them. The dominance of mathematics in Cambridge was established by the 1750s, and changes later in the century simply increased the pressure and intensity of the examination system. The campaigns of John Jebb to widen the curriculum in the 1770s foundered partly on the revelation of his Unitarianism. Within a less contested climate of institutional debate, John Napleton's contemporary proposals for reform at Oxford were less controversial.[11] Oxford reform, however, was meditated and realized at the turn of the century, at the height of conservative fears of secularism and radicalism. The examination statute of 1800 was in large part aimed at containment and control.[12] This was a time when the conservative Anglican establishment was nervous at the prospect of radical intellectual and political activity, and throughout Europe there were fears of the consequences of an overproduction of educated young men. Hence the remark of Sydney Smith in the *Edinburgh Review* article of 1809 which opened that journal's campaign against Oxford. Smith wrote of the Oxford dons that

> To preserve the principles of their pupils they confine them to the safe and elegant imbecilities of classical learning. A genuine Oxford tutor would shudder to hear his young men disputing upon moral and political truth, forming and pulling down theories, and indulging in all the boldness of political discussion. He would augur nothing from it but impiety to God, and treason to Kings.[13]

In Cambridge, resistance to French ideas focused on a disapproval of analytical (algebraic) mathematics by a Newtonian mathematical establishment which had become hidebound. The Senate House Examination was by this time a venerable institution.[14] The successful insertion of French analysis into the curriculum was accomplished in the more relaxed years after the Napoleonic Wars. The addition of classics to the curriculum followed in the early 1820s. Again, the timing was crucial, but perceptions of the social role of knowledge also played a part. In a period of repression and suspicion, the distance of mathematical teaching and learning from social—especially political and religious—practice meant that it attracted much less controversy than classics.

Oxford, Cambridge, and English schooling

In 1800 Oxford and Cambridge were the educational wings of the Anglican church. Many of their students were the sons of clerics; many of their graduates took orders on graduation.[15] Throughout the first half of the century, the Church took the brightest and best of their bachelors. And since Latin and Greek, together with Hebrew, were the languages of the Church, what was at times referred to as 'the classical system'—the domination of elite schooling by the learning of Latin and Greek—was tightly tied to the Anglican system: the domination of education by the Established Church. In the elementary schools, the Anglican National Schools competed for pupils with the dissenting British Schools from around 1810. The public schools and universities of England, on the other hand, were suffused with Anglican belief and practice. When the criteria for ecclesiastical appointments began to shift, towards the end of the eighteenth century, from connection to merit, that merit was measured by prowess in Greek scholarship. Hence that curious phenomenon the 'Greek play bishop'.[16] Conversely, when the editors of Greek plays became bishops, they typically abandoned classical scholarship. Hence Housman's well-known reference in the preface to his edition of Manilius to the 'stroke of doom' of 1824/5 which sent Dobree and Elmsley to their graves, and Blomfield from Cambridge to the bishopric of Chester. In fact, Blomfield had been appointed in 1819 to the rectorate of St Botolph's, Billingsgate (while retaining a rural living). Thomas Gaisford, professor of Greek at Oxford, wrote to his colleague Peter Elmsley on 13 May 1820, 'Whether Blomfield will go on with Aeschylus, or merge himself altogether in divinity is to me rather uncertain'.[17] Similarly, Julius Hare's classical publication ceased completely when he left Cambridge for Hurstmonceaux in 1832.[18]

The word 'system' may suggest a tightly integrated set of institutions, with levels through which pupils progressed. The reality was very different. In contrast with France and Germany, which both had mass schooling systems in place by the early nineteenth century,[19] state intervention in education came very late in England. The first tentative steps toward government involvement in education came in 1833, but consisted merely of establishing a committee of the Privy Council and issuing a few grants; in the 1840s a schools inspectorate was established. The basic legislation was passed only in 1870 for elementary schools, and in 1902 for secondary schools. The public (i.e., fee-paying) schools were united by the middle and upper-class clientele to which they appealed, but it was a clientele for which they competed. Competition fostered differentiation between the schools even as it held them together against the social groups they excluded by charging for their services.

The lack of standardized provision which resulted is evident in the attempts made to combat it in the 1830s and 40s—the period when the expansion of the rail network and the introduction of a cheap postal system enhanced communication. In 1835 Thomas Arnold urged the production of standard Latin grammars, so that a boy who moved from one school to another would not have his schooling disrupted. The novelist Samuel Butler wrote feelingly of his difficulties in having a new Latin grammar beaten into him each time he moved school.[20] Through the century, and after several waves of expansion, the public school sector gradually took shape as a coherent system. The Head Masters' Conference, founded in 1869, provided a talking shop for its leaders.[21] The Oxford and Cambridge School Examinations Board, set up four years later, promoted common standards in assessment, as well as encouraging liaison between the two universities and their feeder schools. Here, too, the pattern had been a ragged one. The schools had developed that curious institution, the sixth form, whose members' average age increased until boys were leaving at 19 or 20. The sixth form was almost an alternative to an undergraduate course.[22] Indeed, there were embarrassments in the 1830s and 1840s, when sixth formers who were applying to enter Oxbridge went in for university classical prizes and won them while still at school. At the same time, the large salaries offered to classical masters at the leading schools, especially those who were in charge of boarding houses, made it difficult for the universities to compete.[23] In short, our modern assumptions about progression from one form of schooling to another do not apply in any straightforward sense.[24]

Oxford was informally integrated with this loose-knit system in a way that Cambridge was not. The elite schools taught almost nothing but classics throughout the first half of the nineteenth century.[25] They thus offered a thorough grounding for the university curriculum at Oxford, similarly dominated by classics, but not for the Cambridge course, which consisted largely of mathematics. Those who went to Cambridge might be prepared in some rural grammar schools (notably those in the north of England, like William Wordsworth's Hawkeshead School), by private tutors—some of them local clergy educated at Cambridge—or at the London colleges. Otherwise they had to begin with the rudiments after matriculating.[26] This informal disjunction between classics and mathematics had a hierarchical dimension reflected in the contrast between the two largest Cambridge colleges. St John's specialized in mathematics and had many sizars (poor students who had originally earned their keep by carrying out menial tasks, but by the nineteenth century were in effect minor scholars). Trinity's strength lay rather in classics, and it drew students, on average, from a higher social stratum. Even at St John's, however, the college examination system (the first to be established in Cambridge, in 1765) included thorough and regular testing of classical knowledge.[27]

Cambridge was, however, integrated with the schools at the college level; it was the colleges which were the sole home of classical teaching until the foundation of the Classical Tripos in 1822, and organized inter-collegiate teaching began only in the late 1860s.[28] It is very difficult to gauge the overall relationship between the schools and the two universities, and hence to answer the question: If the two universities inhabited a competitive field in which their individual identities throve on agonistic differentiation, how did competition actually *happen*? To what extent did students (more likely, their parents and teachers) actually choose between them in the nineteenth century? The available data, scattered and heterogeneous as they are, do not offer a firm basis for generalization. In the first half of the century, many schools had close links to particular colleges—most notably, Winchester to New College, Oxford, and Eton to King's College, Cambridge. It was also common for a college to draw from a particular county or region. Such links were cut by the 1850 Royal Commissions on Oxford and Cambridge, but they took some time to wither away. Oscar Wilde's friend Robert Ross was thrown into a fountain at King's in the 1880s during a tussle between the snobbish old Etonian clique and those they regarded as their social inferiors. The figures assembled by Honey and Curthoys on school-university links suggest a fairly stable relationship, but their comparative data point to a rather greater intake by Oxford from higher social classes—a pattern which it is reasonable to link with the university's classical bias.[29]

Classics at Oxford and Cambridge

In the first half of the nineteenth century, both places had curricular structures which can be described as 'sequential' rather than 'branching'. In Oxford one studied classics, and if successful could then study mathematics; in Cambridge the reverse held true. Choice of subject was thus only available in the negative sense that having studied one subject, one could choose not to study another; or, of course, by going to one university rather than the other. The Cambridge Classical Tripos was not established until 1822, though efforts had been made in that direction by James Monk, the Regius Professor of Greek, in the 1810s. The Oxford examination, as befitted the work of cautious, even nervous, planners, included both the major areas of received high-status knowledge: classics (*literae humaniores*) and mathematics and science (*scientiae naturales*). The preponderance of classics in the new examination reflected the university's existing curricular bias. In Cambridge Christopher Wordsworth, vice-chancellor of the university, master of Trinity and the leading figure behind the Tripos's foundation, had to battle against a dominant mathematical majority. The concessions he had to make to get his measure through show how powerful the opposition was. His original proposal was for an examination to be taken after the mathematics examination, to be compulsory for all except the top ten wranglers (i.e., first class men) in mathematics, and to include original composition in Latin and Greek. The examination which emerged in 1824 was entirely voluntary, and was open only to those who had already achieved honours in mathematics. What is more, it contained no original composition at all. It is true that the university had a series of prizes, some of which were awarded for compositional prowess. But it is probably also true that composition was seen by the mathematicians as the farther shore of classics—the hardest to acquire in a short time, and also the most obvious example of 'taste', as opposed to the intellectual rigour and instant problem-solving on which the Cambridge mathematical establishment prided itself. The new examination, then, was handicapped from the start.

At Oxford, the oral examination in *Literae Humaniores* had by the early 1830s become primarily a written test, examined separately from mathematics and science, and with four classes. Composition in Latin and Greek, not included at first, was added in 1830.[30] It included history and philosophy, and candidates were allowed to illustrate their answers from modern authors. This might be said to reflect the broader vision of classical scholarship imported from Germany: *Altertumswissenschaft* rather than the narrower textual work of men like Porson and Elmsley, Monk and Blomfield. To put it another way, it supported the Germanizing trend of the *Philological Museum*, the journal founded in 1831 by Julius Hare and Connop Thirlwall, rather than the Porsonian aims of its predecessor the *Museum Criticum*, which had ceased publication in 1824. Both journals had been run from Trinity College, Cambridge; but the broader vision of the *Philological Museum* had little effect on the Cambridge classical curriculum. By the mid-1830s, in any case, Hare had left for a rich country living and Thirlwall had been expelled from his college for criticizing compulsory chapel attendance. The tripos continued to test translation and composition, with a scattering of questions arising from the texts set. Not until 1849 was a paper on ancient history added, and by all accounts it was not taken very seriously by undergraduates.

It was also at this point that the mathematical bar on entry was relaxed, though it did not disappear until 1857. Thus for the first 25 years of the tripos's history, those classicists who could not cope with the rigours of Cambridge mathematics were unable to sit the examination. Richard Shilleto, one of the best-known Cambridge scholars in the narrowly linguistic, Porsonian style, just scraped in: he was Wooden Spoon (last in the list of mathematical honours) in 1832. The only compensation was that the possession of an honours degree was not then so essential to academic employment as it became later on. Thomas Evans, one of the unfortunate victims of the system, went on to teach at Shrewsbury School, then the most effective producer of classical students in England, and later became professor of Greek at Durham. Evans was agreed to be one of the half dozen best composers of Greek and Latin in Victorian England. In 1839, while still at Cambridge, he took his revenge on the mathematicians by publishing a poem in Greek called *Mathematogonia, or the Mythological Birth of the Nymph Mathesis*, in which he poured elegant scorn on the curriculum which had blocked his path. His poem, loosely based on Hesiod's Theogony, tells of the fashioning of Mathematics from the triangle and other figures by Hephaestus at Zeus's command. It is borne by the Furies first to the Nile delta ('a country which is triangular') and eventually to the banks of the Cam. Here it is set down 'to generate disputes and sharp provocations to madden [the inhabitants'] minds . . . a Death destroying everything, a second Sphinx, one born to compose inscrutable riddles and generate havoc among mortal kin'.[31]

At Oxford, meanwhile, Greats had in 1850 been recast in the form which would last until 1972: dominated by ancient history and ancient and modern philosophy, and preceded by a Moderations course which concentrated on language and literature. The nature of Greats gave rise in the 1880s to the complaint by Oxford historians that a final school of classics paid very little attention to Latin and Greek. The Cambridge tripos, on the other hand, had been described in Oxford as giving extensive knowledge of those languages, but without any idea of what one might do with that knowledge. In the 1860s and 70s, however, the ancient history paper was expanded, and a paper on ancient philosophy added; but the dominant emphasis was still placed on the accurate knowledge of the wide variety of linguistic styles found in ancient authors, and an ability to reflect these in translation and manipulate them in composition. The Cantabrigian view of Oxford was that it concentrated on literature, not language, and on the rote learning of set books. The contrast was reinforced by the fact that in Oxford a student could choose which books to offer in examination; the number and choice of books offered, in effect, constituted an announcement of the class of degree at which one was aiming. Francis Newman's Oxonian comment on the Cambridge system in 1843 was that 'it is not a very rare thing for students so to concentrate their attention on mere language and style, on the manual called "The Greek Theatre", and on books on Greek and Latin Antiquities, as to be quite unacquainted with the contents of any one work; having perhaps not read a single author through'. He goes on to admit, however, that the Oxford system was liable to promote the rote learning of set books.[32]

The modern form of the Tripos dates only from 1879, when it was divided into two parts. Part I included language and literature, rather like Mods; Part II consisted of five separate courses in literature and criticism, philosophy, history, archaeology, and philology. Two aspects of the new tripos need to be emphasized. The first is the highly specialized nature of Part II. This was progressively accentuated over the next 20 years by the reduction in the number of sections which could be offered by a candidate for examination, and by the reform of 1895 by which the literature section, which had initially been compulsory, became optional. Its range was wider than that of Greats, but it was a specialized rather than an integrated course. The second aspect is that a degree could be obtained on Part I alone. This must have been the price of getting the divided tripos accepted, but it proved almost fatal to Part II, whose numbers by the 1890s were pathetically small— except, embarrassingly, among the women.[33] Public schoolboys came up to read classics, went through more of what they had had at school, then took their degree after Part I, or perhaps changed to another tripos. Despite several attempts by Cambridge classical teachers, this provision was not abandoned till 1918. The Tripos continues in the same form, with Part II consisting of courses A to E.[34] Group F, on Roman Law, was set up in the 1970s and folded when its only teacher retired. X, an interdisciplinary course, began in the 1980s and is flourishing.[35] In its transcending of specialisation it might be thought to approach the nature of Greats, though one of its founders recently referred to Greats as 'a glorious white elephant'.[36] The attitude this suggests comes quite close, paradoxically enough, to the Oxonian delight in being behind the (modern) times. Matthew Arnold famously eulogized Oxford in *Essays in Criticism* (1865) as the 'home of lost causes, and forsaken beliefs, and unpopular names, and impossible loyalties'. More prosaically, the author of a guide to student life in Oxford remarked that

> It is sometimes said that our university, compared with Cambridge, is antiquated, unenterprising, and 'behind the times'. In the modicum of truth which gives force to such criticisms, may be found the secret of Oxford culture.[37]

To summarize, then, the two courses had in common in the last century a basis in the teaching of language and literature; and both of them offered a path from that to the study of history and philosophy. But the status of the basis was different in each case. In Cambridge, it was in effect a full course, sufficient unto itself, to which the specialist sections of Part II were optional add-ons. In Oxford, Moderations was merely a stepping stone to Greats. Their status also differed. In Cambridge, classics emerged in, and long remained under, the shadow of mathematics. Not until the late 1850s was it autonomous, and even then it was never to acquire the status of Greats as the university's premier course. In Oxford, classics dominated university examinations from their foundation. This status surely provided a fruitful basis for the expansive, integrated nature of Greats. Similarly we might suspect a link between the second-rank status of classics in Cambridge and the more specialized curriculum which evolved there.

A mutual regard: contemporary comparisons

In this section I draw on the large, though scattered, corpus of nineteenth-century comparisons of the two universities—largely made from within one or the other—in order to establish the major dimensions of mutual characterization. A very clear-cut contrast between them was offered by John Conington, who was in 1854 appointed the first Professor of Latin at Oxford. He commented that

> Cambridge . . . imparts an education, valuable not so much for itself, as for the excellent discipline which prepares the mind to pass from the investigation of abstract intellectual truth to the contemplation of moral subjects. Oxford, on the contrary, seeks without any such medium to arrive at the higher ground at once . . . leading the mind, before it has been sufficiently disciplined, to investigate the highest and most sacred subjects at once.[38]

This assured judgement was, in fact, uttered eleven years before Conington's election to the chair, when he was a sixth-former at Rugby; presumably his teachers had been discussing university applications with him. It is unclear just which parts of the curriculum he is thinking of, but in the case of Cambridge it must have included mathematics, since at that point the classical tripos was only accessible to those with high mathematical honours. William Whewell, master of Trinity College, Cambridge, wrote in similar terms in 1840 to his friend Julius Hare:

> You say that the Oxford men have come forwards more strenuously than we have in this attempt to purify and elevate the current principles of action. True: but they have come forwards before they know what they have to say.[39]

Both of the above comments were made in the wake of the controversy provoked by the Tractarians in Oxford, and so have to be evaluated as part of that moment.

Others went into more detail on curriculum and pedagogy. Charles Merivale, in his autobiography, remarked that where 'Oxford professed to cultivate the study of the ancient literature, Cambridge's [aim] was to acquire the most accurate appreciation of the ancient languages'.[40] Merivale's testimony is supported by that of the classical archaeologist Percy Gardner, recollecting in the tranquillity of the early 1930s his undergraduate career at Cambridge in the 1860s; his testimony is valuable because he taught at both places.

> The system of Shillito [sic] and other noted teachers of classics was to lay all the stress on words, and to neglect the subject matter of the ancient writers. Exact scholarship was the one thing they aimed at. They liked to see a man, as they put it, translate through a brick wall, turn classical phrases into elegant English, and English prose into readable Greek and Latin, without troubling oneself what was the full bearing of the passage.[41]

Thomas Ethelbert Page, who was at Cambridge a few years after Gardner, fiercely defended the system they had gone through against the reform proposals which led to the addition of Part II. Singing the praises of what was commonly called 'pure scholarship', he urged that the man who acquired a rigorous linguistic grounding was able to traverse the whole range of ancient literature and thus join an international community of civilized men. He was replied to by the Trinity Platonist Henry Jackson, who commented

> I must go back to the old tripos . . . the golden age of 'pure scholarship'. What . . . 'pure scholarship' meant was this. They read Thucydides, but not Grote; they studied the construction of the speeches, but did not confuse themselves with trying to study their drift. They read the Phaedrus, but had no Theory of Ideas.[42]

Jackson himself inherited a developmental conception of the Platonic dialogues based on the work of Schleiermacher, and transmitted through Julius Hare and his own teacher William Hepworth Thompson. In the present context, it is worth noting that in one of the prefaces to his translation of the dialogues the Oxford classicist Benjamin Jowett criticized Jackson for focusing too much on individual passages and thus failing to appreciate the unity of individual dialogues.[43]

The rough and the smooth: Oxford and Cambridge styles

In this section the analysis is broadened to consider social and intellectual styles more generally, as identified both within the universities and without. From the 1850s on, the major focus for public comparisons of the two universities was provided by the annual Boat Race. Hence such comments as the following, which taken out of context might be thought to refer to dress styles: 'The Oxford and Cambridge styles used to be palpably different to the eye by the height of the feather'; 'The feather was cleaner than that of Cambridge'.[44] Characterisations (and stereotypes) are also to be found in fiction: first in novels, in the twentieth century also in films. In some cases these fictional representations are 'without' in more than one sense: beyond the boundaries not just of Oxbridge, but of Britain. The exploits of Oxonians abroad are better known, largely because of their involvement with the British Empire;[45] but Cambridge examples can be found, as in the novel *The Ebb-tide* (1894) written by R. L. Stevenson and his son-in-law Lloyd Osbourne. This concerns a group of young Englishmen stranded in the South Seas: they were 'the three most miserable English-speaking men in Tahiti . . . yet not one of them had figured in a court of justice; two were of kindly virtues; and one had a tattered Virgil in his pocket'. From that rhetorical tricolon we might infer that the habitual reader of Virgil constitutes the moral apex of this miserable triangle. I ascribe this example to Cambridge because one of the three had a boat which he called after his 'old shop', Trinity Hall. Earlier in the book one of the group, surrounded by sailors on the Thames, meets another of the trio and recognizes the style of the university man, latching on to him with relief. The novel thus offers us vignettes of the English university man stranded on a foreign shore—socially on the Thames, geographically in the South Seas. It also reminds us of the colonization of the world by the social and cultural authority which was represented by the ancient universities; it colonization usually thought of in terms of 'Oxford and Empire', but which extended perhaps beyond both of these.

For an Oxford example we can take Edmund Clerihew Bentley's celebrated detective novel of 1913, *Trent's Last Case*. It describes Trent's first meeting with Marlowe, the young secretary of the murdered millionaire Sigsbee Manderson.

In his carriage, inelastic as weariness had made it; in his handsome, regular features; in his short, smooth, yellow hair; and in his voice as he addressed Trent, the influence of a special sort of training was confessed. 'Oxford was your play-ground, I think, my young friend', said Trent to himself.[46]

If it had been appropriate to be more specific, Bentley might have mentioned his own college, Merton. He was himself devoted to his alma mater, his devotion apparently only increased by the sense of shame he felt at gaining only a second in history in 1898. Bentley gained his degree at just the time when the numbers graduating in modern history overtook those in Greats. Greats was for some time after that officially regarded as the premier course in the university, but in the twentieth century it increasingly became one subject among many.

Another Oxonian writer of detective novels, Edmund Crispin (the pseudonym of Bruce Montgomery) gives us a contrast between products of the two universities. His detective, Gervase Fen, is a professor of English at Oxford, and much given to spouting lines of English literature at odd moments—rather like Michael Innes' (i.e. J. I. M. Stewart's) John Appleby, though in a less mannered way. In *Frequent Hearses* (1950), Fen investigates a death at a film studio. The victim has been starring in a historical drama about Alexander Pope, for which a 'small, futile Cambridge don' called Gresson is hired as historical adviser. His stock falls when he is unable to give the date of Queen Anne's death. His only distinction is that he is constantly pursuing starlets.[47] To this fictional film one can add a real one: Alfred Hitchcock's *The Lady Vanishes* (1938). When the smooth Ruritanian officer travelling with two Englishmen is asked where he learned such excellent English, he replies 'at Oxford'. Shortly afterwards, one of them clubs him over the head, remarking 'I'm a Cambridge man myself'.[48]

Here, then, we have two contrasted styles: the smooth confidence of Oxford, the rough energy of Cambridge. Of course the Stevenson example leaves Cambridge undercharacterized, but in a way that is the point: in the shadow of its more prestigious rival, the Cambridge character is often difficult to identify, and sometimes seems to be simply a lack of Oxonian grace. No wonder Thackeray, a Cambridge man, placed his hero in Oxbridge rather than in Camford.

Comparison, contact, and complication

Within Oxford and Cambridge themselves, comparisons were often made of their different intellectual styles. The typical contrast which emerges from such comments is that Oxford men enjoyed arguing about large metaphysical questions on which they split hairs and chopped logic, while Cantabs were more down to earth. The Eton master William Johnson (later Cory),

219

who was at Cambridge in the 1840s with Henry Maine, described a visit Maine made to him at Eton in 1847, two years after they graduated:

> We went through several hard subjects in the old Cambridge way, in that method of minute comparison of opinions, without argument which I believe to be peculiar to the small intellectual aristocracy of Cambridge.[49]

This is, I think, the first occurrence of the phrase 'intellectual aristocracy', which has been given general currency by a well-known paper by Noel Annan.[50] Cory's account is supported, in a way which harks back to Conington's comparison, by Leslie Stephen in his biography of his friend Henry Fawcett. 'The dominant influences of Cambridge in those days', he writes, referring to the mid-1850s, 'were indeed favourable to a masculine but limited type of understanding'. Later on he offers an illuminating comparison of Fawcett with William Gladstone:

> Mr Gladstone . . . was as typical a representative of the Oxford which obeyed the impulse of Newman, as Fawcett of the comparatively plain, practical, and downright Cambridge. Mr Gladstone's astonishing versatility of mind . . . was a source of wondering amusement to Fawcett's strong, but comparatively limited intellect. He was rather scandalised than amused by the singular subtlety and ingenuity in presenting unexpected interpretations of apparently plain doctrines which makes the history of Mr Gladstone's opinions so curious a subject for the psychologist.[51]

Elsewhere, Stephen declared that Gladstone 'with his great abilities somewhat marred by over-acuteness and polish, is an excellent type of the Oxford mind'.[52] Gladstone, of course, was at Oxford at a time when Aristotle had still to be joined, if not dethroned, by Plato.[53] The passionate exactitude, pedantry even, which an Oxford training in Aristotelian logic could produce was exemplified in his reply when asked where the followers of Peel should sit in the House of Commons: 'Taking a seat is an external sign and pledge that ought to follow upon full conviction of the thing it is understood to betoken'.[54]

To mention Gladstone, however, is to invoke a unique phenomenon, and one which reminds us that individuals had their own styles. Not all Oxonians were clones of their alma mater—who was herself internally various. Another example which illustrates the complicating effect of idiosyncrasy comes from a letter written by Roger Fry to his friend James Headlam in 1887. Fry was staying in Lucerne with his friend James McTaggart, a keen Hegelian from Trinity College, Cambridge. In his letter he reports a visit from the brothers Schiller, of Balliol and Magdalen:

[they] rejoice in the title of 'intelligent Philistines' and make great capital out of McTaggart who has been staying here and whom I fear they rather hate . . . [There was an] incessant storm of argument . . . I fear poor McT had rather a hard time of it. It is very interesting to me to find how totally different the Oxford point of view is to ours [:] it is so essentially critical in the sense rather of disbelieving in every thing than of sympathetic criticism. The elder brother believes in ghosts and scientific politics & in nothing else as far as I can see.[55]

Here Hegelian idealism, which was much more at home in Oxford, is represented by a Cambridge man, while the cutting knives of scepticism are wielded by Oxonians.[56]

These contrasts have to do with intellectual style, but of course this can be related to the social style which is so often intertwined with it. Gladstone was a remarkable orator as well as a remarkable constructor of intellectual patterns—a point hinted at by Stephen's reference to his 'presenting' interpretations. It was Oxford that had the orators; it was precisely in 'presenting' ideas that the Oxonians scored. One might say that Oxford typically produced public men, Cambridge private. Another witness who knew both places was Alexander Macmillan, who after selling books in Cambridge for a decade became publisher to Oxford University Press in 1863. Macmillan declared in 1864 that

There is a very marked Oxford manner . . . [a] fine gentlemanliness . . . [the] Cambridge manner—opener and more manly (aliter, rougher and less gentlemanly).[57]

Henry Jackson wrote in much the same vein in 1913, responding to a friend who had remarked what an attractive scholar Gilbert Murray was:

I think that Oxford is very successful in breeding 'attractive' scholars: more than Cambridge. And this is not surprising. For we dare not talk our shop in a mixed company, and even in a scholars' party we are very conscious of our limitations as specialists.[58]

Jackson's knowledge of Oxford came largely from his membership of the joint dining club called the *Ad Eundem*, a title taken from the formula with which the two universities recognized the validity of each other's degrees. He had been going to its dinners since 1869, and thus had more than 40 years' experience of discussions which must often have included a comparing of notes—especially on the two great issues which hung over both places from the 1870s to the early 1920s, the admission of women and the status of compulsory Greek. Others also had sufficient experience of both places to compare them. Some were brothers—Charles and Christopher Wordsworth, Henry and Arthur Sidgwick, for example. Some moved from one place to the other, as in the case of Percy Gardner. In other cases, the gap was bridged by friendship. Oscar Wilde and his friend Robert Ross engaged in a running argument, half serious, half jesting, about the relative merits of Oxford, Wilde's own university, and Ross's Cambridge, which Wilde referred to as 'a kind of preparatory institution for Oxford'. Ross wrote an essay called 'The Brand of Isis' which Linda Dowling has called 'the amusing protest of a Cambridge man at the Oxford ascendancy'.[59] (In the light of my comments on Gladstone, it is interesting to see that in his essay Ross claims the Grand Old Man for Cambridge: 'Mr Gladstone intellectually always seemed to me a Cambridge man in his energy, his enthusiasm, his political outlook. Only in his High Church proclivities is he suspect'.)[60] Further investigation on a wider front would, I think, show that this case is typical, in that the Cambridge literature talks of Oxford, while in Oxford, Cambridge is rarely mentioned.

The example of Gladstone—acclaimed as Oxonian, claimed as Cantabrigian, yet triumphantly sui generis—should remind us not to reify the notion of institutional styles. The specialised Part II curriculum at Cambridge, for example, generated not only specialization, but an ideological reaction to specialization. The Trinity College lecturer J. C. Stobart wrote his two books *The Glory that was Greece* and *The Grandeur that was Rome* (1911–12) in order to bring together the ancient literature, history, and archaeology which were being kept separate in the Tripos. Richard Jebb himself, the fine flower of late-Victorian Cambridge classics, urged the secretary of the new British Academy to encourage links between the committees of its different sections. 'In Cambridge', Jebb declared, 'I have long felt that the extremely rigorous specialization fostered by Part II of the Classical Tripos has had the effect of narrowing our scholarship & partitioning the field in a *rigid* manner which has scarcely a parallel in any other University'.[61] He himself had attempted to teach modern as well as ancient Greek during his tenure of the chair of Greek at Glasgow; and though best known for his work on Sophocles, had energetically supported the foundation of the British School of Archaeology in Athens. As a final example, consider the case of Francis Cornford. Cornford was inspired by Jane Harrison to look at the assumptions underlying explicit philosophical systems; his first book, *Thucydides Mythistoricus*, dealt with the influence of contemporary medical thought and terminology on Thucydides. Yet he never referred in his writing to the modern philosophical work carried on in his life time, some of it by fellow fellows of Trinity like Moore, Whitehead, Russell and Wittgenstein. The next generation of Cambridge ancient philosophers (Guthrie, Kirk, Raven) were positively antagonistic to attempts to liaise with practitioners of philosophy.[62] In the case of Whitehead and Russell's work in mathematical logic, or of Wittgenstein's in epistemology, one could understand this; but Moore's ethics and Whitehead's writing on metaphysics and religion would surely have appealed to Cornford. We know, however, that Cornford was a reserved person who did not mix much with the other fellows of his college. In company he tended to listen rather than talk. So perhaps, as with Gladstone from whom we began, we have to allow for the relative autonomy of the individual. There are certainly Cambridge classical scholars who might have been happier at Oxford: the most obvious example is perhaps the historian, Baptist, and popularizer T. R. Glover, the nearest thing Cambridge could offer to Oxford's A. E. Zimmern.[63]

In making the kind of inter-institutional comparison I am exploring here, we are confronted with what used to be called Galton's problem: i.e., that comparison of distinct entities is contaminated by their interaction. Oxford and Cambridge dons not only interacted with each other, they also frequently compared the curricula, pedagogies, and styles of the two places. There were several mechanisms for this. I have already mentioned that some dons moved from one to another. There were joint dining clubs like the Ad Eundem club to which Jackson belonged, which had been founded by Henry Sidgwick and his friends in the winter of 1864/5. And at crucial points when curriculum change was mooted, hasty checks were carried out on the other place, to gather evidence of what might be copied, because it was a good idea, or avoided, because it wasn't local.[64] In the extensive debates on the classical curriculum in Cambridge in the late 1860s, a standard conservative argument was that both places had their own distinctive styles of work: philosophical in Oxford, philological in Cambridge. Students could thus choose which they preferred—where they had the information and the freedom of action needed for choice—which, as I have suggested above, rather few in fact possessed.

It has been suggested that schools sent their best classicists to Oxford, the less good to Cambridge. That would have made sense while the mathematics bar was in place in Cambridge, that is until 1857. After that, however, such decisions would have better been made on pupils' potentials for different *kinds* of work. We have already seen that Percy Gardner lamented going to the wrong place. More famously, A. E. Housman, who failed Greats, perhaps at his own provocation, would surely have done better in Cambridge. The story is a familiar one, so I summarize: he gained a first in Mods, then devoted himself to textual study, and in his Greats exam sent in such pathetically inadequate answers that instead of being given a fourth, as some others were, he was failed outright.[65] How good the schools were at such strategic decisions is another question. Charles Stevens was a high-achieving pupil at Winchester College, skilled at the language-centred scholarship which still dominated classical teaching there just after the First World War. In 1922, he went up to New College and gained a first in Mods, but then collapsed to a third in Greats. The austere rigours of analytic philosophy, especially as practised by his tutor H. W. B. Joseph, were too much for him. His friend the ancient historian John Myres wrote of him that the catastrophe of his Greats marks scarred him for life.[66] Similarly, the celebrated Greek scholar J. D. Denniston, author of a standard work on Greek particles, who narrowly missed succeeding Gilbert Murray in the Regius chair of Greek in 1936, had achieved only a second-class degree in Greats after a first in Moderations.[67] How many others suffered in this way it is hard to know, partly because the interaction between schools and universities is so little researched.[68] But it is clear that, as in Gardner's case and probably also Stevens's, some public schools established channels of migration with one place or the other and then cultivated them. We thus have a picture of the fundamental flaws in the two systems: at Oxford you could be sucked into a curriculum which first repeated what you had done at school, then hurled you into new fields where you might wither and die. In Cambridge the mathematics requirement could prevent your even getting into classics, unless you gained a high level of knowledge of a very different subject of which you might have learned very little at school.

The picture of Oxford men as more comfortable in society fits well with the university's dominance in the public life of nation and empire. The statistics of imperial appointments, civil service personnel, and bishoprics tell their own story. To take the cabinet as an example, in the period from 1812 to 1940, only between 1828 and 1841 were there more Cambridge members than there were Oxonians.[69] From Jowett's Balliol a conveyor belt took graduates to the higher reaches of the home civil service and to the administration of the Empire. Cambridge had a part in this, but it was both smaller and less organized. Overall, the public profile of Oxford was much higher than that of Cambridge. And from at least the 1850s until the Great War, Greats symbolized Oxford, and was regarded as its premier course. Did this lead to complacence? It is true that the Oxford classical dons managed to make changes in a way which their Cantabrigian colleagues found impossible. The obvious explanation is that the classicists were in a majority at Oxford, a minority at Cambridge. The failure of Part II of the Cambridge Classical Tripos in the 1890s was a publicly admitted fact which its teachers were powerless to do anything about: when they tried, they were outvoted.

Aspects of Oxbridge classics

I. Journals

A different picture emerges, however, if we look at the publication of classical journals, as the table below indicates. In nineteenth-century England they typically collapsed a few years after their foundation for lack of contributors, subscribers or both. By my count, six of these were founded in Cambridge in the nineteenth century, four in London, and only two at Oxford.[70]

Nineteenth-Century English Classical Journals

1810–29	Classical Journal L
1813–24	Museum Criticum C
1831–3	Philological Museum C
1843–9	Classical Museum L
1851–2	Terminalia O
1851–3	Museum of Classical Antiquities L
1854–9	Journal of Classical and Sacred Philology C
1868–1920	Journal of Philology C
1880–	Journal of Hellenic Studies L/C
1882–	Proceedings of Cambridge Philological Society C
1885–	Transactions of Oxford Philological Society O
1887–	Classical Review C

[In some cases, dates differ from those found elsewhere, which are taken from publication in bound volumes subsequent to first publication.]

In other ways, too, Cambridge could claim a higher profile. The Classical Association was founded in 1903 by a Cambridge man, J. P. Postgate, though with the support of an ex-Oxford man teaching in Birmingham, E. A. Sonnenschein. In the Edwardian era Cambridge had a cluster of classical knights—Richard Jebb, John Sandys, William Ridgeway—unmatched in Oxford, though Gilbert Murray was offered and declined a knighthood. Part of the answer perhaps has to do with several features of the Cambridge context. First, the low-church culture of earnest endeavour, here channelled into academic organization. Second, the professionalizing mode of work fostered by a more specialized curriculum. Third, the solidaristic effect on classicists of being in a minority of the academic population, unlike their opposite numbers in Oxford.

II. Gender

I mentioned above the two great issues of late Victorian Oxbridge: whether to admit women to membership and whether to abandon the compulsory Greek requirement for students. The two issues were in fact closely linked, since in each case what was at issue was the universities' right to maintain their autonomy from outside pressures. In the case of compulsory Greek, the histories run roughly parallel, both places abolishing the requirement just after the Great War. The issue of female admission turned out rather differently, for while Oxford gave women full membership in 1920, in Cambridge they had to wait till 1948. This prompts the question, what differences can be seen in the interaction of classics and gender in the two universities?

In her *Hellenism and Homosexuality in Victorian Oxford*, Linda Dowling argued that the discourse of homosexual love developed by Pater and Wilde from the mid-1860s onwards fed on, and was made possible by, the Greats curriculum which had been reoriented toward Plato by Jowett in the previous decade.[71] Plato offered a theorizing of a spiritualized love between men, one which Jowett's suave treatment portrayed as ethically neutral. But in addition, K. O. Müller's book on the Dorians, a product of the German historical school of which Jowett approved, provided a crucial legitimating basis for homosexuality. The civic republican tradition so powerful in nineteenth-century England had revolved round an image of the male citizen warrior, capable of both voting and fighting. In this tradition, the homosexual was effeminate and hence in civic terms a nonperson. What Müller's book had done was to identify the role played by homosexual groups among the warlike Dorians. The love of men became the love of comrades, fighting together for their nation.[72]

In Oxford such views could be developed on the basis of this reading within friendship groups, clubs and the tutorial encounter. What of Cambridge? It is difficult to imagine anyone writing a Cantabrigian equivalent of Dowling's book. She does refer briefly to the writing of Edward Carpenter, who took up the themes developed by John Addington Symonds. Dowling says that 'matriculating at Cambridge, Carpenter developed into a homosexual apologist along the earnest, enthusiastic, activist lines characteristic of that university'.[73] Yet we do not find on the Cam the kind of elaborated discourse of homosexual love based on Greek literature and history which we do at Oxford. One reason for this is that Cambridge did not offer the fused social and intellectual intimacy of the tutorial. Its teaching was conducted through supervisions organized by directors of studies, who were separate from moral tutors. It thus lacked what Tollemache called the 'tutor-worship' . . . which 'does not flourish on the banks of the Cam'.[74] But the major reason is surely that it had no Greats to provide the pervasive ideological underpinning for the emergence of such a discourse. There were classically-educated homosexuals at Cambridge, to be sure, though the names which come most readily to mind—Oscar Browning, Lowes Dickinson, E. M. Forster—were not classicists. But they were not Pater or Wilde. They were, however, all Kingsmen; and King's was certainly, in the late nineteenth century, a place where tutorial relationships were cultivated, in part by migrating or exiled members of the aesthetic minority of Eton College staff. While Plato was studied at Trinity, Platonic love was cultivated at King's.[75] This almost suggests that we might see the college as an outpost of Oxonian values within Cambridge. That it was seen in this way is suggested by a writer in the Cambridge magazine *Varsity* in 1948, who remarked that 'a Kingsman is the nearest thing in Cambridge to an Oxford man, and like him, has a queer accent, lolls about the place and doesn't believe in rowing'.[76] We might compare an anecdote in which Oxford looks at Cambridge. The point is also made by an incident reported by Geoffrey Madan. Raymond Asquith of Balliol visited Cambridge; on his return his college servant asked him 'What sort of place is it, sir? Something in the Keble line?'.[77] This anecdote can be dated to the early 1900s, when Asquith was an undergraduate. Keble was then only thirty years old; the comment implied that Cambridge was a junior and inferior version of Oxford. The general point is clear: in comparing collegiate universities we have to allow for the complicating factor of collegiate points of view.

If we look for intimate relationships in late Victorian Cambridge which might be related to the teaching and learning of classics, we are struck by two phenomena. The first is not confined to classics: several of the young women who came there from the late 1860s onwards married their teachers. John Percival Postgate, for example, proposed to one of his little class at Girton, whose name was Edith, and was accepted. A few months later she broke off the engagement, and he promptly offered his hand to her classmate—also an Edith.[78] There were also, as it were, horizontal marriages within the same generation. James Smith Reid, editor of Cicero and first occupant of the chair of Ancient History, married one of the sisters of the archaeological brothers Ernest and Percy Gardner, while Percy married Reid's sister.

The second phenomenon, however, *is* tied to the study of classics: the series of intimate friendships between Jane Ellen Harrison and several academics, all younger than herself. Of these the best known is her relationship with Francis Cornford, whose *Thucydides Mythistoricus* bears the marks of her influence. None of Harrison's relationships with men lasted; those with women were more successful. What I want to look at here is the link between her relationships and the work she carried out herself and inspired in others on Greek ritual and religion. The illustration shows a Christmas card drawn and sent by Frances Darwin in December 1908 to her fiancé Francis Cornford.

The figures shown are from left to right, the artist, her addressee, her father the botanist Sir Frank Darwin, and Jane Harrison. The drawing is based on a Greek vase painting of a young woman holding a piglet which had been reproduced in Harrison's *Prolegomena to the Study of Greek Religion*.[79] In her biography of Harrison, Sandra Peacock drew on the occasional use of the Greek *choiros* (pig) to refer to the female genitalia to suggest that the figures' poses reflect their attitude to their own sexuality. In these terms we might characterize the pigs in the painting as, from left to right: offered, available, cuddled, on a tight rein.[80] But Peacock seems not to have noticed that the foot of the drawing carries the words ΑΛΑΔΕ ΜΥΣΤΑΙ ('To the sea, mystics!'), the phrase used on the third day of the annual pilgrimage from Athens to Eleusis, when the mystics dipped their sacrificial piglets in the waters of the Corinthian Gulf to purify them.[81] There is a gentle joke on this: a wave at the far left, a towel on Cornford's arm. Other things could be said about the drawing. For example, the choice of the Eleusinian mysteries, whose initiates were sworn to silence, may have been prompted by Francis Cornford's habitual silence when with others, mentioned above. My main

227

Greek vase painting as Edwardian Christmas card: from Frances Darwin to Francis Cornford, December 1908. (Reproduced by courtesy of Professor J. P. Cornford)

concern here, however, is to emphasize that the drawing shows us the close ties between explorers of the mysterious depths of the ancient Greek world, depths then being revealed through excavation. Those depths lay beneath the shining world of white columns and Olympian deities conventionally portrayed by Victorian scholars: they were full of mysteries, curses, irrationalism, and ritual. Harrison and her friends and disciples worked together and, even more unusually, published together on these topics.[82] Here we have a phenomenon which has no parallel in Oxford: a band of scholarly explorers led by a woman.[83] The subject matter of their work can be related to the curriculum of the Classical Tripos, which included the study of myth and ritual.[84] But it might also be suggested that the formation of this loose-knit group was encouraged by the specialized subdivisions of the Part II syllabus, so different from the integrated pattern of Oxford Greats.[85]

Conclusion: tradition, transmission, 'transformission'

I have attempted above to compare the two most prestigious and influential institutional versions of classics in nineteenth-century England. At Oxford classics was dominant, and Greats acknowledged as the university's premier course. The examination tested knowledge of set books which were chosen by students from an official list. Language and literature (Moderations or

'Mods') served as a basis for an integrated course in history and philosophy (*Literae Humaniores* or 'Greats'). The heavy emphasis on Aristotle in the earlier part of the century gave way after the 1850s to a focus on Plato. In Cambridge classics emerged in the shadow of a well-established and prestigious mathematics course, and gained autonomy only in the late 1850s. Its division into two parts produced a course which superficially resembled the Oxford curriculum, but Part II, itself divided into options, was hamstrung until 1918 by the availability of a degree after Part I.

The Oxford man might be seen as a reflection of Aristotle's great-souled man, of Plato's guardian, or as an amalgam of the two. In any case, he was typically comfortable with a place in the public sphere, projecting an image of effortless learning. His Cambridge counterpart preferred the back room, where he worked strenuously to fulfil restricted objectives and specialized tasks. He knew more about the classical languages, but less about literature, then his Oxonian opposite number. Here we have, then, the 'rough' and the 'smooth'. The larger picture in which such comparisons must be located includes the two universities' religious history. Tractarianism, which emerged and occupied minds at Oxford in the 1830s and 40s, had little impact in Cambridge, where fervour ran in Broad Church channels and dissenters could matriculate, though not take degrees. Indeed, among the Tractarians to 'Cambridgize' became a term of opprobrium, rather like 'protestantize' or 'Miltonize'.[86]

In both cases, we need to distinguish ideological projections from reality. In Oxford, as Ian Small has suggested, Pater and Wilde may have been reacting against a perceived turn to professionalized scholarship, of which their writing was respectively subversive and transgressive.[87] What has been called 'Cambridge ritualism'—the work of Harrison and her associates—could be seen as an attempt to raise an integrated chthonic vision against the specialized respectability of the Tripos. Their path might thus be seen as parallel to that of Frazer, who began with a dissertation on Plato and went over to the wild side of antiquity when his eye was caught by the Golden Bough. Here again the religious context has to be taken into account: a concern to subvert conventional Christian belief was certainly present in Frazer's work, as it was in the writing of Arthur Verrall and perhaps with Harrison herself. But as in the case of Gladstone, discussed above, we have to be careful to allow for individual (and idiosyncratic) variations on institutional themes.[88]

The two collegiate universities, when compared, thus offer a number of levels at which differences and similarities can be identified. The pluralistic perspective employed above is, I believe, useful in helping us to resist the various deterministic approaches by which the study of cultural transmission has been plagued. These can be classified under three headings, which I summarize briefly in order of their historical occurrence. The determinism of the *source* assumes that a pure message is transmitted, any change being regarded as incidental impurity. As Grafton has said of the work of Aby Warburg and his colleagues on the classical tradition, they 'treated transmission as a simple, one-directional process. . . . The original message appeared to be pure and perfect. The changes and revisions introduced into it in the course of time were defined as interference . . . a corruption, not an enhancement, of the original'.[89] The romantic reaction against such views gave us a contrary determinism, that of the *receiver*. As Turner has suggested, the 'tyranny of Greece over Germany' might better be seen as the 'tyranny of Germany over Greece'.[90] In the twentieth century, these two determinisms were joined by a third, which we might call the determinism of the *message*. This is exemplified by the structuralism of Roman Jakobson. For example, in his analysis of reported speech, he emphasized the role of what he called 'shifters'. 'I sit on the mat' becomes 'She said she sat on the mat'; 'on the mat' alone does not 'shift'. There is, of course, a certain attraction in the notion that cultural transmission can be analyzed as a kind of reported speech, each successive version constituting an *'oratio'* ever more *'obliqua'*. The crucial weakness of this approach, however, is that change is simply a function of linguistic structure. How and why does it happen? It just does: irrespective of human agency, social context and historical circumstance. (Yet we notice that in this reported speech, 'shifting' itself is prompted by the [social] act of reporting.[91])

Jakobson's writing influenced the work of Basil Bernstein, who though best known for his sociolinguistics also developed a formal sociology of curriculum.[92] Bernstein's approach can be called 'categorical' in more than one sense. Its stress on formal boundaries was Kantian (here the influence of Jakobson was reinforced by that of Durkheim and Lévi-Strauss). But it was also 'categorical' (rather than 'dialectical') in its fundamentally determinist picture of curricular structure and curricular change.[93] For Bernstein, curricular form was an epiphenomenon of deep-structural societal form; hence curricular change reflected societal change. Specifically, he argued that in the 1960s the root principles of English curricula were changing from 'keep things apart' to 'keep things together' (the Kantian strain is very evident here). But change itself seemed to consist (rather as in the contemporary work of Thomas Kuhn) of gestalt switches, as one curricular form/ paradigm was replaced by another. There was no room in such an analysis for politics, or indeed for human agency.[94] The contemporary work of Pierre Bourdieu also had its 'categorical' aspects, though his Kantianism was modified by an allegiance to Marx and Weber.[95] Bourdieu's analysis of the role of education in bourgeois society paints a deterministic picture: he sees a dynamic, not a dialectic. What I particularly want to emphasize here, however, is the absence of the institutional level in the work of both Bourdieu and Bernstein. For both of them, the boundaries of schools and universities seem completely permeable: they are channels of transmission bereft of any power to shape, refract or deflect what is transmitted.[96] On the contrary, I hope to have shown here, by comparing Oxford and Cambridge, that a shared inheritance—in this case, of classical culture—has taken on distinct and different shapes in the two universities. The process involved is, in short, not so much transmission as *transformission*.[97] Further, the differences which can be identified relate not only to details of curriculum and pedagogy, but also to wider issues of social and intellectual style.

This paper has attempted a preliminary comparison of two universities focused on one subject area; much remains to be done. Other comparisons could have been made, among the most interesting that between Oxford classics and Cambridge mathematics, the dominant subject areas, the pride of each university, throughout the nineteenth century. Such a comparison would have gone more directly to the heart of the contrasting styles of the two places; yet the difference between the subject areas takes away opportunities which are the reward for keeping subjects constant. All these comparisons depend on detailed evidence from the institutions compared: and this includes, as I have argued, evidence of their own exercises in comparison. We also need studies of the interaction of such institutions within the wider symbolic markets where cultural capital is created, distributed, and consumed. How, for example, were Oxford and Cambridge curricular and pedagogic ideologies exported to newer institutions? The interests and political contexts of their news homes are likely to have had a profound effect on the precise form in which such transplanted ideas were manifested there. In the 1850s, the classical curricula of the universities of Sydney and Melbourne had significant differences, though both were assembled by men imported from Britain.[98] Again, a study of the use of English defences of classics in South Africa in the late nineteenth century has shown that the use made of these works was very selective indeed.[99]

Thackeray's conflated title, which in 1849 reflected the profound similarities between the two ancient collegiate institutions, by the middle of the twentieth century also implied their common status as against a cluster of newer bodies. To Durham and the two London colleges, founded in the 1820s, had been added a range of civic 'redbrick' universities;[100] in the 1960s 'plate-glass' institutions added to the variety, some of them copying the collegiate structure of Oxbridge. By the 1970s, the university system resembled a geological formation in which status could largely, but not entirely, be read off from age. In the last fifteen years, the irresistible rise of the academic audit has undercut the sedimented hierarchies of that system, imposing a single evaluative mechanism on a wide range of subject areas and institutions. It is perhaps historically apt that at the end of a century whose intellectual production has been dominated by the natural sciences, this juggernaut should flatten those old pretenders, the humanities, beneath wheels which run most comfortably in scientific grooves.[101] Within the humanities, classics had already fallen furthest from its previous glories—but then it had furthest to fall. A subject which had dominated most elite education before 'subjects' were thought of had given way, since the middle of the nineteenth century, to a growing range of new areas of knowledge.[102] The abolition of the compulsory Greek requirement by Oxford and Cambridge in 1919 symbolized a withdrawal from its Victorian status as exemplar of humanistic knowledge;[103] their abolition of the compulsory Latin requirement in 1960 completed the marginalization of classics in English high culture. The coup de grace was delivered by the National Curriculum promulgated in 1988, which drew a new, centrally-defined map of the secondary school curriculum in which classics did not appear.[104] Twenty years later, faced with a diminishing supply of linguistically competent school leavers, Oxford and Cambridge are admitting students to read for classics degrees who have neither Latin nor Greek. The increasing role of fee-based funding has led to a newly systematic recruitment of overseas students; at the peak of the university system Oxford and Cambridge have been joined by two metropolitan institutions which are not universities: Imperial College and University College. In the competitive struggles between such institutions, curricular emphases may well play a part in the agonistic formation of identities—but it is highly unlikely that classics will feature in any important sense.

References

1. I should like to thank Mordechai Feingold and Sheldon Rothblatt for their comments on an early draft of this article.
2. For Germany, see A. T. Grafton, 'Polyhistor into Philolog: Notes on the Transformation of German Classical Scholarship, 1780–1850', *History of Universities* 3 (1983), 159–92. The organization of classics in the Netherlands in an earlier period offers a similar contrast with England: M. Feingold, 'Reversal of Fortunes: the Displacement of Cultural Hegemony from the Netherlands to England in the Seventeenth and Early Eighteenth Centuries', in D. Hoak and M. Feingold (eds.), *The World of William and Mary. Anglo-Dutch Perspectives on the Revolution of 1688–89* (Stanford, 1996), 234–64, at 237–8.
3. The basic secondary sources are the two official university histories. The *History of the University of Oxford* [hereafter *HUO*], in eight multiauthored volumes, was completed in the autumn of 2000 by the publication of volume 7 (1870–1914). The *History of the University of Cambridge* [*HUC*] is on a smaller scale: four single-authored volumes, of which only three have appeared (there appears to be no immediate prospect of publishing volume 2). Understandably, neither pays much attention to the other place. But whereas the Oxford nineteenth-century volumes (6 and 7) include chapters on classics, their Cambridge equivalents, working to a much more restrictive brief, do not. The chapters of *Classics Transformed* (Oxford, 1998) in which I dealt with the subject at university level were largely based on evidence from Cambridge, drawing a justified complaint from a reviewer that I had not taken Oxford classics properly into account (O. Murray, 'Classics in England', *Classical Review*, n.s. 50 (2000), 256–9). The present paper will, I hope, go some way toward redressing this neglect.

4. 'Camford' also appeared there for the first time, but has failed to enter public consciousness: Oxbridge is mentioned 28 times in the text of the *Oxford English Dictionary* to Camford's 8; the score in the text of the *Dictionary of National Biography* is 9–0.

5. Intervention in Scottish universities, however, had begun in 1826: see, for example, G. E. Davie, *The Democratic Intellect. Scotland and Her Universities in the Nineteenth Century* (Edinburgh, 1961), 26–40.

6. L. Campbell, *On the Nationalisation of the Old English Universities* (London, 1901). For the methodological point, see the introductory essay in C. A. Stray (ed.), *The Mushri-English Pronouncing Dictionary. A Chapter in Nineteenth-Century Public-School Lexicography* (Reading, 1995).

7. See M. Feingold, 'The Humanities', in *HUO 4* (Oxford, 1997), 211–357.

8. J. Gascoigne, *Cambridge in the Age of the Enlightenment. Science, Religion and Politics from the Restoration to the French Revolution* (Cambridge, 1989), 7.

9. V. H. H. Green, *Religion at Oxford and Cambridge* (London, 1964), 153.

10. Gascoigne, *Cambridge in the Age of the Enlightenment*, 187.

11. For Jebb's campaigns, see Searby, *HUC 3*, 163–6; for Napleton, V. H. H. Green, 'Reformers and Reform in the University', *HUO 5*, 615–8.

12. This was stressed by W. R. Ward, *Victorian Oxford* (London, 1965), 14; cf. Green, 'Reformers and reform', 622–3; M. Brock 'The Oxford of Peel and Gladstone', *HUO 6*, 8.

13. 'Edgeworth's *Professional Education*', *Edinburgh Review* 15 (Oct. 1809), 40–53; repr. in *Collected Works* (2nd edn, London, 1840), i. 189–95.

14. In a sense its history began in 1730, the year in which the new Senate House was opened; the examination had however been held before then. For a summary, see Searby *HUC 3*, 158–9. For more detailed discussions, see J. Gascoigne, *Cambridge in the Age of the Enlightenment*; A. Warwick, *Masters of Theory* (Chicago, 2001). The term 'mathematical tripos' became possible only after 1824, but 'Senate House Examination' continued in use for some time after that date.

15. Theological colleges existed, but their graduates, though ordained, were not regarded as gentlemen. See A. Haig, *The Victorian Clergy* (London, 1986).

16. Stray, *Classics Transformed*, 39, 41; M. Brock, *HUO 6*, 15.

17. Elmsley papers, Westminster School, box 2.

18. See the bibliography of his publications in N. M. Distad, *Guessing at Truth* (Shepherdstown, 1979).

19. J. A. Armstrong, *The European Administrative Elite* (Princeton, 1973); A. Green, *Education and State Formation* (London, 1990).

20. C. A. Stray, 'Paradigms of Social Order: The Politics of Latin Grammar in Nineteenth-Century England', *Bulletin of the Henry Sweet Society*, 13 (1989), 13–24.

21. It is worth remembering that the HMC was founded by heads of less famous schools as means of resisting the dominance of schools like Eton, Harrow and Winchester. The challenge had been absorbed by the late 1880s.

22. W. A. Reid and J. Filby, *The Sixth: An Essay in Education and Democracy* (Lewes, 1982), 17–43.

23. See, for example, Alfred Marshall's evidence to the (Aberdare) Commission on Higher Education in Wales and Monmouthshire, in P. Groenewegen (ed.), *Official Papers of Alfred Marshall, a Supplement* (Cambridge, 1996), 44 (Question no. 18, 266).

24. This may be why the matriculation rates at Oxbridge levelled off from the mid-1820s to c 1860: adolescents went to, or stayed on at, schools in the expanding public-school sector.

25. M. L. Clarke, *Classical Education in Britain 1500–1900* (Cambridge, 1959), 74–84; Stray, *Classics Transformed*, 31–45.

26. For details, see Warwick, *Masters of Theory*.

27. C. A. Stray, 'The Shift from Oral to Written Examination: Cambridge and Oxford 1700–1914', *Assessment in Education*, 8 (2001), 35–51, on p. 42.

28. It should not however be assumed that such integration guaranteed a progressive course of study, especially as a large proportion of students—in some cases a majority—did not proceed to honours degrees. The evidence on this for Cambridge is unclear, and different estimates are difficult to reconcile. See C. A. Stray, 'Renegotiating Classics: The Politics of Curricular Reform in Late-Victorian Cambridge', *Echos du Monde Classique/Classical Views*, 42 (n.s. 7) (1998), 449–70, on p. 458.

29. J. R. de S. Honey and M. C. Curthoys, 'Oxford and schooling', *HUO 7*, 545–70; this includes some statistical comparisons with Cambridge.

30. Francis Newman ascribed this to the influence of the university scholarships introduced in 1825: V. A. Huber, *The English Universities* (2 vols, London, 1943), ii. 524. But it would not have been possible without the shift to written papers. See further Stray 'The Shift from Oral to Written Examination'.

31. [T. S. Evans], *Mathematogonia, or, the Mythological Birth of the Nymph Mathesis* (Cambridge, 1839). (Translation kindly provided by Christopher Collard).

32. Huber, *English Universities*, ii. 521. The book was translated and edited by Francis Newman, who uses his notes to supplement, correct and often to admonish Huber. The book he refers to is, presumably, *The Theatre of the Greeks*, originally assembled by P. W. Buckham (1825) but later much enlarged and revised by J. W. Donaldson (4th edn 1836, 7th edn 1859).

33. See C. Breay, 'Women and the Classical Tripos 1869–1914', in C. A. Stray (ed.), *Classics in 19th and 20th Century Cambridge, Proceedings of the Cambridge Philological Society*, supplementary vol. 24 (1999), 49–70.

34. In 1918 the label *section* was replaced by *group*—perhaps connotating integration rather than division. One might even detect an Oxonian influence in the new terminology—perhaps imported via Henry Jackson, who spearheaded the reform. See below for Jackson's Oxford links.

35. A characteristic product is W. M. Beard and J. G. Henderson, *A Very Short Introduction to Classics* (Oxford, 1995).

36. W. M. Beard, 'The Invention and Reinvention of "Group D"', in Stray (ed.), *Classics in Cambridge*, 95–134, on p. 133.

37. E. C. Lefroy, *Undergraduate Oxford* (Oxford, 1878), 71. I owe this reference to Linda Dowling.

38. Letter of 19 May 1843: 'Memoir' by H. J. S. Smith, in *Miscellaneous Writings*, ed. J. A. Symonds (London, 1872), i. p. xviii.

39. Whewell to J. C. Hare, 5 November 1840. Trinity College Library, Add. MS a 215/52. Quoted by permission of the Master and Fellows of Trinity College, Cambridge.
40. C. Merivale, *Autobiography of Charles Merivale* (London, 1898), 102.
41. P. Gardner, *Autobiographica* (Oxford, 1933), 13.
42. D. A. Winstanley, *Later Victorian Cambridge* (Cambridge, 1947), 221.
43. B. Jowett, *The Dialogues of Plato*, (2nd edn., Oxford, 1875), i. pp. xxix–xxxvi. There are thus three levels of analysis to consider—the corpus, the dialogue, the passage—in such debates on interpretative strategy.
44. *Pall Mall Gazette*, 16 May 1865; *St James's Gazette*, 28 March 1884. Feathering is the practice of turning oars through 90 degrees when out of the water to decrease wind resistance; the term was later applied to aircraft propellers.
45. R. Symonds, *Oxford and Empire* (London, 1986).
46. Penguin ed. 1937, 48. Bentley wisely does not try to explain how Marlowe's regularity of features and hair colour can be attributed to his Oxford training.
47. 'He conceived the studios to be a kind of stalking-ground for the pandemic Venus . . . [he was] immitigably ensnared by lubricious fancies'. *Frequent Hearses* (London, 1950), 58.
48. I owe this reference to Keith Tribe. The English 'clubman' was Caldicott, played by Naunton Wayne.
49. *Extracts from the Journals of W. Cory*, selected by F. W. Cornish (London, 1897), 46.
50. 'The intellectual aristocracy', now most easily available as the final chapter of his *The Dons* (London, 1999).
51. L. Stephen, *Life of Henry Fawcett* (London, 1885), 90, 244.
52. L. Stephen, *Sketches from Cambridge* (London, 1865, repr. 1932), 95.
53. For a discussion of Coleridge's dictum that 'Every man is born an Aristotelian, or a Platonist' in relation to the contrast between Oxford and Cambridge, see D. Newsome, *Two Classes of Men: Platonism and English Romantic Thought* (London, 1974), 73–8.
54. G. M. Young, *Daylight and Champaign* (London, 1948), 55.
55. Roger Fry to James Headlam, [August 1887], Headlam papers, Churchill Archives Centre, Cambridge.
56. For another surprising contrast of this kind, see the discussion of J. W. Headlam and J. W. Mackail in *Classics Transformed*, 242–6.
57. C. L. Graves, *Life and Letters of Alexander Macmillan* (London, 1910), 228–9.
58. Henry Jackson to J. A. Platt, 15 August 1913: R. St J. Parry, *Henry Jackson OM* (Cambridge, 1926), 184–5.
59. R. Ross, 'The brand of Isis', in *Masques and Phases* (London, 1909), 33–46; Dowling, *Hellenism*, 119 n. 18.
60. Ross 'The brand of Isis', 37. The essay was originally published in 1902.
61. Jebb to Israel Gollancz, 15 December 1902 (British Academy archives).
62. This point was emphasized to me by Myles Burnyeat, another Oxbridge migrant: formerly Professor of Ancient Philosophy at Cambridge, now a fellow of All Souls College, Oxford.

63. On Glover see H. G. Wood, *Terror Reaveley Glover. A Biography* (Cambridge, 1953); on Zimmern, see P. C. Millett, 'Zimmern and his "Greek Commonwealth"', *Arion* (forthcoming).

64. See for example the correspondence between Leonard Whibley of Cambridge and Alfred Godley of Oxford on the Compulsory Greek issue in the 1900s (Whibley papers, Pembroke College, Cambridge).

65. Exhaustive discussion in P. G. Naiditch, *A. E. Housman at University College, London* (Leiden, 1988), 191–203.

66. See my introduction to C. G. Stevens, *Winchester Notions* (London, 1998), 2–7.

67. C. M. Bowra, 'John Dewar Denniston', *Proceedings of the British Academy* 35 (1949), 219–32.

68. A notable recent exception is Honey and Curthoys, 'Oxford and schooling' (cited in note 29 above).

69. M. C. Curthoys, *HUO 6*, 481.

70. For these journals, see P. G. Naiditch, 'Classical Studies in Nineteenth-Century Great Britain as Background to the "Cambridge Ritualists"', in W. M. Calder III (ed.), *The Cambridge Ritualists Reconsidered* (*Illinois Classical Studies*, Supplement 2) (Urbana, 1991), 123–52.

71. Dowling, *Hellenism*.

72. In 'A "plastic structure"', *HUO 7*, 34–8, Michael Brock seems concerned to play down such matters and does not refer to Dowling's book.

73. Dowling, *Hellenism*, 79 n. 5.

74. *Old and Odd Memories* (London, 1908), 181. Cf. the remarks of P. B. Nockles, 'Lost Causes and Impossible Loyalties: The Oxford Movement and the University', *HUO 6*, 195–267, on p. 211.

75. For tutorials and supervisions at Trinity, see J. Smith, 'Carrot and Stick', in J. Smith and C. A. Stray (eds.), *Teaching and Learning in Nineteenth-Century Cambridge* (Woodbridge, 2001).

76. M. Barber *The Captain* (London, 1996), 75. In this case the reference is surely to rowing boats.

77. J. A. Gere and J. Sparrow (eds.), *Geoffrey Madan's Notebooks* (Oxford, 1981), 24.

78. It is difficult to resist the speculation that initially Postgate confused the two Ediths.

79. (Cambridge, 1903), 126. The sacrifice is there identified as part of the Thesmophoria.

80. S. Peacock, *The Mask and the Self* (New Haven, 1988), 160–1. Her interpretation was uncritically taken over by N. G. Annan, *The Dons* (London, 1999), 238–9.

81. There is an obvious clue in J. G. Stewart, *Jane Ellen Harrison. A Portrait from Letters* (London, 1959). Cornford's line drawing is on p. 108. On p. 109 the drawing on which Frances Cornford's picture was based is reproduced, with the caption 'ἅλαδε μύσται To the Sea, Mystics! At the Eleusinian Mysteries "Each man took and bathed with his own pig"'.

82. Harrison's *Themis* (Cambridge, 1912) includes a chapter by Cornford and an excursus by Gilbert Murray.

83. See further W. M. Beard, *The Invention of Jane Harrison* (Cambridge MA, 2000); A. Robinson, *Jane Harrison: Life and Work* (Oxford, 2001).

84. Cf W. M. Beard, 'Learning to Pick the Easy Plums: The Invention of Ancient History in Nineteenth-Century Classics', in Smith and Stray (eds.), *Teaching and Learning*.

85. It is now commonplace to dismiss the identification of a group of 'Cambridge Ritualists' as reification. In the future it may be necessary to go beyond both original construction and subsequent deconstruction. What is beyond dispute is that a dynamic nexus of relationships existed, and that Harrison formed its major node.

86. Nockles, 'Lost causes', 211.

87. I. Small, *Conditions for Criticism: Authority, Knowledge and Literature in the Late Nineteenth Century* (Oxford, 1991).

88. A case in point is the grouping together of Jane Harrison, Francis Cornford and Gilbert Murray as 'the Cambridge Ritualists': on which, see e.g. Beard, *Invention*, 109–28.

89. A. Grafton, 'Introduction: notes from underground on cultural transmission', in A. Grafton and A. Blair (eds.), *Transmission of Culture in Early Modern Europe* (Philadelphia, 1990), 2. The point had been made some time before by J. H. Whitfield, 'Momus and the nature of humanism', in R. R. Bolgar (ed.), *Classical Influences on European Culture 1500–1900* (Cambridge, 1971), 177–81.

90. F. M. Turner, *The Greek Heritage in Victorian Britain* (New Haven, 1981), 8. The reference is to E. M. Butler's influential book *The Tyranny of Greece over Germany* (Cambridge, 1935).

91. R. Jakobson, 'Shifters, Verbal Categories, and the Russian Verb', in *Selected Writings* (The Hague, 1971), ii. 130–47.

92. B Bernstein, 'On the classification and framing of educational knowledge', *Class, Codes and Control 1: Towards a Theoretical Sociology of Language* (London, 1971), 202–30.

93. The former are predicated on the assumption of stability; the latter, of change. See M. C. Albrow, 'Dialectical and Categorical Paradigms of a Science of Society', *Sociological Review*, 22 (1974), 183–201.

94. See the brief discussion in C. A. Stray, 'Beyond Classification—Bernstein and the Grammarians', *History of Education*, 19 (1990), 267–9.

95. P. Bourdieu and J. P. Passeron, *La Réproduction* (Paris, 1970).

96. For a detailed critique of Bernstein and Bourdieu from this point of view, see M. S. Archer, 'Process Without System', *European Journal of Sociology*, 24 (1983), 193–221.

97. Cf. Randall McLeod, 'Information on information', *Text*, 5 (1990), 239–80, on p. 244: 'the text's "transformission"—how it was transformed as it was transmitted'.

98. I. Westbury, 'The Melbourne and Sydney Arts Courses 1852–61', *Melbourne Studies in Education* (1961–2), 256–84.

99. D. Johnson, 'Aspects of a Liberal Education: Late Nineteenth-Century Attitudes to Race, from Cambridge to the Cape Colony', *History Workshop Journal*, 36 (1993), 163–82.

100. The term derives from 'B. Truscot' [E. A. Peers], *Redbrick University* (London, 1943).

101. See M. Strathern, 'From Improvement to Enhancement: An Anthropological Comment on the Audit Culture', *Cambridge Anthropology*, 19 (1996–7), 1–21.

102. 'Subject' is cited by *OED* from 1843, not long after 'classics' first appears as a singular noun. The common source is probably the examination system of the reconstructed University of London (1836–).

103. For a study of the 1906 praelections for the Cambridge Greek chair as a symbolic moment in this process, see C. A. Stray (ed.), *The Owl of Minerva: the Cambridge Praelections of 1906. Proceedings of the Cambridge Philological Society*, supplementary vol. 28, forthcoming 2002.

104. Stray, *Classics Transformed*; M. St J. Forrest, *Modernising the Classics* (Exeter, 1996).

86

EXPERIMENTAL SCIENCE IN EARLY NINETEENTH-CENTURY OXFORD

G. L'E. Turner

Source: *History of Universities* VIII (1989): 117–35.

I

The use of demonstration apparatus to teach experimental philosophy on Baconian principles was practised by individual lecturers at Oxford and Cambridge universities at the end of the seventeenth century. This method of teaching, generally called the lecture-demonstration, brought about the widespread popularization of science during the eighteenth century, a phenomenon recognized in 1789 by James Keir, when he wrote:

> The diffusion of a general knowledge, and of a taste for science, over all classes of men, in every nation of Europe, or of European origin, seems to be the characteristic feature of the present age.[1]

Such wide dissemination resulted in a demand for scientific instructions that gradually became institutionalized. The University of Oxford, because of its examination structure, was comparatively slow to include the experimental sciences formally in its curriculum. There is, however, plenty of evidence that science lectures outside the classical curriculum were enthusiastically attended by a considerable proportion of undergraduates during the eighteenth, and the first half of the nineteenth centuries.[2]

The beginnings of the lecture-demonstration may be seen in the early years of the Royal Society, at the meetings for which Robert Hooke was required to produce 'three or four considerable experiments' on each occasion. William Whiston, Newton's successor in the Lucasian chair at Cambridge, taught the Baconian programme using much apparatus, and his published and illustrated lectures set a pattern for over a century. Because

239

of his supposed heretical views, Whiston left Cambridge for London in 1710 and continued his lecture courses at a coffee-house in conjunction with an instrument maker.[3] The man who began the study of experimental philosophy at Oxford was the Scot, David Gregory, who became Savilian professor of astronomy in 1691. Three years later he was followed from Edinburgh by John Keill, who started in 1700 a lecture course using apparatus, some of his own devising. John Desaguliers, another highly successful lecturer in London, had spent three years lecturing at Hart Hall, Oxford, before his move to the capital in 1713.[4]

The tradition established by Newton remained strong at Cambridge, and the importance of natural philosophy was confirmed in 1782 by the establishment of the Jacksonian professorship of natural and experimental philosophy. The will of the founder actually required an abundance of 'fact' to be demonstrated. The first holder of the chair was Isaac Milner, who, with his successor, Francis Wollaston, concentrated his teaching largely on chemistry. Wollaston began by lecturing alternately on experimental philosophy and chemistry, performing, it is said, no fewer than 300 experiments annually.[5] He handed over his apparatus to Samuel Vince, who was elected in 1796 to the Plumian professorship of astronomy. Vince advertised a course of lectures in 1793 which placed a strong emphasis on mathematics and astronomy, but which relied heavily on practical demonstrations.[6]

Extremely large cabinets of apparatus were acquired by all the lecture-demonstrators, whether at the universities in Britain, Holland, France, and the United States, or by the travelling lecturers such as Stephen Demainbray or Benjamin Martin, and many others.[7] A third class of cabinet 'maker' came from the nobility and wealthy landowners. John Stuart, third earl of Bute (1713–92), was a patron of science as well as of literature and art. He had a very extensive collection of minerals, a library of books on natural history and botany, and a cabinet. This was sold at auction in 1793 in 255 lots, the number of individual items being around 500.[8] The chemical laboratory was sold separately. When the future King George III was born in 1738, Lord Bute was twenty-five, and from the evidence of his correspondence was at that time interested in scientific apparatus. It seems clear that in science as well as in matters of state, Lord Bute had a profound influence on the king. At Kew, the king kept a cabinet of experimental apparatus that numbered well over a thousand items, and much of it remains today in the London Science Museum.[9] Stephen Demainbray was employed as the lecture-demonstrator to the royal household during the 1750s, and he it was who expanded the collection. Eventually, when it was decided to discontinue the maintenance of the Kew Observatory, where the instruments were kept, the mechanical and physical apparatus was sent in 1841 to King's College in the Strand, for use in 'a general course of Experimental Philosophy'. A permanent base for lecture demonstrations was provided in London by the foundation in 1799 of the Royal Institution by the American, Benjamin

Thompson, known as Count Rumford. The prospectus by Rumford, published in 1799, bore the title: *Proposal for forming by subscription in the Metropolis of the British Empire, a Public Institution for diffusing the knowledge and facilitating the general introduction of Useful Mechanical Inventions and Improvements, and for teaching, by Courses of Philosophical Lectures and Experiments, the application of Science to the Common Purposes of Life.*[10] This foundation is world famous for its lecture-demonstrations that continue to the present, and for the fundamental and far-reaching research of Humphry Davy and Michael Faraday, to mention but two. After the departure of Rumford in 1802, Davy came to the Royal Institution from Thomas Beddoes' Pneumatic Institution at Bristol, and his lecture-demonstrations were an immediate success, so much so that the dry and far more theoretical lectures of Thomas Young had to be terminated.[11]

The model was soon followed by the London Institution, founded in the City of London in 1805, which became the largest and best endowed of the new style of scientific establishments of the early nineteenth century.[12] Its purpose was to 'promote the diffusion of Science, Literature, and the Arts'. Large premises were built, which were opened in 1819. In the first year there were five different series of lectures, the subject of one being 'Elements of chemistry and its connection with arts and manufactures', while another was entitled 'Experimental philosophy; or the useful application of natural philosophy to society by hydrostatics, mechanics, optics, and the use of the steam-engine and other machines'. This was just the sort of syllabus taught at Oxford by Charles Daubeny from 1822 (chemistry), and by Stephen Rigaud from 1810 (experimental philosophy), although the location in the Ashmolean building was minute and ill-equipped compared with London.

The skills required by technical advances during the early nineteenth century made it necessary for the workers to understand the principles that underlay the tasks required of them. Craft training had in earlier times been undertaken by the apprentice system of the guilds, but the new era demanded a new approach. A most important movement was that of the Mechanics' Institutes, which became so popular that it has been estimated that 610 existed in England and Wales by 1850.[13] What is regarded as the inspiration for these institutes is the Andersonian Institution at Glasgow, where George Birkbeck, professor of natural philosophy, gave lectures for artisans in around 1800.[14] The first that was formally founded was the Edinburgh School of Arts in 1821, which is now the Heriot-Watt University. Here courses on chemistry, natural philosophy, applied chemistry and applied mechanics were given. The London Mechanics' Institute was founded in 1823 and continues today as Birkbeck College, in the University of London. The syllabus comprised chemistry, mathematics, hydrostatics, applied chemistry, astronomy and electricity.

In North America, the first lecture-demonstrations were performed at Harvard College from 1727.[15] At the end of the century, from 1790,

Transylvania College at Lexington, Kentucky, acquired apparatus, a considerable purchase being made in Paris in 1821.[16] Similar purchases, worth £1446, were made by the college of Charleston, South Carolina, at much the same period.[17] In the 1830s, the Seminary at Quebec bought a consignment of apparatus in London, and later sent staff on buying trips to Paris.[18] These few examples will serve to indicate that a pattern similar to that in Europe was being repeated elsewhere.

II

The world in which the University of Oxford found itself by the beginning of the nineteenth century was, then, full of enthusiasm for science and technology, from the king down to the artisan. In 1800, the university introduced examinations in classics and mathematics, but not in the physical sciences at that time. The latter were included in the examination system in 1849 with the formation of the honour school of Natural Science.[19] It was this that brought about the building of the new University Museum in Parks Road, the Gothic pile erected between 1855 and 1860.[20] Here were housed the science professors (with the exception of those at the Botanic Garden), with their departments of chemistry, experimental philosophy, mineralogy, geology, medicine, and anatomy, plus an observatory for the Savilian professor. Thus the Ashmolean Museum building in Broad Street was finally replaced as the scientific institution of the university.

The Ashmolean Museum, opened in 1683, contained the chemical laboratory and the lecture room for natural history, as it was named.[21] It was in this room that the lecture-demonstrations were performed from 1714 by John Whiteside (1714–29), James Bradley (1730–60), Nathaniel Bliss (1760–2), Thomas Hornsby (1763–1810), and Stephen Rigaud (1810–32).[22] Occasionally an anatomy was performed and teaching of mineralogy and geology was done from time to time. Pressures for the expansion of teaching in science, and for space to hold the growing collection of the museum, forced a series of departures from the old building. The University Press which occupied the Clarendon Building, paid for out of the profits of Lord Clarendon's *History of the Rebellion*, moved to a new site in 1830, leaving space that was taken by the geological collections and by the cabinet of physical apparatus. The initiative was taken by Rigaud, whose title was reader in experimental philosophy, and William Buckland, reader in mineralogy from 1813, and also reader in geology from 1818.

The critical years for Oxford were around 1790, when Thomas Beddoes was lecturing on chemistry. He published a devastating criticism of the Bodleian Library in 1787, pointing out a neglect to keep up with scientific journals and scientific books, comparing it unfavourably with some small-town subscription libraries.[23] From his extensive travels, Beddoes thought the Bodleian to be one of the worst conducted public libraries in Europe, unfit for an institution instructing the youth of a great commercial state. Beddoes himself lectured diligently on chemistry, his income being the students' fees from those who voluntarily attended the lectures. Beddoes was a friend of Dean Jackson of Christ Church, one of the instigators of the new examination system of 1800. Beddoes left Oxford in some disgust in 1792 for Bristol, where he set up the Pneumatic Institute, employing there the young Humphry Davy.

The last of the old style chemical readers was Robert Bourne, who succeeded Beddoes in 1794. His approach to the teaching of chemistry was schoolmasterly and practical: to provide students who were to become MPs, landed gentry, manufacturers, and physicians, with a basic knowledge of the properties of matter. But a change had been initiated by the criticisms of Beddoes, and three new professorships were established under the will of George Aldrich. They were filled in 1803 as follows: professor of the practice of medicine, Robert Bourne; professor of anatomy, Christopher Pegge; professor of chemistry, John Kidd. It is interesting to note that the stipend of the chemical professor was augmented by a grant from the Crown in 1817, as had been the stipends of the readers in experimental philosophy and mineralogy in 1813.

A leading reformer and chemist of the first half of the nineteenth century was Charles Daubeny, who, after taking his BA at Oxford, graduated in medicine in Edinburgh in 1818. Elected to the Aldrichian chair of chemistry in 1822, he immediately asked for and received a large grant to buy chemical apparatus and he tried to undertake research.[24] He added to himself the Sherardian chair of botany in 1834, and in 1840 the chair in rural economy, so had both the means and incentive to move out of the basement of the Ashmolean Museum to a large new building erected at his own expense adjacent to the Botanic Garden. This move occurred in 1848. Daubeny was a campaigner and pamphleteer endeavouring to counter the 'neglect' of science in Oxford, and to promote the educational value of chemistry, apart from its economic value. He was in at the foundation of the British Association for the Advancement of Science, and was responsible for inviting it to meet at Oxford in 1832.[25]

Turning now to what is today called physics, we find Thomas Hornsby, an eighteenth-century pluralist, who collected successively the positions of Savilian professor of astronomy 1763, Radcliffe Observer 1772, Sedleian professor of natural philosophy 1782, and Radcliffe Librarian 1783. He also conducted the lecture-demonstrations on experimental philosophy in the Ashmolean, having a collection of apparatus that was valued in 1790 at £375.[26] The course continued in the tradition of the beginning of the eighteenth century, the subject headings being mechanics, optics, hydrostatics, and pneumatics. Hornsby had reacted quickly to new discoveries, and in 1785 he delivered a course specifically on 'The different Kinds of Air', based on the discoveries of Priestly. It included the theory of balloons, and one should give the Ashmolean extra credit here, because the assistant in the chemical laboratory, James Sadler, had the previous year been the first Englishman to go up in a balloon.[27]

On the death of Hornsby in 1810, Rigaud took over the teaching of experimental philosophy. He had, in fact, been groomed to take over, and had deputized when Hornsby was ill. It is also not surprising that he had experimental skills, since he was the grandson of Stephen Demainbray, the King's astronomer at Kew and the man responsible for keeping the cabinet of physical apparatus there. Rigaud held the Readership till his death in 1839 concurrently with the Savilian chairs first of geometry and then of astronomy, to which he moved in 1827. However, when Robert Walker succeeded Rigaud in 1839 he did so as reader in experimental philosophy in its own right, not now annexed to a Savilian professorship. The full independence and importance of the subject was finally shown by the conversion to a professorship in 1860, the date of the opening of the new University Museum. In effect, Walker was the first professor of physics at Oxford. A quantity of apparatus still exists from his era, and may be seen in the Museum of the History of Science.

III

The account given above has brought in the names of those who lectured in the physical sciences during the first half of the nineteenth century, and has outlined the movements from building to building as pressures increased. What remains to be done is to consider just what was taught, and how far new developments in science were reflected. Also, how did the audience of young men react to the teaching? Here a great deal of work needs to be undertaken. Because experimental sciences were not part of the examination structure, either before or after 1800, there are no statutes to look to for guidance. But there were syllabuses printed for the use of those who attended the lectures, and some of these may be found. They indicate a very traditional scheme of experimental demonstration, one which changes hardly at all until the 1790s, after which some of the new discoveries are inserted. A mathematical approach is apparently deliberately avoided, because few students had sufficient knowledge of mathematics. But there are some lecturers who add some geometrical or analytical workings in smaller type or as an appendix. Rigaud, obviously a very careful and systematic man, who had an informed interest in the history of science, collected syllabuses, and his collection, including some of his own, is now kept (thanks to a donation by the Radcliffe Trustees in the 1930s) in the Oxford Museum of the History of Science.

Examples of Rigaud's printed syllabuses for 1812, 1813, 1821 and 1824 exist, increasing in extent from 20 to 48 pages. The main headings are: introduction, matter and motion, mechanics, hydrostatics, pneumatics and hydraulics, meteorology, optics, electricity, magnetism. Intercomparison shows that novelties and new experiments from the world outside were constantly added in. To pick out a few, one may name the polarization of light, Fraunhofer's spectra, the Italian Professor Amici's reflecting microscope, wave theory, Captain Kater's pendulum experiments and the new standards of length, and the friction of carriages on rail-roads. It is clear that this was the period when natural and experimental philosophy was turning into the physics and applied physics of the end of the nineteenth century. While the teaching of the classics that led to the examinations for the BA was in the hands of the colleges, the university provided unexamined courses in the sciences that attempted to satisfy the intellectual curiosity aroused by the 'taste for science' held to be the 'characteristic feature of the present age'.

The trouble was not the capabilities of most of the science professors, but the attitudes to science of those college men who governed the teaching and the examining for the BA in Literae Humaniores. And the Rudiments of Religion allowed no discretionary power to the examiners; failure here meant no degree at all. As adherence to the Thirty-Nine Articles was required, the university was attacked for religious exclusiveness. Criticizing Oxford, *The Athenaeum* wrote, in 1834, 'The universal spread of extra-academical knowledge, and the tone of utilitarianism . . . render it impossible that the course of education, which was the admiration of our forefathers, can be tolerated by their descendants'.[28] The editor pointed out that science was intimately mixed up with the prosperity and well-being of society, and should be included in every course of liberal education. He went on to complain that Oxford neither encouraged science among its students nor paid its professors as much as 'a pittance sufficient to meet even the most moderate views in life'.

Indeed, critics were all around, even inside the university, and the reason for this was that fundamental changes were taking place. As Arthur Engel puts it, in his even-handed essay,

> crucial to the intellectual conflicts and institutional changes at Oxford in the first half of the nineteenth century was the question of whether the university was to provide careers for academic men, and, if so, what sorts of careers these were to be in terms of functions, status, and income.[29]

It must be remembered that, at the beginning of the century, the Oxford don was by profession a clergyman, not a teacher, for holy orders and celibacy were conditions for holding a fellowship. The pattern was that after ten years or so the fellowship was relinquished for a living generally in the gift of the college, and probably for marriage. But by the end of the nineteenth century, most college fellows were career teachers, spending all their lives in the profession. While this crucial change was in process of taking place, the increasing strictness introduced into the examination statutes led to a growing number of private coaches.[30] This may provide a reason for the complaint that professorial lectures were ill-attended. Professor Daubeny wrote a letter to Convocation on 24 February, 1839, to explain that he had cancelled his chemical course because of low numbers.[31] His high point had been in 1828 with 45 auditors; in 1840, after his cancelled year, he could muster a total of only 10 auditors: 4 graduates, 3 undergraduates, and 3 who were not members of the university. Daubeny thought that professorial lectures ought to be compulsory, and that they should be examined and an attendance certificate issued. Yet another cause for the turning away from science was the onset of the Tractarian movement from 1830 onwards: in the eyes of the Oxford establishment science was just not relevant.

The attitudes within the University of Oxford cannot be completely fathomed by a reading of the statutes, the minutes of the hebdomadal board, or the position papers of those pressing for reform. What is necessary is an investigation into those who did choose to pay up their fee and attend the lectures of the various professors. Attendance registers do, luckily, exist. The late J. M. Edmonds, curator of the geological collections, had amassed a great deal of information on course attendance, and he had also identified most of the names on the registers. His papers have been deposited at the Museum of the History of Science, where they are being edited for publication by the librarian, Mr A. V. Simcock. The brief analysis below is derived from the MSS Edmonds 10–28, but must be taken as preliminary and as an indication only, since the full analysis of the courses is complicated through some being split into parts either in terms of level or in terms of topic. In Tables 1 and 2 the attendance registers of Daubeny's course in chemistry, Rigaud's course in experimental philosophy, Buckland's courses in mineralogy and geology are compared in various ways: total numbers, average per course, the percentage of doctors, MAs, BAs, and undergraduates at

Table 1 Attendance at Oxford Science Lectures, 1818–48.

Subject	Chemistry	Exp. Philos.	Mineralogy	Geology
Years of Lectures	1822–49	1818–39	1814–49	1814–49
Number of Courses	29	40	33	33
Total Attended	439	725	818	1055
*Average Attendance per Course	15	18	25	32
Average Attendance of Non-University Auditors per course	2.7	1.2	1	1

* Rounded figures

Table 2 Average Attendance at Oxford Science Lectures, 1818–48.

Subject	Chemistry		Exp. Philos.		Mineralogy		Geology	
Years of Lectures	1822–49		1818–39		1814–49		1814–49	
	N	%	N	%	N	%	N	%
Doctors	0.2	1	0	0	0.5	2	1	3
MA	5.3	35	1.9	10	7.7	31	7.8	25
BA	4	26	4.7	26	7.6	31	7.9	25
Undergraduates	5.6	37	11.6	64	9	36	15.2	47
*Total	15	100	18	100	25	100	32	100

*Rounded figures

each course, and the numbers of non-university auditors. The information is also presented in the form of histograms in Tables A to D.

Of the members of the university who attended the courses, undergraduates accounted for between one-third and two-thirds in all four subjects. The geology course attracted the largest audience, the chemistry the smallest. On the other hand chemistry always attracted the largest number of non-university auditors (albeit a handful). Geology lost its appeal dramatically after 1840, collecting in that year only 11, to be compared with the 87 of 1824, a peak. Mineralogy doubtless had less of a theological interest, hence lower numbers. It went down from 1834, with only 9 auditors compared with a peak of 57 in 1817. Chemistry hit a low point from 1839 to 1844, when there began a slight rise. But experimental philosophy maintained a very steady interest through all its varied topics and for the whole of the period considered, 1811 to 1831 (i.e., to the end of the Ashmolean period before the move to the Clarendon Building). The peak attendance was 40 in 1818, Lent term, and the lowest 4 in 1827, Easter term, but this is a freak figure. The large numbers of MAs attending is noticeable in all courses, except experimental philosophy (which attracted not a single Doctor).

These figures may be compared with those taken from the register of James Bradley's lectures on experimental philosophy from 1746 to 1760. The average attendance was 37 at a course, and the charge was three guineas, giving an average income of £116. As two or three courses were given each year, the income was appreciable. During the fifteen-year period, 1221 men attended Bradley's lecture-demonstrations.[32] This is a remarkable number considering the size of the university, for around 1750 the average yearly matriculation was just 200, so in fifteen years some 3000 would have entered, thus showing that about one third of the university came to hear and view Bradley's performance.

Little is known about the disposition of the lecture rooms in the Ashmolean Building. A visitor from Denmark made a simple drawing of the horseshoe

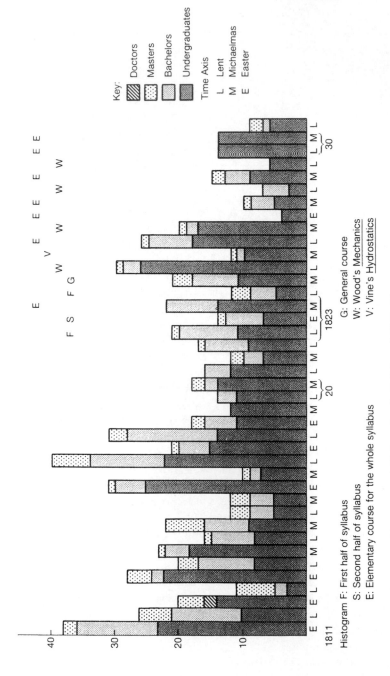

Figure A Courses in Experimental Philosophy, S. P. Rigaud 1811–31.

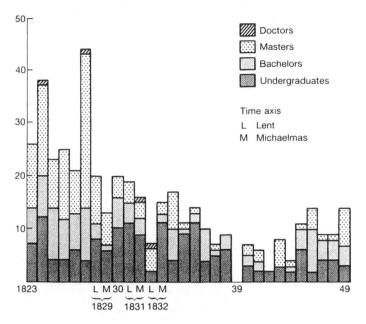

Figure B Courses in Chemistry, C. G. B. Daubeny, 1823–49.

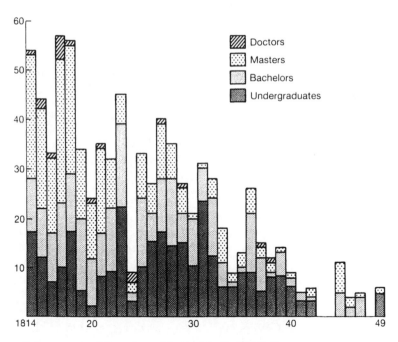

Figure C Lectures in Mineralogy, W. Buckland, 1814–49.

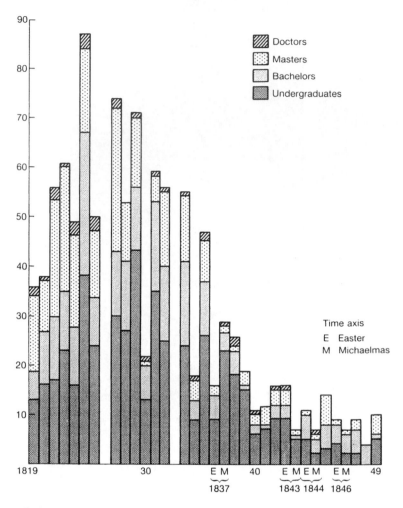

Figure D Lectures in Geology and Palaeontology, W. Buckland, 1819–49.

seating in three tiers during his 1777 visit, but that is all.[33] A lithograph of 1823 is probably the only representation of a lecture given during the first half of the nineteenth century. It shows William Buckland demonstrating fossils to a gathering of 52 in a room on the western side of the upper ground floor of the Ashmolean. An analysis of the auditors has been published in 1976 by the late J. M. Edmonds and the late J. A. Douglas. They showed that the 52 in the audience was composed of 3 heads of colleges, 19 Fellows, 8 BAs not Fellows, 19 undergraduates, and 3 who were not members of the university.[34] The disposition of the facilities for science teaching on the first floor of the Clarendon Building in rooms vacated by the Press is known from a drawing, dated May 1831, done by the architect Sir Robert

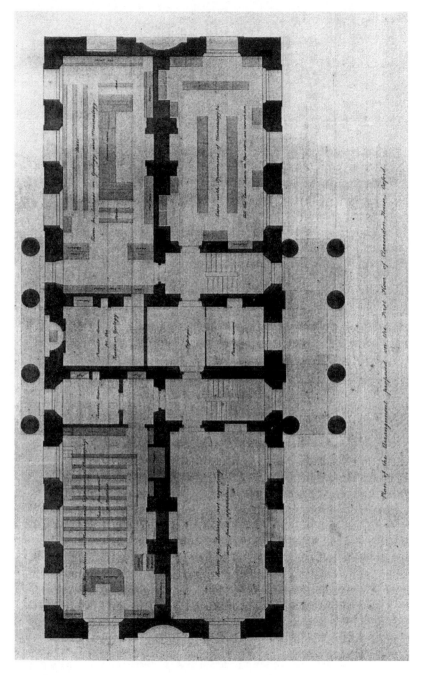

Figure 1 Plan of the Arrangement proposed on the first floor of the Clarendon House, Oxford, 1831.

Smirke.[35] The space given over to Rigaud is labelled: 'Room for Lectures on Natural and Experimental Philosophy'. There is a U-shaped 'Reader's Table', four cases on the walls for apparatus, a book press, and a special table marked: 'Model of Steam Engine'.[36] The lecturer behind his bench faced nine rows of benches, the back five being raked, and Smirke has labelled this part: 'Seats for about 70 Students'. Clearly, there were expectations for the future, for Rigaud had only reached a total of 40 auditors in 1818, and for his elementary course in 1830 had an audience of not more than 14. In the opposite corner of the building was a space marked by Smirke as a 'Room for Lectures on Geology and Mineralogy', which had benches to seat around 65. This space was needed in 1834, but audiences soon fell away (Table D).

It has been shown that during the first half of the nineteenth century there was a very considerable demand for scientific knowledge at all levels throughout the Western world. Should Oxford, as one of the premier universities, have welcomed the teaching of science more wholeheartedly than it did? Or was Oxford right to hold it at arm's length, as had been done with the older professions of medicine and law, by sending students who had completed their course in the *litterae humaniores* to the London hospitals and the Inns of Court? Oxford saw itself as a guardian of knowledge and not a creator of it: science would be better done elsewhere. Reforms in teaching methods, incentives to make students work, the proper design of examinations, these were necessary and were carried out. But if a university is there to train the mind of the young is it also necessarily obliged to fill it with practical facts? If today many universities do just that, is it right to assume that all should do so, and that this is a fair criterion by which to judge the University of Oxford 150 years ago?

References

1. J. K. [James Keir], *The First Part of a Dictionary of Chemistry &c* (Birmingham, 1789), p. iii.
2. G. L'E. Turner, 'The Physical Sciences', in L. S. Sutherland and L. G. Mitchell (eds.), *The History of the University of Oxford* v. The Eighteenth Century (Oxford, 1986), 659–81.
3. W. Whiston, *Memoirs of the Life and Writings of Mr William Whiston, containing memoirs of several of his friends also* (London, 1749), 135ff, 235ff.
4. See the Preface to J. T. Desaguliers, *A Course of Experimental Philosophy* (2 vols.; London, 1734–44). Nicholas Hans, 'The Rosicrucians of the Seventeenth Century and John Theophilus Desaguliers, the Pioneer of Adult Education', *Adult Education*, 7 (1935), 229–40.
5. R. T. Gunther, *Early Science in Cambridge* (Oxford, 1937), 81.
6. Ibid., 82f.
7. A. E. Musson and E. Robinson, *Science and Technology in the Industrial Revolution* (Manchester, 1969), especially chapter 1; Jean Torlais, 'La Physique

expérimentale', in René Taton (ed.), *Enseignement et diffusion des sciences en France au XVIIIe siècle* (Paris, 1964), 619–36; J. R. Millburn, *Benjamin Martin: Author, Instrument-maker and 'Country Showman'* (Leyden, 1976); Geert Vanpaemel, 'Experimental Physics and the Natural Science Curriculum in Eighteenth Century Louvain', *History of Universities* vii (1988) 175–96.

8. G. L'E. Turner, 'The Auction Sale of the Earl of Bute's Instruments, 1793', *Annals of Science*, 23 (1967), 213–42.

9. J. A. Chaldecott, *Handbook of the King George III Collection of Scientific Instruments* (London, 1951).

10. Reprinted in *Proceedings of the Royal Institution*, 6 (1872).

11. References to Beddoes are in Dorothy A. Stansfield, *Thomas Beddoes M.D. 1760–1808: Chemist. Physician, Democrat* (Dordrecht, 1984); Turner, 'Physical Sciences', 666–8; A. V. Simcock, *The Ashmolean Museum and Oxford Science 1683–1983* (Oxford, 1984), 35, n. 91; and D. A. Stansfield and R. G. Stansfield, 'Dr Thomas Beddoes and James Watt: Preparatory Work 1794–96 for the Bristol Pneumatic Institute', *Medical History*, 30 (1986), 276–302. On Young, see G. N. Cantor, 'Thomas Young's Lectures at the Royal Institution', *Notes and Records of the Royal Society*, 25 (1970), 87–112.

12. J. N. Hays, 'Science in the City: The London Institution, 1819–40', *British Journal for the History of Science*, 7 (1974), 146–62.

13. Musson and Robinson, *Science and Technology*, 181f.

14. T. Kelly, *George Birkbeck* (London, 1957).

15. I. Bernard Cohen, *Some Early Tools of American Science: An Account of the Early Scientific Instruments . . . in Harvard University* (Cambridge, Mass., 1950).

16. Leland A. Brown, *Early Philosophical Apparatus at Transylvania College* (Lexington, Kentucky, 1959).

17. Barbara Hughes, *Catalog of the Scientific Apparatus at the College of Charlston: 1800–1940* (Charlston, South Carolina, 1980).

18. Paul Carle, 'Le cabinet de physique et l'enseignement des sciences au Séminaire de Québec', *Cap au Diamant* (revue de la Société historique de Québec), autunm 1985.

19. F. Sherwood Taylor, 'The Teaching of Science at Oxford in the Nineteenth Century', *Annals of Science*, 8 (1952), 82–112. On the development of the examination system at early nineteenth-century Oxford generally, see M. Curthoys, 'The Early Years of the Oxford Examination System, 1800–1830' (unpublished conference paper).

20. A. V. Simcock, *The Ashmolean Museum and Oxford Science 1683–1983* (Oxford, 1984).

21. R. F. Ovenell, *The Ashmolean Museum 1683–1894* (Oxford, 1986).

22. Turner. 'Physical Sciences'; Simcock, *Ashmolean Museum*.

23. E. Robinson, 'Thomas Beddoes, M.D., and the Reform of Science Teaching in Oxford', *Annals of Science*, 11 (1955), 137–41; Thomas Beddoes, *A Memorial Concerning the State of the Bodleian Library* (Oxford, 1787).

24. For many references, see Simcock, *Ashmolean Museum*, 36, n. 93. For the chemistry laboratory and equipment, much of which remains, see C. R. Hill, *Museum of the History of Science: Catalogue 1 Chemical Apparatus* (Oxford, 1971); the Appendix has the 1823 inventory of apparatus bought with a vote of £200.

25. Jack Morrell and Arnold Thackray, *Gentlemen of Science: Early Years of the British Association for the Advancement of Science* (Oxford, 1981).
26. Bodleian Library, MS Top. Oxon. c.236, ff. 3–13; R. T. Gunther, *Early Science in Oxford*, xi (Oxford, 1937), p. 195.
27. J. E. Hodgson, 'James Sadler of Oxford, Aeronaut, Chemist, Engineer and Inventor', *Transactions of the Newcomen Society*, 8 (1927–8).
28. *The Athenaeum*, No. 344, 31 May 1834, in a review of Daubeny's Inaugural Lecture on the Study of Botany.
29. Arthur Engel, 'The Emerging Concept of the Academic Profession at Oxford 1800–1854', in L. Stone (ed.) *The University in Society* (2 vols.; Princeton, N.J., 1975) i. 309.
30. Ibid., p. 313.
31. Charles G. B. Daubeny, 'To the Members of Convocation', 24 February 1839 (Papers relating to the Proceedings of the University, 1839 Bodleian Library, Oxford).
32. Turner, 'Physical Sciences', 673. Bradley's attendance list in the Bodleian Library, MS Bradley 3, is printed in R. T. Gunther, *Early Science in Oxford*, xi, 359–98.
33. Kongelige Bibliotek, Copenhagen, MS Ny kgl. Saml. 377 e, f.67r (The Travel Diary of Thomas Bugge, 1777). The plan, redrawn, is reproduced in Simcock, *Ashmolean Museum*, opposite p. 12.
34. J. M. Edmonds and J. A. Douglas, 'William Buckland, F.R.S. (1784–1856) and an Oxford Geological Lecture 1823', *Notes and Records of the Royal Society*, 30 (1976), 141–67.
35. Oxlord University Archives, UD/11/1/2 & 3.
36. Most likely the working model of a James Watt beam engine by Watkins & Hill of London, now on display in the Museum of the History of Science. It is illustrated in colour on Plate VIII in G. L'E. Turner, *Nineteenth-Century Scientific Instruments* (London, 1983).

87

STRUCTURAL CHANGE IN ENGLISH HIGHER EDUCATION, 1870–1920

Roy Lowe

Source: Detlef K. Müller, Fritz Ringer and Brian Simon (eds) *The Rise of the Modern Educational System, 1870–1920*, Cambridge: Cambridge University Press, 1987, pp. 163–78.

English higher education underwent a complete transformation in the period 1870 to 1920. At the outset provision was unsystematic and, for many social groups, sporadic. The four small existing universities catered for so few of the population that it was left to a plethora of Mechanics' Institutes, Literary and Philosophical Societies and adult schools to provide any sort of post-school facility for the mass of the people. During the fifty years after 1870 the process of growth by which this crisis was relieved involved the creation of a clearly defined and widely recognised hierarchical structure. To what extent this marked a conscious attempt at the segregation of social classes, and to what extent an inexorable response to external pressures, is uncertain, but it is possible to attempt a description of the hierarchies which were established.

In this analysis agencies of higher education must be considered as part of a developing system, in a relationship not only with the emergent secondary and elementary schools but also with the growing industries and professions. Central to the analysis attempted here is a consideration of how far this process was part of the rigid stratification of society by which dominant social groups used the educational system to preserve their position, and the extent to which this was alleviated by a meritocratic function.

At the apex of this emergent system stood the Oxbridge colleges. An important element in the dynamic of change was the fierce determination of those within the two leading universities to ensure that the pre-eminence of these institutions was not eroded. The tokens of that pre-eminence were a continuing strong commitment to a classical education and the maintenance of strict control over admission to the student body.

So fierce were the external pressures for change that there was, naturally enough, a continuing controversy concerning both what should be taught and to whom. Apologists for Oxbridge point out the extent to which traditional curricula were supplemented by new subjects during this period, but, in reality, every proposal to modernise Oxbridge met with a strong groundswell of conservatism. When, in 1907, an appeal was launched at Oxford to finance teaching in modern subjects, particularly the sciences and modern languages, it was emphasised that

> in providing for the endowment of new subjects of a scientific or modern character, the object of this appeal is, while bringing Oxford up to date, not to destroy, but rather to conserve, its old traditions as a university pre-eminently of the 'humane' studies and literary culture.[1]

Similarly, when J. L. Myres, in 1911, proposed a course in Modern Greats, he met a fusilade of criticism. The comment from G. Beardoe Grundy was typical:

> Easy paths to knowledge lead to that worst kind of ignorance which knows nothing well, while pretending to complete knowledge . . . If a man has not brains enough to master Greek sufficiently for the purpose of Lit. Hum. he ought not to be put to the high studies demanded by the examination. The university cannot, without degrading its studies, legislate for those who have had serious defects in their previous education.[2]

This conservatism is explicable in part by the fact that this was the period when the major professions looked increasingly to the ancient universities for entrants who had received either a liberal education or a training in the fundamental sciences. Medicine, the law, architecture and the civil service all began to recruit unprecedented numbers of Oxbridge graduates. Although the new appointments boards of Oxford and Cambridge succeeded in steering many graduates into industry, it must be remembered that many of these graduated in subjects with no immediate links with industrial skills, and that almost all of them went into managerial positions of one sort or another, thus reinforcing an industrial hierarchy.[3]

The more recently founded civic universities all aspired to the status and prestige which was universally afforded to Oxbridge. Their ambitions were summarised in the prospectus of the University of Birmingham, drawn up shortly after the grant of a charter in 1900. 'It is clear', claimed the Birmingham dons,

> that the Chamberlain ideal for the Midland University has always been a school of general culture, specialising in the facilities for

training applied scientists. It is not a technical school; there was already a most excellent one in Birmingham before the university was erected. It is for training 'captains of industry', not the rank and file, or even the non-commissioned officers.[4]

This determination to participate in a competitive scramble for status, which was shared by the other civic universities, and indeed by technical institutions with far less chance of fulfilling their ambitions, was a crucial element in the dynamic of change and helped to precipitate the rigid structuralisation of higher education. It is hardly surprising that institutions sponsored from the profits of a fiercely competitive industrial system and dependent for their well-being and even survival upon attracting students, should succumb to this competitive style from the outset.

What these civic colleges did achieve was to distance themselves from the technical colleges, although in many instances their curricula encroached upon the preserves of those colleges. Equally, they were unable to achieve recognition as first-grade institutions of higher education – this accolade was reserved for Oxbridge, and never truly threatened. Thus, by 1914, a rigidly hierarchical system of higher education had emerged in England.

What made the impact of this development so powerful was the fact that it was geared to a similar hierarchy of secondary schools. The tripartite division foreseen by the Taunton Commissioners in 1868 was, in the event, implemented in a rather different form during the following forty years, with the 'public' schools, the endowed grammar schools and the post-1902 municipal secondary schools becoming the three clearly identified tiers of secondary schooling. Central to this stratification, as to that of higher education, was the notion that able scholars might be promoted on merit through the deployment of a scholarship system. This rationale, which was deployed throughout the period under review, was suspect from its inception. One letter to Joshua Fitch, a Secondary Schools Commissioner, on the Exeter schools indicated the prejudice which from the outset threatened the impartial operation of a scholarship system:

> the creation of exhibitions from elementary schools will not in my opinion give these exhibitions to the poor.
>
> As a rule I take it the poor are of inferior intellect. I take it that the lowest stratum of society is of inferior intellect, or else it would not continue the lowest stratum, and that intellect is hereditary like any other quality.[5]

Within Oxbridge, too, there was some resistance to the opening of access such as was advocated by Mark Pattison. James Bryce, writing to Henry Sidgwick immediately after the publication of *Suggestions on Academical Organisation* in 1868, asked:

Have you seen Pattison's book? It is the clearest and finest thing any of our people has put forth. But all the regular Liberals call out that it is Utopian, some that it is self-interested. Certainly we may fear that if other things have not produced a learned class in England, endowments will not.[6]

Equally, there were those within Oxford who saw the need to dovetail the curriculum to that of the group of schools from which the university would draw. In the protracted debate on the need for geographical studies within the university, which culminated in the appointment of Halford Mackinder to a Readership in 1899, the needs of the Empire were often cited. But, significantly, H. E. Rawlinson, President of the Royal Geographical Society, emphasised in 1871 that

> Geography will become, very shortly, a large and clearly defined part of education in all the Endowed Schools of England, that is to say in the very schools whose boys form the great majority of those affected by the proposed scheme of examination.[7]

On this ground he thought it worthy of addition to the curriculum of the university. Equally, when geography was formally established in the closing years of the century, it was only after the syllabus had been trimmed to meet the demands of traditionalists, such as W. R. Anson of All Souls College, Oxford, who argued that 'if geography is to take its proper place here it must have its root in the Studies of Classical and Modern History'.[8]

It was clear that changes were under way in the secondary schools to which the universities must respond. As early as 1870 the point was emphasised by John Percival at the annual conference of the National Association for the Promotion of Social Science, which was to become an important forum for the discussion of higher education. Percival's remarks are sufficiently pertinent to be worth quoting at length:

> It is this threatening hiatus between the liberal training of our universities and the modern school, as the creation of city life and its requirements, that I see as one of the chief dangers of English education at this time . . . You are no longer content that your boys should spend their time to the age of eighteen in learning portions of a small number of Latin and a still smaller number of Greek authors, something of Latin and Greek grammar and Latin composition, and a smattering withal of elementary mathematics; and yet this is all our universities even profess to exact or enquire about, before a student is admitted to their walls.
>
> They shut out from their influence a whole class of schools, which have sprung up in obedience to what seems a national want, but

which can never grow to anything like full educational stature . . . without some such encouragement as the university alone can give. I speak of the modern school . . . Who frequent our universities? Who are those that come under their influence? Not the men who are directing the life of Manchester, Newcastle, Liverpool, Bristol or Birmingham, but the sons of country gentlemen, or men destined for certain professions, or a few sons of the wealthier merchants and manufacturers; whilst the names of Oxford and Cambridge are strange names to the mass of those who are guiding our industrial and commercial enterprise . . .

Who can fail to lament the want of real living connections between our old universities and the great commercial and industrial centres? A great step will have been taken in this direction if the universities should so reform themselves as to remain closely connected with all middle class schools even those of modern aims and tendencies.

I hope also to see Oxford and Cambridge planning various faculties in every great city, and thus flourishing . . . firmly rooted in the very midst of our industrial and commercial enterprise.[9]

It is significant that Percival did not foresee the creation of new universities as a desirable response to this crisis, but anticipated that the Extension Movement, by which Oxbridge dons visited the provincial cities, could meet the national need. This emphasis, which Percival shared with many influential contemporaries, was to help doom local developments to inferior status.

Significant, too, is the response made to those remarks in discussion by the Rev. Nash Stephenson, who emphasised what was to become a key consideration in any discussion of university reform, the risk of dilution:

I have a misgiving as to the wisdom of opening up a scheme for the advancement of the working classes which might prove illusory, and of raising hopes which could never be realised. There must be 'hewers of wood and drawers of water' . . . If some persons ought to govern the minds of others who looked up to them for guidance, they ought not to open illusory expectations which in the end might inflict injury rather than confer good.[10]

It is in this way that the class exclusivity of the university system was justified.

In this atmosphere it is hardly surprising that change within the existing universities, when it did come, was limited in scope. Indeed, even Mark Pattison, an apologist for university reform, argued in 1876 that unless the English middle classes first reformed themselves, the schools and universities

259

could do nothing for them. For him, intellectual philistinism was the English disease; he lamented

> the wretched destitution of all intellectual nourishment in which the middle classes of England grow up; the absence in middle-class homes of all intelligent interests; the incapacity for ideas which character-ises them; the outer darkness in which their self-complacent exist-ence is passed, while the inexhaustible riches of the several worlds of sciences, of literature, poetry and art are unopened to them, is a modern phenomenon which has now attained the proportions of a social blot . . . The schools will not be improved while the homes remain what they are.[11]

Thus part of the rationale which underpinned the pre-eminence of Oxbridge was the preservation of a gentlemanly ideal in a society evincing increasingly barbaric tendencies. At a conference on secondary education in 1893 the President of Magdalen College stressed that the universities

> must teach those things which have a really educating and elevating effect and teach them in a manner which is really educating and elevating . . . They should ultimately set the standard of the sec-ondary schools . . . all the boys from such schools, nay, all English citizens, should be gentlemen.[12]

But, if the diffusion of cultural values was to be an important function of the universities, reinforcing the significance of a humane education in the liberal arts, it was important, too, that this democratic duty was not taken too far:

> It would be no kindness, no real boon to education or the country if the universities were either to neglect or starve learning and science in the interests of education, or again were to lower their standards and intellectually cheapen their degrees, for the sake of admitting and passing through their midst a number of students from secondary schools. They must hold high the intellectual standard.[13]

This liberal education was justified on the grounds that Oxbridge catered for a particular social group, and this view was shared by critics and apolo-gists alike. On the one hand, Bishop Gore, fighting in 1907 for a Royal Commission on Oxford, complained that 'our university . . . is a playground for the sons of the wealthier classes . . . not in any serious sense a place of study at all'.[14] Among his opponents was Lord Curzon, whose *Principles and Methods of University Reform* argued that changes of too sweeping a nature were unnecessary:

> It is as desirable that Oxford should educate the future country squire, or nobleman, or banker, or member of parliament, or even the guardsman, as that it should sharpen the wits of the school-master or the cultivated artisan . . . We have in our old universities a mechanism for training the well-to-do to a sense of responsibility, and a capacity for public affairs which it would be the height of folly to throw away.[15]

Thus the call of national duty was invoked to justify Oxford's continued ministration to the elite.

In the event, during this period classical and humane studies were deployed to strengthen the bond between the old universities and the more prestigious secondary schools. The outbreak of war in 1914 saw the preeminence of a literary education, offering a route from 'public' school to Oxbridge and thence to the civil service and major professions, reinforced rather than weakened.

Against this background the existing universities attempted to meet the burgeoning demand for higher education through the provision of Extension lectures on an occasional basis. Initiated by James Stuart of Cambridge between 1867 and 1873, it was from the outset foreseen that this movement would bring the universities into contact with social groups they had so far neglected:

> University Extension leads directly . . . to a reconsideration of our course of study. We educate at this place chiefly and almost exclusively clergymen, barristers and country gentlemen to the pro-fession of medicine, to that of a solicitor, to the military and civil service of the state. To those commercial and industrial pursuits which now engage large and increasing numbers of educated men we contribute little. And even of the three classes mentioned above, a large and increasing proportion do not now seek education at this or the sister university. The object of the 'Extension' movement has been to see whether we could not open the gates of the university wider without injury to its proper functions and character.[16]

This note, penned in about 1872, was to prove prophetic; by the 1890s a mass movement had emerged. Its offshoot was the Workers' Educational Association, which was to become the major 'compensatory' route to higher education for the working classes during the first half of the twentieth century. Although the apologists for this system, men such as Albert Mansbridge and R. H. Tawney, emphasised the extent to which it opened a broad 'highway' to the universities for social groups previously excluded, in reality the outcome was that Oxbridge, in particular, was spared the need for extensive internal reform. Further, the WEA was consciously used during the Edwardian period to head off the pressure which was generated by Ruskin College, newly founded in Oxford, for genuine reform of the University. Ruskin, as an independent college catering for working men with a curriculum centred on the social sciences, posed a direct challenge to the University. As early as 1905, within six years of its foundation, discussions were under way among the Oxford professoriate on how to channel this new college.[17] In the event, attempts to emasculate its work failed and it became necessary to sponsor the Workers' Educational Association as an organisation offering teaching more closely aligned to the University model. It is this consideration which helps explain the tone adopted by Lord Curzon, the Chancellor of the University, when he addressed himself to the problem of University Extension. Curzon was one of the Oxford apologists for whom Extension lecturing was vital, allowing them to claim that Oxford was catering for not only 'those who wish to remain in their order, but desire a university education as a means of raising themselves within it', but also for

> the many who hope by means of a university education to rise in the social as well as in the intellectual scale . . . The distinction between the two classes is fundamental. The university will fail in its duty to the nation if it does not endeavour to provide with equal anxiety and liberality for both: but it will require to provide for them by different means.[18]

Thus, for Curzon, the role of the University Extension was critical, since it enabled Oxford to be seen to be catering for social groups it had previously ignored, and could be used therefore to pre-empt demands for sweeping internal reform. Curzon went on to detail his scheme for non-collegiate places, University Extension and tutorial classes, the incorporation of Ruskin and the foundation of a Working Men's College in some detail, and, in a passage which was a direct attack upon what Ruskin College was attempting, emphasised that the curriculum 'should not be confined exclusively to Sociology and Economics since it is doubtful if of themselves these are capable of ensuring a liberal education'.[19]

This hesitance of Oxbridge to cater for the needs of the 'high industrial phase' of development left a lacuna which the embryonic civic colleges were only too keen to fill. Sponsored in the main by industrialists and enthusiasts who keenly proclaimed the need to train the elite of the industrial work force, these colleges took the pure and applied sciences as their province from the outset. Industrial chemistry at Manchester and Leeds, mining at Newcastle and Birmingham, metallurgy at Sheffield, shipbuilding at Newcastle, brewing at Birmingham: by the 1890s the provincial colleges had established an impressive list of specialisms orientated towards the industrial needs of their own areas.

The result was the recruitment of a new clientele, drawn mainly from the localities of the Redbrick university colleges and largely representative of the new middle classes thrown up by this second-phase industrialisation. Direct evidence on the social background of students at differing universities is as yet fairly slight, but there are several pointers which suggest contrasts between the pre-existing universities and those newly established in the industrial towns.

First, they experienced different patterns of growth. While the number of students at Oxford, Cambridge, London and Durham grew eightfold between 1861 and 1931, the student capacity of the new provincial university colleges was nearly thirty times as great in 1931 as it had been in 1861. The growth of technical education in non-university institutions was even more striking: this sector was minute in 1861 (less than 2000 students at one estimate) but rose to almost 1.8 million by 1921, remaining thereafter above the one million level. The vast majority of these students were part-time. These figures have been worked out in greater detail elsewhere, but they suggest, even in their raw form, that the newer institutions were catering for the needs of the new industrial areas and may have drawn largely from them.[20]

There is some evidence, too, that contemporaries thought this was the case. In 1895 the Bryce Report drew attention to the fact that 'Oxford and Cambridge are now largely recruited from sections of society which have had long-standing hereditary connections with them.'[21] This was seen as evidence of a

> separation between the older universities and a branch of Secondary Education which is daily growing in importance . . . Several witnesses laid stress on the imperfect connection between the university [Oxbridge] and many secondary schools of the modern type . . . There is very little contact between the higher and lower grade of secondary education in this country. Thus the headmaster of the higher grade elementary school at Leeds, at which boys and girls are prepared for the universities, stated that he 'cannot get boys to go to Cambridge, and has had no boys express a desire to go to Oxford'.[22]

The Bryce Commission investigated the previous schooling of students at four contrasting universities, and the returns (see Table 1) suggested very clearly that the Victoria University, comprising Manchester, Leeds and Liverpool, had a recruitment base which contrasted with its older counterparts. Strikingly, almost two-thirds of the student body of the Victoria University was recruited from modern secondary schools, from technical schools or from the elementary sector, which for this purpose included the higher-grade schools. The Bryce Report commented favourably on the Leeds Central School, which had limited aspirations for its pupils:

Table 1 Previous places of education of undergraduates, and scholarships awarded.

	The seven major 'public' schools	HMC schools	Schools not represented at HMC	Private tuition	Training college	Technical school	Pupil-teacher centre	Public elementary school
Oxford	469/125	866/434	313/11	292/12	6/0	5/0	4/2	9/3
Cambridge	266/66	838/366	391/135	354/26	15/3	18/10	15/8	10/6
Durham	0/0	28/12	33/10	52/7	1/0	0/0	0/0	4/0
Victoria	18/1	220/37	403/105	71/12	2/2	44/25	9/8	71/43

Source: From Bryce Report, *Secondary Education* (London, 1895), vol. 9, p. 426. In each case the number of students is given first, and the number of scholarships after the stroke.

The classical education aimed at was limited to such requirements as would be needed for the Victorian or London matriculation, and the degree it prepared for was the BSc rather than BA. What was true of the Leeds School was true of many other schools of the same type.[23]

Several factors ensured that, at their inception, these colleges had little chance of rivalling the existing universities in prestige. Much teaching was part-time and the bulk of it below degree level. The annual returns made by the Redbrick universities to the Treasury show that, as late as 1901, some 45 per cent of the student population were on part-time courses. When the first returns were made, in 1893, only a handful of the students in these new civic colleges were completing degree courses. At Manchester, where 123 students graduated from a student body of over 1000, the proportion was unusually high. Most colleges had fewer than 20 graduates. This is explained by the fact that, although some recruits made their way from newly reformed grammar schools, for many these civic colleges offered a part-time rounding-off of an elementary school education, especially during the 1890s as the new higher-grade schools came into their own.

Thus the seeds of a segmented system, by which different sectors of higher education catered for different social groups, were sown before the turn of the century. In the swift expansion of the late nineteenth century, though, there was still some confusion between the role of technical colleges, polytechnics, mechanics' institutes and the new university colleges, as all claimed some responsibility for technical education.

During the first years of the twentieth century this hiatus was resolved as the civic universities distanced themselves from the 'technical' sector and thus, whether consciously or not, became the natural outlet for the products of reformed grammar schools and municipal secondary schools. This occurred through similar changes taking place in both sectors at the same time.

At the schools' level, developments are fairly well documented and are dealt with elsewhere in this volume. In brief, the structuralisation of secondary education, which was speeded by the attempts of the Endowed Schools and Charity Commissioners to construct a tripartite system after 1869, continued through a period of sustained growth into the first years of the twentieth century. The high-prestige 'first-grade' schools, comprising the 'public' schools and some local grammar schools, aspired at least to keep their pupils to the age of 18, to link with the major universities and to offer a broad, humane curriculum as a preamble to university work. Below them the 'second-grade' schools, although reluctant to accept this label, devised curricula centred far more round modern and scientific subjects and, by the turn of the century, were beginning to stand in a clear relationship to the civic universities, an increasing proportion of whose entrants were recruited from this source. By 1916 it was possible for the committee reporting on *Scholarships for Higher Education* to assume that the vast majority of university entrants made their way via secondary schools.

The Secondary School Regulations in 1904, promulgated by R. L. Morant, threatened to blur this hierarchical divide by imposing a broad curriculum upon all secondary schools administered by the Board of Education (effectively, all those below 'public' school status). Thus, the new municipal secondary schools which appeared after 1902 were obliged to follow a curriculum virtually identical with that of the vast majority of long-established grammar schools.

If one outcome of this was to turn the face of the English secondary schools away from technical education for the foreseeable future, another was to keep them in step with the civic universities. For here, at precisely the same historical moment, similar developments were under way. During the first decade of the twentieth century the newly chartered civic universities, securely established as institutions of higher education, turned increasingly to the problem of redressing curricular imbalance. In brief, they retreated from the full-blown 'scientism' which had been used to justify their establishment, towards the 'defining institutions', Oxford and Cambridge. In so doing they remained in step with the secondary schools from whom they fed.

It is worth exploring the reasons for this change to gain clues as to its significance for the structure of the system as a whole. Sanderson has suggested that in the north of England the influence of Manchester was critical, diverting institutions in other towns such as Leeds and Sheffield from the technological model. The influence of London external degrees, of grants from central government after 1893, and the demands of teacher training, all seem to have played a part. This latter, in particular, was an element in the segmentation process by which significant numbers passed through the grammar schools into the arts faculties of the civic universities and thence back to the schools as teachers, where they worked to project others along the same road.

An element which appears to have been unconsidered in this analysis is the extent and nature of the colonisation by Oxbridge of the emergent civic colleges. In the *Reports from the University Colleges* made annually from 1894 to the Treasury it is possible to glimpse something of this development. In 1894, the first year of return, it is clear that Cambridge was more successful than Oxford in securing posts for its alumni in the civic colleges: at Birmingham five Cambridge men had a single Oxford graduate as a colleague, at Newcastle the ratio was six to one. Elsewhere the two major universities were more evenly represented, although Cambridge still tended to preponderate. But these Oxbridge products, although only a minority of the staff, formed in each case a significant proportion of the graduates appointed. The civic colleges did much work below degree level and, during the 1890s, many of their teachers were non-graduates. Newcastle, for example, had 18 non-graduates and 20 graduates, of whom 7 were educated at Oxbridge. By the turn of the century, when the reversion to the arts was about to accelerate, this Oxbridge domination was even more marked. In this year Birmingham submitted a return showing 18 non-graduates and 17 graduates (3 London, 9 Cambridge and 5 Oxford) as its staff complement. The proportions were similar elsewhere.[24]

Hardly surprisingly, it was the most influential posts in the provincial universities which fell to Oxbridge. In 1894, of 13 professors at Liverpool, only 4 were not from the two ancient universities. By 1901 the appointment of two more Cambridge men to chairs had only sharpened this distinction. This example is striking, but far from untypical. Indeed, there is clear evidence that the Oxbridge 'establishment' saw appointments to the new universities as a kind of gift which was theirs to bestow. The correspondence between Henry Sidgwick and James Bryce is informative:

> You may know that the Principalship of Owens College is vacant by the resignation of A. W. Ward. Do you know of anyone at Cambridge likely to be a good man for it? . . . Functions really very important, chiefly administrative, but a man of wide outlook and general intellectual eminence desire [*sic*]. One on the literary side rather than on the scientific is needed, because in Manchester science is sure to take care of itself: it is the humanistic side that needs careful cultivation.[25]

This from Bryce to Sidgwick in 1897; two years later it was the turn of Sidgwick to raise similar issues in discussion of the Birmingham venture:

> As regards Birmingham do you think as I remember you thought in the case of Owens College – that science will take care of itself, and the important thing is to take care of literature? Because, if so, I should be inclined to suggest S. H. Butcher . . . He is a brilliant scholar of the non-pedantic kind, a good speaker, an attractive personality with a fine air of distinguished culture about him. He is

the best possible available man; at least assuming that my brother Arthur would be considered too old.[26]

Ironically, the man appointed to Birmingham, Sir Oliver Lodge, shared with Bryce and Sidgwick a lifelong interest in spiritualism, such were the vagaries of the late Victorian 'old boy network'. Against this background it is hardly surprising that the civic professoriate sought to build their new Zion in the image of the Oxbridge colleges they had so recently left behind them.

It is interesting to consider the response to Oxbridge of this blurring of roles at and after the First World War. On the one hand, there were those radicals, such as R. H. Tawney, who were ready to see the closer identification of the civic universities with Oxbridge as a part of the process of democratising higher education. He told the 1922 Commission on the Ancient Universities:

> It is of capital importance that capacity (wherever it exists) should move freely to the work for which it is best suited. One condition of that movement is easy access to higher education, and any obstacle which makes such education difficult to obtain results in a grave waste of the nation's human resources. There is an immense reservoir of talent in the elementary schools which is not yet drawn on.[27]

Further, Tawney argued, the growth in secondary education, which would foreseeably double from the 8 per cent of the population for whom it then catered, could only sharpen this demand:

> There is a general belief among thoughtful working people that higher education in general, and Oxford and Cambridge in particular, had been organised in the past too largely for the convenience of the well-to-do classes, and that, though a certain number of able boys pass to them, no very persistent and strenuous efforts have been made to remove the financial obstacles. The workman in a mining village or cotton town sees his clever boy prevented from going to university by lack of means, while the son of his employer, even if not conspicuously intelligent, appears to be admitted without difficulty. The ill-will which results is not negligible. Few things would do more to ease the tension between classes than the knowledge that higher education, including university education, is easily accessible to every able boy.[28]

But, for many, what Tawney discerned as an ideal appeared as an increasingly real threat; for them it was important to emphasise the distinctiveness of the ancient universities. Ironically, it was the Vice-Chancellor of a provincial university, George Adami, who did this most forcefully in 1922:

> From their very eminence, irrespective largely of the extent of the stipend, Cambridge and Oxford will always attract teachers and investigators of the first class. Utilise these, not in training the Toms, Dicks, and Harrys of the under-graduate world, but in influencing and advancing the selected best products of the Empire. If universities are to be overcrowded with undergraduates, let it be the provincial universities. It is their duty to minister to the localities in which they are placed; they receive local grants and local benefactions. When Oxford and Cambridge were the only English universities, then of right men came to them from all quarters. It was this that made them national but this particular need exists no longer. It will raise the tone of the provincial universities if they receive a greater proportion of public school boys.[29]

Equally, though, the civic universities were to be kept in an inferior relationship to Oxbridge, since Adami envisaged a system which would 'give every encouragement to select any promising graduates of the provincial and imperial universities to come into residence' at Oxbridge. This view was echoed at the time by C. K. Webster, the Professor of Modern History at Liverpool, who pleaded that Oxford and Cambridge might become 'purely graduate universities drawing their students from amongst those who have acquitted themselves best at the modern universities'.[30]

This rationale could only be sustained if it were supported by the deployment of meritocratic scholarships. It is appropriate, therefore, that Adami, a significant but relatively neglected figure in the early twentieth-century landscape, should have been one of the leading advocates of competitive examinations. An eugenicist, and a leading enthusiast for racial improvement, George Adami used the Consultative Committee of the Board of Education between 1920 and 1924 to popularise selective scholarships. He was one of the authors of the seminal 1924 Report on this subject. But it must be emphasised that the Board of Education was alerted to the need for a more efficient scholarship system into higher education before Adami's involvement. As early as 1916 an Interim Report had emphasised the need to draw 'by whatever means, the better talent from the rural districts and from the rural labouring class for higher education'.[31] In this process scholarships were to be the catalyst. It is significant that, in this Report, the Consultative Committee of the Board of Education defended the structure of the existing scholarship system, involving closed awards from the 'public' schools to Oxbridge, and argued for its augmentation rather than its replacement:

If the Local Education Authorities took a completely independent line in their methods of award they would cut off their pupils from the advantages offered by Oxford and Cambridge, and effect a thorough severance between the public schools and the old universities on the one hand and the new universities and the grant earning schools on the other. Such a severance is not to be desired.[32]

In these terms a 'tracking' system sustained by closed scholarships to Oxbridge and local awards to the civic colleges was defended in 1916.

The classic study by G. S. M. Ellis on the access of poor students to the universities confirmed that, for much of the nineteenth century, scholarships offered no more than 'a narrow gate through which the poor child may infrequently have reached the university'. More significantly, the rise of the new universities, which coincided with the reorganisation of secondary schooling, led to a particularly close relationship between these universities and the new secondary schools: 'The comparatively low range of fees, and the economical standard of living which is becoming a tradition within them, have made them [the new universities] relatively more accessible to the children of poor parents.'[33] This view was confirmed by Glass and Gray, who showed that the proliferation of scholarships immediately before the First World War did offer poor students a chance of aspiring to the ancient universities, but that in reality alumni of the 'public' schools (and particularly those of the 15 most expensive public schools) entered the race for scholarships at an enormous advantage. Of the 432 scholarships offered by the Oxbridge colleges in 1913–14, 374 (86%) were awarded to 'public' school pupils, 27 (6%) to alumni of endowed grammar schools and 29 (7%) to pupils of municipal secondary schools. In brief, 'public' school boys had 12 times the chance of winning an Oxbridge scholarship than their contemporaries in the state sector.[34]

It seems, therefore, that, although the period under review witnessed a vast extension of the scholarship system, this did not represent a wholehearted attempt to democratise higher education; rather, this situation was thought to be defensible on the grounds that different universities had differing functions and served separate social groups, a fact which was to be at least tacitly acknowledged in the working of competitive examinations.

Similarly, at the school level, it was accepted – albeit grudgingly – that a differentiated system of secondary education would necessitate unequal access to higher education. The comments of C. E. Theodosius, a secondary schools inspector, on the grading of education in Bristol, made in 1907, are revealing:

I have recently had occasion to bring to the notice of the Bristol LEA a defect in their educational organisation which had hitherto escaped notice and which I have some reason to believe exists in other large towns. It may be briefly described as a breakdown in the 'educational ladder' at the top.

The old grammar schools of every grade, with all their faults, flattered themselves that they never let the really brilliant boy escape notice, and that every nerve was strained to bring his work to a university scholarship standard. The number of distinguished men who were educated at some of our humbler grammar schools is a confirmation of this claim . . . I suppose it is generally recognised that our new municipal secondary schools are and must remain second grade schools; that the normal leaving age will be 16 or 17 and that the staff will continue for some time at any rate, to consist of elementary teachers who have obtained a London BA or BSc in the interests of their professional work, i.e. by men and women who have ceased to be students at the age of 19 or 20, instead of, as in the first grade schools, by teachers who have had a regular university course, and have only taken up their profession at the age of about 23. It may therefore be assumed that these schools cannot, as a rule, attempt anything like a university scholarship standard of work. The result of this is that our secondary schools must be definitely graded, as indeed they are in practice.[35]

These remarks reflect the 'orthodoxy' preached by the inspectorate in the years before 1914 and are further evidence of a fortuitous dovetailing of the modern schools with the Redbrick universities, where, as the Bryce Commissioners pointed out, the age of entry was commonly 16 or 17, in contrast with Oxbridge, where the age of entry could be 'roughly stated at 19'.[36]

Thus a picture emerges of an educational system which by the time of the First World War had become segmented at various levels, the better to serve the needs of a differentiated society. Distinctive types of secondary school were linked to a hierarchical system of higher education in different ways. The swift growth and transition of the late nineteenth century had only briefly challenged these hierarchies; the adjustments of the early years of the new century served merely to confirm them.

If the period from 1870 to 1914 emphasised the unassailability of English elite institutions despite swift technological and social changes, it was also marked by close parallels between secondary and higher education. Most strikingly, the elite universities and schools (Oxbridge and the 'public' schools) remained aloof from, and relatively unscathed by, the social transformation which impelled traumatic changes at the second level (within the local grammar schools and civic university colleges). Throughout the period controversy centred upon the design and structure of this sector and the role of a technological education within it, rather than upon the refurbishing of elite institutions.

Further, at this more contentious second level, the first years of the twentieth century saw strikingly similar developments, involving a reversion from the modernism of the late nineteenth century towards a more prestigious 'humane' education.

These parallels suggest, at least implicitly, that schools and universities were not simply responding to the same pressures but were making adjustments which confirmed their roles in a clearly structured system. The extent to which these trends involved the clear establishment of a watertight 'tracking' system, by which particular types of school led exclusively to specific areas of higher education, is uncertain. But the evidence assembled here certainly suggests that such a process was under way. At the very least it is possible to conclude that one important element in the dynamic of change was an acute awareness among the English upper and middle classes of the importance of social hierarchies.

Notes

1 *Statement on the Needs of Oxford University, 1907* (Bodleian Library, MS Top Oxon, c. 236).
2 Bodleian Library, MS. LH/Misc/1/1.
3 R. A. Lowe, 'English Elite Education in the Late Nineteenth and Early Twentieth Centuries', in W. Conze and J. Kocka, *Bildungsbürgertum im 19. Jahrhundert* (Stuttgart, 1985), pp. 149–53.
4 *Birmingham University Prospectus* (1904).
5 Letter from John Daw to Joshua Fitch, 2 May 1871 (PRO ED 27/695).
6 Letter from James Bryce to Henry Sidgwick, 4 January 1868 (Bodleian Library, MS Bryce 15).
7 Letter from H. E. Rawlinson (President of the Royal Geographical Society) to the Vice Chancellor, 3 July 1871 (Bodleian Library, MS MR/7/4/1).
8 Letter from W. R. Anson (All Souls) to the Royal Geographical Society, 15 February 1899 (Bodleian Library, MS MR/7/4/4).
9 *Transactions of the National Association for the Promotion of Social Science* (London, 1870), p. 311.
10 *Ibid.*, p. 316.
11 *Trans NAPSS* (London, 1876), p. 44.
12 *Report of a Conference on Secondary Education in England* (Oxford, 1893), p. 11.
13 *Ibid.*
14 *Statement on the Needs of Oxford University, 1907.*
15 Lord Curzon of Kedleston, *Principles and Methods of University Reform* (Oxford, 1909), p. 46.
16 Letter on University Extension (unsigned) (Bodleian Library, MS Eng. Hist. c. 786).
17 R. A. Lowe, 'Some Forerunners of R. H. Tawney's Longton Tutorial Class', *History of Education*, vol. 1, no. 1 (1972), pp. 53–4.
18 Curzon, *Principles and Methods*, p. 49.
19 *Ibid.*, p. 64.
20 See R. A. Lowe, 'The Expansion of Higher Education in England', in K. H. Jarausch (ed.), *The Transformation of Higher Learning, 1860–1930* (Stuttgart, 1982), pp. 37–56.

21 Bryce Report, *Secondary Education* (London, 1895), vol. 1, p. 219.
22 *Ibid.*, vol. 1, p. 234.
23 *Ibid.*, vol. 1, p. 142.
24 Board of Education, *Reports from University Colleges* (London, annually from 1894).
25 Letter from James Bryce to Henry Sidgwick, 21 October 1897 (Bodleian Library, MS Bryce 15).
26 Letter from Henry Sidgwick to James Bryce, 6 November 1899 (*ibid.*).
27 Papers relating to the 1922 Commission on the Reform of the Ancient Universities (Bodleian Library, MSS Top Oxon, b. 104–9, c. 267).
28 *Ibid.*
29 *Ibid.*
30 *Ibid.*
31 Board of Education Consultative Committee, *Interim Report on Scholarships for Higher Education* (London, 1916), p. 66.
32 *Ibid.*, p. 31.
33 G. S. M. Ellis, *The Poor Student and the University* (London, 1942), p. 6.
34 D. V. Glass and J. L. Gray, 'Opportunity and the Older Universities', in L. Hogben, *Political Arithmetic* (London, 1938), pp. 428–33.
35 PRO, ED 12/139.
36 Bryce Report, vol. 1, p. 230.

88

MODERN GREATS

T. D. Weldon

Source: *Universities Quarterly* I (1946–7): 348–57.

I agree entirely with Mr. Gallie's conclusion that it is practicable and desirable to combine philosophical studies with other subjects in both arts and scientific courses. Possibly it may be of some interest to those who are thinking along these lines to consider the experience which has been gained during some twenty years development at Oxford of Modern Greats, officially styled the Final Honour School of Philosophy, Politics and Economics, or P.P.E.

Past history

The School has inevitably been much influenced both for good and ill by its inheritance from *Literae Humaniores* (Greats). It has special problems of its own both theoretical and practical, and now that it is starting in earnest again after an almost complete break during the war period, it is reasonable to attempt some estimate of its aims and problems. In particular it is worth inquiring whether the combination of philosophy with two other branches of study which it sets out to accomplish is educationally sound.

Greats is a two branched School. It comprises Philosophy (of which not less than a third is Greek philosophy) and Ancient History. Most people would probably agree that it was at its best when Ancient History was a compact study relying mainly on written sources for its evidence, and when Philosophy had not yet been disturbed by the intrusion of modern logic and philosophical analysis. It is now decidedly unmanageable and suffers from most if not all of the complaints which will shortly be discussed in connection with Modern Greats. The crucial and most controversial point about the latter has always been its three branched character. Every candidate must offer at least two papers in each of the three branches. He must also take two further subjects of a more specialised type which may but need not be concentrated on a single branch. Hence the usual distribution of papers is, for example, two papers each in Philosophy and Politics, four papers in Economics; but two papers in Philosophy and three each in Politics and Economics is not unusual. It should be noted that the six common subject papers are the same for all candidates so that the student who offers four papers in Economics is required to deal with the same papers on General Philosophy and Moral and Political Philosophy as the candidate who takes two philosophical further subjects.

This arrangement is to some extent the result of deliberate policy and to some extent the consequence of the historical situation at the time when the School was inaugurated. It was a compromise between those who wanted a full Final Honour School in Economics and those who held that something comparable to Greats was needed for the benefit of students whose interests and previous education turned their attention to European civilisation in the nineteenth century rather than to the earlier civilisation of the Mediterranean basin. As a result there has been, and still is some conflict of opinion between the Modern Greats school of thought which considers that the School contains too much economic theory and too little history, and the Economists who think that the time available for the study of their subject is inadequate.

Specialist versus humanist

Before this point can be considered a more general difficulty, on the solution of which in the end it depends, must be taken into account. Modern Greats like other Final Honour Schools has never been quite clear as to what it is trying to do. On the one hand it is attempting to train specialists especially in economic theory and political institutions; and 'specialists' means essentially 'academic specialists', men whose researches will advance these subjects and who will themselves become tutors and professors in them. This entails vigorous training in research technique and intimate acquaintance with the best work which is actually being done by contemporary authorities. It is analytical rather than historical, and those who concentrate their attention on it naturally deplore the amount of energy which their pupils are required to devote to other branches of study and even to immoderate wanderings within a single branch. 'Time is short', they say, 'and we cannot get enough solid training in statistical method into it to qualify a man to undertake research work if he is largely occupied in irrelevant excursions into philosophy, political history and the errors of the classical economists.'

On the other hand we have the Humanists. 'Only a small proportion of the men taking the School are going to be professionals, they urge,' and it is educationally unsound to consider their interests to the detriment of the many who are going into business, the Civil Service or other professions. These men need what Greats used to provide, the comprehensive study of a civilisation as a whole. In this, whatever Marxists may say to the contrary, economic considerations are only one factor. They are not the whole truth and we distort the outlook of future administrators and politicians if we permit or even encourage them to think that it is.'

In the long run this disjunction between the claims of specialists and non-specialists is a false one; but its practical importance for the moment is considerable and should not be overlooked. In Oxford at any rate it has been exaggerated by excessive concentration on the Final Honours School as the only really important factor in education as far as the Humanities are concerned. We have, indeed, awarded so-called "Advanced Degrees", the D.Phil. and the B.Litt., but we have attached no serious weight to them. They have never been considered as essential or even useful qualifications for college tutorships.

The consequence has been that any professor or tutor who wanted to expound the results of his own work had perforce to expound them to undergraduates reading for Final Honour Schools. But undergraduates with few exceptions do not attend lectures or classes which have no cash value. They not unreasonably expect to be remunerated for their trouble by a good chance of a question in Schools; and nobody who knows the facts will deny that this has led to constant pressure for increased specialisation and to a progressive weighting of Modern Greats as well as of other Schools in favour of professional training and against a more general education. This is clearly most unsatisfactory. Whatever we may think about the need for specialist training in universities, the ground for advocating it should not be the very natural desire of existing specialists to attract intelligent audiences.

This trouble which, although it was generally felt, was especially prevalent in Modern Greats, has now we hope been cured. The university, after some doubts and hesitations on the part of the worshippers of the Final Honour School, has at length established a genuine post graduate degree, the B.Phil., which can be taken in one or two years after the B.A. and will deliberately cater for the requirements of those who aim at becoming academic specialists. There will be properly organised classes and seminars, and students are restricted to one branch of study, that is, either Philosophy or Politics or Economics. Specialisation within the branch selected will not be entirely unrestricted, since candidates are required to offer papers which show that their acquaintance with the subject as a whole is up to a high standard, but practically any special subject is legitimate.

This provision enables the case of the specialist *versus* the humanist in the final honour School to be discussed on its merits without the disturbing thought of professors in search of worthy disciples. Without it I am inclined to think that any attempts to extend undergraduate courses beyond the limits of a single branch of study somewhat narrowly interpreted are doomed to frustration; and this reflection is by no means confined to arts courses.

275

Are three subjects justified?

We may now consider more specifically the claim of Modern Greats to exist as a three branched School, and perhaps the best approach to this question is by way of the leading proposals for changing it. The obvious possibilities are either (a) to cut one branch out completely, supporters of this course being divided into (i) those who favour dropping Philosophy and having a School of Politics and Economics, (ii) those who, with Greats in mind, would make it Philosophy and Politics and encourage the economists to start a new School of their own: or (b) to allow candidates to opt for any two branches of the existing School and drop the third. Of these (b) was originally the more popular, largely on the assumption that its adoption would in practice produce (a) (i). No-one in his senses, it was felt, would study philosophy unless he were compelled to do so. Subsequent experience has modified this faith considerably by making it clear that things would not necessarily turn out in that way. There are good empirical grounds for supposing that a high proportion of the best candidates other than those who hope to become professional economists would jettison Economics. This would be a great pity, and the possibility of it naturally predisposes reformers to (a) (i) as such.

This, however, is by the way. What really matters is the main argument in favour of exchanging a three branched for a two branched school, namely that students in the former, like the nation's generators, are overloaded and that the surplus load must somehow be shed. The case is roughly this. Allowing two terms for a preliminary examination of some kind and one for revision before Schools, the undergraduate has only six terms and two long Vacations in which to accomplish his task. But to gain anything more than a superficial and therefore worthless acquaintance with three important branches of study necessarily takes longer than this. The Greats man does only six papers, three in Philosophy and three in Ancient History in the same period of time. His course involves going to a tutor in each of these branches once a week during term so that he gets 24 hours private tuition a year both in Philosophy and in Ancient History. This it is claimed is the bare minimum into which worthwhile instruction on two important subjects can be compressed. Hence either the subjects in Modern Greats are not important, or the instruction given in them is not worthwhile, or both.

I have quoted this argument in the form in which it is commonly advanced by tutors in Greats because this is the variety which I hear most frequently. *Mutatis mutandis* it is put forward by representatives of other arts faculties and is not infrequently heard within the Modern Greats School. It is simple and, I think, fallacious, but it is sufficiently important and widespread to deserve serious consideration. In dealing with it I shall assume without discussion that if Modern Greats as a three branched School is overloaded, then it is inevitable that Philosophy should be the subject excluded from it to reduce the load. Whatever may be the situation as regards earlier civilisations, it simply makes no sense to attempt to divorce politics from economics in the nineteenth and twentieth centuries. Economic theory is meaningless in abstraction from economic organisation, and the latter cannot be studied without considerable knowledge of political institutions and history. Without Philosophy, Politics and Economics are in my opinion seriously weakened, but they are not nonsense. So we reach the questions, 'Is it necessary or desirable that a study of philosophy should be superimposed on that of politics and economics, and, if so, can this be done without overloading the student?' I believe that the answer to these questions is an emphatic affirmative and I will try to justify this view.

Value of philosophy

Many doubts as to the value of philosophy both for the aspiring specialist in other subjects, and for the undergraduate, who wants an education to qualify him for a professional or business career, spring from an out-dated but persistent view of what modern philosophy is about. Systems of metaphysics are indeed a most unprofitable study except for professional philosophers with antiquarian tastes; but they are not the side of philosophical inquiry with which any student of politics and economics needs to concern himself. What he is or should be vitally interested in are problems as to the nature of evidence, and it is these which are also the primary concern of many philosophers. This, of course, is a controversial statement and it is impossible within the limits of this article to give more than a condensed and dogmatic statement of the issues involved. They are fully discussed in standard works on the subject.

Since the days of Aristotle, it has been generally recognised that different kinds of evidence are relevant to different kinds of inquiry. "Proof" is not the same process to a lawyer as it is to a mathematician. It is only within the last half-century, however, that this fact and its implications have been given the attention which they deserve. Even in the exact sciences confusions have frequently arisen, and still sometimes arise from a failure to inquire whether a particular proposition or law is deduced from definitions assumed at the start or whether it is founded on observation of empirical facts. Sometimes the question can be answered as soon as it is formulated, but this is by no means invariably the case. Frequently nothing but careful analysis can establish the correct answer.

Now it will not be disputed that the classical exponents both of economic and political theory proceeded almost entirely by deduction from definitions which purported to be empirically grounded but which were in fact very arbitrarily framed. Some indeed were sufficiently closely related to observable data to lead to conclusions more or less in accordance with experience;

others were less fortunate. Admittedly this situation has now altered. Officially at any rate statistical method has replaced deduction throughout the Social Sciences. This, however, does not remove the possibility of confusing different types of evidence with one another. It merely makes such confusion, when it does occur, considerably harder to detect. Indeed the statistical approach is by no means as completely empirical as it sometimes believes itself to be. We cannot, if we are wise, avoid asking 'What exactly is the value of statistical evidence on sociological problems? Is it comparable with the value of evidence collected by the same method (if it *is* the same method) in the physical and biological sciences?'

This leads to a further consideration. It is now well known that the structure and rules of language exercise a powerful and generally unobserved influence on the direction and nature of our thinking. They suggest definitions which are only too likely to be accepted uncritically as truths about matters of fact. Many of the metaphysical puzzles which were the bane of physics, biology and psychology from the seventeenth to the nineteenth century and which still have their devotees, can be proved to have arisen from assumptions derived from linguistic usage. Neither economics nor politics is immune to this complaint, but a study of logic and general scientific method is a reasonably safe inoculation against it, and such an inoculation has necessity and not merely a luxury for the specialist as well as for the general student. Propagandists have at least a sound empirical knowledge of how to use the wrong kind of evidence to support their case and also of how to make a definition look like a description.

The popular fallacy about philosophy, then, is the belief that it constitutes a separate body of doctrine with a separate subject matter of its own. In fact, however, the problem is not that of studying a third subject connected only arbitrarily with the other two; it is that of studying politics and economics in the most efficient way. Admittedly some of those who have pontificated and who still pontificate about philosophy do not share this view, but believe that they are acquainted with some esoteric and unscientific method of acquiring knowledge superior to that employed by less privileged investigators. This belief is irrelevant to the present discussion. The function of philosophy in Modern Greats is to encourage an analytical inquiry into the methodological and linguistic problems which are involved in scientific procedure in general and in that of the Social Sciences in particular. This need not entail any very burdensome Commitment either in reading or in tutorial work, and it is not difficult to keep it going by occasional classes and lectures (which are not very time-consuming) in terms during which tutorial work is being done in the other two branches of the School. Detailed historical knowledge of the views of our philosophical ancestors is by no means essential, since the development of discovery by scientific methods and not the progress of metaphysical system-building is what matters.

Practical difficulties

I hold, therefore, that Modern Greats as a three branched School is sound in principle and that it is a better education than any two branched altern- ative would be. Any complaint as to overloading should disappear if the B.Phil. is sensibly used and if the scope and function of philosophy is prop- erly understood: but I certainly do not claim that the School as it has actually been administered and taught in Oxford is a perfect instance of what such a course of study ought to be and is capable of becoming. Apart from the well-founded charge of excessive and premature specialisation, which we hope will now disappear, it is certainly true that the teaching of the three branches, especially in the opening stages, is not always as closely integrated as it should be. Many of those who have taken the School might find it difficult to recognise my account of philosophy as a description of what they actually studied under that name.

It would be unprofitable to discuss the explanation of this weakness in detail. Essentially the difficulty has been one of man-power in the teaching staff, and this is a point which should be borne in mind when the possibility of introducing similar courses elsewhere is under consideration. Originally all teaching for Modern Greats both in Philosophy and in Politics and some in Economics had to be provided by existing college tutors as a side-line to their main job, which was that of teaching for Greats and Modern History. As they were already fully occupied, they had no alternative to providing the Modern Greats student with such portions of their existing courses as were more or less relevant to the syllabus of the new School and leaving him to make the best he could of it. Hence it was inevitable that instruction should tend to fall into three water-tight compartments and that the essen- tial unity of the School should be destroyed or at least obscured. This situation has now been partially relieved by the gradual emergence of tutors whose sole or chief interest, as far as teaching is concerned, is confined to Modern Greats, but it is regrettably true that for some undergraduates 'philosophy' still means, 'a nodding acquaintance with theories of knowledge popular in the seventeenth and eighteenth centuries, but now generally discredited, plus a little enquiry into the nature of pleasure and moral obligation'. These really have very little to do with economic theory or political institutions, nor do most students find them interesting in themselves. At best they are a useful introduction to modern philosophical problems; but the function of an introduction is to introduce somebody to something, and in this case what that something is frequently remains obscure to the end. This, how- ever, is not a valid criticism of philosophy as a subject of study.

The practical need for Modern Greats to adapt itself to the teaching resources of other Schools is responsible for another weakness in its present structure. The historical periods, on which attention is focussed in the three branches, are not identical and in some papers they are far too long. The ideal Modern Greats would, in my opinion, be far more restricted in the extent though not in the quality of its historical requirements than is the case at Oxford. I should be quite happy to have it concentrated on philosophical and political developments since 1900. This does not mean that everything prior to that date could be ignored, but simply that such events should form the background of the School and not the substance of it. Locke and Hume are still very good reading and their views deserve considerable respect; but they are an introduction to and not a substitute for the works of Bertrand Russell. I think, too, that the aim of this particular School should be to concentrate on the kind of evidence which can profitably be used in probable predictions of the future rather than on that which is relevant to the establishment of true propositions about the past. There are plenty of other Schools whose concern is primarily with the latter.

My conclusion then is that philosophy is an essential element in the serious study of politics and economics, as it also is of the study of other sciences; and I would emphasise more than Mr. Gallie does that the aim of prescribing it is not to impart 'culture' or general background, but to make both specialists and general students more competent to carry out their own work than they would be without it. Whether it has this effect or not will be judged by the success of its products in competition with those educated on different lines, and I see no reason to be afraid of this empirical test.

89

GENERAL EDUCATION

J. S. Fulton

Source: *Universities Quarterly* V (1950–1): 41–8.

It came as something of a surprise to many of those who took part in the Home Universities Conference in December, 1949, to find that the need for general education won almost unanimous acceptance in a large conference representing university teachers of every grade and faculty, university administrators and lay members of Councils. It is true that two warning notes were sounded. One very properly drew attention to practical difficulties. The other, more concerned with principle, warned those committed to general education that although it might be possible to produce individuals who knew how to talk they would regrettably have nothing to say. "Rien n'est plus dangéreux qu'une idée générale dans une tête vide." This would be a fair and proper criticism if anyone really proposed that general ideas were to have a monopoly of the education of students in our universities. Fortunately, this is not so. We are all committed to the virtues of an educational system in which specialisation offers the key to the mastery of one's own mind through the mastery of one's own subject. The trend towards a comparatively narrow field of inquiry and consequently a narrowing of the field in which education takes place, is too firmly established to be reversed. So the head need not be empty, and under modern conditions there is very little danger that it will be allowed to be so.

One speaker at the Conference very wisely said that, although there was fairly widespread agreement about the need for general education, the chief difficulty arose in knowing how to set about providing it. He was right. It is not a question of clearing a time-table—difficult though that is— so much as the discovery, whenever practical details come up for discussion, that general education means widely differing things to different people. It would be pleasant if progress could be guaranteed by an immediate and successful search for a satisfactory definition. Unfortunately, the discussion has not yet gone far enough to yield the hope that a definition can be found at this stage.

When we agree on the need for general education we seem to be in agreement that something is missing in our present university courses. Either that something which once was there is there no longer; or that changes in society or in the social structure of the population of universities have created a need for something to be done in university education which was rarely or never done in the past. To agree to this does not for most of us involve denying that the constituents of existing university courses are themselves essential elements of a healthy educational diet. In other words, we hold that our undergraduates (or some of them) are suffering from what the doctors call a deficiency disease. What they are getting is all right so far as it goes, but it is not a balanced diet; something which ought to be in the diet is missing. On the other hand, we are not agreed about the answers to the questions—what ingredient of the diet is missing? what is the degree of unbalance? who suffer most from the deficiency? The result is that either nothing gets done or that the reformers are forced to compromise, for example, on what has recently been described, somewhat contemptuously, as a voluntary course of lectures providing a smattering of many subjects, better than nothing, but quite inadequate to the need.

It is the modest aim of this article to discuss briefly three main types of deficiency. If it can be agreed that these are important deficiencies, that will at least be a first stage towards the more important task of determining what kinds of corrective are needed to meet the shortcomings. Two remarks of a general character may not in the meantime be out of place. The first is that although consideration will be given only to the existing content of formal education this is not due to any failure to recognise the immense importance in general education of informal discussion between students engaged in different fields of study, or the importance of social contact between student and student, student and teacher, in a healthy corporate life. Whatever steps might be agreed upon as correctives to existing deficiencies in a university education, these would quite certainly be of greatly increased value if they took place within a university organised by the provision of residence to promote the informal exchange of ideas. Secondly, most of those who are interested in the problem of general education are fully aware of the overcrowding of existing university time-tables. There are, however, two ways of making good a deficiency of diet. One is a crude and wrongly conceived method which simply adds weight or bulk. The other involves the introduction of an ingredient in whose absence the remainder of the diet is only imperfectly assimilated; when it is introduced its presence invigorates the whole system and restores its natural rhythm to the body. It is the second type of corrective which deserves our serious consideration.

Social fragmentation and social unity

A great deal of pioneer work in general education has been done in the United States of America. It should not surprise us that this is so. It is a commonplace about the United States that it is more sectional than smaller and homogeneous states like ours—sectional in geography and climate; in the races and origins of its people; and from these therefore arise political sectionalism and sectional economic interests. Thus sectional or regional interests tend, from time to time, to obscure the consciousness of American unity. It was not always so. The U.S.A. began as thirteen states, homogeneous in almost every respect. Relying on a natural sense of community derived from the possession of a common heritage in a common stock, a common language and a common religion, they committed themselves in the name of freedom to the cult of diversity. The times were favourable, the drive of a new and virile people carried the experiment along at breakneck speed. Great, and indeed breathtaking as the achievement is, it leaves room for doubt whether diversity has not outstripped the sense of community in relation to which diversity alone has meaning. That is why men distinguished in the universities of the United States have asked themselves and are asking still whether university courses do not need a new direction in which greater emphasis should be consciously given than in the past to "the common things". The balance between what is common—what tends to maintain unity—and what encourages diversity (or nonconformity) is a shifting one. At times it will be comparatively safe to neglect the one, at other times, the other. These American educationalists are surely right to take seriously their responsibility to prevent a disastrous overbalance. Their wise judgment in this matter is an indispensable element in the preservation of a sound national health.

It would be possible for British universities to watch with a benevolent neutrality this situation in the United States were it not that circumstances have confronted universities in every modern industrialised society with problems which, if not identical, are closely related in nature and urgency to those of the universities of the U.S.A.

The industrial revolution—a child of science—is more and more deeply influencing our lives with every year that passes. Like science it divides to conquer, and by division it continues to win new material conquests over nature. The result is that problems which were once soluble—or which were thought to be soluble—by laymen have passed into the domain of those who possess expert skill. No modern society which did not produce experts could possibly progress or, indeed, survive. But we cannot shut our eyes to the fact that expert skill is at its highest and most valuable when its range is narrowest. Thus the more we call to our aid the expertness of the expert, the more we are creating a society of men who by virtue of their mastery over a small field are shut off from knowledge and experience of the remainder. Specialised knowledge has as its obverse specialised ignorance.

The result is that functional groups in present-day society are more sharply delineated than at any time in modern history. Because members of particulars groups are so specialised in their training and outlook, they are sharply cut off from other groups and live their lives in detachment from the majority of their fellows. That isolation, the product of a high specialised skill, produces group sympathies and loyalties which turn their owners' eyes inwards to their own group and its sectional welfare, rather than outwards to the larger society which the group exists to serve.

Present day industrialism, then, has by its techniques imposed a partial and restricted experience on modern industrial man. Side by side with that fact another fact of the greatest significance about modern industrial society has become clear, that is, the interdependence of these various expert and partial activities. To make a modern industrial nation-state *go* (leaving out the problems of international politics and trade) needs almost a miracle of cooperation. If these two facts—the fragmentation of modern life and the need for co-operation—are as significant as I am suggesting, the universities have surely questions to ask themselves and decisions to make. Do those trends matter? And if they matter, is it the duty of the universities merely to follow the trends or to offer correctives? No one will gainsay that it is an essential part of their business to produce specialists of the highest order. But to do that and to do nothing else is to minister to the growing fragmentation of our social life. Surely it is another great task of our generation to discover how to produce the intellectual (and no less the moral) qualities needed for a healthy integration of the specialised and sectional activities of modern society; especially when we remember that the very conditions which produce a good specialist tend almost inevitably to destroy his consciousness and awareness of the whole. The specialist needs a mental apparatus through which to achieve some understanding of the relation of his own expert group to other expert groups; to deny him this is to take great risks with the health and sanity of society.

Human relations

A writer in a recent number of this Journal has denied that a university needs to do more than to promote research and to turn out men and women qualified for their professional tasks. Perhaps enough has already been said to record dissent from that view. However, it may be added that men and women who are to lead worthy lives have more than a professional job to do. High among every individual's duties, whatever his education and whatever his profession, are those of thinking rightly about his relations with and responsibilities to other people. While it is certainly true that the universities should not be expected to bear alone the burden of equipping their members for those non-professional aspects of their lives, neither should they be indifferent. At present in each of the main faculties there are courses from which students can emerge without the experience of thinking under disciplined conditions about any but inanimate things. Some students so educated may have little apparent ground for regret since the rest of their career may be spent in further enquiry into the "behaviour of things". But many others will assume responsibilities for discharging which a knowledge of people and of their behaviour forms as important a part as a knowledge of things. They are ill-equipped for these tasks unless at some time during their university careers they have been helped to feel, in the company of well-trained minds, what it is like to think clearly about human institutions and behaviour. At the same time, there is much to be said for the view that people who think only in terms of human organisation and human choice are no more adequately equipped for the modern world. This latter view is, however, one for discussion at another time. What is being argued here is that the important part which human relations must play in the future work and private lives of students should be recognised in the courses provided at universities; and that, for example, philologists and physical scientists should be helped to think about what "may be otherwise" as well as about things that are exact and measurable—about matters of opinion as well as about the subject matter of exact science; about the principles of human organisation and behaviour whether in the fields of morals, politics or economics.

Culture

No satisfactory account has been or perhaps can be given of the qualities which should be possessed by one who is a good product of a university education. We shall all agree that he should have gained a mastery over some field of thought. It is this perfectly right and proper urge to mastery which has led to the narrowing of the field of education which in turn has produced the problem of general education and many of the misgivings about some present trends. There is probably considerable agreement too that while individuals are undergoing university courses they should learn to distinguish between a good book and a worthless one, between slovenly thinking and accuracy in other fields as well as their own; should learn to recognise and hate what is cheap and superficial; and should learn also the habit of appreciating things of beauty.

Until quite recently university students were members of a limited number of families whose sons carried on the university tradition generation after generation. No so long ago, it was a difficult business for a member of a non-university family to break into the charmed circle. A large part of our problem arises from the fact that it is no longer so. The old state of affairs began to come to an end with the dissolution of aristocratic rule and the beginning of the experiment in social democracy. In truth, social democracy itself cannot succeed unless the universities are prepared to receive and to educate in each generation a fresh supply of young men and women whose homes are not university homes. How is this to be done? If the task is taken up at all, it is unlikely to be carried to a successful conclusion unless we are prepared where necessary to modify traditional teaching methods which were better suited to the former order of things. New methods will have to take account of the powerful economic motive with which so many of our students now enter their universities. In itself that motive is harmless and may indeed be laudable. At the same time it is the university's business to transform its owner, in the few years it has got him, into a lover of the subject for its own sake. Nor is the prospect by any means discouraging. As the Vice-Chancellor of Leeds recently pointed out in a broadcast, the science faculties (to speak of them alone) are transforming science students into true scientists with a success that is little short of miraculous.

It is beside the point for the universities and the schools to enter into an unprofitable contest about where responsibility lies in this fundamentally important task. Dr. Eric James said perhaps the last word about it in a recent article when, besides inviting the schools to experiment, he asked the universities to send out to the schools teachers who, whatever their special subjects, were men and women of general culture; if they did so, the universities would receive in turn from the schools more generally cultured freshmen. It might reasonably be suggested that an enquiry into the past history of the Scottish universities in this field would be illuminating. Many a young man came up to the Scottish universities from a home which, though it knew great poverty, had taught him to respect learning and the learned man. He had received a thorough and well drilled training in his school, but he had never moved in a world of wide culture. He knew his Bible and he knew *The Pilgrim's Progress*; there was no family income to spend on other books or on paintings; he certainly did not enter the university after he had made his "grand tour". Yet somehow the Scottish university succeeded, in the short time in which the student remained within its precincts, in turning him into a man of learning. To ask what sort of professors and what sort of courses achieved these results, are questions whose answers might be fruitful for our times.

Some suggestions

It is possible that a number of those concerned with university education would admit the reality—however slight—of the deficiencies briefly discussed above. If so, on what lines would experiments to find remedies suggest themselves? In the short space that remains only the merest sketch of an answer is possible.

At least three main types of "general education" can be broadly distinguished—

(*a*) in which the specialist is persuaded by his developing interest in his own subject not only to probe more deeply but also to follow that interest into kindred or complementary fields;

(*b*) in which the "one-sidedness" of a particular subject is corrected by another kind of intellectual discipline;

(*c*) general "culture" lectures (varying from one lecture to a course) or essays.

Of these (*a*) corresponds to the natural progress of many fine and original minds. Sympathetically translated into terms of Honours courses it can be flexible enough to nourish both the high academic specialist whose interest (and primary function) is to advance the frontiers of his subject; as well as the individual who, starting with a natural and absorbing interest in one branch of learning, broadens that interest into the "relations" of his subject. In this direction there lies probably the best hope of arresting social fragmentation before it passes the danger point.

(*b*) enjoys the protection of a highly respectable ancestry in, for example, Classical Greats. It is not, of course, suggested that every high-flying academic specialist should halt in his tracks and turn e.g. to the formal study of human society. On the contrary, it is arguable that research will be served only by the most single-minded devotion. This type of general education in its modern form might be more appropriate to the less purely academically minded such as might be expected afterwards to assume practical responsibilities involving the management both of men and of things; and who would be ill-prepared for such duties by an education confined to one of the two fields.

(*c*) has caused perhaps more confusion than either of the others. It is fashionable in some quarters to belittle courses of lectures offering "general culture". But only the insensitive can be totally indifferent to the need for them. For the freshmen from non-university homes, windows must be opened. Some will be opened at school, others only at the university stage. The function of such courses is to show the extent and the richness of the country which falls under the domain of men and women of culture and of learning; and to provide maps of a landscape which students will be stimulated to explore later for themselves. In the modern universities where residence (and the interchange of ideas which it makes possible), though accepted as an aim, is only very imperfectly realised in practice, such a stimulus is the more urgently needed.

90

HIGHER EDUCATION SINCE THE WAR

Universities, CATs and technical colleges; Robbins and after

E. E. Robinson

Source: E. E. Robinson, *The New Polytechnics*, London: Cornmarket, 1968, pp. 13–33.

The recent controversy about postponing the raising of the school leaving age exposed our reluctance to recognise the economic importance of education. We regard education not as an industry but as a social service and our priorities in its development are argued in terms of social justice rather than economic return. We are committed to a major reform of secondary education and a massive expansion of the universities on a basis no firmer than a belief that education is a 'good thing' and everybody should have more of it. Social righteousness has been thick in the air and has prevented in this country the hard calculation of priorities that has greatly influenced educational policies in some other countries.

The consequence of this has not been the social levelling in education which might have been expected. Indeed it is possible that an education policy based on economic considerations would have had more egalitarian results.

Propaganda for educational advance has come mainly from the left and has taken the form of seeking for the whole population the education previously enjoyed only by an elite minority.

This is a poor basis for policy not just because its attainment is too expensive but because it fails to discriminate between different forms of education and to recognise the social function of education. The function of the public school and university system has been to train a ruling elite. To model a system of mass education on this is obviously nonsense. But many British educationists, particularly those on the political left, have seemed to be attempting this because they have interpreted the upper class tradition not as a training for leadership but as mere personal liberation and cultivation which should be extended to the working class. Vocational education for the working class has been associated with the bad old days and the progressives have embraced instead the idea of liberal education for the workers. Thus, for example, the Workers Educational Association and the university extra-mural departments have conceived their task in this way and not in providing vocational education. The superficial egalitarianism of this approach in fact conceals a fundamental assumption of a very different kind—that the elite can expect to live through their work but the majority must try to live in spite of their work. Liberal education for the workers is conceived as education for leisure. The ideal that everybody should find self-expression through his economic activity in this society is obviously unacceptable to the left which thus finds itself positively committed to a class structure in education.

Between the wars this went unchallenged because nobody thought there were economic grounds for general educational advance. The prewar discussion of secondary education was conducted with little reference to the need for a highly educated work force.

After the war the most spectacular development in English education— the phenomenal expansion of the technical colleges—was the result not of political decision but of steady pressure from progressive employers and their employees; the employers wanted better workers and the workers wanted better jobs. But to this development the champions of the working class were largely indifferent; the main emphasis in the educational policies of the Labour Party and the TUC was on the improvement of secondary education and expansion of the universities. The overwhelming majority of the adults who were obtaining formal education were doing so in the technical colleges but the Labour Party seemed not even aware of this. One of the party's intellectual leaders, Mr Anthony Crosland, was a member of a party study group which stated with gross inaccuracy in 1963 that most students in technical colleges were under 18 and the work of these colleges was therefore largely irrelevant to a policy statement on higher education.[5] Two years later he committed the Labour Government to basing its policies for education beyond school largely on the expansion and development of this field. What was the cause of this *volte face*, and what are its implications? To answer this question we must first look at the history of our fragmented system of post-school education, with particular reference to the growth of the colleges of advanced technology and the regional technical colleges.

Traditionally British policy in higher education has been based on three institutions—the university, the teachers' training college and the further education college.

The universities were initially developed for the academic education of fee paying upper and middle class children together with 'scholars'—working class children of exceptional ability. Latterly the trend has been to admit a greater number of 'scholars' by extending the system of grants to impecunious students and to reduce the privilege of the children of wealthier parents. Unexpectedly this has not resulted in a significant shift in the class composition of the university population although the university population has greatly increased—as in the case of other social reforms the middle classes have derived much more than their share of the benefit.

The teachers' training colleges were conceived as academically inferior and subordinate to the universities. They trained bright working class children to become teachers of working class children in state schools. Their form of education was conceived as vocational training as distinct from academic education—languages and mathematics have always played an insignificant part in their curriculum. The universities have always been numerically dominated by men and have significantly taken a very small number of working class women: the training colleges have been a traditional form of higher education for working class women.

The further education colleges, which were initially developed within the same institutions as technical and trade schools, have grown astronomically since 1945 as the rag-bag of education beyond school incorporating not only vocational training of workers but also the overflow from the universities. It is the further education colleges which are particularly important for our present purpose.

The demand for university education from potential students is dependent on two factors. The first of these is the number of students who have qualified in school studies for entry to university. The academic standard for university entry is not an absolute but has varied: the number of university entrants is to some extent controlled by the manipulation of entry standards. The standard now required for university entrance (at least two good A level passes in GCE) is much higher than it was 30 years ago (when the standard was 'matric' ie the equivalent of six passes at GCE O level); this emphasises the importance of the second factor. The second factor determining the pressure of university places is the economic one—the availability of financial support for the university student. Between the wars the normal means of entry to a university was either to obtain 'matric' and to have the private financial support to sustain three years of full-time study (which in turn might depend on private financial support to remain at school to the age of 17 or 18) or to obtain a scholarship awarded by the university, the state or a local authority. These university, state and local authority scholarships were available only to students who could achieve an unusually high standard in the Higher School Certificate or similar examination—ie the equivalent of a much higher standard than a bare pass in the present GCE A level examination. Before the war the university entrance level was much lower than at present for those with money but higher than at present for those without money.

Between the wars a number of technical colleges and polytechnics [O] (existing polytechnics are shown polytechnics [O] to distinguish them from the proposed polytechnics), originally providing training for working class boys and derived from the mechanics institutes of the nineteenth century and the trade schools of pre-1914, developed courses for full professional qualifications in engineering and commerce and in some cases for external degrees of the University of London. Generally these courses catered for students who could not afford to go to university and were developed particularly in the large urban centres—the polytechnics [O] of London and the technical colleges in such cities as Bradford, Glasgow and Manchester.

After 1945 a completely different development is discernible. A scheme of students' grants for discharged ex-servicemen (the FET scheme) created new pressures on university places. A large number of men who would never otherwise have contemplated a university education were offered free places to pursue degree courses. They were accorded priority over school leavers for university places (the school leavers were told to complete their national service before entering the university) but the demand was so great that the universities were unable to meet it. The government permitted FET grants to be tenable in degree and other courses in technical colleges and thereby encouraged not only the expansion of existing facilities in the colleges but also the growth of degree courses in colleges which previously had not contemplated work at this level. The unsatisfied demand for courses from ex-servicemen was mainly in the applied sciences and technology and this was acceptable to the government of the day which was well disposed to a crash programme in education for industry. It was at this time that work of university standard became firmly established in great volume in such colleges as Battersea Polytechnic and the Royal Technical College, Salford, in which it had previously existed on a smaller scale and in such colleges as Acton Technical College in which it had not previously existed at all. These were among the colleges which a decade later were to be the nuclei of new technological universities, but they were to pass through a long period of uncertainty before this was achieved.

The wartime Coalition Government had set up the Percy Committee in 1944 to make recommendations about the need for higher technological education. This Committee in its report[6] in 1945 envisaged the expansion of courses in technical colleges as well as in universities, and some of its recommendations closely resembled policies adopted by governments 10 and 20 years later. It suggested, for example, the establishment of the Dip Tech along lines which were adopted in 1955, but the Labour Government of 1945–51 ignored the proposal. The implications of its inaction was that the government regarded the growth of higher education in the technical colleges as a temporary expedient until the universities were able to meet the demand for places.

There followed during the early fifties a period of disillusionment for the leading technical colleges. They had tasted—albeit in a dilute form—the status and delights of university level work and had begun to acquire the teaching staff to sustain it. Now they were to find their student numbers decline and sometimes to see their classes collapse for lack of students. In some cases uneconomic classes of three or four students were forcibly closed on the intervention of Her Majesty's Inspectors—although often against the wishes of local authorities which were proud of their involvement in higher education. The demand for opportunities for part-time study for degrees continued, although diminishing in volume and under increasing difficulty as the University of London raised the standards of its final examinations. In particular the London engineering degree, after a revision of regulations in the mid-fifties, became almost impossible by purely leisure-time study.

The work of the colleges at this period was sustained by two new sources of students demanding courses to prepare them for the new standards of university—students from overseas and students transferring from schools to complete studies at sixth form level. Until and during the war the attainment of the old matric standard (ie the equivalent of GCE O level) had been adequate for university entry and universities offered courses for inter BSc or inter BA to students who had not completed a sixth form course. These courses had been used particularly by private students and overseas students. After 1945 the universities abandoned these courses. In some cases they systematically directed wouldbe students, particularly overseas students, to polytechnics [O] and technical colleges where they could complete courses for inter BA, inter BSc or first MB before entering the university. These technical college courses attracted students from overseas and students from secondary schools inadequately staffed and equipped for sixth form work (often these were private schools). They also attracted students who decided they preferred college to school—a development whose full implications have yet to be realised. These preliminary university courses gave employment to the colleges and provided a source from which the advanced, degree and diploma courses could be sustained. Some students completed the preliminary course and yet failed to obtain a university place. Others preferred to complete the university course in the college in which they were settled. Others who might not have otherwise contemplated a university education were persuaded by the college to continue their education.

The initiative with which the local authorities and principals of the colleges met the difficulties in the early fifties arising from the vacuum in government policy was crucial for their future. For during this period a body of opinion was developing among officials of the Ministry of Education, encouraged by some of the leading officials among the larger local authorities, that a major initiative in higher education was possible in the LEA colleges. When in 1956 Sir David Eccles and the Churchill Government were persuaded of this the colleges which were selected to spearhead this development were generally those which had best survived the troubles of the early fifties. Until this time although no major expansion of the universities had been undertaken (the prewar university colleges such as Leicester had been granted full university status but only one new university—Keele—had been created), the government had assumed that the necessary higher education development could take place within the university sector. In the mid-fifties the climate changed. This was the time when the scale of postwar technological development, particularly in the USA and the USSR, first became apparent to politicians and leading industrialists. Churchill was shaken by his realisation in 1954 or 1955 of Russian industrial potential and Eccles—possibly the most underrated Minister of Education—appreciated the desperate need to modernise British industry and responded to the foresight of his officials. A second factor which justified the 1956 White Paper[7] on technical education was the growing pressure for university places for which the existing universities were quite unprepared. The mid-sixties were to see the effect of the postwar bulge in the birthrate: there would be more young people in school and therefore a greater demand for post-school education.

But even in the fifties the growth of national prosperity was already leading to an increased demand for higher education. Wages and employment were high, the 'embourgeoisement' of the working class was proceeding apace and it was therefore more conceivable to the working man that his son or even his daughter might aim at a university degree. Gradually, at first within the discretion of local authorities, grants for students were more liberally awarded. Most important, though this seems to have been little anticipated, the reform of secondary education introduced by the 1944 Act was beginning to take effect. Grammar school places were being greatly increased, the numbers of pupils in sixth forms were rapidly growing, technical schools were being transferred from mere craft training establishments into quasi-grammar schools and even secondary modern schools were beginning to register GCE successes. Also the continuation of national service probably added a stimulus to academic ambition.

Whatever its *rationale* at the time—and the last word on this must await a detailed study—the White Paper of 1956 was a decisive step not only for the technical colleges immediately affected but ultimately for the whole of higher education. It legitimised for the first time the development of higher education to university level outside the universities. It was the start of the colleges of advanced technology, now well known, and of the polytechnics —ultimately a much greater development but as yet little known.

Like most developments in this field of education this policy statement went practically unnoticed outside the colleges: it was ignored by the education world itself. For several years after 1956 it was common to meet educationists in the traditional sectors—school teachers and university professors—who were totally unaware of the difference between a college of advanced technology and a secondary technical school. In this they were guided by some of the leaders of progressive opinion—the *New Statesman's* only comment on the 1956 White Paper was a mild welcome for a new deal for the technical schools!

The government's first hesitant encouragement to the colleges had been its decision in 1952 to give special grant aid to local authorities in respect of a limited number of colleges doing advanced (ie university level) work. Under the percentage grant arrangements then in operation for educational expenditure the government paid 60%; the new provision was for a 75% grant for the advanced work of selected colleges. Approval for this grant award was jealously sought by college principals and local authorities both as a symbol of status and as tangible encouragement to expand. The 1956 White Paper listed the 24 colleges which at that time had such recognition. This list included most of the colleges which had a significant body of full-time students doing advanced work and was generally interpreted as a provisional list of the colleges of advanced technology to be scheduled for development. Disillusionment for the majority quickly followed when in 1957 the government announced that development of advanced work was to be concentrated in nine colleges, the colleges of advanced technology— soon to be known as the CATs. These were to be institutions with national catchment concentrating on university level work; they were quickly to shed their lower level work and, in the image of the contemporary university, to lose their interest in part-time students. The remaining listed colleges were to be conceived as regional in function. They were to retain a wide range of work with full-time and part-time students and implicitly to continue their traditional role as an overflow receptacle for the established system of higher education. This they were to combine with the provision of courses in which the universities had no interest or which they did not consider their proper province.

It is with the development of these colleges, selected in 1952/56 and excluded in 1957, and others with which they were subsequently associated that we are now primarily concerned. But their development during the decade which was to follow before they were again selected in 1966 cannot be discussed in isolation from the development of the CATs. For the publication of the 1956 White Paper, the formation of an elite group of nine CATs and the relegation of the remaining so-called regional colleges to an ambiguous role left for these colleges—and the local authorities which had committed resources to their development—no alternative but to regard themselves as frustrated, aspirant CATs. One and only one of these 'kittens' succeeded in beating the system. This was Brunel College, now Brunel University, which was designated the tenth CAT in 1962. The remarkable feature of this story is not that Middlesex County Council and Brunel College achieved this but that many of the other regional colleges were able to develop as major institutions of higher education despite their exclusion from the government's 1957 list. Indeed some of the regional colleges which in 1966 were conceived by the government as leading polytechnics-to-be, such as Lanchester College of Technology at Coventry and Hatfield College of Technology in Hertfordshire, were not even in the long list of 1956. The story of the development of higher education in the technical colleges during the last decade is a story of development in spite of government action as much as it is a story of the effect of government policies. One of the problems we have to consider, and one of the problems which is concerning the government of today, is the extent to which future growth can be predicted, planned or controlled. A common and perhaps cynical view is that the problem is conceived by the government as 'how little can we get away with?' If this is true the politicians can derive little encouragement from recent history: the evidence is that if young people exist who want higher education national government must take very drastic action indeed to prevent them getting it.

The 1956 White Paper was pre-occupied with technological education interpreted in a fairly narrow sense. Although the popular image of the technical colleges and the colleges of further education is one of metal bashing, plumbing and woodwork, such work has long constituted much less than a majority element of the work of these colleges.

The education of an engineer or a technologist is primarily an academic matter and properly carried out includes a study of basic physical and social sciences as well as the theories of engineering materials and processes. But the popular misconception of the work of technical colleges also overlooks other fields such as commerce, public administration, art and architecture in which the colleges are heavily involved; and not least their work in general education supplementing the work of the schools and the universities. The staffs in technical colleges include, in addition to engineering graduates and skilled engineering craftsmen, large numbers of graduates in arts and men professionally qualified in law, accountancy, banking, insurance and many other fields.

An important feature of the 1956 White Paper was that it gave the green light for developments in technology—in the applications of physical and biological sciences—but not in the other fields of vocational or general education. Most notably, for this was an omission not to be repaired for eight years, it gave no encouragement to education for commerce. This had traditionally been the poor relation in the technical colleges; commercial employers were notably less enthusiastic about education than the industrialists and consequently many young people had to obtain their qualifications by evening study and correspondence courses whilst their engineering contemporaries were given day-release from work to attend college. In some large cities colleges of commerce existed separately from the technical colleges and were starved of resources whilst the technical colleges were expanded. After 1956 the commerce department of the technical college became even more emphatically deprived than before and even in some cases was banished completely. The development of education for art and design was also overlooked in the 1956 policy but this failure was redeemed by the establishment of the National Advisory Council on Art Education (the Coldstream Council) in 1959 and the National Council for Diplomas in Art and Design (the Summerson Council) in 1961.

By using its power of establishing academic qualifications and making awards to students the government was able to encourage certain fields of study rather than others.

A vital element of the policy was the establishment in 1955 of the National Council for Technological Awards (sometimes known as the Hives Council after Lord Hives its first chairman) along similar lines to those suggested some years earlier by the Percy Committee. This Council was to make awards to students on completion of authorised courses in authorised colleges. The course and the award were to be of honours degree standard, but, in deference to university interests which had long opposed developments of this kind, the award was to be not a degree but a diploma— the Diploma in Technology or Dip Tech as it was familiarly known. The astonishing thing about it was that, during its short lifetime of less than 10 years, it did become known and did obtain recognition despite the initial pessimism of most of the participants in the scheme and the frank contempt of many outside.

A particularly bold step was the establishment of the NCTA not as an examining body to determine syllabuses and set examinations but as an inspecting and supervising body—the colleges themselves had the responsibility of constructing curricula and of conducting examinations. If they were judged by the Council to be inadequate they were simply denied recognition; the Council would not do the job for them. The setting-up of the NCTA along these lines was much more significant as an educational reform than the listing of the colleges and possibly even more significant than the granting of resources. Certainly some unrecognised and ill equipped colleges were able to establish themselves by this machinery. Others despite their advantages of recognition and resources had considerable difficulty in satisfying the Council. Before the NCTA was set up the degree level work of the colleges (with the rare exception of those like Sunderland Technical College, which had arrangements with the University of Durham to enter students for its degree examination in engineering) was aimed at degrees of the University of London (external degrees except in the case of some of the London polytechnics [O]). Permission to run courses for London degrees had to be sought from the University which had to be satisfied about the adequacy of the accommodation facilities and staff available; this requirement was however little more than nominal and approval was given to degree courses in colleges with facilities which were grossly inadequate by any standard. The NCTA set completely new, and for many technical colleges hitherto unknown, standards both in accommodation and in course planning. In the existing literature the greatest importance has been attached to the NCTA's insistence that courses should be of the 'sandwich' pattern and that they should include 'liberal studies' and studies in administration. It was even more important that the Council threw the whole responsibility for courses and examinations on to the staffs of the colleges themselves and set new standards of accommodation, equipment and staffing which the local authorities were compelled to meet. Many local authorities were shocked to be told that their colleges were below the necessary standard for recognition. The Ministry of Education itself had a rude awakening particularly at Loughborough, the one college which it directly controlled: the college was twice rejected by the Council before it improved its facilities and obtained recognition. The NCTA formula has been continued in the Summerson Council (for awards in art) and in the Council for National Academic Awards (CNAA) which incorporated the NCTA after Robbins.

The freedom which the colleges obtained under the NCTA was in sharp contrast with the previous academic arrangements which prevailed in the colleges. It was notably greater than that enjoyed by the university colleges such as Leicester, Nottingham and Hull that had grown up between the wars. These had been restricted to preparing students for London external degrees until the granting of their charters (similar arrangements had been used for university colleges established in the colonies). In the establishment of the new universities after the war (first Keele in 1949 then Sussex, York, Kent, East Anglia, Essex, Lancaster and Warwick) this practice was not adopted and the universities awarded their own degrees from the start. The effects of the difference in procedure can already be seen in the contrast between the respective contributions to new educational thinking of the two generations of new universities. The facility to develop their own distinctive courses has been important in enabling the CATs and the regional colleges to hold their own in a rapidly developing situation even though they have not yet used the opportunity to the full.

The unexpected success in the recognition of the Dip Tech was only partly due to the enlightened government decision on the procedures of the NCTA. The universities, of which I will have many hard things to say, contributed generously to this. A number of eminent university teachers gave time and enthusiasm to the work of the NCTA, discussing courses, visiting colleges and thereby playing an important part in guaranteeing standards. A crucial decision was that of the Vice-Chancellors Committee to recommend the acceptance of the honours Dip Tech as equivalent to an honours degree in admitting students to university study for postgraduate qualifications. Important too was the recognition by the Burnham Committee and the Civil Service Commissioners which was quickly granted. But most important of all was the recognition and the active support given to the Dip Tech by some of the leading industrial firms, particularly those of the electrical engineering industry. Some of the pressures which these firms brought to bear on colleges, particularly Rugby and Stafford which they dominated, went close to infringement of academic freedom and local government autonomy, but this was greatly outweighed on the credit side by their sponsorship of students, their provision of industrial training and their tangible assistance in a dozen ways to the colleges which they supported. Not least important was that they went further than merely recognising the Dip Tech as the equivalent of a BSc but took convincing action to demonstrate in some cases that they positively preferred Dip Tech holders to university graduates. The recognition given by some government departments and some local authorities, as employers of technologists, was far less impressive.

When the Robbins Committee proposed in 1963 to replace the Dip Tech by the bachelor's degree there was little protest from the universities. True, they had other things to worry about when contemplating Robbins but nevertheless the success of the Dip Tech had achieved a significant and remarkable change in the climate of academic opinion.

All this is in retrospect, but at the time things looked rather different. When the Robbins Committee was established in 1961 the CATs were just beginning to acquire the confidence derived from their new status and opportunities. In the early days following designation and the establishment of the Dip Tech they had proceeded cautiously—they had little academic self-government and in some cases little confidence to exercise the freedom they had gained. Many of the proposed Dip Tech courses submitted to the NGTA were based on London BSc syllabuses only slightly modified (in one case not modified at all). The colleges were particularly cautious in advancing proposals for courses in the academic fields, such as production engineering, which were notoriously ignored by most universities and in which they could make an important new contribution. When Robbins started on his work there were progressive voices urging that the CATs be given full status as universities but few people in the colleges themselves believed this was a real possibility—certainly few believed that the individual CATs might obtain charters of their own. No one was more surprised than many of the teachers and students in the CATs when during 1962 and 1963 informed public opinion began to assume that full university status was inevitable. It is interesting to contrast the lack of confidence betrayed in the evidence to Robbins of some of the CAT representatives with the ready acceptance of the Robbins recommendations about the colleges.

This transformation did not apply to the regional colleges. Throughout the pre- and immediate post-Robbins discussions their very existence was virtually ignored. Over and over again, in Hansard and in press comments on Robbins, the term 'institutions of higher education' was used to include only the universities, teachers' training colleges and colleges of advanced technology. The assumption, implicit in existing government policy, that higher education in the technical colleges was a temporary expedient was generally accepted even by the few who recognised that it existed at all. This tendency was encouraged by the terms of reference of the Robbins Committee and by the way in which it interpreted them. The Committee was to make recommendations about *full-time* higher education. This was taken to include the work of the universities and the teachers' training colleges (even though the entry requirements for teachers' training colleges were significantly lower than those for universities) but to include only the full-time work of technical colleges for which the entry qualification was similar to the standards of entry to universities. Although the Robbins Committee considered the education of teachers in detail it felt incompetent to deal with professional education in general and, in particular, with those aspects of professional education in which the technical colleges were mainly interested. Thus the Robbins Committee from the start, partly by the definition of its terms of reference and partly by its interpretation of those terms, excluded from its consideration a sufficiently large body of the work of the regional colleges to render incomplete any recommendations it might make for their future. Worse than this, having disregarded the economic, social and academic implications of the growth of the advanced work of the colleges and having discounted the manpower planning aspect of higher education as incalculable, the Robbins Committee upgraded the CATs to university status in mere recognition of their academic attainment in conventional terms. The Committee thereby emasculated the 1956 policy without any awareness of the implications of its action. It was consistent in its philosophy, if hopelessly awry in its calculation, in asserting that the future of the regional colleges must be as candidates for university status this year, next year, sometime or never.

The Robbins Committee recommended that the regional colleges should continue under local authority control and that they should continue to provide courses in higher (ie university level) education for full-time and part-time students. As far as full-time study was concerned, this was in some measure a temporary expedient pending the adequate provision of university places, although a limited number of the colleges might attain university status by 1980. In this context a figure of 10 was specified but this was to include colleges selected possibly not only from the regional technical colleges and teachers' training colleges in England and Wales but also from colleges in Scotland.

The saving grace of the Robbins Report as far as the regional colleges were concerned was the recommendation that the NCTA should be converted into the Council for National Academic Awards (CNAA) which was to have a royal charter to grant degrees (not merely diplomas) for courses in all fields of study (not merely technology) by all patterns of study (part-time and full-time as well as sandwich). Lord Robbins has subsequently explained that this Council was intended to have a very limited function. It was to concentrate on colleges which were clearly *en route* to full university status. It is likely that, in common with most of his university colleagues inside and outside the Committee, he failed to appreciate the potential of this instrument. This lack of understanding was probably not shared by those members of his committee—particularly Mr (now Sir) Harold Shearman, Sir David Anderson and the representatives of the Ministry of Education—who were more familiar with current trends in the technical colleges.

The immediate reactions to the Robbins Report in the regional colleges were, first, resentment that the CATs which were so little distinguishable from them should receive such greatly preferential treatment and, secondly, a determination in many of the colleges to be among the 10 selected for elevation to university status.

Some of the colleges, notably those at Brighton, Coventry and Hatfield along with some of the London polytechnics [O], could with justification claim to be already as highly developed, physically and academically, as some of the CATs. But these were not the only colleges which obtained the support of their controlling local authorities in the clamour for university status which developed during the first half of 1964. For the 10 university vacancies Robbins said should be filled by 1980 there were more than a score of forceful applications presented to the Minister. Great was the howl when in the spring of 1965 Mr Anthony Crosland reduced the figure to a firm zero, at least until 1975, and added for good measure that none of the colleges would be permitted to become part of existing universities! But all this was yet in the future. Immediately following Robbins the regional colleges, a minor but grossly underestimated section of the whole field, were of little general concern. The CATs went joyfully on their way to glory, the politicians prepared for the counter attack from the university conservatives, which in the event hardly materialised despite frenzied activity in Printing House Square, and two set piece battles were prepared. The first—as to two Ministers of Education or one—despite the conservative line taken by the majority of the Robbins Committee which advocated a separate ministry for the universities, was never a serious issue after Mr Shearman wrote his minority report that set out clearly the hard political reasons for bringing the whole of education under one major department of state. That it remained an issue of political debate for some time after the publication of the Report owed more to the battle for power within the Conservative Party in a pre-election year than to fundamental differences in policy. The issue was resolved by Sir Edward Boyle who conceded to Mr Quintin Hogg the senior post whilst retaining in his own hands the effective control of policy and winning the day on the machinery of control.

The second battle after Robbins, interrupted by the prolonged agony of the 1964 election (which came six months later than generally anticipated), was that for control of the teachers' training colleges now elevated to the title of colleges of education.

Robbins had recommended that these colleges should be transferred to the financial and academic control of the universities—a recommendation which was superficially attractive but politically unrealistic. After Robbins it was inevitable that public expenditure on higher education should be greatly increased and that there should be a greater measure of public control of universities. This would be difficult enough to achieve; to transfer the large and critical sector of teacher training from local authority control to university control at this stage would only increase the difficulty.

Before the general election of 1964 both political parties committed themselves generally to the expansion of higher education and to the elevation of the CATs. They carefully reserved their position on the teachers' training colleges and said nothing about the regional colleges. The Labour Party had on file the 1963 Taylor Report[5] which had recommended the incorporation of training colleges and regional technical colleges into 45 new universities but the party had been careful not to adopt this as policy and to avoid its mention in all election policy statements. If only because neither party could afford to antagonise the local authorities, but also because each could appreciate the economic realities, there was no serious possibility that the transfer of the colleges of education to university control would be implemented by either. When Mr Michael Stewart assumed office as Secretary of State for Education and Science in October 1964 he was strongly in favour of this reform—not surprisingly since he had appeared in person before the Robbins Committee on behalf of the Fabian Society as an advocate of it—but he had no firm backing in the party and found no great support for it among his senior officials. Within three months the idea was stone dead and Mr Stewart had moved on to the Foreign Office. As for the regional colleges few in either party knew or cared (but there were important individual exceptions). Certainly neither party had a policy, public or private.

In the Conservative Party Sir Edward Boyle's appreciation of the problems of this sector of public education—as of so many others—was far ahead of that of his colleagues but he avoided declaring his hand. A Conservative Minister of Education always has difficulties in explaining his problems to his privately educated colleagues. Boyle's difficulty with this sector—which was even too low in the league for the Labour leaders to comprehend—was inevitably very great.

In the Labour Party only one leading figure had made a study of this problem and he was at the crucial time 'hors de combat', much to his bitter frustration. This was Mr Richard Crossman who had emerged during the winter of 1963–64 as the party spokesman on education. His perception of the political importance of the technical colleges was partly inspired and informed by his personal involvement with the curious situation which was developing in his own constituency of Coventry. Beautifully situated alongside the city's celebrated cathedral was possibly the best equipped and educationally most advanced of the regional colleges. Within the city was also one of the leading teachers' training colleges and just outside the boundary were the beginnings of the new University of Warwick. The local authority was amongst the most progressive in the country in its educational administration (although it was typical of a progressive Labour authority that it saw nothing odd in establishing a new university alongside two well established colleges) and each of the three institutions had a capable and progressive principal. A better place to recognise the shortcomings of Robbins could hardly be found. Even worse, in the context of Coventry, were the implications of the fragmentary policies for higher education which were being pressed by civil servants in the name of economic necessity. Mr Crossman became strongly committed in 1964 to a unitary policy for the development of higher education—a policy which would have meant the subordination of the technical colleges to the universities and the subordination of the universities to the Secretary of State for Education and Science. But Mr Crossman signalled his intentions too clearly, the academics and teachers within the party were too strong for him, and in the government formed in October he was found another job. With him went the academics' worst fears of Labour government; with him also went the most serious Labour Party documentation on education, for good or ill. Thereafter policies have been determined off the cuff.

Two new factors influenced the policies of the Labour Government in higher education. The first was the economic crisis—not a mere passing phase but a long term problem which quickly eliminated the possibility of an over optimistic policy for expansion. Even the expansion proposed by Robbins was too expensive and this presumed the continuing provision of places on the cheap in the colleges of education and the regional colleges. A second new factor which intensified the problem was that the Robbins figures for the projected demand for places in higher education, which Robbins had warned were a conservative estimate, proved quickly to be so—the Robbins rate of expansion would not be enough unless many wouldbe students were to be turned away. Even these projections were, in any case, inadequate as measures of demand for they were in fact merely projections of satisfied demand. The actual demand, given the adequate provision of students grants and the availability of suitable courses, could prove to be even greater. Furthermore if the government's plans for the reform of secondary education were to have the results predicted the demand for higher education would be further inflated. Already over half the children obtaining five GCE passes or better (roughly the old matric standard) were not continuing after school in any form of full-time further education. The consequences of further increasing the number of children obtaining GCE and of improving the opportunities for their further education were considerable—and indeed have not yet been calculated.

This was the problem which confronted the government in 1964 and confronts it still. The Robbins expansion of the universities within the available finances was regarded by many university teachers as placing them under severe stress and threatening to lower standards. Yet the demand for higher education by wouldbe students is very greatly increasing and will continue to increase, the need for skilled manpower continues and the flow of money is severely restricted. There is no easy solution to this problem, no political party has a policy for dealing with it and certainly no socialist educational utopia is in sight.

Inheriting Mr Stewart's decision to retain the colleges of education under direct public control Mr Crosland attached first priority to the completion of policy in higher education and defined this in two speeches in the spring of 1965. At the conference of the National Union of Teachers in Douglas at Easter he outlined a crash programme for attacking the problem of teacher training in which he explicitly said that the colleges of education were to be put on an emergency footing—to undertake maximum expansion with the minimum of resources. A week later, in his notorious Woolwich speech, he defined his policy for higher education in technical colleges which was to form the basis for the policy subsequently detailed in the 1966 White Paper. In this speech, drawing freely from a document[8] prepared by the Association of Teachers in Technical Institutions (which had decided to seek the expansion of the maximum number of its colleges outside the university system rather than the promotion of a limited number into the university system), he played on a doubtful dichotomy between the academic education of the universities and the vocational education of the colleges in the public sector to rationalise the government's decision to establish no new universities within the next decade and to encourage and concentrate the growth of higher education in the technical college system under direct public control. The award of degrees by the Council for National Academic Awards, which had been established early in 1964 as recommended by Robbins, was a vital part of this proposal. Together with specific decisions not to permit the incorporation of certain regional colleges into universities and a general embargo on proposals of this kind Mr Crosland's speech constituted a significant modification of the Robbins recommendations. It implied a significant shift of the balance in higher education between the autonomous and public sectors. It meant that within a decade, even if we ignored part-time students, the autonomous sector would become only a minor part of higher education in England and Wales and that the Council for National Academic Awards would become the largest degree awarding body in the country. A further implication of the Woolwich speech, and that which caused the greatest antagonism, for the speech was generally welcomed in the technical colleges and ignored in the universities, was that the colleges of education should be regarded as part of the public sector and should associate more closely than hitherto with the technical colleges. There was an outcry from the colleges of education and the institutes of education, already smarting from the decision not to incorporate them completely into the university system, and a temporary breakdown in relations between the government and the teachers in the colleges.

Despite the government's efforts to placate the teachers in the colleges of education throughout 1965 by hurrying along the proposals for the liberalisation of college government they remained bitterly hostile to the 'binary policy'* for higher education as it came to be known. Their agitation against the threat of association with the despised technical colleges and the CNAA, little though this was understood, found ready allies in the university professors of education and expedited the acceptance by most university senates of the proposals to establish BEd degrees.

The teacher training lobby extended its campaign into the political parties, and had some success in the Labour Party, causing Mr Crosland some embarrassment not only with back bench MPs but also with some of his colleagues—notably Mr Crossman. This did not result in any reversal of policy for the technical colleges but it did lead to the withdrawal of the idea, never more than implicit in the Woolwich speech, of the closer association of the colleges of education with the technical colleges. It also led to a discreet withdrawal by Mr Crosland of his rather crude version of the dichotomy between academic and vocational education.

But for the technical and other colleges of further education (the colleges of commerce were particularly glad now to be firmly in the picture) the plans went ahead. In the spring of 1966 came the publication of the White Paper which proposed the incorporation of some 60 colleges of technology, building, art and commerce into 30 new polytechnics and the concentration, as far as was practicable, of courses of full-time and part-time higher education in these centres. It redefined 'higher education' to include many courses not included by Robbins in his terms of reference, which though not requiring GCE A levels as an entry qualification ultimately overlapped university courses in their academic level†. All the regional colleges were included (one of them only after reconsideration in 1967) together with colleges of commerce and art which had not been eligible for regional designation and a number of colleges of technology which had developed their advanced work substantially since 1962, when the list of regional colleges had last been revised. It is a measure of the speed of the post-Robbins growth of higher education in this sector that by 1966 the Robbins estimate of student numbers for 1970–71 was already exceeded and several colleges judged unready for regional status in 1962 had by 1966 a full-time degree student body of over 500, drawn from a national catchment area.

The statistical basis of the White Paper was unashamedly vague and its financial basis was not apparent. The number of students in the selected colleges following courses now regarded as included in higher education was available neither in the White Paper nor in any publication, official or unofficial. The policy was for the period 1966–1976 but the projected student numbers were given only for 1970–71 and these only for full-time students in the old (Robbins) definition of higher education. The student capacity of the selected colleges was also apparently unknown. No estimate of the cost of the proposed exercise has been published.

In the White Paper the principle was laid down—and subsequently reinforced in ministerial speeches—that the new polytechnics were not to emulate the university pattern, followed slavishly by the CATs, of 'shedding' all courses other than those leading to the award of degrees and of generally disregarding the needs of part-time students. Mr Crosland used the, by now highly emotive, term 'comprehensive' in his exposition of the concept of the polytechnic as an institution catering for a wide range of student ability, student availability and academic subjects. In contrast with the development following the 1956 White Paper, growth was not to be limited to courses in technology. There was one reservation—out of deference to the teacher training lobby the development of teacher training in the polytechnics was to be strictly limited.

The White Paper came under serious attack from three directions. It was attacked first by the technical college lobby because it left the excluded colleges in limbo[9]. Advanced work in these colleges was not to be forbidden but it was clearly to be discouraged—they were to act as the traditional receptacle for 'overflow' from the legitimised colleges. But this time the predicament was more serious because the 'other colleges'—as they were euphemistically dubbed by the White Paper—were simultaneously under pressure from two other directions: developments in secondary education were threatening to denude them of their full-time students in the 16–19 age range and developments in industrial training were threatening to incorporate their students into industrial training establishments on the much detested French pattern. Alarm in the colleges was increased by the apparent lack of concern shown by the Department of Education and Science about their predicament. The ATTI which had initially derived considerable satisfaction from the accord between its own policies and the statement in the Woolwich speech felt that the White Paper repeated the old pattern of the creation of an elite hierarchy and the consequent dangers of submission to the university ideal which it perceived as hostile to the whole technical college tradition. The ATTI had not forgotten the alacrity with which teachers in the CATs had turned their backs on their colleagues in the technical colleges when given the opportunity. Apart from the affront to the ATTI's idealism here was a renewed and much greater threat to its membership and the status of the technical college field as a whole.

The second attack came from the art colleges and the professional artists who had given them strong support in the comparatively recent emergence from the doldrums. During the fifties art education had been seriously neglected in national policy. Many art departments in technical colleges were run down and sometimes completely displaced whilst technical departments were expanded. Culturally their teachers and students had little in common with the 'rude mechanics' alongside them: the two groups often developed a relationship of mutual contempt. Most of the significant new developments in art education under the sponsorship of the Coldstream and Summerson Councils had taken place in art colleges which were independent of technical colleges (from which many of them had sprung). Association with technical colleges was linked with failure, independence with success. Worst of all, partly as a result of the artist's inherent reluctance to organise himself politically, the policy came to many of the art colleges as a complete surprise. The art colleges, like the colleges of education, yearned for association with the universities, at least to the extent of having the much vaunted academic freedom and of having nothing to do with the technical colleges. The Inner London Education Authority quickly yielded to the apartheid demands of its artists. Some of the provincial authorities secured the assent of their art colleges to mergers: they sensed the advantages of conformity and association with a larger organisation. Many others remain reluctant and it seems likely that despite pressures from politicians some of the art colleges will be granted their continued independence though they may find the price is dear. One of the soundest and most important principles of the government's policy is that in the improvement of material standards, particularly amenities, there are large economies of scale.

Finally the policy came under a new attack from the universities, now more keenly aware of their own financial difficulties and belatedly appreciating the possible implications for them of the growth of a new state university system. Their most effective point of attack was that the colleges to be designated as polytechnics were best equipped to provide education in those academic fields which were in least demand—technology and applied physical science. This was the area in which university capacity was not fully taken up: it was also the most expensive to maintain and expand. Therefore to propose the expansion of the polytechnics on economic grounds was clearly a nonsense, they said.

For almost a year following the White Paper the government collected comments on its proposals from interested organisations, relevant local education authorities and regional advisory councils for further education. Delays in further progress were caused by demands from local authorities and their allies for the addition of further polytechnics to the proposed list—in all 12 deputations of this kind were received by the Department of Education and Science. All save two were unsuccessful. Delays were also caused by belated representations on behalf of art colleges wishing to be excluded which were supported by almost all the national bodies concerned with art education. These representations too were unsuccessful.

In April 1967 the Secretary of State issued formal invitations to local authorities to submit proposals for the establishment of polytechnics. This letter of invitation spelled out in some detail the nature of the machinery of college government which was recommended. This incorporated proposals for the liberalisation of college government along the lines proposed by the Robbins Committee and by the 1966 Weaver Committee[10] on the government of colleges of education. It included a great increase in staff participation in college government—a feature notably lacking in local authority colleges—and a significant reduction in the powers in detail which could be reserved by local authority committees and officials. The problems of college government were to be simplified by proposed legislation permitting the powers of governing bodies to be strengthened and permitting the Secretary of State if necessary to force the hand of reluctant local authorities in this matter. Particularly difficult problems were presented by the proposed polytechnics which were to incorporate colleges currently under the control of separate local authorities (in some cases colleges to be amalgamated were 12 miles apart).

In addition to the request for a proposed scheme of government the letter of invitation asked local authorities to outline proposals for the development of courses within the available and already planned accommodation. The letter emphasised that at this stage (ie prior to formal designation of the polytechnic) no long term plan, academic or logistic, was required. The view of the government was that having created guidelines and a broad framework it could leave the matter in the hands of the local authorities. The major problem which then arose, and still exists, is that economic circumstances have largely forced a situation which calls for a formulation of educational policy for the polytechnics. The main purpose of this book is to advance some tentative proposals. But first we re-examine critically the government's policy within the wider context.

Notes

* Many of the attacks were directed at the 'binary system', as though Crosland had invented it. He answered this and defended his policy in his Lancaster speech in January 1967. See Appendix C.
† Mr Crosland's successor as Secretary of State, Mr Patrick Gordon Walker, made the redefinition of 'higher education' more explicit in a speech recorded for the BBC (but not delivered publicly as intended) at Manchester on 1 March 1968. He stated erroneously that the new definition (courses which required five GCE O levels for entry and which went beyond the standard of sixth form work) was the same as that used by Robbins.

Publications and abbreviations

Publications

1 *Secondary Education for All*
    R. H. Tawney   Allen & Unwin 1924
2 *The Education of the Adolescent*

HMSO 1926

3   *Higher Education*

HMSO 1963

4   *A Plan for Polytechnics and Other Colleges*

HMSO 1966

5   *The Years of Crisis*
report of the Labour Party's Study   Labour Party 1963
Group on Higher Education

6   *Higher Technological Education*

HMSO 1945

7   *Technical Education*

HMSO 1956

8   *The Future of Higher Education Within the
Further Education System*

ATTI 1965

9   *Plan for Polytechnics*

ATTI September 1966

10   *Report of the Study Group on the Government
of Colleges of Education*

HMSO 1966

11   *Report of the Committee on University Teaching Methods*

HMSO 1964

12   *Children and Their Primary Schools*

HMSO 1966

13   *Half our Future*

HMSO 1963

14   *Secondary School Examinations Other Than the GCE*

HMSO 1960

15   *Examining at 16+*

Schools Council 1966

16   *The Organisation Man*
William H. Whyte   Penguin Books 1960

17   *New Society*

10 November 1966

18   *A Higher Award for Business Studies*

HMSO 1964

19   *Engineering Design*

HMSO 1963

20   *Where*

January 1967

21   *Contrary Imaginations*
Liam Hudson   Methuen 1966
Penguin Books 1968

22   *The Management and Staffing of Local Government*

HMSO 1966

23   *The Government of Colleges of Education*

HMSO 1966

Abbreviations

AEC	Association of Education Committees
AEU	Amalgamated Engineering Union
AMIMechE	Associate Member of the Intitution of Mechanical Engineers
ASTMS	Association of Scientific, Technical and Managerial Staff
ATTI	Association of Teachers in Technical Institutions
BA	Bachelor of Arts
BEd	Bachelor of Education
BSc	Bachelor of Science
CAT	College of Advanced Technology
CNAA	Council for National Academic Awards
CSE	Certificate of Secondary Education
DATA	Draughtsmen's and Allied Technicians' Association
DES	Department of Education and Science
DipAD	Diploma in Art and Design
Dip Tech	Diploma in Technology
ETU	Electrical Trades Union
FE	Further education
FET	Further Education and Training
GCE	General Certificate of Education
HE	Higher education
HMI	Her Majesty's Inspector
HNC	Higher National Certificate
HND	Higher National Diploma
ILEA	Inner London Education Authority
LEA	Local education authority
LSE	London School of Economics and Political Science
MB	Bachelor of Medicine
MSc	Master of Science
NALGO	National Association of Local Government Officers
NCTA	National Council for Technological Awards
NUPE	National Union of Public Employees
NUS	National Union of Students
NUT	National Union of Teachers
ONC	Ordinary National Certificate
PhD	Doctor of Philosophy
PPE	Philosophy, politics and economics
TUC	Trades Union Congress
UGC	University Grants Committee

91

FROM TECHNICAL SCHOOL TO TECHNOLOGICAL UNIVERSITY

Peter Venables

Source: P. Venables, *Higher Education Developments: The Technological Universities*, London: Faber and Faber, 1978, pp. 11–34.

Like all other educational institutions, technological ones are both the products and the causes of change in society. They cannot be protected from the stresses and strains involved in such change, nor isolated from a wide range of influences, including those of a conforming character. Institutions of higher education have sustained and increased the rate of scientific discovery and its application in the emergence of modern technological nations, and have themselves changed accordingly. Such developments have also profoundly affected the structure of society, the range and kind of employment available, the standard of living and the use of leisure, and indeed the economic and political relationships between nations.

These institutions also ensure the continuity of modern civilisations by preserving and extending culture, science and the arts, and by providing vocational, professional and adult education. In recent times, however, the basis of society has been threatened increasingly by the impact of technological innovation, and this has emphasised the importance of fostering the biological and the social sciences alongside the physical ones.

In the last decade, the purposes and functions of higher educational institutions throughout the world have thus been increasingly the subject of sceptical enquiry, even of hostile attack from without, and of anxious concern and radically divisive philosophies and responses from within. 'Men make institutions, institutions mould men', said Winston Churchill, but it is important to note that the men and women who are thus moulded by institutions are mostly those who did not make them. Moulding constraints are of course indispensable to the continuity of civilised society, but its institutions and their moulding purposes need to be understood and modified in response to the changing needs and aspirations of mankind.

In former times the slow rate of change enabled the moulds to be turned to developing needs at a reasonably commensurate rate. Now the pace and character of change, induced by science and technology, produce problems which cannot be contained or solved within the traditional moulds, and the resulting stresses and strains put a premium on understanding and reasonable action. Men and women are less and less inclined to acquiesce quietly to the institutional moulds designed by their forefathers, as these are keenly felt to embody irritating, not to say highly abrasive, outmoded values and practices. They thus feel compelled to remould their existing institutions – whether they be educational or social, political or religious – to redesign them, and to establish entirely new ones: to require institutions, indeed, that will secure humane objectives and desirable social advances within their own lifetime, and not in some distant future period.

There is one further consideration which underlies this sense of urgency. Education is perforce the basis of a technological society, but it is now beginning to be understood that it is no less an indispensable defence against its abuses if that society is to become truly democratic, and to remain so. 'Without education, human opportunities and lasting satisfactions and the citizen's rights are apt to wither away, a fact not overlooked by dictators. "Power always tends to corrupt, absolute power corrupts absolutely", said Acton. Technological power can all too readily become an absolutely corrupting power, as the last three decades right up to the present bear frequent and terrible witness. Access to education is therefore increasingly felt to be of paramount importance, and it should not be subject to arbitrary, unreasonable or removable barriers on the part of the institutions which provide it.'[1]

This study is concerned with the development of technological institutions in this country during two decades. The first, starting in 1956, when the Colleges of Advanced Technology were designated, covers their progress until 1966 when they became Universities. The second ten years sees them establishing themselves as a definitive section of the University system, both nationally and internationally. This period also saw the designation of the Polytechnics and other major developments in Further Education. The changing character of all these institutions must be seen in relation to the changing nature of the society of which they are a part.

The evolution of human society has taken place sequentially in four main phases: the nomadic, the agrarian, the industrial and, most recently, the technological. Profound changes in economic and social structure, combined with an accelerating rate of change, have characterised the last two phases so that the word 'revolution' rather than 'evolution' comes more readily to mind. The inescapable stresses and strains involved, the adjustments, transformations and innovations of economic, political and social structures to meet changing needs, bear most hardly where the rate of change is fastest and is seemingly compelled from without. This is most evident with

311

the underdeveloped countries in a world increasingly dominated by modern technological societies and systems, mainly those of Europe, Russia and the United States.

The four phases of development are characterised by an increasing withdrawal of labour from the land to towns of increasing size and complexity, which require ever-growing complex services to sustain them. A second characteristic is increasing horsepower/wattage per worker in productive industry with increasing productivity. In turn this leads to a diminution in the proportion of workers in productive industry relative to those in secondary and tertiary occupations as, for example, in engineering and coalmining compared with those employed in commerce and the distributive trades, and in social, governmental and other service occupations and professions. Primary industries become increasingly capital-intensive, agriculture included, while the secondary and tertiary sectors remain labour-intensive.

Such characteristics and trends might indicate an incipient transition from the technological to a sociological phase, a transition towards greater and not less complexity, because of the greater indeterminacy of the sociological problems as compared with the technological ones. In relation to this, we may note that the industrial phase grew out of a scientific empiricism and pragmatism, whereas rigorous scientific research and application is indispensable to the technological phase. By contrast, research, for the incipient psycho-sociological phase has scarcely begun, and is certainly not commensurate with present, let alone future, needs – as witness, for example, the founding of the Department of Scientific and Industrial Research (DSIR) in 1916 (now the Science Research Council – SRC), and the Social Science Research Council (SSRC) as late as 1965.

As expanding cities have coalesced into conurbations, states and nations have combined into supranational groups, almost coincident with continents and with ever-increasing economic power, for which the furtherance of science and technology is vital. In this context science and technology know no frontiers, with the creation perforce of international cartels to exploit them to the full. For all the debate about other aspects, this is the scientific-technological, and therefore economic, reality of being in the Common Market.

The inherent educational implications and consequences have yet to be worked out, though innovations have already begun in British tertiary institutions. Indeed, educational changes are the concomitants of social, political and economic changes. They may frequently be delayed, through unawareness or inertia in institutions, and even through active hostility on the part of their members. The slow, reluctant introduction of science and technology into British Universities, as recounted by Eric Ashby,[2] fully exemplifies such reactions.

Because of their major commitment to technology, the Technological Universities and Polytechnics are open to particularly searching questions, the answers to which are among the close concerns of this book. For example, are Technological Universities, and Polytechnics also, simply service-stations for a technological society, the values of which are beyond question? What are and what should be the relationships of higher educational institutions to society at large, to government, industry, commerce and the professions? What should be the nature of their governance to relate them responsibly to the needs of society and no less to protect their autonomy against undue political and economic pressures? What should be the breadth, specialisation and relevance of their studies, and what is the significance and feasibility of general studies? How far should admission procedures and range of courses take account of the special needs of disadvantaged groups in society?

These questions have acquired a sharper cutting edge because of the changing social conditions and human expectations of the last decade. The attempt to answer some of these questions has led to the emergence of new institutions and the substantial modification or change of direction of others,[3] and calls for comment on related educational terminology.

Long-term pressures, exerted against widespread inertia if not active professional resistance, have impelled us towards the belated recognition of the underlying unity of 'higher education' and 'Further Education' which also includes 'Teacher Education' (formerly 'Teacher Training'), professional education, adult education and leisure activities (in Evening Institutes). All these must be considered as integral parts of the last of the three major phases of the educational system – primary, secondary, tertiary. Tertiary education covers the whole range of educational provision for adult citizens.

Raising of the school-leaving age has always been followed over the years by increased enrolments in Further and higher education. So we may expect that the proportion staying on at school will continue to increase, and that day release will be increasingly supplemented by block release and sandwich courses in schools and Junior Colleges which will share the same educational aims and provide similar social and counselling services for adolescent students. The present overlap between secondary schools and Technical Colleges is likely to be a transient problem and there are sound psychological considerations for marking the attainment of adult citizenship at eighteen in an unambiguous educational way, that is by eligibility for entry to tertiary institutions.

With the exception of Brunel, which began as Acton Technical College in 1928, the Technological Universities stem from part-time classes which started in the nineteenth century, and the earliest of the technological institutions derive from Mechanics' Institutes originating in the period 1820–35. The best history of the origins of the further education colleges is *Mechanics' Institutes of Lancashire and Yorkshire before 1851* by Mabel Tylecote.[4] The Mechanics' Institutes are indeed the spiritual ancestors not only of the Technological Universities but of some Civic Universities as well.[5]

Impetus for change came with the 1851 Exhibition, made more urgent with the unfavourable comparisons in the 1862 Exhibition of British products with those of Continental manufacturers, and strengthened by Lyon Playfair's advocacy of the need to develop technical education. The establishment of the Department of Science and Art in 1853 and of the Education Department, into which it was incorporated, in 1857, were indispensable steps forward.[6] Their examinations proved a positive catalyst of change – an early adumbration of 'the importance of being qualified'[7] – and the same was true of those of the Society of Arts from 1856 and, later still, of the examinations of the City and Guilds of London Institute, founded in 1881. In the north, the Union of Lancashire and Cheshire Institutes, founded in 1839, pioneered examinations from 1847 onwards.

W. H. G. Armytage, commenting on the Paris Exhibition of 1867, writes, 'When English industrialists heard that their exhibits . . . were characterised as "slovenly intruded heaps of raw material mingled with pieces of rusty iron", intimations of their mortality began to dawn on them.'[8] Progress was slow, intermittent and unpredictable, and between 1902 and 1918 no more than ten technical schools were built. The 1914–18 war produced another fitful spurt, but the impulse to establish compulsory part-time day education under the Fisher Acts of 1917 and 1919 petered out except at Rugby.[9]

The ardent advocacy of Lord Eustace Percy over several years raised hopes of substantial progress and in 1929 he felt that 'there were signs that during the next ten years there would be a national development in technical education as broad and far-reaching as that seen during the last twenty years in secondary education.'[10] The world economic blizzard of 1929–30 blighted all such hopes, and developments began again only in the late 1930s, and then on a scale totally inadequate for the enormous load of work so soon to fall upon the Technical Colleges in World War II. The Colleges responded magnificently to wartime tasks, by acquiring and making use of whatever buildings were available, however unsuitable and inadequate for the purpose. 'Make do and mend', a wartime necessity, was highly detrimental to technical education, but the policy continued into the 1950s.

Day courses were soon added to evening classes in arts, crafts and domestic science, but they remained a small proportion of the total enrolments. Secondly, advanced work grew slowly, but derived strength from the London University external degree system. For the then Polytechnics in London, a definitive stage was reached with the University of London Act in 1898, which led to the system of having some of their teachers recognised by the University, enabling their matriculated students to take internal degrees of the University.

Nationally from 1921 onwards part-time day advanced work grew under the National Certificate schemes, with 'endorsements' thereon which exempted holders from the requirements for professional examinations. In due time, however, courses for Ordinary National Certificate were transferred to other local institutions of less standing, while Higher National Certificate courses, and subsequently Higher National Diplomas also, were concentrated in the major technological institutions. Such changes and reorganisations were a normal feature of growth, varying only in detail in the particular institution. It is therefore totally misleading to represent the shedding of courses by the Colleges of Advanced Technology on becoming Universities as a quite novel and unjustifiable aspect of their evolution.

General education and social activities were included from the earliest days. However, with notable exceptions such as the Regent Street Poly-technic, the provision was voluntary and very limited. Official policy changed slowly, but with enlightened developments in various Local Authorities, such as the Essex Technical Colleges under Sir John Sargent's leadership, so that such work and activities became more widely recognised as an integral part of the educational work of a Technical College.

Technical education became a duty of the Local authorities only with the passing of the 1944 Education Act, but it remained a loosely knit system responding variously to the needs of the times under the guidance of the Regional Advisory Councils (RACs). These were established as a result of the Percy Committee Report on Higher Technological Education, which was the first of many post-war reports[11] stressing the increased need for scientists and technologists, especially in industry. The nine RACs had the National Advisory Committee for Industry and Commerce (NACEIC) at the apex. This Council raised the question of creating a central awarding body many times and eventually, in July 1955 the Government established the National Council for Technological Awards (NCTA) under the chair-manship of Lord Hives for the award of the Diploma in Technology (Dip.Tech.). This was not a degree but was to be regarded as a degree equivalent, a limitation which was removed when its successor, the Council for National Academic Awards (CNAA), was established with a Royal Charter in 1964.

1956 white paper on technical education

The Ministry of Education Pamphlet No. 8, *Further Education*, published in 1946, envisaged a new structure for Local Colleges of Further Education and Regional Colleges, with new roles and defined catchment areas, but this did not become official planning policy until the publication of a White Paper ten years later in February 1956.[12] This set out a plan for the Technical Colleges of England and Wales, based on a five-year capital development programme of £70m, with a rapid increase in the capacity of advanced courses from 9,500 to about 15,000. Students in these courses became eligible for State Scholarships.

The Government strongly endorsed a report on sandwich courses by NACEIC[13] which recommended that expansion was to be mainly in courses leading to the award of the Dip.Tech. and that the bulk of full-time or sandwich courses should be carried on in Colleges which concentrated on advanced courses at technological (as distinct from technician) level. The 1956 White Paper listed in para. 68 twenty-four colleges in receipt of 75 per cent grant for certain parts of their advanced work, and the Government confirmed its wish to see 'the proportion of advanced work at these Colleges vigorously increased, so that as many of them as possible may develop speedily into Colleges of Advanced Technology'. Strong governing bodies were essential, with power to spend within the heads of annual estimates approved by the Local Authority. The scale and standard of staffing were to be improved, and the academic staff were to be given 'appropriate freedom to plan their courses'.

The building-up of the Advanced Colleges was not intended to prevent development of advanced courses elsewhere, especially the part-time ones, and the White Paper noted that some 150 Colleges already provided Higher National Certificate and other advanced part-time courses. In retrospect, this can be seen as a serious failure to grasp the nettle of concentration, the lack of which has plagued the development of advanced work ever since. Circular 305 which followed[14] delineated a structure of Local Colleges, Area Colleges, Regional Colleges and, at the apex, the Colleges of Advanced Technology. More specifically, the last group were 'to provide a broad range and substantial volume of work exclusively at advanced level (whether in full-time, sandwich or part-time courses), including postgraduate and research work', and which satisfied conditions set out in the Appendix to the Circular. The Minister considered it important that 'a small number of Colleges should develop as speedily as possible into Colleges of Advanced Technology concentrating entirely on advanced studies and providing a broad range of work of the highest quality . . . such Colleges will be required to comply with certain conditions in respect of administration, finance, staffing and accommodation.' The Minister proposed 'to announce a provisional list of Colleges of Advanced Technology . . . (which) will be formally designated as soon as the Minister is able to satisfy himself the College already fulfils the conditions or will be able to do so in the near future'.

In the event eight were provisionally designated[15] and later confirmed by the Minister:

Birmingham College of Technology
Bradford Technical College
Cardiff College of Technology and Commerce
Loughborough College of Technology
Royal Technical College, Salford

and in London, *Battersea*, *Chelsea* and *Northampton Polytechnics*. Two others were considered: *Bristol College of Technology*, which was later confirmed; and *Rutherford College, Newcastle upon Tyne*, which was not, and which eventually became a Polytechnic. *Brunel College of Technology* was added to this list in 1962. The remainder of the twenty-four institutions in receipt of 75 per cent grant became the nucleus of some twenty-five institutions subsequently recognised as Regional Colleges. The foregoing basic structure is set out in Diagram 1, and it remained broadly the same until after the Robbins Report in 1963. In due course the Regional Colleges named in Diagram 1 became the Polytechnics.[16]

Qualifications		*Present number*	*Likely future number*	*Types of courses*	*Courses for*
Dip.Tech., BSc. London; professional qualifications; postgraduate diplomas; higher degrees & diplomas	Colleges of Advanced Technology	10——→?		PT +FT	University level only TGT +P + research + postgraduate
Some Dip.Tech. & BSc. London; professional qualifications; Higher National Diplomas & Certificates; City & Guilds Final examinations	Regional Colleges	25——→30?		PT +FT	Superior TN + C + some TGT +P +some postgraduate + research
Some Higher and Ordinary National Certificates; some City & Guilds Final and Inter examinations; general education e.g. GCE O- and A-level; domestic and catering courses (*a*)	Area Colleges	155 (*b*)→210 (*b*)		PT +FT	TN +C + some P
Ordinary National Certificates; City and Guilds Inter and some Final examinations; general education e.g. GCE O-level and some A-level; full-time domestic and catering courses, etc. (*a*)	Local Colleges of Further Education	275? (*b*)→ ?(*b*)		PT +FT	TN +C + general education

Note (a): commercial courses not indicated, though many Technical Colleges have commerce departments and courses; the same is true for art courses and schools within Technical Colleges	Four-tier structure – see White Paper on Technical Education (Cmd 9703) and Ministry of Education Circular 305	*Note (b):* no official numbers yet stated	PT =Part-time courses FT =Full-time courses including sandwich courses'	TGT = technologists TN = technicians C =craftsmen P =courses to graduateship of professional institutions

Colleges of Advanced Technology: Battersea (London); Birmingham; Bradford; Bristol; Brunel (Middlesex); Chelsea (London); Loughborough; Northampton (London); Salford; Welsh (Cardiff)

Regional Colleges: Borough (London); Brighton; Brixton (London); Hatfield College of Technology; Huddersfield; Kingston-upon-Thames; Lanchester College of Technology; Coventry; Leeds College of Technology; Leicester; Liverpool (Building); Liverpool (Technology); North Staffordshire; Northern (London); Nottingham; Plymouth and Devonport; Portsmouth; Rugby; Rutherford College of Technology (Newcastle-upon-Tyne); Sir John Cass (London); South East Essex Technical College, School of Art (Dagenham); Sunderland; The Polytechnic (London); Treforest; West Ham; Woolwich (London)

Diagram 1 Structure of technical education at the time of publication of the Robbins Committee Report.

Note: The diagram oversimplifies somewhat by omitting specific reference to separate Colleges of Art, Colleges of Commerce, National Colleges and their various relationships with Technical Colleges, quite a number of which themselves contained Schools of Art and Departments of Commerce and, in a few cases, National Colleges as well.

Technical education had evolved differently in Scotland, with a strong group of central institutions and a less adequate system of Local Colleges compared with England and Wales. The continuance of this structure was accepted in the White Paper, but reinforcement was considered essential especially at local level. A capital grant of £10m was allocated for this purpose. Seven of the central institutions were technical in character, the leading ones being the Royal Technical College, Glasgow, and the Heriot-Watt College, Edinburgh.

The change of status requiring exclusive concentration on advanced work speeded the process of shedding craft, technician and similar courses which was already under way. This in turn meant an increased intake for the Local Colleges, and in some cases the creation of new ones. At Birmingham, for example, it meant the creation of two separate Colleges in 1957–58.

The academic situation in the Colleges up to 1955 had been one of almost total dependence on approval of courses by external bodies. This meant that academic boards, wherever and in whatever form they existed, were largely formal in character. The main examining bodies were London University concerning both external and internal degree courses, and the Ministry of Education joint committees with professional institutions concerning courses for Higher National Certificates and Diplomas. In a relatively few instances College Associateship courses were recognised by the respective professional institutions for full or partial exemption from their own final examinations.

In this respect the National Council for Technological Awards exercised a very powerful and beneficial influence, by making it possible for the Colleges to develop and administer their own Dip.Tech. courses. These were designed by academic staff according to principles generally applicable to whole groups of courses, instead of isolated ones, thus requiring the kind of joint discussion and decision-making appropriate to academic boards. Though the system appeared in some ways to be similar to that used for approving National Diploma courses, in reality contact and fruitful dis-cussion took place directly with the visiting boards appointed by NCTA. Most important of all were the External Examiners, recommended by the College and approved by NCTA.

Unlike the remote, anonymous Assessors of the National Certificate and Diploma system, they worked closely with academic staff in general support of the courses, and specifically in the moderation of examinations set by the College staff. Their appointments were generally for three years but renewable, and this continuity of influence was important. The approval of courses following visitation by NCTA boards was for five years, and this again was another important factor in the growth of confidence and inde-pendence within the colleges. Criteria for approval by NCTA related to the suitability of the curriculum, the qualifications of the staff, the facilities and accommodation within the particular college, and the proportion of advanced work in them. These were applied rigorously but not punitively, and were powerful levers in moving governing bodies and LEAs to improve standards accordingly. After the Robbins Report, the NCTA was replaced by the CNAA, which operates an essentially similar system.

The standard of the Dip.Tech. was set at the level of an honours degree of a British University, and this later came under criticism as being too exclusive. It was generally supposed that Dip.Tech. would be awarded almost wholly for sandwich courses, but in practice over the years the proportion of traditional three-year full-time courses increased, a continuing trend under the CNAA which has been heavily criticised as weakening the commitment of institutions to sandwich courses.

A third substantial criticism was that Dip.Tech. courses too closely resembled University degree courses in content and method. This ignored the fact that within sandwich courses the aim is to make the link between the training for industry and the academic study periods as close and mutually supportive as possible. This unawareness revealed the inertia of past practice but also suggested some sensitivity about the implied criticism of traditional practice. It could also be held to exemplify a quite normal academic (not to say wholly human) feeling when facing change, that any change from the traditional is bound to be a change for the worse; which is perhaps akin to the reaction of administrators that nothing should ever be tried for the first time, especially if it is original.

Before the designation of the Colleges as CATs, their governing bodies (apart from those in the London Polytechnics and Loughborough) shared responsibility with the LEAs who tended to be the dominating partner. The College office was an outpost of the LEA office, and the office staff were responsible ultimately to the Chief Education Officer and not to the Principal. The establishment of posts not only needed approval by the Education Committee but also by the Establishment Committee of the Council.

The consequent rigorous application of existing criteria was felt, for example, very severely in the lack of clerical posts and in the limitation of laboratory technicians. The College was apt to be treated simply as one of many under the LEA and its proposals were subject always to the first consideration in mind: 'If we do it for you, we will have to do it for the others.' Even after achieving special status there was still the external control of establishment, especially of grading and salaries of posts, the control of furniture, apparatus and equipment by the LEA's Sites and Buildings Sub-Committee, and the delay of final approval of expenditure above certain meagre limits (such as £50–£100) until passed by the Further Education Sub-Committee, the Education Committee and the Council. With all this, the frustrations of having a governing body (*sic*) which was simply a sub-committee of a sub-committee of the Education Committee of the Council[17] remained real enough.

The Regional Advisory Councils existed for the approval of courses in the colleges of the particular region and the prevention of wasteful duplication among them. Prior to designation the Advanced Colleges were subject to these procedures and each was treated as one among many, i.e. many institutions with supposedly similar claims; inevitably thereafter they found the regional supervision increasingly irksome. While they endeavoured to assume their special position by informing the Regional Councils of their plans rather than asking for approval, it was not until after independence in 1962 that the Ministry dealt with this problem in their favour. The Advanced Colleges then began to approach the position of the Universities by simply informing the respective Councils of their proposed developments. This has brought the criticism that the Advanced Colleges 'had simply opted for regional irresponsibility',[18] but it was a nonsense to treat the apex in the same way as the rest of the complex pyramid of institutions (as the Polytechnics were themselves later to discover).

Another problem was that of employer-employee relationships, as between LEA-governing body and academic staff. The Principal was the focal point of functioning between these two spheres, passing down policies and instructions from on high and, much less frequently, perhaps even rarely, passing views and recommendations upwards from the staff. Not surprisingly, similar authoritarian relationships were apt to obtain from the Heads of Departments downwards; and the roles and relationships of Principal and Heads especially suffered sharp reorientation, which engendered quite severe strains in the changes of 1962 and 1966–67.

Accommodation problems were acute. Where courses were shed, the workshops and other rooms vacated were seldom appropriate to the new demands. Building plans thus became an early and persistent preoccupation. At Bradford and Birmingham the eventual result was a very substantial expansion of city centre sites despite existing land values,[19] but the far more costly London sites posed altogether more formidable problems of expansion.

Committee of principals

From 1956 onwards the Colleges of Advanced Technology felt the need to establish a common understanding as a basis for joint action where this seemed desirable. The Principals were loyal members of the Association of Principals of Technical Institutions and were reluctant at first to form their own group lest they appear to be separatist and divisive.

However, their common needs prevailed, and the Principals first met together on 6th June 1957.[20] Lack of a voice to represent their interests led them to make a formal announcement of the establishment of their Committee in June 1959. Fifty-four meetings were held, the last being on 13th January 1965, just before the Principals became members of the

Committee of Vice-Chancellors and Principals of the Universities of the United Kingdom (CVCP). The Principals' Committee could not make decisions which were binding on their institutions, but there was a great deal of agreement which resulted in similar action within them, to a far greater degree than they later experienced or witnessed within the admittedly much larger VC's Committee. That was not merely a question of size, but one especially of the rigour of institutional autonomy, whereby the prospect of common action was apt to fade away through a timeless series of interdependent bottlenecks; and the case for the Universities thus went by default.

On a regular basis and additionally as necessity required, the Principals' Committee had invited senior officers of the Ministry to their meetings and this proved invaluable for clarifying if not always resolving common problems. This again was in sharp contrast to the relationship which obtained between the VC's Committee and the UGC at the time the Principals of the Colleges became Vice-Chancellors.

Among the many concerns of the Principals' Committee the lack of higher academic awards was one of the most urgent. Advice was taken as to whether there was any legal barrier to the Colleges awarding their own higher degrees of MTech. and DTech., and finding none, they informed the Ministry accordingly. The reaction was very sharp to the effect that, 'if the Governors, in spite of the advice of the Ministry of Education, decided to support the staff in instituting higher awards carrying the titles suggested, the Ministry would withdraw the financial grant to the College.' This was in May 1961, almost coincident with the founding of the first of the new Universities (Sussex), which were given the right to award degrees before either staff were appointed or students enrolled. In no time at all after this, owing to the impetus of the Robbins Report, degree-granting powers were given to a body which was never to have teaching staff or students of its own – the Council for National Academic Awards. It is arguable that the same impetus was necessary to enable the Colleges to break out of the academic frustration created by the entrenched power of the traditional Universities. There was also a strong disinclination in powerful academic circles to recognise the importance of technology,[21] which increased the resistance against giving University status to technological institutions.

Independent status 1962

Paragraph 71 of the 1956 White Paper reads: 'There are those who argue that a College of Advanced Technology cannot be successfully administered within the framework of local government. The Government do not accept this. Local Authorities take great pride in such Colleges and often have been willing to find more money for them than the pressure on national resources has allowed them to spend. To remove these Colleges from local control against the wishes of the Authorities could be justified neither by past experience nor by the hope of better results from a more central control. This statement is, however, subject to one qualification: the Government rely on the Local Authorities to work effectively together in planning the provision of courses and – just as important – in making it possible for students to attend courses which best suit their needs, whether these courses are in their own or another Authority's area.'

Within a brief five years, however, on 22nd June 1961, Sir David Eccles, Minister of Education, announced in a Parliamentary answer the intention to transfer control of the Colleges to independent governing bodies which would receive a direct grant from the Ministry of Education.[22] He reported this diplomatically to the Annual Conference of the Association of Education Committees the following day:[23] 'Since they were designated, these nine Colleges – and the Local Authorities have been responsible for eight of them – have made remarkable progress . . . All these good results have made me feel that I was justified in taking the decision that I did, against some very influential opposition, to rely on the Local Authorities to shape the first years of the Colleges of Advanced Technology. Now the very success of the CATs has faced us with new problems. In terms of the areas from which they draw their students they have become national institutions.' This action was 'not intended to prejudice any long-term solution. It may be the Robbins Committee will want to go further.' Meanwhile, he proposed to designate one more CAT: Brunel College of Technology.

There was in fact no mention in the 1956 White Paper of the LEAs shaping only the first years, but a brief six years had sufficed to nullify the apparently very strong assertion of confidence in governance by the Local Authorities. The Minister gave the major reason for the change, but there were other powerful factors that it would have been less polite to mention. There was, for example, the dependence on the Local Authority office and their procedures, and the consequent difficulties of initiating developments and of making progress quickly. Good professional and personal relationships, which generally obtained (as, for example, one is glad to record, during this period with Sir Lionel Russell CBE, Chief Education Officer, City of Birmingham Education Committee, in his unqualified support of the emergence of the College of Advanced Technology) helped to surmount the difficulties and frustrations inherent in inadequate and inappropriate procedures and requirements, but that was no reason for continuing them.

The Minister referred to the national catchment of the colleges for students, but did not draw out the consequence that this meant that the Colleges were financed increasingly from the 'Pool'. This was finance contributed to by all LEAs whether they had students on advanced courses or not, which in effect meant that rural areas were paying for technological education in industrial conurbations. Thus one of the major LEAs involved contributed from its own rates less than 3 per cent of the net cost of the College while retaining 100 per cent governance of it. There was considerable ambivalence about these Colleges within the LEAs: pride in their growing achievements mixed with concern about their increasing demands for resources (despite the 'Pool') in comparison with the needs of the growing number of Technical Colleges for which they were also responsible. 'If anyone thinks they're going to take away our Colleges, he can have another think coming', asserted a representative governor at a meeting of the Association of Technical Institutions in the early 1960s, and there was evidence of similar confusion at national level.

A pertinent question, now probably indeterminate, is whether and to what extent problems would have been eased had the Government not insisted on several bites at the one cherry – from College of Technology to College of Advanced Technology to direct-grant-independent-status to University status – but had granted the final stage at the outset. Despite the granting of full University status and commensurate sites to the 'new' Universities, this was never contemplated for the CATs.

The piecemeal approach affected not only sites but the planning and use of the buildings to be set on them. For example, at Birmingham the LEA had planned a site and buildings 'to bring the Colleges of Technology, Art and Commerce into relationship with each other as institutions of comparable standing with promising prospects of interrelating their work.' Work on the building, planned in pre-war days, was started after the war on this policy, but was overtaken by events. The designation of the College of Technology entailed a reallocation of space for its expansion, the consequent transference of the College of Art to separate buildings on the same site, and of the College of Commerce to a building attached as a large wing to the original rectangular building, while another wing was added to the opposite side of the main building.

Architecturally the result was – to say the least – unfortunate, and would hardly have been contemplated had there been the slightest glimmer of the eventual move to University status, whereby the city centre site was expanded from some 1.8 hectares to about 14 hectares. However for some years the Colleges all remained on the same site and some progress was made in establishing interrelationships. These included, for example, a joint Guild of Students and Students' Union for the University and the two Colleges, and courses in architecture and planning of the College of Art leading to degrees of Aston University under a scheme of affiliation – but these relationships were severed by the later rigours of the binary policy.

Another notable instance was that of the Colleges at Loughborough, where a strong attempt was made in 1972–74 to set the binary policy aside and bring the Colleges into relationship as was once the case.[24]

In concluding this account of the period of the CATs, including the difficulties and stresses of the penultimate phase, the impression must not be left that relationships between the Colleges and the Ministry were unsatisfactory. Quite the contrary – working relationships became increasingly close and effective over the years, especially between the senior officials concerned and the Principals' Committee from 1961 to 1964; and a warm tribute is due to Sir Antony Part for his support during the period of transition.

The Robbins Committee

The Committee publicly invited both written and oral evidence, and heard evidence from ninety organisations and thirty-one individual witnesses,[25] and its work of sifting and assessing this cannot of course be repeated here. Only a very short summary of the evidence submitted by the Principals' Committee will be attempted. (Evidence was submitted separately by some of the governing bodies and, not surprisingly, there was a considerable degree of congruence with that of the Principals' Committee.[26])

The statistical picture they presented of changing enrolments is given in Table 1, and their proposals for the balance of studies are shown in Table 2.

It was considered that 'a fully fledged Faculty of Social Sciences is indispensable as a basis for professional studies, industrial administration and management studies. It should probably include Departments of Economics, History, Industrial Sociology, Industrial Psychology, Industrial Administration, and a residential Centre for Management Studies . . . It would also have its own undergraduate full-time and/or sandwich courses in Social Science with increasing specialisation after the first year in Economics, Industrial Sociology and Industrial Psychology. Instead of economists, sociologists and psychologists being trained mainly within Arts Faculties as at present, there would be evident advantage in having some at least of them trained within a predominantly technological institution.'

A proposal to use the terminology 'Royal Colleges' was first bruited in the Percy Committee report and the Principals endorsed this suggestion in their concluding paragraph: 'There is almost a natural inclination on the part of new institutions to strive to become part of the established order. Many would, therefore, urge that we should develop into technological Universities, styled as such. However, we believe in a diversity of institutions, and we are concerned to establish a route in higher education parallel to that of the traditional Universities. We think this would be best secured by fully implementing a suggestion of the Percy Committee Report in the light of modern requirements, namely, that the Colleges should become chartered Royal Colleges of Technology.'

The Robbins Report was published on 23rd October 1963[27] and accepted by the Government in a White Paper.[28]

The Committee stated its conclusions in forthright fashion, as the following key passages in paras. 390 to 395[29] demonstrate:

Table 1 Colleges of Advanced Technology: enrolments before and after designation as CATs.

Types of course	Session 1955–56		Session 1958–59		Session 1959–60		Session 1960–61	
	Lower level	University	Lower level	University	Lower level	University	Lower level	University
Full-time	2,212	3,745 (916)	669	5,154 (1,513)	641	5,804 (1,867)	275	5,347 (1,588)
Sandwich: Dip. Tech.	—	191	—	1,907	—	2,882	—	3,595
Sandwich: professional	172	397	—	713	—	706	—	632
TOTAL: full-time and sandwich	2,384	4,333	669	7,774	641	9,392	275	9,574
Part-time day	10,950	4,896 (201)	3,916	6,528 (566)	3,871	6,935 (585)	412	7,969 (1,839)
Evenings only	13,423 (76)	9,677 (3,811)	5,407 (53)	10,493 (4,097)	5,153 (55)	11,972 (5,910)	2,335 (51)	10,732 (5,188)

Note: Submitted by the Principals' Committee in their evidence to the Robbins Committee. Figures in brackets indicate numbers on short courses included in the totals.

Table 2 Colleges of Advanced Technology: proposed balance of studies.

Study	Percentage of total enrolments
Engineering and Applied sciences	*65*
Pure sciences	*15*
Social sciences	*10*
Other studies	*10*

390. We consider that the present powers and status of the Colleges are not commensurate with the work they are doing.

391. It is anomalous that such colleges should not have the power to grant their own degrees.

392. We recommend that in future these Colleges should in general become Technological Universities, and that this should be recognised in their titles if they so wish.

393. We recommend that the Colleges should have the power to award both first and higher degrees.

394. It also follows that these institutions should have the forms of government appropriate to University status.

395. We recommend that immediate steps be taken to grant charters and to transfer responsibility for finance to the body responsible for University finance.

To those who had tried overseas to explain that a Dip.Tech. was of honours degree standard and therefore equivalent to a degree of a British University (so why not call it a degree?) – or who had striven conscientiously but in vain to establish the MCT, the award at doctorate level of the College of Technologists[30] (that ill-starred offspring of the NCTA) – to all of these the recognition of the anomaly in para. 391, and the resulting recommendation in para. 393, came as balm to the troubled spirit. However much this may be attributed merely to academic snobbishness, nothing could sell an alternative to the traditional degree pattern to any influential group within the Colleges. This was simply because of the need to ensure the necessary supply of able staff and students vital to development. So ARCT, MRCT and FRCT vanished totally, and BTech. etc., hardly survived at all, against the pressures for BSc., MSc. and above all Ph.D.

The reservation that 'the Colleges should *in general* become Technological Universities' in the event covered the cases of Chelsea and Cardiff. Chelsea was an anomalous choice for a College of Advanced *Technology*, having no such courses at all. It was included by virtue of the high standard of its scientific work, but it had long looked in the direction of London

University for incorporation as a constituent College. It had no sandwich courses, and made a small attempt to establish them, but soon abandoned it, partly as a result of difficulties arising from the requirements of the Senate of London University. Thus, Chelsea did not gain its Charter of Incorporation within the University until December 1971.

The reasons why the Cardiff College did not become independent were essentially political, inherent in the context of Wales and Welsh nationalism. It is curious that whereas University expansion in Scotland (population 5,223,600) increased the number of Universities from four to eight, Wales (population 2,724,275) retained a single University. The attempt to found a separate Technological University in Cardiff was stillborn. A further proposal in the Robbins Report for five Special Institutions for Scientific and Technological Education and Research (SISTERS),[31] was not implemented, though three potential candidates[32] were assisted by special grants in the succeeding years.[33]

It would be misleadingly inadequate to record the final stages of transition to University status without recalling the sense of exhilaration and deep satisfaction felt at the time by most staff and students, and by members of Council, Court and Convocation. For many these feelings received adequate even moving expression in the traditional ceremonies, variously modified to reflect their own particular histories and locations, which were arranged to celebrate the granting of the Royal Charters to them. To these celebrations each new University invited other British Universities to send representatives to support them at this definitive, indeed momentous, stage of their development. Despite so many occasions in so short a period of time – unprecedented in the history of British Universities – the response was high, sustaining visually and unequivocally their entry into the wider academic community. The worldwide significance of attaining University status became evident with the attendance of representatives at the Tenth Quinquennial Congress of Commonwealth Universities in Sydney, Australia in August 1968,[34] preceded by the meeting of their Executive Heads in Melbourne.

Some there are who do not value the inner significance of such occasions, and indeed even of customary congregations for the conferment of degrees, and who disparage them on grounds of cost, or of being outmoded and superfluous. To concede such a stance about public ceremonies would entail an aesthetic and emotional impoverishment of our lives. Critics there are also of the holding of quinquennial congresses for similar reasons, but also alleging that they make no impact, commensurate with the time, effort and cost involved, on the political scene or in contributing to the social and educational well-being of the community. This latter image persists probably because it serves ulterior purposes, since the stereotype is in fact quite obsolete. For instance, the ACU Congress, held in Edinburgh in August 1973, concentrated its discussions on five topics: the problems of the environment and the Universities; contemporary culture and the Universities;

resources for higher education; co-operation between Universities; and the government of Universities.[35]

The sense of exhilaration, amounting almost to euphoria, did not last (a quite normal phenomenon) and was soon affected by uncertainties, not least as to how the institutions would fare under the UGC – perhaps very much at the lower end of the traditional list, instead of at the head of the Ministry/DES list as direct grant institutions. Such fears concerned the expansion of and therefore the particular role of the Technological Universities in higher education but in the event, their development was complicated by different factors, most of all by the seriously diminishing response among students to courses in science and technology.[36]

Notes

1 Peter Venables, 'Conflicting patterns and purposes in higher education': The Foundation Oration delivered at Birkbeck College, London, on 20th January 1970; *Universities Quarterly*, Autumn 1970.

2 Eric Ashby, *Technology and the Academics* (Macmillan, London 1958).

3 See Peter Venables, *The Changing Pattern of Technical and Higher Education* (BACIE Golden Jubilee Publications, 1970).

4 (Manchester University Press, 1957.)

5 See W. H. G. Armytage, *Civic Universities* (Ernest Benn, London 1955).

6 For the history of this period concerning technical education see Michael Argles, *South Kensington to Robbins* (Longmans, London 1964), Chapter 2.

7 *15 to 18*, Crowther Report (HMSO, 1959), Chapter 47 and Part VI.

8 *As 5*, Chapter 10.

9 P. I. Kitchen, *From Learning to Earning: Birth and Growth of a Young People's College* (Faber & Faber, London 1944).

10 Reported *TES*, 2nd January 1929.

11 For a detailed appraisal of these see Peter Venables, *Technical Education* (G. Bell & Sons, 1956), Chapter xv, pp. 468–77.

12 *Technical Education* (Cmnd. 9703, HMSO 1956).

13 *Report on Sandwich Training and Education* (NACEIC, February 1956).

14 Circular 305, *The Organisation of Technical Colleges*, 21st June 1956.

15 *Hansard* (House of Commons), 21st June 1956.

16 See Table Aiiif for details.

17 *As 11*, p. 486.

18 Tyrrell Burgess and John Pratt, *Policy and Practice: The Colleges of Advanced Technology* (Allen Lane Penguin Press, 1970), p. 136.

19 K. L. Stretch, 'Academic Ecology: On the Location of Institutions of Higher Education', *Minerva*, Vol. II, 1963–64, pp. 320–35.

20 The author served as Chairman, and Dr (later Sir) James Tait as Hon. Secretary of the Committee throughout the whole of its existence. Secretarial services were provided throughout by Miss G. M. Needham MBE.

21 Eric (Lord) Ashby, *Adapting Universities to a Technological Society* (Jossey-Bass, London 1974).

22 With the exception, already noted, of Loughborough, which gained direct grant status in 1952.

23 *Education*, 30th June 1961, p. 1450.

24 This was partly achieved in 1976. See Brief Histories, App. II.

25 Robbins Report, 'Higher Education' (*as 22*), pp. 303–12.
26 This version was itself based substantially on that originally submitted by the present author when interviewed by the Robbins Committee in May 1961 (Report Annex, para. 17). See also Peter Venables, 'The Colleges of Advanced Technology', *Chemistry and Industry*, 8th September 1962.
27 Cmnd. 2154, HMSO, 1963, with volumes of Appendices.
28 Higher Education: Government Statement (HMSO, 1963).
29 *Ibid.*, p. 131.
30 The illogicality of nomenclature for a higher award beyond Dip.Tech. was recognised – it could hardly be Dippier Tech: nor was the continental solution of Dr.Ing. available in the British context.
31 *Ibid.*, paras. 383–87.
32 Strathclyde, Imperial College and UMIST.
33 See Table AⅢc.
34 *Tenth Congress of the Universities of the Commonwealth 1968 Report of Proceedings, Sydney, August 17–23* (Association of Commonwealth Universities, London 1969).
35 *Report of the Proceedings, Commonwealth Universities and Society* (Association of Commonwealth Universities, 1974).
36 However, changes apparent in 1976 may once again prove that a short-term judgement is not necessarily a sound long-term guide.

92

THE BASIC IDEAS

Walter Perry

Source: W. Perry, *Open University: A Personal Account by the First Vice-Chancellor*, Buckingham: Open University Press, 1976, pp. 1–9.

The concept of the Open University evolved from the convergence of three major postwar educational trends. The first of these concerns developments in the provision for adult education, the second the growth of educational broadcasting and the third the political objective of promoting the spread of egalitarianism in education.

Since the Second World War the educational scene has bubbled with a continuous ferment of new ideas. Established practices have, almost without exception, come under challenge. Educational theorists have advanced radical, even iconoclastic, new philosophies. Amongst them are the concepts of 'education permanente', continuing education and recurrent education. Yet, despite continuing debates at national and international level, the inertia inherent in established educational systems is normally much too strong to permit of high speed change. Inertia stems both from the sheer complexity of educational systems and from the network of vested interests concerned with maintaining them.

Advances have usually been made only by pragmatists, who are prepared to modify and supplement existing systems to bring them more nearly into line with what is theoretically desirable, but who do so in ways that are acceptable to the establishment. Thus a system may, through a series of such piecemeal modifications, undergo radical change. This process takes longer but is much less painful than revolution would be.

In the UK almost every requirement of the total educational system has been scrutinised by government committees with a view to introducing such modifications. The tragedy is that an overall philosophy to provide a framework for change has never been defined and accepted, with the result that the modifications actually introduced have been random rather than designed. A host of good ideas is buried in the reports of the numerous committees – Plowden, Crowther, Hazelgrave, Robbins, James and Russell

– which, if carefully selected and integrated, could provide much of the basis for a splendid new structure of educational provision.

What of the position of education for adults in such a structure? A lot depends on semantics. For administrative purposes in Britain the term 'adult education' covers only the activities of specified agencies, oriented neither towards vocational training nor towards any formal academic qualification; namely the Workers' Educational Association, the extramural departments of the universities, and the classes offered by Local Education Authorities. It does not cover all education offered to and taken up by adults. Adult education, in this sense, has always been the Cinderella of our educational world. Indeed Jennie Lee once described it as 'the patch on the backside of our educational trousers'. The whole spectrum of these activities was reviewed by the Russell Committee in its Report of 1973.[1]

University extramural departments were created primarily to extend the cultural influence of the universities to the adult population in their own localities. From the beginning the adults who enrolled in extramural classes were predominantly middle-class. Many of them had already benefited from higher education and were extending their interests and knowledge. More than 75% of all such classes are in the liberal arts or the social sciences; nearly all are 'non-vocational' and do not offer participants any opportunity of sitting an examination or of obtaining a certificate or diploma. They are, as the Americans put it, 'not for credit', being designed to suit those who want to study solely for their own self-fulfilment.

The pattern of Workers' Educational Association courses had, by this time, evolved into something almost indistinguishable from this. Originally the aim of the WEA was to stimulate and satisfy the demands of adults, and in particular of members of the workers' movements, for education. But over the years WEA classes had come to attract a predominantly middle-class audience, and the majority of classes were now 'non-vocational'. The third provider of adult education, Local Education Authorities, by 1968 undertook the lion's share of the task. In that year nearly 1.7 million adults enrolled for courses of study in LEA classes. Despite the fact that fees were kept at a nominal level, the bulk of the students was again drawn from the middle class; there was little sign of interest from those who were educationally under-privileged. Most of the courses were 'non-vocational' and, as the Russell Report emphasises, 80–90% of the programmes consisted of courses in physical activities, domestic subjects, arts and crafts, music and drama, foreign languages, and practical activities such as woodwork and car maintenance.

The value of all this in filling a need was undoubted; but the fact that the existing provision of 'adult education' was valuable did not mean that it satisfied all the needs for education that were felt by adults. There were two clear gaps.

First, there were very few opportunities offered to the adult who wished to embark upon vocational courses at the higher education level. That there were notable exceptions to this general rule did not invalidate it. My general impression, as a complete newcomer to the adult educational world, was that 'examinations' and 'vocational' were almost dirty words, that somehow study towards a qualification was felt to be intrinsically less worthy than study for the sake of study. This attitude inhibited the development of vocational courses almost everywhere.

If 'adult education' did not include all the provision of education for adults, who then provided the remainder of it? How far did the institutions of initial higher education, at that time the universities, the polytechnics and the colleges, cater for adults, for 'mature students'? British universities, unlike their counterparts in the United States, in Australia and in New Zealand, did not to any significant extent offer evening education, leading to a degree for part-time students. London University offered its external degree but this was a system of examination only. Virtually no teaching programmes were offered and adults scattered throughout the country had to make their own arrangements to prepare themselves for the examinations. Birkbeck College did provide part-time degree programmes for those who, living in London, could attend the College and was the shining exception to the rule. By 1968 it appeared that the polytechnics, which had been founded as Colleges of Advanced Technology with the part-time student very much in mind, were likely to gravitate towards full-time courses for full-time students. The technical colleges, although they had large numbers of part-time students, were catering in the main for people seeking an education at pre-university level, although they also offered courses intended to prepare students for London University examinations.

There was a gap, therefore, in provision. An adult who wished to take a degree, whether he was qualified to start the degree or not, would find it exceptionally hard to gain entrance to any university or polytechnic. This was true even if he was prepared to study full-time. Provision for mature entrants in most universities was extremely limited. There was tremendous demand from school leavers for the limited places available in the universities and most admission authorities gave preference to them. Money was better spent on training them than on training adults who could, at the end of their course, make a contribution to society only for a shorter period. The needs of adults who could not stop work to enter higher education on a full-time basis and who wished to obtain degrees by working part-time were often not met at all.

Such a student could register for a London external degree, study on his own and work towards that degree sometimes without any guidance or help. There are some classic examples of people who succeeded in obtaining qualifications in this way, amongst them Jennie Lee and Margaret Thatcher, but it was an extremely hard road. External students of London University could sometimes receive tuition by registering for part-time courses offered by technical colleges; others could take similar courses offered by the commercial correspondence colleges, but the number of such courses, except in subjects like Commerce and Law, was restricted, and the quality was often open to serious question. Correspondence colleges all too frequently lived on the profits made from those who paid fees but dropped out at an early stage, thereby making very little demand on the system, although the better colleges did provide a good service for those students who lasted the course.

Thus the gap in provision of vocational courses left by 'adult education' was in no real sense filled by other institutions, which provided higher education mainly for school leavers – 'initial higher education'. The existence of the gap was recognised fairly widely, but opinions also differed widely on whether there was any real need to fill it. Many authorities doubted whether there was a sizeable unsatisfied demand among adults for this kind of educational opportunity. Perhaps these doubts were a source of comfort, because few had any faith that it would be practicable successfully to offer vocational higher education on a part-time basis.

The second gap in 'adult education' provision lay in its failure to attract those very members of the adult community for whom much of it had originally been designed: those who, at the stage of their initial education, had been under-privileged and deprived. To them the institutions of initial higher education offered nothing. They were the drop-outs of the educational system. Yet, amongst them, there were many who were highly intelligent and who would undoubtedly benefit from the experience of higher education if given the chance of it on a part-time basis. Yet, whether such an opportunity would be welcomed by the educationally deprived adult or would again be seized only by the middle-class aspirant, was open to question.

This debate was taking place against the background of a remarkable growth in the provision of educational opportunity for the school leaver. The Robbins Report (1963)[2] had made it clear that the universities must expand to meet the increased demand from qualified school leavers, and this expansion was under way. It insisted that places in higher education should be made available to all those capable of profiting from them. There was a growing awareness of the national need for trained brain power, and for the extension of opportunity to all classes of the population, as a positive step towards replacing the elitist system that had been prevalent in Britain for many years. But most people would have given a higher priority to expanding the provision for school leavers than to providing new opportunities for adults who had had the misfortune to be born too soon to benefit from such an expansion.

On the whole the idea that initial education, up to and including university education, was the only way of providing the country with the graduates it required remained unchallenged. It is an easy system to organise. Full-time education has its established patterns, students are stimulated by the companionship of their contemporaries in a residential situation, and student life is full of social distractions that make for a full and enjoyable experience. The alternative idea of part-time study offers none of these advantages. The loneliness of the long-distance learner is hard to bear even for motivated and dedicated adults. It is probable that most 18 year olds would find it intolerable. Yet the idea of 'continuing education' as a viable alternative to initial education was gaining ground, especially on the Continent. The benefits of capitalising upon the greater motivation and sense of purpose that maturity conferred came to be recognised. The national wastage involved in educational drop-out was similarly noted and much was made of this factor in the Crowther Report of 1959[3] and later in the Robbins Report. Yet in Britain the remedy was basically to extend the provision of initial education, while the problems of the adult, though noted, were not tackled with any vigour.

The effects of the Robbins Report on initial higher education in Britain were profound. There was an enormous increase in the size and number of universities. This extension of opportunity was to be welcomed, though some of the traditional and best aspects of the old universities were lost in the process. For the adult, on the other hand, nothing was done. It was hardly surprising that the existing institutions were not interested in their problems. They had enough difficulty in coping with the expansion induced by Robbins. The average academic was much more concerned with increasing the number of undergraduates in his care than with becoming involved in schemes to provide part-time adult education to degree level in the community. Academics regarded part-time education with great scepticism, considering that their vocation lay with full-time students.

It was often argued that an institution such as the Open University would be an unnecessary development, since all that it could do could equally well be done by the other universities acting in concert. This may be so in theory, but the idea that in 1969 the other universities of Britain might seriously have contemplated moving, either singly or collectively, into the field of part-time adult education is unrealistic. It could not have happened. The overriding view in the academic community was that this problem did not concern them; it ought to concern somebody else. It was this view that perpetuated the gap in educational provision.

The second major educational trend contributing to the evolution of the Open University was the growth in educational broadcasting. From its inception the BBC, under John Reith, had given education a high priority among its objectives in planning. As early as 1926, in an internal BBC memorandum, Mr Stobart put a proposal to Lord Reith for 'a wireless university' but there was to be no such formalisation of educational broadcasting at that stage. Even earlier there were moves to offer adult education in an informal way. In 1924 the Adult Education Committee of the Board of Education and the British Institution of Adult Education, together with the BBC, embarked upon a series of regular talks, and 20,000 copies of the printed syllabus were circulated. In 1927 the BBC set up their own adult education section, and later in the same year, possibly as a result of its creation, a committee of enquiry, under the chairmanship of Sir Henry Hadow[4], was set up by the BBC jointly with the British Institution of Adult Education. One of the recommendations of the committee was that there should be a separate radio station devoted to educational purposes, an idea which has survived for nearly 50 years but which has not yet been implemented. The story of this venture has been traced by Asa Briggs in his *History of Broadcasting*.[5] It was successful for a period of about 5 years, but thereafter the scheme faded away, for various reasons which have been analysed by Lord Briggs. It was succeeded by the establishment of a regular service of educational programmes for adults on one of the BBC's radio channels, financed from the Corporation's licence revenue. These were planned with the help of a Further Education Liaison Council, and included systematic language teaching supported by specially written textbooks and gramophone records.

The advent of television gave a renewed boost to the ideas of those who favoured the use of broadcasting for educational purposes. There were numerous experiments and much was written about the potential of the new medium, not only in the United Kingdom. In Britain one of the leading advocates of the use of television for higher education was R. C. G. Williams who over a period of two years (1962–3), while he was Chairman of the Electronics and Communications Section of the Institution of Electrical Engineers, argued strongly and continuously in favour of the creation of what he called a 'televarsity'.[6] Williams was concerned primarily with the field of technology, but his ideas were quite new in the sense that he raised the possibility of linking educational broadcasts with correspondence education and with visits to existing universities. In other words he produced a plan for a multimedia integrated programme rather than one concentrating on isolated educational broadcasts. In 1962 Michael Young wrote a paper[7] in which he estimated the probable growth of demand for higher education in the new decade. Amongst his proposals was one advocating the creation of an 'Open University' which would prepare people for the external degree of London University. He also drew attention to the increasing use of the broadcasting media for educational purposes in the United States and of correspondence teaching in the Soviet Union. He proposed the immediate creation of a National Extension College that would help students to achieve degrees through the London external system. These proposals were to reach fruition in October 1963 when the National Extension College was actually established, in Cambridge, and the first courses began to be designed.

The hours during which the BBC and the ITA were permitted to broadcast were controlled by the Postmaster General. In 1961 Mr Woodrow Wyatt introduced to the House of Commons, under the ten-minute rule, a bill designed to ensure that the Postmaster General would allow programmes of adult education to be broadcast outside the normally permitted hours. He too was concerned mainly with the need to provide further educational programmes for adults in the field of science and technology. No action was taken as a result of Mr Wyatt's bill because the Pilkington Committee on Broadcasting[8] was about to report, and this provided the Government with an excuse for deferring any action. The Report itself was presented to Parliament in June 1962. Although it was in favour of an expansion of formal adult educational television, the general conclusion was that there should be no segregated service of educational broadcasting, for three reasons: first, that an educational channel would isolate educational programmes, depriving other channels of any such component; second, that a separate educational channel would not reach the general public most in need of educational programmes; and third, that the production staff dealing with educational programmes would continue to benefit from association with other producers of more general programmes only if the services were offered on the same channels. These views were by no means confined to the Committee. They were held by the Ministry of Education, the BBC, the Association of Education Committees, the National Union of Teachers, the Workers Educational Association and the Universities Council for Adult Education. Indeed in the evidence submitted to the Committee by the BBC, they stated that 'to the best of the BBC's knowledge there does not at present exist amongst education authorities and organisations any demand for an educational service outside the context of the general services'. Nevertheless there was a contrary view even then. Professor George Catlin, a member of the National Broadcasting Development Committee, put forward to the Pilkington Committee an idea for the establishment of an educational trust which would control a new educational service. This kind of proposal was supported by bodies such as the Viewers' and Listeners' Association, and also, for reasons that were not clear and were almost certainly not wholly altruistic, by the ITA.

In parallel with this public debate about educational broadcasting and its future, things were happening behind the scenes. From 1961 the BBC was negotiating with the Universities Council for Adult Education and other educational bodies about the development of programmes for adult education. John Scupham, then Controller of Educational Broadcasting at the BBC, was anxious to move into this area and the UCAE in 1961 asked the extramural departments of the universities to encourage their staffs both to examine ways in which talks on radio and television could be used for educational purposes, and to make concrete suggestions about such a service. These discussions also involved officials of the Department of Education and Science, resulting by September 1962 in a government memorandum proposing the introduction of adult education programmes on television.[9] Despite some experimental attempts by extramural departments in the country to act on these recommendations there was little evidence of success by the end of 1963. The main hindrance to progress in this whole field was usually the lack of adequate transmission times. It is, however, important to note the valuable experiments carried out under the direction of Harold Wiltshire at the Extramural Department of the University of Nottingham in collaboration with one of the independent television companies, and of Michael Young at the National Extension College in collaboration with the Further Education Department of the BBC, in offering courses that combined radio and TV broadcasts with correspondence education. These were clear forerunners, in the years between 1963 and 1969, of the Open University.

The growth of interest in the potential of educational broadcasting in the United States was no doubt part of a national response to the technological challenge from Russia presented by the success of the 'Sputnik' programme. Enormous advances were made but they were scattered and inchoate. The primary causes of this lay in the national structure of provision both for education and for broadcasting. Education was the responsibility of state legislatures and only indirectly of the Federal government, so that a coherent national programme for education did not emerge. Broadcasting was organised almost entirely by commercial companies. Neither within a state, nor on a federal basis, was there any controlling organisation like the BBC so that, again, there was no coherent national programme, either for broadcasting or for educational broadcasting. The result is that, despite progress and experimentation both earlier and more extensive than that which took place in Britain, nothing comparable to the Open University has emerged so far in the United States.

In the Soviet Union the use of educational broadcasting was extremely limited. They had, however, successfully pioneered the development of education by correspondence for external students and indeed, some 40% of all graduates in the Soviet Union had by 1960–61 followed at least a part of their course by correspondence. There was no comparable provision of correspondence education either in the United States or in Great Britain and this was a factor which had impressed itself on Harold Wilson's mind during his successive visits to the Soviet Union during the early years of the 1960s.

The third major trend was the increasing concern expressed throughout the world (during the 1950s and the early 1960s), about elitism in education and the effects of this on the nature of society. The Crowther report had indicated that the social background of children was a large factor in determining their educational career and that steps should be taken to make opportunities more easily available to the lower socio-economic groups. This point was taken up and developed very fully by Brian Jackson and Dennis Marsden in their book *Education and the Working Class,* first published in 1962.[10] The Robbins Committee, set up in 1961, also tackled the question in some detail. They showed that 45% of young people whose fathers were in the 'higher professional' group entered full-time higher education compared with only 4% for those whose fathers were in skilled manual occupations. In March 1962, the Labour Party, at that time led by Mr Gaitskell, set up a study group under the chairmanship of Lord Taylor to examine Labour's attitude towards higher education, whose report was presented in March 1963.[11] It again drew attention to how greatly the lower socio-economic groups were deprived of opportunities for higher education. Within the report it was proposed that an experiment should be mounted on BBC radio and television and by ITA, in organizing a 'University of the Air' for serious planned adult education; and that, as an alternative, the fourth television channel might be used exclusively for higher education.

By 1963, the time was ripe for someone to grasp the significance of these three trends and to crystallise them into a coherent pattern. It was Harold Wilson who seized the opportunity thus afforded. There was clear evidence of a gap in the provision of part-time higher education for adults; there was a strong political motive for promoting educational egalitarianism, a motive that was particularly suited to Labour Party philosophy; and the developments in educational broadcasting offered a new means both of filling the gap and counteracting elitism.

In a speech delivered in Glasgow on 8 September 1963,[12] as part of the pre-election programme of the Labour Party, Harold Wilson presented his synthesis of the ideas that had been germinating in his mind from all these sources. He proposed a set of nationally organised correspondence courses, primarily for technicians and technologists, designed for adults who had left school at 16 or 17 but who could reasonably be expected to acquire new skills and qualifications by working part-time at home. 'What we envisage,' he said, 'is the creation of a new educational trust representative of the universities and other educational organisations, associations of teachers, the broadcasting authorities, publishers, public and private bodies, producers capable of producing television and other educational material. This trust would be given state financial help and all the government assistance required. Broadcasting time could be found either by the allocation of the fourth television channel together with the appropriate radio facilities or by pre-empting time from the existing three channels and the fourth, when allocated. Educational programmes would be made available for supplementary study at educational institutes such as technical colleges.' In other words, Mr Wilson's plan was for a consortium of various interests, in education and broadcasting, designed to make available study by external means including broadcasting and correspondence. In his speech he laid little stress on educational egalitarianism although, as I have said, the time was ripe for it. He was much more concerned with the need for expanding technological education and for harnessing technological advances in the media of mass communication to the service of education.

338

Mr Wilson's plan for a 'University of the Air' may bear little relation to the Open University as it exists today; but it was to be the key that opened the door. It was the first expression of interest, by a powerful political figure, in the provision of opportunities for higher education to adults, studying part-time while in full employment, through a multimedia system that harnessed educational broadcasting to correspondence teaching and other methods.

Notes

1 DEPARTMENT OF EDUCATION AND SCIENCE (1973) *Adult Education: a plan for development*, HMSO (Russell Report, 1973).
2 PRIME MINISTER'S COMMITTEE ON HIGHER EDUCATION (1963) *Higher Education*, Appendix 1: The demand for places in higher education, Cmnd 2154–1, HMSO (Robbins Report, 1963).
3 MINISTRY OF EDUCATION. CENTRAL ADVISORY COUNCIL FOR EDUCATION (ENGLAND) (1959) *15–18: a Report*, Vol. 1, HMSO (Crowther Report, 1959).
4 BRITISH BROADCASTING CORPORATION (1928) *New Ventures in Broadcasting: a study of adult education*, BBC.
5 BRIGGS, A. (1965) *The Golden Age of Wireless* (Vol. 2 of *The History of Broadcasting in the United Kingdom*), Oxford University Press.
6 WILLIAMS, R. C. G. (1962) in *The Electrical Journal*, 23 Feb 1972; and in a speech at Guildford (1963).
7 YOUNG, M. (1962) 'Is your child in the unlucky generation?', *Where?*, no. 10, Autumn 1962, pp. 3–5.
8 GENERAL POST OFFICE (1962) *Report of the Committee on Broadcasting*, Cmnd 1753, HMSO (Pilkington Report, 1962).
9 GENERAL POST OFFICE (1962) *Broadcasting: memorandum on the Report of the Committee on Broadcasting*, Cmnd 1770, HMSO.
10 JACKSON, B. and MARSDEN, D. (1966) *Education and the Working Class*, Penguin (Rev. edn.).
11 STUDY GROUP ON HIGHER EDUCATION (1963) *Report to the Labour Party*, unpublished (Taylor Report).
12 WILSON, H. (1963) Speech to a Labour Party rally, Glasgow, 8 Sept 1963.

93

MODULAR SYSTEMS
IN BRITAIN

Oliver Fulton

Source: R. O. Berdahl, G. C. Moodie and I. J. Spitzberg (eds) *Quality and Access in Higher Education: Comparing Britain and the United States*, Buckingham: SRHE and Open University Press, 1991, pp. 142–51.

Introduction

The American modular system which Sheldon Rothblatt describes has the qualities of a truly functional arrangement. Its advantages have sufficiently outweighed its defects, in the particular circumstances of mass higher education in American society, to give it a virtually unchallenged acceptance and a taken-for-granted historical inevitability. The same cannot be said for its counterpart in England and Wales,[1] the 'traditional' university system of the single-subject honours degree course, planned – and examined – as a three- or four-year whole by the collective enterprise of a department or a faculty. No doubt the latter has plenty of life left in it, but it has faced repeated challenges since the Second World War, and an opponent might even claim that its end is in sight. Certainly the number of examples of modular courses in Britain is growing very fast.

The previous chapter has set the scene. The fundamental question which Rothblatt poses is the functional one: what is it about our societies that has sustained the particular organizational structures and the cultural and pedagogic assumptions within which we admit young, and not-so-young, people to our universities and colleges, and determine what and how to teach them and how they are to be assessed? I shall argue here that part of the answer, at least, lies in our respective attitudes to and opportunities for access: it is surely not an accident that the single-subject honours course in Britain was first challenged by modular arrangements in the 1960s,[2] and that modularity began to increase much faster and more steadily in the mid-1980s. The tension between access and 'quality' expresses itself in many forms, but the creation of new institutions in the 1960s, when participation rates were rising sharply, and the recently revived concern with access are undoubtedly connected with the move away from traditional course structures. I return to this point in due course.

The traditional English degree structure

The dialectic which Rothblatt and I have adopted as our method has already indicated the essential qualities of the traditional 'English' system. But it may, none the less, be helpful to underline them. The first is specialization, beginning quite early in the secondary schools. In our traditionalist institutions, newly arrived first-year undergraduates have already long abandoned large areas of knowledge, and there is no question of a student of the humanities or social sciences studying even a smattering of science in college, polytechnic, or university: probably they last did so at the age of 15. The typical undergraduate course (using the word to cover the whole three or four years' experience) is restricted to a single discipline, taught within a single department: choice is confined to certain 'electives' (the term is exclusively American, however) or areas of specialization within the discipline: historical periods, say, or topic areas corresponding closely to the specialist interests of particular members of the teaching staff. But there is always a large core area common to all students in the department. Breadth or interdisciplinary study are ruled out.

A basic assumption is that any choice by students can permit variations only in topic and not in level. We do not find the kind of specialist options to which Rothblatt refers, which provide extra opportunities and challenges for the most able students, or safety nets for the weakest. There are of course inexplicit differences between the standards expected in different options, and it is part of the student's task of mastering the hidden curriculum to discover which options, or which staff members, are most highly regarded academically, or which will require the least effort, depending on their own ambitions and needs. But the principle of common standards for all is crucial.

The second element of the traditional system is assessment. The standard form is the final honours examination, set and marked by the faculty, school, or department as a whole, or by their representatives in the larger universities, to be taken in the last term of the course in a whole series of three-hour examination papers consisting of essays on previously unseen questions. Although most papers cover particular sub-areas of the discipline, they will not necessarily be set, and will certainly not be marked, exclusively by the teachers of these specialisms. In the purest form, choice is catered for not by a choice of papers but by a choice of questions within each compulsory paper, and staff take pride in the ingenuity with which they ensure breadth of coverage across the discipline. This diet is still on offer in many British universities – and many polytechnics – today. It is symbolized in the language of prospectuses for potential students which describe the (three- or four-year) course in terms not of topics to be covered but of papers to be sat in the final summer term.

The justification is academic – a belief in the indivisibility of the essential core of the discipline, and a fear that even for final-year students cross-fertilization and continuity between sub-areas of a discipline do not happen spontaneously. So there must be 'general papers' to encourage students to synthesize their separate specialisms into a coherent view: to examine piece-meal would encourage a magpie approach to the acquisition of knowledge. But like the American modular system, the English system also embodies a set of more basic values about the nature of knowledge, the process of learning, and the relations between teacher and taught, as well as the social role of higher education in training and selection. For example, it proclaims a strong belief in the *uniformity* of students' experience – both during the course and before they join it.

As far as the course itself is concerned, the English (and now, generally, British) predilection for 'quality' here shows itself at its strongest. In prac-tice, I suspect that nowadays the main preoccupation is no longer the protection of the unity and coherence of a disciplinary perspective, import-ant though that is to many academics; rather, it is the problem of fairness. Rightly or wrongly, British academics see themselves as members of a strongly meritocratic profession; and they are acutely aware that the society (or at least the specific professions and occupations) into which their graduates will go takes the degree classifications which they apply extremely seriously. There are undoubtedly some quite troubling problems with any of the assessment systems applied by higher education; but whatever their blind spots, British academics are devoted at a rhetorical level to the principles of meritocracy and fairness. And fairness is enshrined not only in elaborate examination regulations, frequently consulted, but in the whole idea of competition against universally applied criteria in a curricular experience which is common to all.

But the uniformity stretches back well before enrolment. The whole sys-tem is also predicated on a homogeneous student body, capable – financially as well as academically – of studying at the same pace, and coming from a common background of preparation. Hence the attachment to full-time study and common, high entry standards – a point to which I return later.

As for teaching and learning, the implication is that learning takes place best when untainted by (continuous) assessment. At Oxford or Cambridge 'tutors' teach, and provide informal feedback on essays which they do not grade: lecturers, drawn in rotation from among tutors and others, examine – without partiality, since they do not know the students.[3] In the jargon of evaluation, the 'formative' and 'summative' tasks of the teacher are completely distinct: tutors wrestle, formatively, with individuals, and deal with their personal as well as their intellectual development and problems;

lecturers examine, without reference to personal circumstances and without the pressure from students that Rothblatt describes.

Defects of the traditional system

To these attitudes and values there are, of course, rejoinders, and even without the preceding description of the American system it might be possible to deduce the main lines of attack. For attacks, or at least experiments with alternatives, there have long been.

The call of interdisciplinary courses

The most longstanding criticism has been aimed at the narrow coverage of the single-subject degree. Excessive and premature specialization has been a central theme of educational reformers, in secondary as well as higher education, for many years. Many of the arguments are familiar enough on both sides of the Atlantic – they correspond to the American debates over liberal or general education: the need for a broad education for citizenship (that is, for both political and cultural participation); the needs of the labour market (many of the criticisms have come from employers of graduates, who recruit more administrator–manager generalists than they do research and development personnel); and, of course, a desire to find failings in the education system on which national economic decline, materialism, ecological disaster, the subversion of the media, or football riots can plausibly be blamed.

Attempts to develop less specialized undergraduate curricula stretch back to the introduction of Greats at Oxford in the nineteenth century, in close parallel with the introduction of broadly based entrance examinations for the home and Indian Civil Services. Particular examples have varied considerably in their emphasis on, on the one hand, combinations of useful disciplines and, on the other, the analytic and integrative skills which interdisciplinary work might develop, regardless of content – 'developing the general powers of the mind', in the Robbins Report's useful phrase. But pleas for reduced specialization have recurred regularly, notably in the Robbins (1963) and Leverhulme (1983) Reports, in the comments of the UGC in the 1960s, and in those of employers' organizations – only to be offset by calls for rigour, depth, high standards and continuity from much the same quarters as the wheel of educational fashion revolves.

But there are other causes than fashion. For one thing, the balance between research and teaching has changed. By the 1960s an increasing number of graduates were being recruited back into higher education as teachers, but the Ph.D. had not yet been adopted as the standard form of training or the required qualification. Thus the first degree began to be expected to bear the brunt of specialist research training for the brightest students, at a time when most academics' own interests in research as opposed to tutoring were in any case growing fast. Proclamations of the need for interdisciplinarity and the dangers of over-specialization at this time were thus also a reaction by those who cared mainly about teaching to what they saw as a deteriorating situation.

Another element was provided by the growth in demand for higher education in the 1950s and 1960s, and in particular by the UGC's decision to meet it in part by creating new universities. These institutions, needing to establish themselves quickly in their own right, looked for some form of distinctiveness with which to attract good students and staff. If the new crusade was in favour of interdisciplinarity, and against the traditional 'redbrick' model in which the department was sovereign, the new universities appointed themselves as its leaders. With self-conscious references to Scotland, and even to 'Balliol-by-the-Sea', they set out to 'redraw the map of learning'.[4]

Student choice

If a preference for interdisciplinarity was partly imposed by staff, there was also – perhaps more strongly after the events of 1968 – an acknowledgement of the desirability of giving students greater freedom of choice. The political challenge to the unquestioned authority of the teacher was reinforced by the resurgence of 'progressive' learning theory – across the age-range from primary schools onwards – which suggested that students' motivation and indeed their intellectual development and comprehension could be enhanced by giving them greater control over the shape of their own curriculum; and by the sense that the increasing competitiveness forced on secondary education by the rising demand for a limited supply of places had damaged students' capacity for self-direction and discovery.

In the 1960s and their aftermath, student choice was proposed in the causes of improving learning and re-humanizing the university. By the mid-1970s, however, the philosophy of the market had begun to erode the confidence of providers of higher education that, as producers, they knew best what not only the students but the nation needed. A rising, politically orchestrated dissatisfaction with 'standards' began to suggest that it was only through consumer power that the entrenched professions could be forced to respond to the popular will. In a situation where real resources were declining fast, institutional leaders began to flirt with the idea of using consumer (i.e. student) demand as a weapon for claiming extra funds, or simply of shifting existing allocations around their institution. Modular structures, with free student choice, began to look attractive: what better reason for closing a course or disposing of an unwanted staff member than failure to recruit viable numbers?

At a more modest level, modular systems at least allow for greater flexibility and responsiveness to external change. It is not so much that curricular flexibility is a great virtue as that inflexibility is an obvious vice – and there have been notorious cases of atrophied curricula in great universities. The modular system, by allowing small-scale, piecemeal development, enhances the potential responsiveness of courses to changes in science and scholarship.

Alternatives to assessment by examination

The third main strand in the web of change was the attack on the traditional assessment system. One element was indeed the sheer dislike of many students for the gruelling three-hour honours examinations: brutal, impersonal (a vice, this, not a virtue in the 1960s) and rigid, putting an unfair premium on performance in a single week at the end of the final year and creating a huge strain for all but the most phlegmatic students. Many staff, too, were at least half-convinced by the occasional catastrophes that these examinations were more of a lottery than was acceptable. The best defence of end-of-course examinations is that there is no alternative: as soon as more humane and flexible possibilities were on the agenda, traditional systems were left with few friends.

These humanitarian considerations were considerably bolstered by psychological research (mainly at school level, but the implications for higher education were obvious) which suggested that this kind of examination rewards or encourages certain kinds of cognitive and intellectual skills at the expense of others – most damagingly, that far from promoting a wide-ranging synthesis at the end of three years of increasingly sophisticated work, it may in fact reward rather primitive types of rote learning; and that 'first-class minds' turn out to possess a rather narrow range of personality traits. Sociologists were quick to add that the later success of those with better classes of degrees was not conclusive evidence that the labels had been, objectively speaking, correctly applied.

Thus 'continuous assessment' began to find its way into higher education. By now the technical arrangements vary considerably, not only between institutions but between departments or even individual teachers within them; and much ingenuity, and not a little confusion for students, is involved in the multiplicity of schemes combining elements of both terminal and continuous assessment. Now in practice continuous assessment is expected to perform a large number of incompatible functions: providing both formative feedback and summative judgement, monitoring progress and, not least, penalizing lazy or disorganized students. The essentially humane motives which led to its adoption are not the whole story. If cunningly devised, it can also be a powerful method of control over students' work styles and indeed motivation. Everyone who endured the traditional system knows of people who devoted most of their student career to the extra-curricular attractions of university life. Sanctions against all but the most grossly idle were informal at best, and largely unenforceable. Continuous assessment tightens the screws. It probably saves quite a few students from the worst consequences of their own character defects, and it also assures the taxpayer that public money, which includes student maintenance grants, is not being frittered away. Rothblatt's defence of 'wasting time' cuts little ice with the promoters of efficiency studies, or those who propose to fit the British near-standard of 90 weeks' residence for a first degree into two calendar years instead of three. The American lack of faith in students has spread as the size of the British system has grown.

Changes in the recruitment of students

It is not only the public's perception of students that has changed as the system has grown: academics, too, have felt compelled to respond to the changing composition and changing preparation of university and polytechnic entrants. Keele University, founded in the late 1940s with an innovative design of a common 'foundation year' followed by major/minor specialization, based its plans not only on the needs of graduates but also on its hopes of attracting students from weaker schools, which could not provide as good a liberal arts foundation as the traditional recruiting ground of élite grammar and public schools. By 1970, the Open University faced the need to develop appropriate introductory courses for its ostensible[5] prime target group of older people with, potentially, no formal qualifications; and in the 1980s large parts of the system, notably the sciences and technology, faced a severe shortage of applicants qualified with the appropriate A-levels, and again had to devise new preparatory courses.[6]

Modular structures as a solution

This brings us back to modularity and its relationship to access. Britain has been uniquely slow, not so much in expanding its system (that is at least a subject for debate) as in adapting it from an élite to a mass character; even at present participation levels of almost fifteen per cent of the 18-year-old age-group (a figure which, not incidentally, refers only to full-time participation) there are many respects in which we are still operating an élite system on a surprisingly large scale. The effect is well represented by the now well-known 'efficiency' of British higher education, indicated by very high and very fast graduation rates by international standards. Nowhere is the élite character better demonstrated than by the assumption, built into course structures, student support systems and so on, that the British student will not be a *Wandervogel*: the norm is still one of continuous full-time attendance at a single institution.

It is, to repeat, not an accident that a modular course structure was pioneered by the Open University, which was created to cater solely for part-time students without 'normal' entry qualifications. I suspect that careful enquiry would show that the introduction of part-time courses was a major inducement to modularity in institutions of all kinds. The other components have, no doubt, all played their parts in specific cases: some modular or 'combined studies' courses at polytechnics, for example, have interdisciplinarity as their main goal. On the other hand, not all modular courses are continuously assessed by their teachers: the Open University is a monument of collective enterprise from course design right through to assessment. But both the presence and the needs of 'mature' and 'non-traditional' students are increasingly preoccupying most institutions; and notable among these are alternative modes of study, credit accumulation and credit transfer. Attempts to graft these onto the traditional system are clumsy and off-putting to all concerned.

If one were to make facile comparisons, it is undoubtedly the polytechnics which look most American in the senses described by Sheldon Rothblatt. In the last few years (up to the point when they gained independence from local government in April 1989) most of them have been strongly pressed by their political controllers to respond to local community needs. Many have developed strong equal opportunity policies, aimed at recruiting members of the various under-represented minorities in their immediate catchment area. And it is the polytechnic sector which has been the driving force behind increased participation in general. Whether out of philosophical commitment or in response to strong financial incentives which national governments first failed to control and then belatedly took credit for, the polytechnics have very substantially increased their enrolments during the 1980s, partly by finding space for students who might earlier have expected to find places in universities, but mainly by creating a new clientele for themselves. Like all British higher education institutions, they suffer from the tension between their desires for market responsiveness and status enhancement. But in the 1980s they almost managed to square the circle.

It would require a substantial research project to establish the present state of play on the various dimensions of modularity: university and poly-technic prospectuses are frequently inexplicit, and certainly inconsistent in the amount of information they provide. But I doubt if one could find a single institution with the range of 'electives' that even a small American college purports to offer: even so-called combined studies courses generally turn out to have a fairly restricted focus. And British institutions go in for much bigger units: the Carnegie unit may be 1/120 of a degree and Berkeley's 1/40, but the Open University's is 1/8: far less freedom here. The ideology of student choice is heavily constrained by subject-based academics' pre-scriptive instincts; and interdisciplinarity seems only precariously in fashion at present, the wheel having revolved another half-turn in the last few years.

On the other hand, government policy, as well as that of most – but not all – institutions in the face of demographic decline, is tilting in favour of mature students and their needs; and credit accumulation and credit transfer seem to be coming in on a slow but irresistible tide. In a research project on admissions policy Susan Ellwood and I discovered that modularization was indeed growing fast (Fulton and Ellwood, 1989). A substantial number of institutions – smaller colleges and polytechnics, but also a few universities – had either already modularized all or part of their courses or were planning or contemplating doing so in the fairly near future. One pressing reason was financial: in contrast to the American experience, modularization can in the early stages bring considerable economies as duplication of courses is reduced and class sizes are increased. The extra administrative burden, though real, is not yet seen as serious enough to threaten this economic rationale. But the main reason given to us was indeed the demand for greater and more varied access. The system allows institutions to take in a wider clientele with much more varied levels of specific or general preparation; it facilitates part-time study; and it creates the possibility not only of admitting students with credit transferred from elsewhere but of giving partial credits, generally certificates or diplomas, for intermediate years, which are portable to other institutions and have a value on the job market.

In a sense, the motives in Britain are more pragmatic than egalitarian: not for us the ideology of upward educational mobility, of the Ph.D. lurking in the book-bag of the remedial student at the community college. Transfer is mainly horizontal (i.e. within the same sector of the system), not vertical, and primarily permits geographical and career mobility in response to new needs for retraining and continuing education. But if we do not (yet) need upward mobility, it will be odd if every institution succumbs. There is already a university–polytechnic divide, with most of the recent developments on the polytechnic side. Quite where the line will be drawn is hard to predict; but I suspect that truly élite status will continue to imply many of the features of the historic English system. (Not, however, traditional examinations. Continuous assessment seems already to have taken over the vast majority of courses.)

Rothblatt has argued that it is external pressures, mainly for access and all the advantages it brings with it, that have been the motive force behind modularization, and not the interests of the academic staff. Modular courses, continuously assessed, undoubtedly put greater control in the hands of individual lecturers, even with all the British paraphernalia of double marking, external examining, validating and moderating that is described elsewhere in this volume. My impression is, however, that in our debates in Britain we have concentrated mainly on the benefits for students and for learning, and not on the rights and privileges of staff.[7] Perhaps undergraduate education is still seen as an appropriately collegial enterprise, one where individualism is less admired. It is more likely, however, that we have fudged, or failed to notice, the distinction between the 1960s' ideal of *inter*disciplinary teaching – which is time-consuming and difficult and makes great demands of teachers as well as students – and *multi*disciplinary opportunities for students, of which modularity is the essence. Here academic staff may well offer their special subjects with little regard for what their colleagues are providing, and it is up to students themselves, sometimes aided and sometimes hindered by administrators and their regulations, to make sense of the result. The levels of collegiality and collaboration which characterized the genuine interdisciplinarity of the 1960s were a reaction against the growing research ethic, and they have been increasingly squeezed as the dominance of research has asserted itself. Cutting up the map of learning is more amenable to busy researchers than redrawing it.

The traditional English system has few defenders. Confusing and confused though some of the newer alternatives may be, it is difficult to regret the changes. We are a long way still from a system which will fit the requirements of mass higher education. Most of our modules, where they exist, are too big to provide crevices for remedial coursework: instead we still insist that every entrant must be fully competent to pass the course before first enrolment, and we pack off doubtful cases on 'access' courses which are provided elsewhere, with neither the cachet nor the financial support which higher education brings with it. Our inflexibility is both a product of, and reinforces, understandable but quite excessive worry about entry standards (Fulton, 1988; Fulton and Ellwood, 1989). Exit standards, too, have been distorted by the traditional system. Collective course design and the quest for integration lead too easily to inertia – the failure to adapt curricula in response to new scholarship or to students' needs. The fixed disciplinary menu has done no better at rounding out our graduates than the laissez-faire cafeteria of the United States: each system has its own pathology. We cannot and certainly will not trade our system piecemeal for the American – but ours is more obviously dysfunctional, and change is in the air. One thing is clear: loose talk about quality and standards, defined by structure and not by process, is not going to get us very far.

Notes

1 The 'traditional' honours degree pattern is specifically English in origin. It has also prevailed in Wales. The old Scottish university tradition – which has been increasingly, but not totally, assimilated to the English pattern – is less specialized and more accessible. In this chapter, references to the tradition use the terms 'England' or 'English', and to current trends and events use 'Britain' or 'British'. (See, also, the general Note on British National Terminology in the preliminaries to this book.)

2 See Church (n.d.). A further, authoritative account which dates the main impetus to the early 1970s is given by Squires (1986).

3 This has not, however, entirely protected them from claims of discrimination – against papers with women's names on them, for instance.

4 These two phrases come from the first years of Sussex University. See Daiches, (1964).

5 Ostensible, because in practice it recruited very largely in the early years from people with substantial sub-degree qualifications (such as school teachers with non-graduate Certificates of Education).

6 See Fulton and Ellwood (1989).

7 Academic freedom is probably far less discussed in Britain than in Germany or the United States, where there is a history of more serious conflict; here it tends to be equated, uncritically if not downright tendentiously, with the mere presence of tenure in academics' contracts of employment.

References

Church, C. H. (n.d.). Modular courses in British higher education: a critical assessment. University of Kent, mimeo.

Daiches, D. (ed.) (1964). *The Idea of a New University*. London: Deutsch.

Fulton, O. (1988). Elite survivals? Entry 'standards' and procedures for higher education admissions, *Studies in Higher Education*, **13**(1).

Fulton, O. and S. Ellwood (1989). *Admissions to Higher Education: Policy and Practice*. Sheffield: Training Agency.

[Leverhulme] (1983) *Excellence in Diversity: Towards a New Strategy for Higher Education* (The Leverhulme Report). Guildford, Society for Research into Higher Education.

[Robbins] (1963) *Report of the Committee on Higher Education*. London, HMSO, Cmnd 2154.

Squires, G. (1986). *Modularisation*. Manchester, CONTACT Paper No. 1.

94

THE PARIS STATUTES OF
1215 RECONSIDERED

Stephen C. Ferruolo

Source: *History of Universities* V (1985): 1–14.

The University in Paris grew; it was not founded. While this often made assertion is essentially true, it should not blind us to the important role played by external authorities — and, above all, by officials of the Church — in the development of the schools in the twelfth century and then in the formation of the university in the early years of the thirteenth century. There is still a useful and valid distinction to be made between the origins of later universities, such as Naples and Toulouse, which were actually founded *ex privilegio* and those of Paris and also of Bologna, which developed *ex consuetudine* or, as some historians would have it, 'spontaneously'.[1] However, in no case was a university able to come into being without some degree of public notice and acceptance. As Jacques Le Goff has rightly argued, even 'the "spontaneously born" universities arose out of situations in which the attitudes and needs of public authorities and the forces they represented always played a fairly large role'.[2] What was spontaneous in this history was the growth of the schools, not the formation of universities. For these novel educational institutions to become securely established, the support, co-operation, and recognition of external authorities were necessary. In this sense, Paris was no different in its origins and early history from any other medieval university.

Neither the king of France, nor the pope, nor any diocesan official planned that Paris should become a — in fact, the — major international centre of education in twelfth-century Europe. But, at the same time, it is important to realise that any one of them could have adopted policies or taken actions which would have made conditions in Paris far less favourable to scholars and which would have impeded the advance of learning in the city's schools. Because of the important role of external conflicts in the later development of the University of Paris, historians have often misinterpreted the developments of this earlier period. It is cooperation, not conflict, with external authorities which characterises the formative years of the 'university of masters and scholars' in Paris. Throughout this vital period, the interests and needs of those in the schools and of the public authorities who watched over them coincided or, at least, they did not yet diverge. With the exception of the single, but often-cited, dispute of 1212–13 between the university and the chancellor, John of Candeilles, over the granting of the *licentia docendi*, this remains true until after both royal and papal recognition of the university's corporate autonomy. Through the formative decades of the university, from before 1150 until after 1215, education in Paris, as I have shown elsewhere, enjoyed the fortuitous advantages of the proximity of ambitious kings, the distance of sympathetic popes, and, above all, the well-informed and active support of learned bishops and chancellors.[3]

It is in the light of this reinterpretation of the formative decades of the university that I propose to reconsider the set of statutes promulgated for the masters and scholars of Paris by Cardinal Robert of Courson, the papal legate to France, during the eventful summer preceding the convocation in Rome of the Fourth Lateran Council. My primary concern here will not be to discuss or explain each of the specific rules and regulations decreed but to examine the statutes as a whole and ask three questions about them. Were there any precedents for the Paris statutes of 1215? How and why were they promulgated? And what do these statutes tell us about the formation of the university?

Although frequently cited as the university's original and first regulations, the statutes of 1215 were not unprecedented. Several years earlier, when several young arts masters had deviated from established norms concerning their dress, the scheduling of lectures and disputations, and attendance at the funerals of deceased colleagues, masters from the faculties of arts, theology, and canon law had together elected eight deputies to formulate the first set of regulations for the schools. The faculties had also agreed that all the masters regent in Paris would be required to submit themselves to these regulations by oath in order to continue teaching. Unfortunately, the regulations do not survive. We only know of this important episode in the early history of the university because, in 1208–9, Innocent III issued a decree *Ex litteris vestre* recognising the right of the Paris masters to reinstate a certain Master G. who had previously been expelled from the university for refusing to swear to abide by the regulations.[4] Given what the decree tells us of the issues of contention, we can nevertheless assume that the regulations must have set standards for academic dress, prescribed some sort of a curriculum or arts masters to follow, and required masters to attend their colleagues' funerals. These were all matters subsequently addressed by Robert Courson in the statutes of 1215. As it seems unlikely that established practices would have changed substantially in the meantime, we can also assume that the legate made use of these earlier regulations as his precedents.

Two preliminary points, then, need to be made about what the statutes are and are not. They are the earliest *extant* regulations of the University of Paris, in fact the first surviving rules of any university. But they were not wholly new or original. The statutes of 1215 had precedents. There can be little doubt that they embodied the substance of the regulations previously formulated by elected deputies of the Paris masters and tacitly approved by the papal decree of 1208–9.

This brings me to a third important point about the statutes, this one having to do with the question of how and why they were promulgated. The Paris statutes of 1215 were not a systematic set of rules imposed upon the university by an external authority. That the statutes are not very systematic is evident to anyone who has read them. But before explaining their striking lack of orderliness, I will need to defend the more controversial assertion I have made that the statutes were not imposed upon the university from the outside.[5]

Most historians, by describing the statutes of 1215 as having been promulgated *for*, or granted *to*, the university, have made the implicit assumption — or even, in some cases, the explicit assertion — that the statutes represent another example of external interference in the internal affairs of Paris masters. However, there is a far more satisfactory explanation of how the statutes came to be legislated. Rather than being a set of externally imposed rules, the statutes of 1215 are more accurately to be described as the results of co-operative efforts between a papal legate who had close ties to the schools, having been educated and having taught in Paris, and the nascent corporation of masters who had, for several years, been organising and trying to regulate their own affairs.

In the prefatory words of the statutes, Robert of Courson explicitly states that, though granted a special mandate from the pope to act, he had depended on the counsel of good men to formulate the statutes. To fulfil his mandate, Courson worked in close consultation with Paris masters and especially — though I hasten to add, not exclusively — with his former colleagues on the theology faculty.[6] Essential to the promulgation of the statutes of 1215 was both the general agreement within the schools of the need for reform as well as the willingness of an influential group of masters to cooperate with the papal legate to set procedures and policies in writing which would thenceforth be enforced independently by the university. Robert of Courson, the papal legate, remains the central figure in the promulgation of these statutes and therefore something more will need to be said about his career.

For at least a dozen years prior to being raised to the cardinalate by Innocent III in 1212, Courson had been a prominent master in the Paris schools and an influential member of the theology faculty. John Baldwin has convincingly shown him to have been an important member of the circle of moral theologians who had been influenced by, and then had carried on the work of, Master Peter the Chanter.[7] While teaching, Courson had proven himself to be especially skilled at finding the means to reconcile the moral principles of those masters who debated theological issues on the theoretical level with the more concrete and practical questions raised in everyday life.[8] As a master, Courson was frequently employed as a papal judge delegate and is also known to have played an active role in school and diocesan affairs. He was involved in the campaign to identify and suppress the followers of masters Amaury of Bène and David of Dinant in Paris. And he participated in the diocesan council of 1210 that imposed a ban on the teaching of Aristotle's *libri naturales* by the arts faculty.[9] Although direct evidence is lacking, it is certainly probable, given his known influence, that Courson had been one of the theology masters involved in the events surrounding the formulation of the rules and the enforcement of the oath mentioned in the decree of 1208–9. Both by training and experience, Courson was ideally suited for the mandated task of reforming the schools of Paris for the better and — no less significant in the wording of the decree — of providing for their future tranquillity.[10]

When I say that he was ideally suited for this task, however, I am not overlooking the well-known difficulties that Courson had previously encountered fulfilling his duties as papal legate. Dispatched to France in April 1213, soon after Innocent III had announced his plan to convene the Fourth Lateran Council, Courson had been given the twofold commission of preparing for the great council by convoking diocesan councils and publicising the new crusade by preaching. After some initial successes enacting reform decrees at councils in Paris (June 1213) and Rouen (February–March 1214), Courson found himself confronting stubborn resistance, growing hostility and, ultimately, widespread and organised opposition to his legateship. Several contemporary chroniclers record complaints about the fairness of Courson's legal decisions or about the severity of his actions.[11] According to the royal chronicler, William the Breton, not only had the legate's indiscriminate preaching of the crusade done more harm than good, his indiscreet attacks on clerical morality had caused so much public scandal and local disorder that the entire French clergy together with the king had been moved to petition the pope for his removal.[12] William might well have had reasons to misrepresent and to exaggerate the extent of Courson's unpopularity. But, as corroborating evidence of the legate's difficulties, we know that, on at least three occasions, Innocent III found it necessary to intervene to annul Courson's decisions or to moderate his actions.[13] Indeed, resentment against the legate finally became so great that the last council he summoned, one scheduled to convene in Bourges in May 1215, never took place. The prelacy and diocesan clergy, apparently with royal support, refused to respond to the legate's summons.[14]

It was in the wake of this humiliation and in the closing months of his legateship just before the convening of the Lateran Council in November 1215 that Robert of Courson returned to Paris to act on the pope's mandate to reform the schools. There Courson met neither opposition nor resistance. The time was clearly right to undertake such action. Paris masters, pleased with what they had achieved so far by acting collectively, had good reason to be encouraged about the prospects of further regulating their own affairs, especially if they acted under the aegis of the papal legate and former member of their guild. Moreover, Robert of Courson had apparently learned something from his previous mistakes trying to mandate policies too strict and reforms too severe to be accepted. This time he also had the advantage of working with former colleagues more sympathetic to his purposes. Together the legate and masters set out to draw up a set of statutes which would secure the corporate achievements and complete the programme of educational reform begun years before when Courson himself had been teaching in Paris.

Before examining the statutes themselves, I again want to emphasise that they were promulgated not at a time of conflict or contention but at one of peace and cooperation in the history of the nascent university's relations with external authorities. By the summer of 1215, even the serious dispute with the chancellor over the license to teach appears to have been largely dismissed by the masters as an unfortunate incident over a matter now resolved and not likely to cause any further disruption within the university. The compromise settlement concluded in August 1213, after months of deliberation, had been one largely favourable to the masters' collective interests. True, the chancellor could still license teachers at his own discretion and this denied the faculties the complete control over the certification of masters later understood to be so vital to the university's corporate autonomy. But, in 1212–13, this had not been the issue of contention. The masters had won the assurance they had wanted that candidates whom they had certified as worthy to teach would be granted the licence of any payments, oaths, or obligations to the chancellor.[15]

However inevitable the serious conflicts which later occurred between the university and the chancellor might appear to have been to us in retrospect, we cannot assume that, in 1215, the masters somehow anticipated these conflicts and acted accordingly. It is far more likely that the masters anticipated that the good relations which they, until then, had usually enjoyed with the bishops and chancellors of Paris had been securely reestablished. We know, again in retrospect, that neither Bishop Philip of Nemours (1208–19) nor his chancellors — and most notably Philip the Chancellor (1218–36) — were ever to be as tolerant and benevolent as their predecessors had been towards the schools since the middle of the twelfth century. But, as of 1215, the serious efforts of diocesan officials to increase their control over the schools and to limit the autonomy of the university were still in the future. The masters could not have foreseen that they would have a bitter struggle to secure their independence and autonomy from local ecclesiastical authorities. In 1215, their more pressing concern was to act collectively to reform and to regulate existing conditions within the schools.

As for the role of the papacy up to that time, it was no doubt important to the masters that Innocent III had come down so firmly on their side in the dispute with the chancellor over the *licentia docendi*.[16] However, as of 1215, the support of the papacy had probably been much more vital in helping the masters to resolve the internal problems and conflicts of the nascent corporation than in defending the university against incursions into its affairs by the chancellor or the bishop of Paris. The decisive precedent for understanding the statutes of 1215 is not the papally negotiated settlement of the university's conflict with the chancellor in 1212–13 over the license to teach. Much more important is the decree of 1208–9 by which Innocent III tacitly recognised the right of the university to make its own statutes and to require oaths from all its members to observe them.

The statutes of 1215 cover an array of matters, some obviously of great importance to the functioning of a university, others seemingly less so. Some matters are treated in great detail, others only in passing. There is no order or system apparent in them. Although the statutes' lack of orderliness has often been commented upon, it has never been satisfactorily explained.

At least partly accountable for the form of the statutes must have been the pressure of time under which the legate and the masters were working. Robert of Courson himself did not arrive in Paris until early summer, he was no doubt expected to arrive in Rome in advance of the opening of the Lateran Council, and he must still have been heavily burdened with the task of resolving the disputes remaining from his previous decisions and actions. This could not have left him very much time to fulfil the pope's mandate. Moreover, the task of convening, consulting, and negotiating with faculties was unlikely to have been any easier then than it is now. Under the circumstances, Courson seems to have wisely decided to limit his efforts to those matters about which there was already substantial consensus about what ought to be done or where established practices and customs, consistent with the objectives of reforming and tranquilising the schools, needed to be formally confirmed. In several cases, existing decrees or privileges were simply restated and renewed. But Courson and the masters also made significant strides in formulating rules for aspects of education which, up to then, had remained unregulated though not uncriticised. In fact, despite their disorder and lack of any apparent unifying principle, the statutes of 1215 succeeded in addressing many of the principal criticisms which had been made of the schools during their previous decades of rapid growth and expansion.

With the expansion of the schools, no single issue had received more attention than the harm being done to education by masters who were too young, morally unworthy, or not adequately trained to teach.[17] It is hardly surprising, given the importance attributed to this issue by critics and earlier reformers, that the statutes of 1215 are most detailed in setting minimal qualifications for teaching in Paris. Strict rules were established for members of both the arts and the theology faculties. In the arts, the statutes stipulated that a candidate for the licence to teach had to be at least twenty-one and had to have studied for a minimum of six years. In theology, the minimal age for a teacher was set at thirty-five and at least eight years of study, including a minimum of five full years of attending theology lectures, were required.[18]

As for determining the worthiness of candidates, the statutes made permanent the certification procedures agreed to in the settlement of August 1213 between the university and the chancellor: theologians needed to be approved by their faculty and masters of arts by an examination panel of six masters appointed by the arts faculty and the chancellor.[19] For arts masters there was a further stipulation that a candidate for the license had to promise to teach in Paris for at least two years. This requirement was probably included not because of any serious concern about a shortage of arts masters but rather as a means of providing a greater degree of stability within the schools.[20]

Next in apparent importance to Courson and the masters was establishing what was and was not to be taught in Paris and when the lectures of the various faculties were to be scheduled. The decrees for the arts faculty approved and provided for instruction in all of the traditional liberal arts. Grammar and dialectic were given precedence in ordinary lectures. But the feast days were reserved for rhetoric, the quadrivium,[21] and ethics. In sum, the statutes of 1215 mandated a broad liberal arts curriculum not very much different from that which humanists like John of Salisbury had promoted decades earlier.[22] For all subjects, except the arts of the quadrivium, specific texts were prescribed for teaching. These include Aristotle's logical writings, both old and new, and his *Ethics*. At the same time, the statutes renewed the legislation of 1210 prohibiting the arts faculty from teaching Aristotle's metaphysics and the *libri naturales* as well as any commentaries on them.[23] In contrast to these detailed provisions for the arts faculty, only one rule was mandated for the teaching of Paris theologians: they were not to begin their lectures before 9:00 a.m.[24] Consistent with the educational ideal that the arts were propaedeutic to theology, this gave the arts masters the opportunity to attend lectures on theology after having taught their own classes earlier in the morning.

In addition to regulating masters and the curriculum, the statutes addressed some specific aspects of academic conduct and deportment that had long been targets of the critics and satirists of the schools. The lavish banquets customarily given by students after their examinations and masters after their inceptions were prohibited. Scholars could still invite their friends and colleagues to these events, but only a few; and there was to be no drinking and feasting. Instead the scholars were encouraged to increase the gifts of clothing and other things customary on these occasions and especially to be mindful of the needs of the poor.[25] Excesses in clothing were also prohibited and a strict dress code established for the arts faculty. These masters, when teaching, were required to wear one simple black and round cope, which should reach the ankles, at least when new, a pallium, and plain shoes without pointed toes.[26] The statutes made no stipulation for the clothing of the theology faculty. But, as most, if not all, theologians were beneficed members of the clergy, they were presumably already subject to a dress code.

Not surprising given his mandate to provide for the future tranquility of the schools, Courson found it necessary to touch upon town-gown relations. Two of the decrees directly addressed matters over which the scholars and citizens of Paris had clashed. In one case, Courson sided decisively with the university. The statutes conceded to the university the rights to the meadow in the bourg Saint-Germain, known as the *Prato clericorum* or Pré-aux-Clercs, which scholars and the abbey of Saint-Germain had contested, at times violently, since at least 1192.[27] In the other case, scholars were admonished not to occupy a room without obtaining the consent of the previous tenant, whenever possible.[28] Such an admonition probably did little to lessen the conflicts caused by the shortage of affordable lodging and suitable teaching space.

Of far more general importance to the future of the university were those statutes providing for the discipline of scholars and the governance of the schools. Here Courson mostly restated or reinforced existing legislation. He began by reconfirming the privilege, long supported by the papacy, that placed students directly under the legal jurisdiction of their masters.[29] However, to improve discipline in the schools, he also decreed that no student was to be allowed to remain in Paris who was not willing to submit to the authority of a specific master.[30] The independence of the masters from external authorities was protected by the renewal of the legislation of 1213 stipulating that no monetary payment, oath, or other precondition was to be required by the chancellor or by any other diocesan official before issuing the *licentia docendi*.[31] And, most important of all, the autonomy of the university was guaranteed by the explicit confirmation of the right of the masters to make and to enforce their own statutes.

The particulars stipulated by Courson in connection with the university's right of self-governance require some comment. According to the statutes, the masters and scholars had the right to make rules and regulations (*obligationes et constitutiones*) enforced by faith, penalty, or oath, determining what action was to be taken were a case involving the murder, mutilation, or serious injury of a scholar to be resolved unjustly and also setting what rents were to be charged for lodgings, both of which clearly concerned town-gown relations, as well as on such internal affairs as academic dress, the burial of colleagues, and the scheduling of lectures and disputations.[32]

Why does Courson mention these several, rather diverse matters and no others? There is no reason to believe that his intention was to limit the university's right of self-governance. Rather than wanting to restrict the university, Courson was seeking to encourage the masters to exercise their responsibilities over those matters known to have previously caused the disruption of the schools. The right was to be exercised, the decree concludes, so that 'the university might not be dissolved or destroyed'. This was probably meant to be both a justification and an exhortation. The right of the Paris masters to regulate their own affairs, tacitly recognised by Innocent III in the bull *Ex litteris vestre*, had been formally confirmed. It would now be up to the masters themselves to complete the reform of the schools.

On no matter other than the qualifications for masters are the statutes more detailed than in establishing the procedures to be followed when a member of the university died. In the case of the death of a student, the statutes prescribed that all the masters were to attend the funeral, half at one time half at another — presumably, so that classes would not be disrupted. When a master died, however, all were to attend the funeral and keep vigil together, and, on the day of burial, all lectures and disputations were to be cancelled.[33] These funerary practices, like the right to make and to enforce their own rules, were important to the ability of the masters of Paris to function and to be recognised as a single corporate body or guild. Here we again see Robert of Courson acting to strengthen the corporate identity and autonomy of the university which he, as master, had been involved in forming.

Most vital of all to the future autonomy of the university were the procedures Courson established for the enforcement of these decrees. The statutes stipulated that any intentional violators of the prescribed rules and regulations were to be excommunicated unless, within fifteen days of their violations, they had appeared to emend their presumption either before the entire university or before some smaller group constituted by the university to hear such cases.[34] Significantly, it made no difference in the procedures whether the violations at issue pertained to a rule applying only to a single faculty or to one binding upon all masters and scholars. Jurisdiction, in all cases, rested within the university as a whole, that is, in all the faculties acting together as a single corporate body. This was not something new. Since before 1208–9, when the pope had recognised their right to readmit the master expelled from the university for refusing to take the oath to abide by their rules, the Paris faculties had been effectively functioning as a single guild or corporation. The established procedures of the nascent university's self-governance had now been clarified and formalised.

In sum, it should be evident that the statutes of 1215 served a dual purpose. First, by establishing rules on the qualifications of masters, the supervision of students, and the curriculum, the statutes fulfilled a programme of educational reform long urged for the schools. Second, by confirming and strengthening the procedures of self-governance, the statutes recognised the corporate autonomy of the university, which had first been formed seven or more years before when the masters had acted independently to attempt to regulate their own affairs. If too late to be the foundation charter, the statutes were the decisive document in confirming the corporate rights, strengthening the corporate identity, and securing the corporate autonomy of the recently established 'university of masters and scholars of Paris'. After 1215, there could be no doubt that the future of learning in Paris depended upon the collective will of the masters and scholars of all the faculties acting together as an essentially autonomous and formally recognised guild.

This brings me to the third and final question. What do the statutes of 1215 tell us about the formation of the university? If, as I have argued, the decades during which the university was formed were characterised by far more peace and co-operation than conflict and contention between those in the schools and external authorities, then there is a serious problem with the long-established explanation that the university was formed as a direct consequence of the struggle of the schools to free themselves from ecclesiastical domination.[35] Given the clear evidence that generally harmonious external relations prevailed until after 1215, the masters of Paris could not have been forced to join together in order to defend their freedom against diocesan officials. Masters of the various Paris faculties and schools joined together to form a single guild, not because they were threatened by external authorities and sought strength in numbers, but because, despite their differences and rivalries, they shared a common professional identity.

Evidence of the nature of this new professional identity can be found in the nascent university's first statutes. The statutes promulgated by Robert of Courson for Paris 1215 — as well as those drawn up sometime before 1208–9 by the masters themselves — were, as we have seen, primarily concerned with teaching. What should be taught in the schools, how, when, and by whom should that teaching be done, and defining the authority masters were to exercise over their students, these were the matters on which the faculties first acted together. Does this not suggest that the professional identity which the Paris masters shared and which originally motivated them to join together to form the university was based on a consciousness of their duties and responsibilities as teachers?

References

An earlier version of this paper was read at the Annual Meeting of the American Historical Association in December 1983. The author especially wishes to thank Professor Alan Bernstein of the University of Arizona for his helpful comments and criticisms.

1. On this distinction see Stephen d'Irsay, *Histoire des universités françaises et etrangères des origines à nos jours* I (Paris, 1933), 129–33, and the more recent article of Laetitia Boehm, 'Die *negotio scholaris*: Zur Entstehung von Berufsbewußtsein und Rechtsstand des Universitätsgelehrten im Mittelalter', in *Festiva Lanx: Johannes Spörl Festgabe*, ed. K. Schnith (Munich, 1966), pp. 29–52.

2. 'The Universities and Public Authorities in the Middle Ages and Renaissance', in *Time, Work and Culture in the Middle Ages*, tr. A. Goldhammer (Chicago, 1980), p. 137.

3. See Ferruolo, *The Origins of the University: The Schools of Paris and Their Critics 1100–1215* (Stanford, 1985), pp. 283–301.

4. *Chartularium Universitatis Parisiensis*, eds. H. Denifle and E. Chatelain (4 vols., Paris, 1889–97), I no. 8, pp. 67–68. Hereafter abbreviated as *CUP*.

5. Cf. the views of Hastings Rashdall, *The Universities of Europe in the Middle Ages*, eds. F. M. Powicke and A. B. Emden (3 vols., Oxford, 1936), I, 309; Gordon Leff, *Paris and Oxford Universities in the Thirteenth and Fourteenth Centuries* (New York, 1968), pp. 25–27; and J. Boussard, *Nouvelle histoire de Paris: De la fin du siège de 885–886 à la mort de Philippe Auguste* (Paris, 1976), p. 341.

6. 'Noverint universi, quod cum domini pape speciale habuissemus mandatum, ut statui Parisiensium scolarium in melius reformando impenderemus operam efficacem, nos de bonorum virorum consilio scolarum tranquillitati volentes in posterum providere, ordinavimus et statuimus . . .' (*CUP* I no. 20, p. 78). Cf. M. Grabmann, *I divieti ecclesiastici di Aristotele sotto Innocenzo III e Gregorio IX*, in *Miscellanea Historiae Pontificiae* V (Rome, 1941), 65–66, who argues that the 'boni viri' referred to were the theologians.

7. John W. Baldwin, *Masters, Princes, and Merchants: The Social Views of Peter the Chanter and His Circle* (2 vols. Princeton, 1970), I, 19–25 and *passim*.

8. Especially notable was Courson's treatment of the issue of academic fees, which is found in his *Summa 'Tota coelestis philosophia'*, Ms. Paris BN lat. 14524, f. 42[ra–b]. This is discussed in Baldwin, *Masters, Princes and Merchants* I, 125–7, and in Ferruolo, *Origins*, pp. 302–3.

9. See M. and C. Dickson, 'Le cardinal Robert de Courson. Sa vie,' *Archives d'histoire doctrinale et littéraire du moyen âge* 9 (1934), 79–80 and 120–24, and Grabmann, *I divieti*, p. 65.

10. See note 6 above.

11. These complaints can be found in Dickson, 'Robert de Courson', pp. 112–14.

12. *Historia de vita et gestis Philippi Augusti*, ed. H. F. Delaborde, *Oeuvres de Rigord et de Guillaume le Bréton* (2 vols., Paris, 1882–1885, I, 303–304).

13. See Dickson, 'Robert de Courson', pp. 97–99.

14. *Ibid.*, pp. 112–14.

15. *CUP* I nos. 16–18, pp. 75–76. Cf. Alan E. Bernstein, 'Magisterium and License: Corporate Autonomy against Papal Authority in the Medieval University of Paris', *Viator* 9 (1978), 291–307.

16. The strongly-worded bull Innocent III had issued on 20 January 1212 (*Miramur non modicum*) has been unambiguous in its support of the masters. Of the chancellor's mistreatment of scholars, the pope had indignantly written, 'Cum igitur tempore, quo vacavimus Parisius studio litterarum, nunquam scolares viderimus sic tractari' (*CUP* I no. 14, p. 73).

17. See, for example, the criticisms made by Stephen of Tournai in his letter to the pope (*CUP* I no. 48, pp. 47–8).
18. The age of thirty-five was significantly higher than the canonical age for ordination and also exceeded the limit of thirty which critics such as Raoul Ardent and Jacques of Vitry had urged for public preaching or teaching. This rather strict age limit reflects the strong concern Robert of Courson himself had expressed when teaching that maturity was especially important for teachers of theology and canon law (*Tota coelestis philosophia*, Ms. Paris BN lat. 14524, ff. 49vb–50ra).
19. *CUP* I no. 18, pp. 75–76.
20. Cf. Leff, *Paris and Oxford Universities*, p. 137. On the numbers of masters teaching in Paris at this time see the estimates in John W. Baldwin's recent article, 'Masters at Paris from 1179 to 1215', in *Renaissance and Renewal in the Twelfth Century*, ed. R. L. Benson and G. Constable (Cambridge, Mass., 1982), pp. 142–8.
21. The list of subjects to be lectured on during feastdays includes the '*quadruvialia*'. Yet, for some reason, Leff (*Paris and Oxford Universities*, p. 138) writes of 'the complete absence of any of the practical sciences of the *quadrivium*'.
22. On the relationship of the university and humanism see my article 'The Twelfth-Century Renaissance', in *Renaissances Before the Renaissance: Cultural Revivals of Late Antiquity and the Middle Ages*, ed. W. Treadgold (Stanford, 1984), pp. 114–43.
23. 'Non legantur libri Aristotelis de *methafisica* et de *naturali philosophia*, nec *summe* de eisdem, aut de doctrina magistri David de Dinant, aut Amalrici heretici, aut Mauricii hyspani' (*CUP* I no. 20, pp. 78–9). On this prohibition see Grabmann, *I divieti*, pp. 65–6.
24. 'Circa statum theologorum statuimus, quod . . . illorum nullus legat ante tertiam in diebus, quando magistri legunt' (*CUP* I no. 20, p. 79). Note than the restriction applies only on those days when arts masters teach.
25. *CUP* I no. 20, p. 79.
26. *Ibid.*
27. On this meadow and the scholarly disputes over it see Boussard, *Nouvelle histoire de Paris*, p. 183, and Pearl Kibre, *Scholarly Privileges in the Middle Ages* (Cambridge, Mass., 1962), pp. 241–3.
28. 'Nullus irrequisito consensu inquilini vel scolas accipiat vel domum, dum facultatem habeat requirendi' (*CUP* I no. 20, p. 79).
29. 'Quilibet magister forum sui scolaris habeat' (*CUP* I no. 20, p. 79). In settling a conflict involving some scholars in Reims in 1170–72, Alexander III had first established the principle that the primary jurisdiction over the conduct of students was in the hands of their masters (*CUP* I intro. no. 5, pp. 5–6). Another precedent can be found in the diocesan decrees promulgated for Paris in 1208 by the previous papal legate, Cardinal Gualo (*CUP* I no. 7, p. 66).
30. 'Nullus sit scolaris Parisius, qui certum magistrum non habeat' (*CUP* I no. 20, p. 79).
31. 'Nullus incipiat licenciatus a cancellario vel ab alio data ei pecunia vel fide prestita, vel alia conventione habita' (*CUP* I no. 20, p. 79).
32. 'Item facere possunt magistri et scolares tam per se quam cum aliis obligationes et constitutiones fide vel pena vel juramento vallatas in hiis casibus, scilicet in interfectione vel mutilatione scolaris, vel in atroci injuria illata scolari, si defuerit

justicia, pro taxandis pretiis hospitiorum, de habitu, de sepultura, de lectionibus et disputationibus, ita tamen, quod propter hec studium non dissolvatur aut destruatur' (*CUP* I no. 20, p. 79).

33. *CUP* I no. 20, p. 79.

34. 'Ut autem ista inviolabiliter observentur, onmes qui contumaciter contra hec statuta nostra venire presumpserint, nisi infra quindecim dies a die transgressionis coram universitate magistrorum et scolarium, vel coram aliquibus ab Universitate constitutis presumptionem suam curaverint emendare, legationis qua fungimur auctoritate vinculo excommunicationis innodavimus' (*CUP* I no. 20, p. 79).

35. The most recent scholar to give this explanation of the university's formation is Alfred B. Cobban: 'Paris University provides both the earliest and the most dramatic example in European history of the struggle for university autonomy in the face of ecclesiastical domination' (*The Medieval Universities: Their Development and Organization* (London, 1975), p. 76).

95

AMERICAN HIGHER EDUCATION IN THE AGE OF THE COLLEGE

Jurgen Herbst

Source: *History of Universities* VII (1988): 37–59.

The historiographical issue

No period in the history of American higher education stands more in need of reappraisal and reinterpretation than the 'age of the college'. Until quite recently historians have treated the decades between the Revolution and 'the emergence of the American university' in the years after the Civil War with faint distaste and little appreciation for what they found in it.[1] They saw it as a time of declining standards and dissipation of energies dominated by large numbers of weak and small institutions, many of which came and went without leaving any permanent trace.[2] The 'old-time college' with its uniform curriculum was the period's typical institution. It smelled of the mustiness of old-fashioned frock coats and brought up images of roll-top desks, their cubbyholes stuffed with yellowing papers in much the same fashion that the 'faculties' of students' minds were to be crammed with the facts and qualities the old-time college professor so faithfully dispensed and promoted.[3]

A newer literature has now appeared that dissents rather strikingly from this traditional interpretation. The old-time college no longer is the only educational institution worth noting in this period. Quite to the contrary, an appreciation of diversity now permits us to recognize a whole series of specialized schools that devoted themselves to some form of post-common school education.[4] To use just one example: in the years before 1855 Illinois reported the existence of female high schools and teacher seminaries, literary and theological institutions, female academies, liberal institutes for the establishment and support of education, and seminaries of learning for the advancement of religion, science, and 'the cause of education generally'.

The state had at least one seminary for the promotion of 'English and German literature', one commercial and mathematical institute to teach 'double-entry bookkeeping and the laws of trade, of commercial calculations and the higher mathematics', as well as manual labour colleges, schools, seminaries, and universities. Then there were medical and literary colleges and universities as well as agricultural and female colleges and universities.[5] To be sure, the differences of what was being taught in these institutions were not always pronounced. They depended, after all, on the students' state of prior education or the lack of it. But they were nonetheless novel and remarkable when contrasted with collegiate education during the colonial period.

It is therefore useful to try to take the measure of the changes that have occurred in the historiography of this period and to investigate a few themes that have now emerged as significant starting points for a re-interpretation of American higher education in the ante-bellum years.[6] After a brief characterization of the traditional view, I want to consider the colleges as they reflected the 'politeia', their society's political orientation and commitment, and to highlight their commitment to tradition within diversity by pointing to the role of the ubiquitous 'college course'. At the same time I want to show that this emphasis on tradition did not rule out a careful and measured response to demands for innovation which took the form of partial and parallel courses and schools.

I should like to argue, too, that what has been called the 'great retrogression' needs to be balanced with a consideration of the progressive social role the colleges performed in ante-bellum America.[7] Academic decline and economic and social stimulus may be seen as two sides of the same coin, each requiring the other to enable higher education to survive and perform its traditional function in a frontier society. Finally, I want to end with a brief sketch of the diversity of institutions that came to characterize American higher education in the ante-bellum period. The search for ways to teach practical and applied science, to train teachers for the common schools, and to open collegiate doors for men and women of middle and working class origins introduced novel institutions into ante-bellum higher education.

The traditional view and its problems

The 'age of the college' was endorsed, if not to say sanctified, as a fixed notion in our historiography by Richard Hofstadter and Walter Metzger in their influential study on the history of academic freedom. They divided their work into an 'age of the college' and an 'age of the university'.[8] The latter was said to have begun somewhere around 1876. In that year the Johns Hopkins University opened its doors in Baltimore, Reconstruction ended in the American South, and at about that time the nation was said to have entered the age of organized or corporate capitalism. With the importation of the German university model for graduate education and the emergence of the research university a new era had begun in the history of American higher education.

The distinction between the 'age of the college' and the 'age of the university' raised all sorts of difficulties. Not only did universities with several faculties, colleges, or schools exist in the United States during the 'age of the college', but colleges as one-faculty institutions continued and continue to thrive in the 'age of the university'. Taken from a curricular rather than an institutional point of view, the distinction was equally problematical. Medical, theological, and legal instruction—i.e, university subjects—were offered already in eighteenth century colleges, and the liberal arts course has never disappeared from American higher education.[9]

But this was not all. The typological distinction was imbued also with a qualitative dimension. The 'age of the university' was the modern age in which was born the academic world we know today and in which we feel at home. By contrast, the 'age of the college' was filled with local institutions out-of-touch with national or state issues, stuck in the past, and, particularly as concerned their curricula, unresponsive to their critics. When compared to the institutions that preceded and that followed them, the colleges of the ante-bellum period came to be portrayed as academic backwaters.

Problematic, too, was the contrast between the fall from grace that Richard Hofstadter attributed to the ante-bellum colleges and the tremendous economic and demographic 'take-off' that many scholars noted for the new nation during the first half of the nineteenth century.[10] Willard Hurst chose the felicitous phrase of 'the release of energy' to characterize the expansion in territory, spirit, and political experience that now buoyed the young democracy.[11] Along with all other institutions colleges, too, proliferated. But Hofstadter wrote of 'the great retrogression' to deplore the disregard for academic standards in the multiplying collegiate institutions and to express regret over the loss of, nay the deliberate disregard for, the presumed academic rigour inherited from the colonial colleges and the European past.

American higher education was criticized not only for the 'great retrogression', but also for the presumed unwillingness or inability of the colleges during the ante-bellum era to respond to the demands of the American people for instruction in practical scientific tasks. Here, too, the colonial and the post-bellum period were made to shine by contrast. In the colonial colleges professorships of mathematics and natural philosophy had usually been established soon after the initial appointment of a professor of divinity. In New York and Philadelphia professorships of medicine had been the first professional faculty appointments outside the colleges proper.[12] The rise of the modern university to scientific eminence obviously needs no additional comment.

By contrast, the colleges of the ante-bellum period were said to have paid mere lip-service to science. 'The scientists remained second-rate citizens in the academic world and their influence was negligible', wrote George P. Schmidt.[13] Frederick Rudolph followed the same line when he declared that in the colleges all the curricular experiments with the teaching of science 'were adopted as props for the classical course'.[14] And the classical course, it was asserted by implication if not explicitly, was dominated by the teaching of Latin and Greek.

Colleges in an age of revolution

This disparaging view of American higher education in the ante-bellum period clouds and misrepresents more than it illuminates our understanding. It portrays the colleges as being out-of-touch with their society when it can be argued that just the opposite was the case. In the decades between 1780 and 1860 the institutions and views of collegiate, Latin-based education underwent far-reaching changes that in their legal, organizational, and curricular aspects reflected the deep-seated transformation of the society in which they existed and which they served. Not only do we during the early years of this period have to face the obvious issue of the American Revolution as a war for national independence, but joined to it was the gradually accelerating struggle for republican forms of government and democratic patterns of social relations. With the victory of Andrew Jackson in 1828 the common people would compete for the spoils of politics on equal terms with the sons of the country's established and wealthy families. Should we not assume that changes of such magnitude in the political and social configurations of a people would have made their impact on collegiate institutions as well?

The events educational historians describe do not exist in a vacuum. In the colonial period as throughout western history higher education had been part of the political and ecclesiastical establishment of empire, province, or nation. As present and future leaders of their society, professors and students in the colonial colleges had closely followed and participated in the momentous events that were to bring independence for a new nation. Faculty members educated their students for public service. Patriotic professors, tutors, and students debated and promoted the propagation of republican principles.[15] None was more engaged in this effort inside and outside his college than Princeton's president John Witherspoon who in 1776 became a member of the Continental Congress. At Yale, Princeton, Harvard, and Brown students took the initiative in founding literary societies which soon became centres for political debate and agitation.

Once independence had been won the colleges, willy-nilly, became drawn into the political battles of the new nation. What financial, foreign, and social policies were appropriate for the new republic? The first presidents of the new nation from Washington to Monroe had themselves belonged to the revolutionary generation and saw to it that republican ways would replace the monarchical traditions of the past. By 1828 the victory of Andrew Jackson signalled the ascendency of democracy over aristocracy and feudalism. Faculty members and students in the established colleges continued debating these national issues in familiar ways. If anything, as Robson has pointed out, they increased the fervour of their partisanship.[16]

For students the professorial and tutorial sermons of a new republicanism and democracy often translated themselves into protests against the collegiate traditions of *in loco parentis*.[17] Students demanded that colleges be seen as civil rather than domestic societies and their rights as citizens be recognized and protected against faculty encroachment. Thus Professor Pearson of Harvard could remind his colleagues in 1789 that if students were taught 'that they are entitled to all the civil rights of freemen . . . it is no wonder that they rebel against the constitution of College which, at present, is not founded on such principles'.[18]

Newly founded colleges in the hinterland and on the frontier were far more likely than their Eastern sister institutions to depend on local support and to respond to local issues. Their students came from rural areas and relatively poor families; they were older on the average and often worked and attended college part-time or intermittently. They were also less likely than their younger classmates to board or room together and to feel themselves as members of a college class.[19] In many cases the institutions themselves were supported by religious groups or were part of a promotional effort to encourage development and attract desirable settlers with families.[20] For these new colleges national issues seemed further removed than for their sister institutions in the older areas along the coast. Missionary concerns for the self-imposed mandate of 'taming a wilderness' and bringing civilization and religion to 'the ends of the world' crowded out a secular, republican political culture that had been cherished in the East.[21]

This new collegiate culture was intimately related to the 'release of energy' on the frontier, a release that created a veritable patchwork of local centres across the country with few unifying strands. Diversity and localism marked the new America and the colleges it established beyond the Appalachians.[22] Here Americans looked outward, not backward to the metropolises of the East. Their republicanism translated itself into a democratic localism that saw no need and felt no love for central direction. Local associations of citizens, frequently held together by bonds of a common religion, acted as godfathers for the new colleges. Tocqueville observed it well in 1831: 'In democratic countries the science of association is the mother of science; the progress of all the rest depends upon the progress it has made.'[23] The new colleges sprang up as evidences of democracy in higher education, just as the colonial colleges had served as the academic incubators of republicanism.

Tradition within diversity: the college course

Despite these differences between East and West, between republican tradition and democratic innovation, the colleges were held together by a common commitment to educating the country's future professional, religious, political, and scientific leaders. In Eastern as well as Western colleges the same questions were raised: how to educate for leadership in a democracy? How to harmonize the urgent need for an educated intelligence that was to seek above all the welfare of the commonwealth with the proud boasts of a rough-hewn democracy that believed in the natural ability of everyone to seek their own best interests?

The complexity and confusion of the answers are mirrored in the pages of James Fenimore Cooper's *The American Democrat*. Writing in 1838 Cooper asked the colleges to graduate students who were to be gentlemen of public or private station, who belonged to a class that was 'the natural repository of the manners, tastes, tone, and to a certain extent, of the principles of a country'. With a paternalism incongruous to his professed preference for democracy Cooper exhorted these gentlemen to be stewards of the liberties of their fellow citizens and to assert at all times the principles of democratic government. In turn, Cooper and like-minded Americans felt, the great masses of Americans ought to respect the college-educated gentlemen for the contributions they made to civilization. 'Where many such are found, the arts are more advanced, and men learn to see that there are tastes more desirable than those of the mere animal . . . He who would honor learning, and taste, and sentiment, and refinement of every sort, ought to respect its possessors, and, in all things but those which affect rights, defer to their superior advantages'.[24]

This, to be sure, was a tall order that was bound to remain unfilled. But the colleges, by and large, accepted it and sought to make it their educational mission. The key to its attempted realization lay in their loyalty to the traditional college course as the required uniform curriculum for candidates for the bachelor of arts degree. That course became the mainstay of a college education in the ante-bellum years. The colleges refuted all accusations that in their adherence to it they were inflexible and impractical and unresponsive to the demands of an expanding country for instruction in modern subjects. To the contrary, they argued that only by preserving the traditional curriculum could they perform their function of educating the country's future leaders.

The manifesto of the ante-bellum college was the 1827 report of the Yale Faculty on their curriculum. President Jeremiah Day, the author of the report's first part, made it clear that colleges were concerned with basic intellectual skills and acquirements in literature and science. When young men were exposed to these they would gain the 'foundation of a superior education,' not a complete edifice. The 'discipline and the furniture of the mind' were the aims, not the myriad details of every conceivable subject. The college would select with care its curriculum, but every part of it had to qualify for a particular mission. Thus mathematics would train the faculty of demonstrative reasoning, the physical sciences would instill respect for facts and give practice in inductive reasoning. Classical literature would develop taste and logic would teach its students how to think, as rhetoric would accomplish the same for the art of speaking. The educated graduate would combine solid learning with skills of eloquence; he would have something to say, and he would know how to say it well. He was the college-bred gentleman whom James Fenimore Cooper would hold up ten years later as the ideal American democrat.

The task of the college was the education of character. But that could be achieved only by a balanced approach that would stress the languages as much as the sciences. Concern for 'a proper symmetry and balance of character' in the students made it improper and unlikely that a college would neglect the modern scientific subjects. The Yale faculty pointed out that chemistry, mineralogy, geology, and political economy had been introduced in recent years. Their study required effort no less 'vigorous and steady and systematic' as the study of all other collegiate subjects. A collegiate education, after all, was an education of mind and character to prepare students for the future proper execution of professional tasks.

Thus the Yale faculty and thereafter the faculties of America's colleges throughout the land rejected the accusations of the impracticality of their studies and of their unwillingness to respond to demands for fundamental curricular changes. What they insisted upon was that college studies had to remain general and theoretical or, as they would put it, preparatory to professional study. They embodied the principles of science which were 'the common foundation of all high intellectual attainments,' which in turn were needed among merchants, manufacturers, and farmers as much as among statesmen and politicians. In a democracy—and here Cooper would later echo the report—the college course was to be open to all who contributed in their different ways to the welfare of the nation.[25]

Tradition and innovation

As much as they upheld tradition, the colleges had not been averse to innovation. Yale had made that point in 1777 when its then president-elect Ezra Stiles had submitted to the college corporation proposals for strengthening the traditional role of the college in educating Connecticut's civic and political leaders. Stiles had urged the creation of professorships in belles lettres, oratory, civil history, and law. The new chairs were to be endowed in the college where they could serve the general education of the students 'in that knowledge which may qualify them to become useful members of society as select men, justices of the peace, members of the legislature, judges of courts, and delegates in Congress'. Legal instruction in government, Stiles emphasized, was general education. It was *'civil history* of the best kind. It is not a dull and unanimated narrative of events—it is tracing great events, great political phenomena to their operative and efficient causes—it is the *true spirit of history'*.[26]

The same endorsement of general and theoretical education applied to the so-called partial and parallel courses that several colleges had introduced into their curriculum. Responding to demands from the outside, partial courses allowed non-degree candidates to enroll for part of the regular college programme, and parallel courses substituted more scientific instruction for one of the classical languages in the regular course. In every case, however, the approach remained preparatory and avoided professional instruction.

The colleges acted with great caution. Afraid that increased or novel offerings would detract from the value of the regular college course leading to the bachelor's degree, Princeton in 1796 and Union College in 1802 permitted only non-degree students to attend lectures in the parallel course. Between 1825 and 1828 more such reforms were discussed and adopted at Harvard, Amherst, the University of Vermont, Columbia, Williams, Union, and Dartmouth.[27] By 1828 only President Nott of Union was adventurous enough to award the BA degree to graduates of the regular as well as of the parallel course.[28]

It cannot be said, then, that the colleges had shut their doors, eyes, and ears to the demands of innovation. They had indeed endorsed curricular experiments. They knew that only thus could they keep open the gates to social mobility for many of their students as they had done in the past with remarkable success. Between 1748 and 1768 half of Princeton's students had been sons of farmers of middling to poor economic status, and three-quarters of them later became clergymen, lawyers, or physicians.[29] And what had been true for Princeton had also been true with only minor variations for the other colleges of the colonial period.

This need for colleges to offer a solid and respected basis for a professional career and to respond to changing times and conditions was even more in evidence after 1800 in the new foundations in the hinterland and on the frontier. Because these institutions were marked by diversity and localism and because their students lacked family connections, apprenticeship arrangements, or access to some proprietary professional school that growing up in an established society might have supplied, the regular college course that led to the bachelor of arts degree was even more a necessity for them than for their Eastern brethren. It was the road to opportunity in a democratic society, the most promising pathway to a professional career.

If the Western colleges were to fulfill their function as gateways to professional opportunity, they had to insist on the regular college course to establish their academic respectability and forge a bond of unity among their students. The education societies of churches and denominations that served as college founders in the West could wholeheartedly endorse its literary and scientific contents. As Douglas Sloan has reminded us, in the ante-bellum years the dispute of science with religion lay yet in the future. Charles G. Finney, the great revivalist at Oberlin College, admonished his students to study works on medicine and natural science 'for all these declare the wonderful works of God'.[30] The course thus became the staple fare of the new students in the colleges of the West.

As in the older colleges in the East, the study of the natural sciences was at times introduced in a partial or parallel course. Many of the western colleges also responded to the urgent call for teachers in private academies and public high schools and introduced teacher training. Eventually they allowed women to enroll as well.[31] Part-time school teaching in conjunction with 'normal instruction' then provided welcome opportunity for the many older students from relatively poor families to help defray their college expenses. But whether full or part-time student, male or female, those who had completed the regular college course had earned the bachelor degree and were full-fledged college graduates.

The philosophy of the Yale Report, then, did not rule out responsiveness to new conditions. In fact, it could be argued that it was the combination of upholding academic standards symbolized by the regular college course and being responsive to new developments that allowed the colleges, old as well as new, to play the role the people wanted and the nation needed. In its fusion of tradition and responsiveness, in its ability to accept the new without discarding the old, lay the strength of the ante-bellum college.

The other side of the coin: the great retrogression

If we thus have stressed the strength of the ante-bellum college in its reliance on the traditional college course and its willingness to respond carefully to the needs and demands of their students, what are we to make of Professor Hofstadter's 'great retrogression', that undermining of academic standards and that dispersal of both financial and intellectual resources in the many new and diverse collegiate institutions in the West? I suggest that we see it as the flip side of the 'take-off' and 'the release of energy', and that we acknowledge it as the inevitable consequence of the local initiatives and the associationist nature that characterized so many of the new foundations. As individuals and associations played ever larger roles when they attempted to meet the demand for ministers, physicians, and lawyers in the expanding country, their efforts could not but lead to dispersion of efforts and a weakening of traditional standards.

The need for trained professionals was huge and urgent, and financial and institutional resources were wanting. Individual ministers would respond by opening Latin schools or academies in their localities to prepare boys and young men for college. In many cases they also offered non-classical instruction for girls and young women. Whenever they thought it feasible, clergymen and laymen would band together and draw on their community's resources to establish a college in their midst. Local initiative and personal commitment rather than organizational policy provided the initiative for these educational boot-strap operations.[32]

Where personal and community resources were insufficient, help was sought from the voluntary societies that had been formed to aid educational efforts in the West. The American Education Society, founded in 1815 as the American Society for the Education of Pious Youth for the Gospel Ministry, sought funds to lend money to students and to supply churches with ministers.[33] Thirty years later the Society for the Promotion of Collegiate and Theological Education at the West would assist the colleges directly rather than funding their students.[34] Americans found that it was easier to summon help from their neighbours and friends and from like-minded associates in their churches and interdenominational societies than to call upon the governments of states and nation. The response would come more quickly and directly.

Keeping in mind, then, that the newer colleges sprang up in newly settled country through largely local initiatives and depended for their survival and continuing support on the college societies, it is easier to understand that in many cases the regular college course leading to the bachelor of arts degree was a hope and a goal rather than a presence to be taken for granted. Colleges stood in want of both qualified instructors and prepared students. While professors and tutors, the great majority of them ministers or students of divinity, had in almost every case themselves been trained in the classics, their liabilities had less to do with the kind of education they had received than with its quality and depth.

But the case was different with students. Here the lack of college preparatory training was the real reason for 'the great retrogression'. Colleges in the hinterland and on the frontier could not rely on Latin-trained freshmen. Thus they had to supply that training in their preparatory departments which also functioned as academies to train teachers for the common schools. For many years such colleges failed to graduate students with degrees. They reported larger enrollments in their preparatory than in their college classes. As one of their professors once remarked: 'We call our institutions colleges on the same principle upon which we call Christians saints; not for what they are but for what we expect they will be'.[35] Thus the charters of the antebellum colleges can best be seen as promissory notes than as certificates of character. Or, to mix metaphors, foundations had to be laid first that later generations might build their colleges and universities.

The lack of preparatory institutions in the new country also contributed to the blurring of the line between what we today define as secondary and higher education. The 'release of energy' gave small room to public ventures. The New England tradition of municipal Latin grammar schools faded out in the West, and Latin education became for all intents and purposes a field for private initiatives and enterprise. The law distinguished the colleges that were authorized by legislatures to grant degrees from institutions or individuals who were not. The latter therefore offered their Latin lessons in parsonages, churches, academies, and other schools of various designations and descriptions. By virtue of their charters the colleges could offer a Latin education on every level. If their students were inadequately prepared, they were admitted to the preparatory course or school; if they passed muster on admission, they enrolled in the college proper. Still, the phrase college or collegiate education encompassed the whole field of Latin instruction whether in preparatory school or class, academy, or college.

In the long view of history the local character of ante-bellum colleges and their founders and initial supporters not only distinguished them from the colleges of the colonial era, but also led most decisively to a legal re-definition of American higher education. The colonial colleges had all been provincial rather than local institutions. Harvard College had been the college of the Massachusetts Bay Colony, Princeton had functioned as the College of New Jersey, and the College of William and Mary had been the college for Virginia. With the single exception of Queen's College in New Jersey, the remaining colonial colleges, too, had each played a similar public role and enjoyed a collegiate monopoly in its province. Together with established or dominant church and with provincial assembly and governor, the colleges had represented public authority—a reminder of the old medieval arrangement of *sacerdotium, regnum, and studium* as the three public powers of the realm.[36]

This, however, could no longer be said of the colleges and churches in the ante-bellum years. The Dartmouth College Case decision of the United States Supreme Court in 1819 had recognized that colleges could be local or community institutions. No longer was it to be taken for granted that a college was a public institution. Its legal status was to depend on its charter of incorporation. The charter would reveal whether a state or other public agency had founded, i.e. funded the college, or whether a private person or group had supplied the first funds. The founder's public or private character would determine the legal status of the college. If the institution were a private foundation, the charter would protect it against interference by public authority without the consent of the college governors.[37]

The Dartmouth decision had ushered in a new era in the legal history of American higher education. By encouraging the private sponsorship of colleges as a means of promoting settlement and economic development, the Supreme Court aided the break with the exclusively public character of European and colonial Latin education. The nature of the new country, the 'release of energy' above all, invited this new departure and ushered in an era in which public and private institutions of higher education would develop side by side.[38] For the ante-bellum period in particular, it is the proliferation of the colleges as private institutions and the 'great retrogression' that accompanied it that catches the attention and the imagination. It is here and then that diversity became the hallmark of American higher education.[39]

The diversity of ante-bellum education

Legally diversity manifested itself in ante-bellum American higher education in the side-by-side existence and appearance of public and non-public colleges. This was the legacy of the Dartmouth decision. From a curricular point of view, the repeated calls for opportunities for the children of 'farmers and mechanics' to receive training in practical and applied scientific fields as well as for teaching in the common schools found only a reluctant hearing in the colleges. But they did result in the creation of various academy and high school level institutions and public as well as private normal schools. This added to 'the great retrogession' and kept fluid the distinction between secondary and higher education.

At the outset of the national period the tradition of the colleges as public institutions continued. The old colonial colleges now emerged as bastions of republicanism. The College of Philadelphia reappeared as the University of Pennsylvania, the Yale Corporation added state officials to its members, and the new state constitution of Massachusetts devoted an entire section to 'the University at Cambridge'. The trustees of Dartmouth College found themselves before the bar of the United States Supreme Court because the New Hampshire legislature had taken it as axiomatic that a provincial college was a public institution and that the legislators had the power to amend its charter.

New public colleges were founded in the young republic. State universities were chartered in Georgia in 1785, in North Carolina in 1789, in Vermont in 1791, and in South Carolina in 1801. Though founded by Presbyterians, Transylvania University in Kentucky as well as Blount College and Cumberland College in Tennessee functioned for years as public institutions.[40] Other state universities followed in Ohio in 1804, in Maryland in 1812, in Michigan in 1817, and in Virginia in 1819. Still more were opened in Alabama, Delaware, Indiana, and Missouri during the thirties, and in Iowa, Wisconsin, and Mississippi during the forties.

Yet Americans, by and large, were relunctant to support their public institutions. Given the similar nature of literary and scientific instruction in the regular college course in public as well as private colleges, few legislatures were ready to vote occasional or regular appropriations for their state universities. A college was a college, most legislators thought, and why should some schools be funded by the public when others were not? The predicament of public institutions was made worse because unlike the denominational and the local booster colleges they could not call for aid on member congregations and communities. In Tennessee President Phillip Lindsley would complain that as he and his University of Nashville belonged to no sect or party, they had no one to stand by and befriend them.[41] In North Carolina the friends of the university had tried in 1793 to persuade others to help: 'Episcopalians, Presbyterians, Methodists, Baptists, Universalists, and Society of Friends, peaceful Quakers, give!' But few of them did. Far too many thought the university to be a secular institution rife with infidelity and harbouring atheism.[42]

Life for public institutions remained precarious until long after the Civil War. Newspaper editorials and popular lecturers accused the public universities of ignoring the demands for a higher education responsive to the needs and interests of farmers and mechanics. In Wisconsin in 1850 the *Southport Telegraph* took the 'stall-fed denizens of Madison' to task for their preference to have the state university train doctors, lawyers, and ministers. 'If the friends of this literary hierarchy wish to find favor for it in the eyes of those who will be compelled to support it', the paper editorialized, 'let them make it an institution that shall be useful to the masses . . . and establish those departments which shall be open for the farmer and mechanic . . .'[43]

The key to the ineffectiveness of the early state universities lay in their failure to forge a bridge between the traditional liberal and professional education and the rising demand for practical studies in the sciences applied to agriculture and mechanics. As the regular college course was everywhere meant to remain scientific in a general and theoretical sense, the attempts to introduce new subjects such as chemistry into the curriculum usually stopped short of practical applications. At the time of its enactment, not even the Morrill Act with its injunction that in each state at least one university teach 'such branches of learning as are related to agriculture and the mechanic arts . . .' brought the desired change.[44]

Agriculture and, to some extent, engineering as well as other applied sciences remained the step-children of American collegiate education during the ante-bellum years. If we are to believe the complaints of President Francis Wayland of Brown, farmers and mechanics in particular desired such instruction for their sons. Wayland stated repeatedly that a college 'must carefully survey the wants of the various classes of the community in its vicinity' and then adapt its courses 'not for the benefit of one class, but for the benefit of all classes'. If Brown University were to offer instruction in agriculture, applied chemistry, and science, Wayland wrote, it would attract 'the agriculturist, the manufacturer, the mechanic, or the merchant . . .'[45]

Crusading for federal aid for a 'a university for the industrial classes', Jonathan Baldwin Turner predicted in Illinois that 'if every farmer's and mechanic's son . . . could now visit such an institution but for a single day in the year, it would do him more good in arousing and directing the dormant energies of mind, than all the cost incurred, and'—getting in his sally at the colleges with their regular course—'far more good than many a six months of professed study of things he will never need and never want to know'.[46]

But it wasn't the colleges or the universities that sought to meet this demand. Academies and high schools, the so-called 'people's colleges', offered agricultural and mechanical studies for students from farming and working class families. The first institution of this kind to become widely and favourably known was a public institution chartered by the Congress in 1802. This was the United States Military Academy at West Point, the country's first genuine scientific school. Engineering, drawing, and French were among the subjects studied.[47] Seventeen years later Captain Alden Partridge opened his Literary, Scientific and Military Academy at Norwich, Vermont, and offered instruction in engineering and linguistic, agricultural, and military studies. Students could take as much or as little time as they wished to finish the certificate course.[48]

A businessman followed where the soldiers had trod. Stephen Van Rensselaer endowed the Polytechnic Institute named after him at Troy, New York, in 1824 to afford 'an opportunity to the farmer, the mechanic, the clergyman, the lawyer, the physician, the merchant, and in short to the man of business or leisure, of any calling whatever, to become practically scientific'.[49] Rensselaer's message was clear: while the colleges would prepare young men for professional careers with the bachelor of arts course, the people's colleges were going to offer practical scientific instruction for vocational and professional purposes for as long and to whatever degree as all those who wanted it desired.

By 1815 proprietary medical schools had entered the list of institutions offering practical instruction without requiring a regular college course. In many ways their establishment paralleled the founding of the many local colleges across the country. Both types of schools suffered from the lack of well prepared students. The medical schools offered their doctoral course without requiring the completion of a prior bachelor of arts or medicine degree. As one historian put it, these proprietary medical colleges 'competed to provide the fastest, cheapest, and easiest education. The college that could make good on its claims to do all three could plan on having its benches filled to overflowing'.[50] Compared to the medical schools of the colonial period, the ante-bellum schools were retrograde indeed.

Gradually, the established colleges began to experiment with new and different ways to expand their scientific instruction. At Yale professorships in agricultural chemistry and in practical chemistry were established in 1846 'for the purpose of giving instruction to graduates and others not members of the undergraduate classes'. Thus began the School of Applied Chemistry and in 1854, after the addition two years earlier of a School of Engineering, the Yale Scientific School.[51] These foundations permitted the additions of new subjects for different students without either overloading or distorting the literary and scientific curriculum of the regular undergraduate course. Similar developments occurred at Harvard with the opening of the Lawrence Scientific School in 1847 and at Dartmouth with the Chandler School of Science.

A new step was taken with the opening in 1857 of one of the earliest public scientific schools. The Agricultural College of the State of Michigan in East Lansing began as a separate institution to train farmers and offer a bachelor's degree. From the start it offered a four-year curriculum of the liberal arts and sciences. Its students, so they, their parents, faculty members, and friends in the state's agricultural society argued, did not need practical instruction in agriculture. That was something they knew firsthand. What they needed was an understanding of scientific principles underlying agriculture so that they might be able to improve their farming practice, crops, and herds, and increase their marketing abilities. The college curriculum therefore stressed traditional college subjects and such practical fields as engineering, surveying, technology, and household economy.[52]

The college faced difficulties on two different fronts. Opposition arose in the legislature and the governing board. In order to hold down expenses, the members of these two bodies pushed for the elimination of the liberal arts curriculum as inappropriate to an agricultural school.[53] The college and its friends, however, successfully resisted and defeated these moves. More perplexing and frustrating because pointing to the heart of the agriculturalists' dilemma was the absence of a true agricultural science and of specialized teaching materials and techniques. For agricultural education on a college or university level to succeed, these had first to be developed.

Thus the real pioneering work of the college took place during the 1850s and 1860s in its laboratories and on its experimental fields where the means and methods for agricultural instruction had first to be created. The pay-off would come much later when by 1885 forty per cent of the graduates had been trained for and had gone into farming, a far higher percentage than achieved by the state universities. Building on the foundations laid in the 1860s the college then demonstrated how instruction in practical applications could be successfully joined to a rigorous collegiate curriculum in the liberal arts and sciences and a base of experimental research.[54]

As these concerns for scientific, agricultural, and medical education led to the founding of the new scientific schools, a similar felt need for professionally trained teachers led to other new initiatives. The new colleges in the West had provided a ready supply of male teachers for the secondary schools. Private academies, public normal schools, and female seminaries had sprung up to prepare teachers for the common schools. As by the 1840s elementary school teaching had become an occupation dominated by young women of college age, a small but growing number of these women teachers had been prepared in normal schools, female seminaries, and colleges. Here, too, as with the scientific schools, sustained growth would set in after the War. The ante-bellum years were years of incubation and hesitant beginnings.[55]

Far from being an age of retardation, retrogression, and stultifying monotony, the 'age of the college' contained in vibrant tension the demands of tradition and innovation. Its educational institutions reflected and served rather directly the varied components of its population in settled urban centres and on the raw agrarian frontier. Colleges took seriously their task of civilizing and humanizing a young and growing population, and scientists and scholars began to glimpse and to experiment with the task of mastering new skills and techniques of applied scientific, agricultural, and mechanical education. The call for teacher education could not be overheard. New institutions set off on their shake-down cruise, and if many of them failed their trials and tests, many others overcame their shortcomings and made permanent contributions.

Above all the ante-bellum years opened the colleges to men and women who until then had never dreamed of entering academic life. The sons and daughters of middle-class and poor families in city and country sought out colleges and normal schools, scientific academies and female seminaries to create for themselves a new place and role in life. Aided by their elders through voluntary education societies they availed themselves of private and of public generosity. They demonstrated their need and their determination to be educated. Together with the founders and supporters of all these colleges, schools, institutes, seminars, and academies in all their variety, haphazardness, and precarious abandon, they translated their faith in a democratic society into educational reality.

References

1. The reference is to Laurence R. Veysey, *The Emergence of the American University* (Chicago, 1965).
2. The classic expression of this view is Donald G. Tewksbury, *The Founding of American Colleges and Universities* (New York, 1932 and 1965); see also the critique, Natalie A. Naylor, 'The Ante-Bellum College Movement: A Reappraisal of Tewksbury's Founding of American Colleges and Universities', *History of Education Quarterly*, XIII (Fall 1973), 261–274.
3. George P. Schmidt, *The Liberal Arts College: A Chapter in American Cultural History* (New Brunswick, 1957). Schmidt uses the phrase 'old-time college' and also published *The Old Time College President* (New York, 1930).
4. For a comprehensive statement of the newer view see Colin B. Burke, *American Collegiate Populations: A Test of the Traditional View* (New York, 1982). If Burke seems less willing than I am to credit the ante-bellum period with the diversification of academic institutions, it is because he compares that period with the decades after the Civil War when institutional diversification increased even more rapidly, whereas I compare the ante-bellum years with the colonial period and stress the diversification that had been unknown in the eighteenth century. On other aspects of contrasting the ante-bellum with the post-bellum period see David Potts, 'Students and the Social History of American Higher Education', *History of Education Quarterly*, XV (Fall 1975), 322.

379

5. I have taken the various names from the Illinois State Statutes of the period. See my 'Diversification in American Higher Education', in Konrad H. Jarausch (ed.), *The Transformation of Higher Learning 1860–1930* (Chicago, 1983), 196–206.

6. Such appraisals have been carried out before; see Douglas Sloan, 'Harmony, Chaos, and Consensus: The American College Curriculum', *Teachers College Record*. LXXIII (1971), 221–251; David Potts, 'American Colleges in the Nineteenth Century: From Localism to Denominationalism', *History of Education Quarterly*, XI (Winter 1971), 363–380; my own, 'American College History: Re-Examination Underway', *History of Education Quarterly*, XIV (Summer 1974), 259–266; and James McLachlan, 'The American College in the Nineteenth Century: Toward a Reappraisal', *Teachers College Record*, LXXX (December 1978), 287–306.

7. 'The great retrogession' is the title of a section in Richard Hofstadter's chapter on 'The Old-Time College' in his and Walter P. Metzger's, *The Development of Academic Freedom in the United States* (New York, 1955).

8. Hofstadter and Metzger, *The Development of Academic Freedom*. Their distinction was first severely criticized by James Axtell in his sparkling essay on 'The Death of the Liberal Arts College', *History of Education Quarterly*, XI (Winter 1971), 339–352.

9. For the latter point see George E. Peterson, *The New England College in the Age of the University* (Amherst, 1964).

10. I refer to the 'take-off' as set forth in W. W. Rostow, *The Stages of Economic Growth* (New York, 1963).

11. See Willard Hurst, *Law and the Conditions of Freedom in the Nineteenth-Century United States* (Madison, 1956), 3–32.

12. Jurgen Herbst, *From Crisis to Crisis: American College Government, 1636–1819* (Cambridge, MA, 1982), 94, 160.

13. Schmidt, *The Liberal Arts College*, 51.

14. Frederick Rudolph, *Curriculum: A History of the Undergraduate Course of Study since 1636* (San Francisco, 1977), p. 115. See also the trenchant critique of Rudolph's approach in David B. Potts, 'Curriculum and Enrollments: Some Thoughts on Assessing the Popularity of Antebellum Colleges', *History of Higher Education Annual*, I (1981), 88–109.

15. See David W. Robson, *Educating Republicans: The College in the Era of the American Revolution, 1750–1800* (Westport, CT, 1985), 29.

16. Robson, *Educating Republicans*, 177.

17. See Steven J. Novak, *The Rights of Youth: American Colleges and Student Revolt, 1798–1815* (Cambridge, MA, 1977).

18. Quoted in James McLachlan, 'The *Choice of Hercules*: American Student Societies in the Early 19th Century'. In Lawrence Stone (ed.), *The University in Society* (2 vols.; Princeton, 1974), ii. 463–464.

19. See David F. Allmendinger, Jr., *Paupers and Scholars: The Transformation of Student Life in Nineteenth Century New England* (New York, 1975), 8–27.

20. See Daniel J. Boorstin, who in his *The Americans: The National Experience* (New York, 1965), 152–161, introduced the concept of the 'booster college'.

21. On the role of colleges on the frontier see the chapter on 'The Small Colleges' in Peter C. Mode, *The Frontier Spirit in American Christianity* (New York, 1923).

22. See David B. Potts, '"College Enthusiasm!" As Public Response, 1800–1860', *Harvard Educational Review*, XLVII (February 1977), 31.

23. Alexis de Tocqueville, *Democracy in America*, ed. Phillips Bradley (2 vols.; New York, 1956), ii. 118.

24. James Fenimore Cooper, *The American Democrat* (New York, 1956), 89, 90.

25. Quotations are from the 'Original Papers in Relation to a Course of Liberal Education', *The American Journal of Science and Arts*, XV (January, 1829), 297–351.

26. Ezra Stiles, *Plan of a University: A Proposal Addressed to the Corporation of Yale College, 3 December 1777* (New Haven, 1953).

27. Stanley M. Guralnick, *Science and the Ante-Bellum American College* (Philadelphia, 1975), 24–41.

28. Codman Hislop, *Eliphalet Nott* (Middletown, CT, 1971), 226–227.

29. McLachlan, 'The American College in the Nineteenth Century', 294.

30. Quoted in Sloan, 'Harmony, Chaos, and Consensus', 236.

31. See James Findlay, '"Western" Colleges, 1830–1870: Educational Institutions in Transition', *History of Higher Education Annual*, II (1982), 37.

32. See Potts, 'American Colleges in the Nineteenth Century', 367, and Timothy L. Smith, 'Uncommon Schools: Christian Colleges and Social Idealism in Midwestern America, 1820–1950', *Lectures 1976–1977: The History of Education in the Middle West* (Indianapolis, 1978), 20.

33. Natalie A. Naylor, '"Holding High the Standard": The Influence of the American Education Society in Ante-Bellum America,' *History of Education Quarterly*, XXIV (Winter 1984), 479–497.

34. James Findlay, 'The SPCTEW and Western Colleges: Religion and Higher Education in Mid-Nineteenth Century America', *History of Education Quarterly*, XVII (Spring 1977), 31–62, and 'Agency, Denominations and the Western Colleges, 1830–1860: Some Connections between Evangelicalism and American Higher Education', *Church History*, L (1981), 64–80.

35. President Merriman of Ripon College, as quoted by J. P. Gulliver, 'Commencement at a Frontier College', in *College Days*, Ripon College, Ripon, Wisconsin, I (September 1868), 107.

36. Herbst, *From Crisis to Crisis*, 2.

37. For the nuances of terminology—whether local, private, or community—see my debate with John Whitehead in Whitehead and Herbst. 'How to Think About the Dartmouth College Case', *History of Education Quarterly*, XXVI (Fall 1986), 333–349.

38. Herbst, *From Crisis to Crisis*, 241–243.

39. See my 'Diversification in American Higher Education', in Jarausch (ed.), *The Transformation of Higher Learning 1860–1930*, 196–206.

40. See Merle Borrowman, 'The False Dawn of the State University', *History of Education Quarterly*, 1 (June 1961), 6–22.

41. From Lindsley's 1848 Commencement Address, quoted in Richard Hofstadter and Wilson Smith (edd.), *American Higher Education: A Documentary History* (Chicago, 1961), i. 378–379.

42. Quoted in Kemp P. Battle, *History of the University of North Carolina* (Raleigh, NC, 1907), i. 17.

43. *Southport Telegraph*, February 15, 1850.

44. Indiana and Wisconsin are cases in point. The legislature scorned Indiana University and gave the land grant funds to newly founded Purdue University, a private institution at Lafayette. In Wisconsin the land-grant state university was to develop the 'Wisconsin Idea' of faculty involvement in agriculture, business, and government in answer to the institution's critics. See Merle Curti and Vernon Carstensen, *The University of Wisconsin: A History, 1848–1925* (Madison, WI, 1949), ii. 109–110. For the Morrill Act see Edward Danforth Eddy, Jr., *Colleges for Our Land and Time: The Land-Grant Idea in American Education* (New York, 1956).

45. From Francis Wayland, 'Report to the Corporation of Brown University (1850)', in Theodore Rawson Crane (ed.), *The Colleges and the Public, 1787–1862* (New York, 1963), 136–141, *passim*.

46. Jonathan Baldwin Turner, 'A State University for the Industrial Classes (1850)', in Richard A. Hatch (ed.), *Some Founding Papers of the University of Illinois* (Urbana, 1967), 41.

47. Sidney Forman, *West Point: A History of the United States Military Academy* (New York, 1950), 51–60; Stephen E. Ambrose, *Duty, Honor, Country: A History of West Point* (Baltimore, 1966), 87–90.

48. William Arba Ellis, (ed.), *Norwich University, 1819–1911: Her History, Her Graduates, Her Roll of Honor*, vol. I *General History 1819–1911* (Montpelier, VT, 1911), 12–13.

49. Palmer C. Ricketts, *History of the Rensselaer Polytechnic Institute, 1824–1894* (New York, 1895), 55.

50. Martin Kaufman, *American Medical Education: The Formative Years, 1765–1910* (Westport, CT, 1976), 42.

51. Brooks Mather Kelley, *Yale: A History* (New Haven and London, 1974), 181–183. In 1861 the Yale Scientific School was renamed the Sheffield Scientific School.

52. Madison Kuhn, *Michigan State: The First Hundred Years, 1855–1955* (East Lansing, 1955), 62–64.

53. Willis F. Dunbar, *The Michigan Record in Higher Education* (Detroit, 1963), 85, 86, and Kuhn, *Michigan State*, 26, 27.

54. Kuhn, *Michigan State*, 118, 119.

55. Maris A. Vinovskis and Richard M. Bernard. 'The Female School Teacher in Ante-Bellum Massachusetts', *Journal of Social History*, X (Spring 1977), 322–345. See also the use of the same data by Carl F. Kaestle and Maris A. Vinovskis, *Education and Social Change in Nineteenth Century Massachusetts* (Cambridge, England, 1980).

96

THE COMMITTEE ON SOCIAL THOUGHT OF THE UNIVERSITY OF CHICAGO

John U. Nef

Source: *Universities Quarterly* III (1948–9): 678–86.

During the past one hundred and fifty years the course taken by history has been in directions different from those which have guided graduate study and scholarship in the world's universities. As a result of the new powers which science and engineering made available, all parts of the globe have been drawn into close interdependence. Each part has been filled with people; moving frontiers, like the one which existed in North America until the 1880's, have disappeared; insofar as the interests of humanity are concerned, political frontiers have become meaningless expressions of an age which the industrial revolution has left behind. The only problems which can arrest the attention of men and women everywhere are universal problems.

The need for a universal language which has resulted will not be satisfied by an Esperanto. Words can acquire a common meaning only when there exists a common understanding of the great experiences which all men and women share. There is no lack of words in the modern world. What are lacking are common sentiments and ideas, a common concept of a word such as the word "democracy." The need is for a substantial agreement on the great recurring issues of religion, philosophy, morality and art.

Yet learning and letters have been concerned increasingly during the past one hundred and fifty years with the particular rather than the general, with small special issues—resulting in regional studies even studies of a special city, town or small community. This movement has been pushed to the point where so universal a medium of expression as music or painting, which everyone can grasp without a knowledge of language, is treated as regional and sectional. Instead of gaining ground, the concept of humanity above all nations, which existed in Europe in the eighteenth century, has lost the serious and informed reality that it once possessed. Two centuries ago Montesquieu wrote, "If I knew of something beneficial to me but harmful to my family, I would eject it from my mind. If I knew of something beneficial to my family, but not to my country, I would try to forget it. If I knew of something beneficial to my country but harmful to Europe, or beneficial to Europe but harmful to the human race, I would regard it as a crime." This lofty sense of the mission of universality was shared by many distinguished eighteenth-century men, such as Burke and Gibbon, who spoke and wrote of Europe as "One great republic."

The disease of specialisation

The narrowing view of the responsibilities of the mind since the French Revolution, has been accompanied by a continued narrowing of the scope of scholarship. The two developments are undoubtedly interrelated. Comte was much troubled about the tendency toward specialisation when he wrote his *Cours de Philosophie Positive*, the last volume of which he finished in 1842. The divisions that have since appeared make the scope of individual research and writing in Comte's time seem very wide, the treatment of subjects very general.

The history of political economy may serve as an example. With Adam Smith the subject was closely knit both with statesmanship and with moral philosophy. In the late nineteenth century the economist was inclined to construe his obligation to be that of showing how goods could be produced in larger quantities, and distributed in the manner best suited to further increases in output. Which people should produce the goods, whether it was desirable in the interests of general happiness to produce some of them at all, were construed as questions for statesmen and philosophers. It was no part of the economist's task to inquire whether the statesmen or philosophers had the mission or the knowledge to settle these questions for the benefit of humanity. By the early twentieth century, economics itself was divided into a number of specialties. In the United States the graduate student, seeking the doctor's degree in economics, is offered a choice of many fields of specialisation, such as theory, money and banking, labour relations, statistics, accounting, economic history, history of economic doctrines, etc. In her recent book on George Eliot, Mrs. Bennett has suggested that specialisation is the occupational disease of the modern university.

Establishment of the Committee on Social Thought

The manifold problems which this disease presents led to the formation seven years ago of the Committee on Social Thought at the University of Chicago. It was started by a small group of men associated with Chancellor

Robert Hutchins, whose work for educational reform is already known in Great Britain. Gradually a small faculty has been built up as an integral part of the University of Chicago, but independent of the departments. Along with this faculty there is now a slightly larger group of graduate students and young scholars, chosen from many applicants. There is a two-fold basis of selection. Candidates are chosen because they have successfully demonstrated by their written work, or in the case of the youngest candidates have shown remarkable promise of demonstrating, a capacity to bring into an appropriate philosophical relationship two or more subjects which are treated separately by modern learning. They are chosen also because there is reason to believe that ideas, scholarship, and literary excellence constitute a life passion for them, and are not mere passing whims.

The movement toward extreme specialisation in scholarship has been accompanied by another movement which prolongs the system of the grammar school into adult life, and almost confounds the preparatory school and the university. Graduate students who may be in their thirties, or even in their forties, are obliged to accumulate what are known in the United States as "course credits"; that is to say, they are obliged to follow a stipulated number of lecture courses and seminars, many of which are prescribed, and at the close of each course to pass an examination on its subject matter. Two or three years of routine labour of this kind, in addition to the composition of a thesis (the subject of which is often set by a professor), are required for the doctor's degree. The notion of the advanced student as a junior colleague, which used to prevail in England, never took hold in the United States. Instead, as the number of graduate students multiplied, universities came to resemble factories, in that work for degrees was fashioned according to a prescribed pattern, under the direction of instructed foremen.

The Committee's aims and organisation

For this system of instruction, the Committee on Social Thought has endeavoured to substitute liberty under guidance and self-discipline. No subject of importance to man is regarded as outside the range of the Committee's work, provided adequate supervision can be found for the student. In this connection the Committee has solicited the help of professors in the humanities, the law school, the theological school, and the natural sciences, as well as in the social sciences, in other universities as well as in the University of Chicago. These professors have shown a most gratifying willingness to co-operate in guiding students.

In choosing their work, the students must have the approval of the Committee and any other professors especially concerned. But there are no "course" or "field" requirements. There is no obligation to attend formal lectures. For the faculty there are no prescribed subjects. Each member chooses the subject upon which he lectures and the number of lectures he gives each year, somewhat after the fashion of the Collège de France in Paris. In addition he accepts responsibility for the guidance of a certain number of students.

Two characteristics of modern knowledge present difficulties which seem almost insuperable to the scholar or thinker who is seeking for the universal in his special subject. One is the enormous quantity of information, of ideas, of theories. The other relates to the almost innumerable divisions into which knowledge and art are split. In the view of the Committee on Social Thought, the possibility of surmounting these difficulties rests in a combination of an instructed view of man and the universe (a view which can be derived from the great intellectual and cultural traditions of which we are heirs) with the creative union of two or more special subjects, which range all the way from physics to economics and from political thought to poetry.

The Committee on Social Thought has established a core of study which is called "The Fundamentals," conceived with the object of binding the independent work done by students and scholars into a common intelligibility. (For example, any student embarking on a study of inter-relations between economic, military, and intellectual history will be at a disadvantage unless he has a thorough general knowledge of—among others—the works of Thucydides, Aristotle, Cicero, Augustine, Aquinas, Grotius, Hobbes, Newton, and Comte.) "The Fundamentals" is conceived with the further object of giving the independent work order, form, and style, which will make it understandable to the serious public, insofar as possible independent of place and time. (Nothing is perhaps more helpful in connection with style than to have constantly before one models provided by Plato, Chaucer, Shakespeare, Bacon, Johnson, Burke, Racine, Goethe, Montaigne.) Students are expected to gain an understanding of philosophy—of both epistemology and ethics—which will permit them to make use of new and particular knowledge in relation to human happiness conceived as a whole, both for individual men and for societies. Students are expected to gain an understanding of history, which will enable them to recognise how all sides of human activity are interrelated.

The master's degree is designed for a new kind of scholarly teacher or leader—a teacher who will be capable of guiding and directing college and university students effectively in a more integrated and general training, such as is now being developed in a number of American colleges and in the British universities; a leader who will be capable, whatever vocation he enters, of approaching its problems on behalf of the general interests of humanity. The doctor's degree is designed for persons who have a flair for creative thought, or even art, who show promise of being able, by their works, to instruct and charm a serious world public with general interests.

Candidates for degrees are tested by a general written examination, which extends over a series of three or four days, and by the presentation of written work of a high order—various papers, if the student is a candidate for the master's degree, and a more extensive and sustained piece of writing if he is a candidate for the doctor's degree. A candidate for the doctor's degree is expected, in addition, to deliver a public lecture, setting forth the contribution which he has made to the objectives for which the Committee exists.

Specialists in interrelations

Comte's proposal for meeting the problems of over-specialisation was to create specialists in interrelations, who would settle all issues by positive methods of handling evidence, derived from the natural sciences. Neo-Comtians, who propose to unify knowledge by specialising in interrelations, are numerous today in the United States. But to specialise in interrelations has frequently meant to adopt the vices of specialisation without the virtues. This form of labour contributes to superficiality. What is needed is not a bit of everything, but an appropriate selection of subject matter and methods in which a man can become a master. Specialisation is fundamental to the achievement of great results; it is only by limiting a subject that there is any possibility of speaking in universal terms. The vital matter is that the subject shall be limited, both as to matter and as to methods of using the matter, by a rational effort to achieve a universal purpose, rather than narrowed, merely for the sake of a result that is novel, regardless of its importance for man.

Unification of knowledge

The Committee on Social Thought is convinced that the problems of universal understanding, to which it aims in all humility and modesty to make a contribution, are not to be met either by the use of scientific methods alone or by the imposition of any of the existing dogmas, whether religious, political or economic. The Committee represents, we hope, a return to the Jeffersonian tradition of freedom of inquiry in which the American Republic was founded. Yet the Committee represents a sharp break with the current American dogma that science and engineering, medicine and surgery provide means of unifying knowledge and human beings. Here, as in the matter of the formalities and methods of graduate instruction, the work of the Committee presents a notable alternative to the accepted procedure in America and in other countries, among them Russia, a procedure which assumes that paradise can be achieved simply by technical progress, the multiplication and the more equitable distribution of this world's goods.

Several religious persuasions are represented in the Committee. These range from Roman Catholicism to agnosticism. Many kinds of scholarship are represented, from philosophy to history and to anthropology. Before long we hope the Committee will have on its staff a natural scientist and a man of letters. We are of the opinion that all these religions and all these learned disciplines have something to contribute to the formation of a universal intellectual community, provided the men who represent them are aware of the limitations of their special institutions and subjects, and are striving to transcend them in their search for Truth.

Studies and research

The time is coming—perhaps it has already arrived—when the Committee on Social Thought must be judged by its fruits. Works have begun to appear. Professor Otto von Simson has just published a book entitled *Sacred Fortress*. In it he has managed to show the relations between art, politics and religion at Ravenna in the time of Justinian. Simson was the first executive secretary of the Committee on Social Thought and he is soon to edit a journal called "Measure," whose board of editors has been chosen from the Committee on Social Thought. Chancellor Hutchins is chairman of this board of editors. Daniel Boorstin's recent book, *The Lost World of Thomas Jefferson*, has received some attention in England. It represents one of the first attempts to consider as a whole the intellectual history of the United States, in its relation to history generally. Professor Robert Redfield, the distinguished anthropologist, is soon to publish a volume in which he examines the position of a small Mexican village in relation to the great industrialised world into which it is being pulled. Further books are on the stocks. One is by David Grene, the new executive secretary, who was trained at Trinity College, Dublin. His book is concerned with the significance of Thucydides and Plato inside of a new interpretation of the Periclean age and its meaning for today. Professor Yves R. Simon, the Thomist philosopher, has nearly ready a "Philosophy of Democratic Government," while P. H. von Blanckenhagen, the classical archæologist, has nearly finished a work called "The Image of Man in Greek and Roman Art." Other books deal with the interrelations between war and industrial civilisation, and with the nature and meaning of "democracy," a word which stands in such dire need of clarification.

Special hope is put by the Committee in the work which its students have in hand. Limits of space prevent me from going into detail. I must confine myself to the studies of two men, each of whom gave up four critical years of his life to army service in the European theatre. One of them is writing on the period of Melville in American letters, and out of his work should emerge a better understanding of the peculiar American sense of time, which led to so much hurry and noise, and gave rise to a neat remark of Henry James, that this is a country where the landscape is made for the railroads. The other book is devoted to late fifteenth-century Florence, and in particular to Lorenzo de Medici. Based on materials in Italian archives, this book should bring out the significance of the view which the Italian mind took of all sides of life as art. The book should help us to understand an attitude which had much to do with keeping warfare within bounds during the three centuries when a modern sense of European community developed, from the time of the Reformation to the French Revolution.

The Committee on Social Thought began its publications two years ago with a volume called *The Works of the Mind*, edited by Robert Heywood. In it a number of eminent men of our time, in art, thought, science, and in affairs, set forth the nature of work in connection with their specialties. Their papers show how work of integrity in the most diverse fields has a common purpose and a common intellectual origin in a combination of what Pascal called the *esprit géométrique* and the *esprit de finesse*. Among the contributors to the volume were Marc Chagall, Arnold Schönberg, Frank Lloyd Wright, Professor Charles McIlwain, ex-Chancellor Bruening, Senator Fulbright, John von Neumann, the mathematician, and Alfeo Faggi, one of the best modern sculptors.

From these names, it is apparent that many nationalities are represented. The community which the Committee would like to serve transcends the universities and the nations. It is the community on behalf of which Montesquieu wrote. During the present year at least five out of the dozen members of the Committee's active staff have been abroad lecturing at the invitation of foreign universities, in England, Germany, Sweden, France, Mexico, and China. One member, Edward A. Shils, who shares with David Grene the duties of executive secretary, has a joint appointment with the London School of Economics which keeps him in Great Britain for a part of each year.

International co-operation

Five or six of our students are in Europe at the present time. In return we are expecting European students who share our objectives here in Chicago. A start has been made with the University of Paris. The Committee will have each year one student whose training began in the University of Paris, while the University of Paris will have each year one student whose training began under the Committee.

Of immense value have been the visits paid the Committee by foreign thinkers, artists and scholars, among them Professor R. H. Tawney, Professor A. P. d'Entrèves, H. S. Bennett, Professor Jacques Maritain, Dr. Artur Schnabel, and Professor Arnold Toynbee.

Continuous international relations of these kinds are vital to the Committee's purpose. One of the causes for intellectual atrophy in university communities is their ingrowing character. The members of the faculty are inclined to think of any problem in terms of the local rules and regulations, even the local social life of their university. They are inclined to forget that unless the university serves the world, it has no reason for existence. By the

389

formation of an international group of sponsors, the Committee should be continually reminded of its responsibility to serve the universal.

It is indispensable that work of the kind the Committee on Social Thought has undertaken should be carried on in an intimate way, independently of the means of mass communication—the radio, the cheap newspapers, and magazines, which have done so much to mechanise what should be natural, to stereotype what should be creative, to cheapen what should be valuable and even sacred. As Henry Adams wrote, "Any large body of students stifles the student. No one can instruct more than half-a-dozen students at once."

With the triumph of industrial civilisation all over the world in the past one hundred and fifty years, the intelligent cultivation of the creative life outside the universities has all but disappeared, at any rate in the United States. It is part of the obligation of the Committee on Social Thought to help in reviving this creative life. The attitude toward knowledge and art which a group like the Committee on Social thought hopes to exemplify, together with the discoveries which it hopes to make, will have to be disseminated in ways that do not destroy their meaning and value. While the members gathered together at any time must remain small, the students will be going out in the world. The Committee will encourage the formation of other groups with similar aims. To the development of these some of the students can contribute. Others, who enter fields such as politics, journalism, or art, can help to humanise, universalise and internationalise these fields. As Voltaire once wrote, "A historian has the duty, without being a pedagogue, to instruct the human race." The same is true of all the other disciplines which are associated in the Committee on Social Thought.

97

THE AMERICAN MODULAR
SYSTEM

Sheldon Rothblatt

Source: R. O. Berdahl, G. C. Moodie and I. J. Spitzberg (eds) *Quality and Access in Higher Education: Comparing Britain and the United States*, Buckingham: SRHE and Open University Press, 1991, pp. 129–41.

Modularity: introduction

The world's first democratic nation is also the world's first mass-access higher education system. The special characteristics of American higher education regarded as a *system* are market discipline; diversified sources of funding; competition for students, faculty and resources; strong presidents and boards and comparatively weak academic senates; a process of 'articulation' allowing students from one kind of college or university to 'transfer' to another without loss of time; and the absence of a common 'idea' of a university except 'service' to 'society'. In the public segment, government action is often intrusive; but it is also confused, contradictory and divided, since government itself is subject to multiple and self-cancelling pressures arising from an unpredictable electorate and shifts in 'public opinion'.

American higher education is also characterized by a great variety of types of institutions and standards and a certain hesitation to proclaim one intrinsically superior to the other, even within what may be defined as the élite sector. A report to the Board of Harvard Overseers written in 1886 cautioned that it was 'well . . . that young men in college should become used to the standards which prevail in the world outside, where a man's rank among his fellows is determined by many different considerations, and anything approaching the mathematical inaccuracy of a college rank list is unknown'.[1] By contrast, the nineteenth-century history of Oxford and Cambridge is characterized by precisely such an effort (especially at the latter) to rank undergraduates by order of merit.

Most of the cardinal features of the American higher education system are captured in the organization of the curriculum, which, with several exceptions, is modular in form. The modular system can only be appreciated as a special creation of American history and society, importing local and national tensions into colleges and universities while also providing for alternatives and digressions.

While a remarkable artefact, the American modular system is virtually taken for granted. It is assumed to be axiomatic, a basic and timeless feature of higher education, although few are conscious of its origins and functions. The system does not even possess a common name. The word 'modular' – at least as applied to the American courses structure – is not in everyday use. Possibly it was first used in connection with the lower levels of the education system; but it may well be a British import, or an import subsequently exported, for in Britain the word is assumed to be American in origin.[2]

In the 1930s, the designations 'unit system' and 'college hour system', or more pejoratively, 'time-exposure system', were used. Americans today frequently say 'course system', but in Britain the word 'course' is more akin to the American academic word 'programme'. The British use of the word 'course' is monotheistic, but the American is polytheistic. Monotheism, it has been said, is characterized by rigour, jealousy and exclusion, while polytheism is relaxed, tolerant, careless and inclusive. Recently, designations like 'credit-unit' or 'course-unit' system have been employed, but neither of these is very precise. (Nevertheless, the University of East Anglia adopted the language 'course-unit system' to describe its teaching.) The word 'modular' is not necessarily less vague. While conveying the necessary meaning of a structure of detachable, separate parts and distinct pieces, its use is nevertheless fraught with semantic difficulties. It may, for example, suggest standardized units of study where none in fact exist. In some respects the word is actually misleading, implying intensive not concurrent units of study, as in the bloc 'modular' inter-sessional curriculum of Colorado College, Colorado Springs.

In so far as any kind of degree programme may be chopped into modular bits, the word 'module' does not automatically convey the American meaning of a degree programme that is actually built upward from the bottom of the curriculum. The degree itself is little more than a container for collecting modules from different parts of the study list, such as the 'major', free electives, and choices from a range of breadth and proficiency requirements. By itself, modularity suggests nothing about 'articulation', early twentieth-century educational jargon used to describe the process by which the module as a unit of exchange facilitates the working of transfer mechanisms. From this feature of American higher education modularity acquired the designation 'credit transfer' system. But if no single word or phrase provides a shortcut for understanding the essential nature of the American higher education curriculum, 'module', 'modularity' and 'modularization' (when properly qualified) will have to suffice.

Modularity: history

That much abused notion 'system' does in truth describe the American curriculum, which is composed of many separate elements of different origin linked together over time. In the beginning (for our purposes) was the old unified (and interdisciplinary) collegiate curriculum or 'class system' influenced by Scottish practice and carried over from the later eighteenth century. Undergraduates were divided into distinct cohorts by year, and the subjects for each year's cohort were specified. The class system persisted right up to the middle of the nineteenth century and beyond, but beginning in the 1820s (or perhaps earlier) a number of institutions began to experiment with alternatives, usually in the form of parallel subject tracks providing students with elective choices. The introduction of electives has been called 'the central educational battle of nineteenth-century America . . . the question which aroused the greatest amount of controversy [and] inflamed passions as no other educational issue was able to do'.[3] The issues were legion: the value of collegiate versus professional or 'university' education; the definition of a liberal culture; the place of religion in the curriculum; character formation versus knowledge for individual consumption and use; discipline versus self-motivation; curricular innovation versus the old-time college class system.[4]

Consumer choice with respect to curriculum is an aspect of the transformation of American society from a grouping of colonies in a virgin wilderness to a self-governing federal union increasingly urban, and what subsequently became known as the 'elective system' was intricately connected to the making and remaking of American society.[5] The exact historical origins of electives are vague. Conceivably electives originated at Edinburgh University in the very early eighteenth century where they were called the 'voluntary' system. Thomas Jefferson, credited by some historians with introducing electives to America, had a Scottish teacher at the College of William and Mary in Virginia, and it was at colonial William and Mary that several scholars find traces of an elective principle in the late eighteenth century. But despite the undeniably great influence of the Scottish university on post-1750 American education, the evidence for a Scottish modular precedent is slight and the specific example fleeting.[6]

Indigenous ideas of democracy and a belief in individual self-reliance were factors in the kind of elective system introduced by Jefferson and the Jeffersonians in the University of Virginia founded in the mid-1820s. Support for variety in the curriculum could also be obtained from German sources on the freedom of teaching and the freedom of learning which penetrated Harvard in the 1820s and resulted in the introduction of a limited amount of choice. In general, many different ideologies associated with voluntarism and consumerism existed in nineteenth-century America, many different ways in which electives could and were used, many different types of elective systems were in operation: systems with no restrictions, with partial restrictions, with choice among alternatives, or choice in some sectors of the curriculum but not in others, or partial or full choice in some undergraduate years but not in others. Choice could exist in sequences and timetabling but not in actual courses. Where introduced, 'parallel' tracks allowed for the coexistence of older programmes of study and curricular experiments, and some tracks led to new types of degrees. As in Victorian Britain, separate degree programmes were used to protect the historic BA standard, but mixtures are also in evidence: compulsory with optional modules or tracks, providing full, limited, or no choice in some tracks. Almost all of the typical curricular forms in use in the United States today – mandatory foundation-year courses, capstone courses, two-year collegiate 'seminars' – were known and experimented with in the last century. Americans have never ceased to tinker with combinations of electives and requirements, with ways of joining or separating modules, ever since that famous (or infamous) day on which the diversified curriculum of the present first revealed its educational and administrative potential.[7]

However, the story of the voluntary curriculum or electives, unquestionably important to the history of undergraduate education, is only one part of a larger development. First, elective parallel tracks had to be completely broken into discrete parts (the American 'courses' of today) in order to become self-contained modules where teaching and examining were combined. As this occurred, degree examinations – the oldest type of American college examinations, extending back into the seventeenth century – diminished in importance. Examinations were more or less uncoupled from the degree and instead attached to modules, where every kind of evaluation was possible. Examinations were also scheduled at the convenience of the individual professor, as happened at the state university of Michigan as early as 1833, and the net effect of this transfer was a reinforcement of the practice of continuous assessment, consisting of frequent exercises, quizzes, recitations and examinations. As American higher education did not yet sit atop a lower system of feeder schools, the college and university environment continued to resemble a school. Not until the influence of the graduate school of the twentieth century was felt in the undergraduate curriculum did the core letters and science college become more like a university.

A second and essential step was providing for articulation, so that students could move modules from one kind of institution to another, generally to improve their social or career opportunities. (The migratory American student is not and never was the *Wandervogel* of German romance, pursuing knowledge in and for itself.) If the student transferred, but without modular credits, then obviously the time to degree as well as expenditures increased, and such prolongation of the years of higher education was unacceptable to families of modest means. Furthermore, to encourage upward academic mobility, it was essential to have institutions of very great variety, of different academic standards, levels of cost and geographical location, responsive to very different kinds of educational markets. Otherwise, no useful service was performed in having the student exchange one kind of educational experience for another.

Very likely in the 1870s, or soon thereafter, modules were assigned an arithmetical equivalent connecting the separate capsules of teaching to hours of instruction, thus creating the banking or trading-stamp system that characterizes the administration of nearly all American modular arrangements. The employment of units of credit appears to have been exclusively internal to begin with, a form of domestic book-keeping to provide some means of determining the relative weighting of modules. Severed from parallel course tracks, modules threatened the higher education system with chaos, and among the list of concerns was the fear that unless limits were assigned to student work loads, undergraduates would be overly taxed. The whole vexed problem of defining a work load was in fact beginning to puzzle the American academy, and credit units were therefore a functional substitute for some kind of overall administrative co-ordination of a curriculum transformed into a riot of courses.

The use of units to define transfer work is a feature of the Progressive Era, the period from about 1900 to the First World War, and enters public debate in tandem with calls for standardized testing. Much of the surviving literature from the period is concerned with units principally as a means of bringing order into the typical disorder of American lower education and of stabilizing the curriculum in secondary schools, whose enormous variability was continuing to trouble a higher education community preoccupied with the problems of regularizing the process of university admissions. Because the newly established Carnegie Foundation for the Advancement of Teaching was particularly active in promoting the idea of a common national measure, the unit of credit became known as the 'Carnegie Unit'. At the time of their introduction, units were frequently attacked as a device for measuring classroom quality and the value of academic work,[8] but such was never the intention of their creators, and units have remained quantitative indicators only, a means of tabulating the amount of time presumably spent in studying a particular subject. A number of years elapsed before a universally recognized definition of unit did in fact take hold.

The history of units is fascinating but essentially obscure. Aetiological detail and how units became entangled with a method of evaluation called 'grade points' are missing from historical narrative and remain puzzling.

It is not absolutely necessary to assign numerical work load equivalents to courses for purposes of transferring modules. The system would work if transfer credit were simply given for whole or half courses, although the problems of defining a 'course' stubbornly remain. Today, some aspects of articulation are actually conducted through courses rather than credit units; but units provide more flexibility, permitting the accumulation of many kinds of partial courses as well as numerical fragments and allowing for the simple calculation of an overall average measure of achievement.

Over a period of approximately half a century, the various elements of the American educational system – electives, modules, units, grade points, transferring, continuous assessment, teaching combined with examining, articulation – grew together to form the everyday curricular structure so familiar today. Accompanying that process, indeed caused by it, was the growth of a complex body of regulatory academic legislation which is often a nightmare to administer; and in the wake of legislation, as only to be expected, came a body of faculty and non-faculty administrators.

A connected account of the origins, growth and variations of the interesting and important history of the expansion of the American modular system does not exist. But after all, the story may not appear so interesting and important to potential readers and auditors. It is administrative history, a tiresome account of tiny details congealing into a system, slowly without an identifiable master artificer carefully shaping a massive educational structure. No heroic personalities combat nearly insurmountable odds. No social classes contend for mastery of the economic machine. No threats of revolution hang in the air. The story is humdrum. Yet the American modular structure is a way of life for millions of young persons and for the entire academic profession. It is the means by which a culture attempts to fulfil the life aspirations of its energetic citizenry, aspirations that range from mere getting-on to happy dreams of personal fulfilment and renown. It is a playing out on the stage of universities and colleges of the story of how the United States has accommodated egalitarian pressures and distributed satisfactions in the form of educational access and opportunity, while attempting to retain – where such attempts are made – examples of excellence, merit and originality which by definition cannot be indiscriminately bestowed.

Modularity today: merits

The merits or advantages of the American modular system as it has evolved in conjunction with other features such as articulation, the combining of teaching and examining in one person, and consumer demand, may be identified as flexibility and *Lehrfreiheit*. Flexibility refers to the capacity of the modular system to alter the curriculum with comparative ease and to accommodate diverse student interests and levels of preparation within a single institution. Programmes and courses for an élite group of students can and do exist side-by-side with courses taken by the majority. The liberal arts, professional and technical studies are all provided for in one fashion or another. Just as the existence of a public sector of higher education in America protects the private sector (by absorbing pressures for admission and expansion), so does the availability of ordinary courses protect and guarantee more demanding courses for a smaller number of high-achieving undergraduates. Rigorous methods of assessment intermingle with routine evaluation. Courses can usually be added to or substracted from the overall curriculum without fuss, provided they are not compulsory and have the imprimatur of a recognized teaching unit.

Modular flexibility also rather directly furthers the American concern for social mobility by allowing for the entry into classrooms of non-traditional students who can be given special assistance or encouragement as time and attitude permit; and the system allows (and sometimes forces) the instructor to adjust the pace of learning to the perceived ability level of the class. Modularity provides a fairly simple solution to the controversial question of admitting underprepared students. Remedial courses can be added without disrupting the 'coherence' of the curriculum because, as critics mockingly notice, the American modular system has no coherence anyway. No course needs to be removed to make room for another, but such seeming generosity has a farcical side. Courses are listed that are seldom taught, and in some institutions many listed courses are never given at all because the resource base is weak. But the fiction is maintained to legitimize the curriculum, especially if the title 'university' has been claimed and the institution feels beholden to the mission of disseminating 'universal knowledge'.

Part-time attendance is possible under a modular system, although an institution may wish to control this traffic with a minimum progress-to-degree rule. The number and variety of courses can be co-ordinated with the admissions policy and adjusted to demand, sometimes quite suddenly, as in the teaching of foreign languages or sections of mathematics, that is to say, wherever prerequisites are essential.

By *Lehrfreiheit* (the word has important historical associations for Americans, for the earliest generations of course reformers were always conscious of the German example) is meant the relative freedom of faculty to create and teach in modules and to assign the corresponding student work load. The content of book lists, lecture presentations and discussion sections can be altered at will, as can certain aspects of the student work load, e.g. the number of intermediate examinations, quizzes, critical essays and term papers. Assignments can be revised, reduced, increased, adjusted; marking standards can be modified en route and so on. However, the changes must not be seen to be sudden or unfair, for students enter the classroom assuming instructors have agreed to a social contract based on the course description distributed in advance.

Because the single instructor is rarely asked to teach to a syllabus designed by a civil service ministry or government agency, a board of studies, or even an academic department composed of peers, the American modular system is *professorial* in the classic Oxbridge sense. Lectures are not linked to a degree examination. Research results can be incorporated into the course without delay, so the connection between teaching and research is as strong as the instructor desires. The only substantial external control on the actual content of a course derives from peer pressure, the internalized standards of the discipline, or student complaints too vociferous to ignore. It is in the hiring of faculty that an institution attempts to assure itself of the quality of teaching, although some further assessment occurs at critical review steps in the academic career ladder. Recently, the members of some state legislatures have raised the possibility of different kinds of assessments, but no debate has yet occurred comparable to the discussions over 'value-added' measurements that took place in the Britain of the 1980s.

Just as modularity can exist without articulation, so can it thrive without continuous assessment, but the two are natural allies and together strengthen the instructor's control over the classroom. The utility of continuous assessment is well understood, especially when contrasted with its customary opposite, the single-subject degree course. A student's progress is easily measured, encouragement and warnings are given on a frequent or regular basis, and because of the instructor's autonomy in the classroom, grades or marks can be adjusted according to a teacher's understanding of improvement. Assignments can be weighted as to their importance (usually progressively, but a final grade can also be awarded on the basis of the two or three best pieces of work the student has done). Compensatory work can be allowed if students are desperate for a second chance. Unlike the single-subject honours degree in Britain, assigned after exhausting combat with unseen questions drawn from 'papers', continuous assessment in modular form allows for a poor performance to be counterbalanced by a more successful one. Mistakes are not fatal. An unfortunate experience is soon over with few lasting consequences. *Amour-propre*, that pleasant cherub, is always to be found lurking on the premises. There is no Judgement Day. For these same reasons, success in examinations does not carry quite the cachet in America that it does in Britain. An 'A' student never acquires the glamour attributed to a 'First-Class Mind', since some of the modules contributing to the 'A' record may have been breathers, inserted into the game to allow even star players a chance to gain a second wind.

In Chapter II, Oliver Fulton points out that critics of the British terminal honours examination system argue that undergraduates have too much time on their hands and are inclined to be idle until the period of count-down commences. Preparation for examinations should be steady and regular, whereas in reality it is no more than cramming. Learning acquired at the last minute is just as readily lost.

Perhaps; but preparation for examinations is always at the eleventh hour in any country, even where continuous assessment exists. For that reason, nineteenth-century teachers spoke about the educational superiority of critical essays or term papers. However that may be, it is a fact of history that 'wasting time' has often been a feature of Anglo-American élite systems of education. Learning takes place within a carefully structured environment where a peer-group culture is as important as classroom instruction. Students are supposed to learn as much from one another as from teachers – this feature is 'designed' into the system. The rationale is clear. Leisure is required to promote peer interaction, to allow students an opportunity for self-discovery, wide reading, and valuable extra-curricular activity, such as acting, journalism, music, games and further networking and contacts. If *Lehrfreiheit* describes the American modular system, then a particular kind of *Lehrfreiheit* describes the single-subject honours degree.

Comprehensive terminal examinations on unseen papers with blind marking can only be usefully employed where undergraduates are known to have the requisite skills and necessary self-discipline to acquire a certain amount of proficiency on their own. Continuous assessment on the American model actually suggests a lack of faith in the ability of undergraduates to work independently, to examine material critically, recognize contradictions, define problems, read widely, or pursue subjects of special interest to them. Wherever faculty direction is obviously loose, student educational choices in America tend to be governed by advertising and fads, the classic means of influencing consumer choice. The 1960s student demand for a wholly elective curriculum on the grounds that the consumer was the best judge of his own interest was not a call for educational freedom so much as another instance of American market economics. But the relatively weak elementary and secondary structures of education in the United States invalidate most student claims to intellectual independence.

Taken together, American modularization and continuous assessment describe a system of higher education that combines student demand with professorial self-interest. Both partners to the teaching relationship have an opportunity to express preferences. Students have a chance to select individual classes, and student preferences are most respected where a campus is particularly vulnerable to market discipline. The faculty have an opportunity to more or less teach the courses they choose in a manner they choose according to methods they select without undue concern for continuity or syncopation with their neighbours' modules.

A signal feature of American forms of modularity is their place in furthering the objectives of a second- and third-chance society, one that attempts to minimize both the actual and perceived results of failure. Where access is universal (or nearly so), the risk of failure is always present. The modular system breaks the fall. Despite students' fears, rarely do their educational or career opportunities rest on the outcome of a single academic adventure. Life generally begins again with another module. While certain courses may weigh more heavily in a given programme of studies than another, in general it is the grade-point average that matters. Students rely upon the invisible hand of the academic market-place to smooth out the aberrations, compensate for the errors and correct the overall academic record. The system is self-adjusting: a poor performance is balanced by a better one, although by the same token a strong showing in one module is compromised by a weak one in another.

Modularity today: drawbacks

No higher education system can meet every objection, nor satisfy every criticism, and each must surely contain drawbacks when compared to another. The drawbacks to modularity are many: they are expense, administration, scheduling, work-load definition, the absence of common standards of achievement and measurement, the burden of uniting teaching with examining, the difficulty of establishing effective academic advising procedures, and competition for the student vote arising from the pressure to attract numbers whenever institutional income is threatened.

The old college or class system with its prescribed and limited curriculum confidently rested on the teaching of a few generalists and could survive considerable faculty turnover. Indeed, such turnover was built into the college system as a means of cost control, younger faculty replacing older ones. But modules require specialists, and free electives imply a great range of subjects and large academic (and non-academic) staffs; and since the fixed costs of higher education depend largely on the investment in people, the expenses associated with modularity are substantial, especially as the knowledge base grows and sub-specialization occurs.

Administrative costs are high. Bringing the modules together into some sort of relationship however tenuous and providing even minimal external co-ordination absorbs the energies of department heads, senate committees, deans and their staff. Evaluating transfer equivalents from several thousand different institutions and educational programmes, keeping track of credits and grade points, making exceptions to the rules, advising students on the myriad of regulations that have accumulated around modularity and hearing appeals require a staggering amount of time and energy. The modular system is also a scheduling nightmare. Generated by the American concern for flexibility, modules are often created but rarely destroyed, and this soon leads to problems of classroom space and competition for hours.

As a measure of learning, the assignment of credit units on a basis of classroom contact hours is meaningless, and on a basis of student work load, arbitrary and nonsensical. Neither uniformity of input nor of output is possible. Substantial writing assignments exist in some social science and humanities courses but not in others. Some faculty are dismayed by student prose, others are satisfied with ball-park approximations. The pace of learning and absorption differs radically from student to student, and faculty demands upon student energies and abilities are so varied as to make even the idea of a common measure nearly ludicrous.

Like any legal or taxation system that is unenforceable as written, the credit-unit system will continue to produce elaborate fictions and evasions.

The *mythos* of a standard measure is maintained while in practice students manipulate study lists and negotiate exceptions with equally frustrated or sceptical faculty. Since there is no effective immediate outside control on the internal quality of a given course, there is really no practical means of preventing downward academic drift in a certain number of courses. (Conversely, there is no external constraint on higher standards if the traffic is willing.)

The very same diversity of achievement levels which permits a flexible overall pedagogical response is also the bane of a single classroom teacher's existence. In a 1980s survey of Berkeley faculty, 90% of the respondents identified uneven student preparation and ability as a hindrance in teaching large lecture courses. Should lectures be designed to bring up the bottom, reach the 'average' student, or attract the ablest?[9]

No feature of the American modular system so disturbs critics as the absence of coherence in the curriculum. Building-block sequences are the natural exception. Connections are strongest in foreign languages and mathematics, weakest in the social sciences and humanities. Hence a perennial cry has been for 'coherence and integrity' in the curriculum.[10] The proposed solutions – team-teaching, interdisciplinary courses, separately housed programmes, or mini-colleges – ironically defeat their intentions, since such innovations are seldom compulsory. Consequently, they merely increase the number of choices, compounding the difficulties of the existing course structure.

Modularity exacerbates tensions in the teaching relationship. Faculty are pulled between different role conceptions. Are they liberal arts teachers responsible for forming character, encouraging learning, inculcating discipline and drawing out the innate powers of the mind, a mixture, that is to say, of academic and 'humane' objectives? Or are the professors patient but stubborn representatives of the Higher Criticism, committed to the very best standards of scholarship and science, unwilling to suffer fools gladly? Is the student only a mind upon which is inscribed bold, soaring and sophisticated ideas, or also a person, distinct and special, if momentarily buried beneath alluvial deposits of academic sediment and bureaucratic dust? Such ambivalences make faculty vulnerable to student plea-bargaining for grades and exceptions. They also interfere with efforts to establish informal and personal teaching relationships, such as those existing in systems where teaching and examining are strictly partitioned.

No system of pedagogy is perfectly free of conflict, if simply because some element of coercion is always present in a process of socialization; but the conflicts are greatest where authority is the most visible. However they may feel about their education – and all the available recent survey data indicate that undergraduates generally approve of the ways in which they have been taught – American students often behave as if their college and more especially their university is a collection of obstacles to be overcome, from impersonal record-keeping officers conspiring to prevent their graduation to faculty who are sometimes defended as themselves the victims of a mysterious bureaucracy. But since a university bureaucracy does not itself examine and assign marks, blame can only be laid upon teachers, whose classroom autonomy is so manifest.

The graduate student instructor adds yet another layer of confusion to the teaching relationship. The instructor enrolled for a degree is an intermediary also caught between roles, being neither a regular member of the faculty nor just a student – an ambivalence that in some institutions is addressed by the formation of collective bargaining unions for graduate students to secure benefits, increase independence and improve status.

A major defect of modularity is the difficulty of establishing a really satisfactory mode of academic advising. There is no lack of trying. Different methods are continually juggled, discarded, reintroduced and modified. The problem is less acute in the major, but even there undergraduates struggle to obtain reliable inside information on courses and faculty. Outside the major, chaos reigns. Modularity in conjunction with specialization has created such a bewildering variety of separate courses that no single adviser can have first-hand information on more than a handful, and much of the information is accidental. Furthermore, suiting the student to the course is even more fitful. Mass-education institutions in the United States have such poor staffing ratios that few undergraduates are well-enough known to teachers to receive tailor-made advice.

Conclusion

The flexibility and openness of the American modular system, those very features which allow it to speedily adapt to new conditions, are also the same reasons why the organization of teaching in America resembles the Ptolemaic cosmology of the later Middle Ages. It too works. It accounts for the backward movements of planets and other puzzling phenomena discernible to the naked eye; but it upsets the rationalist who dislikes fictions, is offended by evasions, demands simplicity, and wants a clear-cut statement of principle to govern the operation of complex systems. Whatever its drawbacks – and these are substantial when viewed both in comparative perspective and against some of the historic objectives of American undergraduate education – the modular system is genuinely popular. It is certainly 'unnatural' for American faculty to consider alternatives to the combination of teaching and examining characteristic of the self-contained module, and students understandably are not aware of other systems. No practical objection to modularity exists. The reasons are clear. Faculty prefer the classroom autonomy provided by modules and electives, and students prefer choice to compulsion.

One argument must be refuted, the argument of current (and past) reformers that modules are wholly or mainly the result of ('narrow') specialism and the departmental organization of faculty. While it is true that modularity is inconceivable in the absence of specialization, and that modules and the departmental organization of disciplines have prospered in tandem, a more accurate explanation of the success of autonomous courses lies within the structure and values of American society generally. Modular courses made a mass market for higher education possible, 'solved' the problem of access by 'solving' the problem of remedial education, made transferring possible, and thus provided a brilliant means of accommodating a very large number of quite different but potent social and political pressures. Modularity evolved and survived (and shows no signs of disappearing) precisely because it possessed the widest possible kind of educational reference in a deepening plural culture.

The contradictions of the modular system are those of American society generally. Its merits are its defects, and its defects its merits. But modularity is not a mere reflection or 'reproduction' of a convenient notion called 'American society'. It is a special compromise within that society, an agreement to tolerate the coexistence of radically different aspects of education. It is a system of trade-offs (not all of equal value) and exchanges that are constantly renegotiated as social and economic conditions change. An account of those renegotiations would itself be a major contribution to our understanding of the actual functioning of institutions; but for the moment we must be satisfied with a descriptive and structural analysis of the purpose and place of modules in American history and culture.

Acknowledgements

My colleague Martin Trow has provided me with his customary assistance and insight.

Notes

1 Mary Lovett Smallwood, *An Historical Study of Examinations and Grading Systems in Early American Universities*, Cambridge, Mass., 1935, p. 84.
2 I am indebted for these remarks to an unpublished paper by Clive H. Church of the University of Kent on 'Modular courses in British higher education: a critical assessment'. An earlier published version appears in the *Higher Education Bulletin*, **3** (1975), 165–84.
3 John S. Brubacher and Willis Rudy, *Higher Education in Transition*, 3rd edn, New York, 1976, p. 100.
4 *Ibid.*, pp. 100–101.
5 The same cannot be said of the present British interest in modules, an interest about thirty years old, but this judgement may be challenged by the events of the 1990s. In the 1960s modules were used in the Science Faculty of the University of London and in the Open University. They are now prominently featured in the curricula of the polytechnics and colleges of education (see Church, *ibid.*), but without the extraordinary range of applications possible in the United States.

6 Sir Alexander Grant, *The Story of the University of Edinburgh*, I, London, 1884, p. 277. As well as in Brubacher and Willis, useful remarks on the history of the elective principle appear in R. Freeman Butts, *The College Charts its Course*, New York and London, 1939; William T. Foster, *Administration of the College Curriculum*, Boston, 1911; G. W. Pierson, 'The elective system and the difficulties of college planning, 1870–1940', in *Journal of General Education*, **4** (April 1950), 165–74. Documents appear in Richard Hofstadter and Wilson Smith (Eds), *American Higher Education*, II, Chicago, 1961, pp. 697–747.

7 It has been estimated that between 1870 and 1940 Yale University attempted 'at least seven rather substantial reorganizations – to say nothing of a long series of minor adjustments and experiments' (Pierson, *ibid.*, p. 168).

8 Howard J. Savage, 'The Carnegie Foundation and the rise of the unit', in 43rd *Annual Report* of the Carnegie Foundation for the Advancement of Teaching (1947–48).

9 Robert C. Wilson, 'Berkeley faculty opinions on teaching quality in large lecture classes' (1985).

10 E.g. Ernest L. Boyer, *College, The Undergraduate Experience in America*, New York, 1987; Robert Zemsky, *Structure and Coherence, Measuring the Undergraduate Curriculum*, Association of American Colleges, 1989.